Numerals

Cardinal

1	un, une	31	trente et un
2	deux	32	trente-deux
3	trois	40	quarante
4	quatre	50	cinquante
5	cinq	60	soixante
6	six	70	soixante-dix
7	sept	71	soixante et onze
8	huit	72	soixante-douze
9	neuf	73	soixante-treize
10	dix	74	soixante-quatorze
11	onze	75	soixante-quinze
12	douze	76	soixante-seize
13	treize	77	soixante-dix-sept
14	quatorze	78	soixante-dix-huit
15	quinze	79	soixante-dix-neuf
16	seize	80	quatre-vingts
17	dix-sept	81	quatre-vingt-un
18	dix-huit	82	quatre-vingt-deux
19	dix-neuf	90	quatre-vingt-dix
20	vingt	91	quatre-vingt-onze
21	vingt et un	92	quatre-vingt-douze
22	vingt-deux	100	cent
23	vingt-trois	101	cent un
24	vingt-quatre	102	cent deux
25	vingt-cinq	200	deux cents
26	vingt-six	300	trois cents
27	vingt-sept	301	trois cent un
28	vingt-huit	1,000	mille
29	vingt-neuf	5,000	cinq mille
30	trente	1,000,000	un million

Ordinal

1st	premier, première	19th	dix-neuvième
2nd	deuxième, second	20th	vingtième
3rd	troisième	21st	vingt-et-unième
4th	quatrième	22nd	vingt-deuxième
5th	cinquième	30th	trentième
6th	sixième	40th	quarantième
7th	septième	50th	cinquantième
8th	huitième	60th	soixantième
9th	neuvième	70th	soixante-dixième
10th	dixième	80th	quatre-vingtième
11th	onzième	90th	quatre-vingt-dixième
12th	douzième		
13th	treizième	100th	centième
14th	quatorzième	101st	cent-unième
15th	quinzième	102nd	cent-deuxième
16th	seizième	300th	trois-centième
17th	dix-septième	1,000th	millième
18th	dix-huitième	1,000,000th	millionième

Days of the Week

Sunday	dimanche
Monday	lundi
Tuesday	mardi
Wednesday	mercredi
Thursday	jeudi
Friday	vendredi
Saturday	samedi

Months

January	janvier
February	février
March	mars
April	avril
May	mai
June	juin
July	juillet
August	août
September	septembre
October	octobre
November	novembre
December	décembre

Weights and Measures

The French use the *Metric System* of weights and measures, a decimal system in which multiples are shown by the prefixes **déci-** (one-tenth); **centi-** (one hundredth); **milli-** (one thousandth); **hecto-** (hundred); and **kilo-** (thousand).

1 centimètre	=	.3937 inch
1 mètre	=	39.37 inches
1 kilomètre	=	.621 mile
1 centigramme	=	.1543 grain
1 gramme	=	15.432 grains
100 grammes	=	3.527 ounces
1 kilogramme	=	2.2046 pounds
1 tonne	=	2,204 pounds
1 centilitre	=	.338 ounce
1 litre	=	1.0567 quart (liquid);
		.908 quart (dry)
1 kilolitre	=	264.18 gallons

The
Random House
French
Dictionary

FRENCH – ENGLISH
ENGLISH – FRENCH

FRANÇAIS – ANGLAIS
ANGLAIS – FRANÇAIS

Edited by
Francesca L. V. Langbaum
University of Virginia

Under the General Editorship of
Professor Robert A. Hall, Jr.
Cornell Unversity

RANDOM HOUSE
NEW YORK

Library of Congress Catalog Card Number: 54-5962

This work was originally published by Random House, Inc., in 1983.

ISBN: 0-394-40054-2
Manufactured in the United States of America

30th Printing
First Vest-Pocket Edition

New York   Toronto   London   Sydney   Auckland

Concise Pronunciation Guide

The following concise guide describes the approximate pronunciation of the letters and frequent combinations of letters occurring in the French language. A study of it will enable the reader to pronounce French adequately most of the time. While the guide cannot list all the exceptions to the established pronunciations, or cover the manner in which adjacent words affect each other in speech, such exceptions and variations will readily be learned as one develops facility in the language.

French Letter	Description of Pronunciation
a, à	Between *a* in *calm* and *a* in *hat*.
â	Like *a* in *calm*.
ai	Like *e* in *bed*.
au	Like *oa* in *coat*.
b	As in English. At end of words, usually silent.
c	Before *e, i, y*, like *s*. Elsewhere, like *k*. When *c* occurs at the end of a word and is preceded by a consonant, it is usually silent.
ç	Like *s*.
cc	Before *e, i*, like *x*. Elsewhere, like *k*.
ch	Usually like *sh* in *short*. *ch* is pronounced like *k* in words of Greek origin before *a, o*, and *u* and before consonants.
d	At beginning and in middle of words, as in English. At end of words, usually silent.
e	At end of words, normally silent; indicates that preceding consonant letter is pronounced. Between two single consonant sounds, usually silent. Elsewhere, like English *a* in *sofa*.
é	Approximately like *a* in *hate*.

French Letter	Description of Pronunciation
è, ê, ei	Like *e* in *bed*.
eau	Like *au*.
ent	Silent when it is the third person plural ending.
er (end of words)	At end of words of more than one syllable, usually like *a* in *hate*, the *r* being silent; otherwise like *air* in *chair*.
es	Silent at end of words.
eu	A vowel sound not found in English; like French *e*, but pronounced with the lips rounded as for *o*.
ez	At end of words, almost always like English *a* in *hate*, the *z* being silent.
f	As in English; silent at the end of a few words.
g	Before *e, i, y*, like *z* in *azure*. Elsewhere, like *g* in *get*. At end of words, usually silent.
gn	Like *ni* in *onion*.
gu	Before *e, i, y*, like *g* in *get*. Elsewhere, like *g* in *get* plus French *u* (see below).
h	In some words, represents a slight tightening of the throat muscles (in French, called "aspiration"). In most words, silent.
i, î	Like *i* in *machine*.
ill	(-il at end of words) like *y* in *yes*, in many but not all words.
j	Like *z* in *azure*.
k	As in English.
l	As in English, but always pronounced "bright," with tongue in front of mouth.
m, n	When double, and when single between two vowel letters or at beginning of word, like English *m* and *n* respectively. When single at end of syllable (at end of word or before another consonant), indicates nasalization of preceding vowel.
o	Usually like *u* in English *mud*, but rounder. When final sound in word, and often before *s* and *z*, like *ô*.
ô	Approximately like *oa* in *coat*.
oe, oeu	Like *eu*.
oi	Approximately like a combination of the consonant *w* and the *a* of *calm*.
ou, oû, où	Like *ou* in *tour*.

French Letter	Description of Pronunciation
p	At end of words, usually silent. Between *m* and *t*, *m* and *s*, *r* and *s*, usually silent. Elsewhere, as in English.
pn, ps	Unlike English, when *pn* and *ps* occur at the beginning of words the *p* is usually sounded.
ph	Like *f*.
qu	Usually like *k*.
r	A vibration either of the uvula, or of the tip of the tongue against the upper front teeth. See above under *er*.
s	Generally, like *s* in *sea*. Single *s* between vowels, like *z* in *zone*. At end of words, normally silent.
sc	Before *e* or *i*, like *s*. Elsewhere, like *sk*.
t	Approximately like English *t*, but pronounced with tongue tip against teeth. At end of words, normally silent. When followed by *ie*, *ion*, *ium*, *ius*, and other diphthongs beginning with a vowel, *t* generally is like English *s* in *sea* (unless the *t* itself is preceded by an *s* or an *x*).
th	Like *t*.
u, û	A vowel sound not found in English; like the *i* in *machine* but with lips rounded as for *ou*.
ue	After *c* or *g* and before *il*, like *eu*.
v	As in English.
w	Usually like *v*; in some people's pronunciation, like English *w*.
x	Generally sounds like *ks*; but when the syllable *ex* begins a word and is followed by a vowel, *x* sounds like *gz*. At end of words, usually silent.
y	Generally like *i* in *machine*; but when between two vowels, like y in *yes*.
z	Like *z* in *zone*. At end of words, often silent (see above under *ez*).

Note on Pronunciation

A few minutes' study of the *Concise Pronunciation Guide* on pages iii–v will enable you to pronounce most French words without having to look each word up in the dictionary. For the relatively few cases in which the pronunciation does not follow the usual pattern, this dictionary provides a transcription in simple and familiar symbols.

ă bat

ā cape

â dare

ä calm

à [a vowel intermediate in quality between the *a* of *cat* and the *a* of *calm*, but closer to the former]

ĕ set

ē bee

ĭ big

ī bite

N [a symbol used to indicate nasalized vowels. There are four such vowels in French, found in *un bon vin blanc* (œN bôN väN bläN)]

ŏ hot

ō no

ô order

œ [a vowel made with the lips rounded in position for *o* as in *over*, while trying to say *a* as in *able*]

oi oil

o͝o book

o͞o ooze

ou loud

ŭ up

ū cute

û burn

Y [a vowel made with the lips rounded in position for *oo* as in *ooze*, while trying to say *e* as in *easy*]

ə [indicates the sound of *a* in *alone*, *e* in *system*, *i* in *easily*, *o* in *gallop*, *u* in *circus*]

Irregular Verbs

Infin-itive	Pres. Part.	Past Part.	Pres. Indic.	Future
aller	allant	allé	vais	irai
asseoir	asseyant	assis	assieds	assiérai
atteindre	atteignant	atteint	atteins	atteindrai
avoir	ayant	eu	ai	aurai
battre	battant	battu	bats	battrai
boire	buvant	bu	bois	boirai
conduire	conduisant	conduit	conduis	conduirai
connaître	connaissant	connu	connais	connaîtrai
courir	courant	couru	cours	courrai
craindre	craignant	craint	crains	craindrai
croire	croyant	cru	crois	croirai
devoir	devant	dû	dois	devrai
dire	disant	dit	dis	dirai
dormir	dormant	dormi	dors	dormirai
écrire	écrivant	écrit	écris	écrirai
envoyer	envoyant	envoyé	envoie	enverrai
être	étant	été	suis	serai
faire	faisant	fait	fais	ferai
falloir	———	fallu	(il) faut	(il) faudra
joindre	joignant	joint	joins	joindrai
lire	lisant	lu	lis	lirai
mettre	mettant	mis	mets	mettrai
mourir	mourant	mort	meurs	mourrai
naître	naissant	né	nais	naîtrai
ouvrir	ouvrant	ouvert	ouvre	ouvrirai
plaire	plaisant	plu	plais	plairai
pleuvoir	pleuvant	plu	(il) pleut	(il) pleuvra
pouvoir	pouvant	pu	peux	pourrai
prendre	prenant	pris	prends	prendrai
recevoir	recevant	reçu	reçois	recevrai
rire	riant	ri	ris	rirai
savoir	sachant	su	sais	saurai
suffire	suffisant	suffi	suffis	suffirai
suivre	suivant	suivi	suis	suivrai
tenir	tenant	tenu	tiens	tiendrai
valoir	valant	valu	vaux	vaudrai
venir	venant	venu	viens	viendrai
vivre	vivant	vécu	vis	vivrai
voir	voyant	vu	vois	verrai
vouloir	voulant	voulu	veux	voudrai

Abbreviations

abbr.	abbreviation
adj.	adjective
adv.	adverb
art.	article
comm.	commercial
conj.	conjunction
eccles.	ecclesiastical
f.	feminine
fig.	figurative
geom.	geometry
gramm.	grammar, grammatical
interj.	interjection
intr.	intransitive
lit.	literal, literally
m.	masculine
med.	medical
mil.	military
n.	noun
naut.	nautical
pl.	plural
pred.	predicate
prep.	preposition
pron.	pronoun
sg.	singular
tr.	transitive (used only with verbs which also have reflexive use to indicate intransitive meaning)
vb.	verb

FRENCH-ENGLISH

A

à, *prep.* at, in, to.

abaisser, *vb.* depress, lower.

abandon, *n.m.* desertion, abandonment.

abandonné, *adj.* forlorn.

abandonner, *vb.* forsake, leave (desert). **s'a.,** give up, resign oneself.

abasourdir, *vb.* astound.

abattage, *n.m.* slaughter.

abattement, *n.m.* depression, dejection.

abattre, *vb.* depress; reduce; slaughter. **s'a.,** alight.

abbaye, *n.f.* abbey.

abbé, *n.m.* abbot.

abbesse, *n.f.* abbess.

abcès, *n.m.* abscess.

abdiquer, *vb.* abdicate.

abdomen, *n.m.* abdomen.

abeille, *n.f.* bee.

aberration, *n.f.* aberration.

abîme, *n.m.* abyss.

abîmer, *vb.* injure, spoil.

abject, *adj.* abject, low.

aboiement, *n.m.* barking.

abolir, *vb.* abolish.

abolition, *n.f.* abolition.

abominable, *adj.* vile, objectionable.

abondamment, *adv.* fully.

abondance, *n.f.* plenty.

abondant, *adj.* plentiful. **peu a.,** scanty.

abonder de, *vb.* abound in.

abonnement, *n.m.* subscription.

abonner, *vb.* **s'a.,** subscribe.

abord, 1. *n.m.* approach. **2.** *adv.* **d'a.,** at first.

aborder, *vb.* accost.

aboutir, *vb.* end (in).

aboyer, *vb.* bark.

abréger, *vb.* abridge, shorten, abbreviate.

abreuver, *vb.* water (animals).

abréviation, *n.f.* abbreviation.

abri, *n.m.* shelter. **à l'a. de,** safe from.

abricot, *n.m.* apricot.

abriter, *vb.* shelter.

abrupt (-pt) *adj.* steep.

absence, *n.f.* absence.

absent, *adj.* absent. **rester a.,** stay away.

absenter, *vb.* **s'a.,** go away.

abside, *n.f.* apse.

absinthe, *n.f.* absinthe.

absolu, *adj.* utter, absolute.

absolution, *n.f.* absolution.

absorbant, *adj. and n.m.* absorbent.

absorbé dans, *adj.* intent on.

absorber, *vb.* engross, absorb. **s'a. dans,** pore over.

absorption, *n.f.* absorption.

absoudre, *vb.* absolve.

abstenir, *vb.* forbear. **s'a. de,** abstain from.

abstinence, *n.f.* abstinence.

abstraction, *n.f.* abstraction.

abstrait, *adj.* abstract.

absurde, *adj.* absurd, preposterous.

absurdité, *n.f.* nonsense, absurdity.

abus, *n.m.* abuse.

abuser de, *vb.* abuse.

académie, *n.f.* academy.

académique, *adj.* academic.

acajou, *n.m.* mahogany.

accablant, *adj.* oppressive.

accabler, *vb.* overwhelm, burden.

accaparer, *vb.* get a corner on.

accélération, *n.f.* acceleration.

accélérer, *vb.* quicken, hurry.

accent, *n.m.* stress, emphasis, accent.

accentuer, *vb.* accentuate, accent, emphasize.

acceptable, *adj.* acceptable.

acceptation, *n.f.* acceptance.

accepter, *vb.* accept, admit.

accepteur, *n.m.* accepter.

accès, *n.m.* access, approach; fit (of anger); bout (of fever).

accessible, *adj.* accessible.

accessoire, *n.m. and adj.* accessory, adjunct.

accident, *n.m.* crash, accident.

accidentel, *adj.* accidental.

acclamation, *n.f.* acclamation.

acclamer, *vb.* acclaim, cheer.

accommoder, *vb.* accommodate.

accompagnement, *n.m.* accompaniment.

accompagner, *vb.* accompany, go with.

accompli, *adj.* accomplished, complete, perfect.

accomplir, *vb.* accomplish, achieve, fulfill, carry out, perform.

accomplissement, *n.m.* performance, fulfillment, achievement, accomplishment.

accord, *n.m.* agreement, harmony; settlement; chord, tune. **être d'a.,** agree, concur.

accorder, *vb.* grant; bestow; allow; tune. **s'a.,** agree.

accouchement, *n.m.* delivery.

accoucher, *vb.* deliver.

accoucheur, *n.m.* **médecin-a.,** obstetrician.

accouder, *vb.* **s'a.,** lean.

accourir, *vb.* flock, run up.

accoutumer, *vb.* accustom.

accréditer, *vb.* accredit.

accrocher, *vb.* hook, hitch.

accroissement, *n.m.* growth, addition.

accroître, *vb.* increase.

accroupir, *vb.* **s'a.,** squat, crouch.

accueil, *n.m.* reception, greeting.

accueillir, *vb.* receive, greet.

accumuler, *vb.* heap up.

accusateur, *n.m.* accuser.

accusatif, *n.m.* accusative.

accusation, *n.f.* accusation.

accusatrice, *n.f.* accuser.

accusé, *n.m.* defendant.

accuser, *vb.* arraign, accuse.

acharné, *adj.* eager, fanatical.

achat, *n.m.* purchase.

acheminer, *vb.* start (toward).

acheter, *vb.* buy.

acheteur, *n.m.* buyer.

achèvement, *n.m.* completion.

achever, *vb.* complete, finish, achieve.

acide, *adj. and n.m.* acid.

acidité, *n.f.* acidity.

acier, *n.m.* steel.

acoustique, *n.f.* acoustics.

acquérir, *vb.* acquire, get, obtain.

acquiescement, *n.m.* acquiescence, compliance.

acquiescer à, *vb.* acquiesce, consent.

acquisition, *n.f.* acquisition, purchase.

acquittement, *n.m.* acquittal.

acquitter, *vb.* acquit.

âcre, *adj.* sharp.

acrobate, *n.m.f.* acrobat.

acte, *n.m.* act. **a. notarié,** deed. **a. de naissance,** birth certificate.

acteur, *n.m.* actor.

actif, 1. *n.m.* assets (comm.). **2.** *adj.* active.

action, *n.f.* action, deed, act; (comm.) share.

action de contrôle en retour, *n.f.* feedback.

actionnaire, *n.m.* shareholder.

actionner, *vb.* operate.

activement, *adv.* busily.

activer, *vb.* activate, fan, hurry.

activité, *n.f.* activity.

actrice, *n.f.* actress.

actualités, *n.f.pl.* newsreel.

actuel, *adj.* present.

actuellement, *adv.* now, at present.

acuponcture, *n.f.* acupuncture.

adaptation, *n.f.* adaptation.

adapter, *vb.* adapt, fit, adjust, suit.

addition, *n.f.* addition, bill.

additionnel, *adj.* additional.

additionner, *vb.* add.

adhérent, *n.m.* adherent.

adhérer, *vb.* cleave, adhere.

adhésif, *adj.* adhesive.

adieu, *n.m. and interj.* good-bye, farewell. **faire ses adieux,** take one's leave.

adjacent, *adj.* adjacent.

adjectif, *n.m.* adjective.

adjoint, *n.m.* fellow-worker, associate.

adjuger, *vb.* grant.

admettre, *vb.* allow, admit, grant.

administrateur, *n.m.* administrator, director, manager.

administratif, *adj.* administrative.

administration, *n.f.* administration, direction.

administrer, *vb.* administer, manage.

admirable, *adj.* admirable.

admirateur, *n.m.* admirer.

admiration, *n.f.* admiration.

admirer, *vb.* admire.

admission, *n.f.* confession, admission.

adolescence, *n.f.* adolescence.

adolescent, *adj. and n.m.f.* adolescent.

adonner, *vb.* s'a. à, indulge in, become addicted to.

adopter, *vb.* adopt.

adoption, *n.f.* adoption.

adoration, *n.f.* adoration.

adorer, *vb.* worship, adore.

adosser, *vb.* s'a. à, lean on.

adoucir, *vb.* soothe.

adresse, *n.f.* address; skill, ability.

adresser, *vb.* address (a letter); direct. **s'a. à,** apply to.

adroit, *adj.* skillful, clever, handy.

adulte, *adj. and n.m.f.* adult.

adultère, *n.m.* adultery.

adultérer, *vb.* adulterate.

adverbe, *n.m.* adverb.

adversaire, *n.m.f.* opponent.

adverse, *adj.* adverse.

adversité, *n.f.* adversity.

aéré, *adj.* airy.

aérer, *vb.* air (a room).

aérien, *adj.* aerial.

aérogare, *n.f.* airline (city) station.

aéroglisseur, *n.m.* hovercraft.

aéroport, *n.m.* airport.

affable, *adj.* affable.

affaiblir, *vb.* weaken.

affaire, *n.f.* affair, matter; deal; *(pl.)* business. **se tirer d'a.,** manage (somehow). **homme d'a.s,** businessman.

affairé, *adj.* busy.

affaissement, *n.m.* collapse.

affaisser, *vb.* s'a., collapse.

affamé, *adj.* hungry, famished.

affamer, *vb.* starve.

affectation, *n.f.* affectation.

affecter, *vb.* affect.

affection, *n.f.* affection.

affectueux, *adj.* affectionate.

affermir, *vb.* strengthen.

affété, *adj.* finicky.

affiche, *n.f.* poster.

afficher, *vb.* post.

affilier, *vb.* affiliate.

affinité, *n.f.* affinity.

affirmatif, *adj.* affirmative.

affirmation, *n.f.* statement.

affirmer, *vb.* assert, state, maintain, testify, affirm.

affliction, *n.f.* affliction.

affligé, *adj.* sorrowful.

affliger, *vb.* distress, afflict, grieve.

affluent, *n.m.* tributary.

affluer, *vb.* flow into.

affoler, *vb.* drive mad.

affranchir, *vb.* free.

affranchissement, *n.m.* postage.

affréter, *vb.* charter (boat).

affreusement, *adv.* terribly.

affreux, *adj.* dreadful, terrible, horrid, dire.

affront, *n.m.* affront, insult.

affronter, *vb.* confront, face.

afin, 1. a. de, *prep.* in order to. **2. conj. a. que,** so that.

Africain, *n.m.* African.

africain, *adj.* African.

Afrique, *n.f.* Africa.

agacer, *vb.* vex, irritate.

âge, *n.m.* age. **d'un certain â.,** elderly. **le moyen â.,** the Middle Ages.

âgé, *adj.* aged.

agence, *n.f. (comm.)* agency.

agenouiller, *vb.* s'a., kneel.

agent, *n.m.* agent. **a. de police,** policeman. **a. de change,** stockbroker.

aggraver, *vb.* aggravate.

agile, *adj.* nimble.

agir, *vb.* act. **s'a. de,** be a question of.

agitateur, *n.m.* agitator.

agitation, *n.f.* excitement, disturbance, commotion, flutter.

agité, *adj.* upset, excited.

agiter, *vb.* agitate, wave, wag, shake, stir. **s'a.,** toss, flutter.

agneau, *n.m.* lamb.

agonie, *n.f.* agony.

agrafe, *n.f.* clasp.

agrafer, *vb.* clasp.

agrandir, *vb.* enlarge.

agréable, *adj.* likable, pleasant, enjoyable, agreeable.

agréer, *vb.* accept, consent.

agrégation, *n.f.* aggregation, fellowship.

agrément, *n.m.* pleasure.

agresseur, *n.m.* aggressor.

agressif, *adj.* aggressive.

agression, *n.f.* aggression.

agricole, *adj.* agricultural.

agriculture, *n.f.* agriculture.
ahurir, *vb.* bewilder, fluster.
aide, *n.f.* help, aid.
aider, *vb.* help, aid.
aïeul (ä yœl), *n.m.* grandfather.
aïeule (ä yœl), *n.f.* grandmother.
aïeux, *n.m.pl.* ancestors.
aigle, *n.m.f.* eagle.
aiglefin, *n.m.* haddock.
aigre, *adj.* sour.
aigu, *adj.* shrill, keen, pointed.
aiguille, *n.f.* needle.
aiguisé, *adj.* keen.
aiguiser, *vb.* sharpen.
ail (ä ē) *n.m.* garlic.
aile, *n.f.* wing.
ailleurs, *adv.* elsewhere. **d'a.,** in addition, anyhow.
aimable, *adj.* kind, pleasant, amiable.
aimant, *n.m.* magnet.
aimer, *vb.* love, like.
aine, *n.f.* groin.
aîné (ē nā), **1.** *adj. and n.m.* elder. **2.** *adj.* eldest, senior.
ainsi, *adv.* thus, so.
air, *n.m.* air, looks. **en plein air,** in the open air.
aire, *n.f.* area.
aise, *n.f.* ease, comfort. **à l'a.,** comfortable.
aisé, *adj.* substantial, well-to-do; easy.
aisselle, *n.f.* armpit.
ajourner, *vb.* put off. **s'a.,** adjourn.
ajoutage, *n.m.* fitting.
ajouter, *vb.* add.
ajuster, *vb.* fit, fix, adjust.
alarme, *n.f.* alarm.
alarmer, *vb.* alarm.
album, *n.m.* album.
alcool (-kôl), *n.m.* alcohol.
alcoolique (-kôl-), *adj.* alcoholic.
alcôve, *n.f.* alcove.
alentours, *n.m.pl.* neighborhood, surroundings.
alerte, *adj.* spry, active, alert.
algèbre, *n.f.* algebra.
aliéné, *n.m.* lunatic.
aliéner, *vb.* alienate.
aligner, *vb.* line up.
aliment, *n.m.* food.
alimentation, *n.f.* feeding.
alimenter, *vb.* feed.
alinéa, *n.m.* paragraph.
allaiter, *vb.* nurse.

allée, *n.f.* path, avenue, aisle.
allégation, *n.f.* allegation.
alléger, *vb.* lighten, soothe.
allégresse, *n.f.* glee, delight, mirth.
alléguer, *vb.* plead, allege.
Allemagne, *n.f.* Germany.
Allemand, *n.m.* German (person).
allemand, 1. *n.m.* German (language). **2.** *adj.* German.
aller, *vb.* go. **s'en a.,** go away. **a. à,** fit. **se laisser a.,** drift. **a. bien,** fare well. **a. mal,** fare ill. **a. et retour,** round trip.
alliage, *n.m.* alloy.
alliance, *n.f.* alliance, union.
allié, 1. *n.m.* ally, relation. **2.** *adj.* allied.
allier, *vb.* ally. **s'a. à,** join with.
allô, *interj.* hello.
allocation, *n.f.* allowance.
allonger, *vb.* lengthen, prolong.
allons, *interj.* well, come now.
allouer, *vb.* grant.
allumer, *vb.* light.
allumette, *n.f.* match.
allure, *n.f.* pace, gait.
allusion, *n.f.* hint, allusion. **faire a. à,** allude to.
almanach (-nä), *n.m.* almanac.
alors, 1. *adv.* then. **2.** *conj.* **a. que,** when.
alouette, *n.f.* lark.
alphabet, *n.m.* alphabet.
altérer, *vb.* change.
alternatif, *adj.* alternate.
alternative, *n.f.* alternative.
alterner, *vb.* alternate.
Altesse, *n.f.* Highness (title).
altitude, *n.f.* altitude.
aluminium, *n.m.* aluminum.
amabilité, *n.f.* kindness.
amalgamer, *vb.* amalgamate.
amande, *n.f.* kernel; almond.
amant, *n.m.* lover.
amas, *n.m.* hoard, mass.
amasser, *vb.* hoard, gather, amass.
amateur, *n.m.* amateur.
ambassade, *n.f.* embassy.
ambassadeur, *n.m.* ambassador.
ambassadrice, *n.f.* ambassadress.
ambigu *m.,* **ambiguë** *f.* *adj.* ambiguous.
ambiguïté, *n.f.* ambiguity.
ambitieux, *adj.* ambitious.

ambition, *n.f.* ambition.
ambre, *n.m.* amber.
ambulance, *n.f.* ambulance.
âme, *n.f.* soul.
amélioration, *n.f.* improvement.
améliorer, *vb.* improve.
aménager, *vb.* fit up.
amende, *n.f.* fine. **mettre à l'a.,** fine.
amendement, *n.m.* amendment.
amender, *vb.* amend.
amener, *vb.* bring, lead.
amer (-r), *adj.* bitter.
Américain, *n.m.* American.
américain, *adj.* American.
Amérique, *n.f.* America. **A. du Nord,** North America. **A. du Sud,** South America.
amertume, *n.f.* bitterness.
ameublement, *n.m.* furniture.
ami *m.,* **amie** *f. n.* friend.
amical, *adj.* friendly, amicable.
amidon, *n.m.* starch.
amiral, *n.m.* admiral.
amitié, *n.f.* friendship.
ammoniaque, *n.f.* ammonia.
amniocentèse, *n.f.* amniocentesis.
amoindrir, *vb.* lessen, reduce.
amollir, *vb.* soften.
amortir, *vb.* deaden, soften.
amour, *n.m.* love.
amoureux, 1. *n.m.* lover. **2.** *adj.* in love, amorous.
amour-propre, *n.m.* vanity, pride, conceit.
ample, *adj.* ample, spacious.
ampleur, *n.f.* plenty, compass.
amplifier, *vb.* increase, enlarge, develop.
ampoule, *n.f.* blister; (electric) bulb.
amputer, *vb.* amputate.
amusement, *n.m.* fun, pastime, entertainment.
amuser, *vb.* entertain. **s'a.,** have a good time.
amygdale, *n.f.* tonsil.
an, *n.m.* year.
analogie, *n.f.* analogy.
analogue, *adj.* similar, analogous.
analyse, *n.f.* analysis.
analyser, *vb.* analyze.
anarchie, *n.f.* anarchy.
anatomie, *n.f.* anatomy.
ancêtre, *n.m.* forefather, ancestor.
anche, *n.f.* reed.

anchois, *n.m.* anchovy.
ancien *m.,* **ancienne** *f. adj.* ancient, old, former.
ancre, *n.f.* anchor.
ancrer, *vb.* anchor.
âne *m.,* **ânesse** *f. n.* ass, donkey.
anéantir, *vb.* annihilate, destroy.
anecdote, *n.f.* anecdote.
anesthésique, *adj. and n.m.* anesthetic.
ange, *n.m.* angel.
Anglais, *n.m.* Englishman.
anglais, *adj. and n.m.* English.
Anglaise, *n.f.* Englishwoman.
angle, *n.m.* angle, corner.
Angleterre, *n.f.* England.
angoissant, *adj.* in anguish.
angoisse, *n.f.* agony, pang, anguish.
anguille, *n.f.* eel.
anguleux, *adj.* angular.
anicroche, *n.f.* hitch.
animal, *n.m. and adj.* animal.
animation, *n.f.* animation.
animer, *vb.* enliven, animate.
animosité, *n.f.* animosity.
anneau, *n.m.* ring, circle.
année, *n.f.* year; vintage.
annexe, *n.f.* annex.
annexer, *vb.* annex.
annexion, *n.f.* annexation.
anniversaire, *n.m.* anniversary, birthday.
annonce, *n.f.* advertisement, announcement.
annoncer, *vb.* advertise, announce.
annotation, *n.f.* annotation.
annoter, *vb.* annotate.
annuaire, *n.m.* directory.
annuel, *adj.* yearly, annual.
annulation, *n.f.* cancellation.
annuler, *vb.* cancel, void, annul.
ânonner, *vb.* stammer.
anonyme, *adj.* anonymous.
anormal, *adj.* irregular, abnormal.
anse, *n.f.* handle; bay.
antagonisme, *n.m.* antagonism.
antarctique, *adj.* antarctic.
antécédent, *adj. and n.m.* antecedent.
antécédents, *n.m.pl.* record.
antenne, *n.f.* antenna.
antérieur, *adj.* previous; fore, front.
anthracite, *n.m.* anthracite.

antichambre, *n.f.* entrance hall.
anticipation, *n.f.* anticipation.
anticiper, *vb.* anticipate.
antidote, *n.m.* antidote.
antilope, *n.f.* antelope.
antinucléaire, *adj.* antinuclear.
antipathie, *n.f.* antipathy.
antiquaire, *n.m.* antique dealer.
antique, *adj.* ancient, antiquated, antique.
antiquité, *n.f.* antiquity.
antiseptique, *adj. and n.m.* antiseptic.
antre, *n.m.* den.
anxiété, *n.f.* anxiety, worry.
anxieux, *adj.* anxious.
août (ōō), *n.m.* August.
apaiser, *vb.* allay, quiet, appease.
apathie, *n.f.* apathy.
apercevoir, *vb.* perceive. **s'a. de,** realize.
aperçu, *n.m.* outline.
apéritif, *n.m.* appetizer.
apitoyer, *vb.* move (emotionally).
aplanir, *vb.* even off.
aplatir, *vb.* flatten.
aplomb, *n.m.* poise, boldness.
apoplexie, *n.f.* apoplexy.
apostolique, *adj.* apostolic.
apôtre, *n.m.* apostle.
apparaître, *vb.* appear.
appareil, *n.m.* gear, appliance, device. **a. photographique,** camera.
apparence, *n.f.* appearance, looks.
apparent, *adj.* noticeable, apparent.
apparition, *n.f.* appearance, ghost.
appartement, *n.m.* apartment.
appartenir, *vb.* belong, pertain.
appât, *n.m.* bait.
appel, *n.m.* call, appeal.
appeler, *vb.* call, summon, appeal. **s'a.,** be named.
appendice, *n.m.* appendix.
appétit, *n.m.* appetite.
applaudir, *vb.* applaud.
applaudissements, *n.m.pl.* applause.
applicable, *adj.* applicable.
application, *n.f.* application, industry.
appliqué, *adj.* industrious.
appliquer, *vb.* apply (put on), stick. **s'a.,** work hard.

appointements, *n.m.pl.* salary.
apporter, *vb.* bring, fetch.
apposer, *vb.* affix.
appréciable, *adj.* appreciable.
appréciation, *n.f.* appreciation.
apprécier, *vb.* appreciate, value.
appréhension, *n.f.* apprehension.
apprendre, *vb.* learn. **a. à,** teach (to). **a. par cœur,** memorize.
apprenti, *n.m.* apprentice.
apprentissage, *n.m.* apprenticeship.
apprêt, *n.m.* preparation.
apprêter, *vb.* **s'a.,** prepare, get ready.
apprivoiser, *vb.* tame.
approbation, *n.f.* endorsement, approval, approbation.
approche, *n.f.* approach.
approcher, *vb.* **s'a. de,** approach, go toward.
approfondir, *vb.* deepen.
appropriation, *n.f.* appropriation.
approprier, *vb.* **s'a.,** take over, appropriate.
approuver, *vb.* approve.
approvisionnement, *n.m.* supply.
approximatif, *adj.* approximate.
appui, *n.m.* support.
appuyer (-pwē-), *vb.* support, endorse, advocate. **a. sur,** emphasize.
après, **1.** *adv., prep.* after. **2.** *conj.* **a. que,** after. **d'a.,** according to.
après-demain, *n.m.* day after tomorrow.
après-midi, *n.m.f.* afternoon.
âpreté, *n.f.* harshness, bitterness.
à-propos, *n.m.* fitness.
apte à, *adj.* apt, suitable for.
aptitude, *n.f.* fitness, ability, aptitude.
aqualit, *n.m.* waterbed.
aquarelle (-kwà-), *n.f.* water color.
aquarium (-kwà-), *n.m.* aquarium.
aquatique (-kwà-), *adj.* aquatic.
aqueux, *adj.* watery.
Arabe, *n.m.f.* Arab, Arabian.
arabe, **1.** *n.m.* Arabic. **2.** *adj.* Arab, Arabian, Arabic.
arachide, *n.f.* peanut.
araignée, *n.f.* spider. **toile d'a.,** cobweb.
arbitrage, *n.m.* arbitration.
arbitraire, *adj.* arbitrary.

arbitre, *n.m.f.* umpire, arbitrator.

arbitrer, *vb.* arbitrate.

arbre, *n.m.* tree.

arbrisseau, *n.m.* shrub.

arc (-k), *n.m.* arc, arch, bow.

arcade, *n.f.* arcade.

arc-boutant, *n.m.* flying buttress.

arc-en-ciel, *n.m.* rainbow.

archaïque (àrk-), *adj.* archaic.

arche, *n.f.* arch (of bridge); ark.

archet, *n.m.* bow.

archevêque, *n.m.* archbishop.

archipel, *n.m.* archipelago.

architecte, *n.m.* architect.

architectural, *adj.* architectural.

architecture, *n.f.* architecture.

archives, *n.f.pl.* files, archives.

arctique, *adj.* arctic.

ardemment, *adv.* eagerly.

ardent, *adj.* eager, fiery, ardent.

ardeur, *n.f.* ardor.

ardoise, *n.f.* slate.

arène, *n.f.* arena, ring.

argent, *n.m.* silver, money.

argenterie, *n.f.* silverware.

Argentin, *n.m.* Argentine.

argentin, *adj.* Argentine.

argile, *n.f.* clay.

argot, *n.m.* slang.

argument, *n.m.* argument (reasoning).

argumenter, *vb.* argue (reason).

aride, *adj.* arid.

aristocrate, *n.m.f.* aristocrat.

aristocratie, *n.f.* aristocracy.

aristocratique, *adj.* aristocratic.

arithmétique, *n.f.* arithmetic.

arme, *n.f.* weapon; arm.

armée, *n.f.* army.

armement, *n.m.* armament.

arme nucléaire, *n.f.* nuclear weapon.

armer, *vb.* arm.

armistice, *n.m.* armistice.

armoire, *n.f.* cupboard, closet, wardrobe.

armure, *n.f.* armor.

aromatique, *adj.* aromatic.

arome, *n.m.* flavor, aroma.

arpenter, *vb.* pace.

arracher, *vb.* snatch.

arrangement, *n.m.* arrangement, settlement.

arranger, *vb.* settle, trim, fix, arrange.

arrestation, *n.f.* arrest, apprehen-

sion. **en état d'a.,** under arrest.

arrêt, *n.m.* stop.

arrêté, *n.m.* decree.

arrêter, *vb.* stop, check, halt, arrest.

arrière, *adv.* behind, back. **en a.,** backward. **marche a.,** reverse (gear).

arriéré, 1. *n.m.* arrear. **2.** *adj.* backward.

arrière-garde, *n.f.* rear guard.

arrivée, *n.f.* arrival.

arriver, *vb.* happen, reach, arrive.

arrogance, *n.f.* arrogance.

arrogant, *adj.* arrogant.

arroger, *vb.* arrogate, assume.

arrondir, *vb.* round off.

arrondissement, *n.m.* district.

arroser, *vb.* water, sprinkle; baste (meat).

arsenal, *n.m.* arsenal.

arsenic, *n.m.* arsenic.

art, *n.m.* art. **beaux-arts,** fine arts.

artère, *n.f.* artery.

artichaut, *n.m.* artichoke.

article, *n.m.* article, item, entry. **a. de fond,** editorial.

articulation, *n.f.* joint, articulation.

articuler, *vb.* articulate.

artifice, *n.m.* artifice.

artificiel, *adj.* artificial.

artificieux, *adj.* artful.

artillerie, *n.f.* artillery.

artisan, *n.m.* craftsman, artisan.

artiste, *n.m.* artist.

artistique, *adj.* artistic.

as (äs), *n.m.* ace.

ascenseur, *n.m.* elevator.

ascension, *n.f.* ascent (of a mountain).

Asiatique, *n.m.f.* Asian.

asiatique, *adj.* Asian.

Asie, *n.f.* Asia.

asile, *n.m.* haven, refuge, asylum.

aspect (-pè), *n.m.* looks, appearance, aspect.

asperger, *vb.* sprinkle.

asperges, *n.f.pl.* asparagus.

asphalte, *n.m.,* asphalt.

aspirateur, *n.m.* vacuum cleaner.

aspiration, *n.f.* aspiration, longing.

aspirer, *vb.* aspire, breathe.

assaillant, *n.m.* assailant.

assaillir, *vb.* assail, attack.

assaisonner, vb. season.

assassin, n.m. assassin, murderer.

assassinat, n.m. assassination, murder.

assassiner, vb. assassinate, murder.

assaut, n.m. assault, attack.

assemblage, n.m. collection.

assemblée, n.f. congregation, assembly.

assembler, vb. convene, gather. **s'a.,** assemble.

assentiment, n.m. assent.

asseoir, vb. seat. **s'a.,** sit down.

assertion, n.f. assertion.

asservir, vb. enslave.

assez (de), n. and adv. enough (of); pretty much.

assidu, adj. assiduous, industrious.

assiduité, n.f. industry.

assiéger, vb. besiege.

assiette, n.f. plate.

assigner, vb. assign.

assimiler, vb. assimilate.

assis, adj. seated.

assistance, n.f. those present.

assister à, vb. attend, be present at.

association, n.f. soccer; association, company; connection.

associé, 1. n.m. partner, associate. **2.** adj. associated.

associer, vb. associate.

assombrir, vb. **s'a.,** grow dark.

assommer, vb. murder, slaughter.

Assomption, n.f. Assumption (eccles.).

assortiment, n.m. assortment.

assortir, vb. match; tune.

assoupir, vb. **s'a.,** get drowsy.

assourdir, vb. deafen.

assujetti, adj. subject.

assujettir, vb. subject.

assumer, vb. assume.

assurance, n.f. assurance, insurance.

assuré, adj. sure.

assurer, vb. insure; assure. **s'a. de,** make certain.

assureur, n.m. insurer.

astérisque, n.m. asterisk.

astre, n.m. star.

astronaute, n.m. astronaut.

astronome, n.m. astronomer.

astronomie, n.f. astronomy.

astucieux, adj. tricky.

atelier, n.m. studio, (work)shop.

athée, n.m.f. atheist.

athlète, n.m.f. athlete.

athlétique, adj. athletic.

atlantique, adj. Atlantic.

atlas (-s), n.m. atlas.

atmosphère, n.f. atmosphere.

atmosphérique, adj. atmospheric.

atome, n.m. atom.

atomique, adj. atomic.

atroce, adj. atrocious, outrageous.

atrocité, n.f. atrocity.

attachement, n.m. attachment, affection.

attacher, vb. tie, fasten, join, attach.

attaque, n.f. attack.

attaquer, vb. attack.

attardé, adj. belated.

attarder, vb. **s'a.,** linger, delay.

atteindre, vb. reach, attain; strike.

atteint, adj. stricken.

atteinte, n.f. reach. **hors d'a.,** out of reach.

attelage, n.m. team.

atteler, vb. hitch up, harness.

attendre, vb. wait (for), await. **s'a. à,** expect.

attendrir, vb. soften, move. **se laisser a.,** relent.

attendrissement, n.m. feeling, emotion.

attentat, n.m. criminal attack, outrage.

attente, n.f. expectation, wait.

attentif, adj. thoughtful, attentive.

attention, n.f. notice, heed, attention. **faire a.,** heed, pay attention.

atténuer, vb. extenuate.

atterrir, vb. land.

attester, vb. attest.

attirer, vb. attract, entice, lure.

attitude, n.f. attitude.

attouchement, n.m. touch.

attraction, n.f. attraction.

attrait, n.m. charm.

attraper, vb. catch.

attrayant, adj. attractive.

attribuer, vb. ascribe, attribute.

attribut, n.m. attribute, characteristic.

attrister, vb. grieve.

au *m.*, **à la** *f.*, **aux** *pl. prep.* to the, in the.
aube, *n.f.* dawn.
auberge, *n.f.* inn.
aubergine, *n.f.* eggplant.
aubergiste, *n.m.* innkeeper.
aucun, *pron.* none.
aucunement, *adv.* not at all.
audace, *n.f.* audacity.
audacieux, *adj.* daring, bold.
au-dessous, **1.** *adv.* below. **2.** *prep.* **au-d. de**, beneath, under.
au-dessus, **1.** *adv.* above. **2.** *prep.* **au-d. de**, over, above.
audience, *n.f.* audience.
audiovisuel, *adj.* audiovisual.
auditoire, *n.m.* audience, assembly.
auge, *n.f.* trough.
augmentation, *n.f.* increase, raise, rise.
augmenter, *vb.* increase.
augure, *n.m.* omen, augury. **de bon a.**, auspicious. **de mauvais a.**, ominous.
augurer, *vb.* augur.
aujourd'hui, *adv.* today.
aumône, *n.f.* alms.
aumônier, *n.m.* chaplain.
auparavant, *adv.* before (time).
auprès de, *prep.* next, near, beside.
auréole, *n.f.* halo.
aurore, *n.f.* dawn.
auspice, *n.m.* auspice.
aussi, *adv.* too, also; so, as; therefore.
austère, *adj.* austere, severe.
austérité, *n.f.* austerity.
Australie, *n.f.* Australia.
Australien, *n.m.* Australian.
australien, *adj.* Australian.
autant, *adv.* so much, as much. **a. que**, as (so) much as. **d'a. que**, since. **a. plus**, so much the more.
autel, *n.m.* altar.
auteur, *n.m.* author, originator.
authentique, *adj.* true, genuine, authentic.
auto, *n.f.* auto.
autobus (-s), *n.m.* bus.
automatique, *adj.* automatic.
automne (-tôn), *n.m.* fall.
automobile, *n.f.* automobile.
autonomie, *n.f.* autonomy.
autorisation, *n.f.* license, authorization.

autoriser, *vb.* authorize.
autoritaire, *adj.* authoritative.
autorité, *n.f.* authority.
autour, **1.** *adv.* around. **2.** *prep.* **a. de**, around.
autre, **1.** *adj.* other. **2.** *pron.* other, else. **l'un l'a.**, one another. **quelqu'un d'a.**, someone else.
autrefois, *adv.* formerly.
autrement, *adv.* otherwise.
Autriche, *n.f.* Austria.
Autrichien, *n.m.* Austrian.
autrichien, *adj.* Austrian.
autruche, *n.f.* ostrich.
autrui, *pron.* someone else, others.
auxiliaire, *adj.* auxiliary.
avalanche, *n.f.* avalanche.
avaler, *vb.* swallow.
avance, *n.f.* advance. **d'a.**, beforehand. **en a.**, fast (clock).
avancé, *adj.* forward, advanced.
avancement, *n.m.* advance; advancement; promotion.
avancer, *vb.* proceed; come or go forward or onward.
avances, *n.f.pl.* advance. **faire des a. à**, make approaches to.
avant, **1.** *adv.* fore, bow. **2.** *adv.*, *prep.* before. **3.** *conj.* **a. que**, before. **en a.**, forward, onward. **en a. de**, ahead of.
avantage, *n.m.* advantage.
avantageux, *adj.* advantageous; favorable; profitable.
avant-bras, *n.m.* forearm.
avant-garde, *n.f.* vanguard.
avant-hier (-yâr), *n.m.* day before yesterday.
avant-toit, *n.m.* eaves.
avare, **1.** *n.m.f.* miser. **2.** *adj.* miserly, stingy.
avarice, *n.f.* avarice.
avec, *prep.* with.
avenant, *adj.* comely. **à l'a.**, accordingly.
avenir, *n.m.* future.
Avent, *n.m.* (eccles.) Advent.
aventure, *n.f.* adventure.
aventurer, *vb.* **s'a.**, take a chance.
aventureux, *adj.* adventurous.
aventurier, *n.m.* adventurer.
avenue, *n.f.* avenue.
averse, *n.f.* shower.
aversion, *n.f.* aversion, dislike.
avertir, *vb.* notify, warn.
avertissement, *n.m.* warning.

avertisseur d'incendie, *n.m.* fire alarm.

aveu, *n.m.* admission, confession.

aveugle, *adj.* blind.

aveuglement, *n.m.* blindness.

aveuglément, *adv.* blindly.

aveugler, *n.f.* blind.

aviateur, *n.m.* flier, aviator.

aviation, *n.f.* air force, aviation.

avide, *adj.* eager, greedy, avid.

avidité, *n.f.* greediness.

avilir, *vb.* debase, disgrace.

avion, *n.m.* airplane. **a. de bombardement**, bomber. **par a.**, via air mail.

avis, *n.m.* notice, opinion, advice (*comm.*).

aviser, *vb.* inform, notify. **s'a. (de)**, decide.

avocat, *n.m.* lawyer; advocate.

avoine, *n.f.* oat.

avoir, *vb.* have. **il y a**, ago.

avortement, *n.m.* abortion.

avoué, *n.m.* attorney, lawyer.

avouer, *vb.* confess, admit, avow.

avril (-l), *n.m.* April.

axe, *n.m.* axis.

ayatollah, *n.m.* ayatollah.

azur, *n.m.* azure, blue.

azuré, *adj.* azure.

B

babeurre, *n.m.* buttermilk.

babil, *n.m.* babble.

babiller, *vb.* babble.

bâbord, *n.m.* (*naut.*) port.

babouin, *n.m.* baboon.

bac, *n.m.* ferryboat. **passage en b.**, ferry.

bachelier, *n.m.* graduate.

bacille (-l), *n.m.* bacillus.

bactérie, *n.f.* bacterium.

bactériologie, *n.f.* bacteriology.

badaud, *adj.* silly.

bagages, *n.m.pl.* luggage.

bagatelle, *n.f.* trifle.

bague, *n.f.* ring.

baguette, *n.f.* wand, stick; long, thin loaf of bread.

baie, *n.f.* bay, creek; berry.

baigner, *vb.* bathe.

baigneur, *n.m.* bather.

baignoire (bēn wär), *n.f.* bathtub.

bail, *n.m.* lease.

bâillement, *n.m.* yawn.

bâiller, *vb.* yawn.

bâillon, *n.m.* gag.

bain, *n.m.* bath.

baïonnette, *n.f.* bayonet.

baiser, *n.m.* and *vb.* kiss.

baissé, *adj.* downcast.

baisser, *vb.* lower, sink.

bal, *n.m.* ball.

balai, *n.m.* broom. **b. à laver**, mop.

balance, *n.f.* scales, balance.

balancement, *n.m.* rocking, swinging.

balancer, *vb.* rock, swing, sway. **se b.**, roll, hover.

balayer, *vb.* sweep.

balbutier, *vb.* stammer.

balcon, *n.m.* balcony.

baldaquin, *n.m.* canopy.

baleine, *n.f.* whale.

ballade, *n.f.* ballad.

balle, *n.f.* bullet, ball; bale.

ballet, *n.m.* ballet.

ballon, *n.m.* balloon.

ballot, *n.m.* bundle.

ballotter, *vb.* shake.

balsamique, *adj.* balmy.

bambou, *n.m.* bamboo.

ban, *n.m.* ban. **mettre au b.**, ban.

banal, *adj.* trite.

banane, *n.f.* banana.

banc, *n.m.* bench.

bandage, *n.m.* bandage.

bande, *n.f.* strip, stripe; pack, gang, band.

bande vidéo, *n.f.* videotape.

bandit, *n.m.* bandit, robber, knave.

banlieue, *n.f.* suburbs.

bannière, *n.f.* banner.

bannir, *vb.* banish.

bannissement, *n.m.* banishment.

banque, *n.f.* bank. **billet de b.**, banknote.

banqueroute, *n.f.* bankruptcy.

banqueroutier, *n.* bankrupt.

banquet, *n.m.* banquet, feast.

banquier, *n.m.* banker.

baptême (bä tĕm), *n.m.* christening, baptism.

baptiser (bä tēt), *vb.* christen, baptize.

Baptiste (bä tēt), *n.m.* Baptist.

baptistère (bä tēs-), *n.m.* baptistery.

bar, *n.m.* bar; bass (fish).

baraque, *n.f.* booth, stall.

baratter, vb. churn.

barbare, 1. n.m.f. barbarian. 2. adj. barbarian, barbarous, wild.

barbarie, n.f. cruelty.

barbe, n.f. beard.

barbouiller, vb. daub, blur.

baromètre, n.m. barometer.

baron, n.m. baron.

barque, n.f. boat.

barrage, n.m. dam.

barre, n.f. bar, rail(ing). **b. du gouvernail**, helm.

barreau, n.m. bar.

barrer, vb. shut out.

barricade, n.f. barricade.

barrière, n.f. gate; bar, barrier; fence.

barrique, n.f. barrel, cask.

bas, n.m. stocking.

bas m., **basse** f. adj. base, low, soft. **en b.**, down(ward), downstairs. **b. côté**, aisle.

bascule, n.f. seesaw. **chaise à b.**, rocking-chair.

base, n.f. base, basis.

basse, n.f. bass (voice).

basse-cour, n.f. barnyard.

bassesse, n.f. baseness.

bassin, n.m. basin, dock.

bataille, n.f. battle.

bataillon, n.m. battalion.

bâtard, adj. and n.m. bastard.

bateau, n.m. boat.

bâtiment, n.m. building.

bâtir, vb. build.

bâton, n.m. stick, staff.

battant, n.m. flap, door.

batte, n.f. bat.

battement, n.m. beat.

batterie, n.f. battery.

battre, vb. beat, strike; flap, pulsate. **se b.**, fight.

baume, n.m. balm.

bavard, adj. talkative, gossipy.

bavardage, n.m. gossip, chatter.

bavarder, vb. gossip, chat(ter).

bavette, n.f. bib.

bazar, n.m. bazaar.

béatitude, n.f. bliss.

beau, bel m., **belle** f. adj. beautiful, handsome, fair, lovely, fine. **avoir beau**, (to do something) in vain. **faire beau**, be fine (weather).

beaucoup (de), adj. a lot, a great deal; much, many. **de b.**, by far.

beau-frère, n.m. brother-in-law.

beau-père, n.m. father-in-law.

beauté, n.f. beauty. **grain de b.**, mole.

bébé, n.m. baby.

bec, n.m. beak, bill; spot; burner.

bêche, n.f. spade.

bêcher, vb. dig.

becqueter, vb. peck.

bée, adj. **rester bouche b.**, stand gaping.

bégayer, vb. stammer.

bêler, vb. bleat.

Belge, n.m.f. Belgian.

belge, adj. Belgian.

Belgique, n.f. Belgium.

bélier, n.m. ram.

belle-fille, n.f. daughter-in-law.

belle-mère, n.f. mother-in-law; stepmother.

belligérant, adj. and n.m. belligerent.

bénédiction, n.f. blsessing, benediction.

bénéfice, n.m. benefit, advantage, profit.

bénéficier, vb. benefit, profit.

bénin m., **bénigne** f. adj. benign.

bénir, vb. bless.

béquille, n.f. crutch.

berceau, n.m. cradle, bower.

bercer, vb. rock.

berge, n.f. bank.

berger, n.m. shepherd.

besogne, n.f. (piece of) work.

besoin, n.m. need, want. **avoir b.**, need.

bestiaux, n.m.pl. cattle.

bétail, n.m. cattle, animals.

bête, 1. n.f. beast, animal. 2. adj. stupid, dumb.

bêtise, n.f. nonsense.

béton, n.m. concrete.

betterave, n.f. beet.

beurre, n.m. butter.

bévue, n.f. blunder, boner.

biais, n.m. slant; bias. **en b.**, at an angle.

bibelot, n.m. trinket.

biberon, n.m. baby's bottle.

Bible, n.f. Bible.

bibliothèque, n.f. library; bookcase.

biblique, adj. biblical.

bicyclette, n.f. bicycle. **faire de la b.**, cycle.

bidon, n.m. can.

bien, n.m. good; (pl.) goods,

property, estate. **faire du b. à**, benefit.

bien, *adv.* well. **b. entendu**, of course. **aller b.**, be well. **vouloir b.**, be willing. **b. que**, although.

bien-aimé, *n.m.f. and adj.* darling.

bien-être, *n.m.* welfare.

bienfaisant, *adj.* beneficent, kind, humane.

bienfait, *n.m.* benefit.

bienfaiteur, *n.m.* benefactor.

bienheureux, *adj.* blessed.

bientôt, *adv.* soon.

bienveillance, *n.f.* benevolence, kindness.

bienveillant, *adj.* benevolent, kindly.

bienvenu, *adj.* welcome.

bière, *n.f.* beer, ale.

biffer, *vb.* cancel, erase.

bifteck, *n.m.* beefsteak.

bigamie, *n.f.* bigamy.

bigot, *n.m.* bigot.

bigoterie, *n.f.* bigotry.

bijou, *n.m.* jewel.

bijouterie, *n.f.* jewelry.

bile, *n.f.* bile. **se faire de la b.**, worry.

billard, *n.m.* billiards.

bille, *n.f.* marble (toy).

billet, *n.m.* ticket, note. **b. de banque**, banknote.

billion (-l-), *n.m.* billion.

biographie, *n.f.* biography.

biologie, *n.f.* biology.

biscuit, *n.m.* biscuit.

bizarre, *adj.* queer, odd, strange.

blâme, *n.m.* blame.

blâmer, *vb.* blame.

blanc *m.,* **blanche** *f. adj.* white, blank. **en b.**, blank.

blancheur, *n.f.* whiteness.

blanchir, *vb.* whiten.

blanchisserie, *n.f.* laundry.

blasé, *adj.* sophisticated.

blasphème, *n.m.* blasphemy.

blasphémer, *vb.* curse, blaspheme.

blatte, *n.f.* cockroach.

blé, *n.m.* wheat.

blême, *adj.* pale.

blesser, *vb.* wound, hurt, injure.

blessure, *n.f.* wound, hurt, injury.

bleu, *adj.* blue; extremely rare (meat).

bloc, *n.m.* pad, block.

blocus (-s), *n.m.* blockade.

blond, *adj.* fair, blond(e).

bloquer, *vb.* block.

blottir, *vb.* **se b.**, cower.

blouse, *n.f.* blouse.

blue jeans, *n.m.pl.* blue jeans.

bluff, *n.m.* bluff.

bluffeur, *n.m.* bluffer.

bobine, *n.f.* spool, reel.

bœuf (bœf), *n.m.* ox, beef. **jeune b.**, steer.

Bohème, *n.f.* Bohemia.

bohème, **1.** *n.m.f.* bohemian, happy-go-lucky person. **2.** *n.f.* artistic underworld. **3.** *adj.* bohemian.

Bohémien, *n.m.* Bohemian; gypsy.

bohémien, *adj.* Bohemian.

boire, *vb.* drink. **b. à petits coups**, sip.

bois, *n.m.* wood, forest, lumber.

boiserie, *n.f.* woodwork.

boisseau, *n.m.* bushel.

boisson, *n.f.* beverage, drink.

boîte, *n.f.* box; can (food). **b. aux lettres**, mail-box.

boiter, *vb.* limp.

boiteux, *adj.* lame.

bol, *n.m.* bowl.

bombardement, *n.m.* bombardment.

bombarder, *vb.* bomb, bombard.

bombe, *n.f.* bomb, shell.

bombe à neutrons, *n.f.* neutron bomb.

bon *m.,* **bonne** *f. adj.* good, kind. **de b. heure**, early. **b. marché**, cheap.

bon, *n.m.* bond.

bonbon, *n.m.* candy, bonbon.

bond, *n.m.* bound, leap.

bonder, *vb.* overcrowd, jam.

bondir, *vb.* bound, leap, spring.

bonheur, *n.m.* happiness.

bonhomme, *n.m.* fellow.

bonjour, *interj. and n.m.* good morning.

bonne, *n.f.* maid.

bonnement, *adv.* simply.

bonnet, *n.m.* cap, hood.

bonsoir, *interj. and n.m.* good evening.

bonté, *n.f.* kindness, goodness.

bord, *n.m.* edge, rim, brim. **b. du toit**, eaves.

border, *vb.* bound, edge, border, hem.

borne, *n.f.* bound, limit.

borner, *vb.* bound, limit.

bosquet, *n.m.* clump (trees).

bosse, *n.f.* bump.

bosselure, *n.f.* dent.

bossu, *adj.* hunchbacked.

botanique, *n.f.* botany.

botte, *n.f.* boot; bunch.

bottine, *n.f.* boot.

bouche, *n.f.* mouth.

boucher, *vb.* stop up.

boucher, *n.m.* butcher.

boucherie, *n.f.* butcher shop.

bouchon, *n.m.* cork.

boucle, *n.f.* curl, loop, buckle. **b. d'oreille,** earring.

boucler, *vb.* curl.

bouclier, *n.m.* shield.

bouder, *vb.* sulk.

boue, *n.f.* mud.

bouée, *n.f.* buoy.

boueur, *n.m.* scavenger.

boueux, *adj.* muddy.

bouffée, *n.f.* puff.

bouffon, *n.m.* clown, fool.

bouffonerie, *n.f.* antic(s).

bouger, *vb.* stir, move, budge.

bougie, *n.f.* candle.

bouillir, *vb.* boil.

bouilloire, *n.f.* kettle.

bouillon, *n.m.* broth.

bouillonner, *vb.* bubble.

bouillotte, *n.f.* kettle.

boulanger, *n.m.* baker.

boulangerie, *n.f.* bakery.

boule, *n.f.* ball.

bouleau, *n.m.* birch.

bouledogue, *n.m.* bulldog.

boulevard, *n.m.* boulevard.

bouleversement, *n.m.* upset.

bouleverser, *vb.* upset, overturn.

bouquet, *n.m.* cluster, bunch, bouquet.

bouquiniste, *n.m.* (second-hand) bookseller.

bourbeux, *adj.* sloppy.

bourdon, *n.m.* bumblebee.

bourdonnement, *n.m.* buzz.

bourdonner, *vb.* hum, buzz.

bourg, *n.m.* borough, village.

bourgeois, *adj.* middle-class, bourgeois.

bourgeoisie, *n.f.* middle class.

bourgeon, *n.m.* bud.

bourgeonner, *vb.* bud.

bourre, *n.f.* stuffing.

bourreau, *n.m.* executioner, hangman; brute.

bourrelet, *n.m.* pad.

bourrer, *vb.* stuff, pad.

bourru, *adj.* gruff.

bourse, *n.f.* purse, bag; stock exchange; scholarship, fellowship.

boursoufler, *vb.* bloat.

bousculer, *vb.* jostle.

bousiller, *vb.* bungle.

boussole, *n.f.* compass.

bout, *n.m.* end, tip, butt, stub.

bouteille, *n.f.* bottle.

boutique, *n.f.* shop.

bouton, *n.m.* button, bud; pimple.

boutonnière, *n.f.* buttonhole.

boxe, *n.f.* boxing.

boxeur, *n.m.* boxer.

boycotter, *vb.* boycott.

bracelet, *n.m.* bracelet.

braconnier, *n.m.* poacher.

brailler, *vb.* bawl.

braise, *n.f.* coals, embers.

brancard, *n.m.* stretcher.

branche, *n.f.* branch, bough, limb.

brandir, *vb.* brandish.

branler, *vb.* waver.

braquer, *vb.* aim, point.

bras, *n.m.* arm.

brasse, *n.f.* fathom.

brasser, *vb.* brew.

brasserie, *n.f.* brewery, beer-joint.

bravade, *n.f.* bravado.

brave, *adj.* fine, good, brave.

braver, *vb.* brave, face, defy.

bravoure, *n.f.* courage.

brebis, *n.f.* lamb.

brèche, *n.f.* breach, gap.

bref, 1. *adj.m.,* **brève** *f.* brief, short. **2.** *adv.* in short.

Brésil, *n.m.* Brazil.

brevet, *n.m.* commission. **b. d'invention,** patent.

bribe, *n.f.* scrap, bit.

bride, *n.f.* bridle.

brider, *vb.* curb.

bridge, *n.m.* bridge (game).

brièveté, *n.f.* brevity.

brigade, *n.f.* brigade.

brigadier, *n.m.* corporal.

brigant, *n.m.* robber, knave.

brillant, *adj.* brilliant, bright, glowing.

briller, *vb.* shine, glisten, glare.
brin, *n.m.* blade (grass).
brindille, *n.f.* twig.
brioche, *n.f.* bun.
brique, *n.f.* brick.
briquet, *n.m.* lighter. **pierre à b.,** flint.
brise, *n.f.* breeze.
briser, *vb.* break, shatter, smash.
britannique, *adj.* British.
brocart, *n.m.* brocade.
broche, *n.f.* spit, spindle; brooch.
brochure, *n.f.* pamphlet.
broder, *vb.* embroider.
broderie, *n.f.* embroidery.
bronchite, *n.f.* bronchitis.
bronze, *n.m.* bronze.
broquette, *n.f.* tack.
brosse, *n.f.* brush.
brouhaha, *n.m.* uproar.
brouillard, *n.m.* fog, mist.
brouiller, *vb.* jumble, embroil; scramble (eggs). **se b.,** quarrel.
brouillon, *n.m.* (rough) draft.
broussailles, *n.f.pl.* brushwood.
brouter, *vb.* browse.
broyer, *vb.* crush.
bruine, *n.f.* drizzle.
bruiner, *vb.* drizzle.
bruissement, *n.m.* rustle.
bruit, *n.m.* noise, clatter; report, rumor.
brûler, *vb.* burn.
brume, *n.f.* mist. **b. légère,** haze.
brumeux, *adj.* foggy, misty.
brun, *adj.* brown.
brune, *adj. and n.f.* brunette.
brusque, *adj.* abrupt, curt, blunt, gruff, brusque.
brut, *adj.* crude, gross.
brutal, *adj.* brutal, savage.
brutalité, *n.f.* brutality.
brute, *n.f.* brute.
bruyant, *adj.* noisy, loud.
bruyère, *n.f.* heath, heather.
bûche, *n.f.* log.
bûcheron, *n.m.* wood-cutter.
budget, *n.m.* budget.
buffet, *n.m.* buffet.
buffle, *n.m.* buffalo.
buis, *n.m.* box (tree).
buisson, *n.m.* bush, thicket.
buissonneux, *adj.* bushy.
bulbe, *n.m.* bulb.
bulle, *n.f.* bubble; (papal) bull.
bulletin, *n.m.* bulletin, ticket.

bureau, *n.m.* office, bureau; desk.
 b. de location, box-office.
burin, *n.m.* chisel.
burlesque, *adj.* ludicrous.
buste, *n.m.* bust.
but, *n.m.* aim, goal, purpose.
butin, *n.m.* spoils, booty.
butte, *n.f.* hill, knoll.
buvard, *n.m.* blotter.

C

ça, *pron.* that.
cabane, *n.f.* cabin, hut.
cabaret, *n.m.* cabaret, tavern.
cabine, *n.f.* cabin, booth.
cabinet, *n.m.* closet; office. **c. de toilette,** lavatory. **c. de travail,** study.
câble, *n.m.* cable, rope.
câbler, *vb.* cable.
câblogramme, *n.m.* cablegram.
cacao, *n.m.* cocoa.
cacher, *vb.* hide, conceal. **se c.,** lurk.
cachet, *n.m.* seal.
cadavre, *n.m.* corpse.
cadeau, *n.m.* gift, present.
cadence, *n.f.* cadence.
cadet, 1. *n.m.* cadet. **2.** *adj.* junior.
cadran, *n.m.* dial.
cadre, *n.m.* frame.
café, *n.m.* coffee; café.
cage, *n.f.* cage.
cahier, *n.m.* notebook.
caille, *n.f.* quail.
caillot, *n.m.* clot.
caillou, *n.m.* pebble.
caisse, *n.f.* crate, case, box.
caissier, *n.m.* cashier, teller.
cajoler, *vb.* coax.
calamité, *n.f.* calamity.
calcium, *n.m.* calcium.
calcul, *n.m.* calculation.
calculer, *vb.* figure, reckon, calculate.
cale, *n.f.* hold.
calembour, *n.m.* pun.
calendrier, *n.m.* calendar.
calibre, *n.m.* caliber.
calicot, *n.m.* calico.
callosité, *n.f.* callus.
calme, *n.m. and adj.* quiet, calm.
calmer, *vb.* soothe, quiet, calm.
calomnie, *n.f.* slander.

calomnier, *vb.* slander.

calorie, *n.f.* calorie.

calotte, *n.f.* crown (of hat).

Calvaire, *n.m.* Calvary.

camarade, *n.m.f.* comrade, companion, mate.

camaraderie, *n.f.* companionship, fellowship.

cambrioleur, *n.m.* burglar.

camion, *n.m.* truck.

camoufler, *vb.* camouflage.

camp, *n.m.* camp.

campagnard, 1. *n.m.* countryman, peasant. **2.** *adj.* peasant.

campagne, *n.f.* country; campaign.

camper, *vb.* camp.

camphre, *n.m.* camphor.

Canada, *n.m.* Canada.

Canadien, *n.m.* Canadian.

canadien, *adj.* Canadian.

canaille, *n.f.* rabble; scoundrel.

canal, *n.m.* channel, canal.

canapé, *n.m.* sofa, couch; canapé.

canard, *n.m.* duck.

canari, *n.m.* canary.

cancer (-r), *n.m.* cancer.

cancérogène, *adj.* carcinogenic.

candeur, *n.f.* purity; candor.

candidat, *n.m.* candidate, applicant.

candidature, *n.f.* candidacy.

candide, *adj.* frank, open, candid.

canevas, *n.m.* canvas. **gros c.,** burlap.

canin, *adj.* canine.

canne, *n.f.* cane, stick.

canneberge, *n.f.* cranberry.

cannelle, *n.f.* cinnamon.

cannibale, *adj.* and *n.m.f.* cannibal.

canoë (-ō ā), *n.m.* canoe.

canon, *n.m.* cannon.

canot, *n.m.* boat, canoe. **c. automobile,** motorboat.

cantaloup, *n.m.* cantaloupe.

cantique, *n.m.* hymn.

canton, *n.m.* district, canton.

caoútchouc (-chŏō), *n.m.* rubber.

cap (-p), *n.m.* cape (headland).

capable, *adj.* efficient, fit, capable, competent.

capacité, *n.f.* capability, capacity.

cape, *n.f.* cape (clothing).

capitaine, *n.m.* captain.

capital, *n.m.* and *adj.* capital.

capitale, *n.f.* capital (city).

capitaliser, *vb.* capitalize.

capitalisme, *n.m.* capitalism.

capitaliste, *n.m.f.* capitalist.

caporal, *n.m.* corporal.

capote, *n.f.* hood.

câpre, *n.f.* caper.

caprice, *n.m.* whim, fancy.

capricieux, *adj.* fickle, capricious.

capsule, *n.f.* capsule.

captif, *adj.* and *n.m.* captive.

captiver, *vb.* captivate, charm.

captivité, *n.f.* captivity.

capture, *n.f.* capture.

capturer, *vb.* capture.

capuchon, *n.m.* hood.

car, *conj.* for.

caractère, *n.m.* character, nature, disposition; type.

caractériser, *vb.* characterize; distinguish; mark.

caractéristique, *adj.* characteristic.

carafe, *n.f.* decanter, water-bottle.

caramel, *n.m.* caramel.

carat, *n.m.* carat.

caravane, *n.f.* caravan.

carbone, *n.m.* carbon.

carboniser, *vb.* char.

carburateur, *n.m.* carburetor.

carcasse, *n.f.* shell; carcass.

cardinal, *n.m.* cardinal.

carême, *n.m.* Lent.

caresse, *n.f.* caress.

caresser, *vb.* fondle, stroke, caress.

cargaison, *n.f.* cargo.

caricature, *n.f.* caricature.

carie, *n.f.* decay.

carillon, *n.m.* chime.

carillonner, *vb.* chime.

carnaval, *n.m.* carnival.

carnet, *n.m.* notebook.

carnivore, *adj.* carnivorous.

carotte, *n.f.* carrot.

carré, *n.m.* and *adj.* square.

carreau, *n.m.* diamond (cards); pane; tile.

carrefour, *n.m.* crossroads.

carrière, *n.f.* career; scope; quarry.

carriole, *n.f.* (light) cart.

carrosse, *n.m.* coach.

carte, *n.f.* chart, map, card. **c. de crédit,** *n.f.* credit card. **c. du jour,** bill of fare.

carton, *n.m.* cardboard; box, carton.

cartouche, *n.f.* cartridge.

cas, *n.m.* case; event.

case, *n.f.* pigeonhole; hut, shed.

caserne, *n.f.* barracks.

casque, *n.m.* helmet.

casquette, *n.f.* cap.

cassable, *adj.* breakable.

casse-croûte, *n.m.* snack.

casser, *vb.* break, crack.

casserole, *n.f.* pan.

cassette, *n.f.* **1.** casket. **2.** cassette.

cassis, *n.m.* black currant.

caste, *n.f.* caste.

castor, *n.m.* beaver.

casuel, *adj.* casual.

catalogue, *n.m.* catalogue.

cataracte, *n.f.* cataract.

catarrhe, *n.m.* catarrh.

catastrophe, *n.f.* disaster, catastrophe.

catéchisme, *n.m.* catechism.

catégorie, *n.f.* category.

cathédrale, *n.f.* cathedral.

catholicisme, *n.m.* Catholicism.

catholique, *adj.* Catholic.

cauchemar, *n.m.* nightmare.

cause, *n.f.* case; cause.

causer, *vb.* chat; cause.

causerie, *n.f.* chat, talk.

causette, *n.f.* chat.

caution, *n.f.* bail, security.

cavalerie, *n.f.* cavalry.

cavalier, *n.m.* rider, horseman; escort.

cave, *n.f.* cellar, cavern.

cavité, *n.f.* cavity.

ce (sə), **cet** (sĕt) *m.,* **cette** (sĕt) *f.,* **ces** (sā) *pl. adj.* that, this.

ceci, *pron.* this.

cécité, *n.f.* blindness.

céder, *vb.* yield, give in, cede.

cèdre, *n.m.* cedar.

ceindre, *vb.* gird.

ceinture, *n.f.* belt, sash.

cela, *pron.* that.

célébration, *n.f.* celebration.

célèbre, *adj.* famous, noted.

célébrer, *vb.* celebrate.

célébrité, *n.f.* celebrity.

céleri, *n.m.* celery.

céleste, *adj.* heavenly, celestial.

célibataire, 1. *n.m.* bachelor. **2.** *adj.* single.

celle, *pron. f.* See **celui.**

cellule, *n.f.* cell.

celluloïd (-lô ēd), *n.m.* celluloid.

celtique, *adj.* Celtic.

celui *m.,* **celle** *f.,* **ceux** *m.pl.,* **celles** *f.pl. pron.* the one. **celui-ci,** this one; the latter. **celui-là,** that one; the former.

cendre, *n.f.* ashes, cinders.

cendrier, *n.m.* ash-tray.

censeur, *n.m.* censor.

censure, *n.f.* censure.

censurer, *vb.* censor.

cent, *adj.* and *n.m.* hundred. **pour c.,** percent.

centaine, *n.f.* hundred.

centenaire, *adj.* and *n.m.* centenary, centennial.

centième, *adj.* hundredth.

centigrade, *adj.* centigrade.

centimètre, *n.m.* centimeter.

central, *adj.* central.

centraliser, *vb.* centralize.

centre, *n.m.* center.

cependant, *adv.* however, still, yet.

cercle, *n.m.* circle, ring, hoop; club.

cercueil, *n.m.* coffin.

céréale, *adj.* and *n.f.* cereal.

cérémonial, *adj.* and *n.m.* ceremonial.

cérémonie, *n.f.* ceremony. **sans c.,** informal.

cérémonieux, *adj.* formal, ceremonious.

cerf (sĕr), *n.m.* deer.

cerf-volant, *n.m.* kite.

cerise, *n.f.* cherry.

certain, *adj.* certain, sure; *(pl.)* some.

certes, *adv.* indeed.

certificat, *n.m.* credentials; certificate.

certifier, *vb.* certify.

certitude, *n.f.* certainty, assurance.

cerveau, *n.m.* brain.

cervelle, *n.f.* brains.

cessation, *n.f.* stopping, cessation.

cesser, *vb.* stop, desist, cease.

cession, *n.f.* assignment (law).

cet, cette, *pron.* See **ce.**

chacun, *pron.* everybody, everyone; each; apiece.

chagrin, 1. *n.m.* grief, vexation. **2.** *adj.* fretful.

chagriner, vb. grieve.
chaîne, n.f. chain; range.
chaînon, n.m. link.
chair, n.f. flesh.
chaire, n.f. pulpit, rostrum.
chaise, n.f. chair.
chaland, n.m. barge.
châle, n.m. shawl.
chaleur, n.f. warmth, heat, glow.
chaloupe, n.f. launch.
chambre, n.f. room; chamber;
House (parliament). **c. à cou-**
cher, bedroom.
chameau, n.m. camel.
chamois, n.m. chamois.
champ, n.m. field.
champignon, n.m. mushroom.
champion, n.m. champion.
championnat, n.m. championship.
chance, n.f. luck, risk, chance.
chanceler, vb. stagger, reel.
chancelier, n.m. chancellor.
chandail, n.m. sweater.
chandelier, n.m. candlestick.
chandelle, n.f. candle.
change, n.m. exchange.
changeant, adj. changeable.
changement, n.m. change, shift.
changer, vb. alter, shift, change.
chanson, n.f. song.
chant, n.m. song, chant. **c. du**
coq, cock-crow.
chantage, n.m. blackmail.
chanter, vb. sing, chant.
chanteur, n.m. singer.
chantier, n.m. (work)yard.
chaos (k-), n.m. chaos.
chaotique (k-), adj. chaotic.
chapeau, n.m. hat, bonnet.
chapelle, n.f. chapel.
chaperon, n.m. chaperon.
chapiteau, n.m. capital.
chapitre, n.m. chapter.
chapon, n.m. capon.
chaque, adj. every, each.
char, n.m. chariot. **c. d'assaut,**
(military) tank.
charbon, n.m. coal. **c. de bois,**
charcoal.
charcuterie, n.f. delicatessen.
charge, n.f. load, charge.
charger, vb. load, burden, charge.
chariot, n.m. wagon; baggage
cart.
charisme, n.m. charisma.
charitable, adj. charitable.

charité, n.f. charity.
charlatan, n.m. charlatan.
charmant, adj. delightful, lovely,
charming.
charme, n.m. spell, charm.
charmer, vb. charm.
charnel, adj. carnal.
charnu, adj. fleshy.
charpente, n.f. framework.
charpentier, n.m. carpenter.
charretier, n.m. carter.
charrette, n.f. cart.
charrue, n.f. plow.
charte, n.f. charter.
chasse, n.f. hunt(ing), chase.
châsse, n.f. shrine.
chasser, vb. hunt, chase; drive
away.
chasseur, n.m. hunter; bellboy.
châssis, n.m. (window) sash.
chaste, adj. chaste.
chasteté, n.f. chastity.
chat m., **chatte** f. n. cat.
châtaigne, n.f. chestnut.
château, n.m. mansion, castle.
châtier, vb. punish, chastise.
chatouiller, vb. tickle.
chatouilleux, adj. ticklish.
chaud, adj. hot, warm.
chaudière, n.f. boiler.
chauffage, n.m. heating.
chauffer, vb. heat, warm.
chauffeur, n.m. driver, chauffeur.
chaumière, n.f. cottage.
chaussée, n.f. road.
chausser, vb. wear shoes. **se c.,**
put on shoes.
chaussette, n.f. sock.
chaussure, n.f. footgear.
chauve, adj. bald.
chauve-souris, n.f. bat.
chaux, n.f. lime.
chavirer, vb. capsize.
chef, n.m. leader, chief.
chef-d'œuvre (shě-), n.m. masterpiece.
chemin, n.m. road. **c. de fer,** railway. **à mi-c.,** halfway. **c. de ta-**
ble, table-runner.
chemineau, n.m. tramp.
cheminée, n.f. fireplace, chimney; funnel.
chemise, n.f. shirt. **c. de nuit,**
nightgown.
chêne, n.m. oak.
chenille, n.f. caterpillar.
chèque, n.m. check.

chèque de voyage, *n.m.* traveler's check.

cher (-r), *adj.* dear, expensive.

chercher, *vb.* seek, look for, search. **aller c.,** fetch.

chère, *n.f.* fare.

chéri, *adj. and n.m.* beloved, darling.

chérir, *vb.* cherish.

cheval, *n.m.* horse. **à c.,** on horseback. **monter à c.,** ride (horseback). **fer à c.,** horseshoe.

chevaleresque, *adj.* chivalrous.

chevalerie, *n.f.* chivalry.

chevalet, *n.m.* easel; knight.

chevalier, *n.m.* knight.

cheveu, *n.m., pl.* **cheveux,** hair.

cheville, *n.f.* ankle; peg.

chèvre, *n.f.* goat.

chevreau, *n.m.* kid.

chevreuil, *n.m.* roe.

chevron, *n.m.* rafter.

chevroter, *vb.* quaver.

chevrotine, *n.f.* buckshot.

chez, *prep.* at . . .'s (house, office, shop, etc.).

chic, *adj.* stylish.

chien, *n.m.* dog.

chienne, *n.f.* bitch.

chiffon, *n.m.* rag.

chiffonner, *vb.* crumple.

chiffre, *n.m.* figure.

chiffrer, *vb.* figure.

Chili, *n.m.* Chile.

Chilien, *n.m.* Chilean.

chilien, *adj.* Chilean.

chimie, *n.f.* chemistry.

chimiothérapie, *n.f.* chemotherapy.

chimique, *adj.* chemical.

chimiste, *n.m.f.* chemist.

Chine, *n.f.* China.

Chinois, *n.m.* Chinese (person).

chinois, 1. *n.m.* Chinese (language). **2.** *adj.* Chinese.

chiquenaude, *n.f.* flip.

chirurgie, *n.f.* surgery.

chirurgien, *n.m.* surgeon.

chloroforme (k-), *n.m.* chloroform.

choc, *n.m.* shock, clash, brunt.

chocolat, *n.m.* chocolate.

chœur (k-), *n.m.* choir, chorus.

choisir, *vb.* choose, select, pick.

choix, *n.m.* choice.

chômage, *n.m.* stoppage (of work).

choquer, *vb.* shock, clash.

choral (k-), *adj.* choral.

chose, *n.f.* thing, matter. **quelque c.,** anything.

chou, *n.m.* cabbage.

chou-fleur, *n.m.* cauliflower.

choyer, *vb.* pamper.

chrétien (k-), *adj. and n.m.* Christian.

chrétienté (k-), *n.f.* Christendom.

christianisme (k-), *n.m.* Christianity.

chronique (k-), **1.** *n.f.* chronicle. **2.** *adj.* chronic.

chronologique (k-), *adj.* chronological.

chrysanthème (k-), *n.m.* chrysanthemum.

chuchoter, *vb.* whisper.

chute, *n.f.* fall, drop, downfall.

cible, *n.f.* target.

cicatrice, *n.f.* scar.

cidre, *n.m.* cider.

ciel, *n.m., pl.* **cieux,** heaven, sky.

cierge, *n.m.* (church) candle.

cigale, *n.f.* locust.

cigare, *n.m.* cigar.

cigarette, *n.f.* cigarette.

cigogne, *n.f.* stork.

ci-joint, *adj.* enclosed.

cil (-l), *n.m.* eyelash.

cime, *n.f.* top, summit.

ciment, *n.m.* cement.

cimenter, *vb.* cement.

cimetière, *n.m.* churchyard, cemetery.

cinéma, *n.m.* cinema.

cinglant, *adj.* scathing.

cinq (-k), *adj. and n.m.* five.

cinquante, *adj. and n.m.* fifty.

cinquième, *adj. and n.m.* fifth.

cintre, *n.m.* semicircle; arch.

circonférence, *n.f.* circumference.

circonscription, *n.f.* **c. électorale,** borough.

circonscrire, *vb.* circumscribe.

circonstance, *n.f.* event, circumstance. **c. critique,** emergency.

circuit, *n.m.* circuit. **hors c.,** disconnected.

circulaire, *adj.* circular.

circulation, *n.f.* traffic, circulation.

circuler, *vb.* circulate, turn, revolve.

cire, *n.f.* wax.

cirer, *vb.* polish, shine.

cireur, *n.m.* bootblack.

cirque, *n.m.* circus.

cisailles, *n.f.pl.* shears.

ciseau, *n.m.* chisel; *(pl.)* scissors.

ciseler, *vb.* chisel.

citadelle, *n.f.* citadel.

citation, *n.f.* quotation, citation.

cité, *n.f.* city. **droit de c.,** citizenship.

citer, *vb.* quote, cite.

citoyen, *n.m.* citizen.

citron, *n.m.* lemon. **c. pressé,** lemonade.

citrouille, *n.f.* pumpkin.

civil (-l), **1.** *n.m.* civilian. **2.** *adj.* civil.

civilisation, *n.f.* civilization.

civilisé, *adj.* civilized.

civiliser, *vb.* civilize.

civique, *adj.* civic.

clair, *adj.* clear, bright. **c. de lune,** moonlight.

clairière, *n.f.* glade, clearing.

clairon, *n.m.* bugle.

clameur, *n.f.* clamor, outcry.

clandestin, *adj.* clandestine.

clapoteux, *adj.* choppy (sea).

claque, *n.f.* slap.

claquement, *n.m.* smack.

claquer, *vb.* slap, smack, chatter (teeth), bang.

clarifier, *vb.* clarify.

clarinette, *n.f.* clarinet.

clarté, *n.f.* clarity; light.

classe, *n.f.* class.

classement, *n.m.* classification.

classer, *vb.* classify, order, file, grade.

classeur, *n.m.* file.

classification, *n.f.* classification.

classifier, *vb.* classify.

classique, *adj.* classic, classical.

clause, *n.f.* clause.

clavicule, *n.f.* collarbone.

clef (klā), clé, *n.f.* key.

clémence, *n.f.* clemency.

clément, *adj.* merciful.

clerc, *n.m.* clerk.

clergé, *n.m.* clergy.

clérical, *adj.* clerical.

cliché, *n.m.* cliché; snapshot.

client, *n.m.* customer, patron, client.

clientèle, *n.f.* customers, practice.

cligner (de l'œil), *vb.* wink.

clignoter, *vb.* blink, wink.

climat, *n.m.* climate.

climatisation, *n.f.* air-conditioning.

climatiser, *vb.* air-condition.

clin, *n.m.* **c. d'œil,** wink.

clinique, 1. *n.f.* clinic. **2.** *adj.* clinical.

cloche, *n.f.* bell.

clocher, *n.m.* belfry. **de c.,** parochial.

cloison, *n.f.* partition.

cloître, *n.m.* cloister, convent.

clôture, *n.f.* fence.

clou, *n.m.* nail.

clouer, *vb.* nail, tack.

club (-b), *n.m.* club.

coaguler, *vb.* coagulate.

coalition, *n.f.* coalition.

coasser, *vb.* croak (frogs).

cocaïne, *n.f.* cocaine.

cochon, *n.m.* pig.

coco, *n.m.* **noix de c.,** coconut.

cocon, *n.m.* cocoon.

code, *n.m.* code; laws.

code postal, *n.m.* zip code.

cœur, *n.m.* heart.

coffre, *n.m.* bin; coffer.

cogner, *vb.* bump, strike, run into, knock (down).

cohérent, *adj.* coherent.

cohésion, *n.f.* cohesion.

coiffer, *vb.* dress (hair).

coiffeur, *n.m.* hairdresser, barber.

coiffure, *n.f.* hair-do.

coin, *n.m.* corner, wedge.

coïncidence (kō ăn-), *n.f.* coincidence.

coïncider (kō ăn-), *vb.* coincide.

col, *n.m.* collar; pass.

colère, *n.f.* anger, temper. **en c.,** angry.

colimaçon, *n.m.* snail.

colis, *n.m.* parcel.

collaborateur, *n.m.* fellow-worker.

collaboration, *n.f.* assistance, collaboration.

collaborer, *vb.* work together, collaborate.

collant, *n.m.* panty hose.

collatéral, *adj. and n.m.* collateral.

colle, *n.f.* glue, paste.

collecte, *n.f.* collection.

collectif, *adj.* collective.

collection, *n.f.* collection.

collectionneur, *n.m.* collector.

collège, *n.m.* college.

collègue, *n.m.f.* colleague.
coller, *vb.* glue, paste, stick.
collier, *n.m.* necklace; collar (dog).
colline, *n.f.* hill.
collision, *n.f.* collision.
colombe, *n.f.* dove.
colon, *n.m.* settler, colonist.
colonel, *n.m.* colonel.
colonial, *adj.* colonial.
colonie, *n.f.* settlement, colony.
coloniser, *vb.* colonize.
colonne, *n.f.* column.
coloré, *adj.* colorful.
colorer, *vb.* color.
colossal, *adj.* huge, colossal.
colosse, *n.m.* giant, colossus.
colporter, *n.m.* peddle.
colporteur, *n.m.* peddler.
combat, *n.m.* fight, battle. **hors de c.,** disabled.
combattant, *adj. and n.m.* combatant.
combattre, *vb.* fight.
combien (de), *adv.* how much, how many.
combinaison, *n.f.* combination, slip, B.V.D.'s.
combiner, *vb.* devise, combine.
comble, *n.m.* climax, top.
combler, *vb.* heap up, fill.
combustible, 1. *n.m.* fuel. **2.** *adj.* combustible.
combustion, *n.f.* combustion.
comédie, *n.f.* comedy.
comédien, *n.m.* actor, comedian.
comestible, *adj.* edible.
comète, *n.f.* comet.
comique, *adj.* funny, comic(al).
comité, *n.m.* committee.
commandant, *n.m.* major, commander.
commande, *n.f.* order; commission.
commandement, *n.m.* command, commandment.
commander, *vb.* order, command.
commanditer, *vb.* finance.
comme, 1. *adv.* as, how. **2.** *prep.* as, like. **c. il faut,** proper, decent.
commémoratif, *adj.* memorial.
commémorer, *vb.* commemorate.
commençant, *n.m.* beginner.
commencement, *n.m.* beginning, start.
commencer, *vb.* begin, start.
comment, *adv.* how.

commentaire, *n.m.* comment, commentary.
commentateur, *n.m.* commentator.
commenter, *vb.* comment on.
commerçant, *n.m.* trader.
commerce, *n.m.* trade, commerce.
commercer, *vb.* trade.
commercial, *adj.* commercial.
commettre, *vb.* commit.
commis, *n.m.* clerk.
commissaire, *n.m.* commissary, commissioner.
commission, *n.f.* errand, commission.
commode, 1. *n.f.* dresser, bureau. **2.** *adj.* handy, convenient, comfortable.
commodité, *n.f.* convenience.
commun, *adj.* joint, common.
communauté, *n.f.* community.
commune, *n.f.* commune, town(ship).
communicatif, *adj.* communicative.
communication, *n.f.* communication.
communion, *n.f.* communion.
communiquer, *vb.* communicate.
communisme, *n.m.* communism.
communiste, *adj. and n.m.f.* communist.
compacité, *n.f.* compactness.
compact (-kt), *adj.* compact.
compagne, *n.f.* mate, companion.
compagnie, *n.f.* company.
compagnon, *n.m.* mate, fellow, companion.
comparable, *adj.* comparable.
comparaison, *n.f.* comparison.
comparaître, *vb.* appear.
comparatif, *adj. and n.m.* comparative.
comparer, *vb.* compare.
compartiment, *n.m.* compartment.
compas, *n.m.* compass.
compassion, *n.f.* sympathy, compassion.
compatible, *adj.* compatible.
compatissant, *adj.* sympathetic, compassionate.
compatriote, *n.m.f.* compatriot.
compensation, *n.f.* amends; compensation.
compenser, *vb.* compensate.

compétence, *n.f.* qualification, efficiency, competence.

compiler, *vb.* compile.

complaire, *vb.* please.

complaisance, *n.f.* kindness, compliance.

complaisant, *adj.* obliging, kind.

complément, *n.m.* object; complement.

complet, 1. *n.m.* suit. **2.** *adj.* full, thorough, complete.

compléter, *vb.* complete.

complexe, *adj. and n.m.* complex.

complexité, *n.f.* complexity.

complication, *n.f.* complication.

complice, *n.m.f.* party to, accomplice.

compliqué, *adj.* intricate, involved, complicated.

compliquer, *vb.* complicate.

complot, *n.m.* plot.

comporter, *vb.* **se c.,** act, behave.

composant, *adj. and n.m.* component.

composé, *adj. and n.m.* compound.

composer, *vb.* compound, compose.

compositeur, *n.m.* composer.

composition, *n.f.* essay, theme, composition.

compote, *n.f.* stewed fruit.

compréhensif, *adj.* comprehensive.

compréhension, *n.f.* comprehension.

comprendre, *vb.* understand, realize, comprise, include. **c. mal,** misunderstand.

compresse, *n.f.* compress.

compression, *n.f.* compression.

comprimer, *vb.* compress.

compromettre, *vb.* compromise.

compromis, *n.m.* compromise.

comptabilité, *n.f.* accounting, bookkeeping.

comptable, *n.m.* accountant.

compte, *n.m.* account, count. **rendre c. de,** account for. **tenir c. de,** allow for.

compter, *vb.* count, reckon. **c. sur,** rely on.

compteur, *n.m.* meter.

comptoir, *n.m.* counter.

comte, *n.m.* count.

comtesse, *n.f.* countess.

concave, *adj.* concave.

concéder, *vb.* grant, concede.

concentration, *n.f.* concentration.

concentrer, *vb.* condense, concentrate.

concept (-pt), *n.m.* concept.

conception, *n.f.* conception.

concernant, *prep.* concerning.

concerner, *vb.* concern.

concert, *n.m.* concert.

concession, *n.f.* grant, license, admission, concession.

concevable, *adj.* conceivable.

concevoir, *vb.* conceive, imagine.

concierge, *n.m.f.* janitor, doorkeeper, porter.

concile, *n.m.* council.

conciliation, *n.f.* conciliation.

concilier, *vb.* reconcile, conciliate.

concis, *adj.* concise.

concision, *n.f.* conciseness.

concluant, *adj.* conclusive.

conclure, *vb.* complete, conclude, infer.

conclusion, *n.f.* conclusion.

concombre, *n.m.* cucumber.

concourir, *vb.* concur, contribute, contend.

concours, *n.m.* contest.

concret, *adj.* concrete.

concurrence, *n.f.* competition.

concurrent, *n.m.* rival, competitor.

condamnation (-dä nä-), *n.f.* conviction, condemnation, sentence.

condamner (-dä nä), *vb.* convict, doom, condemn, sentence.

condensation, *n.f.* condensation.

condenser, *vb.* condense.

condescendance, *n.f.* condescension.

condescendre, *vb.* condescend.

condition, *n.f.* condition.

conditionnel, *adj. and n.m.* conditional.

conditionner, *vb.* condition.

condoléance, *n.f.* condolence. **faire ses c.s à,** condole with.

condominium, *n.m.* condominium.

conducteur, *n.m.* conductor.

conduire, *vb.* lead, take, drive, conduct. **se c.,** behave, act.

conduite, *n.f.* behavior, conduct.

cône, *n.m.* cone.

cône de charge, *n.m.* warhead.

confection, *n.f.* making (e.g. clothes); ready-made garment.

confédération, *n.f.* confederacy, confederation.

confédéré, *adj. and n.m.* confederate.

conférence, *n.f.* lecture, talk, conference.

conférer, *vb.* confer, grant.

confesser, *vb.* confess, admit.

confesseur, *n.m.* confessor.

confession, *n.f.* denomination; confession.

confiance, *n.f.* trust, belief, confidence. **digne de c.,** dependable.

confiant, *adj.* confident.

confidence, *n.f.* confidence.

confident, *n.m.* confidant.

confidentiel, *adj.* confidential.

confier, *vb.* confide, entrust. **se c. à,** trust.

confiner, *vb.* confine, limit.

confirmation, *n.f.* confirmation.

confirmer, *vb.* confirm.

confiserie, *n.f.* confectionery.

confisquer, *vb.* confiscate.

confiture, *n.f.* jam, jelly.

conflit, *n.m.* conflict.

confondre, *vb.* confuse, confound.

conforme, *adj.* similar.

conformer, *vb.* conform. **se c. à,** comply with.

conformité, *n.f.* accordance.

confort, *n.m.* comfort.

confortable, *adj.* cozy, snug, comfortable.

confronter, *vb.* confront.

confus, *adj.* confused.

confusion, *n.f.* confusion.

congé, *n.m.* discharge; leave of absence.

congédier, *vb.* discharge, dismiss.

congélateur, *n.m.* freezer.

congeler, *vb.* congeal.

congestion, *n.f.* congestion.

conglomération, *n.f.* conglomeration.

congrès, *n.m.* congress, assembly, conference.

conjecture, *n.f.* guess, conjecture.

conjonction, *n.f.* conjunction.

conjugaison, *n.f.* conjugation.

conjuguer, *vb.* conjugate.

conjuration, *n.f.* conspiracy.

conjurer, *vb.* conspire, plot.

connaissance, *n.f.* knowledge, acquaintance. **sans c.,** unconscious. **faire la c. de,** meet.

connaisseur, *n.m.* connoisseur.

connaître, *vb.* be acquainted with, know.

connexion, *n.f.* connection.

conquérir, *vb.* conquer.

conquête, *n.f.* conquest.

consacrer, *vb.* consecrate, devote, dedicate, hallow.

conscience, *n.f.* conscience, consciousness.

consciencieux, *adj.* conscientious.

conscient, *adj.* conscious.

conscription, *n.f.* draft.

conscrit, *adj. and n.m.* conscript.

consécration, *n.f.* consecration.

consécutif, *adj.* consecutive.

conseil, *n.m.* advice, counsel; council, board; staff.

conseiller, 1. *vb.* advise, counsel. **2.** *n.m.* advisor.

consentement, *n.m.* consent.

consentir, *vb.* consent, assent, accede.

conséquence, *n.f.* outgrowth, result, consequence.

conséquent, *adj.* consequent, consistent. **par c.,** consequently.

conservateur, *adj. and n.m.* conservative.

conservation, *n.f.* conservation.

conserve, *n.f.* conserve, pickle.

conserver, *vb.* conserve, keep; preserve, can.

considérable, *adj.* considerable.

considération, *n.f.* consideration.

considérer, *vb.* consider.

consigne, *n.m.* check-room; *(mil.)* orders.

consigne automatique, *n.f.* (luggage) locker.

consigner, *vb.* consign.

consistance, *n.f.* consistency.

consistant, *adj.* consistent.

consister, *vb.* consist.

consolateur, *n.m.* comforter.

consolation, *n.f.* comfort, solace.

console, *n.f.* bracket.

consoler, *vb.* comfort, console.

consolider, *vb.* consolidate, strengthen.

consommateur, *n.m.* consumer.

consommation, *n.f.* consumption; end, consummation.

consommé, *adj.* consummate.

consommer, *vb.* consummate, complete, consume.

consomption, *n.f.* consumption.

consonne, *n.f.* consonant.

conspirateur, *n.m.* conspirator.

conspiration, *n.f.* conspiration.

conspirer, *vb.* conspire.

constamment, *adv.* continually, constantly.

constance, *n.f.* constancy, firmness.

constant, *adj.* constant, firm.

constater, *vb.* observe, state as a fact.

constellation, *n.f.* constellation.

consternation, *n.f.* dismay.

consterné, *adj.* aghast.

consterner, *vb.* dismay.

constipation, *n.f.* constipation.

constituant, *adj.* constituent.

constituer, *vb.* constitute.

constitution, *n.f.* constitution.

constitutionnel, *adj.* constitutional.

constructeur, *n.m.* builder.

constructif, *adj.* constructive.

construction, *n.f.* construction.

construire, *vb.* construct, build.

consul, *n.m.* consul.

consulat, *n.m.* consulate.

consultation, *n.f.* consultation.

consulter, *vb.* consult.

consumer, *vb.* consume.

contact (-kt), *n.m.* touch, contact.

contagieux, *adj.* contagious.

contagion, *n.f.* contagion.

contaminer, *vb.* contaminate.

conte, *n.m.* tale, story.

contemplation, *n.f.* contemplation.

contempler, *vb.* survey, observe, contemplate.

contemporain, *adj.* contemporary.

contenance, *n.f.* compass, capacity.

contenir, *vb.* hold, restrain, contain.

content de, *adj.* glad of, contented with. **c. de soi-même,** complacent.

contentement, *n.m.* contentment), satisfaction. **c. de soi-même,** complacency.

contenter, *vb.* please, satisfy.

contenu, *n.m.* contents.

conter, *vb.* tell.

contester, *vb.* challenge (dispute), object to, contest.

contexte, *n.m.* context.

contigu, *adj.* adjoining.

continent, *n.m.* continent.

continental, *adj.* continental.

contingent, *n.m.* quota.

continu, *adj.* continuous.

continuation, *n.f.* continuation, continuance.

continuel, *adj.* continual.

continuer, *vb.* carry on, keep on, go on, continue.

continuité, *n.f.* continuity.

contour, *n.m.* outline.

contourner, *vb.* go round.

contracter, *vb.* contract.

contraction, *n.f.* contraction.

contradiction, *n.f.* discrepancy, contradiction.

contradictoire, *adj.* contradictory.

contraindre, *vb.* coerce, force.

contrainte, *n.f.* compulsion.

contraire, 1. *n.m.* reverse. **2.** *adj.* contrary. **au c.,** on the contrary.

contrarier, *vb.* thwart, vex, annoy, oppose, keep (from).

contrariété, *n.f.* annoyance.

contraste, *n.m.* contrast.

contraster, *vb.* contrast.

contrat, *n.m.* contract.

contre, *prep.* against.

contre-balancer, *vb.* counterbalance.

contrebande, *n.f.* smuggling; contraband.

contre-cœur, *adv.* **à c.,** unwillingly.

contredire, *vb.* contradict.

contrée, *n.f.* district, province.

contrefaire, *vb.* forge, counterfeit.

contrefort, *n.m.* buttress.

contremaître, *n.m.* foreman.

contre-partie, *n.f.* counterpart.

contrepoids (-pwä), *n.m.* counterbalance.

contribuer, *vb.* contribute.

contribution, *n.f.* share, contribution; tax.

contrôle, *n.m.* check.

contrôle des naissances, *n.m.* birth control, contraception.

contrôler, *vb.* control, check.

contrôleur, *n.m.* checker, collector.

controverse, *n.f.* controversy.

convaincre, vb. convince.

convaincu, adj. positive.

convalescence, n.f. convalescence.

convenable, adj. becoming, appropriate, suitable, congenial.

convenance, n.f. convenience.

convenir à, vb. suit, fit, befit, agree.

convention, n.f. convention; contract.

conventionnel, adj. conventional.

converger, vb. converge.

conversation, n.f. talk, conversation.

converser, vb. talk, converse.

conversion, n.f. conversion, change.

convertir, vb. convert, transform.

convexe, adj. convex.

conviction, n.f. conviction.

convive, n.m. guest, companion.

convoi, n.m. convoy, funeral procession.

convoiter, vb. covet.

convoitise, n.f. covetousness.

convoquer, vb. summon, call.

convulsion, n.f. convulsion.

coopératif (kō ô-), adj. coöperative.

coopération (kō ô-), n.f. coöperation.

coopérative (kō ô-), n.f. coöperative.

coopérer (kō ô-), vb. coöperate.

coordonner (kō ôr-), vb. coördinate.

copie, n.f. copy.

copier, vb. copy.

copieux, adj. copious.

coq (-k), n.m. rooster.

coque, n.f. œuf à la c., boiled egg.

coquille, n.f. shell.

coquin, adj. and n.m. rogue, rascal.

cor, n.m. horn; corn.

corail, n.m., pl. coraux, coral.

corbeau, n.m. raven, crow.

corbeille, n.f. basket.

corde, n.f. rope, string, cord.

cordial, adj. hearty, cordial.

cordon, n.m. rope.

cordonnier, n.m. shoemaker.

Corée, n.f. Korea.

corne, n.f. horn.

corneille, n.f. crow.

cornemuse, n.f. bagpipe.

cornichon, n.m. gherkin.

corporation, n.f. corporation.

corporel, adj. bodily.

corps, n.m. body.

corpulent, adj. burly.

corpuscule (-sk-), n.m. corpuscle.

correct (-kt), adj. right, correct.

correction, n.f. correction, correctness.

corrélation, n.f. correlation.

correspondance, n.f. (train) connection: similarity; correspondence.

correspondant, 1. n.m. correspondent. 2. adj. similar, corresponding.

correspondre, vb. correspond.

corriger, vb. mend, reclaim, correct.

corroborer, vb. corroborate.

corroder, vb. corrode.

corrompre, vb. bribe, corrupt.

corrompu, adj. corrupt.

corruption, n.f. bribery, graft, corruption.

corsage, n.m. bodice.

corset, n.m. corset.

cortège, n.m. procession.

cosmétique, adj. and n.m. cosmetic.

cosmopolite, adj. and n.m.f. cosmopolitan.

costume, n.m. attire, dress.

cote, n.f. quotation.

côte, n.f. rib; coast.

côté, n.f. side, way. mettre de c., put to one side (save; discard). à c. de, beside.

côtelette, n.f. chop, cutlet.

coton, n.m. cotton.

cou, n.m. neck.

couche, n.f. layer, bed; stratum; diaper.

coucher, vb. put to bed. se c., lie down; set.

couchette, n.f. bunk, berth.

coucou, n.m. cuckoo.

coude, n.m. elbow.

coudoyer, vb. jostle.

coudre, vb. sew, stitch.

couler, vb. flow, sink, run; cast (metal).

couleur, n.f. hue, color; suit (cards).

couloir, n.m. corridor.

coup, n.m. blow, stroke, hit, bump, knock, cast. c. de feu, discharge (gun). **c. d'œil**, glance, look. **c. de pied**, kick. **c. de poing**, punch.

coupable, *adj.* guilty, to blame.

coupe, *n.f.* cut; goblet. **c. de cheveux**, haircut.

couper, *vb.* cut.

couple, *n.f.* couple, pair.

coupler, *vb.* couple.

coupon, *n.m.* remnant; coupon.

coupure, *n.f.* cut, clipping.

cour, *n.f.* court(yard).

courage, *n.m.* bravery, pluck, courage.

courageux, *adj.* brave.

couramment, *adv.* fluently.

courant, 1. *adj.* current. **peu c.**, unusual. **au c.**, well informed. **2.** *n.m.* stream, current. **c. d'air**, draft.

courbe, *n.f.* curve, sweep.

courber, *vb.* bend, curve.

courbure, *n.f.* curvature.

coureur, *n.m.* runner.

courir, *vb.* run.

couronne, *n.f.* crown, wreath.

couronnement, *n.m.* coronation.

couronner, *vb.* crown.

courrier, *n.m.* mail.

courroie, *n.f.* strap.

courroux, *n.m.* wrath.

cours, *n.m.* course.

course, *n.f.* race, errand.

court, *adj.* short.

courtepointe, *n.f.* quilt.

courtier, *n.m.* broker.

courtisan, *n.m.* courtier.

courtois, *adj.* courteous.

courtoisie, *n.f.* courtesy.

cousin, *n.m.* cousin.

coussin, *n.m.* cushion.

coussinet, *n.m.* bearing.

coût, *n.m.* cost.

couteau, *n.m.* knife.

coutellerie, *n.f.* cutlery.

coûter, *vb.* cost.

coûteux, *adj.* expensive, costly.

coutume, *n.f.* custom.

couture, *n.f.* seam. **haute couture**, high fashion.

couturière, *n.f.* dressmaker.

couvée, *n.f.* brood.

couvent, *n.m.* convent.

couver, *vb.* brood, hatch; smolder.

couvercle, *n.m.* lid, cover.

couvert, 1. *n.m.* cover. **2.** *adj.* covered, cloudy.

couverture, *n.f.* blanket; cover; (*pl.*) bedclothes.

couvrir, *vb.* cover.

crabe, *n.m.* crab.

crachat, *n.m.* spit.

cracher, *vb.* spit.

craie, *n.f.* chalk.

craindre, *vb.* fear.

crainte, *n.f.* fear, dread, awe.

craintif, *adj.* fearful.

cramoisi, *adj. and n.m.* crimson.

crampe, *n.f.* cramp.

crampon, *n.m.* clamp, cramp iron.

cramponner, *vb.* **se c.**, cling.

crâne, *n.m.* skull.

crapaud, *n.m.* toad.

craquement, *n.m.* crack.

craquer, *vb.* crack.

cratère, *n.m.* crater.

cravate, *n.f.* necktie.

crayon, *n.m.* pencil.

créance, *n.f.* belief. **lettres de c.**, credentials.

créancier, *n.m.* creditor.

créateur *m.*, **créatrice** *f.* **1.** *adj.* creative. **2.** *n.* creator.

création, *n.f.* creation.

créature, *n.f.* creature.

crédit, *n.m.* credit.

credo, *n.m.* creed.

crédule, *adj.* credulous.

créer, *vb.* create.

crème, *n.f.* cream, custard.

crémerie, *n.f.* dairy store.

crêpe, *n.f.* pancake; crepe.

crépuscule (-sk-), *n.m.* dusk.

crête, *n.f.* ridge, crest.

crétin, *n.m.* dunce.

cretonne, *n.f.* cretonne.

creuser, *vb.* dig.

creuset, *n.m.* crucible.

creux, *adj. and n.m.* hollow.

crevasse, *n.f.* crevice.

crever, *vb.* burst; die.

crevette, *n.f.* shrimp.

cri, *n.m.* cry, call.

crible, *n.m.* sieve.

crier, *vb.* yell, shout.

crime, *n.m.* crime.

criminel, *adj.* criminal.

crinière, *n.f.* mane.

crise, *n.f.* crisis.

cristal, *n.m.* crystal.

cristallin, *adj.* crystalline.

cristalliser, *vb.* crystallize.
critérium, *n.m.* criterion.
critique, 1. *n.m.* critic. **2.** *n.f.* criticism. **3.** *adj.* critical.
critiquer, *vb.* criticize.
croasser, *vb.* croak.
croc (-ō), *n.m.* hook.
croche, *n.f.* quaver (music).
crochet, *n.m.* bracket, hook.
crochu, *adj.* hooked.
crocodile, *n.m.* crocodile.
croire, *vb.* believe.
croisade, *n.f.* crusade.
croisé, *n.m.* crusader.
croiser, *vb.* cross.
croiseur, *n.m.* cruiser.
croisière, *n.f.* cruise.
croissance, *n.f.* growth.
croissant, *n.m.* crescent.
croître, *vb.* grow.
croix, *n.f.* cross.
croquant, *adj.* crisp.
croquet, *n.m.* croquet.
croquis, *n.m.* sketch.
crosse, *n.f.* (golf) club.
crotale, *n.m.* rattlesnake.
crouler, *vb.* fall apart.
croup, *n.m.* croup.
croupir, *vb.* wallow.
croûte, *n.f.* crust.
croûton, *n.m.* crouton.
croyable, *adj.* believable.
croyance, *n.f.* belief.
croyant, *n.m.* believer.
cru, *adj.* raw.
cruauté, *n.f.* cruelty.
cruche, *n.f.* pitcher.
crucifier, *vb.* crucify.
crucifix, *n.m.* crucifix.
cruel, *adj.* cruel.
cryochirurgie, *n.f.* cryosurgery.
Cuba, *n.m.* Cuba.
Cubain, *n.m.* Cuban.
cubain, *adj.* Cuban.
cube, *n.m.* cube.
cubique, *adj.* cubic.
cueillir, *vb.* pick.
cuiller, *n.f.* spoon. **c. à thé,** teaspoon. **c. à bouche,** tablespoon.
cuillerée, *n.f.* spoonful.
cuir, *n.m.* leather.
cuirassé, *n.m.* battleship.
cuire, *vb.* cook; sting, smart.
cuisine, *n.f.* kitchen, cooking.
cuisinier, *n.m.* cook.
cuisse, *n.f.* thigh.

cuivre, *n.m.* copper. **c. jaune,** brass.
cul-de-sac, *n.m.* blind alley.
culotte, *n.f.* breeches.
culpabilité, *n.f.* guilt.
culte, *n.m.* worship; cult.
cultiver, *vb.* cultivate; grow, raise.
culture, *n.f.* culture, cultivation; farming.
cure, *n.f.* cure.
curé, *n.m.* (parish) priest.
curieux, *adj.* curious.
curiosité, *n.f.* curiosity, curio.
cursif, *adj.* cursive.
cuticule, *n.f.* cuticle.
cuve, *n.f.* vat.
cuver, *vb.* ferment.
cuvette, *n.f.* (wash) basin.
cuvier, *n.m.* washtub.
cycle, *n.m.* cycle.
cycliste, *n.m.f.* cyclist.
cyclomoteur, *n.m.* moped.
cyclone, *n.m.* cyclone.
cygne, *n.m.* swan.
cylindre, *n.m.* cylinder.
cylindrique, *adj.* cylindrical.
cymbale, *n.f.* cymbal.
cynique, 1. *n.m.* cynic. **2.** *adj.* cynical.
cynisme, *n.m.* cynicism.
cyprès, *n.m.* cypress.
czar, *n.m.* czar.

D

dactylographe, *n.m.f.* typist.
daigner, *vb.* deign.
daim, *n.m.* buck.
daine, *n.f.* doe.
dais, *n.m.* canopy.
dalle, *n.f.* slab, flag(stone).
dame, *n.f.* lady.
damner (dä nä), *vb.* damn.
Danemark, *n.m.* Denmark.
danger, *n.m.* danger.
dangereux, *adj.* dangerous.
Danois, *n.m.* Dane.
danois, *adj. and n.m.* Danish.
dans, *prep.* in, into.
danse, *n.f.* dance.
danser, *vb.* dance.
danseur, *n.m.* dancer.
dard, *n.m.* dart.
date, *n.f.* date.
dater, *vb.* date.

datte, *n.f.* date.

davantage, *adv.* more, further.

de, *prep.* of, from, by, about; some.

dé, *n.m.* die; thimble.

débarquer, *vb.* land.

débarrasser, *vb.* rid.

débat, *n.m.* debate.

débattre, *vb.* canvass; debate.

débit, *n.m.* delivery (speech); sale; debit.

débiter, *vb.* sell (retail).

débiteur, *n.m.* debtor.

déblayer, *vb.* clear.

déborder, *vb.* overflow.

déboucher, *vb.* flow (into).

débourser, *vb.* disburse.

debout, *adv.* up. **être d.,** stand.

débris, *n.m.pl.* wreck, debris.

début, *n.m.* beginning, first appearance, debut.

débuter, *vb.* make one's first appearance; begin.

décadence, *n.f.* decay, decadence.

décaféiné, *adj.* decaffeinated.

décapiter, *vb.* behead.

décéder, *vb.* die.

décembre, *n.m.* December.

décence, *n.f.* decency.

décent, *adj.* decent.

déception, *n.f.* disappointment.

décerner, *vb.* award.

décès, *n.m.* death.

décevoir, *vb.* disappoint.

décharge, *n.f.* discharge.

décharger, *vb.* unload, discharge.

décharné, *adj.* gaunt.

déchausser, *vb.* take off shoes.

déchets (-ā), *n.m.pl.* waste.

déchets nucléaires, *n.m.pl.* nuclear waste.

déchiffrer, *vb.* decipher.

déchirer, *vb.* tear, rend.

déchirure, *n.f.* tear, rent.

décibel, *n.m.* decibel.

décider, *vb.* prevail upon, decide.

décimal, *adj.* decimal.

décisif, *adj.* decisive.

décision, *n.f.* decision.

déclamer, *vb.* recite.

déclaration, *n.f.* statement, declaration.

déclarer, *vb.* state, declare.

déclin, *n.m.* ebb.

décliner, *vb.* decline.

décolorer, *vb.* bleach, fade.

décomposer, *vb.* spoil, decompose.

déconcerter, *vb.* baffle, disconcert, embarrass.

décongestionnant, *adj.* decongestant.

décontracté, *adj.* relaxed.

décoratif, *adj.* decorative.

décoration, *n.f.* decoration, trimming.

décorer, *vb.* decorate.

décors, *n.m.pl.* scenery.

découper, *vb.* carve (meat).

découragé, *adj.* despondent.

découragement, *n.m.* discouragement.

décourager, *vb.* dishearten, discourage.

découverte, *n.f.* discovery.

découvreur, *n.m.* discoverer.

découvrir, *vb.* uncover detect, discover.

décrépit, *adj.* decrepit.

décret, *n.m.* decree.

décréter, *vb.* enact.

décrire, *vb.* describe.

dédaigneux, *adj.* scornful.

dédain, *n.m.* scorn, disdain.

dedans, *n.m.* inside, within.

dédicace, *n.f.* dedication.

dédier, *vb.* dedicate.

déduction, *n.f.* deduction.

déduire, *vb.* infer, deduce, deduct.

défaire, *vb.* undo.

défaite, *n.f.* defeat.

défaut, *n.m.* flaw, fault, failure, lack. **à d. de,** for want of.

défectueux, *adj.* faulty, defective.

défendeur, *n.m.* defendant.

défendre, *vb.* forbid, defend.

défense, *n.f.* prohibition, plea, defense.

défenseur, *n.m.* advocate, defender.

défensif, *adj.* defensive.

déférer, *vb.* defer.

défi, *n.m.* challenge, defiance.

défiance, *n.f.* mistrust.

déficit (-t), *n.m.* deficit.

défier, *vb.* challenge, defy. **se d. de,** mistrust.

défigurer, *vb.* deface.

défiler, *vb.* march off.

défini, *adj.* definite.

définir, *vb.* define.

définitif, *adj.* final, definitive.

définition, *n.f.* definition.
déformer, *vb.* distort, deform.
défraîchi, *adj.* dingy.
défricher, *vb.* reclaim.
défunt, *n.m. and adj.* deceased.
dégagé, *adj.* breezy.
dégât, *n.m.* damage.
dégénérer, *vb.* degenerate.
dégoût, *n.m.* distaste, disgust.
dégoûtant, *adj.* foul, disgusting.
dégoûter, *vb.* disgust.
dégoutter, *vb.* drip.
dégradation, *n.f.* degradation.
dégrader, *vb.* degrade.
degré, *n.m.* degree, step.
déguisement, *n.m.* disguise.
déguiser, *vb.* disguise.
dehors, *adv.* (out)doors, outside.
 en d. de, apart from.
déifier, *vb.* deify.
déité, *n.f.* deity.
déjà, *adv.* already.
déjeter, *vb.* make unsymmetrical.
déjeuner, *n.m. and vb.* lunch,
 breakfast. **petit d.,** breakfast.
déjouer, *vb.* foil, thwart.
delà, *adv.* beyond. **au d. de,** over,
 past, beyond.
délabrement, *n.m.* decay.
délabrer, *vb.* ruin, wreck.
délacer, *vb.* unlace.
délai, *n.m.* delay.
délaissement, *n.m.* desertion.
délaisser, *vb.* desert.
délassement, *n.m.* relaxation.
délasser, *vb.* refresh.
délateur, *n.m.* informer.
délavé, *adj.* faded, pallid.
délayer, *vb.* dilute with water.
délectable, *adj.* delicious.
délectation, *n.f.* enjoyment.
délecter, *vb.* delight.
délégation, *n.f.* delegation.
délégué, *n.m.* delegate.
déléguer, *vb.* delegate.
délester, *vb.* relieve of ballast.
délétère, *adj.* harmful; offensive.
délibératif, *adj.* deliberative.
délibération, *n.f.* deliberation.
délibéré, *adj.* deliberate.
délibérer, *vb.* deliberate.
délicat, *adj.* dainty, delicate.
délicatesse, *n.f.* delicacy.
délices, *n.f.pl.* delight.
délicieux, *adj.* delicious.
délié, *adj.* slender; keen.
délier, *vb.* untie.

délimiter, *vb.* mark the limits of.
délinéer, *vb.* delineate.
délinquant, 1. *n.m.* delinquent,
 offender. **2.** *adj.* delinquent.
délirant, *adj.* delirious.
délire, *n.m.* frenzy.
délirer, *vb.* rave.
délit, *n.m.* offense, crime.
délivrance, *n.f.* rescue, deliverance.
délivrer, *vb.* rescue, set free, deliver.
déloger, *vb.* dislodge.
déloyal, *adj.* disloyal.
déloyauté, *n.f.* disloyalty.
déluge, *n.m.* deluge.
déluré, *adj.* clever, cute.
démagogue, *n.m.* demagogue.
demain, *adv.* tomorrow.
demande, *n.f.* application, request, inquiry, claim. **d. en mariage,** proposal.
demander, *vb.* ask, request. **se d.,**
 wonder.
demandeur, *n.m.* plaintiff.
démangeaison, *n.f.* itch.
démanger, *vb.* itch.
démanteler, *vb.* dismantle.
démarcation, *n.f.* demarcation.
démarche, *n.f.* walk, bearing;
 step.
démarrage, *n.m.* start.
démarrer, *vb.* unmoor; start off.
démarreur, *n.m.* (self)-starter.
démasquer, *vb.* unmask; expose,
 reveal.
démêler, *vb.* disentangle.
démembrement, *n.m.* dismem-
 berment.
démembrer, *vb.* dismember.
déménagement, *n.m.* moving.
déménager, *vb.* move.
déménageur, *n.m.* furniture
 mover.
démence, *n.f.* insanity.
démener, *vb.* struggle.
dément, *adj.* insane.
démenti, *n.m.* denial.
démentir, *vb.* give the lie to.
démesuré, *adj.* measureless, immense.
démettre, *vb.* **se d. (de),** resign.
demeure, *n.f.* abode.
demeurer, *vb.* dwell.
demi, *n.m. and adj.* half.
demi-cercle, *n.m.* semicircle.
demi-dieu, *n.m.* demigod.

demi-frère, *n.m.* stepbrother.

demi-heure, *n.f.* half an hour.

démilitariser, *vb.* demilitarize.

demi-place, *n.f.* half price; half fare.

demi-saison, *adj.* between-season.

demi-sœur, *n.f.* stepsister.

demi-solde, *n.f.* half-pay.

démission, *n.f.* resignation.

démobilisation, *n.f.* demobilization.

démobiliser, *vb.* demobilize.

démocrate, *n.m.f.* democrat.

démocratie, *n.f.* democracy.

démocratique, *adj.* democratic.

démodé, *adj.* old-fashioned.

demoiselle, *n.f.* young lady. **d. d'honneur**, bridesmaid.

démolir, *vb.* demolish.

démolition, *n.f.* demolition.

démon, *n.m.* demon.

démonétiser, *vb.* demonetize.

démoniaque, *adj.* demonic.

démonstratif, *adj.* effusive, demonstrative.

démonstration, *n.f.* demonstration.

démonter, *vb.* unhorse; dismantle.

démontrable, *adj.* demonstrable.

démontrer, *vb.* demonstrate.

démoralisation, *n.f.* demoralization.

démoraliser, *vb.* demoralize.

démouler, *vb.* remove from a mold.

démuni, *adj.* short of, lacking.

dénationaliser, *vb.* denationalize.

dénaturer, *vb.* denature.

dénégation, *n.f.* denial.

dénigrer, *vb.* disparage.

dénivelé, *adj.* not level.

dénombrement, *n.m.* enumeration; census.

dénombrer, *vb.* count.

dénomination, *n.f.* denomination.

dénommer, *vb.* name.

dénoncer, *vb.* report, denounce.

dénonciation, *n.f.* denunciation.

dénoter, *vb.* denote.

dénouement, *n.m.* result, outcome.

dénouer, *vb.* untie.

denrée, *n.f.* ware, produce.

dense, *adj.* dense.

densité, *n.f.* density.

dent, *n.f.* tooth. **mal de d.s**, toothache. **brosse à d.s**, toothbrush.

dentaire, *adj.* dental.

denté, *adj.* cogged.

dentelle, *n.f.* lace.

dentifrice, *n.m.* tooth paste or powder.

dentiste, *n.m.* dentist.

dentition, *n.f.* dentition.

denture, *n.f.* set of natural teeth.

dénuder, *vb.* denude.

dénué, *adj.* destitute, bare.

dénuement, *n.m.* destitution.

dénuer, *vb.* divest.

dépannage, *n.m.* emergency repairs.

dépareillé, *adj.* odd (unmatched).

départ, *n.m.* departure.

département, *n.m.* department.

départir, *vb.* divide in shares.

dépasser, *vb.* outrun, pass.

dépayser, *vb.* bewilder, confuse.

dépêche, *n.f.* dispatch.

dépêcher, *vb.* **se d.**, hurry.

dépeindre, *vb.* portray.

dépendance, *n.f.* annex (to a building).

dépendant, *adj.* dependent.

dépendre, *vb.* depend.

dépens, *n.m.pl.* expenses.

dépense, *n.f.* expenditure, expense.

dépenser, *vb.* spend, expend.

dépérir, *vb.* waste away; decline.

dépiécer, *vb.* dismember.

dépit, *n.m.* spite. **en d. de**, despite.

déplacement, *n.m.* displacement.

déplacer, *vb.* displace, move, shift.

déplaire à, *vb.* displease.

déplaisant, *adj.* displeasing.

déplanter, *vb.* transplant.

déplantoir, *n.m.* trowel.

déplier, *vb.* unfold.

déploiement, *n.m.* deployment.

déplorable, *adj.* wretched, deplorable.

déplorer, *vb.* deplore.

déployer, *vb.* deploy.

déplumer, *vb.* pluck.

déportation, *n.f.* deportation.

déportements, *n.m.pl.* misconduct.

déporter, *vb.* deport.

déposant, *n.m.* depositor.

déposer, vb. deposit, set down, depose.

dépositaire, n.m.f. trustee.

déposséder, vb. oust; dispossess.

dépôt, n.m. deposit, depot. **d. de vivres,** commissary.

dépouille, n.f. hide, skin, pelt.

dépouiller, vb. strip. **se d. de,** shed.

dépourvu, adj. devoid; needy.

dépoussiéreur, n.m. vacuum cleaner.

dépravation, n.f. depravity.

dépraver, vb. deprave.

dépréciation, n.f. depreciation.

déprécier, vb. depreciate, cheapen.

déprédation, n.f. depredation.

dépression, n.f. depression.

déprimer, vb. depress.

depuis, adv. and prep. since. **d. que,** conj. since.

députation, n.f. delegation.

député, n.m. representative, deputy.

déraciner, vb. uproot, eradicate.

déraison, n.f. unreason.

déraisonnable, adj. unreasonable.

dérangement, n.m. disturbance.

déranger, vb. disturb, trouble.

derechef, adv. once again.

dérégler, vb. upset, disorder.

dérider, vb. smooth; cheer up.

dérision, n.f. derision. **tourner en d.,** deride.

dérivation, n.f. derivation, etymology.

dérive, n.f. drift. **à la d.,** adrift.

dériver, vb. derive; drift.

dernier, adj. last, latter.

dernièrement, adv. lately.

dérober, vb. rob. **se d.,** steal away.

dérouiller, vb. remove the rust from.

dérouler, vb. unroll, unfold.

déroute, n.f. rout.

dérouter, vb. mislead; confuse.

derrière, n.m., adv. and prep. behind.

derviche, n.m. dervish.

dès, prep. since. **d. que,** conj. as soon as.

désabuser, vb. disillusion.

désaccord, n.m. disagreement.

désaccoutumer, vb. break of a habit.

désaffecter, vb. put (church) to secular use.

désagréable, adj. nasty, distasteful.

désagrégation, n.f. disintegration.

désaligné, adj. out of alignment.

désaltérer, vb. quench (one's) thirst.

désappointement, n.m. disappointment.

désappointer, vb. disappoint.

désapprobation, n.f. disapproval.

désapprouver, vb. disapprove.

désarmement, n.m. disarmament.

désarmer, vb. disarm.

désarroi, n.m. disorder.

désastre, n.m. disaster.

désastreux, adj. disastrous.

désavantage, n.m. disadvantage.

désaveu, n.m. denial.

désavouer, vb. disown.

descendance, n.f. descent.

descendant, 1. n.m. offspring, descendant. **2.** adj. downward, descending.

descendre, vb. go down, come down, alight, descend.

descente, n.f. raid; descent.

descriptif, adj. descriptive.

description, n.f. description.

désembarquer, vb. disembark, unload.

désenchanter, vb. disenchant.

désenivrer, vb. sober up.

désert, n.m. wilderness, desert.

déserter, vb. desert.

déserteur, n.m. deserter.

désertion, n.f. desertion.

désespéré, adj. hopeless, forlorn, desperate.

désespérer, vb. despair.

désespoir, n.m. desperation, despair.

déshabiller, vb. undress.

déshériter, vb. disinherit.

déshonnête, adj. improper, indecent.

déshonneur, n.m. disgrace, dishonor.

déshonorant, adj. dishonorable.

déshonorer, vb. disgrace, dishonor.

déshydrater, vb. dehydrate.

désignation, n.f. nomination.

désigner, vb. appoint, nominate; point out; designate.

désillusion, n.f. disillusion.

désinfectant, *n.m.* disinfectant.
désinfecter, *vb.* disinfect, fumigate.
désinfection, *n.f.* disinfection.
désintégration, *n.f.* disintegration.
désintegrer, *vb.* disintegrate.
désintéressé, *adj.* unselfish.
désintéressement, *n.m.* unselfishness.
désir, *n.m.* desire, wish.
désirable, *adj.* desirable.
désirer, *vb.* desire, wish.
désireux, *adj.* desirous.
désistement, *n.m.* withdrawal.
désobéir à, *vb.* disobey.
désobéissance, *n.f.* disobedience.
désobéissant, *adj.* disobedient.
désœuvré, *adj.* idle.
désolation, *n.f.* desolation.
désolé, *adj.* disconsolate; desolate.
désoler, *vb.* desolate.
désordonné, *adj.* disorderly.
désordonner, *vb.* upset, confuse.
désordre, *n.m.* disorder.
désorganisation, *n.f.* disorganization.
désorganiser, *vb.* disorganize.
désormais, *adv.* henceforth.
despote, *n.m.* despot.
despotique, *adj.* despotic.
despotisme, *n.m.* despotism.
dessécher, *vb.* dry out, parch; drain.
dessein, *n.m.* plan, intent.
desserrer, *vb.* loosen.
dessert, *n.m.* dessert.
dessin, *n.m.* drawing, design, sketch.
dessinateur, *n.m.* designer.
dessiner, *vb.* draw, design. **se d.,** loom.
dessous, *n.m.* underside. **en d., au-d. de,** beneath, underneath.
dessus, *n.m.* top. **en d., au-d. de,** above. **d. de lit,** bedspread.
destin, *n.m.* fate, destiny.
destinataire, *n.m.f.* addressee.
destination, *n.f.* destination. **à d. de,** bound for.
destinée, *n.f.* destiny.
destiner, *vb.* destine, intend.
destituer, *vb.* dismiss.
destructif, *adj.* destructive.
destruction, *n.f.* destruction.
désuet, *adj.* obsolete.

désuétude, *n.f.* disuse.
désunion, *n.f.* disunion.
désunir, *vb.* disconnect.
détaché, *adj.* loose.
détachement, *n.m.* detachment.
détacher, *vb.* detach. **se d.,** stand out.
détail, *n.m.* item, particular, detail. **au d.,** at retail.
détective, *n.m.* detective.
déteindre, *vb.* run (of colors).
détenir, *vb.* detain.
détente, *n.f.* 1. trigger. 2. (politics) détente.
détention, *n.f.* custody, detention.
détérioration, *n.f.* deterioration.
détériorer, *vb.* deteriorate.
détermination, *n.f.* determination.
déterminer, *vb.* determine, fix.
détestable, *adj.* detestable, hateful.
détester, *vb.* abhor, loathe, detest.
détonation, *n.f.* detonation.
détoner, *vb.* detonate.
détour, *n.m.* turn; detour.
détourné, *adj.* devious.
détourner, *vb.* turn away; divert; avert; embezzle.
détresse, *n.f.* trouble, distress.
détriment, *n.m.* detriment.
détroit, *n.m.* strait.
détruire, *vb.* destroy.
dette, *n.f.* debt.
deuil, *n.m.* mourning.
deux, *adj. and n.m.* two. **tous les d.,** both.
deuxième, *adj.* second.
deux-points, *n.m.* colon.
dévaliser, *vb.* rob.
dévaliseur, *n.m.* robber.
devancer, *vb.* be ahead of.
devant, 1. *n.m.* front. 2. *prep.* before, in front of.
devanture, *n.f.* window, (shop) front.
dévastation, *n.* devastation.
dévaster, *vb.* devastate.
déveine, *n.f.* bad luck.
développement, *n.m.* development.
développer, *vb.* develop.
devenir, *vb.* become.
déverser, *vb.* divert.
dévêtir, *vb.* undress, disrobe.

déviation, *n.f.* deviation.
dévider, *vb.* unwind.
dévier, *vb.* turn away.
deviner, *vb.* guess.
devinette, *n.f.* puzzle, riddle.
devis, *n.m.* estimate.
devise, *n.f.* motto.
dévisser, *vb.* unscrew.
dévoiler, *vb.* unveil, disclose, reveal.
devoir, *n.m.* duty.
devoir, *vb.* owe; be supposed to; have to; (conditional) ought.
dévorer, *vb.* devour.
dévot, *adj.* devout.
dévotion, *n.f.* devotion.
dévoué, *adj.* devoted.
dévouement, *n.m.* devotion.
dévouer, *vb.* dedicate, devote.
dextérité, *n.f.* dexterity.
diabétique, *adj. and n.* diabetic.
diable, *n.m.* devil.
diablerie, *n.f.* mischief.
diabolique, *adj.* diabolic.
diacre, *n.m.* deacon.
diacritique, *adj.* diacritic.
diadème, *n.m.* diadem.
diagnostic, *n.m.* diagnosis.
diagnostiquer, *vb.* diagnose.
diagonal, *adj.* diagonal.
diagramme, *n.m.* diagram.
dialectal, *adj.* dialect.
dialecte, *n.m.* dialect.
dialogue, *n.m.* dialogue.
dialoguer, *vb.* converse, talk together.
diamant, *n.m.* diamond.
diamétral, *adj.* diametric.
diamètre, *n.m.* diameter.
diaphane, *adj.* diaphanous.
diaphragme, *n.m.* diaphragm.
diarrhée, *n.f.* diarrhea.
diathermie, *n.f.* diathermy.
diatribe, *n.f.* diatribe.
dictateur, *n.m.* dictator.
dictature, *n.f.* dictatorship.
dictée, *n.f.* dictation.
dicter, *vb.* dictate.
diction, *n.f.* diction.
dictionnaire, *n.m.* dictionary.
dicton, *n.m.* maxim, proverb.
didactique, *adj.* didactic.
dièse, *adj. and n.m.* sharp.
diète, *n.f.* diet.
diététique, *adj.* dietetic.
Dieu, *n.m.* God.
diffamant, *adj.* libelous.

diffamateur, *n.m.* libeler.
diffamation, *n.f.* libel.
diffamer, *vb.* defame.
différence, *n.f.* difference.
différenciation, *n.f.* differentiation.
différencier, *vb.* differentiate.
différend, *n.m.* difference, dispute.
différent, *adj.* different.
différer, *vb.* defer; differ.
difficile, *adj.* arduous, hard; difficult; fastidious.
difficilement, *adv.* with difficulty.
difficulté, *n.f.* trouble; difficulty.
difficulté psychologique, *n.f.* hangup.
difforme, *adj.* deformed.
difformité, *n.f.* deformity.
diffus, *adj.* diffuse.
diffusion, *n.f.* spread, diffusion.
digérer, *vb.* digest.
digestible, *adj.* digestible.
digestif, *adj. and n.m.* digestive.
digestion, *n.f.* digestion.
digital, *adj.* digital.
digitaline, *n.f.* digitalis.
digne, *adj.* worthy.
dignitaire, *n.m.* dignitary.
dignité, *n.f.* dignity.
digression, *n.f.* digression.
digue, *n.f.* dike, dam.
dilapidation, *n.f.* waste.
dilater, *vb.* expand, dilate.
dilemme, *n.m.* dilemma.
dilettante, *n.m.* amateur.
diligence, *n.f.* diligence.
diligent, *adj.* diligent.
diluer, *vb.* dilute.
dilution, *n.f.* dilution.
dimanche, *n.m.* Sunday.
dimension, *n.f.* dimension.
diminuer, *vb.* lessen, decrease, diminish.
diminutif, *adj. and n.m.* diminutive.
diminution, *n.f.* decrease.
dindon, *n.m.* turkey.
dîner, 1. *n.m.* dinner. **2.** *vb.* dine.
dîneur, *n.m.* diner.
diphtérie, *n.f.* diphtheria.
diphtongue, *n.f.* diphthong.
diplomate, *n.m.* diplomat.
diplomatie, *n.f.* diplomacy.
diplomatique, *adj.* diplomatic.
diplôme, *n.m.* diploma.
dipsomane, *n.* dipsomaniac.

dipsomanie, *n.f.* dipsomania.

dire, *vb.* say, tell. **vouloir d.** mean. **c'est-à-d.,** namely; that is.

direct, *adj.* direct.

directement, *adv.* directly.

directeur, *n.m.* manager, director.

directif, *adj.* guiding.

direction, *n.f.* management, leadership, direction.

directorate, *n.m.* directorate.

dirigeable, *adj.* and *n.m.* dirigible.

dirigeant, *adj.* ruling.

diriger, *vb.* manage, boss, steer, direct.

discernable, *adj.* barely visible.

discernement, *n.m.* discernment, judgment.

discerner, *vb.* discern.

disciple, *n.m.* follower, disciple.

disciplinaire, *adj.* disciplinary.

discipline, *n.f.* discipline.

discipliner, *vb.* discipline.

disco, *n.m.* disco.

discontinuer, *vb.* discontinue.

disconvenance, *n.f.* unsuitability.

discordance, *n.f.* discord.

discorde, *n.f.* discord.

discothèque, *n.f.* discotheque.

discourir, *vb.* speak one's views.

discours, *n.m.* speech, oration, talk, discourse.

discourtois, *adj.* discourteous.

discrédit, *n.m.* disrepute.

discréditer, *vb.* disparage.

discret, *adj.* discreet.

discrétion, *n.f.* discretion.

disculper, *vb.* exonerate.

discursif, *adj.* discursive.

discussion, *n.f.* argument, discussion.

discutable, *adj.* debatable.

discuter, *vb.* argue, debate, discuss.

disette, *n.f.* famine.

diseur, *n.m.* talker.

disgrâce, *n.f.* disgrace.

disgracier, *vb.* put out of favor.

disjoindre, *vb.* sever, disjoint.

dislocation, *n.f.* dislocation.

disloquer, *vb.* dislocate.

disparaître, *vb.* disappear.

disparate, *adj.* unlike; badly matched.

disparition, *n.f.* disappearance.

dispendieux, *adj.* expensive.

dispensaire, *n.m.* dispensary.

dispensation, *n.f.* dispensation.

dispense, *n.f.* military exemption.

dispenser, *vb.* dispense.

disperser, *vb.* scatter, disperse.

dispersion, *n.f.* dispersal.

disponible, *adj.* available.

disposé, *adj.* disposed. **d. d'avance,** predisposed. **peu d.,** reluctant.

disposer, *vb.* dispose, settle.

dispositif, *n.m.* device.

disposition, *n.f.* arrangement, disposal, disposition.

disproportionné, *adj.* disproportionate.

dispute, *n.f.* row, fight, quarrel, dispute.

disputer, *vb.* dispute. **se d.,** quarrel.

disqualifier, *vb.* disqualify.

disque, *n.m.* disk, record.

dissemblable, *adj.* unlike.

dissemblance, *n.f.* dissimilarity.

dissension, *n.f.* dissension.

dissentiment, *n.m.* dissent.

disséquer, *vb.* dissect.

dissertation, *n.f.* essay.

dissimulation, *n.f.* pretense.

dissimuler, *vb.* dissemble, pretend.

dissipation, *n.f.* dissipation.

dissiper, *vb.* dispel, waste, dissipate.

dissolu, *adj.* dissolute.

dissolution, *n.f.* dissolution.

dissoudre, *vb.* dissolve.

dissuader, *vb.* dissuade.

distance, *n.f.* distance.

distancer, *vb.* outdistance.

distant, *adj.* distant.

distillation (-l-), *n.f.* distillation.

distiller (-l-), *vb.* distill.

distillerie (-l-), *n.f.* distillery.

distinct (-kt), *adj.* distinct.

distinctif, *adj.* distinctive.

distinction, *n.f.* distinction.

distingué, *adj.* distinguished.

distinguer, *vb.* discriminate; make out; distinguish.

distraction, *n.f.* distraction, pastime.

distraire, *vb.* distract, amuse. **se d.,** have fun.

distrait, *adj.* absent-minded.

distribuer, *vb.* give out, deal out, distribute.

distributeur, *n.m.* distributor.

distribution, *n.f.* distribution; delivery; cast.

district (-trèk), *n.m.* district.

dit, *adj.* called.

divaguer, *vb.* ramble.

divan, *n.m.* davenport, couch.

divergence, *n.f.* divergence.

diverger, *vb.* diverge.

divers, *adj.* various.

diversion, *n.f.* diversion.

diversité, *n.f.* diversity.

divertir, *vb.* divert, entertain. **se d.,** enjoy oneself.

divertissement, *n.m.* diversion.

dividende, *n.m.* dividend.

divin, *adj.* divine.

divinateur, *n.m.* soothsayer.

divinité, *n.f.* divinity.

diviser, *vb.* part, divide.

divisible, *adj.* divisible.

division, *n.f.* division.

divorce, *n.m.* divorce.

divorcer, *vb.* divorce.

divulguer, *vb.* divulge.

dix (-s), *adj. and n.m.* ten.

dix-huit (-z-), *adj. and n.m.* eighteen.

dix-huitième (-z-), *adj. and n.m.f.* eighteenth.

dixième (-z-), *adj. and n.m.* tenth.

dix-neuf (-z-), *adj. and n.m.* nineteen.

dix-sept (-s-), *adj. and n.m.* seventeen.

dizaine. *n.f.* (group of) ten.

docile, *adj.* docile.

docilité, *n.f.* docility.

docte, *adj.* learned, wise.

docteur, *n.m.* doctor.

doctorat, *n.m.* doctorate.

doctrine, *n.f.* doctrine.

document, *n.m.* document.

documenter, *vb.* document.

dodu, *adj.* plump.

dogmatique, *adj.* dogmatic.

dogma, *n.m.* dogma.

dogue, *n.m.* watchdog.

doigt (dwä), *n.m.* finger. **d. de pied,** toe.

doit, *n.m.* debit.

dollar, *n.m.* dollar.

domaine. *n.f.* domain, property.

dôme, *n.m.* dome.

domestique, 1. *n.m.f.* servant. **2.** *adj.* domestic.

domicile, *n.m.* residence.

dominant, *adj.* dominant.

domination, *n.f.* sway, domination, dominion.

dominer, *vb.* rule, dominate.

domino, *n.m.* domino.

dommage, *n.m.* injury, damage. **c'est d.,** that's too bad. **quel d.!,** what a pity!

dompter, *vb.* tame, subdue.

don, *n.m.* gift.

donateur, *n.m.* donor.

donation, *n.f.* donation.

donc (-k), *adv.* therefore.

donjon, *n.m.* dungeon.

donne, *n.f.* deal (cards).

donner, *vb.* give.

donneur, *n.m.* giver.

dont, *pron.* whose.

dorénavant, *adv.* hereafter.

dorer, *vb.* gild.

dorloter, *vb.* coddle.

dormant, *adj.* dormant; asleep.

dormir, *vb.* sleep.

dos, *n.m.* back.

dose, *n.f.* dose.

doser, *vb.* decide the amount.

dossier, *n.m.* record.

dot (-t), *n.f.* dowry.

doter, *vb.* endow.

douane, *n.f.* customs, custom house.

douanier, *n.m.* customs officer.

double, *adj. and n.m.* double. **faire le d. de,** duplicate.

doubler, *vb.* double.

doublure, *n.f.* lining.

doucement, *adv.* gently.

doucereux, *adj.* sugary; oversweet.

douceur, *n.f.* sweetness, gentleness, meekness.

douche, *n.f.* shower bath; douche.

douer, *vb.* endow.

douille, *n.f.* socket.

douleur, *n.f.* pain, ache, sorrow, grief.

douloureux, *adj.* painful.

doute, *n.m.* doubt.

douter, *vb.* doubt. **se d. de,** suspect.

douteux, *adj.* dubious, doubtful, questionable.

douve, *n.f.* ditch.

doux *m.,* **douce** *f. adj.* soft, sweet, gentle, mild, meek.

douzaine, *n.f.* dozen.

douze, *adj. and n.m.* twelve.
douzième, *adj. and n.m.* twelfth.
doyen, *n.m.* dean.
dragon, *n.m.* dragon; dragoon.
draguer, *vb.* dredge.
drainage, *n.m.* drainage.
drainer, *vb.* drain.
dramatique, *adj.* dramatic.
dramatiser, *vb.* dramatize.
dramaturge, *n.m.* playwright.
drame, *n.m.* drama.
drap, *n.m.* sheet.
drapeau, *n.m.* flag.
draper, *vb.* drape.
draperie, *n.f.* drapery.
drapier, *n.m.* clothier.
dresser, *vb.* draw up.
dressoir, *n.m.* dresser.
drogue, *n.f.* drug.
droguer, *vb.* drug.
droit, 1. *n.m.* right; law; claim. **2.** *adj. and adv.* (up)right, straight, fair. **d. d'auteur,** copyright.
droite, *n.f.* right. **à d.,** (to the) right.
drôle, *adj.* funny.
du, *m.,* **de la,** *f.,* **des,** *pl. prep.* some, any.
dû *m.,* **due** *f. adj.* due.
duc, *n.m.* duke.
duché, *n.m.* dukedom.
duchesse, *n.f.* duchess.
ductile, *adj.* ductile.
duel, *n.m.* duel.
duelliste, *n.m.* duellist.
dûment, *adv.* duly.
dune, *n.f.* dune.
duo, *n.m.* duet.
dupe, *n.f.* dupe.
duper, *vb.* trick.
duperie, *n.f.* trickery.
duplicité, *n.f.* duplicity.
dur, *adj.* hard, tough.
durabilité, *n.f.* durability.
durable, *adj.* lasting, durable.
durant, *prep.* during.
durcir, *vb.* harden.
durcissement, *n.m.* hardening.
durée, *n.f.* duration.
durement, *adv.* hard, harshly, strongly.
durer, *vb.* last.
dureté, *n.f.* hardness.
duvet, *n.m.* down.
duveté, *adj.* downy.
dynamique, *adj.* dynamic.
dynamite, *n.f.* dynamite.

dynamo, *n.f.* dynamo.
dynastie, *n.f.* dynasty.
dynastique, *adj.* dynastic.
dysenterie, *n.f.* dysentery.
dyslexie, *n.f.* dyslexia.
dyspepsie, *n.f.* dyspepsia.

E

eau, *n.f.* water. **faire e.,** leak.
eau-de-vie, *n.f.* brandy.
eau-forte, *n.f.* nitric acid.
ébahir, *vb.* amaze.
ébahissement, *n.m.* amazement.
ébarber, *vb.* trim, clip.
ébauche, *n.f.* outline.
ébaucher, *vb.* outline.
ébène, *n.m.* ebony.
ébénisterie, *n.f.* cabinet work.
éblouir, *vb.* dazzle.
éboulement, *n.m.* cave-in.
ébouriffer, *vb.* ruffle.
ébranler, *vb.* shake.
ébriété, *n.f.* drunkenness.
écaille, *n.f.* scale.
écarlate, *adj. and n.f.* scarlet.
écart, *n.m.* separation. **à l'é.,** aloof.
écarté, *adj.* isolated; lonely.
écartement, *n.m.* gap, separation.
écarter, *vb.* set aside.
ecclésiastique, *adj. and n.m.* ecclesiastic.
écervelé, *adj.* scatterbrained.
échafaud, *n.m.* scaffold.
échafaudage, *n.m.* scaffolding.
échancrer, *vb.* scallop, notch.
échange, *n.m.* exchange.
échangeable, *adj.* exchangeable.
échanger, *vb.* exchange.
échantillon, *n.m.* sample.
échappatoire, *n.f.* loophole.
échappement, *n.m.* exhaust.
échapper, *vb.* escape.
écharde, *n.f.* splinter.
écharpe, *n.f.* scarf, sling.
échasse, *n.f.* stilt.
échauder, *vb.* scald.
échauffer, *vb.* heat up.
échéance, *n.f.* maturity.
échecs (-shè), *n.m.pl.* chess.
échelle, *n.f.* ladder, scale.
échelon, *n.m.* step; echelon.
échevelé, *adj.* dishevelled.
échine, *n.f.* spine.
échiner, *vb.* work like a slave.

écho (-kō), n.m. echo.
échoir, vb. fall due.
échoppe, n.f. booth, stall.
échouer, vb. fail. **faire é.**, frustrate.
éclabousser, vb. splash.
éclair, n.m. flash.
éclairage, n.m. lighting.
éclaircie, n.f. clearing.
éclaircir, vb. clear up.
éclairer, vb. (en)lighten, light, clear up, clarify.
éclaireur, n.m. scout.
éclat, n.m. chip, splinter; burst; brilliance, radiance, glamour.
éclatant, adj. bursting; loud; brilliant.
éclatement (de pneu), n.m. blowout.
éclater, vb. burst out.
éclectique, adj. eclectic.
éclipse, n.f. eclipse.
éclipser, vb. eclipse.
éclore, vb. hatch, open, blossom.
écluse, n.f. lock.
écœurer, vb. disgust.
école, n.f. school.
écolier, n.m. schoolboy.
écologie, n.f. ecology.
écologique, adj. ecological.
écologiste, n.m. ecologist; environmentalist.
économe, adj. economical.
économie, n.f. economy. **é. politique**, economics.
économique, adj. economic(al).
économiser, vb. economize.
économiste, n.m. economist.
écope, n.f. ladle.
écoper, vb. ladle or bail out.
écorce, n.f. bark.
écorcher, vb. skin.
écorchure, n.f. gall.
Écossais, n.m. Scotchman, Scotsman.
écossais, adj. Scotch, Scottish.
Écosse, n.f. Scotland.
écot, n.m. share.
écouler, vb. drain. **s'é.**, flow, elapse.
écouter, vb. listen (to).
écouteur, n.m. listener.
écran, n.m. screen.
écraser, vb. crush.
écrémer, vb. skim.
écrevisse, n.f. crayfish.
écrier, vb. **s'é.**, exclaim.

écrin, n.m. case, box.
écrire, vb. write. **machine à é.**, typewriter.
écrit, adj. written.
écriteau, n.m. notice.
écritoire, n.f. inkstand.
écriture, n.f. writing, scripture.
écrivain, n.m. writer.
écrou, n.m. nut.
écrouler, vb. **s'é.**, fall to pieces.
écru, adj. natural.
écu, n.m. shield.
écuelle, n.f. bowl, dish.
écume, n.f. lather, foam.
écuménique, adj. ecumenical.
écureuil, n.m. squirrel.
écurie, n.f. stable.
écusson, n.m. escutcheon.
écuyer (-kwē-), n.m. squire.
édenté, adj. toothless.
édifice, n.m. building.
édifier, vb. build; edify.
édit, n.m. edict.
éditeur, n.m. publisher.
édition, n.f. edition.
éditorial, adj. editorial.
éducateur, n.m. educator.
éducation, n.f. breeding, education.
éduquer, vb. educate.
effacer, vb. erase, efface.
effectif, adj. effective, actual.
effectivement, adv. effectively.
effectuer, vb. effect.
efféminé, adj. effeminate.
effet, n.m. effect; (pl.) belongings. **en e.**, as a matter of fact, indeed.
efficace, adj. effective.
efficacité, n.f. efficacy.
effigie, n.f. effigy.
effleurer, vb. skim, graze.
effondrement, n.m. collapse.
effondrer, vb. **s'e.**, collapse, sink.
efforcer, vb. **s'e.**, endeavor, try hard.
effort, n.m. endeavor, strain, exertion, effort.
effrayant, adj. fearful.
effrayer, vb. frighten, scare, startle.
effréné, adj. unrestrained; frantic.
effroi, n.m. fright.
effronté, adj. brazen.
effronterie, n.f. effrontery.
effusion, n.f. shedding.

égal, *adj.* even, equal, same.

également, *adv.* equally.

égaler, *vb.* equal.

égaliser, *vb.* equalize.

égalité, *n.f.* equality, evenness.

égard, *n.m.* regard, consideration, esteem. **à l'é. de,** as for. **plein d'é.s,** considerate.

égaré, *adj.* astray.

égarement, *n.m.* aberration.

égarer, *vb.* mislay, bewilder. **s'é.,** go astray, get lost.

égayer, *vb.* cheer up.

église, *n.f.* church.

égoïsme, *n.m.* selfishness, egoism.

égoïste, *adj.* selfish.

égorger, *vb.* kill.

égotisme, *n.m.* egotism.

égout, *n.m.* sewer.

égoutter, *vb.* drain; drip.

égratignure, *n.f.* scratch.

Égypte, *n.m.* Egypt.

Égyptien, *n.m.* Egyptian.

égyptien, *adj.* Egyptian.

éhonté, *adj.* brazen, shameless.

élaboration, *n.f.* working out, elaboration; data processing.

élaborer, *vb.* draft, elaborate.

élan, *n.m.* elk; zest.

élancer, *vb.* **s'é.,** dash.

élargir, *vb.* widen, increase, enlarge.

élasticité, *n.f.* elasticity.

élastique, *adj. and n.m.* elastic.

électeur, *n.m.* voter.

électif, *adj.* elective.

élection, *n.f.* election.

électoral, *adj.* electoral.

électricien, *n.m.* electrician.

électricité, *n.f.* electricity.

électrique, *adj.* electric, electrical.

électrocardiogramme, *n.m.* electrocardiogram.

électrocuter, *vb.* electrocute.

élégance, *n.f.* elegance.

élégant, *adj.* elegant, smart, stylish.

élégie, *n.f.* elegy.

élément, *n.m.* element.

élémentaire, *adj.* elementary.

éléphant, *n.m.* elephant.

élevage, *n.m.* breeding.

élévation, *n.f.* elevation.

élève, *n.m.f.* pupil.

élevé, *adj.* lofty.

élever, *vb.* raise. **s'é.,** arise, soar.

éleveur, *n.m.* breeder.

élider, *vb.* elide.

éligibilité, *n.f.* eligibility.

éligible, *adj.* eligible.

élimination, *n.f.* elimination.

éliminer, *vb.* eliminate.

élire, *vb.* elect.

élite, *n.f.* elite.

elle, *pron.f.* she, her; (*pl.*) they, them (*f.*).

elle-même, *pron.* herself.

éloge, *n.m.* praise.

éloigné, *adj.* remote.

éloignement, *n.m.* distance.

éloigner, *vb.* take away. **s'é.,** go away, recede.

éloquence, *n.f.* eloquence.

éloquent, *adj.* eloquent.

élu, *adj.* chosen.

éluder, *vb.* evade, elude.

émacié, *adj.* emaciated.

émail, *n.m.,* *pl.* **émaux,** enamel.

émancipation, *n.f.* emancipation.

émanciper, *vb.* emancipate.

émaner, *vb.* emanate.

emballer, *vb.* pack.

embarcation, *n.f.* craft.

embargo, *n.m.* embargo.

embarquer, *vb.* embark.

embarras, *n.m.* embarrassment, trouble, fix.

embarrassant, *adj.* embarassing, awkward.

embarrasser, *vb.* embarrass.

embaumé, *adj.* balmy.

embaumer, *vb.* perfume, embalm.

embellir, *vb.* beautify.

embêter, *vb.* bore, irritate.

emblème, *n.m.* emblem.

embolie, *n.f.* embolism.

embouchure, *n.f.* mouth.

embourber, *vb.* bog.

embranchement, *n.m.* junction.

embrasser, *vb.* embrace, kiss.

embrayage, *n.m.* clutch.

embrouillement, *n.m.* tangle, mix-up.

embrouiller, *vb.* perplex, entangle.

embrun, *n.m.* spray.

embuscade, *n.f.* ambush.

émeraude, *n.f.* emerald.

émerger, *vb.* emerge.

émerveiller, *vb.* astonish.

émettre, *vb.* emit, send forth, issue.

émeute, *n.f.* riot.
émietter, *vb.* crumble.
émigrant, *n.m.* emigrant.
émigration, *n.f.* emigration.
émigré, *n.m.* political exile.
émigrer, *vb.* (e)migrate.
éminemment, *adv.* eminently.
éminence, *n.f.* eminence.
éminent, *adj.* eminent.
émission, *n.f.* issue.
emmagasinage, *n.m.* storage.
emmagasiner, *vb.* store.
emmener, *vb.* take away.
émotif, *adj.* emotional.
émotion, *n.f.* emotion, feeling.
émotionnable, *adj.* emotional.
émotionner, *vb.* thrill.
émoussé, *adj.* blunt.
émouvant, *adj.* moving.
émouvoir, *vb.* move.
empaler, *vb.* impale.
empan, *n.m.* span.
emparer, *vb.* s'e. de, take possession of.
empêchement, *n.m.* prevention.
empêcher, *vb.* prevent, stop, hinder, inhibit.
empereur, *n.m.* emperor.
empêtrer, *vb.* entangle.
emphase, *n.f.* emphasis.
emphatique, *adj.* emphatic.
empiéter, *vb.* encroach, trespass.
empire, *n.m.* empire.
empirique, *adj.* empirical.
emplette, *n.f.* purchase. **faire des
e.s,** shop.
emploi, *n.m.* employment, use;
job.
employé, *n.m.* employee, clerk,
(public) servant.
employer, *vb.* employ, use.
employeur, *n.m.* employer.
empois, *n.m.* starch.
empoisonné, *adj.* poisonous.
empoisonner, *vb.* poison.
emporter, *vb.* take away. **s'e.,** get
angry.
empreinte, *n.f.* print, impression.
empressé, *adj.* solicitous.
empressement, *n.m.* eagerness.
empresser, *vb.* **s'e.,** be eager.
emprise, *n.f.* expropriation.
emprisonnement, *n.m.* imprisonment.
emprisonner, *vb.* imprison.
emprunt, *n.m.* loan.
emprunter à, *vb.* borrow from.

emprunteur, *n.m.* borrower.
ému, *adj.* touched, stirred.
émule, *n.m.* rival, competitor.
en, 1. *prep.* in, into. **2.** *adv.*
thence; of it; some, any.
encadrer, *vb.* frame.
en-cas, *n.m.* reserve.
enceinte, *adj.f.* pregnant.
encens, *n.m.* incense.
enchaîner, *vb.* chain.
enchantement, *n.m.* enchantment.
enchanter, *vb.* delight, charm, enchant.
enchère, *n.f.* bid. **vente aux e.s,**
auction.
enclore, *vb.* fence in, enclose.
enclos, 1. *n.m.* enclosure. **2.** *adj.*
shut in.
enclume, *n.f.* anvil.
encoche, *n.f.* notch.
encoller, *vb.* paste.
encombrant, *adj.* cumbersome.
encombré, *adj.* crowded.
encombrement, *n.m.* congestion.
encombrer, *vb.* crowd, clutter,
block up.
encontre, *adv.* **à l'e.,** toward,
counter (to).
encore, *adv.* still, yet, again.
encourageant, *adj.* encouraging.
encouragement, *n.m.* encouragement.
encourager, *vb.* encourage, urge,
promote.
encourir, *vb.* incur.
encre, *n.f.* ink.
encrier, *n.m.* inkwell.
encyclopédie, *n.f.* encyclopedia.
endetté, *adj.* indebted.
endiguer, *vb.* dam up.
endive, *n.f.* chicory.
endolori, *adj.* painful.
endommager, *vb.* damage.
endormi, *adj.* asleep.
endormir, *vb.* put to sleep. **s'e.,**
go to sleep.
endossement, *n.m.* endorsement.
endosser, *vb.* endorse.
endroit, *n.m.* place.
enduire, *vb.* smear, daub.
endurance, *n.f.* endurance.
endurant, *adj.* patient.
endurcir, *vb.* harden.
endurcissement, *n.m.* hardening.
énergie, *n.f.* energy.
énergique, *adj.* energetic.

énervant, *adj.* enervating.

énervé, *adj.* nervous.

enfance, *n.f.* childhood. **première e.,** infancy.

enfant, *n.m.f.* child.

enfantement, *n.m.* childbirth.

enfanter, *vb.* bear (children).

enfantillage, *n.m.* childishness.

enfantin, *adj.* childish.

enfariner, *vb.* coat with flour.

enfer (-r), *n.m.* hell.

enfermer, *vb.* shut in.

enfiévrer, *vb.* excite, inspire.

enfin, *adv.* finally, at last.

enflammer, *vb.* inflame.

enfler, *vb.* swell.

enflure, *n.f.* swelling.

enfoncer, *vb.* sink.

enfouir, *vb.* bury.

enfourchure, *n.f.* bifurcation; crotch of a tree.

enfreindre, *vb.* violate.

enfuir, *vb.* **s'e.,** run away, flee, elope.

enfumer, *vb.* fill or cover with smoke.

engageant, *adj.* personable, charming.

engagement, *n.m.* pledge, agreement, engagement.

engager, *vb.* hire, engage. **s'e.,** volunteer.

engelure, *n.f.* chilblain.

engendrer, *vb.* beget.

engin, *n.m.* machine; engine, motor.

englober, *vb.* include.

engloutir, *vb.* devour.

engorgement, *n.m.* choking.

engouement, *n.m.* infatuation.

engouffrer, *vb.* engulf.

engourdir, *vb.* dull.

engrais, *n.m.* fertilizer.

engraisser, *vb.* fatten.

engraver, *vb.* strand or ground (a ship).

engrenage, *n.m.* gear.

engrener, *vb.* engage (gears).

enhardir, *vb.* make bolder.

énigmatique, *adj.* enigmatic.

énigme, *n.f.* riddle, puzzle, enigma.

enivrant, *adj.* intoxicating.

enivrement, *n.m.* intoxication.

enivrer, *vb.* intoxicate. **s'e.,** get drunk.

enjambée, *n.f.* stride.

enjamber, *vb.* stride.

enjeu, *n.m.* stake.

enjoindre, *vb.* enjoin; call upon.

enjôlement, *n.m.* cajolery.

enjôler, *vb.* cajole.

enjoliver, *vb.* beautify.

enjoué, *adj.* playful.

enjouement, *n.m.* playfulness.

enlacer, *vb.* entwine; interlace; embrace.

enlaidir, *vb.* make or become ugly.

enlevable, *adj.* detachable.

enlèvement, *n.m.* removal, abduction.

enlever, *vb.* take away, remove, abduct.

enneigé, *adj.* snow-covered.

ennemi, *adj. and n.m.* enemy.

ennoblir, *vb.* exalt; ennoble.

ennui (-nwē), *n.m.* nuisance, bore, bother; boredom.

ennuyer, *vb.* bore, annoy, vex, bother, irk.

ennuyeux, *adj.* boring, tedious, dull.

énoncer, *vb.* enunciate.

énonciation, *n.f.* enunciation.

énorme, *adj.* enormous.

énormité, *n.f.* enormity.

enquérir, *vb.* inquire.

enquête, *n.f.* inquiry.

enraciner, *vb.* root. **s'e.,** take root.

enragé, *adj.* rabid.

enrageant, *adj.* infuriating.

enrager, *vb.* be, go mad. **s'e.,** get angry.

enregistrement, *n.m.* registration, recording; checking.

enregistrer, *vb.* record, register, list; check (luggage).

enrichir, *vb.* enrich.

enrober, *vb.* coat, envelop.

enrôlement, *n.m.* enlistment, enrollment.

enrôler, *vb.* enlist, enroll.

enroué, *adj.* hoarse.

enrouement, *n.m.* hoarseness.

enrouler, *vb.* **s'e.,** roll up, twist, wind.

enseigne, *n.f.* sign, ensign.

enseignement, *n.m.* teaching, instruction.

enseigner, *vb.* teach.

ensemble, 1. *n.m.* set. **2.** *adv.* together.

ensevelir, *vb.* bury.
ensoleillé, *adj.* sunny.
ensommeillé, *adj.* sleepy.
ensuite, *adv.* then, next, afterwards.
ensuivre, *vb.* s'e., ensue.
entablement, *n.m.* entablature.
entacher, *vb.* taint, besmirch.
entailler, *vb.* hack (notch).
entamer, *vb.* begin.
entassement, *n.m.* accumulation.
entasser, *vb.* heap up.
ente, *n.f.* scion (horticulture).
entendement, *n.m.* understanding, sense.
entendre, *vb.* hear, understand. s'e., get on together.
entendu, *adj.* understood, agreed. **bien e.,** of course.
enténébré, *adj.* gloomy.
entente, *n.f.* understanding, agreement.
enterrement, *n.m.* burial.
enterrer, *vb.* bury.
entêté, *adj.* perverse.
entêtement, *n.m.* stubbornness.
entêter, *vb.* s'e., be stubborn, insist.
enthousiasme, *n.m.* enthusiasm.
enthousiaste, 1. *n.m.f.* enthusiast. 2. *adj.* enthusiastic. **e. de,** keen on.
entichement, *n.m.* infatuation.
entier, *adj.* whole, complete, entire.
entité, *n.f.* entity.
entonnoir, *n.m.* funnel.
entorse, *n.f.* sprain.
entourage, *n.m.* circle of friends; surroundings.
entourer, *vb.* surround, encircle.
entournure, *n.f.* armhole.
entr'acte, *n.m.* intermission.
entr'aide, *n.f.* mutual assistance.
entrailles, *n.f.pl.* bowels.
entrain, *n.m.* zest.
entraîner, *vb.* draw along; involve, entail; coach, train.
entraîneur, *n.m.* coach.
entrant, *adj.* incoming.
entraver, *vb.* clog.
entre, *prep.* among, between.
entre-clos, *adj.* ajar.
entre-deux, *n.m.* interval.
entrée, *n.f.* admission; entry; main course.
entreface, *n.f.* interface.

entregent, *n.m.* tact; spirit.
entrelacer, *vb.* interlace.
entremets (-mè), *n.m.* (side) dish.
entremetteur, *n.m.* intermediary.
entreposer, *vb.* store.
entreposeur, *n.m.* warehouseman.
entrepôt, *n.m.* warehouse.
entreprenant, *adj.* enterprising.
entreprendre, *vb.* undertake.
entrepreneur, *n.m.* contractor. **e. de pompes funèbres,** undertaker.
entreprise, *n.f.* concern, undertaking.
entrer (dans), *vb.* enter, come in, go in. **laisser e.,** admit.
entretenir, *vb.* entertain. s'e., converse.
entretien, *n.m.* maintenance; conference; talk, conversation.
entrevoir, *vb.* glimpse.
entrevue, *n.f.* interview.
entr'ouvert, *adj.* ajar.
entr'ouvrir, *vb.* open halfway.
énumération, *n.f.* enumeration.
énumérer, *vb.* enumerate.
envahir, *vb.* invade.
envahissement, *n.m.* invasion.
enveloppe, *n.f.* envelope, wrapping.
envelopper, *vb.* envelop, wrap, enfold.
envers, 1. *n.m.* wrong side. 2. *prep.* toward.
enviable, *adj.* enviable.
envie, *n.f.* envy, desire. **avoir e. de,** want to, feel like.
envier, *vb.* envy.
envieux, *adj.* envious.
environ, *prep. and adv.* around; about; approximately.
environnement, *n.m.* surroundings.
environnementaliste, *n.m.* environmentalist.
environner, *vb.* surround.
envisager, *vb.* consider.
envoi, *n.m.* shipment, sending.
envoler, *vb.* s'e., fly away.
envoyé, *n.m.* envoy.
envoyer, *vb.* send.
enzyme, *n.f.* enzyme.
éon, *n.m.* eon.
épais, *adj.* thick.
épaisseur, *n.f.* thickness.
épaissir, *vb.* thicken.
épancher, *vb.* shed (blood).

épanouir, vb. **s'é.,** bloom.

épargne, n.f. savings.

épargner, vb. save, spare.

éparpiller, vb. scatter.

épars, adj. scattered, sparse.

éparvin, n.m. spavin.

épatant, adj. (colloq.) grand.

épate, n.f. swagger.

épatement, n.m. amazement.

épater, vb. amaze.

épaule, n.f. shoulder.

épaulette, n.f. epaulette.

épée, n.f. sword.

épeler, vb. spell.

épellation, n.f. spelling.

éperdu, adj. distracted.

éperlan, n.m. smelt.

éperon, n.m. spur.

éperonner, vb. spur.

épervier, n.m. hawk.

épeuré, adj. frightened.

éphémère, adj. ephemeral, fleeting.

épice, n.f. spice.

épicé, adj. spicy.

épicerie, n.f. grocery.

épicier, n.m. grocer.

épidémie, n.f. epidemic.

épiderme, n.m. epidermis.

épidermique, adj. epidermal.

épier, vb. spy.

épigramme, n.f. epigram.

épilatoire, n.m. and adj. depilatory.

épilepsie, n.f. epilepsy.

épileptique, adj. and n. epileptic.

épilogue, n.m. epilogue.

épinards (-nar), n.m.pl. spinach.

épine, n.f. spine, thorn. **é. dorsale,** spinal column.

épinet, n.f. spinet.

épineux, adj. thorny.

épingle, n.f. pin. **é. à cheveux,** hairpin. **é. anglaise,** safety pin.

épingler, vb. pin.

épique, adj. epic.

épiscopal, adj. Episcopal.

épisode, n.m. episode.

épisodique, adj. episodic.

épistolaire, adj. epistolary.

épitaphe, n.f. epitaph.

épithète, n.f. epithet.

épitomé, n.m. epitome.

épitre, n.f. epistle.

éploré, adj. tearful.

éponge, n.f. sponge.

éponger, vb. sponge up.

épopée, n.f. epic.

époque, n.f. epoch.

épouffé, adj. breathless, panting.

épouiller, vb. delouse.

épouse, n.f. wife.

épouser, vb. marry.

épouseur, n.m. suitor.

épousseter, vb. dust.

époussette, n.f. duster.

épouvantable, adj. terrible.

épouvante, n.f. fright.

épouvanter, vb. frighten.

époux, n.m. husband.

épreindre, vb. squeeze.

éprendre, vb. **s'é.,** fall in love.

épreuve, n.f. trial, test, ordeal, proof.

éprouver, vb. experience.

éprouvette, n.f. test tube.

épuisant, adj. exhausting.

épuisement, n.m. exhaustion.

épuiser, vb. exhaust.

épuration, n.f. purification.

épurer, vb. purify.

équanimité (-kwà-), n.f. equanimity.

équateur (-kwà-), n.m. equator.

équation (-kwà-), n.f. equation.

équatorial (-kwà-), adj. equatorial.

équestre, adj. equestrian.

équidistant, adj. equidistant.

équilibre, n.m. poise.

équilibrer, vb. balance.

équilibriste, n. tight-rope walker.

équinoxe, n.m. equinox.

équinoxial, adj. equinoctial.

équipage, n.m. crew.

équipe, n.f. team, crew, gang, shift.

équipement, n.m. equipment.

équiper, vb. equip.

équitable, adj. fair.

équité, n.f. equity.

équivalent, adj. and n.m. equivalent.

équivaloir, vb. equal in value.

équivoque, adj. equivocal.

érable, n.m. maple.

éradication, n.f. eradication.

éraflure, n.m. scratch; graze.

érailler, vb. unravel.

ère, n.f. era.

érection, n.f. erection; construction.

éreintant, adj. exhausting.

éreinter, vb. exhaust.

erg, n.m. erg.

ériger, vb. erect.

ermitage, n.m. hermitage.

ermite, n.m. hermit.

éroder, vb. erode.

érosif, adj. erosive.

érosion, n.f. erosion.

érotique, adj. erotic.

errant, adj. wandering.

erratique, adj. erratic.

errer, vb. wander; err.

erreur, n.f. mistake, error.

erroné, adj. erroneous.

éructation, n.f. belch.

éructer, vb. belch.

érudit, adj. learned, scholarly.

érudition, n.f. learning.

éruption, n.f. rash, eruption.

érysipèle, n.m. erysipelas.

escabeau, n.m. stool.

escadrille, n.f. (ships) flotilla; (airplanes) squadron.

escadron, n.m. squadron.

escalader, vb. scale; escalate.

escalier, n.m. stairs.

escalope, n.f. cutlet.

escamotage, n.m. legerdemain.

escamoteur, n.m. conjurer, magician.

escapade, n.f. escapade.

escarcelle, n.f. wallet.

escargot, n.m. snail.

escarole, n.f. endive.

escarpé, adj. abrupt.

escarpement, n.m. steepness.

eschare, n.f. scab; bedsore.

esclandre, n.m. slander.

esclavage, n.m. slavery.

esclave, n.m.f. slave.

escompte, n.m. discount.

escorte, n.f. escort.

escorter, vb. escort.

escouade, n.f. squad.

escrime, n.f. fencing.

escrimer, vb. fight.

escrimeur, n.m. swordsman.

escroc (-ō), n.m. swindler.

escroquer, vb. swindle.

escroquerie, n.f. swindle.

esculent, adj. esculent.

espace, n.m. space.

espacé, adj. at great intervals.

espacer, vb. space out.

espadon, n.m. swordfish.

Espagne, n.f. Spain.

Espagnol, n.m. Spaniard.

espagnol, adj. and n.m. Spanish.

espalier, n.m. espalier.

espèce, n.f. species, kind; (pl.) cash.

espérance, n.f. hope.

espéranto, n.m. Esperanto.

espérer, vb. hope.

espiègle, adj. mischievous.

espièglerie, n.f. mischief.

espion, n.m. spy.

espionnage, n.m. espionage.

espionner, vb. spy on.

esplanade, n.f. esplanade.

espoir, n.m. hope.

esprit, n.m. spirit, mind, wit. Saint-E., Holy Ghost.

esquif, n.m. skiff.

Esquimau m., Esquimaude f. n. Eskimo.

esquimau, adj. Eskimo.

esquinancie, n.f. quinsy.

esquinter, vb. exhaust, tire out.

esquisse, n.f. sketch.

esquisser, vb. sketch.

esquiver, vb. shirk.

essai, n.m. essay, attempt; experiment; assay.

essaim, n.m. swarm.

essaimer, vb. swarm.

essayer, vb. try; assay.

essence, n.f. gasoline; essence.

essentiel, adj. essential.

esseulement, n.m. solitude.

essieu, n.m. axle.

essor, n.m. flight.

essorer, vb. dry.

essoufflé, adj. breathless.

essoufflement, n.m. breathlessness.

essuie-glace, n.m. windshield wiper.

essuyer, vb. wipe.

est (-t), n.m. east.

estacade, n.f. stockade.

estafette, n.f. courier.

estafier, n.m. bodyguard.

estagnon, n.m. oil drum.

estaminet, n.m. bar, taproom.

estampe, n.f. engraving.

estampille, n.f. trademark.

esthète, n.m. esthete.

esthétique, adj. aesthetic.

estimable, adj. estimable.

estimateur, n.m. estimator; appraiser.

estimatif, adj. estimated.

estimation, n.f. estimate.

estime, *n.f.* esteem; estimation.

estimer, *vb.* esteem; estimate, value, rate.

estival, *adj.* of summer.

estivant, *n.m.* summer tourist.

estiver, *vb.* spend the summer.

estoc, *n.m.* tree trunk.

estomac (mä), *n.m.* stomach.

estourbir, *vb.* kill.

estrade, *n.f.* platform; stage.

estropié, 1. *n.m.* cripple. **2.** *adj.* crippled.

estropier, *vb.* cripple.

estuaire, *n.m.* estuary.

esturgeon, *n.m.* sturgeon.

et, *conj.* and.

étable, *n.f.* barn.

établi, *n.m.* worktable.

établir, *vb.* settle, establish.

établissement, *n.m.* establishment.

étage, *n.m.* floor, story.

étagère, *n.f.* whatnot shelf.

étain, *n.m.* tin.

étal, *n.m.* butcher shop.

étalage, *n.m.* display.

étalager, *vb.* display.

étaler, *vb.* display, spread.

étalon, *n.m.* standard.

étameur, *n.m.* tinsmith.

étamine, *n.f.* coarse muslin; stamen.

étampe, *n.f.* stamp.

étamper, *vb.* stamp.

étanche, *adj.* impervious.

étancher, *vb.* quench, stanch.

étang, *n.m.* pond.

étape, *n.f.* stage.

état, *n.m.* state.

état-major, *n.m.* staff.

États-Unis, *n.m.pl.* United States.

été, *n.m.* summer.

éteindre, *vb.* extinguish, put out.

éteint, *adj.* extinct.

étendage, *n.m.* clotheslines.

étendard, *n.m.* standard.

étendre, *vb.* extend, spread, reach.

étendu, *adj.* extensive.

étendue, *n.f.* extent.

éternel, *adj.* everlasting.

éterniser, *vb.* perpetuate.

éternité, *n.f.* eternity.

éternuement, *n.m.* sneeze.

éternuer, *vb.* sneeze.

éther (-r), *n.m.* ether.

éthéré, *adj.* ethereal.

Éthiopie, *n.f.* Ethiopia.

éthique, *n.f.* ethics.

ethnique, *adj.* ethnic.

étinceler, *vb.* sparkle.

étincelle, *n.f.* spark, sparkle.

étincellement, *n.m.* sparkle, glitter.

étiolement, *n.m.* atrophy.

étioler, *vb.* blanch.

étiqueter, *vb.* label.

étiquette, *n.f.* label, tag; etiquette.

étirer, *vb.* stretch out.

étoffe, *n.f.* stuff, material, cloth.

étoffer, *vb.* stuff.

étoile, *n.f.* star.

étoiler, *vb.* bespangle.

étonnement, *n.m.* astonishment.

étonner, *vb.* astonish.

étouffé, *adj.* braised.

étouffer, *vb.* smother.

étourdi, *adj.* thoughtless.

étourdir, *vb.* daze.

étourdissant, *adj.* dazing.

étourdissement, *n.m.* dizziness.

étrange, *adj.* strange.

étranger, *n.* and *adj.* alien.

étranglement, *n.m.* strangulation.

étrangler, *vb.* strangle.

étrave, *n.f.* stem, bow.

être, 1. *n.m.* being. **2.** *vb.* be.

étrécir, *vb.* shrink.

étreindre, *vb.* clasp.

étreinte, *n.f.* clasp, hug, embrace.

étrier, *n.m.* stirrup.

étrille, *n.f.* currycomb.

étroit, *adj.* narrow.

Étrusque, *n.m.f.* Etruscan.

étrusque, *adj.* Etruscan.

étude, *n.f.* study.

étudiant, *n.m.* student.

étudier, *vb.* study.

étui, *n.m.* **1.** case. **2.** needle case.

étuve, *n.f.* steam room.

étymologie, *n.f.* etymology.

étymologique, *adj.* etymological.

eucalyptus, *n.m.* eucalyptus.

eucharistie, *n.f.* eucharist.

eunuque, *n.m.* eunuch.

euphémique, *adj.* euphemistic.

euphémisme, *n.m.* euphemism.

euphonie, *n.f.* euphony.

euphonique, *adj.* euphonic.

euphorie, *n.f.* euphoria.

Europe, *n.f.* Europe.

Européen, *n.m.* European.

européen, *adj.* European.
euthanasie, *n.f.* euthanasia.
eux, *pron.m.* them.
évacuable, *adj.* able to be evacuated.
évacuation, *n.f.* evacuation.
évacuer, *vb.* evacuate.
évader, *vb.* s'é., escape.
évaluateur, *n.m.* appraiser.
évaluation, *n.f.* appraisal.
évaluer, *vb.* evaluate, rate, assess.
évangélique, *adj.* evangelic.
évangéliste, *n.m.* evangelist.
évangile, *n.m.* gospel.
évanouir, *vb.* s'é., fade away; faint.
évaporation, *n.f.* evaporation.
évaporer, *vb.* evaporate.
évasif, *adj.* evasive.
évasion, *n.f.* escape.
évêché, *n.m.* bishopric.
éveil, *n.m.* alertness.
éveillé, *adj.* sprightly.
éveiller, *vb.* wake.
événement, *n.m.* event.
éventail, *n.m.* fan.
éventrer, *vb.* disembowel.
éventualité, *n.f.* eventuality.
éventuel, *adj.* possible.
éventuellement, *adv.* eventually.
évêque, *n.m.* bishop.
éviction, *n.f.* eviction.
évidemment, *adv.* evidently.
évidence, *n.f.* evidence. **en é.,** conspicuous.
évident, *adj.* obvious, evident.
évider, *vb.* scoop out.
évier, *n.m.* sink.
évincer, *vb.* oust.
éviscérer, *vb.* eviscerate, disembowel.
évitable, *adj.* avoidable.
éviter, *vb.* avoid.
évocation, *n.f.* evocation.
évolution, *n.f.* evolution.
évoquer, *vb.* evoke.
exact (-kt), *adj.* exact, precise.
exactement, *adv.* exactly.
exactitude, *n.f.* precision.
exagération, *n.f.* exaggeration.
exagérer, *vb.* exaggerate.
exaltant, *adj.* exciting.
exaltation, *n.f.* exaltation.
exalté, *adj.* impassioned.
exalter, *vb.* exalt, elate.
examen, *n.m.* examination.
examiner, *vb.* examine.

exaspération, *n.f.* exasperation.
exaspérer, *vb.* exasperate, aggravate.
excavateur, *n.m.* steam shovel.
excavation, *n.f.* excavation.
excaver, *vb.* excavate.
excédent, *n.m.* excess; overweight.
excéder, *vb.* exceed.
excellence, *n.f.* excellence, excellency, highness.
excellent, *adj.* excellent.
exceller, *vb.* excel.
excentrique, *adj.* eccentric.
excepté, *prep.* except.
excepter, *vb.* except.
exception, *n.f.* exception.
exceptionnel, *adj.* exceptional.
excès, *n.m.* excess.
excessif, *adj.* excessive, extreme.
exciser, *vb.* excise; cut out.
excitabilité, *n.f.* excitability.
excitable, *adj.* excitable.
excitant, *adj.* exciting.
exciter, *vb.* excite.
exclamatif, *adj.* exclamatory.
exclamation, *n.f.* exclamation.
exclamer, *vb.* exclaim.
exclure, *vb.* exclude.
exclusif, *adj.* exclusive.
exclusion, *n.f.* exclusion.
excommunication, *n.f.* excommunication.
excommunier, *vb.* excommunicate.
excorier, *vb.* excoriate.
excrément, *n.m.* excrement.
excréter, *vb.* excrete.
excrétion, *n.f.* excretion.
excursion, *n.f.* excursion.
excursionniste, *n.* excursionist.
excusable, *adj.* excusable.
excuse, *n.f.* plea, excuse.
excuser, *vb.* excuse. **s'e. de,** apologize for.
exécuter, *vb.* perform, enforce.
exécuteur, *n.m.* executor.
exécutif, *adj. and adv.* executive.
exécution, *n.f.* performance, enforcement, execution.
exemplaire, **1.** *n.m.* copy. **2.** *adj.* exemplary.
exemple, *n.m.* instance, example.
exempt, *adj.* exempt.
exempt de droits, *adj.* duty-free.
exempter, *vb.* exempt.
exemption, *n.f.* exemption.

exerçant, *adj.* practicing.
exercer, *vb.* exercise, drill, train. **s'e.,** practice.
exercice, *n.m.* exercise, drill, practice.
exhalation, *n.f.* exhalation.
exhaler, *vb.* exhale.
exhaustion, *n.f.* exhaust.
exhiber, *vb.* show, present; exhibit.
exhibition, *n.f.* exhibition.
exhortation, *n.f.* exhortation.
exhorter, *vb.* exhort.
exhumer, *vb.* exhume.
exigence, *n.f.* requirement.
exiger, *vb.* require, exact, demand.
exil (-l), *n.m.* exile.
exilé, *n.m.* exile.
exiler, *vb.* banish.
existant, *adj.* existent.
existence, *n.f.* existence.
exister, *vb.* exist.
exode, *n.m.* exodus.
exonération, *n.f.* exoneration.
exonérer, *vb.* exonerate.
exorbitant, *adj.* exorbitant.
exorciser, *vb.* exorcise.
exotique, *adj.* exotic.
expansible, *adj.* expansible.
expansif, *adj.* expansive.
expansion, *n.f.* expansion.
expatriation, *n.f.* expatriation.
expatrié, *n.* exile, expatriate.
expectorant, *n.m. and adj.* expectorant.
expectorer, *vb.* expectorate.
expédient, *n.m.* makeshift.
expédier, *vb.* dispatch.
expéditif, *adj.* expeditious.
expédition, *n.f.* dispatch; expedition, shipment.
expérience, *n.f.* experience, experiment.
expérimental, *adj.* experimental.
expérimentation, *n.f.* experimentation.
expérimenté, *adj.* practiced, experienced.
expert, *adj. and n.m.* expert.
expiable, *adj.* expiable.
expiation, *n.f.* atonement.
expier, *vb.* atone for.
expiration, *n.f.* expiration.
expirer, *vb.* expire.
explétif, *n. and adj.* expletive.
explicatif, *adj.* explanatory.

explication, *n.f.* explanation.
explicite, *adj.* explicit, clear.
expliquer, *vb.* explain.
exploit, *n.m.* feat, exploit.
exploitation, *n.f.* exploitation, working.
exploiter, *vb.* exploit.
explorateur, *n.m.* explorer.
exploratif, *adj.* exploratory.
exploration, *n.f.* exploration.
explorer, *vb.* explore.
explosible, *adj.* explosible.
explosif, *adj. and n.m.* explosive.
explosion, *n.f.* blast, explosion.
exportation, *n.f.* export, exportation.
exporter, *vb.* export.
exposé, *n.m.* account, statement.
exposer, *vb.* expound, expose, exhibit.
exposition, *n.f.* exposition, exposure, show, display.
exprès, 1. *n.m.* special delivery. **2.** *adj.* express. **3.** *adv.* on purpose.
expressif, *adj.* expressive.
expression, *n.f.* expression.
exprimable, *adj.* expressible.
exprimer, *vb.* express.
exproprier, *vb.* expropriate.
expulser, *vb.* expel.
expulsion, *n.f.* expulsion.
expurgation, *n.f.* expurgation.
expurger, *vb.* expurgate.
exquis, *adj.* exquisite.
exsuder, *vb.* exude.
extase, *n.f.* ecstasy.
extasier, *vb.* **s'e. sur,** rave about.
extatique, *adj.* ecstatic.
extensif, *adj.* extensive.
extension, *n.f.* extension.
exténuation, *n.f.* extenuation.
exténuer, *vb.* extenuate, exhaust.
extérieur, 1. *n.m.* exterior. **2.** *adj.* exterior, outer.
extérieurement, *adv.* externally.
extermination, *n.f.* extermination.
exterminer, *vb.* exterminate.
externat, *n.m.* day school.
externe, *adj.* external.
exterritorialité, *n.f.* extraterritoriality.
extincteur, *n.m.* fire extinguisher.
extinction, *n.f.* extinction.
extirper, *vb.* extirpate, root out.
extorquer, *vb.* extort.

extorsion, *n.f.* extortion.
extra-, *prefix* extra.
extraction, *n.f.* extraction; descent.
extrader, *vb.* extradite.
extradition, *n.f.* extradition.
extra-fin, *adj.* extremely fine.
extraire, *vb.* extract.
extrait, *n.m.* extract, abstract.
extraordinaire, *adj.* extraordinary, unusual.
extraordinairement, *adv.* extraordinarily.
extravagance, *n.f.* extravagance.
extravagant, *adj.* extravagant.
extrême, *adj. and n.m.* extreme.
extrémiste, *n.* extremist.
extrémité, *n.f.* extremity.
extrinsèque, *adj.* extrinsic.
extroverti, *n.* extrovert.
extrusion, *n.f.* extrusion.
exubérance, *n.f.* exuberance.
exubérant, *adj.* exuberant.
exultation, *n.f.* exultation.
exulter, *vb.* exult.

F

fable, *n.f.* fable.
fabliau, *n.m.* fabliau.
fabricant, *n.m.* maker, manufacturer.
fabricateur, *n.m.* forger.
fabrication, *n.f.* make.
fabrique, *n.f.* factory.
fabriquer, *vb.* manufacture.
fabuleux, *adj.* fabulous.
fabuliste, *n.m.* fabulist.
façade, *n.f.* front.
face, *n.f.* face. **en f. de,** opposite.
faire f. à, confront.
facétie, *n.f.* joke, prank.
facétieux, *adj.* facetious.
facette, *n.f.* facet.
fâché, *j.* angry; sorry.
fâcher, *vb.* anger, offend, grieve.
se f., get angry.
fâcherie, *n.f.* quarrel, argument.
fâcheux, *adj.* upleasant.
facial, *adj.* facial.
facile, *adj.* easy.
facilité, *n.f.* fluency, ease.
faciliter, *vb.* facilitate, make easy.
façon, *n.f.* way, manner, fashion.
de f. à, so as to.
faconde, *n.f.* glibness; fluency.

façonner, *vb.* shape, fashion.
facsimilé, *n.m.* facsimile.
facteur, *n.m.* factor, element; mailman.
factice, *adj.* artificial.
factieux, *adj.* factious; quarrelsome.
faction, *n.f.* faction, party.
factionnaire, *n.m.* sentry.
facture, *n.f.* invoice, bill.
facturer, *vb.* bill; send an invoice to.
facultatif, *adj.* optional.
faculté, *n.f.* faculty.
fadaise, *n.f.* nonsense.
fade, *adj.* insipid.
fadeur, *n.f.* insipidity.
fagot, *n.m.* bundle.
faible, *adj.* weak, faint, dim, feeble.
faiblement, *adv.* feebly, weakly.
faiblesse, *n.f.* weakness, frailty, dimness.
faiblir, *vb.* weaken.
failli, *adj. and n.m.* bankrupt.
faillibilité, *n.f.* fallibility.
faillible, *adj.* fallible.
faillir, *vb.* fail.
faillite, *n.f.* bankrupcy.
faim, *n.f.* hunger.
fainéant, *n.m.* loafer.
faire, *vb.* make, do. **f. part,** inform. **f. mal à,** hurt. **f. voir,** show.
faisable, *adj.* feasible.
faisan, *n.m.* pheasant.
fait, *n.m.* fact. **tout à f.,** wholly.
falaise, *n.f.* cliff.
fallacieux, *adj.* fallacious.
falloir, *vb.* be necessary. **comme il faut,** decent.
falot, *n.m.* lamp.
falsificateur, *n.m.* forger; falsifier.
falsification, *n.f.* falsification.
falsifier, *vb.* falsify.
fameux, *adj.* famous.
familiariser, *vb.* familiarize.
familiarité, *n.f.* familiarity.
familier, *adj.* familiar.
familièrement, *adv.* familiarly.
famille, *n.f.* family, household.
famine, *n.f.* famine.
fanatique, *adj. and n.m.* fanatic.
fanatisme, *n.m.* fanaticism.
faner, *vb.* fade.
fanfare, *n.f.* fanfare.
fanfaronnade, *n.f.* boast.
fange, *n.f.* filth; vice.

fantaisie, *n.f.* fancy, fantasy.
fantastique, *adj.* fantastic.
fantoche, *n.m.* puppet.
fantôme, *n.m.* phantom, ghost.
faon, *n.m.* fawn.
farce, *n.f.* stuffing; farce.
farceur, *n.m.* jokester.
farcir, *vb.* stuff.
fard, *n.m.* facial makeup.
fardeau, *n.m.* burden.
farinacé, *adj.* farinaceous.
farine, *n.f.* meal, flour.
farniente, *n.m.* idleness.
farouche, *adj.* fierce, sullen, shy.
fascinant, *adj.* fascinating.
fascination, *n.f.* fascination.
fascine, *n.f.* faggot (of wood).
fasciner, *vb.* fascinate.
fascisme, *n.m.* fascism.
fasciste, *n.m.* fascist.
faste, *n.m.* ostentation.
fastidieux, *adj.* dull.
fat, *adj.* foppish.
fatal, *adj.* mortal; fatal.
fatalisme, *n.m.* fatalism.
fataliste, *n.m.f.* fatalist.
fatalité, *n.f.* fatality; misfortune.
fatigant, *adj.* tiring.
fatigue, *n.f.* weariness.
fatiguer, *vb.* tire.
fatuité, *n.f.* smugness.
faubourg, *n.m.* suburb.
faubourien, *adj.* suburban.
faucher, *vb.* mow.
faucheur, *n.m.* reaper, mower.
faucille, *n.f.* sickle.
faucon, *n.m.* hawk.
fauconneau, *n.m.* young falcon.
fauconnerie, *n.f.* falconry.
faufil, *n.m.* basting thread.
faufiler, *vb.* baste.
faune, *n.f.* fauna; wildlife.
faussaire, *n.f.* forger; liar.
faussement, *adv.* falsely.
fausser, *vb.* pervert, warp, distort.
fausset, *n.m.* falsetto; spigot, faucet.
fausseté, *n.f.* falseness.
faute, *n.f.* fault, mistake. **f. de,** for want of.
fauteuil, *n.m.* armchair.
fautif, *adv.* faulty, wrong.
fauve, *adj.* wild.
faux, 1. *n.m.* forgery. **2.** *f.* scythe.
faux *m.,* **fausse** *f. adj.* false, wrong, spurious, counterfeit.

faux-filet, *n.m.* sirloin.
faveur, *n.f.* favor. **en f. de,** on behalf of.
favorable, *adj.* conducive, favorable.
favorablement, *adv.* favorably.
favori, *n.m.* whisker.
favori *m.,* **favorite** *f. adj. and n.* favorite.
favoriser, *vb.* favor.
favoritisme, *n.m.* favoritism.
fayot, *n.m.* kidney bean.
féal, *adj.* faithful.
fébrile, *adj.* feverish.
fécal, *adj.* fecal.
fécond, *adj.* fertile.
féconder, *vb.* fertilize.
fécondité, *n.f.* fertility.
féculent, *adj.* starchy.
fédéral, *adj.* federal.
fédéraliser, *vb.* federalize.
fédéraliste, *n. and adj.* federalist.
fédération, *n.f.* confederacy, federation.
fédérer, *vb.* federate.
fée, *n.f.* fairy.
féerie, *n.f.* fairyland.
féerique, *adj.* fairylike.
feindre, *vb.* feign, pretend.
fêler, *vb.* crack.
félicitation, *n.f.* congratulation.
félicité, *n.f.* bliss.
féliciter (de), *vb.* congratulate (on).
félin, *adj.* feline.
félon, *adj.* disloyal.
femelle, *adj. and n.f.* female.
féminin, *adj.* female, feminine.
femme, *n.f.* woman, wife. **f. de chambre,** chambermaid.
fémoral, *adj.* femoral.
fendille, *n.f.* crack.
fendiller, *vb.* **se f.,** crack.
fendoir, *n.m.* cleaver.
fendre, *vb.* split, rip.
fenêtre, *n.f.* window.
fenil, *n.m.* hayloft.
fente, *n.f.* crack, rip, split.
féodal, *adj.* feudal.
féodalité, *n.f.* feudalism.
fer (-r), *n.m.* iron. **chemin de f.,** railway. **fil de f.,** wire. **f. à cheval,** horseshoe.
fermail, *n.m.* brooch, clasp.
ferme, *n.f.* farm. **maison de f.,** farmhouse.
ferme, *adj.* firm, steady, fast.

fermement, *adv.* firmly.

fermentation, *n.f.* fermentation.

fermenter, *vb.* ferment.

fermer, *vb.* close. **f. à clef,** lock.

fermeté, *n.f.* firmness.

fermier, *n.m.* farmer.

féroce, *adj.* fierce.

férocité, *n.f.* ferocity.

ferraille, *n.f.* old iron.

ferreux, *adj.* ferrous.

ferrique, *adj.* ferric.

fertile, *adj.* fertile.

fertilisant, *n.m.* fertilizer.

fertilisation, *n.f.* fertilization.

fertiliser, *vb.* fertilize.

fertilité, *n.f.* fertility.

férule, *n.f.* cane, rod.

fervemment, *adv.* fervently.

fervent, *adj.* fervent.

ferveur, *n.f.* fervor.

fesse, *n.f.* buttock.

fessée, *n.f.* spanking.

fesser, *vb.* spank.

festin, *n.m.* feast.

festiner, *vb.* feast.

feston, *n.m.* festoon.

fête, *n.f.* feast, party. **jour de f.,** holiday.

fêter, *vb.* fete.

fétiche, *n.m.* fetish.

fétide, *adj.* fetid.

feu, *n.m.* fire. **f. de joie,** bonfire. **f. d'artifice,** fireworks. **prendre f.,** catch fire. **coup de f.,** shot.

feu, *adj.* late (deceased).

feuillage, *n.m.* foliage.

feuille, *n.f.* leaf, sheet, foil.

feuilleter, *vb.* skim (book).

feutre, *n.m.* felt.

fève, *n.f.* bean.

février, *n.m.* February.

fez, *n.m.* fez.

fi, *interj.* fie!

fiacre, *n.m.* cab.

fiançailles, *n.f.pl.* engagement, betrothal.

fiancé, *n.m.* fiancé.

fiancer, *vb.* betroth.

fiasco, *n.m.* fiasco.

fibre, *n.f.* fiber.

fibreux, *adj.* fibrous.

ficelle, *n.f.* string, twine.

fiche, *n.f.* slip (of paper).

ficher, *vb.* **se f. de,** care nothing about.

fichier, *n.m.* card index.

fichu, *adj.* ruined.

fictif, *adj.* fictitious.

fiction, *n.f.* fiction.

fidèle, *adj.* faithful.

fidélité, *n.f.* fidelity, loyalty, allegiance.

fief, *n.m.* feud.

fiel, *n.m.* gall.

fiente, *n.f.* dung.

fier (-r), *adj.* proud.

fier, *vb.* **se f.,** trust.

fierté, *n.f.* trust.

fièvre, *n.f.* fever.

fiévreux, *adj.* feverish.

fifre, *n.m.* fife(r).

figer, *vb.* coagulate.

figue, *n.f.* fig.

figuratif, *adj.* figurative.

figure, *n.f.* face, figure.

figurer, *vb.* figure, imagine. **se f.,** fancy.

fil, *n.m.* thread, string. **f. de fer,** wire.

filament, *n.m.* filament.

filature, *n.f.* spinning-mill.

file, *n.f.* file.

filer, *vb.* spin.

filet, *n.m.* net.

filial, *adj.* filial.

filin, *n.m.* rope.

fille, *n.f.* daughter. **jeune f.,** girl. **vieille f.,** old maid.

film, *n.m.* film.

filmer, *vb.* film.

filou, *n.m.* thief.

fils (fês), *n.m.* son.

filtrant, *adj.* filterable.

filtration, *n.f.* filtration.

filtre, *n.m.* filter.

filtrer, *vb.* filter.

fin, 1. *n.f.* end. **2.** *adj.* fine; sharp; clever.

final, *adj.* final.

finaliste, *n.* finalist.

finalité, *n.f.* finality.

finance, *n.f.* finance.

financer, *vb.* finance.

financier, 1. *n.m.* financier. **2.** *adj.* financial.

finasser, *vb.* finesse.

finir, *vb.* finish.

Finlande, *n.f.* Finland.

Finnois, *n.m.* Finn.

finnois, *adj.* and *n.m.* Finnish.

firmament, *n.m.* firmament.

firme, *n.f.* company.

fiscal, *adj.* fiscal.

fissure, *n.f.* fissure.

fixation, *n.f.* fixation.

fixe, *adj.* set, fixed.

fixer, *vb.* fix, secure, settle.

fixité, *n.f.* fixity.

flaccidité, *n.f.* flabbiness.

flacon, *n.m.* bottle.

flagellation, *n.f.* flagellation.

flageller, *vb.* flog.

flagrant, *adj.* flagrant.

flair, *n.m.* flair.

flairer, *vb.* smell.

flamand, *adj.* Flemish.

flambant, *adj.* flaming.

flambeau, *n.m.* torch.

flambée, *n.f.* blaze.

flamber, *vb.* blaze.

flamboyant, *adj.* flaming; flamboyant.

flamboyer, *vb.* flame, flare.

flamme, *n.f.* flame.

flanc, *n.m.* side, flank.

flanchet, *n.m.* flank (of beef).

flanelle, *n.f.* flannel.

flâner, *vb.* saunter, stroll, loiter, loaf.

flâneur, *n.m.* idler.

flanquer, *vb.* flank.

flaque, *n.f.* puddle.

flasque, *adj.* flabby.

flatter, *vb.* flatter.

flatterie, *n.f.* flattery.

flatteur, *n.m.* flatterer.

fléau, *n.m.* scourge, plague.

flèche, *n.f.* arrow.

fléchir, *vb.* bend.

flegmatique, *adj.* phlegmatic.

flegme, *n.m.* phlegm.

flet, *n.m.* flounder.

flétan, *n.m.* halibut.

flétrir, *vb.* wilt, wither.

fleur, *n.m.* flower, blossom, bloom.

fleuret, *n.m.* foil.

fleuri, *adj.* flowery.

fleurir, *vb.* flower, bloom, blossom.

fleuriste, *n.m.f.* florist.

fleuve, *n.m.* river.

flexibilité, *n.f.* flexibility.

flexible, *adj.* flexible.

flirt (-t), *n.m.* flirtation.

flirter, *vb.* flirt.

flocon, *n.m.* flake.

florissant, *adj.* prosperous, flourishing.

flot, *n.m.* wave. **à flot,** afloat.

flottant, *adj.* floating; irresolute.

flotte, *n.f.* fleet.

flottement, *n.m.* fluctuation; wavering.

flotter, *vb.* float.

flou, *adj.* hazy, indistinct.

fluctuation, *n.f.* fluctuation.

fluctuer, *vb.* fluctuate.

fluet *m.*, **fluette** *f.* *adj.* thin, delicate.

fluide, *adj. and n.m.* fluid, liquid.

fluidité, *n.f.* fluidity.

flûte, *n.f.* flute.

flûté, *adj.* soft; flute-like.

flux, *n.m.* flow, flux.

fluxion, *n.f.* inflammation.

foi, *n.f.* faith; trust.

foie, *n.m.* liver.

foin, *n.m.* hay.

foire, *n.f.* fair.

fois, *n.f.* time. **à la f.,** at once.

foison, *n.f.* abundance.

foisonner, *vb.* abound.

folâtre, *adj.* frisky.

folâtrer, *vb.* frolic.

folichon, *adj.* playful.

folie, *n.f.* mania, madness, folly.

folklore, *n.m.* folklore.

follement, *adv.* foolishly.

follet, *adj.* merry, playful.

fomenter, *vb.* foment.

foncé, *adj.* dark.

foncer, *vb.* deepen.

fonction, *n.f.* function.

fonctionnaire, *n.m.* official, civil servant.

fonctionnement, *n.m.* operation, working.

fonctionner, *vb.* function, work.

fonctions, *n.f.pl.* office.

fond, *n.m.* bottom, (back)ground. **à f.,** thorough(ly). **au f.,** fundamentally.

fondamental, *adj.* basic, fundamental.

fondateur, *n.m.* founder.

fondation, *n.f.* foundation, establishment.

fondé, *adj.* authentic; (*comm.*) funded.

fondement, *n.m.* foundation.

fonder, *vb.* found.

fonderie, *n.f.* foundry.

fondre, *vb.* melt, fuse.

fondrière, *n.f.* bog.

fonds, *n.m.* fund.

fongus (-s), *n.m.* fungus.

fontaine, *n.f.* fountain.

fonte, *n.f.* melting.

fonts, *n.m.pl.* font.

football, *n.m.* football.

footing, *n.m.* walking.

forain, *n.m.* peddler.

forçat, *n.m.* convict.

force, *n.f.* strength, force; emphasis.

forcé, *adj.* forced, far-fetched.

forcément, *adv.* of necessity.

forcené, *adj.* frantic.

forcer, *vb.* force, compel.

forcir, *vb.* thrive.

forer, *vb.* bore, drill.

forestier, *n.m.* forest ranger.

foret, *n.m.* drill.

forêt, *n.f.* forest.

foreuse, *n.f.* drill.

forfait, *n.m.* crime; forfeit; contract.

forfaiture, *n.f.* mishandling.

forfanterie, *n.f.* bragging.

forge, *n.f.* forge.

forger, *vb.* forge.

forgeron, *n.m.* blacksmith.

forgeur, *n.m.* forger; inventor.

formaliser, *vb.* offend.

formaliste, *adj.* formal; precise.

formalité, *n.f.* formality, ceremony.

formation, *n.f.* formation.

forme, *n.f.* shape, form.

formel, *adj.* formal.

former, *vb.* form, shape.

formidable, *adj.* terrible, formidable.

formule, *n.f.* formula, form.

formuler, *vb.* formulate, draw up.

fort, **1.** *n.m.* fort. **2.** *adj.* strong, loud. **3.** *adv.* hard.

forteresse, *n.f.* fort(ress).

fortifiant, *adj.* strengthening.

fortification, *n.f.* fortification.

fortifier, *vb.* strengthen.

fortuit, *adj.* accidental.

fortuité, *n.f.* fortuitousness.

fortune, *n.f.* fortune.

fortuné, *adj.* lucky, fortunate.

fosse, *n.f.* pit.

fossé, *n.m.* ditch; dike.

fossette, *n.f.* dimple.

fossile, *n.m.* fossil.

fossoyer, *vb.* dig a trench.

fou *m.,* **folle** *f. adj.* mad, crazy, demented.

foudre, *n.m.* thunderbolt.

foudroyant, *adj.* terrifying, crushing.

foudroyer, *vb.* crush, blast.

fouet, *n.m.* whip, lash.

fouetter, *vb.* flog, whip.

fougère, *n.f.* fern.

fougue, *n.f.* dash.

fougueux, *adj.* fiery, impetuous.

fouille, *n.f.* excavation.

fouiller, *vb.* ransack.

fouillis, *n.m.* litter, mess.

fouir, *vb.* dig, burrow.

foulard, *n.m.* scarf.

foule, *n.f.* crowd, mob.

fouler, *vb.* trample.

foulure, *n.f.* sprain, wrench.

four, *n.m.* oven.

fourbe, **1.** *n.m.* knave. **2.** *adj.* scheming.

fourberie, *n.f.* knavery.

fourbir, *vb.* polish.

fourche, *n.f.* fork.

fourchette, *n.f.* fork.

fourgon, *n.m.* wagon.

fourmi, *n.f.* ant.

fourmillement, *n.m.* swarming; tingling.

fourmiller, *vb.* mill; swarm.

fourneau, *n.m.* stove, furnace.

fournée, *n.f.* batch.

fourniment, *n.m.* equipment.

fournir de, *vb.* supply, furnish.

fournisseur, *n.m.* tradesman.

fournitures, *n.f.pl.* supplies.

fourrage, *n.m.* fodder, forage.

fourrager, *vb.* forage.

fourré, *adj.* lined (of clothing); thick; wooded.

fourreau, *n.m.* sheath.

fourrer, *vb.* thrust in. **se f.,** interfere, meddle.

fourreur, *n.m.* furrier.

fourrure, *n.f.* fur.

fourvoyer, *vb.* mislead.

foyer, *n.m.* focus, hearth. **f. domestique,** home.

frac, *n.m.* dress coat.

fracas, *n.m.* crash; rattle; noise; ado.

fracasser, *vb.* **se f.,** shatter.

fraction, *n.f.* fraction.

fracture, *n.f.* fracture.

fracturer, *vb.* break, fracture.

fragile, *adj.* brittle, delicate, frail, fragile.

fragilité, *n.f.* fragility.

fragment, *n.m.* fragment.

fragmenter, vb. divide up.

fraîcheur, n.f. freshness, coolness.

fraîchir, vb. freshen.

frais, n.m.pl. expense(s), cost, fee.

frais m., **fraîche** f. adj. fresh, cool.

fraise, n.f. strawberry; ruffle.

framboise, n.f. raspberry.

franc, 1. n.m. franc. **2.** adj.m., **franche** f. frank, open.

Français, n.m. Frenchman.

français, adj. and n.m. French.

Française, n.f. Frenchwoman.

France, n.f. France.

franchement, adv. frankly.

franchir, vb. clear, cross.

franchise, n.f. frankness.

franciser, vb. make French.

franc-maçon, n.m. Freemason.

franc-parler, n.m. frankness.

franc-tireur, n.m. sniper; free-lancer.

frange, n.f. fringe.

frangible, adj. breakable.

frapper, vb. strike, hit, rap, knock. **f. du pied,** stamp.

frasque, n.f. prank.

fraternel, adj. brotherly.

fraterniser, vb. fraternize.

fraternité, n.f. brotherhood.

fraude, n.f. fraud.

frauder, vb. defraud.

fraudeur, n.m. smuggler.

frauduleux, adj. fraudulent.

frayer, vb. open up; rub.

frayeur, n.f. fright.

fredaine, n.f. prank.

fredonner, vb. hum.

frégate, n.f. frigate.

frein, n.m. brake, check.

freiner, vb. brake; restrain.

frelater, vb. adulterate.

frêle, adj. frail.

frelon, n.m. hornet.

frémir, vb. tremble. **faire f.,** thrill.

frémissement, n.m. shiver, thrill.

frêne, n.m. ash (tree).

frénésie, n.f. frenzy.

frénétique, adj. frantic.

fréquemment, adv. often.

fréquence, n.f. frequency.

fréquent, adj. frequent.

fréquenter, vb. frequent, associate with.

frère, n.m. brother.

fresque, n.f. fresco.

fret, n.m. freight.

fréter, vb. charter (ship); freight.

frétillant, adj. lively.

frétiller, vb. wag; quiver.

fretin, n.m. young fish.

frette, n.f. hoop.

friand, adj. dainty; fond (of).

friandise, n.f. love of delicacies.

fricoter, vb. cook, stew.

friction, n.f. friction.

frictionner, vb. chafe.

frigo, n.m. frozen meat.

frigorifier, vb. freeze, refrigerate.

frileux, adj. chilly; susceptible to cold.

frime, n.f. pretense, sham.

fringant, adj. lively, frisky.

friper, vb. crush, rumple.

fripier, n.m. second-hand clothing dealer.

fripon, 1. adj. knavish. **2.** n.m. rascal.

friponnerie, n.f. roguery.

fripouille, n.f. rascal.

frire, vb. fry.

frisé, adj. curly.

friser, vb. curl.

frisoir, n.m. (hair) curler.

frisson, n.m. shudder, shiver.

frissonnement, n.m. shudder; shivering.

frissonner, vb. shudder, shiver.

frites, n.f.pl. (potato) chips.

friture, n.f. frying.

frivole, adj. frivolous.

frivolité, n.f. frivolity.

froc, n.m. (monk's) frock.

froid, n.m. and adj. cold. **un peu f.,** chilly. **avoir f.,** be cold.

froideur, n.f. coldness.

froissé, adj. bruised. **être f. de,** resent.

froissement, n.m. crumpling, rustling, jostling.

froisser, vb. crease, wrinkle; bruise, hurt.

frôler, vb. graze.

fromage, n.m. cheese.

froment, n.m. wheat.

froncement, n.m. puckering, contraction.

froncer, vb. pucker. **f. les sourcils,** frown.

frondaison, n.f. foliage.

fronde, n.f. sling.

fronder, vb. sling; censure.

front, n.m. forehead.

frontière, *n.f.* boundary, border, frontier.

frottement, *n.m.* rubbing.

frotter, *vb.* rub.

frou-frou, *n.m.* rustle.

fructueux, *adj.* fruitful.

frugal, *adj.* frugal.

frugalité, *n.f.* frugality.

fruit, *n.m.* fruit.

fruiterie, *n.f.* fruit store.

fruitier, *n.f.* fruit seller.

fugace, *adj.* fleeting.

fugitif, *adj.* fugitive.

fuir, *vb.* flee; shun; leak.

fuite, *n.f.* escape, flight; leak.

fumée, *n.f.* smoke.

fumer, *vb.* smoke.

fumeur, *n.m.* one who smokes.

fumeux, *adj.* smoky.

fumier, *n.m.* dung.

funèbre, *adj.* funereal.

funérailles, *n.f.pl.* funeral.

funeste, *adj.* disastrous.

fureter, *vb.* pry.

fureur, *n.f.* fury.

furie, *n.f.* fury.

furieux, *adj.* furious.

furtif, *adj.* sly.

fuseau, *n.m.* spindle.

fusée, *n.f.* rocket.

fuser, *vb.* melt, spread.

fusil, *n.m.* rifle.

fusiller (-zēl yā), *vb.* shoot.

fusion, *n.f.* merger; meltdown.

fusionner, *vb.* merge.

futé, *adj.* cunning, crafty.

futile, *adj.* futile.

futur, *n.m. and adj.* future.

futurologie, *n.f.* futurology.

fuyant, *adj.* passing, transitory, fugitive.

fuyard, *n.* fugitive.

G

gâcher, *vb.* mess.

gâchette, *n.f.* trigger.

gage, *n.m.* pledge, wage.

gageure, *n.f.* bet.

gagnant, *n.m.* winner.

gagner, *vb.* earn, gain, win, beat (in a game).

gai, *adj.* cheerful, cheery, merry, gay.

gaieté, *n.f.* mirth, cheer, merriment, gaiety.

gaillard, *adj.* hearty, sound.

gain, *n.m.* gain, profit.

gaine, *n.f.* girdle.

galant, 1. *n.m.* beau. **2.** *adj.* gallant, civil, courteous. **g. homme,** gentleman.

galanterie, *n.f.* courtesy, compliment.

galbe, *n.m.* outline, contour.

galère, *n.f.* galley, ship.

galerie, *n.f.* gallery, balcony (theater).

galet, *n.m.* boulder.

gallon, *n.m.* gallon.

galon, *n.m.* stripe, braid.

galop, *n.m.* gallop.

galoper, *vb.* gallop.

gambader, *vb.* frolic.

gamin, *n.m.* boy, urchin.

gamme, *n.f.* scale.

gangster (-r), *n.m.* gangster.

gant, *n.m.* glove.

ganterie, *n.f.* glove shop.

garage, *n.m.* garage.

garagiste, *n.m.* garage keeper.

garant, *n.m.* sponsor.

garantie, *n.f.* guarantee, pledge.

garantir, *vb.* guarantee, pledge, warrant.

garçon, *n.m.* boy; waiter; bachelor; flight attendant.

garçonnière, *n.f.* bachelor's apartment.

garde, *n.f.* watch, guard, custody. **prendre g. à,** beware of. **avant-g.,** vanguard. **g. du corps,** bodyguard.

garde-boue, *n.m.* fender.

garde-feu, *n.m.* fender (fireplace).

garde-manger, *n.m.* pantry.

garder, *vb.* guard, keep, mind.

gardeur, *n.m.* keeper.

gardien, *n.m.* keeper, guard, watchman, guardian.

gare, 1. *n.f.* station. **2.** *interj.* look out!

garer, *vb.* garage, park.

gargariser, *vb.* se g., gargle.

gargarisme, *n.m.* gargle.

garni, *adj.* furnished, garnished.

garnir, *vb.* trim, garnish.

garnison, *n.f.* garrison.

garniture, *n.f.* fittings.

gars, *n.m.* chap.

gaspillage, *n.m.* waste.

gaspiller, *vb.* waste, squander.

gâteau, *n.m.* cake. **g. de miel,** honeycomb. **g. sec,** cookie.

gâter, *vb.* spoil.

gâterie, *n.f.* excessive indulgence.

gâteux, *adj.* senile.

gauche, *adj. and n.f.* left. **à g.,** on *or* to the left. *adj.* awkward, clumsy.

gaucherie, *n.f.* clumsiness.

gaufre, *n.f.* waffle.

gaule, *n.f.* pole.

gausser, se g. de, mock, banter.

gaz (-z), *n.m.* gas.

gaze, *n.f.* gauze.

gazeux, *adj.* gassy, gaseous.

gazon, *n.m.* turf, lawn.

gazouillement, *n.m.* warble, twitter.

géant, *n.m.* giant.

geindre, *vb.* moan, whine.

gelé, *adj.* frozen.

gelée, *n.f.* jelly, frost.

geler, *vb.* freeze.

gémir, *vb.* groan, wail, moan.

gémissement, *n.m.* groan, moan.

gênant, *adj.* troublesome, bothersome.

gencive, *n.f.* gum.

gendarme, *n.m.* policeman.

gendarmerie, *n.f.* police force.

gendre, *n.m.* son-in-law.

gêne, *n.f.* trouble, uneasiness. **être à la g.,** be uneasy.

gêné, *adj.* uneasy.

généalogie, *n.f.* pedigree.

gêner, *vb.* hinder, be in the way, embarrass, bother.

général, *n.m. and adj.* general, overhead *(comm.).* **quartier g.,** headquarters.

généraliser, *vb.* generalize.

généralissime, *n.m.* commander-in-chief.

généralité, *n.f.* generality.

génération, *n.f.* generation.

généreusement, *adv.* generously.

généreux, *adj.* generous, liberal.

générosité, *n.f.* generosity.

génial, *adj.* of genius, highly original.

génie, *n.m.* genius; engineer corps. **soldat du g.,** engineer.

genièvre, *n.m.* gin.

génisse, *n.f.* heifer.

genou, *n.m.* knee; *(pl.)* lap.

genre, *n.m.* kind, gender.

gens, *n.m.f.pl.* people, persons, folk.

gentiane, *n.f.* gentian.

gentil *m.,* **gentille** *f.* *adj.* pleasant, nice.

gentilhomme, *n.m.* nobleman, peer.

gentillesse, *n.f.* prettiness, gracefulness.

géographie, *n.f.* geography.

géographique, *adj.* geographical.

géologie, *n.f.* geology.

géométrie, *n.f.* geometry.

géométrique, *adj.* geometric.

gérance, *n.f.* managership.

géranium, *n.m.* geranium.

gérant, *n.m.* manager, director, superintendent.

gerbe, *n.f.* sheaf.

gerçure, *n.f.* chap.

gérer, *vb.* manage.

germain, *adj.* first (of cousins).

germe, *n.f.* germ.

germer, *vb.* sprout.

gésir, *vb.* lie.

geste, *n.m.* gesture.

gesticuler, *vb.* gesticulate.

gestion, *n.f.* management.

gibier, *n.m.* game.

giboulée, *n.f.* sudden storm.

gicler, *vb.* spurt.

gifler, *vb.* slap.

gigantesque, *adj.* great, huge.

gigot, *n.m.* leg (of meat).

gigue, *n.f.* leg; jig.

gilet, *n.m.* vest. **g. de dessous,** undershirt.

gingembre, *n.m.* ginger.

girofle, *n.m.* **clou de g.,** clove.

giron, *n.m.* lap.

gitane, *n.m.f.* gypsy.

gîte, *n.m.* lodging, bed.

givre, *n.m.* frost.

glabre, *adj.* smooth-shaven.

glaçage, *n.m.* frosting.

glace, *n.f.* ice, ice cream; mirror.

glacer, *vb.* freeze.

glacial, *adj.* icy.

glacier, *n.m.* glacier.

glacière, *n.f.* icebox.

glacis, *n.m.* slope.

glaçon, *n.m.* block of ice.

glaise, *n.f.* clay.

gland, *n.m.* acorn.

glande, *n.f.* gland.

glaner, *vb.* glean.

glapir, *vb.* yelp; screech.

glas, *n.m.* knell.
glissade, *n.f.* slide, slip.
glissant, *adj.* slippery.
glisser, *vb.* slide, slip. **se g.,** creep, sneak.
global, *adj.* entire.
globe, *n.m.* globe. **g. de l'œil,** eyeball.
gloire, *n.f.* glory.
glorieux, *adj.* glorious.
glorifier, *vb.* glorify.
glose, *n.f.* criticism; gloss.
glossaire, *n.m.* glossary.
glousser, *vb.* cluck.
gluant, *adj.* sticky.
gobelet, *n.m.* goblet.
gober, *vb.* swallow.
goéland, *n.m.* seagull.
golfe, *n.m.* gulf.
gomme, *n.f.* gum; eraser.
gommeux, *adj.* gummy.
gond, *n.m.* hinge.
gonfler, *vb.* inflate; swell.
gonfleur, *n.m.* tire pump.
gorge, *n.f.* throat; gorge.
gorger, *vb.* cram.
gosier, *n.m.* throat.
gosse, *n.m.f.* kid (child).
gothique, *adj.* Gothic.
goudron, *n.m.* tar.
gouffre, *n.m.* gulf, abyss.
goulu, *adj.* gluttonous.
gourde, *n.f.* flask.
gourmand, 1. *n.m.* glutton. **2.** *adj.* greedy.
gourmander, *vb.* scold.
gourmandise, *n.f.* greediness.
gourmer, *vb.* curb.
gourmet, *n.m.* epicure.
gourmette, *n.f.* curb (horse).
gourou, *n.m.* guru.
gousse, *n.f.* shell, pod.
goût, *n.m.* taste, relish.
goûter, 1. *n.m.* snack. **2.** *vb.* taste, relish.
goutte, *n.f.* drop; gout.
goutteux, *adj.* gouty.
gouttière, *n.f.* gutter.
gouvernail, *n.m.* rudder, helm.
gouvernante, *n.f.* governess, housekeeper.
gouvernement, *n.m.* government.
gouverner, *vb.* govern, rule, steer.
gouverneur, *n.m.* governor.
grabuge, *n.m.* squabble.
grâce, *n.f.* grace. **faire g. de,** spare.

gracier, *vb.* pardon.
gracieux, *adj.* graceful, gracious.
grade, *n.m.* grade, rank.
gradin, *n.m.* step, tier.
graduel, *adj.* gradual.
graduer, *vb.* graduate.
grain, *n.m.* grain, seed, berry, kernel. **g. de beauté,** mole.
graine, *n.f.* seed, berry.
graissage, *n.m.* greasing.
graisse, *n.f.* grease, fat.
graisser, *vb.* grease.
grammaire, *n.f.* grammar.
gramme, *n.m.* gram.
grand, *adj.* big, great, tall.
grand'chose, much.
grandement, *adv.* grandly, greatly.
grandeur, *n.f.* size, height, greatness.
grandiose, *adj.* grand.
grandir, *vb.* grow.
grand'mère, *n.f.* grandmother.
grand-père, *n.m.* grandfather.
grange, *n.f.* barn.
granit (-t), *n.m.* granite.
graphique, *n.m.* chart.
grappe, *n.f.* bunch, cluster.
gras *m.*, **grasse** *f.* *adj.* fat, stout.
grassement, *adj.* plentifully.
grasset, *adj.* plump.
grassouillet, *adj.* plump.
gratification, *n.f.* bonus.
gratifier, *vb.* bestow.
gratin, *n.m.* burnt part.
gratitude, *n.f.* gratitude.
gratte-ciel, *n.m.* skyscraper.
gratter, *vb.* scrape, scratch.
gratuit, *adj.* free.
grave, *adj.* grave.
graveleux, *adj.* gritty.
graver, *vb.* engrave.
graveur, *n.m.* engraver.
gravier, *n.m.* gravel.
gravir, *vb.* climb.
gravité, *n.f.* gravity.
graviter, *vb.* gravitate.
gravure, *n.f.* engraving. **g. à l'eauforte,** etching.
gré, *n.m.* pleasure.
Grec *m.*, **Grecque** *f.* *n.* Greek (person).
grec, *n.m.* Greek (language).
grec *m.*, **grecque** *f.* *adj.* Greek.
Grèce, *n.f.* Greece.
gréement, *n.m.* rig.
gréer, *vb.* rig.

greffier, *n.m.* clerk.
grêle, 1. *n.f.* hail. 2. *adj.* thin, slight.
grêler, *vb.* hail.
grêlon, *n.m.* hailstone.
grelotter, *vb.* shiver.
grenier, *n.m.* attic.
grenouille, *n.f.* frog.
grève, *n.f.* strike. se mettre en g., strike, *vb.*
gréviste, *n.m.f.* striker.
gribouiller, *vb.* scribble.
grief, *n.m.* grievance.
grièvement, *adv.* seriously.
griffe, *n.f.* claw, clutch.
griffer, *vb.* seize; scratch.
griffonner, *vb.* scribble.
grignoter, *vb.* nibble.
gril, *n.m.* grill.
grillade, *n.f.* broiling.
grille, *n.f.* grate, gate.
griller, *vb.* broil, roast, toast.
grillon, *n.m.* cricket.
grimace, *n.f.* grimace.
grimacer, *vb.* make faces.
grimer, *vb.* make up.
grimper, *vb.* climb.
grincer, *vb.* creak, grate, grind.
gris, *adj.* gray; drab; drunk.
griser, *vb.* get drunk.
grive, *n.f.* thrush.
grogner, *vb.* growl, snarl, grumble.
grommeler, *vb.* mutter.
gronder, *vb.* scold, nag; roar, rumble.
gros *m.*, grosse *f.* *adj.* overly large; gross, stout, rough. en g., wholesale.
groseille, *n.f.* currant.
grosseur, *n.f.* size, thickness.
grossier, *adj.* coarse, crude, gross.
grossièreté, *n.f.* coarseness.
grossir, *vb.* magnify, grow.
grotesque, *adj.* grotesque.
grouiller, *vb.* stir, swarm.
groupe, *n.m.* group, party; cluster.
groupement, *n.m.* grouping.
grouper, *vb.* group.
grue, *n.f.* crane.
gué, *n.m.* ford. traverser à g., wade.
guêpe, *n.f.* wasp.
guère, *adv.* hardly.
guérir, *vb.* cure, heal.

guérison, *n.f.* cure.
guerre, *n.f.* war.
guerrier, *adj.* warlike.
guetter, *vb.* watch (for).
gueule, *n.f.* mouth.
gueux, *n.m.* beggar, tramp.
guichet, *n.m.* ticket-window.
guide, *n.m.* guide(book).
guider, *vb.* guide.
guillotine, *n.f.* guillotine.
guingan, *n.m.* gingham.
guirlande, *n.f.* garland.
guise, *n.f.* way, manner.
guitare, *n.f.* guitar.
gymnase, *n.m.* gymnasium.

H

habile, *adj.* clever, skillful, smart, able.
habileté, *n.f.* craft, ability.
habillement, *n.m.* apparel.
habillements masculins, *n.m.pl.* menswear.
habiller, *vb.* dress.
habilleur *m.*, habilleuse *f.* *n.* dresser.
habit, *n.m.* coat; attire; (*pl.*) clothes.
habitant, *n.m.* inhabitant, resident.
habitation, *n.f.* dwelling.
habiter, *vb.* inhabit, live.
habitude, *n.f.* habit, practice. d'h., customarily. avoir l'h. de, be accustomed to.
habituel, *adj.* customary, usual.
habituer, *vb.* get used to.
hâbleur, *n.m.* boaster.
hache, *n.f.* ax.
hacher, *vb.* mince, chop, hack up.
hachette, *n.f.* hatchet.
hachis, *n.m.* hash.
hagard, *adj.* haggard.
haie, *n.f.* hedge.
haillon, *n.m.* rag.
haine, *n.f.* hatred.
haineux, *adj.* hating.
haïr, *vb.* hate.
haïssable, *adj.* hateful.
halage, *n.m.* towage.
hâle, *n.m.* tan, sunburn.
haleine, *n.f.* breath.
haler, *vb.* haul, tow.
hâler, *vb.* tan. se h., become sunburned.

haleter, *vb.* pant, gasp.

halle, *n.f.* market.

halte, *n.f.* halt.

hamac, *n.m?* hammock.

hameau, *n.m.* hamlet.

hameçon, *n.m.* hook.

hampe, *n.f.* handle.

hanche, *n.f.* hip.

hangar, *n.m.* shed.

hanter, *vb.* haunt.

hantise, *n.f.* obsession.

happer, *vb.* snap.

harcèlement, *n.m.* hassle, harassment.

harceler, *vb.* worry, bother; hassle; harass.

hardes, *n.f.pl.* togs.

hardi, *adj.* bold.

hardiesse, *n.f.* boldness.

hareng, *n.m.* herring.

hargneux, *adj.* cross, snarling.

haricot, *n.m.* bean.

harmonie, *n.f.* harmony.

harmonieux, *adj.* harmonious.

harmoniser, *vb.* put in tune, harmonize.

harnacher, *vb.* harness.

harnais, *n.m.* harness.

harpe, *n.f.* harp.

harpin, *n.m.* boat hook.

hasard, *n.m.* chance. **au h.** or **par h.**, at random.

hasarder, *vb.* venture.

hasardeux, *adj.* hazardous, unsafe.

hâte, *n.f.* haste, hurry. **à la h.**, hastily.

hâter, *vb.* hasten, hurry.

hâtif, *adj.* early, hasty.

haussement, *n.m.* raising; shrug.

hausser, *vb.* raise; shrug.

haussier, *n.m.* bull (stock exchange).

haut, **1.** *n.m.* top. **2.** *adj.* high, loud. **à haute voix**, aloud. **en haut**, up, above.

hautain, *adj.* haughty, lofty, proud.

hautbois, *n.m.* oboe.

haute fidélité, *n.f.* high fidelity.

hauteur, *n.f.* height; haughtiness. **être à la h. de**, be up to.

hauturier, *adj.* sea-going.

hâve, *adj.* wan, gaunt.

havre, *n.m.* haven.

havresac, *n.m.* knapsack.

hebdomadaire, *adj.* weekly.

héberger, *vb.* shelter.

hébété, *adj.* dull.

hébreu, **1.** *n.m.* Hebrew (language). **2.** *adj.* Hebrew.

hein, *interj.* huh?

hélas (-s), *interj.* alas!

héler, *vb.* call, hail.

hélice, *n.f.* propeller.

hélicoptère, *n.m.* helicopter.

helvétique, *adj.* Swiss.

hémisphère, *n.m.* hemisphere.

hémorragie, *n.f.* hemorrhage.

hennir, *vb.* neigh.

héraut, *n.m.* herald.

herbage, *n.m.* grass, pasture.

herbe, *n.f.* grass, herb; marijuana. **mauvaise h.**, weed.

herbeux, *adj.* grassy.

héréditaire, *adj.* hereditary.

hérésie, *n.f.* heresy.

hérétique, **1.** *n.m.f.* heretic. **2.** *adj.* heretic, heretical.

hérisser, *vb.* bristle.

hérisson, *n.m.* hedgehog.

héritage, *n.m.* inheritance.

hériter, *vb.* inherit.

héritier, *n.m.* heir.

hermétique, *adj.* (sealed) tight.

hermine, *n.f.* ermine.

hernie, *n.f.* hernia.

héroïne, *n.f.* heroine.

héroïque, *adj.* heroic.

héroïsme, *n.m.* heroism.

héros, *n.m.* hero.

hertz, *n.m.* hertz.

hésitation, *n.f.* hesitation.

hésiter, *vb.* hesitate, waver, falter.

hétérosexuel, *adj.* heterosexual.

hêtre, *n.m.* beech.

heure, *n.f.* hour; time. **de bonne h.**, early.

heureusement, *adv.* happily, luckily.

heureux, *adj.* glad, happy; lucky, fortunate; successful.

heurt, *n.m.* blow, shock.

heurter, *vb.* collide (with).

heurtoir, *n.m.* (door) knocker.

hibou, *n.m.* owl.

hideux, *adj.* hideous.

hier (-r), *adv.* yesterday.

hilare, *adj.* hilarious.

hilarité, *n.f.* hilarity.

Hindou, *n.m.* Hindu.

hindou, *adj.* Hindu.

hippodrome, *n.m.* race course.

hippopotame, *n.m.* hippopotamus.

hirondelle, *n.f.* swallow.

hispanique, *adj.* Hispanic.

hisser, *vb.* hoist.

histoire, *n.f.* history. story; to-do, fuss.

historien, *n.m.* historian.

historique, *adj.* historic.

hiver (-r), *n.m.* winter.

hiverner, *vb.* **s'h.,** hibernate.

hocher, *vb.* shake, nod.

hochet, *n.m.* rattle.

hoirie, *n.f.* inheritance.

Hollandais, *n.m.* Hollander, Dutchman.

hollandais, *adj. and n.m.* Dutch.

Hollande, *n.f.* Holland; the Netherlands.

hologramme, *n.m.* hologram.

holographie, *n.f.* holography.

homard, *n.m.* lobster.

hommage, *n.m.* homage.

hommasse, *adj.* mannish.

homme, *n.m.* man. **h. d'affaires,** businessman.

homogène, *adj.* of the same kind, homogeneous.

homosexuel, *adj.* homosexual.

Hongrie, *n.f.* Hungary.

Hongrois, *n.m.* Hungarian (person).

hongrois, 1. *n.m.* Hungarian (language). **2.** *adj.* Hungarian.

honnête, *adj.* honest.

honnêteté, *n.f.* honesty, fairness.

honneur, *n.m.* honor, credit.

honorable, *adj.* honorable.

honoraires, *n.m.pl.* fee.

honorer, *vb.* honor.

honte, *n.f.* shame. **avoir h. de,** be ashamed of. **faire h. à.,** shame.

honteux, *adj.* ashamed; shameful.

hôpital, *n.m.* hospital.

hoquet, *n.m.* hiccup.

horaire, *n.m.* timetable.

horde, *n.f.* horde.

horizon, *n.m.* horizon.

horizontal, *adj.* horizontal.

horloge, *n.f.* clock.

horloger, *n.m.* watchmaker.

hormis, *prep.* except.

horreur, *n.f.* horror.

horrible, *adj.* horrible, ghastly.

horrifier, *vb.* horrify.

horrifique, *adj.* hair-raising.

horripiler, *vb.* annoy.

hors-bord, *n.m.* outboard boat.

hors de, *prep.* out of, outside.

horticole, *adj.* horticultural.

hospice, *n.m.* refuge.

hospitalier, *adj.* hospitable.

hospitaliser, *vb.* hospitalize; shelter.

hospitalité, *n.f.* hospitality.

hostie, *n.f. (eccles.)* host.

hostile, *adj.* hostile.

hostilité, *n.f.* hostility.

hôte, *n.m.* host; guest.

hôtel, *n.m.* hotel; mansion. **h. de ville,** city hall.

hôtelier, *n.m.* innkeeper.

hôtesse, *n.f.* hostess.

hôtesse de l'air, *n.f.* stewardess, flight attendant.

hotte, *n.f.* basket carried on back.

houblon, *n.m.* hop.

houe, *n.f.* hoe.

houer, *vb.* hoe.

houille, *n.f.* coal.

houillère, *n.f.* coal mine.

houle, *n.f.* surge.

houleux, *adj.* stormy, rough.

houppe, *n.f.* tuft; powder puff.

hourra, *n.m.* cheer.

housse, *n.f.* covering.

houx, *n.m.* holly.

hublot, *n.m.* porthole.

huer, *vb.* shout, hoot.

huile, *n.f.* oil.

huiler, *vb.* oil.

huileux, *adj.* oily.

huissier, *n.m.* usher.

huit, *adj. and n.m.* eight.

huitième, *adj. and n.m.f.* eighth.

huître, *n.f.* oyster.

humain, *adj.* human, humane.

humanitaire, *adj.* humanitarian.

humanité, *n.f.* humanity.

humble, *adj.* lowly, humble.

humecter, *vb.* moisten.

humer, *vb.* suck up, sniff up.

humeur, *n.f.* humor; mood, temper.

humide, *adj.* damp, humid.

humidité, *n.f.* moisture.

humiliation, *n.f.* humiliation.

humilier, *vb.* humiliate, humble.

humilité, *n.f.* humility.

humoristique, *adj.* humorous.

humour, *n.m.* humor.

hune, *n.f. (naut.)* top.

huppe, *n.f.* tuft, crest.
hurlement, *n.m.* noise, howling.
hurler, *vb.* howl, roar, yell.
hutte, *n.f.* hut, shed.
hybride, *adj. and n.m.* hybrid.
hydrogène, *n.m.* hydrogen.
hyène, *n.f.* hyena.
hygiène, *n.f.* sanitation, hygiene.
hygiénique, *adj.* hygienic.
hymne, *n.m.* hymn; *n.f.* church hymn.
hypnotiser, *vb.* hypnotize.
hypocondriaque, *adj. and n.* hypochondriac.
hypocrisie, *n.f.* hypocrisy.
hypocrite, **1.** *n.m.f.* hypocrite. **2.** *adj.* hypocritical.
hypothèque, *n.f.* mortgage.
hypothéquer, *vb.* mortgage.
hypothèse, *n.f.* hypothesis.
hystérectomie, *n.f.* hysterectomy.
hystérie, *n.f.* hysteria.
hystérique, *adj.* hysterical.

I

ici, *adv.* here. **d'i.**, hence.
ictère, *n.m.* jaundice.
idéal, *adj. and n.m.* ideal.
idéaliser, *vb.* idealize.
idéalisme, *n.m.* idealism.
idéaliste, *n.m.f.* idealist.
idée, *n.f.* idea, notion.
identification, *n.f.* identification.
identifier, *vb.* identify.
identique (à), *adj.* identical (with).
identité, *n.f.* identity.
idéologie, *n.f.* ideology.
idiome, *n.m.* idiom.
idiot, *adj. and n.m.* idiot(ic).
idiotie, *n.f.* idiocy.
idiotisme, *n.m.* idiom.
idolâtrer, *vb.* idolize.
idole, *n.f.* idol.
idyllique, *adj.* idyllic.
if, *n.m.* yew.
ignare, *adj.* ignorant.
ignoble, *adj.* ignoble.
ignorance, *n.f.* ignorance.
ignorant, *adj.* ignorant.
ignorer, *vb.* not know.
il (ēl), *pron.* he, it; *(pl.)* they.
île, *n.f.* island.
illégal (-l-), *adj.* illegal.
illégitime (-l-), *adj.* illegitimate.

illettré (-l-), *adj.* illiterate.
illicite (-l-), *adj.* illicit.
illimité (-l-), *adj.* boundless.
illogique (-l-), *adj.* illogical.
illuminer (-l-), *vb.* light, illuminate.
illusion (-l-), *n.f.* illusion, delusion.
illustration (-l-), *n.f.* illustration.
illustre (-l-), *adj.* illustrious, famous.
illustrer (-l-), *vb.* illustrate.
image, *n.f.* picture.
imaginaire, *adj.* fancied, imaginary.
imaginatif, *adj.* imaginative.
imagination, *n.f.* imagination.
imaginer, *vb.* imagine.
imam, *n.m.* imam.
imbattable, *adj.* unbeatable.
imbécillité, *n.f.* imbecility; stupidity.
imberbe, *adj.* beardless.
imbiber, *vb.* soak, steep.
imbu, *adj.* imbued; steeped.
imitation, *n.f.* imitation, copy.
imiter, *vb.* imitate, copy; mimic.
immaculé, *adj.* immaculate.
immangeable, *adj.* uneatable.
immatériel, *adj.* incorporeal.
immatriculer, *vb.* matriculate.
immédiat, *adj.* immediate.
immense, *adj.* immense, great, huge.
immensité, *n.f.* immensity.
immeuble, *n.m.* real estate.
imminent, *adj.* imminent.
immiscer, *vb.* **s'i.**, meddle, interfere.
immixtion, *n.f.* mixing; interference.
immobile, *adj.* motionless.
immoler, *vb.* sacrifice. **s'i.**, sacrifice oneself.
immonde, *adj.* filthy.
immoral, *adj.* immoral.
immortaliser, *vb.* immortalize.
immortalité, *n.f.* immortality.
immortel, *adj. and n.m.* immortal.
immuable, *adj.* unchangeable.
immunité, *n.f.* immunity.
impair, *adj.* odd.
impalpable, *adj.* intangible.
imparfait, *adj. and n.m.* imperfect.
impartial, *adj.* impartial.

impasse, *n.f.* dead end.

impassible, *adj.* impassive.

impatience, *n.f.* impatience.

impatient, *adj.* impatient.

impatienter, *vb.* provoke.

impayable, *adj.* invaluable; very funny.

impeccable, *adj.* faultless.

impécunieux, *adj.* impecunious.

impénétrable, *adj.* impenetrable.

impératif, *adj. and n.m.* imperative.

impératrice, *n.f.* empress.

imperceptible, *adj.* imperceptible.

impérial, *adj.* imperial.

impérialisme, *n.m.* imperialism.

impérieux, *adj.* domineering.

impérissable, *adj.* imperishable.

imperméabiliser, *vb.* waterproof.

imperméable, 1. *n.m.* raincoat. **2.** *adj.* waterproof.

impertinence, *n.f.* impertinence.

impertinent, *adj.* saucy.

impétueux, *adj.* headlong, impetuous.

impie, *adj.* impious.

impitoyable, *adj.* merciless, pitiless, ruthless.

impliquer, *vb.* involve, imply.

implorer, *vb.* implore, beg.

impoli, *adj.* rude, impolite, discourteous.

impolitesse, *n.f.* discourtesy.

impopulaire, *adj.* unpopular.

importance, *n.f.* significance, importance.

important, *adj.* momentous, important.

importateur, *n.m.* importer.

importation, *n.f.* import.

importer, *vb.* matter; import.

importun, *adj.* tiresome, bothersome, importunate.

importuner, *vb.* pester, keep bothering.

importunité, *n.f.* importunity.

imposable, *adj.* taxable.

imposer (à), *vb.* impose (on); tax; enforce.

imposition, *n.f.* imposition.

impossibilité, *n.f.* impossibility.

dans l'i. de, unable to.

impossible, *adj.* impossible.

imposteur, *n.m.* fraud (person), faker, impostor.

imposture, *n.f.* imposture, deception.

impôt, *n.m.* tax, tariff.

impotent, *adj.* weak, infirm.

impôt sur les ventes, *n.m.* sales tax.

imprécis, *adj.* imprecise.

imprégner, *vb.* impregnate, imbue.

imprenable, *adj.* impregnable.

impression, *n.f.* print, impression.

impressionnable, *adj.* sensitive, impressionable.

impressionnant, *adj.* impressive.

impressionner, *vb.* affect.

imprévoyance, *n.f.* improvidence.

imprévoyant, *adj.* not foresighted.

imprévu, *adj.* unexpected, unforeseen.

imprimé, *n.m.* printed matter.

imprimer, *vb.* impress; print.

imprimerie, *n.f.* printery, printing.

imprimeur, *n.m.* printer.

improbable, *adj.* improbable.

improbité, *n.f.* dishonesty.

improductif, *adj.* unproductive.

impromptu, *adv., adj. and n.m.* impromptu.

impropre, *adv.* improper, unfit.

improviste, adv. à l'i., all of a sudden.

imprudence, *n.f.* indiscretion.

impudence, *n.f.* impudence.

impudicité, *n.f.* lewdness.

impuissance, *n.f.* impotence.

impuissant, *adj.* impotent, powerless, helpless.

impulsif, *adj.* impulsive.

impulsion, *n.f.* impulse, spur.

impunément, *adv.* with impunity.

impunité, *n.f.* impunity.

impur, *adj.* impure.

impureté, *n.f.* impurity.

imputer, *vb.* impute.

inabordable, *adj.* inaccessible.

inaccoutumé, *adj.* unusual.

inachevé, *adj.* unfinished.

inactif, *adj.* inactive, indolent.

inadvertance, *n.f.* oversight.

inanimé, *adj.* lifeless.

inanité, *n.f.* uselessness.

inaperçu, *adj.* unperceived.

inattaquable, *adj.* unassailable.

inattendu, *adj.* unexpected.

inaugurer, *vb.* inaugurate.

inavouable, *adj.* unavowable, shameful.

incalculable, *adj.* countless, incalculable.

incapable, *adj.* unable.

incarcérer, *vb.* imprison.

incarnat, *adj.* flesh-colored, rosy.

incarner, *vb.* embody.

incartade, *n.f.* insult, prank.

incendie, *n.m.* fire.

incendier, *vb.* set fire to.

incertain, *adj.* uncertain.

incertitude, *n.f.* suspense.

incessamment, *adv.* incessantly; immediately.

inceste, *n.m.* incest.

incident, *n.m.* incident.

incinérer, *vb.* cremate; incinerate.

incision, *n.f.* incision.

inciter, *vb.* incite.

inclinaison, *n.f.* slope.

inclination, *n.f.* bow, nod; propensity.

incliner *vb.* slant, nod, bow. **s'i.,** lean.

inclure, *vb.* include, enclose.

inclus, *adj.* included. **ci-inclus,** enclosed, herewith.

inclusif, *adj.* inclusive.

incolore, *adj.* colorless.

incomber, *vb.* devolve upon.

incommode, *adj.* uncomfortable, inconvenient.

incommoder, *vb.* inconvenience.

incomparable, *adj.* incomparable.

incompatible, *adj.* incompatible.

incompétence, *n.f.* incompetence.

incomplet, *adj.* imperfect, unfinished.

incompris, *adj.* unappreciated, not understood.

inconduite, *n.f.* misconduct.

inconnu, *adj.* unknown.

inconscient, *adj. and n.m.* unconscious.

inconséquent, *adj.* inconsistent.

inconsidéré, *adj.* thoughtless.

inconsistant, *adj.* weak, inconsistent.

inconstant, *adj.* inconstant.

incontestable, *adj.* unquestionable.

incontesté, *adj.* unquestioned.

incontinent, 1. *adj.* incontinent. **2.** *adv.* immediately.

incontrôlable, *adj.* not verifiable.

inconvenance, *n.f.* impropriety.

inconvénient, *n.m.* inconvenience.

incorporer, *vb.* embody.

incorrect, *adj.* incorrect.

incriminer, *vb.* accuse.

incroyable, *adj.* incredible.

incroyant, *n.m.* unbeliever.

inculper, *vb.* charge, accuse.

inculte, *adj.* uncultivated, unkempt.

incurable, *adj.* incurable.

incurie, *n.f.* carelessness, neglect.

Inde, *n.f.* India.

indécis, *adj.* doubtful, vague, dim.

indéfini, *adj.* indefinite.

indéfinissable, *adj.* nondescript.

indéfrisable, *n.f.* permanent wave.

indélicat, *adj.* indelicate.

indélicatesse, *n.f.* indelicacy; blunder.

indépendance, *n.f.* independence.

indépendant, *adj.* independent.

index (-ks), *n.m.* index; forefinger.

indicateur, *n.m.* timetable.

indicatif, *adj. and n.m.* indicative.

indicatif interurbain, *n.m.* area code.

indication, *n.f.* indication.

indice, *n.m.* sign, proof.

indicible, *adj.* unspeakable, inexpressible.

Indien, *n.m.* Indian.

indien, *adj.* Indian.

indifférence, *n.f.* indifference.

indifférent, *adj.* indifferent.

indigène, *n.m.f.* native.

indigent, *adj.* destitute.

indigeste, *adj.* indigestible.

indignation, *n.f.* indignation, anger.

indigne, *adj.* worthless, unworthy.

indigné, *adj.* indignant.

indigner, *vb.* anger.

indiquer, *vb.* indicate, point out.

indirect, *adj.* indirect.

indiscret, *adj.* indiscreet.

indiscutable, *adj.* indisputable.

indispensable, *adj.* indispensable, essential.

indisposer, *vb.* indispose; set against.

indisposition, *n.f.* ailment.

indistinct, *adj.* indistinct.

individu, *n.m.* individual, person.

individuel, *adj.* individual.

indomptable, *adj.* adamant, unconquerable.

indu, *adj.* undue; not ordinary.

induire, *vb.* induce; infer.

indulgence, *n.f.* indulgence.

indulgent, *adj.* lenient, indulgent.

indûment, *adv.* unduly.

industrie, *n.f.* industry.

industriel, *adj.* industrial.

inébranlable, *adj.* immovable, firm.

inédit, *adj.* unpublished.

inefficace, *adj.* ineffectual.

inégal, *adj.* uneven, unequal.

inégalité, *n.f.* inequality, irregularity.

inepte, *adj.* inept, stupid.

ineptie, *n.f.* inept action.

inépuisable, *n.f.* inexhaustible.

inertie, *n.f.* inertia.

inestimable, *adj.* priceless.

inévitable, *adj.* inevitable.

inexact, *adj.* inexact.

inexécutable, *adj.* impracticable.

inexplicable, *adj.* inexplicable.

inexprimable, *adj.* inexpressible.

infaillible, *adj.* infallible.

infâme, *adj.* infamous.

infamie, *n.f.* infamy.

infanterie, *n.f.* infantry.

infatigable, *adj.* untiring.

infécond, *adj.* barren, sterile.

infect, *adj.* infected, rotten.

infecter, *vb.* infect.

infection, *n.f.* infection.

inférieur, *adj. and n.m.* inferior, low(er).

infernal, *adj.* infernal.

infester, *vb.* infest.

infidèle, *adj.* disloyal, unfaithful, false.

infidélité, *n.f.* infidelity.

infime, *adj.* lowest; mean.

infini, *adj. and n.m.* infinite.

infinité, *n.f.* infinity.

infirme, *adj. and n.m.f.* invalid.

infirmer, *vb.* invalidate, weaken.

infirmière, *n.f.* nurse.

infirmité, *n.f.* infirmity.

inflammation, *n.f.* inflammation.

inflation, *n.f.* inflation.

infliger, *vb.* inflict.

influence, *n.f.* influence.

influent, *adj.* influential.

information, *n.f.* inquiry; (*pl.*) news.

informatique, *n.f.* computer science.

informatiser, *vb.* computerize.

informe, *adj.* shapeless.

informer, *vb.* inform. **i. de.** acquaint with.

infraction, *n.f.* breach.

infructueux, *adj.* fruitless.

infuser, *vb.* infuse. **faire i.,** brew.

ingambe, *adj.* nimble.

ingénieur, *n.m.* engineer.

ingénieux, *adj.* ingenious.

ingéniosité, *n.f.* ingenuity.

ingénu, *adj.* naïve, ingenuous.

ingrat, *adj.* ungrateful.

ingrédient, *n.m.* ingredient.

inguérissable, *adj.* incurable.

inhabile, *adj.* awkward, incapable.

inhiber, *vb.* inhibit.

inhospitalier, *adj.* inhospitable.

inhumain, *adj.* cruel, inhuman.

inimitié, *n.f.* enmity.

inique, *adj.* unfair.

initial, *adj.* initial.

initiale, *n.f.* initial.

initiative, *n.f.* initiative.

initier, *vb.* initiate.

injecté, *adj.* **i. de sang,** bloodshot.

injecter, *vb.* inject.

injection, *n.f.* injection.

injonction, *n.f.* injunction.

injures, *n.f.pl.* abuse.

injurier, *vb.* abuse, insult.

injurieux, *adj.* abusive, insulting, offensive.

injuste, *adj.* unfair.

injustice, *n.f.* injustice.

inlassable, *adj.* untiring.

inné, *adj.* innate.

innocence, *n.f.* innocence.

innocent, *adj.* innocent.

innocenter, *vb.* declare innocent.

innombrable, *adj.* countless.

innovation, *n.f.* innovation.

inoccupé, *adj.* idle; unoccupied.

inoculer, *vb.* inoculate.

inodore, *adj.* odorless.

inoffensif, *adj.* innocuous, harmless.

inondation, *n.f.* flood.

inonder, *vb.* flood.

inopiné, *adj.* unexpected.

inoubliable, *adj.* unforgettable.

inouï, *adj.* unheard-of.

inquiet, *adj.* restless, anxious, uneasy.

inquiéter, *vb.* trouble. **s'i.,** worry.

inquiétude, *n.f.* misgiving, worry.

insaisissable, *adj.* imperceptible.

insalubre, *adj.* unhealthy.

inscription, *n.f.* incription, entry.

inscrire, *vb.* inscribe; enter.

insecte, *n.m.* bug, insect.

insensé, *adj.* mad.

insensible, *adj.* insensible; unfeeling.

inséparable, *adj.* inseparable.

insérer, *vb.* insert.

insigne, *n.m.* badge, sign.

insignifiant, *adj.* petty, insignificant.

insinuer, *vb.* hint.

insipide, *adj.* tasteless, dull.

insistance, *n.f.* insistence.

insister, *vb.* insist.

insolation, *n.f.* susntroke.

insolence, *n.f.* insolence.

insolite, *adj.* unusual.

insomnie, *n.f.* insomnia.

insondable, *adj.* bottomless.

insouciant, *adj.* casual, careless.

insoumis, *adj.* unsubdued.

inspecter, *vb.* examine, survey.

inspecteur, *n.m.* inspector.

inspection, *n.f.* inspection.

inspiration, *n.f.* inspiration.

inspirer, *vb.* inspire.

instable, *adj.* temperamental, unsteady, unstable.

installer, *vb.* install.

instamment, *adv.* urgently.

instance, *n.f.* entreaty; instance.

instant, *n.m.* instant. **à l'i.,** at once.

instantané, *adj.* instantaneous.

instinct, *n.m.* instinct.

instinctif, *adj.* instinctive.

instituer, *vb.* institute.

instituteur, *n.m.* teacher.

institution, *n.f.* institution, institute.

institutrice, *n.f.* teacher.

instructeur, *n.m.* teacher.

instructif, *adj.* instructive.

instruction, *n.f.* education, instruction; (*pl.*) directions.

instruire, *vb.* educate, teach, instruct.

instrument, *n.m.* instrument.

instrumentation, *n.f.* orchestration.

insu, *n.m.* **à l'i. de,** unknown to.

insuccès, *n.m.* failure.

insuffisance, *n.f.* deficiency.

insuffisant, *adj.* deficient.

insulaire, 1. *n.m.* islander. **2.** *adj.* insular.

insulte, *n.f.* affront, insult.

insulter, *vb.* affront, insult.

insurgé, *adj. and n.m.* insurgent.

insurger, *vb.* **s'i.,** revolt.

insurmontable, *adj.* insuperable.

intact (-kt), *adj.* intact.

intarissable, *adj.* inexhaustible.

intègre, *adj.* upright.

intégrité, *n.f.* integrity.

intellect, *n.m.* intellect.

intellectuel, *adj. and n.m.* intellectual.

intelligence, *n.f.* intelligence.

intelligent, *adj.* intelligent.

intelligible, *adj.* intelligible; audible.

intempérie, *n.f.* inclemency (of weather).

intempestif, *adj.* untimely.

intendance, *n.f.* administration.

intendant, *n.m.* director.

intendante, *n.f.* matron.

intense, *adj.* intense.

intensif, *adj.* intensive.

intensité, *n.f.* intensity.

intention, *n.f.* intention.

intentionné, *adj.* intentioned.

intentionnel, *adj.* intentional.

intercéder, *vb.* intercede.

intercepter, *vb.* intercept.

interdire, *vb.* forbid.

intéressant, *adj.* interesting.

intéresser, *vb.* interest, concern, affect.

intérêt, *n.m.* interest.

intérieur, *adj. and n.m.* interior.

interjection, *n.f.* interjection.

interloquer, *vb.* embarrass.

intermède, *n.m.* interlude.

intermédiaire, *adj. and n.m.f.* intermediate.

interminable, *adj.* interminable.

internat, *n.m.* boarding school.

international, *adj.* international.

interne, 1. *adj.* internal. **2.** *n.m.* resident student.

interner, *vb.* intern.

interpellation, *n.f.* questioning.

interpeller, *vb.* ask.

interposer, vb. interpose.
interprétation, n.f. interpretation.
interprète, n.m.f. interpreter.
interpréter, vb. interpret.
interrogateur, 1. n.m. examiner. **2.** adj. questioning.
interrogation, n.f. interrogation.
interrogatoire, n.m. cross-examination.
interroger, vb. question.
interrompre, vb. interrupt.
interrupteur, n.m. switch.
interruption, n.f. break, intermission, interruption.
intervalle, n.m. interval.
intervenir, vb. interfere.
intervention, n.f. interference.
intervertir, vb. transpose.
interview, n.m. or f. interview.
interviewer, vb. interview.
intestin, n.m. bowels.
intimation, n.f. notification.
intime, adj. intimate.
intimer, vb. notify.
intimider, vb. daunt, intimidate.
intimité, n.f. intimacy.
intituler, vb. entitle.
intolérance, n.f. intolerance.
intonation, n.f. intonation.
intoxication, n.f. poisoning.
intoxiquer, vb. poison.
intraitable, adj. intractable, difficult to deal with.
intrépide, adj. fearless.
intrigant, 1. adj. intriguing. **2.** n.m. schemer.
intrigue, n.f. plot, intrigue.
intriguer, vb. intrigue; puzzle.
introduction, n.f. introduction.
introduire, vb. introduce, insert.
introuvable, adj. unfindable.
intrus, n.m. intruder.
intrusion, n.f. intrusion; trespass.
intuitif, adj. intuitive.
intuition, n.f. intuition.
inusité, adj. unusual.
inutile, adj. useless, needless.
invalide, 1. n.m.f. invalid. **2.** adj. disabled, invalid.
invalider, vb. invalidate.
invasion, n.f. invasion.
invective, vb. abuse, revile.
inventaire, n.m. inventory.
inventer, vb. invent.
inventeur, n.m. inventor.
invention, n.f. invention.

inventorier, vb. inventory, catalogue.
inverse, adj. inverted, inverse.
investigateur, 1. adj. searching. **2.** n.m. investigator.
investigation, n.f. investigation, inquiry.
investir, vb. invest.
invétéré, adj. inveterate.
invincible, adj. invincible.
invisible, adj. invisible.
invitation, n.f. invitation.
invité, n.m. guest.
inviter, vb. invite, ask.
involontaire, adj. involuntary.
invoquer, vb. call upon.
invraisemblable, adj. improbable.
iode, n.m. iodine.
Irak, n.m. Iraq.
Iran, n.m. Iran.
iris (-s), n.m. iris.
irisé, adj. iridescent.
Irlandais, n.m. Irishman.
irlandais, adj. Irish.
Irlande, n.f. Ireland.
ironie, n.f. irony.
ironique, adj. ironical.
irradier, vb. radiate.
irraisonnable, adj. irrational.
irréfléchi, adj. thoughtless, rash.
irrégulier, adj. irregular.
irréligieux, adj. irreligious.
irrésistible, adj. irresistible.
irrésolu, adj. irresolute.
irrespectueux, adj. disrespectful.
irrévérence, n.f. direspect.
irrigation, n.f. irrigation.
irriguer, vb. irrigate.
irritation, n.f. irritation.
irriter, vb. irritate, anger, provoke.
Islam, n.m. Islam.
islamique, adj. Islamic.
isolateur, adj. insulating.
isolement, n.m. isolation.
isoler, vb. isolate.
Israël, n.m. Israel.
Israëli, n.m. Israeli.
issue, n.f. issue, outlet, outcome.
isthme, n.m. isthmus.
Italie, n.f. Italy.
Italien, n.m. Italian (person.)
italien, 1. n.m. Italian (language). **2.** adj. Italian.
italique, 1. n.m. italics. **2.** adj. italic.
itinéraire, n.m. route, itinerary.

ivoire, *n.m.* ivory.

ivre, *adj.* drunk, intoxicated.

ivresse, *n.f.* drunkenness, intoxication.

ivrogne, *n.m.* drunkard.

ivrognerie, *n.f.* drunkenness.

J

jaboter, *vb.* prattle.

jacasser, *vb.* chatter.

jachère, *n.f.* fallow.

jacinthe, *n.f.* hyacinth.

jadis (-s), *adv.* formerly.

jaillir, *vb.* gush, spurt.

jaillissement, *n.m.* gush, spurt.

jais, *n.m.* jet (mineral).

jalon, *n.m.* staff; landmark.

jalonner, *vb.* mark out.

jalouser, *vb.* envy.

jalousie, *n.f.* jealousy.

jaloux, *adj.* jealous.

jamais, *adv.* ever, never.

jambe, *n.f.* leg.

jambière, *n.f.* legging.

jambon, *n.m.* ham.

jante, *n.f.* rim.

janvier, *n.m.* January.

Japon, *n.m.* Japan.

Japonais, *n.m.* Japanese (person).

japonais, 1. *n.m.* Japanese (language). **2.** *adj.* Japanese.

japper, *vb.* yelp.

jaquette, *n.f.* jacket.

jardin, *n.m.* garden.

jardinage, *n.m.* gardening.

jardinier, *n.m.* gardener.

jarre, *n.f.* jar.

jarretière, *n.f.* garter.

jaser, *vb.* jabber.

jatte, *n.f.* bowl.

jaunâtre, *adj.* yellowish.

jaune, 1. *adj.* yellow. **2.** *n.m.* yolk (of egg).

jaunir, *vb.* turn yellow.

jaunisse, *n.f.* jaundice.

jazz, *n.m.* jazz.

je (jə), *pron.* I.

jeans, *n.m.pl.* jeans.

jésuite, *n.m.* Jesuit.

jet, *n.m.* jet (water, gas).

jetée, *n.f.* pier.

jeter, *vb.* throw.

jeton, *n.m.* token.

jeu, *n.m.* play, game. **mettre en j.,** stake.

jeudi, *n.m.* Thursday.

jeune, *adj.* young, youthful.

jeûne, *n.m.* fast.

jeûner, *vb.* fast.

jeunesse, *n.f.* youth.

joaillerie, *n.f.* jewelry.

joaillier, *n.m.* jeweler.

jobard, *n.m.* fool.

joie, *n.f.* joy.

joindre, *vb.* join.

joint, *n.m.* joint.

jointure, *n.f.* joint (esp. of the body).

joli, *adj.* pretty.

joliment, *adv.* prettily; awfully.

jonc, *n.m.* rush.

joncher, *vb.* scatter.

jonction, *n.f.* junction.

jongler, *vb.* juggle.

jongleur, *n.m.* juggler.

jonquille, *n.f.* jonquil.

joue, *n.f.* cheek.

jouer, *vb.* play.

jouet, *n.m.* toy.

joueur, *n.m.* player.

joufflu, *adj.* chubby.

joug (-g), *n.m.* yoke.

jouir de, *vb.* enjoy.

jouissance, *n.f.* enjoyment.

jouisseur, *n.m.* pleasure-seeker.

jour, *n.m.* day, daylight. **j. de fête,** holiday. **point du j.,** dawn.

journal, *n.m.* newspaper, jounal, diary.

journalier, *adj.* daily.

journalisme, *n.m.* journalism.

journaliste, *n.m.* journalist.

journée, *n.f.* day.

journellement, *adv.* daily.

joute, *n.f.* joust.

jovialité, *n.f.* jollity.

joyau, *n.m.* jewel.

joyeux, *adj.* joyful.

jubilé, *n.m.* jubilee.

jubiler, *vb.* exult.

judaïsme, *n.m.* Judaism.

judiciare, *adj.* judicial, legal.

judicieux, *adj.* wise, judicious.

juge, *n.m.* judge.

jugement, *n.m.* judgment, reason. **mettre en j.,** try.

juger, *vb.* judge.

jugulaire, *adj.* jugular.

Juif *m.,* **Juive** *f. n.* Jew.

juif *m.,* **juive** *f. adj.* Jewish.

juillet, *n.m.* July.
juin, *n.m.* June.
jumeau *m.,* **jumelle** *f. adj. and n.* twin.
jumeler, *vb.* couple, join.
jumelles, *n.f.pl.* opera glasses.
jument, *n.f.* mare.
jupe, *n.f.* skirt.
jupon, *n.m.* petticoat.
jurer, *vb.* swear.
juridiction, *n.f.* jurisdiction.
juridique, *adj.* judicial.
jurisconsulte, *n.m.* jurist, lawyer.
jurisprudence, *n.f.* jurisprudence.
juriste, *n.m.* jurist.
juron, *n.m.* oath.
jury, *n.m.* jury.
jus, *n.m.* juice, gravy.
jusque, *prep.* up to. **jusqu'à,** as far as, until. **jusqu'ici,** hitherto.
juste, 1. *adj.* just, fair, right. **2.** *adv.* just.
justement, *adv.* precisely, exactly.
justesse, *n.f.* accuracy, precision.
justice, *n.f.* justice, fairness.
justifiant, *adj.* justifying.
justification, *n.f.* justification.
justifier, *vb.* justify.
juteux, *adj.* juicy.
juvénile, *adj.* juvenile.

K

kangourou, *n.m.* kangaroo.
karaté, *n.m.* karate.
képi, *n.m.* cap.
kermesse, *n.f.* fair.
kif, *n.m.* marijuana.
kilogramme, *n.m.* kilogram.
kilohertz, *n.m.* kilohertz.
kilométrage, *n.m.* mileage.
kilomètre, *n.m.* kilometer.
kilométrique, *adj.* kilometric.
kiosque, *n.m.* kiosk; newsstand; bandstand.
klaxon, *n.m.* car horn.
kyrielle, *n.f.* litany.

L

la, *pron.* her.
là, *adv.* there.
là-bas, *adv.* yonder, out there.
labeur, *n.m.* labor.
laboratoire, *n.m.* laboratory.

laborieux, *adj.* industrious, laborious.
labour, *n.m.* plowing.
labourer, *vb.* plow.
labyrinthe, *n.m.* maze.
lac, *n.m.* lake.
lacérer, *vb.* lacerate; tear up.
lacet, *n.m.* shoelace; winding.
lâche, 1. *n.m.f.* coward. **2.** *adj.* cowardly, loose.
lâchement, *adv.* loosely, shamefully.
lâcher, *vb.* loosen, let go. **l. pied,** give ground, flee.
lâcheté, *n.f.* cowardice.
lacis, *n.m.* network.
laconique, *adj.* laconic.
lacrymogène, *adj.* **gaz l.,** tear gas.
lacté, *adj.* milky.
lacune, *n.f.* gap, blank.
ladre, *adj.* stingy, mean.
lagune, *n.f.* lagoon.
laid, *adj.* ugly.
laideron, *n.m.* ugly person.
laideur, *n.f.* ugliness.
lainage, *n.m.* woolen goods.
laine, *n.f.* wool.
laineux, *adj.* wooly; downy.
laïque (lä ēk), *n.m.* layman.
laisse, *n.f.* leash.
laisser, *vb.* let, leave.
laisser-aller, *n.m.* freedom, negligence.
laissez-passer, *n.m.* pass.
lait, *n.m.* milk.
laitage, *n.m.* dairy foods.
laiterie, *n.f.* dairy.
laiteux, *adj.* milky.
laitier, *n.m.* milkman.
laiton, *n.m.* brass.
laitue, *n.f.* lettuce.
lambeau, *n.m.* rag.
lambin, *adj.* slow, dawdling.
lame, *n.f.* blade.
lamé, *adj.* gold- or silver-trimmed.
lamelle, *n.f.* (microscope) slide.
lamentable, *adj.* sad, grievous.
lamentation, *n.f.* lamentation.
lamenter, *vb.* mourn, lament.
laminer, *vb.* laminate.
lampe, *n.f.* lamp. **l. de poche,** flashlight.
lamper, *vb.* drink, gulp.
lampion, *n.m.* Chinese lantern.
lampiste, *n.m.* lamplighter.
lance, *n.f.* lance.

lancer, *vb.* hurl; launch.
lanceur, *n.m.* pitcher.
lancinant, *adj.* throbbing (of pain).
lande, *n.f.* wasteland, moor.
langage, *n.m.* language.
langoureux, *adj.* languishing.
langue, *n.f.* tongue, language.
languette, *n.f.* tonguelike strip.
langueur, *n.f.* languor.
languir, *vb.* pine, languish.
languissant, *adj.* languid.
lanière, *n.f.* strap, thong.
lanterne, *n.f.* lantern.
lapider, *vb.* stone; abuse.
lapin, *n.m.* rabbit.
laps, *n.m.* lapse of time.
lapsus (-sys), *n.m.* slip.
laquais, *n.m.* footman, lackey.
laque, *n.f.* shellac; hairspray.
larcin, *n.m.* larceny, theft.
lard, *n.m.* bacon, fat.
larder, *vb.* lard; pierce.
large, *adj.* wide.
largeur, *n.f.* width.
larguer, *vb.* loosen, let go.
larme, *n.f.* tear.
larmoyer, *vb.* weep, whimper.
larron, *n.m.* thief.
las, *adj.* weary.
lascif, *adj.* lewd, wanton.
laser, *n.m.* laser.
lasser, *vb.* weary.
latéral, *adj.* lateral.
Latin, *n.m.* Latin (person).
latin, 1. *n.m.* Latin (language). **2.** *adj.* Latin.
latte, *n.f.* lath.
laurier, *n.m.* bay, laurel.
lavabo, *n.m.* lavatory.
lavande, *n.f.* lavender.
lavandière, *n.f.* laundress.
lavement, *n.m.* enema.
laver, *vb.* wash.
lavette, *n.f.* dishrag.
laxatif, *n.m.* laxative.
le (lǝ) *m.,* **la** *f.,* **les** *pl.* **1.** *art.* the. **2.** *pron.* him, her, it.
lécher, *vb.* lick.
leçon, *n.f.* lesson.
lecteur, *n.m.* reader.
lecture, *n.f.* reading.
légal, *adj.* lawful, legal.
légaliser, *vb.* legalize.
légalité, *n.f.* legality.
légataire, *n.f.* legatee.
légation, *n.f.* legation.

légendaire, *adj.* legendary.
légende, *n.f.* legend; inscription.
léger, *adj.* light.
légèreté, *n.f.* lightness.
légion, *n.f.* legion.
législateur, *n.m.* legislator.
législatif, *adj.* legislative.
législation, *n.f.* legislation.
législature, *n.f.* legislature.
légitime, *adj.* legitimate, lawful.
legs, *n.m.* bequest.
léguer, *vb.* bequeath.
légume, *n.m.* vegetable.
lendemain, *n.m.* the next day.
lent, *adj.* slow.
lenteur, *n.f.* slowness.
lentille, *n.f.* lentil; lens.
lèpre, *n.f.* leprosy.
lépreux, 1. *adj.* leprous. **2.** *n.* leper.
lequel, *pron.* which, who.
les, *pron.* them.
lesbien, *adj.* Lesbian.
lesbienne, *n.f.* Lesbian.
léser, *vb.* wrong, hurt.
lésine, *n.f.* stinginess.
lésion, *n.f.* wrong; lesion.
lessive, *n.f.* laundry.
lessiveuse, *n.f.* washing machine.
lest (-t), *n.m.* ballast.
leste, *adj.* nimble, clever.
lettre, *n.f.* letter.
lettré, *adj.* lettered, literate.
leur, 1. *pron.* to them; **le leur, la leur,** theirs. **2. leur** *m.f.,* **leurs** *pl.* their.
leurre, *n.m.* lure, trap.
leurrer, *vb.* lure.
levain, *n.m.* yeast, leaven.
levée, *n.f.* embankment, levy.
lever, *vb.* raise. **se l.,** get up.
levier, *n.m.* lever.
lèvre, *n.f.* lip.
lévrier, *n.m.* greyhound.
lexique, *n.m.* lexicon.
lézard, *n.m.* lizard.
lézarde, *n.f.* crevice.
liaison, *n.f.* connection, linkage.
liant, *adj.* supple; affable.
liasse, *n.f.* file.
libelle, *n.m.* libel.
libeller, *vb.* draw up, word.
libéral, *adj.* liberal.
libérateur, *n.m.* rescuer.
libérer, *vb.* free.
liberté, *n.f.* freedom, liberty.

libertin, 1. adj. wanton. **2.** n. libertine.

libraire, n.m. bookseller.

librairie, n.f. bookstore.

libre, adj. free.

libre-échange, n.m. free trade.

licence, n.f. license.

licencié, n.m. licensee; holder of university degree.

licencieux, adj. licentious.

licite, adj. lawful.

licorne, n.f. unicorn.

licou, n.m. halter.

lie, n.f. dreg.

liège, n.m. cork.

lien, n.m. bond, link, tie.

lier, vb. bind, tie, link.

lierre, n.m. ivy.

lieu, n.m. place. **au l. de,** instead of.

lieu-commun, n.m. commonplace.

lieue, n.f. league.

lieutenant, n.m. lieutenant.

lièvre, n.m. hare.

ligne, n.f. line.

lignée, n.f. offspring.

ligoter, vb. bind up.

ligue, n.f. league.

liguer, vb. league.

lilas, n.m. lilac.

limaçon, n.m. snail.

lime, n.f. file; lime (fruit).

limer, vb. file.

limier, n.m. bloodhound.

limitation, n.f. limitation.

limitation des naissances, n.f. birth control, contraception.

limite, n.f. limit, border.

limiter, vb. limit, confine.

limon, n.m. mud, slime.

limonade, n.f. lemon soda.

limoneux, adj. muddy.

limpide, adj. clear, limpid.

lin, n.m. flax.

linceul, n.m. shroud.

linéaire, adj. lineal.

linge, n.m. linen, wash.

lingerie, n.f. linen goods, underwear.

linguistique, adj. linguistic.

linon, n.m. lawn (sheer linen).

linteau, n.m. lintel.

lion, n.m. lion.

lippu, adj. thick-lipped.

liqueur, n.f. liquid, liqueur.

liquidation, n.f. liquidation, settling.

liquide, adj. and n.m. liquid, fluid.

liquider, vb. liquidate.

liquoreux, adj. sweet.

lire, vb. read.

lis (-s), n.m. lily.

liséré, n.m. piping, border.

liseur, n.m. reader.

liseuse, n.f. bookmark.

lisible, adj. legible.

lisière, n.f. edge.

lisse, adj. smooth.

lisser, vb. smooth.

liste, n.f. list, roll.

lit, n.m. bed.

litanie, n.f. litany.

lit-cage, n.m. (folding) cot.

lit de la mer, n.m. seabed.

literie, n.f. bedding.

litière, n.f. litter.

litige, n.m. litigation.

litigieux, adj. litigious.

litre, n.m. liter.

littéraire, adj. literary.

littéral, adj. literal.

littérature, n.f. literature.

liturgie, n.f. liturgy.

livide, adj. livid.

livraison, n.f. delivery. **l. contre remboursement,** C.O.D.

livre, n.f. pound.

livre, n.m. book.

livre broché, n.m. paperback.

livrée, n.f. livery.

livrer, vb. deliver.

livresque, adj. bookish, from books.

livreur, n.m. delivery man.

local, adj. local.

localiser, vb. locate.

localité, n.f. locality.

locataire, n.m.f. tenant.

location, n.f. action or price of renting.

loch (-k), n.m. log.

locomotive, n.f. locomotive.

locuste, n.f. locust.

locution, n.f. locution, phrase.

loge, n.f. box.

logement, n.m. lodging.

loger, vb. lodge.

logique, 1. n.f. logic. **2.** adj. logical.

logis, n.m. dwelling.

loi, n.f. law.

loin, *adv.* far, away.
lointain, *adj.* distant.
loir, *n.m.* dormouse.
loisible, *adj.* optional, allowable.
loisir, *n.m.* leisure.
Londres, *n.m.* London.
long *m.,* **longue** *f. adj.* long.
longe, *n.f.* leash; loin (of veal).
longer, *vb.* go along.
longeron, *n.m.* beam, girder.
longitude, *n.f.* longitude.
longtemps, *adv.* long.
longueur, *n.f.* length.
lopin, *n.m.* small piece, plot.
loquace, *adj.* talkative.
loque, *n.f.* morsel, rag.
loquet, *n.m.* latch.
loqueteux, *adj.* tattered.
lorgner, *vb.* glance at; ogle.
lorgnon, *n.m.* glasses.
loriot, *n.m.* oriole.
lors, *adv.* then. **l. de,** at the time of.
lorsque, *conj.* when.
losange, *n.m.* diamond, lozenge.
lot, *n.m.* lot, prize.
loterie, *n.f.* raffle, lottery.
lotion, *n.f.* lotion.
lotir, *vb.* divide, apportion.
louable, *adj.* praiseworthy.
louage, *n.m.* hire.
louange, *n.f.* praise.
louche, *adj.* shady.
loucher, *vb.* squint.
louer, *vb.* praise; hire, rent.
loueur, *n.m.* one who rents.
loup, *n.m.* wolf.
loupe, *n.f.* magnifying glass.
louper, *vb.* spoil, botch.
loup-garou, *n.m.* werewolf.
lourd, *adj.* heavy.
lourdaud, *n.m.* clod.
lourdeur, *n.f.* heaviness, dullness.
loyal, *adj.* loyal.
loyauté, *n.f.* loyalty.
loyer, *n.m.* rent.
lubricité, *n.f.* lewdness.
lubrifier, *vb.* lubricate.
lucarne, *n.f.* attic window.
lucide, *adj.* lucid.
lucidité, *n.f.* clearness.
luciole, *n.f.* firefly.
lueur, *n.f.* gleam.
lugubre, *adj.* doleful, dismal, lugubrious.
lui, *pron.* he; to him, to her.
lui-même, *pron.* himself, itself.

luire, *vb.* gleam.
luisant, *adj.* shiny.
lumière, *n.f.* light.
lumineux, *adj.* luminous.
lunaire, *adj.* lunar.
lunatique, *adj.* whimsical.
lundi, *n.m.* Monday.
lune, *n.f.* moon. **l. de miel,** honeymoon. **clair de l.,** moonlight.
lunetier, *n.m.* optician.
lunettes, *n.f.pl.* glasses.
lustre, *n.m.* chandelier; luster; five-year period.
lustrer, *vb.* polish, gloss.
luth, *n.m.* lute.
lutiner, *vb.* tease.
lutte, *n.f.* strife, struggle, contest.
lutter, *vb.* struggle, contend.
luxe, *n.m.* luxury.
luxer, *vb.* dislocate.
luxueux, *adj.* luxurious.
luxure, *n.f.* lust.
luzerne, *n.f.* alfalfa.
lycée, *n.m.* high school.
lycéen, *n.m.* high-school student.
lymphatique, *adj.* lymphatic.
lynchage, *n.m.* lynching.
lyncher, *vb.* lynch.
lyre, *n.f.* lyre.
lyrique, *adj.* lyric.

M

M. (abbr. for **Monsieur**), *n.m.* Mr.
macabre, *adj.* macabre, ghastly.
macédoine, *n.f.* salad; mixture.
macérer, *vb.* macerate, soak.
mâcher, *vb.* chew.
machin, *n.m.* thing, gadget.
machinal, *adj.* mechanical.
machination, *n.f.* plot, scheme.
machine, *n.f.* machine. **m. à copier,** copier. **m. à écrire,** typewriter.
machiner, *vb.* plot.
machiniste, *n.m.* machinist.
mâchoire, *n.f.* jaw.
mâchonner, *vb.* mumble, munch.
maçon, *n.m.* mason.
maculer, *vb.* spot, blot.
madame, *n.f.* madam, Mrs.
madeleine, *n.f.* light cake.
mademoiselle, *n.f.* Miss.
madone, *n.f.* Madonna.
mafia, *n.f.* mafia.

magasin, *n.m.* store.
mages, *n.m.pl.* wise men.
magicien, *n.m.* magician.
magie, *n.f.* magic.
magique, *adj.* magic.
magistrat, *n.m.* magistrate.
magnanime, *adj.* magnanimous.
magnat, *n.m.* magnate.
magnétique, *adj.* magnetic.
magnétophone, *n.m.* tape recorder.
magnificence, *n.f.* magnificence.
magnifique, *adj.* magnificent.
mahométan, *adj.* Mohammedan.
mai, *n.m.* May.
maigre, *adj.* lean, thin, meager.
maigrir, *vb.* lose weight.
maille, *n.f.* stitch; mesh.
maillot, *n.m.* shorts; T-shirt.
main, *n.f.* hand. **sous la m.,** handy.
main-d'œuvre, *n.f.* manpower.
maintenant, *adv.* now. **dès m.,** henceforth.
maintenir, *vb.* maintain.
maintien, *n.m.* upkeep; behavior.
maire, *n.m.* mayor.
mairie, *n.f.* city hall.
mais, *conj.* but.
maïs (mä ēs), *n.m.* corn.
maison, *n.f.* house.
maisonnée, *n.f.* household.
maître, *n.m.* master, teacher.
maîtresse, *n.f.* mistress, teacher.
maîtrise, *n.f.* mastery.
maîtriser, *vb.* master, overcome.
majesté, *n.f.* majesty.
majestueux, *adj.* majestic.
majeur, *adj.* major.
majordome, *n.m.* majordomo.
majorer, *vb.* increase price, overprice.
majorité, *n.f.* majority.
majuscule, *n.f.* capital.
mal, 1. *n.m.* harm, ill, evil. **2.** *adv.* badly. **faire m. à,** hurt. **avoir m. à,** have a pain in.
malade, 1. *n.m.f.* sick person, patient. **2.** *adj.* sick.
maladie, *n.f.* disease, illness, sickness.
maladif, *adj.* sickly.
maladresse, *n.f.* awkwardness.
maladroit, *adj.* awkward.
malaise, *n.m.* discomfort.
malappris, *adj.* ill-bred.
malaria, *n.f.* malaria.

malavisé, *adj.* indiscreet, ill-advised.
malchance, *n.f.* bad luck, mishap.
maldonne, *n.f.* misdeal.
mâle, *adj. and n.m.* male.
malédiction, *n.f.* curse.
maléfice, *n.m.* witchery, evil spell.
malencontre, *n.f.* unlucky incident.
malencontreux, *adj.* unlucky.
malentendu, *n.m.* misunderstanding.
malfaiteur, *n.m.* malefactor.
malfamé, *adj.* ill-famed.
malgré, *prep.* despite.
malhabile, *adj.* awkward, dull.
malheur, *n.m.* misfortune, accident.
malheureux, *adj.* unfortunate, unhappy, miserable.
malhonnête, *adj.* dishonest.
malhonnêteté, *n.f.* dishonesty.
malice, *n.f.* mischief, malice.
malicieux, *adj.* malicious, roguish.
malin *m.,* **maligne** *f. adj.* malignant; sharp, sly.
malingre, *adj.* sickly, puny.
malintentionné, *adj.* ill-disposed.
malle, *n.f.* trunk.
mallette, *n.f.* small suitcase.
malotru, *n.m.* boor, lout.
malpropre, *adj.* messy.
malpropreté, *n.f.* messiness.
malsain, *adj.* unhealthy.
malséant, *adj.* improper.
maltraiter, *vb.* misuse.
malveillant, *adj.* malevolent.
malvenu, *adj.* without any right.
malversation, *n.f.* embezzlement.
maman, *n.f.* mamma.
mamelle, *n.f.* udder.
mammifère, *n.m.* mammal.
manche, *n.m.* handle. *f.* sleeve. **La M.,** the English Channel.
manchette, *n.f.* cuff.
manchon, *n.m.* muff.
mandarine, *n.f.* tangerine.
mandat, *n.m.* warrant, writ, mandate. **m.-poste,** money order.
mandataire, *n.m.* agent, proxy.
mander, *vb.* send for, inform.
manège, *n.m.* horsemanship.
manette, *n.f.* handle, lever.
mangeable, *adj.* eatable.
mangeoire, *n.f.* manger.

manger, *vb.* eat.
maniable, *adj.* manageable; easy-going.
maniaque, 1. *n.m.* maniac. **2.** *adj.* maniac, maniacal.
manie, *n.f.* mania.
manier, *vb.* handle, wield.
manière, *n.f.* manner.
maniéré, *adj.* affected.
manière de vivre, *n.f.* life style.
manifestation, *n.f.* demonstration.
manifeste, *adj.* manifest, evident, overt.
manifester, *vb.* manifest, show.
manigance, *n.f.* trick, intrigue.
manipuler, *adj.* manipulate.
manivelle, *n.f.* crank; winch.
mannequin, *n.m.* dummy.
manœuvre, *n.f.* maneuver.
manoir, *n.m.* country house, estate.
manquant, 1. *adj.* missing. **2.** *n.m.* absentee.
manque, *n.m.* lack.
manquer, *vb.* miss, lack, fail.
mansarde, *n.f.* attic.
mansuétude, *n.f.* mildness, kindness.
manteau, *n.m.* cloak, coat.
manucure, *n.f.* manicurist.
manuel, *adj. and n.m.* manual.
manufacture, *n.f.* manufacture.
manuscrit, *adj. and n.m.* manuscript.
manutention, *n.f.* management.
maquereau, *n.m.* mackerel.
maquette, *n.f.* preliminary sketch or model.
maquillage, *n.m.* make-up.
maquis, *n.m.* scrub land; guerrilla fighters.
maquisard, *n.m.* guerrilla fighter.
marais, *n.m.* marsh.
marâtre, *n.f.* stepmother.
maraude, *n.f.* marauding.
marbre, *n.m.* marble.
marchand, *n.m.* merchant.
marchander, *vb.* bargain, haggle.
marchandises, *n.f.pl.* goods.
marche, *n.f.* march, step.
marché, *n.m.* market, bargain. **bon m.,** cheap.
marchepied, *n.m.* runningboard.
marcher, *vb.* walk, step, march, run (machine).
marcheur, *n.m.* pedestrian.

mardi, *n.m.* Tuesday.
mare, *n.f.* pool.
marécage, *n.m.* bog.
marécageux, *adj.* marshy.
maréchal, *n.m.* marshal.
marée, *n.f.* tide.
mareyeur, *n.m.* fish seller.
margarine, *n.f.* margarine.
marge, *n.f.* margin.
margelle, *n.f.* edge, brink.
marguerite, *n.f.* daisy.
mari, *n.m.* husband.
mariage, *n.m.* marriage.
marié, 1. *n.m.* bridegroom. **2.** *adj.* married.
mariée, *n.f.* bride.
marie-jeanne, *n.f.* marijuana.
marier, *vb.* marry.
marijuana, *n.f.* marijuana.
marin, 1. *n.m.* sailor. **2.** *adj.* marine. **fusilier m.,** marine.
marinade, *n.f.* mixture for pickling.
marine, *n.f.* navy.
mariner, *vb.* pickle.
marionnette, *n.f.* puppet.
maritime, *adj.* marine.
marmite, *n.f.* pot.
marmiter, *vb.* blast (with gunfire).
marmot, *n.m.* urchin, brat.
marmotter, *vb.* mumble.
marotte, *n.f.* fad.
marque, *n.f.* brand, mark.
marquer, *vb.* mark.
marqueur, *n.m.* marker, scorekeeper.
marquis, *n.m.* marquis.
marraine, *n.f.* godmother; sponsor.
marron, *n.m.* chestnut; brown.
marronier, *n.m.* chestnut tree.
mars (-s), *n.m.* March.
marteau, *n.m.* hammer.
marteler, *vb.* hammer.
martial, *adj.* warlike.
martre, *n.m.* marten.
martyr, *n.m.* martyr.
martyre, *n.m.* martyrdom.
marxisme, *n.m.* marxism.
mascarade, *n.f.* masquerade.
mascotte, *n.f.* mascot.
masculin, *adj.* masculine.
masque, *n.m.* mask.
masquer, *vb.* mask.
massacre, *n.m.* slaughter.
massage, *n.m.* massage.

masse, *n.f.* mass.

masser, *vb.* mass; massage.

massif, *adj.* massive, solid.

massue, *n.f.* club.

mastiquer, *vb.* chew.

mat (-t), *adj.* dull.

mât (mä), *n.m.* mast.

matelas, *n.m.* mattress.

matelot, *n.m.* sailor.

matérialiser, *vb.* materialize.

matérialisme, *n.m.* materialism.

matérialiste, *adj. and n.m.f.* materialist, materialistic.

matériaux, *n.m.pl.* stuff, materials.

matériel, *adj.* material, real.

maternel, *adj.* native; maternal.

maternité, *n.f.* maternity.

mathématique, *adj.* mathematical.

mathématiques, *n.f.pl.* mathematics.

matière, *n.f.* matter. **table des m.s,** index.

matin, *n.m.* morning.

mâtin, *n.m.* big dog.

matinal, *adj.* early.

matinée, *n.f.* morning.

matineux, *adj.* rising early.

matois, *adj.* cunning, sly.

matou, *n.m.* tomcat.

matraque, *n.f.* heavy club.

matrice, *n.f.* womb.

matricule, *n.f.* roster, registration.

matriculer, *vb.* enroll, register.

matrimonial, *adj.* marital.

mâture, *n.f.* masts (of boats).

maturité, *n.f.* maturity.

maudire, *vb.* curse.

maudit, *adj.* cursed, miserable.

maugréer, *vb.* curse, grumble.

maussade, *adj.* glum, sullen, cross.

mauvais, *adj.* bad.

maxime, *n.f.* maxim.

maximum, *n.m.* maximum.

me (ma), *pron.* me, myself.

méandre, *n.m.* winding.

mécanicien, *n.m.* mechanic, engineer.

mécanique, *adj.* mechanical.

mécaniser, *vb.* mechanize.

mécanisme, *n.m.* mechanism, machinery.

mécano, *n.m.* mechanic.

méchamment, *adv.* maliciously.

méchanceté, *n.f.* wickedness, malice.

méchant, *adj.* wicked, malicious.

mèche, *n.f.* lock; wick, fuse.

mécompte, *n.m.* error, disappointment.

méconnaissable, *adj.* unrecognizable.

méconnaître, *vb.* fail to recognize.

mécontent, *adj.* discontented.

mécontentement, *n.m.* discontent.

mécontenter, *vb.* dissatisfy.

mécréant, *n.m.* unbeliever.

médaille, *n.f.* medal.

médaillon, *n.m.* locket.

médecin, *n.m.* physician.

médecine, *n.f.* medicine.

médiateur, *n.m.* mediator; ombudsman (in France).

médiation, *n.f.* mediation.

médical, *adj.* medical.

médicament, *n.m.* medicament.

médicinal, *adj.* medicinal.

médiéval, *adj.* medieval.

médiocre, *adj.* mediocre.

médiocrité, *n.f.* mediocrity.

médire, *vb.* slander, defame.

médisance, *n.f.* slander.

méditation, *n.f.* meditation.

méditer, *vb.* meditate, muse, brood.

méditerrané, *adj.* Mediterranean.

médium, *n.m.* medium.

méduse, *n.f.* jellyfish.

méduser, *vb.* stupefy.

méfait, *n.m.* crime, misdeed.

méfiance, *n.f.* distrust.

méfiant, *adj.* distrustful.

méfier, *vb.* **se m. de,** distrust.

mégarde, *n.f.* heedlessness.

mégère, *n.f.* vixen, shrew.

mégot, *n.m.* cigarette butt.

meilleur, *adj.* better, best.

mélancolie, *n.f.* melancholy.

mélancolique, *adj.* melancholy.

mélange, *n.m.* mixture.

mélasse, *n.f.* molasses.

mêlée, *n.f.* struggle.

mêler, *vb.* mix. **se m. de,** meddle in.

mélèze, *n.m.* larch.

melliflu, *adj.* sweet, honeyed.

mélodie, *n.f.* melody.

mélodieux, *adj.* melodious.

mélodique, *adj.* melodic.

mélodrame, *n.m.* melodrama.

mélomane, *n.m.* lover of music.

melon, *n.m.* melon.

membrane, *n.f.* membrane.

membre, **1.** *adj.* member, limb.

membrure, *n.f.* frame, limbs.

même, **1.** *adj.* same, very, self. **moi-m.**, myself; **lui-m.**, himself, etc. **2.** *adv.* even. **de m.**, likewise. **tout de m.**, notwithstanding. **mettre à m. de**, enable to.

mémento, *n.m.* memento, notebook.

mémoire, *n.f.* memory, memoir.

mémorable, *adj.* memorable.

mémorandum, *n.m.* memorandum.

mémorial, *n.m.* memorial; memoirs.

menaçant, *adj.* threatening.

menace, *n.f.* threat.

menacer, *vb.* threaten.

ménage, *n.m.* household.

ménagement, *n.m.* discretion.

ménager, **1.** *n.m.* manager. **2.** *vb.* manage.

ménagère, *n.f.* housewife, housekeeper.

ménagerie, *n.f.* menagerie.

mendiant, *n.m.* beggar.

mendicité, *n.f.* begging.

mendier, *vb.* beg.

menées, *n.f.pl.* schemes.

mener, *vb.* lead.

ménestrel, *n.m.* minstrel.

ménétrier, *n.m.* country fiddler.

meneur, *n.m.* leader, ringleader.

méningite, *n.f.* meningitis.

menottes, *n.f.pl.* handcuffs.

mensonge, *n.m.* falsehood, lie.

mensonger, *adj.* false, deceptive.

mensualité, *n.f.* remittance paid monthly.

mensuel, *adj.* monthly.

mensurable, *adj.* measurable.

mental, *adj.* mental.

mentalité, *n.f.* mentality.

menterie, *n.f.* lie.

menteur, *n.m.* liar.

menthe, *n.f.* mint.

mention, *n.f.* mention.

mentionner, *vb.* mention.

mentir, *vb.* lie.

menton, *n.m.* chin.

menu, **1.** *n.m.* menu. **2.** *adj.* little, minute.

menuet, *n.m.* minuet.

menuiserie, *n.f.* woodwork.

menuisier, *n.m.* carpenter.

méprendre, *vb.* **se m.**, be mistaken.

mépris, *n.m.* contempt, scorn.

méprisable, *adj.* mean, contemptible.

méprisant, *adj.* contemptuous.

méprise, *n.f.* mistake, misunderstanding.

mépriser, *vb.* scorn, despise.

mer (-r), *n.f.* sea. **mal de m.**, seasickness.

mercanti, *n.m.* profiteer.

mercantile, *adj.* mercantile.

mercenaire, *adj. and n.m.* mercenary.

mercerie, *n.f.* haberdashery.

merci, *n.m.* thanks, mercy.

mercredi, *n.m.* Wednesday.

mercure, *n.m.* mercury.

mère, *n.f.* mother.

méridien, *n.m.* meridian.

méridional, *adj.* southern.

meringue, *n.f.* meringue.

méritant, *adj.* meritorious.

mérite, *n.m.* merit, desert.

mériter, *vb.* merit, deserve.

méritoire, *adj.* meritorious.

merle, *n.m.* blackbird.

merveille, *n.f.* marvel.

merveilleux, *adj.* wonderful, marvelous.

mésalliance, *n.f.* misalliance.

mésallier, *vb.* marry badly.

mésaventure, *n.f.* accident, mishap.

mesdames, *pl.* of **madame**.

mesdemoiselles, *pl.* of **mademoiselle**.

mésestime, *n.f.* low opinion or repute.

mésintelligence, *n.f.* difficulty, discord.

mesquin, *adj.* shabby, mean, stingy.

mesquinerie, *n.f.* meanness.

message, *n.m.* message.

messager, *n.m.* messenger.

messe, *n.f.* Mass.

Messie, *n.m.* Messiah.

messieurs, *pl.* of **monsieur**.

mesurage, *n.m.* measurement.

mesure, *n.f.* measure. **à m. que**, as.

mesuré, *adj.* measured, cautious.

mesurer, *vb.* measure.

métairie, *n.f.* small farm.
métal, *n.m.* metal.
métallique, *adj.* metallic.
métallurgie, *n.f.* metallurgy.
métamorphose, *n.f.* transformation.
métaphore, *n.f.* metaphor.
métaphysique, 1. *n.f.* metaphysics. **2.** *adj.* metaphysical.
métayer, *n.m.* small farmer.
météore, *n.m.* meteor.
météorologie, *n.f.* meteorology.
métèque, *n.m.* alien.
méthode, *n.f.* method.
méthodique, *adj.* methodical, systematic.
méticuleux, *adj.* meticulous.
métier, *n.m.* loom; craft, trade.
métis, *adj.* hybrid, crossbred.
métrage, *n.m.* measurement.
mètre, *n.m.* meter.
métrique, *adj.* metric.
métro, *n.m.* subway.
métropole, *n.f.* metropolis; native land.
métropolitain, *adj.* metropolitan.
mets, *n.m.* food, dish.
mettable, *adj.* wearable.
metteur, *n.m.* **m. en scène,** play director.
mettre, *vb.* put, place, set. **se m. à,** begin.
meuble, *n.m.* piece of furniture; (*pl.*) furniture.
meubler, *vb.* furnish, outfit.
meule, *n.f.* stack.
meunier, *n.m.* miller.
meurtre, *n.m.* murder.
meurtrier, *n.m.* murderer.
meurtrière, *n.f.* murderess.
meurtrir, *vb.* bruise.
meurtrissure, *n.f.* bruise.
meute, *n.f.* dog pack; mob.
Mexicain, *n.m.* Mexican.
mexicain, *adj.* Mexican.
Mexique, *n.m.* Mexico.
mezzanine, *n.f.* mezzanine.
mi, *adj.* mid, half.
miaou, *n.m.* mew.
miauler, *vb.* mew.
mica, *n.m.* mica.
miche, *n.f.* loaf of bread.
micro, *n.m.* microphone.
microbe, *n.m.* microbe.
microfiche, *n.f.* microfiche.
microforme, *n.f.* microform.
microphone, *n.m.* microphone.

microscope, *n.m.* microscope.
microscopique, *adj.* microscopic.
midi, *n.m.* noon; south.
midinette, *n.f.* young saleswoman, business woman.
mie, *n.f.* crumb.
miel, *n.m.* honey.
mielleux, *adj.* honeyed, sweet.
mien, *pron.* **le mien, la mienne,** mine.
miette, *n.f.* crumb.
mieux, *adv.* better, best.
mièvre, *adj.* affected.
mignard, *adj.* dainty, mincing.
mignon, 1. *adj.* delicate, dainty. **2.** *n.m.f.* darling.
migraine, *n.f.* headache.
migration, *n.f.* migration.
mijoter, *vb.* cook slowly, simmer.
mil (mēl), *num.* thousand.
milice, *n.f.* militia.
milieu, *n.m.* middle, center, environment.
militaire, *adj.* military.
militant, *adj.* militant.
militarisme, *n.m.* militarism.
militer, *vb.* militate.
mille (-l), **1.** *n.m.* mile. **2.** *adj.* and *n.m.* thousand.
millet, *n.m.* millet.
millier (-l-), *n.m.* thousand.
milligramme (-l-), *n.m.* milligram.
million (-l-), *n.m.* million.
millionnaire (-l-), *adj.* and *n.m.f.* millionaire.
mime, *n.m.* mime, mimic.
mimique, *adj.* mimic.
minable, *adj.* shabby, poor.
minauder, *vb.* simper.
mince, *adj.* slender, slight, thin.
minceur, *n.f.* slimness.
mine, *n.f.* mine; mien; lead.
miner, *vb.* mine; wear away; weaken.
minerai, *n.m.* ore.
minéral, *adj.* and *n.m.* mineral.
mineur, 1. *n.m.* miner. **2.** *adj.* and *n.m.* minor.
miniature, *n.f.* miniature.
miniaturiser, *vb.* miniaturize.
minier, *adj.* of mines.
minime, *adj.* very small.
minimum, *n.m.* minimum.
ministère, *n.m.* ministry, department, board.
ministériel, *adj.* ministerial.

ministre, *n.m.* minister. **premier m.,** premier.

minorité, *n.f.* minority.

minotier, *n.m.* miller.

minuit, *n.m.* midnight.

minuscule, *adj.* minute.

minute, *n.f.* minute.

minutie, *n.f.* trifle; care with details.

minutieux, *adj.* minute.

mioche, *n.m.f.* urchin.

miracle, *n.m.* miracle.

miraculeux, *adj.* miraculous.

mirage, *n.m.* mirage.

mirer, *vb.* aim at, look at.

mirifique, *adj.* wonderful.

miroir, *n.m.* mirror.

miroiter, *vb.* glisten.

misanthrope, 1. *n.m.* misanthrope. **2.** *adj.* misanthropic.

mise, *n.f.* putting; mode. **mise en scène,** setting.

miser, *vb.* bid.

misérable, *adj.* miserable, wretched, squalid.

misère, *n.f.* misery.

miséreux, *adj.* poor, miserable.

miséricorde, *n.f.* mercy.

miséricordieux, *adj.* merciful.

misogyne, 1. *n.m.* misogynist. **2.** *adj.* woman-hating; misogynist.

missel, *n.m.* missal.

mission, *n.f.* mission.

missionnaire, *adj. and n.m.f.* missionary.

missive, *n.f.* missive.

mitaine, *n.f.* mitten.

mite, *n.f.* moth.

miteux, *adj.* shabby.

mitiger, *vb.* moderate.

mitoyen, *adj.* midway; jointly owned.

mitrailleuse, *n.f.* machine gun.

mixte, *adj.* mixed, joint.

Mlle. (abbr. for **Mademoiselle**), *n.f.* Miss.

Mme. (abbr. for **Madame**), *n.f.* Mrs.

mobile, *adj.* movable.

mobilier, *adj.* movable.

mobilisation, *n.f.* mobilization.

mobiliser, *vb.* mobilize.

mobilité, *n.f.* mobility; instability.

mode, *n.f.* fashion, mode, mood; (*pl.*) millinery. **à la m.,** fashionable.

modèle, *n.m.* model, pattern.

modeler, *vb.* model, shape.

modelliste, *n.m.f.* dress designer.

modérateur, *n.m.* moderator.

modération, *n.f.* moderation.

modéré, *adj.* moderate.

modérer, *vb.* check, moderate.

moderne, *adj.* modern.

moderniser, *vb.* modernize.

modernité, *n.f.* modernity.

modeste, *adj.* modest.

modestie, *n.f.* modesty.

modicité, *n.f.* small quantity.

modification, *n.f.* alteration.

modifier, *vb.* modify, qualify.

modique, *adj.* moderate, unimportant.

modiste, *n.f.* milliner.

modulation, *n.f.* modulation.

moduler, *vb.* modulate.

moelle, *n.f.* marrow.

moelleux (mwä ly), *adj.* mellow, soft.

mœurs (-s), *n.f.pl.* manner(s), custom.

moi, 1. *n.m.* ego. **2.** *pron.* me.

moignon, *n.m.* stump.

moindre, *adj.* less, lesser, least.

moine, *n.m.* monk.

moineau, *n.m.* sparrow.

moins, *adv.* less, least. **au m.,** at least. **à m. que,** unless.

moire, *n.f.* watered silk.

mois, *n.m.* month.

moisi, *adj.* moldy.

moisir, *vb.* mold.

moisissure, *n.f.* mold.

moisson, *n.f.* harvest, crop.

moissonner, *vb.* reap, harvest.

moissonneur, *n.m.* harvester.

moissonneuse, *n.f.* reaping machine.

moite, *adj.* moist.

moiteur, *n.f.* dampness.

moitié, *n.f.* half. **à m.,** half, *adv.*

molaire, *adj. and n.f.* molar.

môle, *n.m.* pier.

molécule, *n.f.* molecule.

molester, *vb.* molest.

mollah, *n.m.* mullah.

mollasse, *adj.* flabby, soft.

mollesse, *n.f.* softness, weakness.

mollet, 1. *adj.* soft. **œufs mollets,** soft-boiled eggs. **2.** *n.m.* calf of leg.

molletière, *n.f.* legging.

molleton, *n.m.* heavy flannel.

mollir, *vb.* soften, slacken.

mollusque, *n.m.* mollusc.

moment, *n.m.* moment.

momentané, *adj.* momentary.

mon *m.,* **ma** *f.,* **mes** *pl.* *adj.* my.

monacal, *adj.* pertaining to monks.

monarchie, *n.f.* monarchy.

monarchiste, *n.m.* monarchist.

monarque, *n.m.* monarch.

monastère, *n.m.* monastery.

monastique, *adj.* monastic.

monceau, *n.m.* pile.

mondain, *adj.* worldly.

monde, *n.m.* world, people. **tout le m.,** everybody, everyone. **mettre au m.,** bear.

mondial, *adj.* world-wide.

monétaire, *adj.* monetary.

moniteur, *n.m.* monitor.

monnaie, *n.f.* money, change, currency. **Hôtel de la M.,** mint.

monnayer, *vb.* mint.

monocle, *n.m.* monocle.

monogramme, *n.m.* monogram.

monologue, *n.m.* monologue.

monologuer, *vb.* soliloquize.

monoplan, *n.m.* monoplane.

monopole, *n.m.* monopoly.

monopoliser, *vb.* monopolize.

monosyllabe, *n.m.* monosyllable.

monosyllabique, *adj.* monosyllabic.

monotone, *adj.* monotonous.

monotonie, *n.f.* monotony, dullness.

monseigneur, *n.m.* title of honor; My Lord.

monsieur, *n.m.,* **messieurs,** *pl.* gentleman, sir; Mr.

monstre, *n.m.* monster.

monstrueux, *adj.* monstrous.

monstruosité, *n.f.* monstrosity.

mont, *n.m.* mountain, hill.

montage, *n.m.* carrying up.

montagnard, *n.m.* mountaineer.

montagne, *n.f.* mountain.

montagneux, *adj.* mountainous.

montant, *n.m.* amount.

mont-de-piété, *n.m.* pawnshop.

monté, *adj.* mounted, supplied.

montée, *n.f.* ascent, rise, climb.

monter, *vb.* go up, mount, climb, rise.

montre, *n.f.* watch; display. **m.-bracelet,** wrist watch.

montrer, *vb.* show.

montreur, *n.m.* showman.

montueux, *adj.* hilly.

monture, *n.f.* mount.

monument, *n.m.* monument.

monumental, *adj.* monumental.

moquer, *vb.* **se m. de,** make fun of, mock, laugh at.

moquerie, *n.f.* mockery, ridicule.

moqueur, *adj.* mocking.

moral, *adj.* ethical, moral.

morale, *n.f.* morals, morality, morale.

moraliser, *vb.* moralize.

moraliste, *n.m.f.* moralist.

moralité, *n.f.* morals, morality.

morbide, *adj.* morbid.

morceau, *n.m.* piece, bit, morsel. **gros m.,** lump, chunk.

morceler, *vb.* cut up.

mordant, *adj.* pointed.

mordiller, *vb.* nibble.

mordre, *vb.* bite.

morfondre, *vb.* chill.

morgue, *n.f.* morgue.

moribond, *adj.* dying.

morne, *adj.* bleak, dismal, dreary.

morose, *adj.* morose.

morosité, *n.f.* moroseness.

morphine, *n.f.* morphine.

morphinomane, *n.* drug addict.

morphologie, *n.f.* morphology.

mors, *n.m.* horse's bit.

morse, *n.m.* walrus.

morsure, *n.f.* bite.

mort, 1. *n.m.* dummy, dead man. **2.** *n.f.* death. **3.** *adj.* dead.

mortaise, *n.f.* mortise.

mortalité, *n.f.* mortality.

mortel, 1. *adj.* deadly, mortal.

morte-saison, *n.f.* off season.

mortier, *n.m.* mortar.

mortifier, *vb.* mortify.

mort-né, *adj.* still-born.

mortuaire, *adj.* mortuary.

morue, *n.f.* cod.

mosaïque (-ä ēk), *n.f.* mosaic.

Moscou, *n.m.* Moscow.

mosquée, *n.f.* mosque.

mot, *n.m.* word; cue.

moteur, *n.m.* motor.

motif, *n.m.* motive.

motion, *n.f.* motion.

motiver, *vb.* motivate, justify.

motocyclette, *n.f.* motorcycle.

motocycliste, *n.m.* motorcyclist.

motte, *n.f.* clod.

mou *m.,* **molle** *f. adj.* soft.
mouchard, *n.m.* spy.
moucharder, *vb.* spy.
mouche, *n.f.* fly.
moucher, *vb.* blow the nose.
moucheron, *n.m.* gnat.
moucheté, *adj.* spotted.
moucheture, *n.f.* spot.
mouchoir, *n.m.* handkerchief.
moudre, *vb.* grind.
moue, *n.f.* pout, wry face.
mouette, *n.f.* gull.
moufette, *n.f.* skunk.
moufle, *n.f.* mitten.
mouillage, *n.m.* wetting.
mouillé, *adj.* wet.
mouiller, *vb.* soak.
moulage, *n.m.* cast (from mold).
moule, *n.m.* mold.
mouler, *vb.* mold.
mouleur, *n.m.* molder.
moulin, *n.m.* mill.
moulure, *n.f.* molding.
mourant, *adj.* dying.
mourir, *vb.* die.
mouron, *n.m.* pimpernel.
mousquetaire, *n.m.* musketeer.
mousse, *n.f.* moss; foam, lather.
mousseline, *n.f.* muslin.
mousser, *vb.* foam, froth.
mousseux, *adj.* foaming.
mousson, *n.m.* monsoon.
moustache, *n.f.* mustache, whisker.
moustiquaire, *n.f.* mosquito net.
moustique, *n.m.* mosquito.
moutarde, *n.f.* mustard.
mouton, *n.m.* sheep; mutton.
moutonner, *vb.* curl; make wooly.
mouture, *n.f.* grinding.
mouvant, *adj.* moving, shifting.
mouvement, *n.m.* movement, stir.
mouvoir, *vb.* move.
moyen, **1.** *n.m.* means, medium.
2. *adj.* middle, average.
moyennant, *prep.* by means of.
moyenne, *n.f.* average.
Moyen Orient, *n.m.* Middle East.
muabilité, *n.f.* changeability.
mucilage, *n.m.* mucilage.
mue, *n.f.* molting; changing (esp. of voice).
muer, *vb.* molt (animals); break, change (voice).
muet *m.,* **muette** *f. adj.* dumb, mute.
mufle, *n.m.* cad.

mugir, *vb.* roar, bellow.
mugissement, *n.m.* roaring, bellowing.
muguet, *n.m.* lily of the valley.
mulâtre, *n.m. and adj.* mulatto.
mulet, *n.m.* mule.
muletier, *n.m.* muleteer.
mulot, *n.m.* field mouse.
multinational, *adj.* multinational.
multiple, *adj.* multiple, manifold.
multiplicande, *n.m.* multiplicand.
multiplication, *n.f.* multiplication.
multiplicité, *n.f.* multiplicity.
multiplier, *vb.* multiply.
multitude, *n.f.* multitude.
municipal, *adj.* municipal.
municipalité, *n.f.* municipality.
munificence, *n.f.* munificence, liberality.
munificent, *adj.* very generous.
munir, *vb.* provide, supply.
munitionner, *vb.* provision, supply.
munitions (de guerre), *n.f.pl.* ammunition.
muqueux, *adj.* mucous.
mur, *n.m.* wall.
mûr, *adj.* ripe, mature.
muraille, *n.f.* wall.
mural, *adj.* mural.
mûre (de ronce), *n.f.* blackberry.
mûrier, *n.m.* mulberry tree.
mûrir, *vb.* ripen, mature.
murmure, *n.m.* murmur.
murmurer, *vb.* murmur.
musarder, *vb.* waste time, dawdle.
muscade, *n.f.* nutmeg.
muscle, *n.m.* muscle.
musculaire, *adj.* muscular.
musculeux, *adj.* muscular.
muse, *n.f.* muse.
museau, *n.m.* muzzle.
musée, *n.m.* museum.
museler, *vb.* muzzle; gag.
muselière, *n.f.* muzzle.
muser, *vb.* trifle, dawdle.
musical, *adj.* musical.
musicien, *adj. and n.m.* musical, musician.
musique, *n.f.* music.
musulman, *adj. and n.m.* Mohammedan.
mutabilité, *n.f.* mutability.
mutation, *n.f.* change, replacement.

mutilation, *n.f.* mutilation.
mutiler, *vb.* mutilate, mangle, mar.
mutin, *adj.* refractory, mutinous.
mutiner, *vb.* **se m.,** mutiny, revolt.
mutinerie, *n.f.* mutiny.
mutisme, *n.m.* muteness, lack of speech.
mutuel, *adj.* mutual.
myope, *adj.* near-sighted.
myopie, *n.f.* near-sightedness.
myosotis, *n.m.* forget-me-not.
myriade, *n.f.* myriad.
myrrhe, *n.f.* myrrh.
myrte, *n.m.* myrtle.
mystère, *n.m.* mystery.
mystérieux, *adj.* mysterious, weird.
mysticisme, *n.m.* mysticism.
mystification, *n.f.* hoax.
mystifier, *vb.* mystify.
mystique, *adj.* mystic.
mythe, *n.m.* myth.
mythique, *adj.* mythical.
mythologie, *n.f.* mythology.

N

nabot, *n.m.* dwarf.
nacre, *n.f.* mother-of-pearl.
nacré, *adj.* pearly.
nage, *n.f.* act of swimming.
nageoire, *n.f.* fin.
nager, *vb.* swim.
nageur, *n.m.* swimmer.
naguère, *adv.* a short time ago.
naïf (nä ēf) *m.,* **naïve** *f. adj.* naïve.
nain, *n.m.* dwarf.
naissance, *n.f.* birth.
naissant, *adj.* beginning, newborn.
naître, *vb.* be born.
naïveté (nä ēv-), *n.f.* simplicity.
nantir, *vb.* give as security; furnish.
nantissement, *n.m.* pledge, guarantee.
naphte, *n.m.* naphtha.
nappe, *n.f.* tablecloth.
narcisse, *n.m.* daffodil.
narcotique, *n.m.* narcotic.
narguer, *vb.* defy, flout.
narine, *n.f.* nostril.
narrateur, *n.m.* narrator, storyteller.

narration, *n.f.* narrative, recital.
narrer, *vb.* narrate, relate.
nasal, *adj.* nasal.
naseau, *n.m.* nostril.
nasiller, *vb.* talk with a nasal voice.
nasse, *n.f.* fish trap.
natal, *adj.* native.
natalité, *n.f.* rate of birth.
natation, *n.f.* swimming.
natif, *n.m. and adj.* native.
nation, *n.f.* nation.
national, *adj.* national.
nationalisation, *n.f.* nationalization.
nationaliser, *vb.* nationalize.
nationalisme, *n.m.* nationalism.
nationalité, *n.f.* nationality.
nativité, *n.f.* nativity.
naturaliser, *vb.* naturalize; (of animals) stuff.
naturalisme, *n.m.* naturalism, naturalness.
naturaliste, *n.m.* naturalist.
nature, *n.f.* nature.
naturel, 1. *n.m.* nature. **2.** *adj.* natural.
naufrage, *n.m.* shipwreck.
naufragé, *adj.* shipwrecked.
nauséabond, *adj.* nauseous, offensive.
nausée, *n.f.* nausea.
nautique, *adj.* nautical.
naval, *adj.* naval.
navet, *n.m.* turnip.
navette spatiale, *n.f.* space shuttle.
navigable, *adj.* navigable.
navigateur, *n.m.* navigator, seaman.
navigation, *n.f.* seafaring, navigation.
naviguer, *vb.* sail, navigate.
navire, *n.m.* ship.
navrant, *adj.* distressing, causing grief.
navrer, *vb.* wound, grieve.
né, *adj.* born.
néanmoins, *adv.* yet, nevertheless, however.
néant, *n.m.* nothing(ness).
nébuleux, *adj.* cloudy; worried.
nécessaire, *adj.* requisite, necessary.
nécessité, *n.f.* necessity. **n. préalable,** prerequisite.

nécessiter, *vb.* make necessary or imperative.

nécessiteux, *adj.* needy.

nécrologe, *n.m.* obituary.

nef, *n.f.* nave.

néfaste, *adj.* ill-omened, unlucky.

négatif, *adj.* negative.

négation, *n.f.* negation; negative word.

négative, *n.f.* negative argument or opinion.

négligé, 1. *adj.* neglected, sloppy. **2.** *n.m.* state of undress.

négligeable, *adj.* negligible.

négligence, *n.f.* neglect.

négligent, *adj.* negligent.

négliger, *vb.* overlook, neglect.

négoce, *n.m.* commerce, trade.

négociable, *adj.* negotiable.

négociant, *n.m.* merchant.

négociation, *n.f.* negotiation.

négocier, *vb.* negotiate.

nègre, *adj. and n.m.* Black.

négresse, *n.f.* Black.

neige, *n.f.* snow.

neiger, *vb.* snow.

neigeux, *adj.* snowy.

néon, *n.m.* neon.

néophyte, *n.m.* neophyte, convert.

néphrite, *n.f.* nephritis.

nerf (nĕr), *n.m.* nerve.

nerveux, *adj.* nervous.

nervosité, *n.f.* nervousness.

net (-t) *m.,* **nette** *f. adj.* net, clear, clean, neat.

netteté, *n.f.* clearness, neatness.

nettoyer, *vb.* clean, cleanse, scour.

nettoyeur, *n.m.* one who or that which cleans.

neuf, *adj. and n.m.* nine.

neuf *m.,* **neuve** *f. adj.* brand-new.

neutraliser, *vb.* counteract.

neutralité, *n.f.* neutrality.

neutre, *adj. and n.m.* neutral.

neutron, *n.m.* neutron.

neuvième, *adj. and n.m.* ninth.

neveu, *n.m.* nephew.

névralgie, *n.f.* neuralgia.

névrite, *n.f.* neuritis.

névrose, *n.f.* neurosis.

névrosé, *adj. and n.m.* neurotic.

nez, *n.m.* nose.

ni, *conj.* nor. **ni . . . ni . . .,** neither . . . nor . . . .

niais, *adj.* foolish.

niaiserie, *n.f.* silliness, trifle.

niche, *n.f.* alcove.

nichée, *n.f.* brood.

nicher, *vb.* **se n.,** nestle.

nickel, *n.m.* nickel.

nid, *n.m.* nest.

nièce, *n.f.* niece.

nielle, *n.f.* wheat blight.

nier, *vb.* deny.

nigaud, *n.m.* fool, simpleton.

nihilisme, *n.m.* nihilism.

nimbe, *n.m.* halo.

n'importe, *interj.* never mind.

nippes, *n.f.pl.* old clothes.

nitrate, *n.m.* nitrate.

niveau, *n.m.* level. **au n. de,** level with.

niveler, *vb.* make level; survey.

nivellement, *n.m.* leveling, surveying.

noble, 1. *n.m.* nobleman, peer. **2.** *adj.* noble.

noblesse, *n.f.* nobility.

noce, *n.f.* wedding. **faire la n.,** revel.

noceur, *n.m.* gay blade.

nocif, *adj.* harmful.

noctambule, *n.m.* sleep-walker, prowler.

nocturne, *adj.* nocturnal.

Noël (nō ĕl), *n.m.* Christmas; carol.

nœud (nœ), *n.m.* knot.

noir, *adj. and n.m.* black.

noircir, *vb.* blacken.

noisetier, *n.m.* hazel (tree).

noisette, 1. *n.f.* hazelnut. **2.** *adj.* light reddish brown.

noix, *n.f.* nut, walnut.

nolis, *n.m.* freight.

nom, *n.m.* name; noun.

nomade, *adj.* wandering, roaming.

nombre, *n.m.* number.

nombrer, *vb.* number.

nombreux, *adj.* numerous, manifold.

nombril, *n.m.* navel.

nominal, *adj.* nominal.

nominatif, *adj. and n.m.* nominative.

nomination, *n.f.* nomination, appointment.

nommément, *adv.* particularly, namely.

nommer, *vb.* name, nominate, appoint.

non, *adv.* no. **non plus,** neither.
non-aligné, *adj.* non-aligned.
nonchalamment, *adv.* carelessly, nonchalantly.
nonchalant, *adj.* nonchalant.
non-combattant, *adj. and n.m.* non-combatant.
nonne, *n.f.* nun.
nonobstant, *prep.* in spite of, notwithstanding.
nonpareil, *adj.* unequaled.
non-sens, *n.m.* nonsense.
nord, *n.m.* north.
normal, *adj.* normal.
normand, *adj.* Norman; equivocal.
norme, *n.f.* norm.
Norvège, *n.f.* Norway.
Norvégien, *n.m.* Norwegian (person).
norvégien, 1. *n.m.* Norwegian (language). **2.** *adj.* Norwegian.
nostalgie, *n.f.* nostalgia.
notabilité, *n.f.* notability.
notable, 1. *n.m.* notable. **2.** *adj.* remarkable, notable.
notaire, *n.m.* lawyer, notary.
notamment, *adv.* particularly.
notation, *n.f.* notation.
note, *n.f.* note, bill.
noter, *vb.* note.
notice, *n.f.* notice, review.
notification, *n.f.* notification.
notifier, *vb.* notify.
notion, *n.f.* notion.
notoire, *adj.* notorious.
notoriété, *n.f.* notoriety.
notre *sg.,* **nos** *pl. adj.* our.
nôtre, *pron.* **le n.,** ours.
nouer, *vb.* tie.
noueux, *adj.* knotty.
nouilles, *n.f.pl.* noodles.
nourrice, *n.f.* (wet-)nurse.
nourricier, *adj.* nourishing; of nursing.
nourrir, *vb.* feed, nourish, foster.
nourriture, *n.f.* food, nourishment.
nous, *pron.* we, us, ourselves.
nouveau *m.,* **nouvelle** *f. adj.* new, fresh. **de n.,** anew.
nouveauté, *n.f.* novelty.
nouvel an, *n.m.* new year.
nouvelle, *n.f.* news.
nouvellement, *adv.* recently, newly.
novembre, *n.m.* November.

novice, *n.m.f.* novice.
noviciat, *n.m.* novitiate.
noyade, *n.f.* drowning.
noyau, *n.m.* kernel, nucleus.
noyer, *vb.* drown.
noyer, *n.m.* walnut (tree).
nu, *adj.* naked, bare.
nuage, *n.m.* cloud; gloom.
nuageux, *adj.* cloudy.
nuance, *n.m.* shade, degree.
nucléaire, *adj.* nuclear.
nudité, *n.f.* bareness.
nuire à, *vb.* injure, harm.
nuisible, *adj.* injurious, hurtful.
nuit, *n.f.* night.
nul, *adj.* no, none; void. **nulle part,** nowhere.
nullement, *adv.* not at all.
nullité, *n.f.* nonentity.
numéral, *adj. and n.m.* numeral.
numérique, *adj.* numerical.
numéro, *n.m.* number.
nu-pieds, *adv.* barefoot.
nuptial, *adj.* bridal.
nuque, *n.f.* nape.
nutritif, *adj.* nutritious.
nutrition, *n.f.* nutrition.
nylon, *n.m.* nylon.
nymphe, *n.f.* nymph.

O

oasis (-s), *n.f.* oasis.
obéir à, *vb.* obey.
obéissance, *n.f.* obedience.
obéissant, *adj.* obedient.
obélisque, *n.m.* obelisk.
obérer, *vb.* burden with debt.
obèse, *adj.* obese.
obésité, *n.f.* obesity.
objecter, *vb.* object.
objectif, *adj. and n.m.* objective.
objection, *n.f.* objection.
objet, *n.m.* object.
obligation, *n.f.* obligation.
obligatoire, *adj.* compulsory, mandatory, binding.
obligeance, *n.f.* obligingness.
obliger, *vb.* oblige, accommodate.
oblique, *adj.* slanting; devious.
oblitération, *n.f.* obliteration.
oblitérer, *vb.* obliterate.
oblong, *adj.* oblong.
obscène, *adj.* filthy, obscene.
obscénité, *n.f.* obscenity.

obscur, *adj.* obscure, dark, dim.

obscurcir, *vb.* darken, obscure.

obscurcissement, *n.m.* darkening, state of being obscure.

obscurément, *adv.* obscurely.

obscurité, *n.f.* darkness, dimness, obscurity.

obséder, *vb.* harass, haunt.

obsèques, *n.f.pl.* funeral.

obséquieusement, *adv.* obsequiously.

obséquieux, *adj.* obsequious.

observance, *n.f.* observance.

observateur, *n.m.* observer.

observation, *n.f.* observation, remark.

observer, *vb.* observe, watch.

obsession, *n.f.* obsession.

obstacle, *n.m.* obstacle, bar.

obstétrical, *adj.* obstetrical.

obstination, *n.f.* stubbornness.

obstiné, *adj.* obstinate, stubborn.

obstiner, *vb.* s'o., persist.

obstruction, *n.f.* obstruction.

obstruer, *vb.* obstruct, stop up.

obtempérer, *vb.* obey.

obtenir, *vb.* obtain, get.

obtention, *n.f.* obtaining.

obtus, *adj.* obtuse, dull, stupid.

obus (-s), *n.m.* shell.

obusier, *n.m.* howitzer.

occasion, *n.f.* opportunity, chance; bargain.

occasionnel, *adj.* occasional.

occasionner, *vb.* cause, bring about.

occident, *n.m.* west.

occidental, *adj.* western.

occulte, *adj.* occult.

occupant, *n.m.* occupant, tenant.

occupation, *n.f.* pursuit, occupation.

occupé, *adj.* busy.

occuper, *vb.* occupy, busy. s'o. de, attend to.

occurrence, *n.f.* occurrence.

océan, *n.m.* ocean.

océanique, *adj.* oceanic.

ocre, *n.f.* ochre.

octave, *n.f.* octave.

octobre, *n.m.* October.

octroyer, *vb.* grant.

oculaire, *adj.* ocular.

oculiste, *n.m.* oculist.

ode, *n.f.* ode.

odeur, *n.f.* odor, scent, perfume.

odieux, *adj.* hateful, obnoxious, odious.

odorant, *adj.* having a fragrant odor.

odorat, *n.m.* (sense of) smell.

œil, *n.m.*, *pl.* **yeux,** eye. **coup d'o.,** glance.

œillade, *n.f.* wink, quick look.

œillère, *n.f.* eyetooth.

œillet, *n.m.* carnation.

œuf, *n.m.* egg.

œuvre, *n.f.* work.

offensant, *adj.* offensive.

offense, *n.f.* offense.

offenser, *vb.* offend.

offenseur, *n.m* offender.

offensif, *adj.* offensive.

offensive, *n.f.* offensive.

offensivement, *adv.* offensively.

office, *n.m.* office, pantry; (church) service.

officiant, *n.m.* one who officiates.

officiel, *adj.* official.

officier, 1. *n.m.* officer; mate. **2.** *vb.* officiate.

officieux, *adj.* officious.

offrande, *n.f.* offering.

offre, *n.f.* offer.

offrir, *vb.* offer, present.

offusquer, *vb.* obscure, shadow, irritate.

ogre, *n.m.* ogre.

oie, *n.f.* goose.

oignon (ô nyŏN), *n.m.* onion, bulb.

oindre, *vb.* anoint.

oiseau, *n.m.* bird.

oiselet, *n.m.* small bird.

oiseux, *adj.* idle, empty, useless.

oisif, *adj.* idle.

oisillon, *n.m.* young bird.

oisiveté, *n.f.* idleness.

oléagineux, *adj.* oily.

olivâtre, *adj.* olive-colored.

olive, *n.f.* olive.

olivier, *n.m.* olive tree.

olympique, *adj.* Olympic.

ombilical, *adj.* umbilical.

ombrage, *n.m.* shade.

ombragé, *adj.* shady.

ombrager, *vb.* shade.

ombrageux, *adj.* suspicious, doubtful.

ombre, *n.f.* shade, shadow.

ombreux, *adj.* shady.

omelette, *n.f.* omelet.

omettre, *vb.* omit.

omission, *n.f.* omission.
omnibus (-s), *n.m.* bus.
omnipotent, *adj.* omnipotent.
omoplate, *n.f.* shoulder blade.
on, *pron.* one (indef. subj.).
once, *n.f.* ounce.
oncle, *n.m.* uncle.
onction, *n.f.* unction.
onctueux, *adj.* unctuous.
onde, *n.f.* wave.
ondé, *adj.* wavy.
ondoyer, *vb.* wave.
ondulation, *n.f.* wave. **o. perma-**
nente, permanent wave.
onduler, *vb.* wave.
onéreux, *adj.* burdensome.
ongle, *n.m.* (finger)nail.
onglée, *n.f.* numb feeling.
onguent, *n.m.* salve, ointment.
onomatopée, *n.f.* onomatopœia.
onze, *adj. and n.m.* eleven.
onzième, *adj. and n.m.f.* eleventh.
opacité, *n.f.* opacity.
opale, *n.f.* opal.
opaque, *adj.* opaque.
opéra, *n.m.* opera.
opérateur, *n.m.* operator.
opération, *n.f.* operation, transaction.
opératoire, *adj.* operative.
opéré, *n.* patient undergoing surgery.
opérer, *vb.* operate.
opérette, *n.f.* operetta.
opiner, *vb.* hold or express an
opinion.
opiniâtre, *adj.* stubborn.
opiniâtreté, *n.f.* stubbornness.
opinion, *n.f.* opinion.
opium, *n.m.* opium.
opportun, *adj.* timely.
opportunité, *n.f.* timeliness.
opposé, *adj.* opposite, averse.
opposer, *vb.* oppose. **s'o. à,** oppose, resist.
opposition, *n.f.* opposition.
oppresser, *vb.* weigh heavily on.
oppresseur, *n.m.* oppressor.
oppressif, *adj.* oppressive.
oppression, *n.f.* oppression.
opprimer, *vb.* oppress.
opprobre, *n.m.* disgrace, infamy.
opter, *vb.* select, decide.
opticien, *n.m.* optician.
optimisme, *n.m.* optimism.
optimiste, 1. *adj.* optimistic. **2.**
n.m.f. optimist.

option, *n.f.* option.
optique, *adj.* optic.
opulence, *n.f.* opulence, riches.
opuscule, *n.m.* small work.
or, 1. *n.m.* gold. **2.** *conj.* now.
oracle, *n.m.* oracle.
orage, *n.m.* storm.
orageusement, *adv.* turbulently,
stormily.
orageux, *adj.* stormy.
oraison, *n.f.* prayer, oration.
oral, *adj.* oral.
orange, *n.f.* orange.
oranger, *n.m.* orange tree.
orateur, *n.m.* speaker, orator.
oratoire, *adj.* oratorical. **art o.,**
oratory.
orbe, *n.m.* orb, sphere.
orbite, *n.m.* orbit, socket (as of
eye).
orchestre (-k-), *n.m.* orchestra,
band.
orchestrer (-k-), *vb.* orchestrate.
orchidée, *n.f.* orchid.
ordinaire, *adj. and n.m.* ordinary.
ordinal, *adj. and n.m.* ordinal.
ordinateur, *n.m.* computer.
ordonnance, *n.f.* prescription, ordinance, decree.
ordonné, *adj.* orderly, tidy.
ordonner, *vb.* order, ordain, bid,
command.
ordre, *n.m.* order. **de premier o.,**
first-rate.
ordure, *n.f.* filth, garbage, refuse.
ordurier, *adj.* foul.
oreille, *n.f.* ear.
oreiller, *n.m.* pillow.
oreillons, *n.m.pl.* mumps.
orfèvrerie, *n.f.* gold or silver jewelry.
organdi, *n.m.* organdy.
organe, *n.m.* organ.
organique, *adj.* organic.
organisateur, 1. *n.m.* organizer. **2.**
adj. organizing.
organisation, *n.f.* organization,
arrangement.
organiser, *vb.* organize.
organisme, *n.m.* organism.
organiste, *n.m.f.* organist.
orge, *n.f.* barley.
orgelet, *n.m.* sty (of eye).
orgie, *n.f.* orgy.
orgue, *n.m.* organ.
orgueil, *n.m.* pride.

orgueilleux, *adj.* proud, haughty.

Orient, *n.m.* Orient, East.

Oriental, *n.m.* Oriental.

oriental, *adj.* Oriental, eastern.

orienter, *vb.* orient.

orifice, *n.m.* orifice, hole.

originaire, *adj.* original, native.

originairement, *adv.* originally.

original, 1. *n.m.* queer person. **2.** *adj.* original.

originalement, *adv.* originally; unusually.

originalité, *n.f.* originality.

origine, *n.f.* origin, source.

originel, *adj.* original.

oripeau, *n.m.* tinsel, showy clothes.

orme, *n.m.* elm.

orné, *adj.* ornate.

ornement, *n.m.* ornament, adornment, trimming.

ornemental, *adj.* ornamental.

ornementation, *n.f.* ornamentation.

orner, *vb.* adorn, trim.

ornière, *n.f.* rut, track.

ornithologie, *n.f.* ornithology.

orphelin, *n.m.* orphan.

orphelinat, *n.m.* orphanage.

orphéon, *n.m.* choral group.

orteil, *n.m.* toe.

orthodoxe, *adj.* orthodox.

orthodoxie, *n.f.* orthodoxy.

orthographe, *n.f.* spelling, orthography.

orthographier, *vb.* spell.

ortie, *n.f.* nettle.

os, *n.m.* bone.

oscillant, *adj.* oscillating.

oscillation, *n.f.* sway.

osciller, *vb.* fluctuate, oscillate.

osé, *adj.* attempted, bold.

oser, *vb.* dare.

osier, *n.m.* willow.

ossature, *n.f.* bony structure, skeleton.

ossements, *n.m.pl.* human remains.

osseux, *adj.* bony.

ossifier, *vb.* ossify.

ostensible, *adj.* ostensible.

ostentation, *n.f.* ostentation.

ostraciser, *vb.* ostracize.

otage, *n.m.* hostage.

ôter, *vb.* take off, take away.

ou, *conj.* or. **ou . . . ou . . .,** either . . . or . . . .

où, *adv.* where.

ouailles, *n.f.pl.* religious congregation.

ouater (wä-), *vb.* pad.

oubli, *n.m.* forgetfulness, oblivion.

oublier, *vb.* forget.

oublieux, *adj.* forgetful.

ouest (wĕst), *n.m.* west.

oui (wē), *adv.* yes.

ouï-dire, *n.m.* gossip, hearsay.

ouïe, *n.f.* gill.

ouïr, *vb.* hear.

ouragan, *n.m.* hurricane.

ourler, *vb.* hem.

ourlet, *n.m.* hem.

ours (-s), *n.m.* bear. **o. blanc,** polar bear.

ourson, *n.m.* bear cub.

outil, *n.m.* tool, implement.

outillage, *n.m.* quantity of tools, plant.

outiller, *vb.* supply with tools.

outrage, *n.m.* outrage.

outrageant, *adj.* outrageous.

outrager, *vb.* outrage, affront.

outrance, *n.f.* extreme degree. **à o.** to the very end.

outre, *adv. and prep.* beyond. **en o.,** besides, furthermore.

outré, *adj.* excessive, extreme.

outrecuidant, *adj.* excessively bold and forward.

outre-mer, *adv.* across the seas.

outrer, *vb.* overdo, irritate.

ouvert, *adj.* open.

ouverture, *n.f.* opening, gap; overture.

ouvrable, *adj.* work, workable.

ouvrage, *n.m.* work.

ouvrer, *vb.* work.

ouvreuse, *n.f.* usher or usherette.

ouvrier, *n.m.* workman; (*pl.*) labor.

ouvrir, *vb.* open.

ouvroir, *n.m.* work room or shop.

ovaire, *n.m.* ovary.

ovale, *adj. and n.m.* oval.

ovation, *n.f.* ovation.

oxygène, *n.m.* oxygen.

P

pacage, *n.m.* land used for pasture.

pacificateur, 1. *adj.* pacifying. **2.** *n.m.* peacemaker.

pacification, *n.f.* peace-making.

pacifier, *vb.* pacify, appease, soothe.

pacifique, *adj.* pacific, peaceful, peaceable.

pacifisme, *n.m.* pacifism.

pacotille, *n.f.* small wares.

pacte, *n.m.* covenant, pact.

pactiser, *vb.* make a pact, compromise.

pagaie, *n.f.* paddle.

pagale, *n.f.* disorder, rush.

paganisme, *n.m.* paganism.

pagayer, *vb.* paddle.

pagayeur, *n.m.* paddler.

page, 1. *n.m.* page (boy). **2.** *n.f.* page (in book).

pages centrales, *n.f.pl.* centerfold.

pagination, *n.f.* pagination.

paginer, *vb.* number pages.

pagode, *n.f.* pagoda.

paiement, payement, *n.m.* payment.

païen, *adj. and n.m.* pagan, heathen.

paillard, *adj.* lewd, indecent.

paillasse, *n.f.* mattress of straw, ticking.

paillasson, *n.m.* (door-)mat.

paille, *n.f.* straw; defect (in gems).

paillette, *n.f.* spangle; defect.

pain, *n.m.* bread, loaf. **petit p.,** roll.

pair, 1. *n.m.* peer. **2.** *adj.* even, equal.

paire, *n.f.* pair.

pairesse, *n.f.* peeress.

pairie, *n.f.* peerage.

paisible, *adj.* peaceful.

paître, *vb.* graze.

paix, *n.f.* peace.

palabre, *n.m.* palaver.

palais, *n.m.* palace; palate.

palan, *n.m.* gear for hoisting.

palatal, *adj. and n.f.* palatal.

pale, *n.f.* blade, stake.

pâle, *adj.* pale.

palefrenier, *n.m.* groom.

palet, *n.m.* quoit.

paletot, *n.m.* overcoat.

pâleur, *n.f.* paleness.

palier, *n.m.* stair landing.

pâlir, *vb.* grow pale or dim.

palissade, *n.f.* paling, fence.

pâlissant, *adj.* becoming pale.

palme, *n.f.* palm.

palmier, *n.m.* palm (tree).

palpable, *adj.* palpable.

palper, *vb.* touch, feel.

palpitant, *adj.* fluttering, palpitating.

palpiter, *vb.* flutter, beat, palpitate.

paludéen, *adj.* marshy.

pâmer, *vb.* se p., faint.

pamphlet, *n.m.* pamphlet, satire.

pamphlétaire, *n.m.* pamphleteer.

pamplemousse, *n.m.* grapefruit.

pan, *n.m.* side, piece, flap.

panacée, *n.f.* panacea.

panache, *n.m.* plume.

panais, *n.m.* parsnip.

pandit, *n.m.* pundit.

pané, *adj.* dotted with bread crumbs.

panier, *n.m.* basket.

panique, *n.f. and adj.* panic.

panne, *n.f.* fat, lard; accident.

panneau, *n.m.* panel.

panse, *n.f.* paunch, cud.

pansement, *n.m.* dressing.

panser, *vb.* groom; dress.

pantalon, *n.m.* trousers.

panteler, *vb.* pant, gasp.

panthère, *n.f.* panther.

pantomime, *n.f.* pantomime.

pantoufle, *n.f.* slipper.

pantoufler, *vb.* act silly.

paon (pän), *n.m.* peacock.

papal, *adj.* papal.

papauté, *n.f.* papacy.

pape, *n.m.* pope.

paperasse, *n.f.* waste paper; official documents.

paperassier, *adj.* scribbling, petty.

papeterie, *n.f.* stationery.

papetier, *n.m.* stationer.

papier, *n.m.* paper.

papier à notes, *n.m.* notepaper.

papier à tapisser, *n.m.* wallpaper.

papier peint, *n.m.* wallpaper.

papillon, *n.m.* butterfly.

papillonner, *vb.* flutter, trifle.

papoter, *vb.* prate, prattle.

pâque, *n.f.* Passover.

paquebot, *n.m.* small liner, packet.

pâquerette, *n.f.* daisy.

Pâques, *n.m.* Easter.

paquet, *n.m.* package, parcel, bundle; deck (cards).
par, *prep.* by; through.
parabole, *n.f.* parabola; parable.
parachute, *n.m.* parachute.
parade, *n.f.* parade, procession.
parader, *vb.* parade, show off.
paradis, *n.m.* paradise.
paradoxal, *adj.* paradoxical.
paradoxe, *n.m.* paradox.
paraffine, *n.f.* paraffin.
parage, *n.m.* ancestry, descent; locality.
paragraphe, *n.m.* paragraph.
paraître, *vb.* appear, seem.
parallèle, *adj.* and *n.m.f.* parallel.
paralyser, *vb.* paralyze.
paralysie, *n.f.* paralysis.
paralytique, *adj.* and *n.m.f.* paralytic.
paramètre, *n.m.* parameter.
parangon, *n.m.* model, paragon.
paraphraser, *vb.* paraphrase.
parapluie, *n.m.* umbrella.
parasite, *n.m.* parasite.
paratonnerre, *n.m.* lightning rod.
paravent, *n.m.* screen.
parc (-k), *n.m.* park.
parcelle, *n.f.* part, instalment.
parce que, *conj.* because.
parchemin, *n.m.* parchment.
parcimonie, *n.f.* parsimony.
parcourir, *vb.* run through.
parcours, *n.m.* course, journey.
pardessus, *n.m.* overcoat.
par-dessus, *adv.* and *prep.* above, over.
pardon, 1. *n.m.* pardon, forgiveness. **2.** *interj.* sorry!
pardonner (à), *vb.* forgive, pardon.
pardonneur, *n.m.* pardoner.
pare-boue, *n.m.* mudguard.
pare-chocs, *n.m.* bumper.
pareil, *adj.* like.
parent, *n.m.* relative; (*pl.*) parents.
parenté, *n.f.* relationship.
parenthèse, *n.f.* parenthesis.
parer, *vb.* attire, deck out; parry.
paresse, *n.f.* sloth.
paresser, *vb.* laze, waste time.
paresseux, *adj.* lazy.
parfaire, *vb.* complete, finish up.
parfait, *adj.* perfect.
parfois, *adv.* sometimes.
parfum, *n.m.* perfume.

parfumé, *adj.* fragrant.
parfumer, *vb.* perfume.
parfumerie, *n.f.* perfumery.
pari, *n.m.* bet.
parier, *vb.* bet.
parieur, *n.m.* one who bets.
Parisien, *n.m.* Parisian.
parisien, *adj.* Parisian.
parité, *n.f.* equality, parity.
parjure, *n.m.* perjury.
parjurer, *vb.* se p., commit perjury.
parlant, *adj.* speaking, chatty.
parlement, *n.m.* parliament.
parlementaire, *adj.* parliamentary.
parlementer, *vb.* parley.
parler, *vb.* talk, speak.
parleur, *n.m.* one who speaks or talks.
parloir, *n.m.* parlor.
parmi, *prep.* among.
parodie, *n.f.* parody.
parodier, *vb.* parody, imitate.
paroi, *n.f.* wall lining.
paroisse, *n.f.* parish.
paroissial, *adj.* parochial.
parole, *n.f.* speech, word. **prendre la p.,** take the floor.
paroxysme, *n.m.* fit of violence.
parquer, *vb.* park, enclose.
parquet, *n.m.* floor.
parqueterie, *n.f.* parquetry.
parrain, *n.m.* godfather.
parsemer, *vb.* spread, strew.
part, *n.f.* share, part. **de la p. de,** on behalf of. **quelque p.,** somewhere. **nulle p.,** nowhere. **faire p. à,** share; inform.
partage, *n.m.* partition, sharing, share.
partager, *vb.* share, divide.
partance, *n.f.* going, sailing.
partant, *n.m.* one who leaves.
partenaire, *n.m.f.* partner.
parti, *n.m.* party.
partial, *adj.* partial.
partialité, *n.f.* bias, partiality.
participant, *adj.* and *n.m.* participant.
participation, *n.f.* participation, share.
participe, *n.m.* participle.
participer à, *vb.* partake of, take part in.
particularité, *n.f.* peculiarity.
particule, *n.f.* particle.

particulier, *adj.* particular, private, peculiar, special.

partie, *n.f.* part, party.

partiel, *adj.* partial.

partir, *vb.* depart, leave, go (come) away, sail.

partisan, *n.m.* partisan, follower.

partitif, *adj.* partitive.

partition, *n.f.* score.

partout, *adv.* everywhere, throughout. **p. où,** wherever.

parure, *n.f.* ornament.

parvenir, *vb.* reach.

parvenu, *adj.* upstart.

pas, 1. *n.m.* step, pace. **faux p.,** slip. **2.** *adv.* not. **p. du tout,** not at all.

passable, *adj.* fair.

passage, *n.m.* aisle, passage, alley.

passager, 1. *n.m.* passenger. **2.** *adj.* passing, fugitive.

passant, *n.m.* passer-by.

passavant, *n.m.* permit.

passe, *n.f.* passing, permit.

passé, *adj.* and *n.m.* past.

passe-partout, *n.m.* skeleton key, passport.

passeport, *n.m.* passport.

passer, *vb.* pass; go by; spend; strain. **se p. de,** go without.

passereau, *n.m.* sparrow.

passerelle, *n.f.* bridge.

passe-temps, *n.m.* pastime.

passible, *adj.* capable of feeling.

passif, *adj.* and *n.m.* passive.

passion, *n.f.* passion.

passionné, *adj.* passionate.

passionnel, *adj.* concerning or due to passion.

passionner, *vb.* interest, excite. **se p.,** be eager or excited over.

passoire, *n.f.* device for straining.

pastel, *n.m.* crayon.

pastèque, *n.f.* watermelon.

pasteur, *n.m.* pastor.

pasteuriser, *vb.* pasteurize.

pastille, *n.f.* lozenge, cough drop.

pastoral, *adj.* pastoral.

pataud, *adj.* awkward.

patauger, *vb.* flounder.

pâte, *n.f.* paste, dough, batter.

pâté, *n.m.* block; pie.

patenôtre, *n.f.* (Lord's) prayer.

patent, *adj.* patent, evident.

patente, *n.f.* license.

patenter, *vb.* license.

paterne, *adj.* paternal.

paternel, *adj.* paternal.

paternité, *n.f.* fatherhood.

pâteux, *adj.* pasty, thick, muddy.

pathétique, *adj.* pathetic.

pathologie, *n.f.* pathology.

patience, *n.f.* patience.

patient, *adj.* and *n.m.* patient.

patin, *n.m.* skate.

patiner, *vb.* skate.

patineur, *n.m.* skater.

pâtir, *vb.* suffer.

pâtisserie, *n.f.* pastry.

pâtre, *n.m.* shepherd.

patriarche, *n.m.* patriarch.

patricien, *adj.* and *n.m.* patrician.

patrie, *n.f.* native country, homeland.

patrimoine, *n.m.* patrimony.

patriote, *n.m.f.* patriot.

patriotique, *adj.* patriotic.

patriotisme, *n.m.* patriotism.

patron, *n.m.* employer; boss; model, pattern; patron.

patronat, *n.m.* management, employers.

patronner, *vb.* patronize, provide for.

patrouille, *n.f.* patrol.

patrouiller, *vb.* patrol.

patte, *n.f.* paw, leg, flap.

pâturage, *n.m.* pasture.

pâture, *n.f.* fodder, pasture.

paume, *n.f.* palm.

paupière, *n.f.* eyelid.

pause, *n.f.* pause.

pauvre, *adj.* poor.

pauvreté, *n.f.* poverty.

pavaner, *vb.* **se p.,** swagger, strut.

pavé, *n.m.* pavement.

paver, *vb.* pave.

pavillon, *n.m.* pavilion.

pavot, *n.m.* poppy.

paye, *n.f.* payment, salary.

payement, *n.m.* payment.

payer, *vb.* pay, settle.

payeur, *n.m.* payer.

pays, *n.m.* country.

paysage, *n.m.* landscape, scenery.

paysager, *adj.* of the country, rural.

paysan, *n.m.* peasant.

Pays-Bas, les, *n.m.pl.* Holland; the Netherlands.

péage, *n.m.* toll.

peau, *n.f.* skin, hide.

pêche, n.f. peach; fishing.

péché, n.m. sin.

pécher, vb. sin.

pêcher, 1. vb. fish. 2. n.m. peach tree.

pêcherie, n.f. fishing place.

pécheur m., pécheresse f. 1. n. sinner. 2. adj. sinful.

pêcheur, n.m. fisherman.

pécule, n.m. savings.

pécuniaire, adj. pecuniary.

pédagogie, n.f. pedagogy.

pédale, n.f. pedal.

pédant, adj. and n.m.f. pedant, pedantic.

pédanterie, n.f. pedantry.

pédé(raste), n.m. homosexual.

pédestre, adj. pedestrian.

pédiatre, n.m. pediatrician.

pédicure, n.m. chiropodist.

peigne, n.m. comb.

peigner, vb. comb.

peignoir, n.m. dressing-gown.

peindre, vb. paint, portray, depict.

peine, n.f. pain, penalty. à p., hardly, barely; faire de la p. à, pain, vb.; valoir la p. de, be worth while to; se donner la p., take the trouble.

peiner, vb. labor; grieve.

peintre, n.m. painter.

peinture, n.f. paint, painting.

pelage, n.m. coat.

pelé, adj. bald, uncovered.

pêle-mêle, adv. pell-mell.

peler, vb. peel, pare.

pèlerin, n.m. pilgrim.

pèlerinage, n.m. pilgrimage.

pèlerine, n.f. cape.

pélican, n.m. pelican.

pelle, n.f. shovel.

pelletier, n.m. furrier.

pellicule, n.f. film.

pelote, n.f. ball, pellet.

peloton, n.m. ball; group of soldiers.

pelure, n.f. peel.

pénal, adj. penal.

pénalité, n.f. penalty.

penaud, adj. awkwardly bashful or embarrassed.

penchant, n.m. bent, liking, tendency.

pencher, vb. tilt, lean, droop. se p., bend.

pendaison, n.f. hanging (execution).

pendant, prep. during, pending. p. que, as, while.

pendiller, vb. dangle.

pendre, vb. hang.

pendule, n.m. clock; pendulum.

pénétrable, adj. penetrable.

pénétrant, adj. keen.

pénétration, n.f. penetration.

pénétrer, vb. penetrate, pervade.

pénible, adj. painful.

péninsule, n.f. peninsula.

pénitence, n.f. penance.

pénitencier, n.m. penitentiary.

pénitent, adj. and n.m. penitent.

penne, n.f. feather.

pénombre, n.f. gloom, shadow.

pensée, n.f. thought; pansy.

penser (à), vb. think (of).

penseur, n.m. thinker.

pensif, adj. thoughtful, pensive.

pension, n.f. board, pension.

pensionnaire, n.m.f. boarder.

pensionnat, n.m. boarding school.

pente, n.f. slope, slant.

pénurie, n.f. penury, scarcity.

pépier, vb. chirp.

pépin, n.m. pip, kernel.

pépinière, n.f. nursery.

pépite, n.f. nugget.

perçant, adj. sharp.

perce, n.f. boring tool.

perce-neige, n.f. snowdrop.

percepteur, n.m. tax collector.

perception, n.f. perception, collecting.

percer, vb. pierce, bore.

percevoir, vb. collect, amass, perceive.

perche, n.f. pole, perch.

percher, vb. se p., perch.

perchoir, n.m. perch.

perclus, adj. lame, crippled.

percussion, n.f. percussion.

percuter, vb. hit, strike.

perdition, n.f. perdition.

perdre, vb. lose; waste.

perdrix, n.f. partridge.

père, n.m. father.

péremptoire, adj. peremptory.

perfection, n.f. perfection.

perfectionnement, n.m. improvement, finishing.

perfectionner, vb. perfect, finish.

perfide, adj. treacherous.

perfidie, *n.f.* treachery.

perforation, *n.f.* perforation.

perforer, *vb.* perforate, drill.

péricliter, *vb.* be in danger, shake.

péril (-l), *n.m.* peril, danger.

périlleux, *adj.* perilous, dangerous.

périmètre, *n.m.* perimeter.

période, *n.f.* period, term, stage.

périodique, *adj.* periodic.

péripétie, *n.f.* shift of luck.

périr, *vb.* perish.

périscope, *n.m.* periscope.

périssable, *adj.* perishable.

perle, *n.f.* pearl, bead.

perlé, *adj.* pearly, perfect.

permanence, *n.f.* permanence.

permanent, *adj.* permanent.

perméable, *adj.* permeable.

permettre, *vb.* permit, allow.

permis, *n.m.* permit, license.

permission, *n.f.* permission, leave (of absence), furlough.

permissionnaire, *n.m.* one having a permit; one on leave.

permuter, *vb.* change, exchange.

pernicieux, *adj.* pernicious.

pérorer, *vb.* harangue, argue.

perpétrer, *vb.* commit.

perpétuel, *adj.* perpetual.

perpétuer, *vb.* perpetuate.

perplexe, *adj.* perplexed, undecided.

perplexité, *n.f.* perplexity.

perquisition, *n.f.* exploration, search.

perron, *n.m.* flight of steps.

perroquet, *n.m.* parrot.

perruque, *n.f./g.* wig.

perse, *adj.* Persian.

persécuter, *vb.* persecute.

persécution, *n.f.* persecution.

persévérance, *n.f.* perseverance.

persévérant, *adj.* persevering, resolute.

persévérer, *vb.* persevere.

persienne, *n.f.* blind, shutter.

persifler, *vb.* banter, ridicule.

persil, *n.m.* parsley.

persistance, *n.f.* persistence.

persistant, *adj.* persistent.

persister, *vb.* persist.

personnage, *n.m.* personage; character.

personnalité, *n.f.* personality.

personne, 1. *n.f.* person. 2. *pron.* nobody.

personnel, 1. *n.m.* personnel, staff. 2. *adj.* personal.

personnifier, *vb.* personify.

perspective, *n.f.* perspective, prospect.

perspicace, *adj.* discerning.

perspicacité, *n.f.* insight.

persuader, *vb.* persuade, convince, induce.

persuasif, *adj.* persuasive.

perte, *n.f.* loss, waste; (*pl.*) casualties.

pertinence, *n.f.* pertinence.

pertinent, *adj.* relevant, pertinent.

perturbateur, *n.m.* agitator, disturber.

pervers, *adj.* perverse, contrary.

pervertir, *vb.* pervert.

pesant, *adj.* heavy, ponderous.

pesanteur, *n.f.* weight, dullness.

peser, *vb.* weigh.

pessimisme, *n.m.* pessimism.

pessimiste, *n.m.* pessimist.

peste, *n.f.* pestilence; nuisance.

pestilence, *n.f.* pestilence, plague, nuisance.

pétale, *n.m.* petal.

pétiller, *vb.* twinkle, crackle.

petit, 1. *adj.* little, small, petty. 2. *n.m.* cub.

petite-fille, *n.f.* granddaughter.

petitesse, *n.f.* smallness, pettiness.

petit-fils (-fēs), *n.m.* grandson.

petit-gris, *n.m.* fur of the squirrel.

pétition, *n.f.* petition.

pétitionner, *vb.* request, ask.

petits-enfants, *n.m.pl.* grandchildren.

pétrifiant, *adj.* petrifying.

pétrifier, *vb.* petrify or (**se p.**) become petrified.

pétrir, *vb.* knead, mold.

pétrole, *n.m.* petroleum, kerosene.

pétulance, *n.f.* petulance.

peu, 1. *n.m.* little; few. 2. *adv.* not. **p. à p.,** gradually.

peuplade, *n.f.* tribe, clan.

peuple, *n.m.* people.

peupler, *vb.* people.

peuplier, *n.m.* poplar.

peur, *n.f.* fear. **avoir p.,** be afraid. **de p. que . . . ne,** lest.

peureux, *adj.* shy, timid.
peut-être, *adv.* perhaps, maybe.
phallocratie, *n.f.* machismo.
phallocrate, *adj.* macho.
phare, *n.m.* beacon, lighthouse; headlight.
pharmacie, *n.f.* drug store, pharmacy.
pharmacien, *n.m.* druggist.
phase, *n.f.* phase.
phénix, *n.m.* phoenix; superior person.
phénoménal, *adj.* phenomenal.
phénomène, *n.m.* phenomenon; freak.
philanthrope, *n.m.* philanthropist.
philanthropie, *n.f.* philanthropy.
philatélie, *n.f.* stamp-collecting.
philosophe, *n.m.* philosopher.
philosophie, *n.f.* philosophy.
philosophique, *adj.* philosophical.
phobie, *n.f.* phobia.
phonéticien, *n.m.* phonetician.
phonétique, *adj. and n.f.* phonetic, phonetics.
phonographe, *n.m.* phonograph.
phoque, *n.m.* seal.
photocopie, *n.f.* photocopy.
photocopieur, *n.m.* photocopier.
photographe, *n.m.* photographer.
photographie, *n.f.* photograph, photography.
phrase, *n.f.* sentence.
phtisie, *n.f.* consumption.
phtisique, *adj. and n.m.* consumptive.
physicien, *n.m.* physical scientist.
physionomie, *n.f.* looks, expression.
physique, 1. *n.f.* physics. **2.** *adj.* physical.
piailler, *vb.* peep, squeal.
pianiste, *n.m.f.* pianist.
piano, *n.m.* piano.
pic, *n.m.* peak.
picoter, *vb.* prick, peck.
pièce, *n.f.* piece, coin, patch, room. **p. de théâtre,** play.
pied, *n.m.* foot. **aller à p.,** walk. **coup de p.,** kick.
pied-à-terre, *n.m.* temporary quarters.
piédestal, *n.m.* pedestal.
piège, *n.m.* snare, trap.
pierre, *n.f.* stone.
pierreries, *n.f.pl.* jewelry, gems.

pierreux, *adj.* full of stone or grit.
pierrot, *n.m.* clown in pantomime.
piété, *n.f.* piety.
piétiner, *vb.* trample.
piéton, *n.m.* pedestrian.
piètre, *adj.* pitiful, mean, wretched.
pieu, *n.m.* stake, pile.
pieuvre, *n.f.* octopus.
pieux, *adj.* pious.
pigeon, *n.m.* pigeon, dove.
pile, *n.f.* stack; battery.
piler, *vb.* crush, blast.
pilier, *n.m.* pillar, column.
pillage, *n.m.* plundering.
piller, *vb.* plunder.
pilotage, *n.m.* piloting; driving piles.
pilote, *n.m.* pilot.
piloter, *vb.* pilot, lead.
pilule, *n.f.* pill.
piment, *n.m.* chili.
pimenter, *vb.* flavor, season.
pimpant, *adj.* stylish, smart.
pin, *n.m.* pine.
pinacle, *n.m.* pinnacle.
pince, *n.f.* clip; (*pl.*) pliers.
pinceau, *n.m.* paint-brush.
pince-nez, *n.m.* eyeglasses.
pincer, *vb.* pinch, nip.
pinte, *n.f.* pint.
pioche, *n.f.* pickax.
piocher, *vb.* dig.
piocheur, *n.m.* digger.
pion, *n.m.* pawn, peon.
pioncer, *vb.* nap, sleep.
pionnier, *n.m.* pioneer.
pipe, *n.f.* pipe.
piper, *vb.* catch, decoy, trick.
piquant, *adj.* sharp. **mot p.,** quip.
pique, *n.m.* spade.
pique-nique, *n.m.* picnic.
piquer, *vb.* prick, sting.
piquet, *n.m.* picket, peg, stake.
piqûre, *n.f.* prick, sting, puncture.
pirate, *n.m.* pirate.
pirate de l'air, *n.m.* hijacker.
piraterie, *n.f.* piracy.
pire, *adj.* worse, worst.
pirouette, *n.f.* pirouette, shift.
pis, *adv.* worse, worst.
piscine, *n.f.* pool.
pissenlit, *n.m.* dandelion.
pistache, *n.f.* pistachio.
piste, *n.f.* track.
pistolet, *n.m.* pistol.

piston, *n.m.* piston.

pistonner, *vb.* help, push.

pitance, *n.f.* meager amount, as of food.

piteux, *adj.* pitiful.

pitié, *n.f.* pity, mercy.

pitoyable, *adj.* pitiful, miserable.

pitre, *n.m.* clown.

pittoresque, *adj.* picturesque, colorful.

pivoine, *n.f.* peony.

pivot, *n.m.* pivot.

pivoter, *vb.* turn, pivot, revolve.

pizza, *n.f.* pizza.

placard, *n.m.* closet; poster.

placarder, *vb.* post, display.

place, *n.f.* place, room.

placement, *n.m.* investment, placing.

placer, *vb.* invest, place.

placet, *n.m.* petition, demand.

placide, *adj.* placid.

placidité, *n.f.* placidness.

plafond, *n.m.* ceiling.

plage, *n.f.* beach.

plagiaire, *n.m.* one who plagiarizes.

plagiat, *n.m.* plagiarism.

plagier, *vb.* plagiarize.

plaid, *n.m.* plaid.

plaider, *vb.* plead.

plaideur, *n.m.* pleader.

plaidoirie, *n.f.* lawyer's speech.

plaie, *n.f.* wound, sore.

plaignant, *n.m.* plaintiff.

plaindre, *vb.* pity. **se p.,** complain.

plaine, *n.f.* plain.

plainte, *n.f.* complaint.

plaintif, *adj.* mournful.

plaire à, *vb.* please. **s'il vous plaît,** if you please.

plaisance, *n.f.* pleasure, ease.

plaisant, *adj.* joking.

plaisanter, *vb.* joke.

plaisanterie, *n.f.* joke.

plaisir, *n.m.* pleasure.

plan, *n.m.* plan; plane; schedule, scheme. **premier p.,** foreground.

planche, *n.f.* board, shelf, plank.

planche à roulettes, *n.f.* skateboard.

plancher, *n.m.* floor.

planer, *vb.* glide; hover.

planétaire, 1. *adj.* planetary. **2.** *n.m.* planetarium.

planète, *n.f.* planet.

planeur, *n.m.* glider (plane).

plantation, *n.f.* plantation.

plante, *n.f.* plant; sole.

planter, *vb.* plant.

planteur, *n.m.* planter.

planton, *n.m.* military orderly.

plantureux, *adj.* fertile, rich.

plaque, *n.f.* plate, slab. **p. de projection,** lantern-slide.

plaquer, *vb.* plate; abandon.

plaquette, *n.f.* booklet, medal.

plastique, *adj.* plastic.

plastronner, *vb.* pose, strut jauntily.

plat, 1. *n.m.* dish, platter. **2.** *adj.* flat. **œuf sur le p.,** fried egg.

platane, *n.m.* plane-tree.

plat-bord, *n.m.* gunwale.

plateau, *n.m.* plateau, tray.

plate-bande, *n.f.* flower bed.

plate-forme, *n.f.* platform.

platine, 1. *n.m.* platen, plate. **2.** *n.m.* platinum.

platitude, *n.f.* flatness.

plâtras, *n.m.* rubbish, rubble.

plâtre, *n.m.* plaster.

plausible, *adj.* plausible.

plébéien, *adj.* ignoble.

plébiscite, *n.m.* plebiscite.

plein, *adj.* full, crowded.

plénier, *adj.* complete, plenary.

plénitude, *n.f.* fullness.

pleurer, *vb.* cry, weep, lament, mourn.

pleurésie, *n.f.* pleurisy.

pleurnicher, *vb.* complain, whine.

pleurs, *n.m.pl.* tears, weeping.

pleutre, *n.m.* cad, coward.

pleuvoir, *vb.* rain.

pli, *n.m.* fold, envelope, pleat, crease.

pliable, *adj.* pliable.

pliant, *n.m.* folding chair.

plier, *vb.* fold, bend.

plissement, *n.m.* fold, folding.

plisser, *vb.* pleat.

plomb, *n.m.* lead.

plomberie, *n.f.* plumbing.

plombier, *n.m.* plumber.

plongeon, *n.m.* plunge.

plonger, *vb.* plunge, dive, dip.

plongeur, *n.m.* diver; dishwasher.

plouf, *interj. and n.m.* splash, plop.

ploutocrate, *n.m.* plutocrat.

ployer, *vb.* incline, bend.

pluie, *n.f.* rain.

pluie radioactive, *n.f.* fallout.
plumage, *n.m.* feathers.
plume, *n.f.* pen, feather.
plumeau, *n.m.* feather duster.
plumer, *vb.* pluck.
plumet, *n.m.* plume.
plumeux, *adj.* feathery.
plumier, *n.m.* pen or pencil case.
plupart, *n.f.* greater part, majority. **pour la p.,** mostly.
pluralité, *n.f.* plurality.
pluriel, *adj. and n.m.* plural.
plus, *adv.* more, most. **ne . . . p.,** no more. **non p.,** neither. **en p.,** extra.
plusieurs, *adj. and pron.* several.
plus-que-parfait, *n.m. (gramm.)* pluperfect.
plutôt, *adv.* rather.
pluvieux, *adj.* rainy, wet.
pneumatique, *abbr.* **pneu,** *n.m.* tire.
pneumonie, *n.f.* pneumonia.
pochade, *n.f.* hasty sketch.
poche, *n.f.* pocket.
pocher, *vb.* poach.
pocheter, *vb.* pocket.
pochette, *n.f.* little pocket, handkerchief.
pochoir, *n.m.* stencil.
poêle, *n.m.* stove.
poème, *n.m.* poem.
poésie, *n.f.* poem, poetry.
poète, *n.f.* poet.
poétique, *adj.* poetic.
poids (pwä), *n.m.* weight.
poignant, *adj.* poignant, keen.
poignard, *n.m.* dagger.
poignarder, *vb.* stab.
poigne, *n.f.* grip, power.
poignée, *n.f.* handful; handle.
poignet, *n.m.* wrist; cuff.
poil (pwäl), *n.m.* hair.
poilu, 1. *adj.* hairy, strong. **2.** *n.m.* French soldier.
poinçon, *n.m.* punch.
poing, *n.m.* fist.
point, *n.m.* point, dot, period, stitch. **p. de vue,** point of view. **p. du jour,** dawn. **ne . . . p.,** none. **être sur le p. de,** be about to. **au p.,** in focus. **deux p,s.** colon. **p. d'interrogation,** question mark.
pointage, *n.m.* pointing; *(mil.)* sighting.
pointe, *n.f.* point, tip, touch (small amount).

pointer, *vb.* point, aim.
pointeur, *n.m.* pointer, checker.
pointillage, *n.m.* dotting.
pointiller, *vb.* dot; tease.
pointilleux, *adj.* fussy, precise.
pointu, *adj.* pointed.
pointure, *n.f.* size.
poire, *n.f.* pear.
poireau, *n.m.* leek.
poirier, *n.m.* pear tree.
pois, *n.m.* pea.
poison, *n.m.* poison.
poisser, *vb.* make gluey or sticky.
poisson, *n.m.* fish.
poissonnerie, *n.f.* fish store.
poissonneux, *adj.* filled with fish.
poissonnier, *n.m.* fish dealer.
poitrinaire, *adj. and n.m.* consumptive.
poitrine, *n.f.* chest.
poivre, *n.m.* pepper.
poivrer, *vb.* spice with pepper.
poivrier, *n.m.* pepper plant.
poix, *n.f.* pitch.
polaire, *adj.* polar.
pôle, *n.m.* pole.
polémique, *n.f.* argument.
poli, 1. *adj.* civil, polite. **2.** *n.m.* polish.
police, *n.f.* police; (insurance) policy.
policer, *vb.* refine.
polichinelle, *n.m.* Punch (puppet).
policier, *n.m.* policeman. **roman p.,** detective story.
polir, *vb.* polish.
polisseur, *n.m.* polisher.
polisson, 1. *n.m.* gamin, scamp. **2.** *adj.* running wild.
polissonnerie, *n.f.* naughty action or remark.
politesse, *n.f.* good manners.
politicien, *n.m.* politician.
politique, 1. *n.f.* policy, politics. **2.** *adj.* politic, political.
polka, *n.f.* polka.
pollen, *n.m.* pollen.
polluer, *vb.* pollute.
pollution, *n.f.* pollution.
Pologne, *n.f.* Poland.
Polonais, *n.m.* Pole.
polonais, *adj. and n.m.* Polish.
poltron, 1. *adj.* craven, cowardly. **2.** *n.m.f.* coward.
poltronnerie, *n.f.* cowardly behavior.

polygame, 1. *n.m.* polygamist. **2.** *adj.* polygamous.

polygamie, *n.f.* polygamy.

polygone, *n.m.* polygon.

pommade, *n.f.* pomade, salve.

pomme, *n.f.* apple. **p. de terre,** potato.

pommeau, *n.m.* pommel.

pommette, *n.f.* cheekbone.

pommier, *n.m.* apple tree.

pompe, *n.f.* pump; pomp.

pomper, *vb.* pump.

pompeux, *adj.* pompous.

pompier, *n.m.* fireman.

pompon, *n.m.* pompon, tuft.

ponce, *n.f.* pumice.

ponctualité, *n.f.* punctuality.

ponctuation, *n.f.* punctuation.

ponctuel, *adj.* punctual.

ponctuer, *vb.* punctuate.

poney, *n.m.* pony.

pont, *n.m.* bridge; deck.

pontife, *n.m.* pontiff.

pont-levis, *n.m.* drawbridge.

ponton, *n.m.* pontoon.

popeline, *n.f.* poplin.

popote, *n.f.* mess (military).

populace, *n.f.* mob.

populaire, *adj.* popular.

populariser, *vb.* popularize.

popularité, *n.f.* popularity.

population, *n.f.* population.

populeux, *adj.* populous.

porc, *n.m.* pig, pork.

porcelaine, *n.f.* china.

porc-épic, *n.m.* porcupine.

porche, *n.m.* porch.

porcherie, *n.f.* pigpen.

pore, *n.m.* pore.

poreux, *adj.* porous.

pornographie, *n.f.* pornography.

port, *n.m.* port, harbor; carrying; postage.

portable, *adj.* wearable.

portail, *n.m.* portal.

portatif, *adj.* portable.

porte, *n.f.* door, gate.

porte-affiches, *n.m.* billboard.

porte-avions, *n.m.* aircraft carrier.

portée, *n.f.* range, import, scope, reach; litter. **hors de p.,** out of reach.

portefaix, *n.m.* porter.

portefeuille, *n.m.* wallet, case, portfolio.

portemanteau, *n.m.* cloak rack.

portement, *n.m.* carrying.

porte-monnaie, *n.m.* purse.

porter, *vb.* carry, bear; wear. **se p.,** be (in health).

porte-rame, *n.m.* oarlock.

porteur, *n.m.* porter, bearer.

portier, *n.m.* doorman, porter.

portière, *n.f.* door-curtain.

portion, *n.f.* portion, share.

portique, *n.m.* portico, porch.

porto, *n.m.* port wine.

portrait, *n.m.* portrait.

portraitiste, *n.m.* painter of portraits.

Portugais, *n.m.* Portuguese (person).

portugais, 1. *n.m.* Portuguese (language). **2.** *adj.* Portuguese.

Portugal, *n.m.* Portugal.

pose, *n.f.* pose, attitude.

posé, *n.f.* poised, set.

poser, *vb.* place, stand, set, lay. **se p.,** settle, alight.

poseur, *n.m.* person or thing that places or applies; affected person.

positif, *adj. and n.m.* positive.

position, *n.f.* stand, place, position.

positiviste, *n.m.f.* positivist.

posséder, *vb.* own, possess.

possesseur, *n.m.* possessor.

possessif, *adj. and n.m.* possessive.

possession, *n.f.* possession.

possibilité, *n.f.* possibility.

possible, *adj.* possible. **tout son p.,** one's utmost.

postal, *adj.* postal.

poste, *n.f.* mail. **mettre à la p.,** mail. **p. restante,** general delivery.

poste, *n.m.* post. **p. d'essence,** gas station. **p. de secours,** first-aid station.

poster, *vb.* post (letter); place.

postérieur, *adj.* rear, posterior.

postérité, *n.f.* posterity.

posthume, *adj.* posthumous.

postiche, *adj.* false, unnecessary.

post-scriptum, *n.m.* postscript.

postulant, *n.m.* applicant.

postuler, *vb.* apply for.

posture, *n.f.* posture.

pot, *n.m.* pot, pitcher, jar.

potable, *adj.* drinkable.

potage, *n.m.* soup.

potager, *adj.* vegetable.
potasse, *n.f.* potash.
pot-de-vin, *n.m.* tip, bribe.
poteau, *n.m.* post.
potée, *n.f.* potful.
potence, *n.f.* gallows.
potentat, *n.m.* potentate.
potentiel, *adj. and n.m.* potential.
poterie, *n.f.* pottery.
poterne, *n.f.* postern.
potier, *n.m.* potter.
potion, *n.f.* potion.
potiron, *n.m.* pumpkin.
pou, *n.m.* louse.
pouce, *n.m.* thumb; inch.
pouding, *n.m.* pudding.
poudre, *n.f.* powder.
poudrer, *vb.* powder.
poudreux, *adj.* full of powder or dust.
poudrier, *n.m.* compact (cosmetic).
poudroyer, *vb.* be dusty.
pouilleux, *adj.* infected with lice.
poulailler, *n.m.* hen-house.
poulain, *n.m.* colt.
poule, *n.f.* hen, chicken.
poulet, *n.m.* chicken.
poulette, *n.f.* pullet.
poulie, *n.f.* pulley.
poulpe, *n.m.* octopus.
pouls, *n.m.* pulse.
poumon, *n.m.* lung.
poupe, *n.f.* poop (of ship).
poupée, *n.f.* doll.
poupin, *adj.* smart, chic.
pour, *prep.* for; in order to. **p. que,** so that.
pourboire, *n.m.* tip, gratuity.
pourceau, *n.m.* hog.
pour-cent, *n.m.* percent.
pourcentage, *n.m.* percentage.
pourchasser, *vb.* pursue.
pourfendeur, *n.m.* killer, bully.
pourparler, *n.m.* discussion, parley.
pourpoint, *n.m.* doublet.
pourpre, *adj.* purple.
pourquoi, *adv.* why.
pourri, *adj.* rotten.
pourrir, *vb.* rot, spoil.
pourriture, *n.f.* rot.
poursuite, *n.f.* pursuit.
poursuivant, *n.m.* one who sues or prosecutes.
poursuivre, *vb.* pursue, sue, prosecute.

pourtant, *adv.* however.
pourvoi, *n.m.* appeal (at court).
pourvoir (de), *vb.* provide (with), supply. **p. à,** cater to.
pourvoyeur, *n.m.* caterer, purveyor.
pourvu que, *conj.* provided that.
pousse, *n.f.* shoot, sprouting.
poussée, *n.f.* push.
pousser, *vb.* push, urge, drive; grow.
poussier, *n.m.* coal dust.
poussière, *n.f.* dust.
poussiéreux, *adj.* dusty.
poussin, *n.m.* newly-hatched chick.
poussoir, *n.m.* push-button.
poutre, *n.f.* beam.
pouvoir, 1. *vb.* be able, can, may. **2.** *n.m.* power.
prairie, *n.f.* meadow.
praline, *n.f.* burnt almond.
praticable, *adj.* practicable.
praticien, *n.m.* practitioner.
pratique, 1. *n.f.* practice, exercise. **2.** *adj.* practical.
pratiquer, *vb.* practice, exercise.
pré, *n.m.* meadow.
préalable, *adj.* preliminary.
préambule, *n.m.* preamble.
préau, *n.m.* yard, as of a prison.
préavis, *n.m.* advance notice.
précaire, *adj.* precarious.
précaution, *n.f.* precaution, discretion.
précédent, *n.m.* precedent.
précéder, *vb.* precede; come (go) before.
précepte, *n.m.* precept.
précepteur, *n.m.* tutor.
prêche, *n.m.* sermon; the Protestant religion.
prêcher, *vb.* preach.
précieux, *adj.* precious, valuable.
préciosité, *n.f.* preciosity.
précipice, *n.m.* precipice.
précipitamment, *adv.* headlong.
précipitation, *n.f.* hurry.
précipité, *adj.* hasty.
précipiter, *vb.* precipitate. **se p.,** rush, hasten.
précis, *adj.* precise, exact, accurate.
précisément, *adv.* precisely, definitely, just so.
préciser, *vb.* state.

précision, *n.f.* accuracy, precision.
précité, *adj.* previously cited.
précoce, *adj.* precocious.
précocité, *n.f.* precociousness.
précompter, *vb.* deduct in advance.
préconçu, *adj.* preconceived.
préconiser, *vb.* extol, praise.
préconnaissance, *n.f.* foreknowledge.
précurseur, *n.m.* precursor.
prédécesseur, *n.m.* predecessor.
prédestination, *n.f.* predestination.
prédicateur, *n.m.* preacher.
prédiction, *n.f.* prediction.
prédilection, *n.f.* preference, predilection.
prédire, *vb.* foretell, predict.
prédisposer, *vb.* predispose.
prédisposition, *n.f.* predisposition.
prédominant, *adj.* predominant.
prééminence, *n.f.* preëminence.
préface, *n.f.* preface.
préfecture, *n.f.* prefecture, district.
préférable, *adj.* preferable.
préférence, *n.f.* preference.
préférer, *vb.* prefer.
préfet, *n.m.* prefect.
préfixe, *n.m.* prefix.
préfixer, *vb.* fix in advance.
prégnant, *adj.* pregnant.
préhistorique, *adj.* prehistoric.
préjudice, *n.m.* injury.
préjudiciel, *adj.* interlocutory (as in law).
préjugé, *n.m.* prejudice.
préjuger, *vb.* prejudge.
prélasser, *vb.* **se p.**, bask, lounge.
prélat, *n.m.* prelate.
prélèvement, *n.m.* deduction in advance.
prélever, *vb.* deduct previously.
préliminaire, *adj.* preliminary.
prélude, *n.m.* prelude.
prématuré, *adj.* premature.
préméditation, *n.f.* premeditation.
préméditer, *vb.* premeditate.
prémices, *n.f.pl.* first fruits, first works.
premier, *adj.* first, foremost; early; former.
prémisse, *n.f.* premise.

prémunir, *vb.* warn, take precautions.
prendre, *vb.* take.
prénom, *n.m.* given name.
prénommé, *adj.* previously named.
préoccupation, *n.f.* care, worry.
préoccuper, *vb.* worry.
prépaiement, *n.m.* prepayment.
préparatifs, *n.m.pl.* preparation.
préparation, *n.f.* preparation.
préparatoire, *adj.* preparatory.
préparer, *vb.* prepare.
prépondérance, *n.f.* preponderance.
prépondérant, *adj.* preponderant.
préposé, *n.m.* one in charge.
préposition, *n.f.* preposition.
prérogative, *n.f.* prerogative.
près, 1. *adv.* near. 2. *prep.* **p. de**, near. **de p.**, nearby.
présage, *n.m.* omen.
présager, *vb.* (fore)bode.
presbyte, *adj.* far-sighted.
presbytère, *n.m.* parsonage, presbytery.
prescription, *n.f.* prescription.
prescrire, *vb.* prescribe.
préséance, *n.f.* precedence.
présélection, *n.f.* triage.
présence, *n.f.* presence, attendance.
présent, *adj. and n.m.* present.
présentable, *adj.* presentable.
présentation, *n.f.* presentation, introduction.
présentement, *adv.* now, at present.
présenter, *vb.* present, introduce.
se p. à l'esprit, come to mind.
préservatif, *adj. and n.m.* preservative.
préservation, *n.f.* preservation.
préserver, *vb.* preserve.
présidence, *n.f.* presidency.
président, *n.m.* president, chairman.
présidente, *n.f.* chairwoman.
présidentiel, *adj.* presidential.
présider, *vb.* preside.
présomptif, *adj.* apparent, presumed.
présomptueux, *adj.* presumptuous.
presque, *adv.* almost, nearly.
presqu'île, *n.f.* peninsula.
pressage, *n.m.* pressing.

pressant, *adj.* urgent.

presse, *n.f.* press, crowd.

pressentiment, *n.m.* foreboding, misgiving.

pressentir, *vb.* foresee.

presse-papiers, *n.m.* paperweight.

presser, *vb.* press; urge; hurry.

pression, *n.f.* pressure.

pressoir, *n.m.* machine or device for squeezing.

pressurer, *vb.* squeeze, put pressure on.

prestance, *n.f.* imposing appearance.

preste, *adj.* dexterous, nimble.

prestesse, *n.f.* vivacity, nimbleness.

prestige, *n.m.* prestige, illusion.

prestigieux, *adj.* enchanting.

présumer, *vb.* presume.

présupposer, *vb.* presuppose.

prêt, 1. *n.m.* loan. 2. *adj.* ready.

prêtable, *adj.* lendable.

prétendant, *n.m.* claimant.

prétendre, *vb.* claim.

prétendu, *adj.* supposed, so-called.

prétentieux, *adj.* pretentious.

prétention, *n.f.* claim.

prêter, *vb.* lend.

prêteur, *n.m.* lender.

prétexte, *n.m.* pretext.

prétexter, *vb.* pretend, feign.

prêtre, *n.m.* priest.

prêtresse, *n.f.* priestess.

preuve, *n.f.* proof.

preux, *adj. and n.m.* gallant, brave.

prévaloir, *vb.* prevail.

prévenance, *n.f.* attentiveness, obligingness.

prévenant, *adj.* prepossessing, obliging.

prévenir, *vb.* prevent; warn.

préventif, 1. *adj.* preventive. 2. *n.m.* deterrent.

prévention, *n.f.* bias; prevention.

prévenu, *adj.* partial, biased.

prévision, *n.f.* forecast, expectation.

prévoir, *vb.* foresee.

prévôt, *n.m.* provost.

prévoyance, *n.f.* foresight.

prévoyant, *adj.* farseeing, prudent.

prier, *vb.* beg; pray.

prière, *n.f.* prayer.

prieur, *n.m.* prior.

prieuré, *n.m.* priory.

primaire, *adj.* primary.

primauté, *n.f.* preëminence, primacy.

prime, 1. *n.f.* premium, subsidy. 2. *adj.* first; accented.

primer, *vb.* outdo, excel.

primeur, *n.f.* freshness, earliness.

primitif, *adj.* primitive; original.

primordial, *adj.* primordial.

prince, *n.m.* prince.

princesse, *n.f.* princess.

princier, *adj.* princely.

principal, *adj.* chief, main, principal.

principauté, *n.f.* principality.

principe, *n.m.* principle.

printanier, *adj.* of spring.

printemps, *n.m.* spring.

priorité, *n.f.* priority.

prisable, *adj.* estimable.

prise, *n.f.* grasp, hold, grip. **p. de courant**, (electric) plug.

prisée, *n.f.* appraisal.

priser, *vb.* appraise.

priseur, *n.m.* auctioneer, appraiser.

prisme, *n.m.* prism.

prison, *n.f.* jail, prison.

prisonnier, *n.m.* prisoner.

privation, *n.f.* privation, want, hardship.

privé, *adj.* private.

priver, *vb.* deprive.

privilège, *n.m.* privilege, license.

privilégier, *vb.* license.

prix, *n.m.* price, charge, fare; prize, award.

prix-courant, *n.m.* list of prices.

probabilité, *n.f.* probability, chances.

probable, *adj.* likely, probable.

probité, *n.f.* probity.

problématique, *adj.* problematical.

problème, *n.m.* problem.

procédé, *n.m.* procedure, process.

procéder, *vb.* proceed.

procédure, *n.f.* proceeding.

procès, *n.m.* trial; (law)suit.

procession, *n.f.* procession.

processionnel, *adj.* processional.

procès-verbal, *n.m.* minutes (of meeting).

prochain, 1. *n.m.* neighbor. 2. *adj.* next.

prochainement, *adv.* soon.
proche, *adj.* near, close.
proclamation, *n.f.* proclamation.
proclamer, *vb.* proclaim.
procréation, *n.f.* procreation.
procurer, *vb.* procure, get.
procureur, *n.m.* attorney.
prodigalement, *adv.* prodigally.
prodigalité, *n.f.* extravagance.
prodige, *n.m.* prodigy.
prodigieux, *adj.* wondrous.
prodigue, *adj.* extravagant, lavish, profuse,
prodiguer, *vb.* lavish.
producteur, *n.m.* producer.
productif, *adj.* productive.
production, *n.f.* production.
productivité, *n.f.* productivity.
produire, *vb.* produce, yield, breed.
produit, *n.m.* product, commodity.
proéminence, *n.f.* prominence.
proéminent, *adj.* prominent, standing out.
profane, *adj.* profane.
profaner, *vb.* misuse, debase, profane.
proférer, *vb.* say, utter.
professer, *vb.* profess.
professeur, *n.m.* professor, teacher.
profession, *n.f.* profession.
professionnel, *adj.* professional.
professoral, *adj.* professorial.
professorat, *n.m.* professorship.
profil (-1), *n.m.* profile.
profiler, *vb.* show a profile of.
profit, *n.m.* profit.
profitable, *adj.* profitable.
profiter, *vb.* profit.
profiteur, *n.m.* profiteer.
profond, *adj.* deep, profound; indepth.
profondeur, *n.f.* depth.
profus, *adj.* profuse.
profusion, *n.f.* profusion, excess.
progéniture, *n.f.* offspring.
programme, *n.m.* program.
progrès, *n.m.* progress, advance.
progresser, *vb.* progress.
progressif, *adj.* progressive.
progressiste, *n.m.* progressive.
prohiber, *vb.* prohibit.
prohibitif, *adj.* prohibitive.
prohibition, *n.f.* prohibition.
proie, *n.f.* prey.

projecteur, *n.m.* projector.
projectile, *n.m.* missile.
projection, *n.f.* projection.
projet, *n.m.* project. **p. de loi,** bill.
projeter, *vb.* project, plan.
prolétaire, *adj. and n.m.* proletarian.
prolétariat, *n.m.* proletariat.
prolifération, *n.f.* proliferation.
prolifique, *adj.* prolific.
prolixe, *adj.* prolix, wordy.
prologue, *n.m.* prologue.
prolongation, *n.f.* extension, prolongation.
prolonger, *vb.* extend, prolong.
promenade, *n.f.* excursion; walk; ride.
promener, *vb.* take out. **se p.,** take a walk (ride).
promeneur, *n.m.* walker.
promesse, *n.f.* promise.
promettre, *vb.* promise.
promontoire, *n.m.* promontory.
promoteur, *n.m.* promoter.
promotion, *n.f.* promotion.
promouvoir, *vb.* promote.
prompt, *adj.* prompt.
promptitude, *n.f.* quickness.
promulguer, *vb.* promulgate.
prôner, *vb.* lecture to, praise.
pronom, *n.m.* pronoun.
prononcer, *vb.* pronounce, utter; deliver.
prononciation, *n.f.* pronunciation.
pronostic, *n.m.* prognosis, prediction.
propagande, *n.f.* propaganda.
propagandiste, *n.m.* propagandist.
propagateur, *n.m.* propagator.
propagation, *n.f.* propagation.
propager, *vb.* propagate.
propension, *n.f.* inclination, propensity.
prophète, *n.m.* prophet.
prophétie, *n.f.* prophecy.
prophétique, *adj.* prophetic.
prophétiser, *vb.* prophesy.
propice, *adj.* favorable. **peu p.,** unfavorable.
propitiation, *n.f.* propitiation, conciliation.
proportion, *n.f.* proportion.
proportionné, *adj.* proportionate.
proportionnel, *adj.* proportional.

proportionner, *vb.* keep in proportion.

propos, *n.m.* subject; discourse. **à p.,** relevant. **à p. de,** with regard to.

proposable, *adj.* suitable, appropriate.

proposer, *vb.* propose; move. **se p. de,** intend, mean.

proposition, *n.f.* proposal, proposition.

propre, *adj.* proper; clean, neat; own. **peu p.,** unfit.

propreté, *n.f.* cleanliness, neatness.

propriétaire, *n.m.f.* proprietor.

propriété, *n.f.* property (landed), estate.

propulser, *vb.* push, propel.

propulseur, *n.m.* propeller.

propulsion, *n.f.* propulsion.

proroger, *vb.* postpone, extend time limit.

prosaïque (-zä ĕk), *adj.* prosaic.

prosaïsme, *n.m.* prosaicness, dullness.

prosateur, *n.m.* writer of prose.

proscription, *n.f.* proscription.

proscrire, *vb.* outlaw, proscribe.

proscrit, *adj. and n.m.* exile(d); forbidden.

prose, *n.f.* prose.

prosodie, *n.f.* prosody.

prospecter, *vb.* search, as for gold.

prospecteur, *n.m.* prospector.

prospère, *adj.* prosperous.

prospérer, *vb.* flourish, thrive, prosper.

prospérité, *n.f.* prosperity.

prosterner, *vb.* prostrate.

prostituée, *n.f.* prostitute.

prostitution, *n.f.* prostitution.

protecteur, 1. *n.m.* protector; patron. **2.** *adj.* protective.

protecteur du citoyen, *n.m.* ombudsman (in Quebec).

protection, *n.f.* protection.

protectorat, *n.m.* protectorate.

protéger, *vb.* protect, patronize, foster.

protéine, *n.f.* protein.

protestant, *adj. and n.m.* Protestant.

protestantisme, *n.m.* Protestantism.

protestation, *n.f.* protest.

protester. *vb.* protest.

protêt, *n.m.* protest.

prothèse, *n.f.* artificial aid, as a denture.

protocole, *n.m.* protocol.

protubérance, *n.f.* protuberance.

proue, *n.f.* prow, front.

prouesse, *n.f.* prowess.

prouver, *vb.* prove.

provenance, *n.f.* place of origin; product.

provençal, 1. *adj.* of Provence. **2.** *n.m.* language of Provence.

provende, *n.f.* provender, foodstuffs.

provenir, *vb.* come from.

proverbe, *n.m.* proverb, saying.

proverbial, *adj.* proverbial.

providence, *n.f.* providence.

providentiel, *adj.* providential.

province, *n.f.* province.

provincial, *adj. and n.m.* provincial.

provincialisme, *n.m.* provincialism.

provision, *n.f.* supply, store, provision.

provisoire, *adj.* temporary.

provocateur, *n.m.* one who provokes action.

provocation, *n.f.* provocation.

provoquer, *vb.* provoke.

proximité, *n.f.* closeness, proximity.

prude, 1. *n.f.* prude. **2.** *adj.* like a prude.

prudence, *n.f.* caution, prudence.

prudent, *adj.* cautious, prudent.

pruderie, *n.f.* prudishness.

prune, *n.f.* plum.

pruneau, *n.m.* prune.

prunelle, *n.f.* pupil (of eye).

prunier, *n.m.* plum tree.

Prusse, *n.f.* Prussia.

Prussien, *n.m.* Prussian.

prussien, *adj.* Prussian.

psalmiste, *n.m.* psalmist.

psaume, *n.m.* psalm.

psautier, *n.m.* psalm book.

pseudonyme, *n.m.* pseudonym.

psychanalyse (-k-), *n.f.* psychoanalysis.

psychédélique (-k-), *adj.* psychedelic.

psychiatre (-k-), *n.m.* psychiatrist.

psychiatrie (-k-), *n.f.* psychiatry.

psychique (-k-), *adj.* psychic.

psychologie (-k-), *n.f.* psychology.

psychologique (-k-), *adj.* psychological.

psychologue (-k-), *n.m.* psychologist.

psychose (-k-), *n.f.* psychosis.

puant, *adj.* foul, shameful.

puberté, *n.f.* puberty.

public, **1.** *adj. m.*, **publique** *f.* public. **2.** *n.m.* public.

publication, *n.f.* publication.

publiciste, *n.m.* publicist.

publicité, *n.f.* publicity, advertisement(s).

publier, *vb.* publish, issue.

puce, *n.f.* flea.

pucelle, *n.f.* young girl, virgin.

pudeur, *n.f.* modesty.

pudique, *adj.* modest.

puer, *vb.* smell, have an offensive odor.

puéril (-l), *adj.* childish.

pugiliste, *m.* boxer.

puîné, *adj.* younger (of a brother or sister).

puis, *adv.* then.

puisard, *n.m.* cesspool.

puisatier, *n.m.* well-digger.

puiser, *vb.* draw up, derive.

puisque, *conj.* since, as.

puissamment, *adv.* very, powerfully.

puissance, *n.f.* power.

puissant, *adj.* potent, powerful, mighty.

puits (pwē), *n.m.* well; shaft.

pulluler, *vb.* breed abundantly, multiply.

pulmonaire, *adj.* pulmonary.

pulpe, *n.f.* pulp.

pulpeux, *adj.* pulpy.

pulsar, *n.m.* pulsar.

pulsation, *n.f.* pulsation, beating.

pulvérisateur, *n.m.* vaporizer, spray.

pulvériser, *vb.* spray, pulverize.

punaise, *n.f.* bedbug.

punir, *vb.* punish.

punitif, *adj.* punitive.

punition, *n.f.* punishment.

pupille (-l), *n.m.f.* ward: pupil (of the eye).

pupitre, *n.m.* desk.

pur, *adj.* pure.

purée, *n.f.* mash.

purement, *adv.* purely, solely.

pureté, *n.f.* purity.

purgatoire, *n.m.* purgatory.

purge, *n.f.* purge.

purger, *vb.* purge.

purification, *n.f.* purification.

purifier, *vb.* purify, cleanse.

puritain, *adj. and n.m.* Puritan.

purulent, *adj.* purulent.

pustule, *n.f.* pimple.

putois, *n.m.* skunk, polecat.

putréfier, *vb.* corrupt, rot, spoil.

putride, *adj.* putrid.

pygmée, *n.m.* Pygmy.

pyjama, *n.m.* pajamas.

pyramidal, *adj.* pyramidal, overwhelming.

pyramide, *n.f.* pyramid.

Q

quadrangle (kw-), *n.m.* quadrangle.

quadrillé, *adj.* checked, ruled off.

quadriphonique (kw-), *adj.* quadraphonic.

quadrupède (kw-), *n.m. and adj.* quadruped.

quadruple (kw-), *adj.* quadruple.

quai, *n.m.* pier, dock; (station) platform.

qualification, *n.f.* qualification.

qualifier, *vb.* qualify.

qualité, *n.f.* quality, nature, grade.

quand, *adv.* when.

quant à, *prep.* as to, as for.

quantité, *n.f.* amount, quantity.

quarantaine, *n.f.* quarantine.

quarante, *adj. and n.m.* forty.

quart, *n.m.* fourth, quarter.

quartier, *n.m.* district, quarter. **q. général**, headquarters.

quartz (kw-), *n.m.* quartz.

quasar (kw-), *n.m.* quasar.

quasi, *adv.* nearly, quasi.

quatorze, *adj. and n.m.* fourteen.

quatrain, *n.m.* quatrain.

quatre, *adj. and n.m.* four.

quatre-vingt-dix, *adj. and n.m.* ninety.

quatre-vingts, *adj. and n.m.* eighty.

quatrième, *adj. and n.m.* fourth.

quatuor (kw-), *n.m.* quartet.

que, 1. *pron.* whom, which, that. **2.** *conj.* that, than.

quel, *adj.* which, what; of what kind.

quelconque, *adj.* of any kind.

quelque, *adj.* some, any. **q. chose,** something. **q. part,** somewhere.

quelquefois, *adv.* sometimes.

quelques, *adj.* a few.

quelques-uns, *pron.* a few.

quelqu'un, *pron.* somebody.

querelle, *n.f.* quarrel.

quereller, *vb.* quarrel (with); scold.

querelleur, 1. *n.m.* quarreler. **2.** *adj.* inclined to quarrel.

question, *n.f.* question, issue, matter.

questionner, *vb.* question.

quête, *n.f.* quest, seeking.

quêter, *vb.* seek, look for.

queue (kœ), *n.f.* tail; line. **faire la q.,** stand in line.

qui, 1. *interr. pron.* who, whom. **2.** *rel. pron.* who, which. **q. que,** whoever.

quiconque, *pron.* whoever.

quignon, *n.m.* large piece of bread.

quincaillerie, *n.f.* hardware.

quinine, *n.f.* quinine.

quintal, *n.m.* unit of weight (100 kilograms).

quinze, *adj. and n.m.* fifteen.

quinzième, *adj. and n.m.* fifteenth.

quittance, *n.f.* receipt.

quitte, *adj.* free, quit, released.

quitter, *vb.* quit, leave.

quoi, *pron. and interj.* what.

quoique, *conj.* though.

quote-part, *n.f.* quota.

quotidien, *adj.* daily.

R

rabais, *n.m.* reduction.

rabaisser, *vb.* diminish, lower.

rabattre, *vb.* put down, suppress, quell.

rabbin, *n.m.* rabbi.

rabbinique, *adj.* rabbinical.

rabot, *n.m.* plane.

raboter, *vb.* plane, perfect.

raboteux, *adj.* rugged.

rabougri, *adj.* puny, stunted.

raccommodage, *n.m.* fixing, mending.

raccommoder, *vb.* mend.

raccorder, *vb.* join, bring together.

raccourcir, *vb.* shorten, curtail.

raccourcissement, *n.m.* shortening, curtailing.

raccrocher, *vb.* hook up; recover.

race, *n.f.* race.

rachat, *n.m.* redemption.

racheter, *vb.* redeem.

rachitique, *adj.* rickety, affected with rickets.

rachitisme, *n.m.* rickets.

racine, *n.f.* root.

raclage, *n.m.* action of scraping.

racler, *vb.* scrape.

racoler, *vb.* recruit, esp. by fraud.

raconter, *vb.* tell, narrate, recount.

raconteur, *n.m.* story-teller.

radar, *n.m.* radar.

radeau, *n.m.* raft.

radiant, *adj.* radiant.

radiateur, *n.m.* radiator.

radical, *adj. and n.m.* radical.

radier, *vb.* radiate; erase.

radieux, *adj.* radiant, beaming, glorious.

radio, *n.f.* radio; wireless.

radio-actif, *adj.* radioactive.

radiodiffuser, *vb.* broadcast.

radio-émission, *n.f.* broadcast.

radiogramme, *n.m.* radiogram.

radiographie, *n.f.* radiography.

radis, *n.m.* radish.

radium, *n.m.* radium.

radoter, *vb.* babble, drivel.

radoub, *n.m.* refitting (of ship).

radoucir, *vb.* quiet, soften, appease.

rafale, *n.f.* blast, gust, squall.

raffermir, *vb.* make stronger or more secure.

raffinement, *n.m.* refinement.

raffiner, *vb.* refine.

raffinerie, *n.f.* refinery.

raffoler, *vb.* dote on, be mad about.

rafistoler, *vb.* mend, patch.

rafler, *vb.* carry off.

rafraîchir, *vb.* refresh.

rafraîchissement, *n.m.* refreshment.

rage, *n.f.* rage, fury.

rager, *vb.* be angry, rage.

rageur, *n.m.* irritable person.

ragoût, *n.m.* stew.

ragoûtant, *adj.* tasty, pleasing.

ragréer, *vb.* refinish, renovate.

raid, *n.m.* raid.

raide, *adj.* stiff; taut; steep.

raideur, *n.f.* stiffness.

raidir, *vb.* stiffen.

raie, *n.f.* streak; part (in hair).

raifort, *n.m.* horseradish.

rail, *n.m.* rail.

railler, *vb.* make fun of.

raillerie, *n.f.* jesting.

railleur, *n.m.* scoffer, jester.

rainure, *n.f.* groove.

rais, *n.m.* ray, spoke.

raisin, *n.m.* grape(s). **r. sec,** raisin.

raison, *n.f.* reason, judgment. **avoir r.,** be right.

raisonnable, *adj.* reasonable, rational.

raisonnement, *n.m.* reason, argument.

raisonner, *vb.* reason.

rajeunir, *vb.* rejuvenate.

rajuster, *vb.* readjust.

râle, *n.m.* rail (bird); rattle in throat.

ralentir, *vb.* slacken, slow down.

râler, *vb.* rattle (in dying).

rallier, *vb.* rally.

rallonger, *vb.* make an addition to, lengthen.

ramage, *n.m.* flower pattern; chirping; babble.

ramassé, *adj.* thick-set, dumpy.

ramasser, *vb.* pick up.

ramasseur, *n.m.* collector.

rame, *n.f.* oar.

rameau, *n.m.* branch.

ramener, *vb.* bring (take) back.

rameneur, *n.m.* restorer.

ramer, *vb.* row.

rameur, *n.m.* rower.

ramifier, *vb.* divide into branches, ramify.

ramille, *n.f.* twig.

ramollir, *vb.* soften, weaken.

rampe, *n.f.* banister; ramp.

ramper, *vb.* crawl, creep.

rance, *adj. and n.m.* rancid, rancidness.

rancœur, *n.f.* rancor.

rançon, *n.f.* ransom.

rancune, *n.f.* grudge, spite, ran-

cor. **garder de la r.,** bear a grudge.

rancunier, *adj.* rancorous, bitter.

rang, *n.m.* row; rank.

rangée, *n.f.* file, row.

ranger, *vb.* rank, array, (ar)range.

rapace, *adj.* predatory, greedy.

râpe, *n.f.* file, rasp.

râper, *vb.* grate.

rapide, 1. *n.m.* rapid. **2.** *adj.* rapid, fast, quick.

rapidité, *n.f.* rapidity.

rapiécer, *vb.* patch.

rapière, *n.f.* rapier.

rapin, *n.m.* art student, pupil

rapiner, *vb.* plunder, rob.

rappel, *n.m.* recall, repeal, reminder.

rappeler, *vb.* recall, remind. **se r.,** remember.

rapport, *n.m.* report; relation.

rapporter, *vb.* bring back; report. **se r. à,** relate to, refer to.

rapporteur, *n.m.* reporter, tattletale.

rapprochement, *n.m.* bringing close, junction.

rapprocher, *vb.* bring together. **se r. de,** approximate.

rapt, *n.m.* rape, kidnapping.

raquette, *n.f.* racket.

rare, *adj.* scarce, rare.

raréfier, *vb.* rarefy.

rarement, *adv.* seldom.

rareté, *n.f.* rarity, uniqueness, scarcity.

ras, *adj.* smooth-shaven, open.

raser, *vb.* shave.

rasoir, *n.m.* razor.

rassasier, *vb.* cloy, sate.

rassemblement, *n.m.* rally.

rassembler, *vb.* gather, congregate, muster.

rasseoir, *vb.* reseat. **se r.,** be seated again.

rasséréner, *vb.* clear up (weather).

rassis, *adj.* stale.

rassurer, *vb.* reassure, comfort.

rat, *n.m.* rat.

ratatiner, *vb.* shrivel, shrink.

rate, *n.f.* spleen.

râteau, *n.m.* rake.

râteler, *vb.* rake.

râtelier, *n.m.* rack.

rater, *vb.* miss.

ratière, *n.f.* rat trap.

ratifier, vb. ratify.

ration, n.f. ration.

rationnel, adj. rational.

rationnement, n.m. rationing.

rationner, vb. ration.

ratissoire, n.f. scraper, rake.

rattacher, vb. fasten.

rattraper, vb. overtake.

rature, n.f. erasure.

raturer, vb. erase, blot out.

rauque, adj. hoarse, raucous.

ravage, n.m. havoc.

ravager, vb. lay waste.

ravauder, vb. mend, patch.

ravigoter, vb. enliven, refresh.

ravin, n.m. ravine.

ravir, vb. ravish; delight.

ravissant, adj. ravishing, charming; ravenous.

ravissement, n.m. rapture.

ravisseur, n.m. ravisher, robber.

raviver, vb. revive.

rayer, vb. streak; cross out.

rayon, n.m. ray, beam; shelf. **r. X,** X-ray.

rayonnant, adj. beaming.

rayonne, n.f. rayon.

rayonnement, n.m. radiation; radiance.

rayonner, vb. radiate, beam.

rayure, n.f. streak, blemish.

re-, ré-, prefix. re-, again.

réabonnement, n.m. renewal of subscription.

réabonner, vb. renew, resubscribe.

réaction, n.f. reaction. **avion à r.,** jet-plane.

réactionnaire, adj. and n. reactionary.

réagir, vb. react.

réalisable, adj. realizable.

réalisation, n.f. attainment, carrying out.

réaliser, vb. realize. **se r.,** materialize.

réaliste, 1. n.m.f. realist. **2.** adj. realist, realistic.

réalité, n.f. reality.

réassurer, vb. reinsure.

rébarbatif, adj. forbidding.

rebattre, vb. repeat, beat again.

rebattu, adj. trite.

rebelle, 1. n.m.f. rebel. **2.** adj. rebel, rebellious.

rebeller, vb. **se r.,** rebel.

rébellion, n.f. rebellion.

rebondi, adj. plump.

rebondir, vb. bounce.

rebord, n.m. border, edge.

rebuffade, n.f. rebuff, rebuke.

rebut, n.m. trash, refuse, junk, rubbish.

rebuter, vb. rebuke, discard.

recéler, vb. accept stolen goods, hide.

récemment, adv. recently.

recensement, n.m. census.

recenser, vb. make a census.

récent, adj. recent.

réceptacle, n.m. receptacle.

récepteur, n.m. receiver.

réceptif, adj. receptive.

réception, n.f. reception, receipt.

recette, n.f. recipe, receipt; (pl.) returns.

receveur, n.m. conductor; receiver.

recevoir, vb. receive, get; entertain.

réchapper, vb. escape, get out.

réchaud, n.m. food warmer, chafing dish.

réchauffer, vb. warm again, excite.

recherche, n.f. inquiry, (re)search; quest.

rechercher, vb. seek again, investigate.

rechute, n.f. relapse.

récif, n.m. reef.

récipient, n.m. container.

réciproque, adj. mutual.

récit, n.m. account.

réciter, vb. recite, tell.

réclamation, n.f. complaint.

réclame, n.f. advertisement.

réclamer, vb. claim, demand.

reclus, 1. adj. withdrawn, secluded. **2.** n.m. recluse.

réclusion, n.f. (solitary) confinement.

recoin, n.m. recess, corner.

récolte, n.f. crop, harvest.

récolter, vb. harvest. gather.

recommandable, adj. advisable.

recommandation, n.f. recommendation.

recommander, vb. recommend; register (letter).

recommencer, vb. start again.

récompense, n.f. reward.

récompenser, vb. reward.

réconcilier, vb. reconcile.

réconduire, vb. accompany, show out, dismiss.

reconnaissance, n.f. recognition; gratitude.

reconnaissant. adj. grateful.

reconnaître, vb. recognize; admit, acknowledge.

reconstituer, vb. rebuild, restore.

recourir, vb. resort (to).

recours, n.m. resort, recourse.
avoir r. á, resort to; appeal to.

recouvrement, n.f. recovery.

recouvrer, vb. recover, retrieve.

recouvrir, vb. re-cover, cover completely.

récréation, n.f. amusement.

récréer, vb. entertain. se r., amuse oneself.

recrue, n.f. recruit.

recruter, vb. recruit.

rectangle, n.m. rectangle.

recteur, n.m. rector.

rectifier, vb. rectify, correct.

reçu, n.m. receipt.

recueil, n.m. collection, compilation.

recueillir, vb. gather, collect, glean.

recul, n.m. kick, recoil.

reculade, n.f. backing, retreat.

reculer, vb. recoil, draw back, go back.

récuser, vb. challenge, reject.

recycler, vb. recycle.

rédacteur, n.m. editor.

rédaction, n.f. editorial staff.

reddition, n.f. surrendering.

rédemption. n.f. redemption.

rédiger, vb. draw up.

redingote, n.f. frock-coat.

redire, vb. repeat, echo, reveal.

redoutable, adj. redoubtable, alarming.

redouter, vb. dread.

redresser, vb. straighten.

réduction, n.f. reduction, decrease, cut.

réduire, vb. reduce. se r. à, amount to.

réduit, n.m. retreat, hovel.

réel, adj. real, actual.

réfection, n.f. reconstruction, refreshments.

réfectoire, n.m. dining-room.

référence, n.f. reference.

référer, vb. refer.

refermer, vb. close up or again.

réfléchir, vb. reflect, consider, ponder.

reflet, n.m. reflection.

refléter, vb. reflect.

réflexe, adj. and n.m. reflex.

réflexion, n.f. reflection, consideration, thought.

refluer, vb. return to source, ebb.

reflux, n.m. ebb.

refondre, vb. cast gain; remodel, improve.

réformateur, 1. adj. reforming. **2.** n.m. reformer, crusader.

réforme, n.f. reform, reformation.

réformer, vb. reform.

refoulement, n.m. forcing back, retreat.

refouler, vb. drive back, repel.

réfractaire, adj. refractory.

rafraîchir, vb. freshen.

réfrigérant, n.m. refrigerator.

réfrigérer, vb. put under refrigeration.

refroidir, vb. chill, cool.

refroidissement, n.m. cooling, refrigeration, chill.

refuge, n.m. refuge.

réfugié, n.m. refugee.

réfugier, vb. se r., take refuge.

refus, n.m. refusal, denial.

refuser, vb. refuse, withhold, deny.

réfutation, n.f. rebuttal.

réfuter, vb. disprove, refute.

regagner, vb. regain, recover.

regain, n.m. regrowth, renewal.

régal, n.m. feast, repast.

régaler, vb. entertain, treat.

regard, n.m. look.

regarder, vb. look (at); concern.

régence, n.f. regency.

régénerer, vb. regenerate.

régent, adj. and n.m. regent.

régenter, vb. direct, dominate.

régime, n.m. diet; government; direction.

régiment, n.m. regiment.

région, n.f. area, region.

régional, adj. regional.

régir, vb. rule.

régisseur, n.m. manager.

registre, n.m. register, record.

règle, n.f. rule; ruler.

règlement, n.m. regulation; settlement.

réglementaire, *adj.* according to regulations.

régler, *vb.* regulate; rule; settle.

règne, *n.m.* reign.

régner, *vb.* reign.

régression, *n.f.* regression.

regret, *n.m.* regret.

regrettable, *adj.* regrettable.

regretter, *vb.* regret, be sorry for.

régulariser, *vb.* regularize.

régularité, *n.f.* regularity.

régulateur, *n.m.* regulator.

régulier, *adj.* regular.

réhabiliter, *vb.* rehabilitate.

rehausser, *vb.* enhance.

rein, *n.m.* kidney; (*pl.*) loins, back.

reine, *n.f.* queen.

réitérer, *vb.* reiterate.

rejet, *n.m.* rejection.

rejeter, *vb.* reject.

rejeton, *n.m.* plant shoot; scion.

rejoindre, *vb.* rejoin; catch up with, overtake.

réjouir, *vb.* rejoice, delight, cheer up.

réjouissance, *n.f.* festivity.

relâche, *adj.* loose.

relâcher, *vb.* relax, slacken.

relais, *n.m.* relay.

relater, *vb.* relate.

relatif, *adj.* relative.

relation, *n.f.* relation, connection.

relaxation, *n.f.* relaxation, release.

relayer, *vb.* relay.

reléguer, *vb.* relegate, banish.

relève, *n.f. (mil.)* relief, replacement.

relèvement, *n.m.* bearing.

relever, *vb.* lift; relieve; point out.

relief, *n.m.* relief. **mettre en r.,** emphasize.

relier, *vb.* bind; link.

relieur, *n.m.* binder, esp. of books.

religieuse, *n.f.* nun.

religieux, *adj.* religious.

religion, *n.f.* religion.

reliquaire, *n.m.* receptacle for relic.

relique, *n.f.* relic.

reliure, *n.f.* binding.

reluire, *vb.* shine, glisten.

remanier, *vb.* redo, modify.

remarquable, *adj.* remarkable; noticeable.

remarque, *n.f.* remark.

remarquer, *vb.* remark; notice.

rembarrer, *vb.* drive back; put in one's place.

remblai, *n.m.* embankment.

remboursement, *n.m.* refund.

rembourser, *vb.* repay, refund.

remède, *n.m.* remedy, cure.

remédiable, *adj.* remediable.

remédier à, *vb.* remedy.

remerciement, *n.m.* thanks.

remercier, *vb.* thank.

remettre, *vb.* put back; restore; remit; pardon; deliver. **se r.,** recover.

remise, *n.f.* discount; delivery.

rémission, *n.f.* remission.

remontrance, *n.f.* remonstrance.

remontrer, *vb.* show anew, point out error.

remords (-môr), *n.m.* remorse.

remorquer, *vb.* tow.

remorqueur, *n.m.* tug(boat).

rémouleur, *n.m.* sharpener, grinder.

remous, *n.m.* eddy.

rempart, *n.m.* bulwark, rampart.

remplaçant, *n.m.* substitute.

remplacer, *vb.* replace, substitute.

rempli, *n.m.* tuck, hitch.

remplier, *vb.* take a tuck in.

remplir, *vb.* fill; carry out; crowd.

remporter, *vb.* take away, bring back.

remuer, *vb.* stir. **se r.,** bustle.

renaissance, *n.f.* rebirth, revival.

renaître, *vb.* be reborn, get new life.

renard, *n.m.* fox; sly person.

rencontre, *n.f.* meeting. **aller à la r. de,** go to meet.

rencontrer, *vb.* meet; come across.

rendement, *n.m.* output.

rendez-vous, *n.m.* date, appointment.

rendre, *vb.* give back; repay; surrender. **se r. compte de,** realize.

rendu, *adj.* tired out, all in.

rêne, *n.f.* rein.

rené, *adj.* born-again.

renégat, *adj. and n.m.* renegade.

renfermer, *vb.* enclose.

renfler, *vb.* swell, inflate.

renforcer, vb. reinforce.

renfort, n.m. reinforcement, aid.

renfrogner, vb. **se r.** scowl, frown.

rengaine, n.f. often-told story.

renne, n.m. reindeer.

renom, n.m. renown, repute.

renommée, n.f. fame, renown.

renoncer à, vb. renounce, give up, forego.

renonciation, n.f. renunciation.

renouement, n.m. renewing, retying.

renouveau, n.m. springtime.

renouveler, vb. renew, renovate.

renouvellement, n.m. renewal.

renseignements, n.m.pl. information.

renseigner, vb. inform. **se r.,** inquire.

rente, n.f. income; interest; annuity.

rentier, n.m. one who lives off interest on investments.

rentrée, n.f. return.

rentrer, vb. go back, go home.

renversant, adj. amazing, overwhelming.

renverser, vb. overthrow, overturn; reverse.

renvoi, n.m. dismissal; return.

renvoyer, vb. send back, return; dismiss.

repaire, n.m. den, animal's lair.

repaître, vb. feed, feast.

répandre, vb. diffuse, scatter, spill.

répandu, adj. prevalent, widespread.

reparaître, vb. reappear.

réparateur, n.m. restorer, repairer.

réparation, n.f. repair; amends.

réparer, vb. repair, make up for, make amends for.

repartie, n.f. reply, quick retort.

repartir, vb. leave again; retort.

répartir, vb. apportion, allot, distribute.

repas, n.m. meal.

repasser, vb. press; pass; look over.

repentir, 1. n.m. repentance. **2.** vb. **se r.,** repent.

répercussion, n.f. repercussion.

répercuter, vb. reverberate, echo.

repère, n.m. guiding mark.

repertoire, n.m. list, repertory.

répéter, vb. repeat; rehearse.

répétition, n.f. repetition.

répit, n.m. respite.

replacer, vb. replace.

replier, vb. fold again or up.

réplique, n.f. rejoinder; cue.

répliquer, vb. rejoin.

répondant, n.m. respondent, bail.

répondre, vb. answer, reply. **r. de,** vouch for.

réponse, n.f. answer, reply.

report, n.m. (in bookkeeping) amount brought forward.

reportage, n.m. reporting.

reporter, 1. n.m. reporter. **2.** vb. carry or take back.

repos, n.m. rest.

reposer, vb. rest, repose.

repousser, vb. push back, repel; spurn.

repoussoir, n.m. foil.

répréhensible, adj. objectionable.

répréhension, n.f. reprehension, censure.

reprendre, vb. take back, resume.

représailles, n.f.pl. retaliation.

représentant, n.m. representative.

représentatif, adj. representative.

représentation, n.f. representation, performance.

représenter, adj. represent.

répressif, adj. repressive.

répression, n.f. repression.

réprimande, n.f. reproof, rebuke, reprimand.

réprimander, vb. chide, reprove, reprimand.

réprimer, vb. quell.

reprise, n.f. recovery; turn; darn. **à plusieurs r.s,** repeatedly.

repriser, vb. darn.

réprobation, n.f. reprobation.

reproche, n.m. reproach.

reprocher, vb. reproach.

reproduction, n.f. reproduction.

reproduction exacte, n.f. clone.

reproduire, vb. reproduce.

réprouver, vb. censure.

reptile, n.m. reptile.

républicain, adj. and n.m. republican.

république, n.f. republic.

répudier, vb. repudiate.

répugnance, n.f. repugnance.

répulsion, n.f. repulsion.

réputation, n.f. reputation.

réputer, vb. consider, esteem.

requête, n.f. request, plea.
requin, n.m. shark.
requis, adj. required, necessary.
réquisition, n.f. requisition.
rescousse, n.f. rescue.
réseau, n.m. network.
réserve, n.f. reserve, reservation; qualification. **de r.,** spare, extra.
réservé, adj. aloof, reticent.
réserver, vb. reserve.
réserviste, n.m. reservist (mil.).
réservoir, n.m. tank, reservoir.
résidant, adj. resident.
résidence, n.f. residence, dwelling.
résider, vb. reside.
résidu, n.m. residue.
résignation, n.f. resignation.
résigner, vb. resign.
résiliation, n.f. cancelling.
résine, n.f. resin.
résistance, n.f. endurance, resistance.
résister (à), vb. resist.
résolu, adj. resolute.
résolument, adv. resolutely.
résolution, n.f. resolution.
résonnance, n.f. resonance.
résonnant, adj. resonant.
résonner, vb. resound.
résoudre, vb. resolve, solve.
respect (-spè), n.m. respect.
respectable, adj. decent, respectable.
respecter, vb. respect.
respectif, adj. respective.
respectueux, adj. respectful.
respiration, n.f. respiration, breathing.
respirer, vb. breathe.
resplendir, vb. gleam resplendently.
responsabilité, n.f. responsibility.
responsable, adj. responsible; accountable, liable.
ressaisir, vb. regain possession.
ressemblance, n.f. likeness.
ressembler (à), vb. resemble. **se r.,** look alike.
ressentiment, n.m. resentment.
ressentir, vb. feel, resent, show.
resserrer, vb. tighten, compress.
ressort, n.m. spring, elasticity.
ressortir, vb. stand out.
ressource, n.f. resort, resource.
ressusciter, vb. revive, resuscitate.

restaurant, n.m. restaurant.
restaurateur, n.m. restorer; restaurant man.
restauration, n.f. restoration.
restaurer, vb. restore.
reste, n.m. remainder, rest, remnant.
rester, vb. remain, stay.
restituer, vb. give back, restore.
restreindre, vb. restrict.
restrictif, adj. restrictive.
restriction, n.f. restriction.
résultat, n.m. outcome, upshot, result.
résulter, vb. result.
résumé, n.m. summing up.
résumer, vb. sum up.
rétablir, vb. restore, reëstablish. **se r.,** recover.
rétablissement, n.m. recovery.
retard, n.m. delay. **en r.,** late; slow.
retarder, vb. delay, retard; be slow.
retenir, vb. retain; keep; hold (back); detain. **se r. de,** refrain from.
rétentif, adj. retentive.
retentir, vb. resound.
retentissant, adj. reëchoing.
réticence, n.f. silence, reticence.
retirer, vb. withdraw. **se r.,** retire, retreat.
retoucher, vb. retouch, alter.
retour, n.m. return. **de r.,** back.
retourner, vb. go back, invert, return. **se r.,** turn around.
retrait, n.m. contraction, retraction.
retraite, n.f. retreat; privacy.
retrancher, vb. cut off, curtail.
rétrécir, vb. shrink, contract.
rétribution, n.f. salary, recompense.
retrousser, vb. turn up.
retrouver, vb. find; recover.
réunion, n.f. meeting, convention, reunion.
réunir, vb. unite. **se r.,** assemble.
réussir, vb. succeed.
réussite, n.f. successful outcome.
revanche, n.f. revenge. **en r.,** in return.
rêve, n.m. dream.
réveil, n.m. awaking; revival.
réveiller, vb. wake (up), rouse, arouse.

révélateur, 1. *adj.* revealing. **2.** *n.m.* revealer.

révélation, *n.f.* revelation.

révéler, *vb.* disclose, reveal.

revenant, *n.m.* ghost, specter.

revendeur, *n.m.* retailer, old-clothes dealer.

revendiquer, *vb.* claim.

revenir, *vb.* come back, return, recur; amount to.

revenu, *n.m.* income, revenue.

rêver, *vb.* dream.

réverbérer, *vb.* reverberate.

révéremment, *adv.* reverently.

révérence, *n.f.* reverence; bow, curtsy.

révérend, *adj.* reverend.

révérer, *vb.* revere.

rêverie, *n.f.* dreaming, reverie.

revers, *n.m.* reverse, wrong side; lapel.

revêtir, *vb.* clothe; assume.

rêveur, 1. *n.m.* dreamer. **2.** *adj.* pensive.

réviser, *vb.* revise.

réviseur, *n.m.* reviser, inspector.

révision, *n.f.* revision, review.

revivre, *vb.* revive.

révocation, *n.f.* revocation, annulment.

revoir, *vb.* see again. **au r.,** good-bye.

révolte, *n.f.* revolt.

révolter, se r., *vb.* revolt.

révolution, *n.f.* revolution, turn.

révolutionnaire, *adj.* and *n.m.* revolutionary.

revolver, *n.m.* revolver.

révoquer, *vb.* revoke.

revue, *n.f.* review, magazine.

rez-de-chaussée, *n.m.* ground floor.

rhétorique, *n.f.* rhetoric.

rhinocéros, *n.m.* rhinoceros.

rhubarbe, *n.f.* rhubarb.

rhum, *n.m.* rum.

rhumatisme, *n.m.* rheumatism.

rhume, *n.m.* cold.

ricaner, *vb.* laugh objectionably.

riche, *adj.* rich, wealthy.

richesse, *n.f.* wealth.

ricocher, *vb.* ricochet, spring back.

rictus, *n.m.* grin.

ride, *n.f.* wrinkle, ripple.

rideau, *n.m.* curtain.

rider, *vb.* ripple, wrinkle.

ridicule, 1. *n.m.* ridicule. **2.** *adj.* ridiculous.

ridiculiser, *vb.* ridicule.

rien, *pron.* nothing.

rieur, *n.m.* laugher.

rigide, *adj.* rigid.

rigidité, *n.f.* rigidity.

rigole, *n.f.* ditch, gutter.

rigoler, *vb.* laugh.

rigoureux, *adj.* rigorous.

rigueur, *n.f.* rigor.

rime, *n.f.* rhyme.

rimer, *vb.* rhyme.

rince-doigts, *n.m.* finger bowl.

rincer, *vb.* rinse.

ripaille, *n.f.* feasting, revelry.

riposte, *n.f.* retort.

rire, 1. *n.m.* laugh, laughter. **2.** *vb.* laugh.

ris, *n.m.* laugh; reef in a sail; sweetbread.

risée, *n.f.* laugh, mocking.

risible, *adj.* laughable.

risque, *n.m.* risk.

risquer, *vb.* risk.

risque-tout, *n.m.* daredevil.

rissoler, *vb.* brown, as in cooking.

rite, *n.m.* rite.

rituel, *adj.* ritual.

rivage, *n.m.* shore, bank.

rival, *adj.* and *n.m.* rival.

rivaliser, *vb.* compete, rival.

rivalité, *n.f.* rivalry.

rive, *n.f.* bank.

river, *vb.* clinch.

rivet, *n.m.* rivet.

rivière, *n.f.* river.

rixe, *n.f.* brawl.

riz, *n.m.* rice.

rizière, *n.f.* rice field.

robe, *n.f.* dress, gown, frock, robe.

robinet, *n.m.* faucet, tap.

robuste, *adj.* hardy, strong, robust.

roc, *n.m.* rock.

rocailleux, *adj.* rocky, rough.

rocher, *n.m.* rock.

rocheux, *adj.* rocky.

rock, *adj.* rock (music).

rôder, *vb.* prowl.

rôdeur, *n.m.* prowler.

rogner, *vb.* pare, trim down.

rognon, *n.m.* kidney.

rogue, *adj.* proud, arrogant.

roi, *n.m.* king.

rôle, *n.m.* role, part.

Romain, *n.m.* Roman.
romain, *adj.* Roman.
roman, *n.m.* novel.
romance, *n.f.* ballad.
romancier, *n.m.* novelist.
roman-feuilleton, *n.m.* serial.
romanichel, *n.m.* gypsy.
romantique, *adj.* romantic.
romarin, *n.m.* rosemary.
rompre, *vb.* break.
ronce, *n.f.* bramble.
rond, 1. *n.m.* round; circle. **2.** *adj.* round.
ronde, *n.f.* round, patrol.
rondeur, *n.f.* roundness.
ronflement, *n.m.* snoring, roar.
ronfler, *vb.* snore.
ronger, *vb.* gnaw; fret.
rongeur, *adj. and n.m.* rodent.
ronronner, *vb.* purr, murmur.
rosaire, *n.m.* rosary.
rosbif, *n.m.* roast beef.
rose, 1. *n.f.* rose. **2.** *adj.* pink.
roseau, *n.m.* reed.
rosée, *n.f.* dew.
rosier, *n.m.* rosebush.
rossignol, *n.m.* nightingale.
rôt, *n.m.* roast (meat).
rotation, *n.f.* rotation.
rotatoire, *adj.* rotary.
roter, *vb.* belch.
rôti, *n.m.* roast.
rôtir, *vb.* roast.
rotondité, *n.f.* rotundity.
rotule, *n.f.* kneecap.
roturier, *adj.* commonplace, vulgar.
roublardise, *n.f.* cunningness.
roue, *n.f.* wheel.
roué, 1. *n.m.* rake, debauchee. **2.** *adj.* crafty.
rouge, 1. *n.m.* rouge. **2.** *adj.* red. **r. foncé,** maroon.
rouge-gorge, *n.m.* robin.
rougeole, *n.f.* measles.
rougeur, *n.f.* flush, blush.
rougir, *vb.* blush.
rouille, *n.f.* rust.
rouiller, *vb.* rust.
rouir, *vb.* soak.
rouleau, *n.m.* roll, roller, scroll, coil.
roulement, *n.m.* rolling, winding; rotation.
rouler, *vb.* roll, wind.

roulette, *n.f.* little wheel, caster.
roulis, *n.m.* roll.
Roumain, *n.m.* Rumanian (person).
roumain, 1. *n.m.* Rumanian (language). **2.** *adj.* Rumanian.
Roumanie, *n.f.* Rumania.
rousseur, *n.f.* redness. **tache de r.,** freckle.
roussir, *vb.* scorch.
route, *n.f.* road, way, course, route. **en r.,** under way. **en r. de,** on the way to.
routine, *n.f.* routine.
routinier, *adj.* routine.
roux, *adj. and n.m.* red, reddish-brown.
royal, *adj.* royal, regal.
royaliste, *adj. and n.m.f.* royalist.
royaume, *n.m.* kingdom.
royauté, *n.f.* royalty.
ruban, *n.m.* ribbon, tape.
rubis, *n.m.* ruby.
rubrique, *n.f.* red ocher; heading.
ruche, *n.f.* hive.
rude, *adj.* rough, gruff, harsh; rugged.
rudesse, *n.f.* harshness.
rudiment, *n.m.* rudiment, element.
rudimentaire, *adj.* rudimentary.
rudoyer, *vb.* bully.
rue, *n.f.* street, road.
ruée, *n.f.* rush.
ruelle, *n.f.* lane, alley.
ruer, *vb.* **se r.,** rush.
rugir, *vb.* roar.
rugissement, *n.m.* roar.
rugueux, *adj.* rugged, harsh.
ruine, *n.f.* ruin.
ruiner, *vb.* ruin.
ruineux, *adj.* ruinous.
ruisseau, *n.m.* brook, creek, gutter.
ruisseler, *vb.* stream, flow.
rumeur, *n.f.* rumor, noise.
ruminant, *adj. and n.m.* ruminant.
ruminer, *vb.* chew the cud.
rupture, *n.f.* break, rupture.
rural, *adj.* rural.
ruse, *n.f.* trick; cunning.
rusé, *adj.* sly, cunning.
Russe, *n.m.f.* Russian (person).
russe, 1. *n.m.* Russian (language). **2.** *adj.* Russian.
Russie, *n.f.* Russia.

rusticité, n.f. rusticity, uncouthness.

rustique, adj. rustic.

rustre, adj. and n.m. boor, boorish.

rythme, n.m. rhythm.

rythmique, adj. rhythmical.

S

sabbat, n.m. Sabbath.

sable, n.m. sand.

sabler, vb. sand; quaff.

sablier, n.m. sandbox, sandman; hourglass.

sablonneux, adj. sandy.

sablonnière, n.f. sand pit.

sabord, n.m. porthole.

sabot, n.m. hoof; wooden shoe.

sabotage, n.m. sabotage.

saboter, vb. sabotage.

saboteur, n.m. saboteur; awkward bungler.

sabre, n.m. saber.

sac, n.m. sack, bag. **s. à main,** pocketbook. **s. à air,** airbag.

saccade, n.f. jerk.

saccager, vb. ransack, sack, plunder.

sacerdoce, n.m. priesthood.

sachet, n.m. sachet.

sacre, n.m. consecration, coronation.

sacré, adj. sacred.

sacrement, n.m. sacrament.

sacrer, vb. crown, consecrate; curse.

sacrifice, n.m. sacrifice.

sacrifier, vb. sacrifice.

sacrilège, n.m. sacrilege.

sacristain, n.m. sexton.

sac tyrolien, n.m. backpack.

sadisme, n.m. sadism.

sagace, adj. shrewd.

sagacité, n.f. sagacity.

sage, 1. n.m. sage. **2.** adj. wise, good.

sage-femme, n.f. midwife.

sagesse, n.f. wisdom.

saignée, n.f. bleeding.

saigner, vb. bleed.

saillant, adj. prominent, projecting.

saillie, n.f. projection.

saillir, vb. protrude.

sain, adj. healthy, sound, wholesome. **s. d'esprit,** sane.

saindoux, n.m. lard.

saint, 1. n.m. saint. **2.** adj. holy.

Saint-Esprit, n.m. Holy Ghost.

sainteté, n.f. holiness.

saisie, n.f. seizure.

saisir, vb. seize, grasp, snatch, grab.

saisissement, n.m. chill, seizure.

saison, n.f. season.

salade, n.f. salad.

saladier, n.m. salad bowl or dish.

salaire, n.m. wages, earnings, pay.

salarié, 1. adj. salaried. **2.** n.m.f. person earning a salary.

sale, adj. dirty.

saler, vb. salt.

saleté, n.f. dirt.

salière, n.f. saltcellar.

salin, adj. salt, salty.

salir, vb. get dirty.

salive, n.f. saliva.

salle, n.f. (large) room, hall, auditorium, (hospital) ward. **s. de classe,** classroom. **s. de bain,** bathroom.

salon, n.m. parlor.

saltimbanque, n.m. charlatan, buffoon.

salubre, adj. healthful.

salubrité, n.f. healthfulness.

saluer, vb. bow, greet, salute.

salut, n.m. bow, salute; salvation.

salutaire, adj. wholesome, beneficial.

salutation, n.f. greeting.

salve, n.f. salvo, salute.

samedi, n.m. Saturday.

sanctifier, vb. hallow.

sanction, n.f. sanction.

sanctionner, vb. sanction, countenance.

sanctuaire, n.m. sanctuary.

sandale, n.f. sandal.

sang, n.m. blood.

sang-froid, n.m. calmness, composure.

sanglant, adj. bloody.

sangler, vb. strap, fasten.

sanglier, n.m. (wild) boar.

sanglot, n.m. sob.

sangloter, vb. sob.

sangsue, n.f. leech.

sanguin, adj. pertaining to blood.

sanguinaire, adj. bloodthirsty.

sanitaire, *adj.* sanitary.

sans, *prep.* without, out of. **s. doute,** without doubt. **s. plomb,** unleaded. **s. repos,** restless. **s. valeur,** worthless. **s. nom,** nameless.

sans-souci, *adj.* carefree, careless.

santé, *n.f.* health.

saper, *vb.* sap, weaken.

saphir, *n.m.* sapphire.

sapin, *n.m.* fir.

sarcasme, *n.m.* sarcasm.

sarcastique, *adj.* sarcastic.

sarcler, *vb.* weed, root out.

sardine, *n.f.* sardine.

sardonique, *adj.* sardonic.

satanique, *adj.* satanic.

satellite, *n.m.* satellite.

satin, *n.m.* satin.

satire, *n.f.* satire.

satiriser, *vb.* satirize.

satisfaction, *n.f.* satisfaction.

satisfaire, *vb.* satisfy.

satisfaisant, *adj.* satisfactory.

saturer, *vb.* saturate.

satyre, *n.m.* satyr.

sauce, *n.f.* sauce. **s. piquante,** catsup.

saucisse, *n.f.* sausage.

sauf, 1. *prep.* but. **2.** *adj.* safe. **sain et sauf,** safe and sound.

sauf-conduit, *n.m.* safe-conduct pass.

sauge, *n.f.* sage.

saugrenu, *adj.* absurd, preposterous.

saule, *n.f.* willow.

saumon, *n.m.* salmon.

saumure, *n.f.* brine.

saut, *n.m.* spring, jump.

saute, *n.f.* wind shift.

sauter, *vb.* spring, jump, leap, skip. **faire s.,** blow up.

sauterelle, *n.f.* grasshopper.

sautiller, *vb.* hop.

sauvage, 1. *n.m.f.* savage. **2.** *adj.* wild, savage.

sauvegarde, *n.f.* safeguard.

sauvegarder, *vb.* safeguard.

sauve-qui-peut, *n.m.* stampede, panic.

sauver, *vb.* save. **se s.,** run away.

sauvetage, *n.m.* salvage.

sauveteur, *n.m.* rescuer, saver.

sauveur, *n.m.* savior, Saviour.

savane, *n.f.* prairie.

savant, 1. *n.m.* scholar. **2.** *adj.* learned.

saveur, *n.f.* flavor, savor, zest.

savoir, 1. *vb.* know, be aware, have knowledge. **vouloir s.,** wonder. **2.** *n.m.* knowledge.

savoir-faire, *n.m.* poise, ability.

savoir-vivre, *n.m.* breeding, manners.

savon, *n.m.* soap.

savonner, *vb.* soap, lather.

savourer, *vb.* relish.

savoureux, *adj.* tasty.

scabreux, *adj.* improper; risky.

scalper, *vb.* scalp.

scandale, *n.m.* scandal.

scandaleux, *adj.* scandalous.

scandaliser, *vb.* shock.

scander, *vb.* scan.

Scandinave, *n.m.f.* Scandinavian.

scandinave, *adj.* Scandinavian.

Scandinavie, *n.f.* Scandinavia.

scarabée, *n.m.* beetle.

scarlatine, *n.f.* scarlet fever.

sceau, *n.m.* seal.

scélérat, *n.m.* villain, criminal, knave, ruffian.

sceller, *vb.* seal.

scénario, *n.m.* scenario.

scène, *n.f.* scene, stage.

scénique, *adj.* scenic.

scepticisme, *n.m.* skepticism.

sceptique, 1. *n.m.f.* skeptic. **2.** *adj.* skeptical.

sceptre, *n.m.* scepter.

schampooing, *n.m.* shampoo.

schisme, *n.m.* schism.

sciatique, *n.f.* sciatica.

scie, *n.f.* saw.

science, *n.f.* science.

science-fiction, *n.f.* science fiction.

scientifique, 1. *adj.* scientific. **2.** *n.m.f.* scientist.

scier, *vb.* saw.

scinder, *vb.* divide.

scintiller, *vb.* twinkle.

scission, *n.f.* cutting, division.

sclérose, *n.f.* sclerosis.

scolaire, *adj.* scholastic. **système s.,** school system.

scolastique, *adj.* scholastic.

scrofule, *n.f.* scrofula.

scrupule, *n.m.* scruple.

scrupuleux, *adj.* scrupulous.

scruter, *vb.* scan, scrutinize.

scrutin, *n.m.* ballot, poll.

sculpter (-lt-), *vb.* carve.
sculpteur (-lt-), *n.m.* sculptor.
sculpture (-lt-), *n.f.* sculpture.
se (sə), *pron.* himself, herself, itself, oneself, themselves, each other.
séance, *n.f.* sitting; session; meeting.
séant, *adj.* sitting, proper.
seau, *n.m.* pail, bucket.
sec (g), **sèche** *f. adj.* dry.
sécession, *n.f.* secession.
sécher, *vb.* dry.
sécheresse, *n.f.* dryness, drought.
second (-g-), *adj.* second.
secondaire (-g-), *adj.* secondary.
seconde (-g-), *n.f.* second.
seconder (-g-), *vb.* second, help.
secouer, *vb.* shake, rouse.
secourir, *vb.* relieve, succor, help.
secours, *n.m.* help, relief. **premiers s.**, first aid. **poste de s.**, first aid station. **au s.!**, help!
secousse, *n.f.* jar, shock.
secret, *adj. and n.m.* secret.
secrétaire, *n.m.f.* secretary.
sécréter, *vb.* secrete.
sécrétion, *n.f.* secretion.
sectaire, *adj.* sectarian.
secte, *n.f.* sect.
secteur, *n.m.* district, sector.
section, *n.f.* section.
sectionner, *vb.* cut into sections.
séculaire, *adj.* secular.
séculier, *adj.* secular, lay.
sécurité, *n.f.* safety.
sédatif, *adj. and n.m.* sedative.
sédentaire, *adj.* sedentary, stationary.
séditieux, *adj.* seditious.
sédition, *n.f.* sedition.
séduction, *n.f.* seduction.
séduire, *vb.* seduce, attract, allure.
séduisant, *adj.* attractive.
segment, *n.m.* segment.
ségrégation, *n.f.* segregation.
seigle, *n.m.* rye.
seigneur, *n.m.* lord, peer.
seigneurie, *n.f.* lordship.
sein, *n.m.* bosom, breast.
seize, *adj. and n.m.* sixteen.
seizième, *adj. and n.m.* sixteenth.
séjour, *n.m.* stay. **lieu de s.**, resort.
séjourner, *vb.* sojourn.
sel, *n.m.* salt.

sélection, *n.f.* selection.
selle, *n.f.* saddle.
seller, *vb.* saddle.
sellette, *n.f.* little stool or saddle.
selon, *prep.* according to.
seltz, *n.m.* **eau de s.**, soda water.
semailles, *n.f.pl.* sowing.
semaine, *n.f.* week; weekly pay.
semblable, *adj.* similar, alike.
semblant, *n.m.* show; appearance. **faire s.**, make believe.
sembler, *vb.* seem, appear.
semelle, *n.f.* sole.
semence, *n.f.* seed.
semer, *vb.* sow.
semestre, *n.m.* semester.
semeur, *n.m.* sower.
sémillance, *n.f.* briskness, liveliness.
sémitique, *adj.* Semitic.
semoncer, *vb.* lecture, scold.
sénat, *n.m.* senate.
sénateur, *n.m.* senator.
sénile, *adj.* senile.
sénilité, *n.f.* senility.
sens (-s), *n.m.* meaning; sense; direction.
sensation, *n.f.* sensation, feeling.
sensationnel, *adj.* sensational.
sensé, *adj.* sensible.
sensibilité, *n.f.* sensitivity.
sensible, *adj.* sensible, sensitive; conscious (of).
sensitif, *adj.* sensitive.
sensualisme, *n.m.* sensualism.
sensualité, *n.f.* sensuality.
sensuel, *adj.* sensual.
sentence, *n.f.* sentence.
sentencieux, *adj.* sententious.
senteur, *n.f.* smell.
sentier, *n.m.* path.
sentiment, *n.m.* feeling.
sentimental, *adj.* sentimental.
sentimentalité, *n.f.* sentimentality.
sentinelle, *n.f.* sentry.
sentir, *vb.* feel; smell.
séparable, *adj.* separable.
séparation, *n.f.* separation, parting.
séparé, *adj.* separate.
séparer, *vb.* separate, segregate. **se s.**, part.
sept (sèt), *adj. and n.m.* seven.
septembre, *n.m.* September.
septième (sèt-), *adj. and n.m.* seventh.

septique, *adj.* septic.

sépulcre, *n.m.* sepulcher.

séquestrer, *vb.* withdraw.

serein, *adj.* serene, placid.

sérénade, *n.f.* serenade.

sérénité, *n.f.* serenity.

serf, 1. *n.m.* serf. **2.** *adj.* in serfdom or the like.

sergent, *n.m.* sergeant.

série, *n.f.* series.

sérieux, 1. *adj.* serious, sober, grave. **2.** *n.m.* gravity.

serin, *n.m.* canary.

seringue, *n.f.* syringe.

serment, *n.m.* oath.

sermon, *n.m.* sermon.

sermonner, *vb.* lecture, preach.

serpent, *n.m.* snake, serpent.

serpenter, *vb.* wind, wander.

serre, *n.f.* green-house; claw.

serré, *adj.* tight.

serre-joint, *n.m.* clamp.

serrer, *vb.* tighten, squeeze, press, crowd, shake (hands). **s. dans ses bras,** hug.

serrure, *n.f.* lock.

sérum, *n.m.* serum.

servage, *n.m.* servitude.

servant, 1. *adj.* serving. **2.** *n.m.* server, gunner.

servante, *n.f.* maid.

serveuse, *n.f.* waitress.

serviable, *adj.* helpful.

service, *n.m.* service, favor. **être de s.,** be on duty.

serviette, *n.f.* napkin; towel; brief case.

servile, *adj.* menial.

servilité, *n.f.* servility.

servir, *vb.* serve. **se s. de,** use. **ne s. à rien,** be of no use.

serviteur, *n.m.* attendant, servant.

servitude, *n.f.* slavery.

session, *n.f.* session.

seuil, *n.m.* threshold.

seul, *adj.* alone, only, single.

seulement, *adv.* only, solely.

sève, *n.f.* sap.

sévère, *adj.* severe, stern.

sévérité, *n.f.* severity, rigor.

sévir, *vb.* punish, rage.

sevrer, *vb.* wean, withhold.

sexe, *n.m.* sex.

sexisme, *n.m.* sexism.

sexiste, *adj.* sexist.

sexuel, *adj.* sexual.

seyant, *adj.* becoming.

shrapnel, *n.m.* shrapnel.

si, 1. *adv.* so, so much, yes. **si . . . que,** however (+ *adj.*). **2.** *conj.* if, whether.

siècle, *n.m.* century.

siège, *n.m.* seat; siege.

siéger, *vb.* sit, convene, reside.

sien, *pron.* **le sien, la sienne,** his, hers, its.

sieste, *n.f.* siesta.

siffler, *vb.* whistle, hiss.

sifflerie, *n.f.* hissing, whistling.

sifflet, *n.m.* whistle.

signal, *n.m.* signal.

signalement, *n.m.* description, details.

signaler, *vb.* point out.

signature, *n.f.* signature.

signe, *n.m.* sign. **s. de la tête,** nod. **faire s. à,** beckon.

signer, *vb.* sign. **se s.,** cross oneself.

significatif, *adj.* significant, meaningful.

signification, *n.f.* significance, meaning.

signifier, *vb.* signify, mean.

silence, *n.m.* silence.

silencieux, *adj.* noiseless, silent.

silex, *n.m.* flint.

sillage, *n.m.* wake, course.

sillon, *n.m.* furrow.

sillonner, *vb.* plow.

similaire, *adj.* similar.

simple, *adj.* plain, simple, mere; no-frills.

simplicité, *n.f.* simplicity.

simplifier, *vb.* simplify.

simulation, *n.f.* simulation.

simuler, *vb.* pretend.

simultané, *adj.* simultaneous.

sincère, *adj.* candid, sincere.

sincérité, *n.f.* candor, sincerity.

singe, *n.m.* monkey; imitator.

singularité, *n.f.* singularity; peculiar trait.

singulier, *adj. and n.m.* singular; peculiar, strange.

sinistre, 1. *n.m.* disaster. **2.** *adj.* sinister.

sinon, *conj.* otherwise.

sinueux, *adj.* winding, sinuous.

sirène, *n.f.* siren.

sirop, *n.m.* syrup.

siroter, *vb.* sip.

site, *n.m.* site.

sitôt, *adv.* as soon (as).

situation, *n.f.* situation, position, location, office.

situer, *vb.* situate, locate.

six (sês), *adj. and n.m.* six.

sixième (-z-), *adj. and n.m.* sixth.

ski, *n.m.* ski. **faire du s.,** ski, *vb.*

skieur, *n.m.* skier.

smoking, *n.m.* dinner-jacket, tuxedo.

sobre, *adj.* temperate, sober.

sobriété, *n.f.* moderation, temperance.

sobriquet, *n.m.* nickname.

soc, *n.m.* plowshare.

sociable, *adj.* sociable.

social, *adj.* social.

socialisme, *n.m.* socialism.

socialiste, *adj. and n.m.f.* socialist.

société, *n.f.* society; company.

sociologie, *n.f.* sociology.

sociologiste, *n.m.* sociologist.

sœur, *n.f.* sister.

soi-disant, *adj.* so-called.

soie, *n.f.* silk; bristle.

soierie, *n.f.* silk goods.

soif, *n.f.* thirst. **avoir s.,** be thirsty.

soigné, *adj.* trim. **mal s.,** sloppy.

soigner, *vb.* tend, look after, take care of.

soigneux, *adj.* careful.

soi-même, *pron.* oneself.

soin, *n.m.* care. **prendre s. de,** take care of.

soir, *n.m.* evening. **hier s.,** last night. **ce s.,** tonight. **le s.,** at night.

soirée, *n.f.* evening.

soit, *vb.* so be it. **s. . . . s.,** whether . . . or. **s. que,** whether.

soixante (-s-), *adj. and n.m.* sixty.

soixante-dix, *adj. and n.m.* seventy.

sol, *n.m.* earth, soil, ground.

solaire, *adj.* solar.

soldat, *n.m.* soldier.

solde, *n.m.* balance.

sole, *n.f.* sole.

solécisme, *n.m.* solecism.

soleil, *n.m.* sun, sunshine. **coucher du s.,** sunset. **lever du s.,** sunrise.

solennel, *adj.* solemn.

solenniser, *vb.* solemnize.

solennité, *n.f.* solemnity.

solidaire, *adj.* jointly binding.

solidariser, *vb.* **se s.,** unite, join together.

solidarité, *n.f.* joint responsibility.

solide, *adj. and n.m.* solid.

solidifier, *vb.* solidify.

solidité, *n.f.* solidity.

soliloque, *n.m.* soliloquy.

soliste, *n.m.* soloist.

solitaire, *adj.* lonely, lonesome.

solitude, *n.f.* solitude.

solliciter, *vb.* solicit, ask, apply.

sollicitude, *n.f.* solicitude.

soluble, *adj.* soluble.

solution, *n.f.* solution.

solvable, *adj.* solvent.

sombre, *adj.* dark, dim, gloomy, somber.

sombrer, *vb.* sink.

sommaire, *n.m.* summary.

sommation, *n.f.* appeal, summons.

somme, 1. *n.f.* amount, sum. **2.** *n.m.* nap.

sommeil, *n.m.* sleep. **avoir s.,** be sleepy.

sommeiller, *vb.* doze, slumber.

sommer, *vb.* summon.

sommet, *n.m.* top, peak, summit.

somnolence, *n.f.* drowsiness.

somnolent, *adj.* drowsy, sleepy.

somptueux, *adj.* lavish, sumptuous.

son *m.,* **sa** *f.,* **ses** *pl. adj.* his, her, its.

son, *n.m.* sound, ring; bran.

sonate, *n.f.* sonata.

sonder, *vb.* fathom; probe.

songe, *n.m.* dream.

songer à, *vb.* think of, dream.

songeur, *adj.* dreamy, thoughtful. **2.** *n.m.* dreamer.

sonner, *vb.* sound, ring, strike.

sonnerie, *n.f.* ringing.

sonnette, *n.f.* bell.

sonore, *adj.* sonorous.

sophiste, *n.m.* sophist.

soprano, *n.m.* soprano.

sorcellerie, *n.f.* sorcery.

sorcier, *n.m.* wizard.

sorcière, *n.f.* witch.

sordide, *adj.* sordid.

sort, *n.m.* lot.

sorte, *n.f.* sort, kind. **de s. que,** so that.

sortie, *n.f.* exit, way out.

sortilège, *n.m.* sorcery.

sortir, *vb.* go (come, get) out.

sot *m.,* **sotte** *f. adj.* silly, stupid, foolish, dumb.

sottise, *n.f.* foolishness.

sou, *n.m.* cent. **sans le s.,** penniless.

soubassement, *n.m.* basement.

soubresaut, *n.m.* bound, jerk.

souche, *n.f.* stub, stump.

souci, *n.m.* care, worry, concern.

soucier, *vb.* **se s. (de),** care, worry (about).

soucieux, *adj.* anxious.

soucoupe, *n.f.* saucer.

soudain, *adj.* sudden.

soudaineté, *n.f.* suddenness.

soude, *n.f.* soda.

souder, *vb.* solder, fuse.

souffle, *n.m.* breath.

souffler, *vb.* blow.

soufflet, *n.m.* bellows; blow, slap.

souffleter, *vb.* slap one's face.

souffrance(s), *n.f. (pl.)* misery, pain, suffering.

souffrir, *vb.* suffer, bear.

soufre, *n.m.* sulphur.

souhait, *n.m.* wish.

souhaiter, *vb.* wish for.

souiller, *vb.* soil, defile.

souillure, *n.f.* stain, dirt.

soulager, *vb.* relieve, alleviate.

soûler, *vb.* fill with food and drink, inebriate.

soulever, *vb.* lift, raise, arouse.

soulier, *n.m.* shoe.

souligner, *vb.* underline.

soumettre, *vb.* submit, subdue.

soumis, *adj.* obedient, submissive.

soumission, *n.f.* submission.

soupape, *n.f.* valve.

soupçon, *n.m.* suspicion.

soupçonner, *vb.* suspect.

soupçonneux, *adj.* suspicious.

soupe, *n.f.* soup.

souper, *n.m.* supper.

soupir, *n.m.* sigh.

soupirer, *vb.* sigh. **s. après,** yearn for.

souple, *adj.* flexible.

souplesse, *n.f.* suppleness, pliability.

source, *n.f.* source; spring.

sourcil, *n.m.* eyebrow.

sourciller, *vb.* frown.

sourcilleux, *adj.* haughty, disdainful.

sourd, *adj.* deaf.

sourd-muet, *n.m.* deaf mute.

souricière, *n.f.* (mouse)trap.

sourire, *n.m. and vb.* smile.

souris, *n.f.* mouse.

sournois, *adj.* sly.

sous, *prep.* under.

souscription, *n.f.* subscription.

souscrire, *vb.* subscribe.

sous-estimer, *vb.* underestimate.

sous-louer, *vb.* sublet.

sous-marin, *n.m.* submarine.

sous-produit, *n.m.* by-product.

soussigné, *adj.* undersigned.

sous-sol, *n.m.* basement.

sous-titre, *n.m.* subtitle.

soustraction, *n.f.* subtraction.

soustraire, *vb.* subtract.

soutane, *n.f.* cassock.

soute, *n.f.* storeroom.

soutenir, *vb.* support, uphold, maintain; claim; back up.

soutenu, *adj.* steady.

souterrain, *adj.* underground.

soutien, *n.m.* support.

soutien-gorge, *n.m.* brassière.

souvenance, *n.f.* recall, recollection.

souvenir, 1. *n.m.* remembrance, memory. **2.** *vb.* **se s. de,** remember.

souvent, *adv.* often.

souverain, *n.m.* ruler, sovereign.

souveraineté, *n.f.* sovereignty.

soyeux, *adj.* silky.

spacieux, *adj.* spacious.

spasme, *n.m.* spasm.

spatule, *n.f.* spatula.

spécial, *adj.* special.

spécialiser, *vb.* specialize.

spécialiste, *n.m.f.* specialist.

spécialité, *n.f.* specialty.

spécifier, *vb.* specify.

spécifique, *adj.* specific.

spécimen, *n.m.* specimen.

spectacle, *n.m.* sight, show.

spectaculaire, *adj.* spectacular.

spectateur, *n.m.* spectator.

spectre, *n.m.* ghost; spectrum.

spéculation, *n.f.* speculation.

spéculer, *vb.* speculate.

sphère, *n.f.* sphere.

spinal, *adj.* spinal.

spiral, *adj.* spiral.

spirale, *n.f.* spiral.

spirite, *n.m.f.* spiritualist.
spiritisme, *n.m.* spiritualism.
spirituel, *adj.* spiritual; witty.
spiritueux, *adj.* pertaining to alcohol.
splendeur, *n.f.* splendor.
splendide, *adj.* splendid.
spolier, *vb.* plunder, pillage.
spontané, *adj.* spontaneous.
spontanéité, *n.f.* spontaneity.
sporadique, *adj.* sporadic.
sport, *n.m.* sport.
sportif, *adj.* of sport.
squelette, *n.m.* skeleton.
stabiliser, *vb.* stabilize.
stabilité, *n.f.* stability.
stable, *adj.* stable, steady.
stage, *n.m.* period of probation.
stagflation, *n.f.* stagflation.
stagnant, *adj.* stagnant.
stalle, *n.f.* stall.
stance, *n.f.* stanza.
standardiste, *n.m.f.* phone operator.
station, *n.f.* stand, stop, station (subway).
stationnaire, *adj.* stationary.
stationner, *vb.* park.
statique, *adj.* static.
statistique, *n.f.* statistics.
statue, *n.f.* statue.
statuer, *vb.* decree, decide.
stature, *n.f.* stature.
statut, *n.m.* statute.
sténographe, *n.m.f.* stenographer.
sténographie, *n.f.* stenography.
stéréophonique, *adj.* stereophonic.
stérile, *adj.* barren.
stériliser, *vb.* sterilize.
stéthoscope, *n.m.* stethoscope.
stigmatiser, *vb.* mark, stigmatize.
stimulant, *n.m.* stimulus.
stimuler, *vb.* stimulate.
stipuler, *vb.* stipulate.
stoïque, *adj.* and *n.m.f.* stoic.
store, *n.m.* (window) shade, blind.
stratagème, *n.m.* stratagem.
stratégie, *n.f.* strategy.
stratégique, *adj.* strategic.
strict (-kt), *adj.* severe, strict.
strier, *vb.* mark, streak, groove.
structure, *n.f.* structure.
stuc, *n.m.* stucco.
studieux, *adj.* studious.
stupéfait, *adj.* astounded.
stupéfiant, *n.m.* narcotic, dope.

stupéfier, *vb.* astound.
stupeur, *n.f.* amazement.
stupide, *adj.* stupid.
stupidité, *n.f.* stupidity.
style, *n.m.* style.
styler, *vb.* train, teach.
stylet, *n.m.* stiletto.
stylographe, stylo, *n.m.* fountain pen.
suavité, *n.f.* suavity.
subalterne, *adj.* and *n.m.f.* junior (rank).
subdiviser, *vb.* subdivide.
subir, *vb.* undergo, bear.
subit, *adj.* sudden.
subjectif, *adj.* subjective.
subjonctif, *adj.* and *n.m.* subjunctive.
subjuguer, *vb.* subdue, overcome.
sublime, *adj.* sublime, exalted.
submerger, *vb.* submerge, flood.
subordonné, *adj.* and *n.m.* subordinate.
subordonner, *vb.* subordinate.
subreptice, *adj.* surreptitious.
subséquent, *adj.* subsequent.
subside, *n.m.* subsidy.
subsister, *vb.* subsist, live.
substance, *n.f.* substance.
substantiel, *adj.* substantial.
substantif, *n.m.* noun.
substituer, *vb.* substitute.
substitution, *n.f.* substitution.
subtil (-l), *adj.* subtle.
subtilité, *n.f.* subtlety.
subvention, *n.f.* grant, subsidy.
subventionner, *vb.* subsidize.
subversif, *adj.* subversive.
suc, *n.m.* juice.
succéder à, *vb.* succeed, follow.
succès, *n.m.* success; hit.
successeur, *n.m.* successor.
successif, *adj.* successive.
succession, *n.f.* succession.
succion, *n.f.* suction.
succomber, *vb.* succumb.
succursale, *n.f.* branch office.
sucer, *vb.* suck.
sucre, *n.m.* sugar.
sucrer, *vb.* add sugar.
sud (-d), *n.m.* south.
sudation, *n.f.* sweating.
sud-est, *n.m.* southeast.
sud-ouest, *n.m.* southwest.
Suède, *n.f.* Sweden.
Suédois, *n.m.* Swede.
suédois, *adj.* and *n.m.* Swedish.

suer, *vb.* sweat.

sueur, *n.m.* sweat.

suffire, *vb.* suffice.

suffisance, *n.f.* adequacy, conceit.

suffisant, *adj.* sufficient, adequate; conceited.

suffixe, *n.m.* suffix.

suffoquer, *vb.* suffocate.

suffrage, *n.m.* suffrage.

suggérer, *vb.* suggest.

suggestion, *n.f.* suggestion.

suicide, *n.m.* suicide.

suicider, *vb.* se s., kill oneself.

suie, *n.f.* soot.

suif, *n.m.* tallow.

suinter, *vb.* seep.

Suisse, 1. *n.m.* Swiss. **2.** *n.f.* Switzerland.

suisse, *adj.* Swiss.

suite, *n.f.* sequence; retinue; *(pl.)* results, aftermath. **et ainsi de s.,** and so on. **tout de s.,** at once.

suivant, 1. *n.m.* follower. **2.** *adj.* next, following, subsequent. **3.** *prep.* by, according to.

suivi, *adj.* followed, coherent.

suivre, *vb.* follow; attend. **faire s.,** forward.

sujet, 1. *n.m.* subject; topic. **2.** *adj.* subject. **s. à,** liable to.

sujétion, *n.f.* subjection, slavery.

superbe, *adj.* superb, magnificent.

superficie, *n.f.* surface.

superficiel, *adj.* superficial, shallow.

superflu, *adj.* superfluous.

supérieur, *adj. and n.m.* superior, higher, upper; senior.

supériorité, *n.f.* superiority.

superlatif, *adj. and n.m.* superlative.

superstar, *n.m.* superstar.

superstitieux, *adj.* superstitious.

superstition, *n.f.* superstition.

suppléant, *adj. and n.m.* assistant, substitute.

suppléer, *vb.* substitute.

supplément, *n.m.* supplement.

supplémentaire, *adj.* extra. **heures s.s,** overtime.

supplice, *n.m.* punishment, torture.

supplier, *vb.* beseech, entreat, beg, supplicate.

support, *n.m.* support, stand.

supporter, *vb.* support, bear, stand, endure.

supposer, *vb.* suppose, assume.

supposition, *n.f.* assumption, conjecture, supposition.

suppôt, *n.m.* implement, tool, agent.

suppression, *n.f.* suppression.

supprimer, *vb.* suppress, put down, take out.

supputation, *n.f.* computation.

supputer, *vb.* compute.

suprématie, *n.f.* supremacy.

suprême, *adj.* supreme.

sur, *prep.* on, upon, over.

surabonder, *vb.* be very abundant.

suranné, *adj.* out-of-date.

surcroît, *n.m.* addition.

surdité, *n.f.* deafness.

suret, *adj.* sour.

sûreté, *n.f.* safety, security, reliability.

surface, *n.f.* surface, area.

surgélateur, *n.m.* deep freeze.

surgir, *vb.* spring up, arise.

surhumain, *adj.* superhuman.

surintendant, *n.m.* superintendent.

sur-le-champ, *adv.* at once, immediately.

surmener, *vb.* overwork.

surmonter, *vb.* overcome, surmount.

surnaturel, *adj. and n.m.* supernatural.

surnom, *n.m.* nickname.

surpasser, *vb.* surpass.

surplis, *n.m.* surplice.

surplomber, *vb.* overhang.

surplus, *n.m.* surplus, excess.

surprendre, *vb.* surprise.

surprise, *n.f.* surprise.

sursaut, *n.m.* start.

sursauter, *vb.* give a start.

sursis, *n.m.* delay, putting off.

surtaxe, *n.f.* surtax.

surtout, 1. *n.m.* overcoat. **2.** *adv.* above all.

surveillance, *n.f.* supervision, watch.

surveillant, *n.m.* superintendent.

surveiller, *vb.* supervise, watch over.

survenir, *vb.* happen.

survie, *n.f.* survival.

survivance, *n.f.* survival.
survivre, *vb.* survive.
susceptible, *adj.* susceptible; liable.
suspect (-kt), *adj.* suspicious.
suspecter, *vb.* suspect.
suspendre, *vb.* suspend, hang, sling.
suspension, *n.f.* suspension.
suspicion, *n.f.* suspicion.
sustenter, *vb.* sustain, bulwark.
svelte, *adj.* slender, slim.
syllabe, *n.f.* syllable.
sylphide, *n.f.* sylph.
sylvestre, *adj.* sylvan, woody.
sylviculture, *n.f.* forestry.
symbole, *n.m.* symbol.
symboliser, *vb.* symbolize.
symétrie, *n.f.* symmetry.
sympathie, *n.f.* sympathy. **avoir de la s. pour,** like.
sympathique, *adj.* congenial, likeable.
sympathiser, *vb.* sympathize.
symphonie, *n.f.* symphony.
symptôme, *n.m.* symptom.
synchroniser, *vb.* synchronize.
syndical, *adj.* of a trade-union.
syndicat, *n.m.* syndicate. **s. ouvrier,** trade-union.
syndrome, *n.m.* syndrome.
synonyme, *n.m.* synonym.
syntaxe, *n.f.* syntax.
synthèse, *n.f.* synthesis.
synthétique, *adj.* synthetic.
systématique, *adj.* systematic.
système, *n.m.* system.

T

tabac (-bä), *n.m.* tobacco.
tabernacle, *n.m.* tabernacle.
table, *n.f.* table. **t. des matières,** index.
tableau, *n.m.* picture. **t. noir,** blackboard.
tabler, *vb.* count on, depend.
tablette, *n.f.* tablet.
tablier, *n.m.* apron.
tabou, *n.m.* taboo.
tabouret, *n.m.* stool.
tache, *n.f.* spot, stain, blot, smear.
tâche, *n.f.* task; assignment.
tacher, *vb.* spot, stain, blot.
tâcher, *vb.* try.

tacite, *adj.* tacit, silent.
taciturne, *adj.* unspeaking.
tact (-kt), *n.m.* tact.
tacticien, *n.m.* tactician.
tactique, 1. *adj.* of tactics, tactical. **2.** *n.f.* tactics.
taffetas, *n.m.* taffeta.
taie, *n.f.* pillowcase.
taillade, *n.f.* slash.
taille, *n.f.* waist, figure, size.
tailler, *vb.* trim, cut.
tailleur, *n.m.* tailor.
taire, *vb.* keep quiet. **se t.,** be silent.
talent, *n.m.* ability, talent.
talon, *n.m.* heel.
talus, *n.m.* slope.
tambour, *n.m.* drum.
tambourin, *n.m.* tambourine.
tamis, *n.m.* sieve.
tampon, *n.m.* plug, pad.
tamponner, *vb.* plug; run together.
tan, *n.m.* tan (leather).
tandis que, *conj.* while, whereas.
tangible, *adj.* tangible.
tanguer, *vb.* cover with pitch.
tant, *adv.* so much, so many. **t. que,** as long as.
tante, *n.f.* aunt.
tantième, *n.m.* part, percentage.
tantôt, *adv.* presently, soon.
tapage, *n.m.* din.
tapageur, *adj.* rowdy.
taper, *vb.* pat, knock, tap; type.
tapir, *vb.* **se t.,** squat, cower, lurk.
tapis, *n.m.* carpet, rug.
tapisserie, *n.f.* tapestry.
tapissier, *n.m.* upholsterer.
taquiner, *vb.* tease.
taquinerie, *n.f.* teasing.
tard, *adv.* late.
tarder, *vb.* delay.
tardif, *adj.* slow, tardy, late.
tarière, *n.f.* auger.
tarif, *n.m.* scale of charges; rate; fare. **t. douanier,** tariff.
tartan, *n.m.* plaid.
tarte, *n.f.* pie.
tartre, *n.m.* tartar.
tas, *n.m.* heap, pile.
tasse, *n.f.* cup.
tasser, *vb.* pack, fill up.
tâter, *vb.* feel.
tâtonner, *vb.* grope.
taudis, *n.m.* hovel.
taupe, *n.f.* mole.

taureau, *n.m.* bull.

taux, *n.m.* rate.

taverne, *n.f.* tavern.

taxe, *n.f.* tax. **t. (à la) valeur ajou-tée,** value-added tax.

taxer, *vb.* tax, assess.

taxi, *n.m.* cab, taxi.

te, *n.m.* cab, taxi.

te (tə), *pron.* you, yourself.

technicien, *n.m.* technician.

technique, 1. *n.f.* technique. **2.** *adj.* technical.

technologie, *n.f.* technology.

teindre, *vb.* dye.

teint, *n.m.* complexion.

teinte, *n.f.* tint, shade.

teinter, *vb.* tint, stain.

teinture, *n.f.* dye.

teinturier, *n.m.* dry-cleaner, dyer.

tel, *adj.* such.

télégramme, *n.m.* telegram.

télégraphe, *n.m.* telegraph.

télégraphie, *n.f.* telegraphy. **t. sans fil,** *abbrev.* **T.S.F.,** radio, wireless.

télégraphier, *vb.* telegraph.

téléphone, *n.m.* telephone. **coup de t.,** ring.

téléphoner, *vb.* telephone.

télescope, *n.m.* telescope.

télescoper, *vb.* crash, run to-gether.

télévision, *n.f.* television.

tellement, *adv.* so much.

téméraire, *adj.* rash.

témoignage, *n.m.* testimony, to-ken.

témoigner, *vb.* testify.

témoin, *n.m.* witness.

tempe, *n.f.* temple.

tempérament, *n.m.* temper, tem-perament.

tempérance, *n.f.* temperance.

tempérant, *adj.* temperate.

température, *n.f.* temperature.

tempéré, *adj.* temperate.

tempérer, *vb.* moderate, calm, lessen.

tempête, *n.f.* storm, tempest.

tempétueux, *adj.* tempestuous.

temple, *n.m.* temple.

temporaire, *adj.* temporary.

temporiser, *vb.* temporize, evade.

temps (tän), *n.m.* time; weather.

tenace, *adj.* tenacious.

ténacité, *n.f.* tenacity.

tenailles, *n.f.pl.* tongs.

tendance, *n.f.* tendency, trend, leaning.

tendre, 1. *adj.* tender, fond, lov-ing. **2.** *vb.* tend, extend.

tendresse, *n.f.* tenderness, fond-ness.

tendu, *adj.* tense; uptight.

ténèbres, *n.f.pl.* gloom, darkness.

ténébreux, *adj.* dismal.

teneur, *n.m.* **t. de livres,** book-keeper.

tenir, *vb.* hold.

tennis (-s), *n.m.* tennis.

ténor, *n.m.* tenor.

tension, *n.f.* strain; stress.

tentacule, *n.m.* tentacle.

tentatif, *adj.* tentative.

tentation, *n.f.* temptation.

tentative, *n.f.* attempt.

tente, *n.f.* tent; awning.

tenter, *vb.* tempt, try, attract.

tenture, *n.f.* wallcovering.

tenue, *n.f.* rig; conduct, manners.

ténuité, *n.f.* tenuity, unimpor-tance.

térébenthine, *n.f.* turpentine.

terme, *n.m.* term, period; end.

terminaison, *n.f.* ending.

terminer, *vb.* end.

terminologie, *n.f.* terminology.

terminus, *n.m.* terminus.

terne, *adj.* drab, dull, dim, dingy.

ternir, *vb.* tarnish, dull.

terrain, *n.m.* ground(s).

terrasse, *n.f.* terrace.

terrasser, *vb.* heap up, embank; knock down, conquer.

terre, *n.f.* earth, ground, land. **pomme de t.,** potato. **à t.,** ashore.

terrestre, *adj.* earthly.

terreur, *n.f.* terror, fright, fear.

terrible, *adj.* terrible, awful, tre-mendous.

terrifier, *vb.* terrify.

territoire, *n.m.* territory.

terroir, *n.m.* soil.

terroriser, *vb.* terrorize.

tertre, *n.m.* mound.

tesson, *n.m.* broken piece, frag-ment.

testament, *n.m.* testament, will.

testateur, *n.m.* testator.

tête, *n.f.* head. **tenir t. à,** cope with.

téter, *vb.* suck.

téton, *n.m.* breast.

texte, *n.m.* text.

textile, *adj.* textile.

textuel, *adj.* textual.

texture, *n.f.* texture.

thé, *n.m.* tea.

théâtral, *adj.* theatrical.

théâtre, *n.m.* theater.

théière, *n.f.* teapot.

thème, *n.m.* theme.

théologie, *n.f.* theology.

théorie, *n.f.* theory.

théorique, *adj.* theoretical.

thermomètre, *n.m.* thermometer.

thésauriser, *vb.* hoard.

thèse, *n.f.* thesis.

thym, *n.m.* thyme.

ticket, *n.m.* check, ticket, coupon.

tiède, *adj.* lukewarm.

tiédir, *vb.* make or become cool.

tien, *pron.* **le tien, la tienne,** yours.

tiers, *n.m.* third.

Tiers Monde, *n.m.* Third World.

tige, *n.f.* stem, stalk.

tigre, *n.m.* tiger.

tilleul, *n.m.* linden, limetree.

timbre, *n.m.* stamp. **t.-poste,** postage stamp.

timbrer, *vb.* stamp.

timide, *adj.* timid, shy, coy, bashful.

timidité, *n.f.* timidity.

timoré, *adj.* timorous.

tintamarre, *n.m.* racket.

tinter, *vb.* ring, knell, tinkle.

tirailleur, *n.m.* sharpshooter.

tire, *n.f.* pull, yank.

tire-bouchon, *n.m.* corkscrew.

tirer, *vb.* draw, pull; shoot.

tiret, *n.m.* blank.

tiroir, *n.m.* drawer.

tisane, *n.f.* drink, broth.

tisser, *vb.* weave.

tisserand, *n.m.* weaver.

tissu, *n.m.* web; cloth, fabric.

titre, *n.m.* title, right.

titrer, *vb.* invest with a title.

toast (-t), *n.m.* toast.

toaster, *vb.* toast.

toile, *n.f.* web; canvas; linen.

toilette, *n.f.* toilet; dressing, dress.

toison, *n.f.* fleece.

toit, *n.m.* roof.

toiture, *n.f.* roofing.

tolérance, *n.f.* tolerance.

tolérer, *vb.* tolerate, bear.

tomate, *n.f.* tomato.

tombe, *n.f.* grave.

tombeau, *n.m.* tomb.

tombée, *n.f.* fall, decline.

tomber, *vb.* fall. **laisser t.,** drop.

ton, *n.m.* tone, pitch.

ton *m.,* **ta** *f.,* **tes** *pl. adj.* your.

tondeuse, *n.f.* (lawn) mower.

tondre, *vb.* shear; mow.

tonique, *adj. and n.m.* tonic.

tonne, *n.f.* ton; barrel.

tonneau, *n.m.* cask, barrel.

tonner, *vb.* thunder.

tonnerre, *n.m.* thunder.

topaze, *n.f.* topaz.

topographie, *n.f.* topography.

torche, *n.f.* torch.

tordre, *vb.* twist, wrench, wring. **se t.,** writhe.

torpeur, *n.f.* torpor.

torpille, *n.f.* torpedo.

torrent, *n.m.* torrent.

torride, *adj.* torrid.

torse, *n.m.* torso.

tort, *n.m.* wrong. **avoir t.,** be wrong.

tortiller, *vb.* twist, wiggle.

tortu, *adj.* crooked.

tortue, *n.f.* turtle, tortoise.

torture, *n.f.* torture.

torturer, *vb.* torture.

tôt, *adv.* soon, early.

total, *adj. and n.m.* total.

totalisateur, *n.m.* adding machine.

totaliser, *vb.* total, add up.

totalitaire, *adj.* totalitarian.

totalité, *n.f.* entirety.

touchant, *prep.* concerning.

touche, *n.f.* key.

toucher, 1. *n.m.* touch. **2.** *vb.* touch; collect; affect; border on.

touffe, *n.f.* tuft, bunch.

touffu, *adj.* bushy.

toujours, *adv.* always, still, ever, yet.

toupie, *n.f.* top (child's toy).

tour, 1. *n.m.* turn; trick; stroll. **faire le t. de,** go around. **2.** *n.f.* tower.

tourbe, *n.f.* rabble.

tourbillon, *n.m.* whirl. **t. d'eau,** whirlpool. **t. de vent,** whirlwind.

tourbillonner, *vb.* whirl.

tourelle, *n.f.* turret.

touriste, *n.m.f.* tourist.

tourment, *n.m.* torment.

tourmenter, *vb.* torment.
tourne-disques, *n.m.* record player.
tournedos, *n.f.* beefsteak.
tournée, *n.f.* round.
tourner, *vb.* turn, revolve, spin.
tournesol, *n.m.* sunflower.
tournevis, *n.m.* screwdriver.
tournoi, *n.m.* tournament.
tournure, *n.f.* figure.
tousser, *vb.* cough.
tout, 1. *adj.m.*, **toute** *f.*, **tous** *m.pl.*, **toutes** *f.pl.* all, each, every. 2. *pron.* everything. **t. les deux**, both. **t. d'un coup**, all at once. **t. de même**, all the same. **pas du t.**, not at all.
toutefois, *adv.* however.
tout-puissant, *adj.* almighty.
toux, *n.f.* cough.
toxique, *adj.* toxic.
tracasser, *vb.* worry.
trace, *n.f.* trace, step, track, footprint.
tracer, *vb.* outline, trace.
tracteur, *n.m.* tractor.
traction, *n.f.* traction.
tradition, *n.f.* tradition.
traditionnel, *adj.* traditional.
traducteur, *n.m.* translator.
traduction, *n.f.* translation.
traduire, *vb.* translate.
trafic, *n.m.* traffic.
trafiquer, *vb.* traffic, carry on dealings.
tragédie, *n.f.* tragedy.
tragique, *adj.* tragic.
trahir, *vb.* betray.
trahison, *n.f.* treason.
train, *n.m.* train.
traînard, *n.m.* loiterer, dawdler.
traîne, *n.f.* train of dress.
traîneau, *n.m.* sled, sleigh.
traîner, *vb.* drag, haul.
traire, *vb.* milk.
trait, *n.m.* feature; draft; shot. **t. d'union**, hyphen.
traité, *n.m.* treaty.
traitement, *n.m.* treatment.
traiter, *vb.* treat, deal.
traître, *n.m.* traitor.
traîtrise, *n.f.* treachery.
trajet, *n.m.* crossing.
trame, *n.f.* web (woof); plan, plot.
tramer, *vb.* devise.
tramway, *n.m.* streetcar.

tranchant, *adj.* sharp, crisp.
tranche, *n.f.* slice.
tranchée, *n.f.* trench.
trancher, *vb.* cut.
tranquille (-l-), *adj.* quiet. **laisser t.**, leave alone.
tranquilliser (-l-l-), *vb.* soothe, make tranquil.
tranquillité (-l-l-), *n.f.* quiet, stillness.
transaction, *n.f.* transaction.
transe, *n.f.* fright, fear.
transférer, *vb.* transfer.
transformer, *vb.* transform.
transfuser, *vb.* transfuse.
transfusion, *n.f.* transfusion.
transition (-z-), *n.f.* transition.
transitoire (-z-), *adj.* transitory.
transmettre, *vb.* transmit, convey, send.
transparent, *adj.* transparent.
transpiration, *n.f.* perspiration.
transpirer, *vb.* perspire.
transplanter, *vb.* transplant.
transport, *n.m.* transfer, transport, transportation; bliss, ecstasy.
transporter, *vb.* transport, transfer, convey.
transposer, *vb.* transpose.
transsexuel, *adj.* transsexual.
travail, *n.m.* work, job, labor.
travailler, *vb.* work.
travailleur, 1. *n.m.* worker, laborer. 2. *adj.* industrious.
travée, *n.f.* span.
travers, *n.m.* breadth. **à t.**, across, through. **de t.**, askance, awry.
traversée, *n.f.* crossing.
traverser, *vb.* cross.
traversin, *n.m.* bolster.
travesti, *adj.* transvestite.
travestir, *vb.* disguise.
trébucher, *vb.* stumble, trip.
trèfle, *n.m.* clover; club (cards).
treillis, *n.m.* denim.
treize, *adj. and n.m.* thirteen.
tréma, *n.m.* dieresis.
tremblement, *n.m.* trembling. **t. de terre**, earthquake.
trembler, *vb.* tremble, shake, quake.
trembloter, *vb.* quiver.
trémousser, *vb.* flutter.
trempe, *n.f.* temper, cast.
tremper, *vb.* soak, drench, temper.

trente, *adj. and n.m.* thirty.

trépasser, *vb.* die.

trépied, *n.m.* tripod, trivet.

très, *adv.* very.

trésor, *n.m.* treasure, treasury; darling.

trésorier, *n.m.* treasurer.

tressaillement, *n.m.* thrill; start.

tressaillir, *vb.* thrill; start.

tresse, *n.f.* braid.

tresser, *vb.* braid.

tréteau, *n.m.* trestle.

trève, *n.f.* truce.

triangle, *n.m.* triangle.

tribade, *n.f.* Lesbian.

tribu, *n.f.* tribe.

tribulation, *n.f.* tribulation.

tribut, *n.m.* tribute.

tributaire, *adj.* tributary.

tricher, *vb.* cheat.

tricherie, *n.f.* cheating.

tricoter, *vb.* knit.

trier, *vb.* sort.

trimestre, *n.m.* term.

trimestriel, *adj.* quarterly.

trinquer, *vb.* touch glasses in making a toast.

triomphant, *adj.* triumphant.

triomphe, *n.m.* triumph.

triompher, *vb.* triumph.

triple, *adj. and n.m.* triple.

tripoter, *vb.* fiddle with, dabble in; bother.

triste, *adj.* sad.

tristesse, *n.f.* sadness.

trivial, *adj.* trivial.

trivialité, *n.f.* triviality.

troc, *n.m.* barter.

trois, *adj. and n.m.* three.

troisième, *adj.* third.

trompe, *n.f.* horn, trumpet, elephant's trunk.

trompe l'œil, *n.m.* make-believe, sham.

tromper, *vb.* deceive, cheat. **se t.,** be wrong, make a mistake.

tromperie, *n.f.* deceit.

trompette, *n.f.* trumpet.

trompeur, *adj.* deceitful.

tronc, *n.m.* trunk.

trône, *n.m.* throne.

trop, *adv.* too; too much, too many.

trophée, *n.m.* trophy.

tropical, *adj.* tropical.

tropique, *n.m.* tropic.

troquer, *vb.* barter, dicker, trade.

trot, *n.m.* trot.

trotter, *vb.* trot.

trottiner, *vb.* trot, jog.

trottoir, *n.m.* sidewalk.

trou, *n.m.* hole.

trouble, *n.m.* disturbance, riot.

troublé, *adj.* anxious, worried.

troubler, *vb.* perturb.

trouer, *vb.* pierce, bore.

troupe, *n.f.* troop.

troupeau, *n.m.* herd, flock, drove.

troupier, *n.m.* soldier, trooper.

trousseau, *n.m.* bunch; outfit.

trousser, *vb.* truss up, turn up.

trouvaille, *n.f.* discovery.

trouver, *vb.* find. **se t.,** be located.

truc, *n.m.* trick; thing.

truelle, *n.f.* trowel.

truite, *n.f.* trout.

truquer, *vb.* fake.

trust, *n.m.* trust.

T.S.F., *n.f.* radio.

tu, *pron.* you.

tube, *n.m.* tube, pipe.

tuberculeux, *adj.* tuberculous.

tuberculose, *n.f.* tuberculosis.

tuer, *vb.* kill.

tuerie, *n.f.* slaughter, massacre.

tuile, *n.f.* tile.

tulipe, *n.f.* tulip.

tuméfier, *vb.* make swollen.

tumulte, *n.m.* tumult, turmoil, uproar.

tunique, *n.f.* tunic.

tunnel, *n.m.* tunnel.

Turc *m.,* **Turque** *f. n.* Turk.

turc, *n.m.* Turkish (language).

turc *m.,* **turque** *f. adj.* Turkish.

Turquie, *n.f.* Turkey.

tutelle, *n.f.* tutelage, protection.

tuteur, *n.m.* guardian.

tutoyer, *vb.* use "tu" (familiar form) to.

tuyau, *n.f.* pipe; hose.

tympan, *n.m.* eardrum.

type, *n.m.* type; fellow, guy.

typique, *adj.* typical.

tyran, *n.m.* tyrant.

tyrannie, *n.f.* tyranny.

tyranniser, *vb.* tyrannize.

tzigane, *n.* gypsy.

U

ubiquité, *n.f.* ubiquity.

ulcère, *n.m.* ulcer.

ultérieur, *adj.* ulterior, further.
ultime, *adj.* ultimate, last.
un *m.,* **une** *f.* **1.** *art. a.* **2.** *adj. and n.m.* one.
unanime, *adj.* unanimous.
unanimité, *n.f.* unanimity.
unifier, *vb.* unify.
uniforme, *adj. and n.m.* uniform.
union, *n.f.* union.
unique, *adj.* unique; only.
unir, *vb.* unite.
unisexuel, *adj.* unisex.
unisson, *n.m.* unison.
unité, *n.f.* unit, unity.
univers, *n.m.* universe.
universel, *adj.* universal.
université, *n.f.* university, college.
urbain, *adj.* urban.
urgence, *n.f.* urgency.
urgent, *adj.* urgent, pressing.
urne, *n.f.* urn; ballot box.
urticaire, *n.f.* hives.
usage, *n.m.* use; custom.
usager, *adj.* for daily use.
usé, *adj.* shabby, worn-out.
user, *vb.* wear out.
usine, *n.f.* factory.
ustensile, *n.f.* utensil.
usuel, *adj.* usual.
usure, *n.f.* wear and tear; usury; interest.
usurper, *vb.* usurp.
utile, *adj.* helpful, useful.
utilisation, *n.f.* use.
utiliser, *vb.* use.
utilité, *n.f.* utility.
utopie, *n.f.* utopia.

V

vacance, *n.* vacancy; *(pl.)* vacation.
vacarme, *n.m.* uproar.
vaccin, *n.m.* vaccine.
vacciner, *vb.* vaccinate.
vache, *n.f.* cow.
vaciller (-l-), *vb.* waver.
vacuité, *n.f.* emptiness, vacuity.
vagabond, *adj.* vagrant.
vagabonder, *vb.* roam, tramp.
vague, 1. *n.f.* wave. **2.** *adj.* vague.
vaguer, *vb.* wander.
vaillant, *adj.* valiant, brave, gallant.
vain, *adj.* idle, vain, futile.
vaincre, *vb.* defeat.

vainqueur, *n.m.* victor.
vaisseau, *n.m.* ship.
vaisselle, *n.f.* dishes.
valeur, *n.f.* valor; value, worth; *(pl.)* securities.
valeureux, *adj.* brave, valorous.
valide, *adj.* valid.
valise, *n.f.* suitcase.
vallée, *n.f.* valley.
vallon, *n.m.* valley, vale.
valoir, *vb.* be worth. **v. mieux,** be better.
valse, *n.f.* waltz.
vandale, *n.m.f.* vandal.
vanille, *n.f.* vanilla.
vanité, *n.f.* conceit, vanity.
vaniteux, *adj.* vain.
vantard, *adj.* boastful.
vanter, *vb.* extol. **se v.,** boast, brag.
vapeur, 1. *n.m.* steamship. **2.** *n.f.* vapor, steam.
vaporisateur, *n.f.* vaporizer, spray.
variation, *n.f.* variation, change.
varicelle, *n.f.* chicken-pox.
varier, *vb.* vary.
variété, *n.f.* variety.
variole, *n.f.* smallpox.
vase, *n.m.* vase, jar, pot.
vasectomie, *n.f.* vasectomy.
vaseux, *adj.* slimy.
vassal, *n.m.* vassal.
vaste, *adj.* vast, spacious.
vaurien, *n.m.* worthless person, idler.
veau, *n.m.* calf.
végéter, *vb.* vegetate.
véhicule, *n.m.* vehicle.
veille, *n.f.* eve, day before.
veiller, *vb.* watch over, sit up.
veine, *n.f.* vein; luck.
velours, *n.m.* velvet. **v. côtelé,** corduroy.
velouté, *adj.* like velvet.
velu, *adj.* hairy.
vendange, *n.f.* vintage.
vendeur, *n.m.* seller; clerk, salesman.
vendre, *vb.* sell.
vendredi, *n.m.* Friday.
vénéneux, *adj.* poisonous.
vénérer, *vb.* venerate.
vengeance, *n.f.* revenge.
venger, *vb.* avenge. **se v.,** get revenge.
venimeux, *adj.* poisonous.

venin, *n.m.* poison.

venir, *vb.* come. **v. de,** have just. **. . . à v.,** forthcoming.

vent, *n.m.* wind.

vente, *n.f.* sale.

venteux, *adj.* windy.

ventilateur, *n.m.* fan.

ventiler, *vb.* ventilate.

ventre, *n.m.* belly.

venue, *n.f.* advent, arrival.

vêpres, *n.f.pl.* vespers.

ver (-r), *n.m.* worm.

véracité, *n.f.* veracity.

véranda, *n.f.* porch.

verbe, *n.m.* verb.

verbeux, *adj.* wordy, verbose.

verdeur, *n.f.* greenness, sharpness, vigor.

verdict (-kt), *n.m.* verdict.

verdir, *vb.* make or become green.

verge, *n.f.* rod.

verger, *n.m.* orchard.

vérification, *n.f.* check.

vérifier, *vb.* check, confirm.

véritable, *adj.* genuine, real.

vérité, *n.f.* truth.

vermine, *n.f.* vermin.

vernir, *vb.* varnish.

vernis, *n.m.* varnish.

vérole, *n.f.* **petite v.,** smallpox.

verre, *n.m.* glass.

verrou, *n.m.* bolt.

verrouiller, *vb.* bolt.

vers, 1. *n.m.* verse. **2.** *prep.* toward.

verse, *adj.* **tomber à v.,** pour.

verser, *vb.* pour, shed.

versifier, *vb.* versify.

version, *n.f.* version, translation.

vert, *adj.* green.

vertical, *adj.* upright, vertical.

vertige, *n.m.* dizziness.

vertigineux, *adj.* dizzy.

vertu, *n.f.* virtue.

vertueux, *adj.* virtuous.

verveux, *adj.* lively, animated.

vessie, *n.f.* bladder.

veste, *n.f.* jacket.

vestiaire, *n.m.* cloak-room.

vestibule, *n.m.* hall, lobby.

vestige, *n.m.* vestige, remains.

veston, *n.m.* jacket, coat.

vêtement, *n.m.* garment; *(pl.)* clothes.

vétéran, *n.m.* veteran.

vétérinaire, *adj.* veterinary.

vêtir, *vb.* clothe.

véto, *n.m.* veto.

veuf, *n.m.* widower.

veuve, *n.f.* widow.

vexation, *n.f.* vexation.

vexer, *vb.* vex.

viaduc, *n.m.* viaduct.

viande, *n.f.* meat.

vibrant, *adj.* vibrant, vibrating.

vibration, *n.f.* vibration.

vibrer, *vb.* vibrate.

vicaire, *n.m.* vicar.

vice, *n.m.* vice.

vice-roi, *n.m.* viceroy.

vicieux, *adj.* vicious.

vicomte, *n.m.* viscount.

victime, *n.f.* victim.

victoire, *n.f.* victory.

victorieux, *adj.* victorious.

vidange, *n.f.* emptying, cleaning.

vide, 1. *n.m.* emptiness, vacuum, blank, gap. **2.** *adj.* empty, void, vacant, blank.

vidéodisque, *n.m.* videodisc.

vider, *vb.* empty, drain.

vie, *n.f.* life.

vieil, *adj.* old.

vieillard, *n.m.* old man.

vieille, 1. *n.f.* old woman. **2.** *adj. (f.)* old.

vieillesse, *n.f.* old age.

vieillir, *vb.* age.

vierge, *n.f.* virgin.

vieux, *adj.m.* old.

vif *m.,* **vive** *f. adj.* lively, quick, brisk, bright, vivacious.

vif-argent, *n.m.* quicksilver.

vigie, *n.f.* lookout man or station.

vigilance, *n.f.* vigilance.

vigilant, *adj.* watchful.

vigne, *n.f.* vine; vineyard.

vigoureux, *adj.* lusty, hardy, vigorous.

vigueur, *n.f.* vigor, force.

vil (-l), *adj.* vile.

vilain, *adj.* ugly, mean, wicked.

village (-l-), *n.m.* village.

ville (-l), *n.f.* city, town.

villégiature (-l-), *n.f.* country holiday.

vin, *n.m.* wine.

vinaigre, *n.m.* vinegar.

vindicatif, *adj.* vindictive.

vingt (văn), *adj.* and *n.m.* twenty.

vingtaine (văn-), *n.f.* score.

vingtième (văn-), *adj.* and *n.m.* twentieth.

violateur, *n.m.* violator.
violation, *n.f.* violation.
violemment, *adj.* violently.
violence, *n.f.* violence.
violent, *adj.* violent.
violer, *vb.* violate.
violet, *adj.* purple, violet.
violette, *n.f.* violet.
violon, *n.m.* violin.
vipère, *n.f.* viper.
virgule, *n.f.* comma.
viril (-l), *adj.* manly.
virilité, *n.f.* manhood.
virtuel, *adj.* virtual.
virtuose, *n.m.f.* virtuoso.
virus (-s), *n.m.* virus.
vis (-s), *n.f.* screw.
visa, *n.m.* visa.
visage, *n.m.* face.
vis-à-vis, *adv.* opposite, across
from.
viser, *vb.* aim.
visibilité, *n.f.* visibility.
visible, *adj.* visible.
visière, *n.f.* visor; keenness.
vision, *n.f.* vision.
visionnaire, *adj. and n.m.f.* vi-
sionary.
visite, *n.f.* call, visit.
visiter, *vb.* visit.
visiteur, *n.m.* visitor.
visqueux, *adj.* viscous, sticky.
visser, *vb.* screw.
visuel, *adj.* visual.
vital, *adj.* vital.
vitalité, *n.f.* vitality.
vitamine, *n.f.* vitamin.
vite, *adv.* quick, fast.
vitesse, *n.f.* speed, rate; gear.
changer de v., shift gears.
vitrail, *n.m.* (church) window.
vitre, *n.f.* pane.
vitrine, *n.f.* display case, shop-
window.
vitupération, *n.f.* vituperation.
vivace, *adj.* long-lived; perennial
(of plant).
vivacité, *n.f.* vivacity.
vivant, *adj.* alive.
vivement, *adv.* quickly, smartly,
vividly.
vivre, *vb.* live.
vocabulaire, *n.m.* vocabulary.
vocal, *adj.* vocal.
vocation, *n.f.* vocation.
vœu (vœ), *n.m.* vow.
vogue, *n.f.* vogue.

voici, *vb.* here is, behold.
voie, *n.f.* track, road. **v. d'eau,**
leak.
voilà, *vb.* there is; behold.
voile, *n.m.* veil; sail.
voiler, *vb.* veil, hide.
voilure, *n.f.* sails.
voir, *vb.* see. **faire v.,** show.
voirie, *n.f.* dump.
voisin, 1. *n.m.* neighbor. **2.** *adj.*
nearby, adjoining.
voisinage, *n.m.* neighborhood.
voisiner, *vb.* act like a neighbor.
voiture, *n.f.* car, carriage. **en v.!,**
all aboard!
voix, *n.f.* voice.
vol, *n.m.* flight; theft, robbery;
ripoff.
volage, *adj.* fickle.
volaille, *n.f.* fowl, poultry.
volatil, *adj.* volatile.
volcan, *n.m.* volcano.
volcanique, *adj.* volcanic.
volée, *n.f.* flight, covey; herd.
voler, *vb.* fly; steal, rob; rip off.
volet, *n.m.* shutter, blind.
voleur, *n.m.* thief, robber.
vol frété, *n.m.* charter flight.
volontaire, 1. *n.m.* volunteer. **2.**
adj. voluntary, volunteer.
volonté, *n.f.* will.
volontiers, *adv.* gladly, willingly.
voltigement, *n.m.* flutter.
voltiger, *vb.* flutter; hover.
volubilité, *n.f.* volubility, glibness.
volume, *n.m.* volume.
volumineux, *adj.* bulky.
volupté, *n.f.* pleasure, voluptu-
ousness.
vomir, *vb.* vomit.
vorace, *adj.* voracious.
votant, *n.m.* voter.
vote, *n.m.* vote.
voter, *vb.* vote.
votre *sg.,* **vos** *pl. adj.* your.
vôtre, *pron.* **le v.,** yours.
vouer, *vb.* vow.
vouloir, *vb.* want, wish, will. **v.
dire,** mean. **v. savoir,** wonder. **v.
bien,** be willing. **en v. à,** bear a
grudge against.
vous, *pron.* you, yourself.
voûte, *n.f.* vault.
voûter, *vb.* arch.
voyage, *n.m.* journey, trip.
voyager, *vb.* travel.

voyageur, *n.m.* traveler, passenger.

voyageur de banlieue, *n.m.* commuter.

voyant, 1. *n.m.* clairvoyant. **2.** *adj.* gaudy, flashy.

voyelle, *n.f.* vowel.

vrai, *adj.* true, real.

vraisemblable, *adj.* probable, likely.

vraisemblance, *n.f.* probability.

vue, *n.f.* view, sight.

vue d'ensemble, *n.f.* overview.

vulcaniser, *vb.* vulcanize.

vulgaire, *adj.* vulgar, coarse, rude.

vulgarité, *n.f.* vulgarity.

vulnérable, *adj.* vulnerable.

W, X, Y, Z

wagon, *n.m.* coach, car.

wagon-lits, *n.m.* sleeping car.

wagon-restaurant, *n.m.* diner, dining-car.

watt, *n.m.* watt.

xérès (ks-), *n.m.* sherry.

xylophone (ks-), *n.m.* xylophone.

y, *adv.* there, in it, to it.

yacht, *n.m.* yacht.

zèbre, *n.m.* zebra.

zèle, *n.m.* zeal.

zélé, *adj.* zealous.

zénith, *n.m.* zenith.

zéro, *n.m.* zero.

zézayer, *vb.* lisp.

zibeline, *n.f.* sable.

zigzaguer, *vb.* zigzag.

zodiaque, *n.m.* zodiac.

zone, *n.f.* zone, district.

zoologie, *n.f.* zoology.

zoologique, *adj.* zoological. **jardin z.,** zoo.

ENGLISH-FRENCH

A

a, *art.* un *m.*, une *f.*
aardvark, *n.* aardvark *m.*
abacus, *n.* abaque *m.*
abandon, *vb.* abandonner.
abandon, *n.* abandon *m.*
abandoned, *adj.* abandonné.
abandonment, *n.* abandon *m.*
abase, *vb.* abaisser; avilir.
abasement, *n.* abaissement *m.*; avilissement *m.*
abash, *vb.* déconcerter.
abate, *vb.* diminuer.
abatement, *n.* diminution *f.*
abbess, *n.* abbesse *f.*
abbey, *n.* abbaye *f.*
abbot, *n.* abbé *m.*
abbreviate, *vb.* abréger.
abbreviation, *n.* abréviation *f.*
abdicate, *vb.* abdiquer.
abdication, *n.* abdication *f.*
abdomen, *n.* abdomen *m.*
abdominal, *adj.* abdominal.
abduct, *vb.* enlever.
abduction, *n.* enlèvement *m.*
abductor, *n.* ravisseur *m.*
aberrant, *adj.* aberrant, égaré.
aberration, *n.* égarement *m.*
abet, *vb.* aider, encourager, appuyer.
abetment, *n.* encouragement *m.*, appui *m.*
abettor, *n.* aide *m.*, complice *m.*
abeyance, *n.* suspension *f.*
abhor, *vb.* détester.
abhorrence, *n.* aversion extrême *f.*, horreur *f.*
abhorrent, *adj.* odieux, répugnant (à).
abide, *vb.* (tolerate) supporter; (remain) demeurer; (a. by the law) respecter la loi.
abiding, *adj.* constant, durable.
ability, *n.* talent *m.*
abject, *adj.* abject.
abjuration, *n.* abjuration *f.*
abjure, *vb.* abjurer, renoncer à.
abjurer, *n.* personne *f.* qui abjure.
ablative, *adj. and n.* ablatif *m.*

ablaze, *adj.* en feu, en flammes.
able, *adj.* capable; (to be a.) pouvoir.
able-bodied, *adj.* fort, robuste.
able-bodied seaman, *n.* marin de première classe *m.*
ablution, *n.* ablution *f.*
ably, *adv.* capablement.
abnegate, *vb.* nier.
abnegation, *n.* abnégation *f.*
abnormal, *adj.* anormal.
abnormality, *n.* irrégularité *f.*
abnormally, *adv.* anormalement.
aboard, 1. *adv.* (*naut.*) à bord; (all a.) en voiture. **2.** *prep.* à bord de.
abode, *n.* demeure *f.*
abolish, *vb.* abolir.
abolishment, *n.* abolissement *m.*
abolition, *n.* abolition *f.*
abominable, *adj.* abominable.
abominate, *vb.* abominer.
abomination, *n.* abomination *f.*
aboriginal, *adj.* aborigène, primitif.
abortion, *n.* avortement *m.*
abortive, *adj.* abortif, manqué.
abound, *vb.* abonder (en).
about, 1. *adv.* (approximately) à peu près; (around) autour; (to be a. to) être sur le point de. **2.** *prep.* (concerning) au sujet de; (near) auprès de; (around) autour de.
about-face, *n.* volte-face *f.*
above, 1. *adv.* au-dessus. **2.** *prep.* (higher than) au-dessus de; (more than) plus de.
aboveboard, *adj. and adv.* ouvertement, franchement.
abrasion, *n.* abrasion *f.*
abrasive, *adj.* abrasif.
abreast, *adv.* de front.
abridge, *vb.* abréger.
abridgment, *n.* abrégé *m.*, réduction *f.*
abroad, *adv.* à l'étranger.
abrogate, *vb.* abroger.
abrogation, *n.* abrogation *f.*
abrupt, *adj.* brusque; (steep) escarpé.

abruptly, *adv.* brusquement, subitement.

abruptness, *n.* brusquerie *f.,* précipitation *f.*

abscess, *n.* abcès *m.*

abscond, *vb.* disparaître, se dérober.

absence, *n.* absence *f.*

absent, *adj.* absent.

absentee, *n.* absent *m.,* manquant *m.*

absinthe, *n.* absinthe *f.*

absolute, *adj.* absolu.

absolutely, *adv.* absolument.

absoluteness, *n.* pouvoir absolu *m.;* arbitraire *m.*

absolution, *n.* absolution *f.*

absolutism, *n.* absolutisme *m.*

absolve, *vb.* absoudre.

absorb, *vb.* absorber.

absorbed, *adj.* absorbé, préoccupé.

absorbent, *n. and adj.* absorbant *m.*

absorbing, *adj.* absorbant, préoccupant.

absorption, *n.* absorption *f.*

abstain from, *vb.* s'abstenir de.

abstemious, *adj.* abstème.

abstinence, *n.* abstinence *f.*

abstract, 1. *n.* (book) extrait *m.* **2.** *adj.* abstrait.

abstracted, *adj.* détaché, pensif.

abstraction, *n.* abstraction *f.*

abstruse, *adj.* caché, abstrus.

abundance, *n.* abondance *f.*

abundant, *adj.* abondant.

abundantly, *adv.* abondamment.

absurd, *adj.* absurde.

absurdity, *n.* absurdité *f.*

absurdly, *adv.* absurdement.

abuse, 1. *n.* (misuse) abus *m.;* (insult) injures *f.pl.* **2.** *vb.* abuser de, injurier.

abusive, *adj.* (insulting) injurieux.

abusively, *adv.* abusivement, injurieusement.

abut, *vb.* s'embrancher (sur), aboutir (à).

abutment, *n.* contrefort *m.;* (of a bridge) culée *f.*

abyss, *n.* abîme *m.*

academic, *adj.* académique.

academic freedom, *n.* liberté de l'enseignement *f.*

academy, *n.* académie *f.*

acanthus, *n.* acanthe *f.*

accede, *vb.* consentir.

accelerate, *vb.* accélérer.

acceleration, *n.* accélération *f.*

accelerator, *n.* accélérateur *m.*

accent, *n.* accent *m.*

accentuate, *vb.* accentuer.

accept, *vb.* accepter.

acceptability, *n.* acceptabilité *f.*

acceptable, *adj.* acceptable.

acceptably, *adv.* agréablement.

acceptance, *n.* acceptation *f.*

access, *n.* accès *m.*

accessible, *adj.* accessible.

accessory, *n. and adj.* accessoire *m.*

accident, *n.* accident *m.*

accidental, *adj.* accidentel.

accidentally, *adv.* accidentellement, par hasard.

acclaim, *vb.* acclamer.

acclamation, *n.* acclamation *f.*

acclimate, *vb.* acclimater.

acclivity, *n.* montée *f.,* rampe *f.*

accolade, *n.* accolade *f.*

accommodate, *vb.* (lodge) loger; (oblige) obliger.

accommodating, *adj.* accommodant, obligeant.

accommodation, *n.* (lodging) logement *m.*

accompaniment, *n.* accompagnement *m.*

accompanist, *n.* accompagnateur *m.,* accompagnatrice *f.*

accompany, *vb.* accompagner.

accomplice, *n.* complice *m.f.*

accomplish, *vb.* accomplir.

accomplished, *adj.* accompli, achevé.

accord, *n.* accord *m.*

accordance, *n.* conformité *f.*

accordingly, *adv.* (correspondingly) à l'avenant; (therefore) donc.

according to, *prep.* selon.

accordion, *n.* accordéon *m.*

accost, *vb.* aborder.

account, *n.* (comm.) compte *m.;* (narrative) récit *m.*

accountable for, *adj.* responsable de.

accountant, *n.* comptable *m.*

account for, *vb.* rendre compte de.

accounting, *n.* comptabilité *f.*

accouter, *vb.* habiller, équiper.

accouterments, n. équipements m.pl., accoutrements m.pl.

accredit, vb. accréditer.

accretion, n. accroissement m.

accrual, n. accroissement m.

accrue, vb. provenir.

accumulate, vb. entasser.

accumulation, n. entassement m.

accumulative, adj. (thing) qui s'accumule, (person) qui accumule.

accumulator, n. accumulateur m., accumulatrice f.

accuracy, n. précision f.

accurate, adj. précis.

accursed, adj. maudit, exécrable.

accusation, n. accusation f.

accusative, n. and adj. accusatif m.

accuse, vb. accuser.

accused, n. and adj. accusé m., accusée f.

accuser, n. accusateur m., accusatrice f.

accustom, vb. accoutumer.

accustomed, adj. accoutumé, habituel.

ace, n. as m.

acerbity, n. acerbité f., âpreté f.

acetate, n. acétate m.

acetic acid, n. acide acétique m.

acetylene, n. acétylène m.

ache, 1. n. douleur f. **2.** vb. faire mal à.

achieve, vb. accomplir.

achievement, n. accomplissement m.

acid, adj. and n. acide m.

acidify, vb. acidifier.

acidity, n. acidité f.

acidosis, n. acidose f.

acid test, n. épreuve concluante f.

acidulous, adj. acidulé.

acknowledge, vb. reconnaître; (a. receipt of) accuser réception de.

acme, n. comble m., apogée m.

acne, n. acné f.

acolyte, n. acolyte m.

acorn, n. gland m.

acoustics, n. acoustique f.

acquaint, vb. informer (de); (be a.d with) connaître.

acquaintance, n. connaissance f.

acquainted, adj. connu, familier (avec).

acquiesce in, vb. acquiescer à.

acquiescence, n. acquiescement m.

acquire, vb. acquérir.

acquirement, n. acquis m., acquisition f.

acquisition, n. acquisition f.

acquisitive, adj. porté à acquérir.

acquit, vb. acquitter.

acquittal, n. acquittement m.

acre, n. arpent m., acre f.

acreage, n. superficie f.

acrid, adj. âcre.

acrimonious, adj. acrimonieux.

acrimony, n. acrimonie f., aigreur f.

acrobat, n. acrobate m.f.

across, 1. prep. à travers; (on the other side of) de l'autre côté de. **2.** adv. en travers.

acrostic, n. acrostiche m.

act, 1. n. acte m. **2.** vb. (do) agir; (play) jouer; (behave) se conduire.

acting, 1. n. (theater) jeu m.; feinte f. **2.** adj. (taking the place of) suppléant; (comm.) gérant.

actinism, n. actinisme m.

actinium, n. actinium m.

action, n. action f.

activate, vb. activer.

activation, n. activation f.

activator, n. activateur m.

active, adj. actif.

activity, n. activité f.

actor, n. acteur m.

actress, n. actrice f.

actual, adj. réel.

actuality, n. réalité f., actualité f.

actually, adv. réellement, véritablement, en effet.

actuary, n. actuaire m.

actuate, vb. mettre en action, animer.

acumen, n. finesse f., pénétration f.

acupuncture, n. acuponcture f.

acute, adj. (geom.) aigu m., aiguë f.; (mind) fin.

acutely, adv. vivement, d'une manière poignante.

acuteness, n. finesse f., vivacité f.

adage, n. adage m., proverbe m.

adamant, adj. indomptable.

Adam's apple, n. pomme d'Adam f.

adapt, vb. adapter.

adaptable, adj. adaptable.

adaptability, n. faculté d'adaptation f.

adaptation, n. adaptation f.

adapter, n. qui adapte.

adaptive, adj. adaptable.

add, vb. (join) ajouter; (arith.) additionner.

adder, n. vipère f.

addict, n. personne adonnée à f.

addict oneself to, vb. s'adonner à.

addition, n. addition f.

additional, adj. additionel.

addle, 1. vb. corrompre, rendre couvi (of eggs). **2.** adj. couvi, pourri.

address, 1. n. (on letters, etc.) adresse f.; (speech) discours m. **2.** vb. (a letter) adresser; (a person) adresser la parole à.

addressee, n. destinataire m.f.

adduce, vb. alléguer, avancer.

adenoid, adj. and n. adénoïde f.

adeptly, adv. habilement, adeptement.

adeptness, n. habileté f.

adequacy, n. suffisance f.

adequate, adj. suffisant.

adequately, adv. suffisamment, convenablement.

adhere, vb. adhérer.

adherence, n. adhérence f., attachement m.

adherent, n. adhérent m.

adhesion, n. adhésion f.

adhesive, adj. adhésif.

adhesiveness, n. propriété d'adhérer f.

adieu, n. and adv. adieu m.

adjacent, adj. adjacent.

adjective, n. adjectif m.

adjoin, vb. adjoindre, être contigu (à).

adjourn, vb. ajourner, tr. s'ajourner, intr.

adjournment, n. ajournement m.

adjunct, n. and adj. adjoint m., accessoire m.

adjust, vb. ajuster, arranger, régler.

adjuster, n. ajusteur m.

adjustment, n. ajustement m., accommodement m.

adjutant, n. capitaine adjudant major m.

administer, vb. administrer.

administration, n. administration f.

administrative, adj. administratif.

administrator, n. administrateur m.

admirable, adj. admirable.

admirably, adv. admirablement.

admiral, n. amiral m.

admiralty, n. amirauté f.

admiration, n. admiration f.

admire, vb. admirer.

admirer, n. admirateur m.

admiringly, adv. avec admiration.

admissible, adj. admissible.

admission, n. (entrance) entrée f.; (confession) aveu m.

admit, vb. (let in) laisser entrer; (confess) avouer.

admittance, n. entrée f.

admittedly, adv. de l'aveu de tout le monde.

admixture, n. mélange m.

admonish, vb. réprimander.

admonition, n. admonition f., avertissement m.

ado, n. fracas m.

adolescence, n. adolescence f.

adolescent, adj. and n. adolescent m.f.

adopt, vb. adopter.

adoption, n. adoption f.

adorable, adj. adorable.

adoration, n. adoration f.

adore, vb. adorer.

adorn, vb. orner.

adornment, n. ornement m.

adrenal glands, n.pl. capsules surrénales f.pl.

adrenalin, n. adrénaline f.

adrift, adv. (naut.) à la dérive.

adroit, adj. adroit.

adulate, vb. aduler.

adulation, n. adulation f.

adult, adj. and n. adulte m.f.

adulterant, n. adultérant m.

adulterate, vb. adultérer; (of wines, milk, etc.) frelater.

adulterer, n. adultère m.

adulteress, n. femme adultère f.

adultery, n. adultère m.

advance, 1. n. (motion forward) avancement m.; (progress) progrès m.; (pay) avances f.pl.; (in a.) d'avance. **2.** vb. avancer.

advanced, adj. avancé.

advancement, n. avancement m., progrès m.

advantage, n. avantage m.

advantageous, adj. avantageux.

advantageously, adv. avantageusement.

advent, n. venue f.; (eccles.) Avent m.

adventitious, adj. adventice, fortuit.

adventure, n. aventure f.

adventurer, n. aventurier m.

adventurous, adj. aventureux.

adventurously, adv. aventureusement.

adverb, n. adverbe m.

adverbial, adj. adverbial.

adversary, n. adversaire m.

adverse, adj. adverse.

adversely, adv. défavorablement, d'une manière hostile.

adversity, n. adversité f.

advert, vb. faire allusion (à).

advertise, vb. annoncer; **(a. a product)** faire de la réclame pour un produit.

advertisement, n. publicité f.; (in a paper) annonce f.; (on a wall) affiche f.

advertiser, n. personne qui fait de la réclame f.

advertising, n. publicité f., annonce (newspaper) f.

advice, n. conseil m.; (comm.) avis m.

advisability, n. convenance f., utilité f.

advisable, adj. recommandable.

advisably, adv. convenablement.

advise, vb. conseiller.

advisedly, adv. de propos délibéré.

advisement, n. délibération.

advocacy, n. défense f., plaidoyer m.

advocate, 1. n. (law) avocat m.; (supporter) défenseur m. **2.** vb. appuyer.

aegis, n. égide f.

aerate, vb. aérer.

aeration, n. aération f.

aerial, adj. aérien.

aerially, adv. d'une manière aérienne.

aerie, n. aire f.

aeronautics, n. aéronautique f.

aesthetic, adj. esthétique.

afar, adv. loin, de loin.

affability, n. affabilité f.

affable, adj. affable.

affably, adv. affablement.

affair, n. affair f.

affect, vb. (move) toucher; (concern) intéresser; (pretend) affecter.

affectation, n. affectation f.

affected, adj. maniéré.

affecting, adj. touchant, émouvant.

affection, n. affection f.

affectionate, adj. affectueux.

affectionately, adv. affectueusement.

afferent, adj. afférent.

affiance, vb. fiancer.

affidavit, n. attestation (sous serment) f.

affiliate, vb. affilier.

affiliation, n. affiliation f.

affinity, n. affinité f.

affirm, vb. affirmer.

affirmation, n. affirmation f.

affirmative, adj. affirmatif.

affirmatively, adv. affirmativement.

affix, vb. apposer.

afflict, vb. affliger (de).

affliction, n. affliction f.

affluence, n. affluence f., opulence f.

affluent, adj. affluent, opulent.

afford, vb. (have the means to) avoir les moyens de.

affray, n. bagarre m., tumulte m.

affront, 1. n. affront m. **2.** vb. insulter.

afield, adv. aux champs, en campagne.

afire, adv. en feu.

afloat, adv. à flot, en train.

aforementioned, adj. mentionné plus haut, susdit.

aforesaid, adj. susdit, ledit.

afraid, pred. adj. (be afraid) avoir peur.

Africa, n. Afrique f.

African, 1. n. Africain m. **2.** adj. africain.

aft, adv. à l'arrière.

after, 1. adv. and prep. après. **2.** conj. après que.

aftereffect, n. effet m.

aftermath, n. suites f. pl.

afternoon, n. après-midi m. or f.

afterthought, n. réflexion tardive f.

afterward, adv. ensuite.

again, adv. de nouveau, encore;

(again and again) maintes et maintes fois.

against, *prep.* contre.

agape, *adv.* bouche bée.

agate, *n.* agate *f.*

age, **1.** *n.* âge *m.* **2.** *vb.* vieillir.

aged, *adj.* vieux, âgé.

ageism, *n.* attitude discriminative basée sur l'âge *f.*

ageless, *adj.* qui ne vieillit jamais.

agency, *n.* (*comm.*) agence *f.*

agenda, *n.* ordre du jour *m.*, agenda *m.*

agent, *n.* agent *m.*

agglutinate, *vb.* agglutiner.

agglutination, *n.* agglutination *f.*

aggrandize, *vb.* agrandir.

aggrandizement, *n.* agrandissement *m.*

aggravate, *vb.* (intensify) aggraver; (exasperate) exaspérer.

aggravation, *n.* aggravation *f.*, agacement *m.*

aggregate, *n.* masse *f.*

aggregation, *n.* agrégation *f.*, assemblage *m.*

aggression, *n.* agression *f.*

aggressive, *adj.* agressif.

aggressively, *adv.* agressivement.

aggressiveness, *n.* caractère agressif *m.*

aggressor, *n.* agresseur *m.*

aghast, *adj.* consterné.

agile, *adj.* agile.

agility, *n.* agilité *f.*

agitate, *vb.* agiter.

agitation, *n.* agitation *f.*

agitator, *n.* agitateur *m.*

agnostic, *n. and adj.* agnostique *m.*

ago, *adv.* il y a (*always precedes*).

agonized, *adj.* torturé, déchirant.

agony, *n.* (anguish) angoisse *f.*; (death agony) agonie *f.*

agrarian, *adj.* agraire, agrarien.

agree, *vb.* être d'accord.

agreeable, *adj.* agréable.

agreeably, *adv.* agréablement.

agreement, *n.* accord *m.*

agriculture, *n.* agriculture *f.*

ahead, **1.** *adv. and interj.* en avant. **2.** *prep.* (ahead of) en avant de.

aid, **1.** *n.* aide *f.*; (first aid) premiers secours; (first-aid station) poste de secours. **2.** *vb.* aider.

aide, *n.* aide *m.*, assistant *m.*

ail, *vb. intr.* être souffrant.

ailment, *n.* indisposition *f.*

aim, **1.** *n.* (*fig.*) but *m.* **2.** *vb.* viser.

aimless, *adj.* sans but.

aimlessly, *adv.* sans but, à la dérive.

air, **1.** *n.* air *m.*; (**a. force**) aviation *f.*; (**by a. mail**) par avion; (**in the open a.**) en plein air. **2.** *vb.* aérer.

airbag, *n.* (in automobiles) sac à air *m.*

air base, *n.* champs d'aviation *m.*

airborne, *adj.* par voie de l'air.

air-condition, *vb.* climatiser.

air conditioner, *n.* climatiseur *m.*

air-conditioning, *n.* climatisation *f.*

aircraft, *n.* avions *m.pl.*; (**aircraft carrier**) porte-avions *m.*

air gun, *n.* fusil à vent.

airing, *n.* aérage *m.*, tour *m.*

air line, *n.* ligne aérienne *f.*

air liner, *n.* avion *m.*

air mail, *n.* poste aérienne *f.*

airplane, *n.* avion *m.*

air pollution, *n.* pollution de l'air *f.*

airport, *n.* aéroport *m.*

air pressure, *n.* pression d'air *f.*

air raid, *n.* raid aérien *m.*

airsick, *adj.* (**to be a.**) avoir le mal d'air.

airtight, *adj.* imperméable à l'air, étanche.

airy, *adj.* (well aired) aéré; (light) léger.

aisle, *n.* (passageway) passage *m.*; (*arch.*) bas côté *m.*

ajar, *adv.* entr'ouvert.

akin, *adj.* allié (à), parent (de).

alacrity, *n.* empressement *m.*

alarm, *n.* alarme *f.*

alarmist, *n.* alarmiste *m.*

albino, *n.* albinos *m.*

album, *n.* album *m.*

alcohol, *n.* alcool *m.*

alcoholic, *adj.* alcoolique.

alcove, *n.* (recess) niche *f.*; (sleeping alcove) alcôve *f.*

ale, *n.* bière *f.*

alert, *adj.* alerte.

alfalfa, *n.* luzerne *f.*

algebra, *n.* algèbre *f.*

alias, **1.** *n.* nom d'emprunt *m.* **2.** *adv.* autrement nommé, dit.

alibi, *n.* alibi *m.*

alien, *adj.* étranger.

alienate, *vb.* aliéner.

alight, *vb.* (descend) descendre; (stop after descent) s'abattre.

align, *vb.* aligner.

alike, 1. *adj.* semblable; (**be alike**) se ressembler. **2.** *adv.* également.

alimentary canal, *n.* canal alimentaire *m.*

alive, *adj.* vivant.

alkali, *n.* alcali *m.*

alkaline, *adj.* alcalin.

all, 1. *adj.* tout *m.sg.,* toute *f.sg.,* tous *m.pl.,* toutes *f.pl.* **2.** *adv. and pron.* (everything) tout *m.sg.* (above all) surtout; (all at once) tout d'un coup; (all the same) tout de même; (that's all!) c'est tout; (not at all) pas du tout; (everybody) tous; (all of you) vous tous.

allay, *vb.* apaiser.

allegation, *n.* allégation *f.*

allege, *vb.* alléguer.

allegiance, *n.* fidélité *f.*

allegory, *n.* allégorie *f.*

allergy, *n.* allergie *f.*

alleviate, *vb.* soulager.

alley, *n.* (in town) ruelle *f.;* (blind alley) cul-de-sac *m.*

alliance, *n.* alliance *f.*

allied, *adj.* allié.

alligator, *n.* alligator *m.*

allocate, *vb.* assigner.

allot, *vb.* (grant) accorder; (distribute) répartir.

allotment, *n.* partage *m.,* lot *m.*

allow, *vb.* (permit) permettre; (admit) admettre; (grant) accorder; (allow for) tenir compte de.

allowance, *n.* (money granted) allocation *f.;* (food) ration *f.;* (tolerance) tolérance *f.;* (pension) rente *f.;* (weekly allowance) semaine *f.*

alloy, *n.* alliage *m.*

all right, *adv.* très bien.

allude to, *vb.* faire allusion à.

allure, *vb.* séduire.

allusion, *n.* allusion *f.*

ally, 1. *n.* allié *m.* **2.** *vb.* allier.

almanac, *n.* almanach *m.*

almighty, *adj.* tout-puissant.

almond, *n.* amande *f.*

almost, *adv.* presque.

alms, *n.* aumône *f.*

aloft, *adv.* en haut.

alone, *adj.* seul; (let alone) laisser tranquille.

along, 1. *prep.* le long de. **2.** *adv.* (come along!) venez donc!

alongside, *prep.* le long de.

aloof, 1. *adv.* à l'écart. **2.** *adj.* réservé.

aloud, *adv.* à haute voix.

alpaca, *n.* alpaga (fabric) *m.;* alpaca (animal) *m.*

alphabet, *n.* alphabet *m.*

alphabetical, *adj.* alphabétique.

alphabetize, *vb.* alphabétiser.

Alps, *n.pl.* Alpes *f.pl.*

already, *adv.* déjà.

also, *adv.* aussi.

altar, *n.* autel *m.*

alter, *vb.* changer.

alteration, *n.* modification *f.*

alternate, 1. *vb.* remplaçant *m.* **2.** *adj.* alternatif. **3.** *vb.* alterner.

alternative, *n.* alternative *f.*

although, *conj.* bien que.

altitude, *n.* altitude *f.*

altogether, *adv.* tout à fait.

altruism, *n.* altruisme *m.*

alum, *n.* alun *m.*

aluminum, *n.* aluminium *m.*

always, *adv.* toujours.

amalgam, *n.* amalgame *n.*

amalgamate, *vb.* amalgamer.

amass, *vb.* amasser.

amateur, *n.* amateur *f.*

amaze, *vb.* étonner.

amazement, *n.* stupeur *f.*

amazing, *adj.* étonnant.

ambassador, *n.* ambassadeur *m.,* ambassadrice *f.*

amber, *n.* ambre *m.*

ambidextrous, *adj.* ambidextre.

ambiguity, *n.* ambiguïté *f.*

ambiguous, *adj.* ambigu *m.,* biguë *f.*

ambition, *n.* ambition *f.*

ambitious, *adj.* ambitieux.

ambulance, *n.* ambulance *f.*

ambulatory, *adj.* ambulatoire.

ambush, *n.* embuscade *f.*

ameliorate, *vb.* améliorer.

amenable, *adj.* responsable, soumis (à), sujet (à).

amend, *vb.* amender.

amendment, *n.* amendement *m.*

amenity, *n.* aménité *f.,* agrément *m.*

America, *n.* Amérique *f.;* (North

A.) A. du Nord; (South A.) A. du Sud.

American, 1. n. Américain m. **2.** adj. américain.

amethyst, n. améthyste f.

amiable, adj. aimable.

amicable, adj. amical.

amid, prep. au milieu de.

amidships, adv. par le travers.

amiss, adv. de travers.

amity, n. amitié f.

ammonia, n. ammoniaque f

ammunition, n. munitions (f.pl.) de guerre.

amnesia, n. amnésie f.

amnesty, n. amnistie f.

amniocentesis, n. amniocentèse f.

amoeba, n. amibe f.

among, prep. parmi, entre.

amoral, adj. amoral.

amorous, adj. amoureux.

amorphous, adj. amorphe.

amortize, vb. amortir.

amount, 1. n. (sum) somme f.; (quantity) quantité f. **2.** vb. (amount to) se réduire à.

ampere, n. ampère m.

amphibian, n. amphibie m.

amphibious, adj. amphibie.

amphitheater, n. amphithéâtre m.

ample, adj. ample.

amplify, vb. amplifier.

amputate, vb. amputer.

amputee, n. amputé m.

amuse, vb. amuser.

amusement, n. amusement m.

an, art. un m., une f.

anachronism, n. anachronisme m.

analogous, adj. analogue.

analogy, n. analogie f.

analysis, n. analyse f.

analyst, n. analyste m.

analytic, adj. analytique.

analyze, vb. analyser.

anarchy, n. anarchie f.

anatomy, n. anatomie f.

ancestor, n. ancêtre m.

ancestral, adj. d'ancêtres, héréditaire.

ancestry, n. aïeux, m.pl.

anchor, 1. vb. ancrer. **2.** n. ancre f.

anchorage, n. mouillage m., ancrage m.

anchovy, n. anchois m.

ancient, adj. ancien m., ancienne f.

and, conj. et.

anecdote, n. anecdote f.

anemia, n. anémie f.

anesthetic, adj. and n. anesthésique m.

anesthetist, n. anesthésiste m.

anew, adv. de nouveau.

angel, n. ange m.

anger, n. colère f.

angle, 1. n. angle m.; (at an angle) en biais. **2.** vb. (fish) pêcher à la ligne.

angry, adj. fâché; (to get angry) se fâcher.

anguish, n. angoisse f.

angular, adj. anguleux.

aniline, n. aniline f.

animal, n. and adj. animal m.

animate, vb. animer.

animated, adj. animé.

animated cartoon, n. dessin animé m.

animation, n. animation f.

animosity, n. animosité f.

anise, n. anis m.

ankle, n. cheville f.

annals, n.pl. annales f.pl.

annex, n. (to a building) dépendance f.

annexation, n. annexion f.

annihilate, vb. anéantir.

anniversary, n. anniversaire m.

annotate, vb. annoter.

annotation, n. annotation f.

announce, vb. annoncer.

announcement, n. annonce f.

announcer, n. speaker m.

annoy, vb. (vex) contrarier; (bore) ennuyer.

annoyance, n. contrariété f.

annual, adj. annuel.

annuity, n. annuité f., rente annuelle f.

annul, vb. annuler.

anode, n. anode f.

anoint, vb. oindre.

anomalous, adj. anomal, irrégulier.

anonymous, adj. anonyme.

another, adj. and pron. un autre m., une autre f.; (one another) l'un l'autre.

answer, vb. répondre.

answer, n. réponse f.

answerable, adj. responsable (de), susceptible de réponse.

ant, n. fourmi f.

antacid, *adj.* antiacide.

antagonism, *n.* antagonisme *m.*

antagonist, *n.* antagoniste *m.*

antagonistic, *adj.* en opposition (à), hostile (à), opposé (à).

antagonize, *vb.* s'opposer à.

antarctic, *adj.* antarctique.

antecedent, *adj. and n.* antécédent *m.*

antedate, *vb.* antidater.

antelope, *n.* antilope *f.*

antenna, *n.* antenne *f.*

anterior, *adj.* antérieur.

anteroom, *n.* antichambre *m. or f.*

anthem, *n.* (national) hymne national *m.*

anthology, *n.* anthologie *f.*

anthracite, *n.* anthracite *m.*

anthrax, *n.* anthrax *m.*

anthropology, *n.* anthropologie *f.*

antiaircraft, *adj.* contre-avion.

antibody, *n.* anticorps *m.*

antic, *n.* bouffonerie *f.*

anticipate, *vb.* (advance) anticiper; (expect) s'attendre à; (foresee) prévoir.

anticipation, *n.* anticipation *f.*

anticlerical, *adj.* anticlérical.

anticlimax, *n.* anticlimax *m.*

antidote, *n.* antidote *m.*

antimony, *n.* antimoine *m.*

antinuclear, *adj.* antinucléaire.

antipathy, *n.* antipathie *f.*

antiquated, *adj.* antique.

antique, 1. *n.* antique *m.; (antique dealer)* antiquaire *m.*

antiquity, *n.* antiquité *f.*

antiseptic, *adj. and n.* antiseptique *m.*

antisocial, *adj.* antisocial.

antitoxin, *n.* antitoxine *f.*

antler, *n.* andouiller *m.*

anvil, *n.* enclume *f.*

anxiety, *n.* anxiété *f.*

anxious, *adj.* inquiet *m.,* inquiète *f.*

any, 1. *adj.* (in questions, for "some") du *m.sg.,* de la *f.sg.,* des *pl.;* **(not . . . any)** ne . . . pas de; (no matter which) n'importe quel; (every) tout. **2.** *pron. (any of it or* them, with verb) en.

anybody, *pron.* (somebody) quelqu'un; (somebody, implying negation) personne; **(not . . . anybody)** ne . . . personne; (no matter who) n'importe qui.

anyhow, *adv.* en tout cas; d'une manière quelconque.

anyone, *pron. see* **anybody.**

anything, *pron.* (something) quelque chose; (something, implying negation) rien; **(not . . . anything)** ne . . . rien; (no matter what) n'importe quoi.

anyway, *adv. see* **anyhow.**

anywhere, *adv.* n'importe où.

apart, 1. *adv.* à part. **2.** *prep.* **(apart from)** en dehors de.

apartheid, *n.* ségrégation des populations noire et blanche, *f.*

apartment, *n.* appartement *m.*

apathetic, *adj.* apathique.

apathy, *n.* apathie *f.*

ape, 1. *n.* singe *m.* **2.** *vb.* singer.

aperture, *n.* ouverture *f.*

apex, *n.* sommet *m.*

aphorism, *n.* aphorisme *m.*

apiary, *n.* rucher *m.*

apiece, *adv.* chacun.

apologetic, *adj. use verb* s'excuser.

apologist, *n.* apologiste *m.*

apologize for, *vb.* s'excuser de.

apology, *n.* excuses *f. pl.*

apoplectic, *adj.* apoplectique.

apoplexy, *n.* apoplexie *f.*

apostate, *n.* apostat *m.*

apostle, *n.* apôtre *m.*

apostolic, *adj.* apostolique.

appall, *vb.* épouvanter.

apparatus, *n.* appareil *m.*

apparel, *n.* habillement *m.*

apparent, *adj.* apparent.

apparition, *n.* apparition *f.*

appeal, 1. *n.* appel *m.* **2.** *vb.* **(a. to)** en appeler à.

appear, *vb.* (become visible) apparaître; (seem) sembler.

appearance, *n.* (apparition) apparition *f.;* (semblance) apparence *f.;* (aspect) aspect *m.*

appease, *vb.* apaiser.

appeaser, *n.* personne qui apaise.

appellant, *n.* appelant *m.*

appellate, *adj.* d'appel.

appendage, *n.* accessoire *m.,* apanage *m.*

appendectomy, *n.* appendéctomie *f.*

appendicitis, *n.* appendicite *f.*

appendix, *n.* appendice *m.*

appetite, *n.* appétit *m.*

appetizer, *n.* (drink) apéritif *m.*

appetizing, *adj.* appétissant.

applaud, *vb.* applaudir.

applause, *n.* applaudissements *m.pl.*

apple, *n.* pomme *f.*

applesauce, *n.* compote (*f.*) de pommes.

appliance, *n.* appareil *m.*

applicable, *adj.* applicable.

applicant, *n.* postulant *m.*

application, *n.* (request) demande *f.*

applied, *adj.* appliqué.

apply, *vb.* (a. to somebody) s'adresser à; (a. for a job) solliciter; (put on) appliquer; (a. oneself) s'appliquer.

appoint, *vb.* (a person) nommer; (time, place) désigner.

appointment, *n.* (meeting) rendez-vous *m.;* (make an a. with) donner un rendez-vous à; (nomination) nomination *f.*

apportion, *vb.* répartir.

apposition, *n.* apposition *f.*

appraisal, *n.* évaluation *f.*

appraise, *vb.* priser.

appreciable, *adj.* appréciable.

appreciate, *vb.* apprécier.

appreciation, *n.* appréciation *f.*

apprehend, *vb.* saisir.

apprehension, *n.* (seizure) arrestation *f.;* (understanding) compréhension *f.;* (fear) appréhension *f.*

apprehensive, *adj.* craintif.

apprentice, *n.* apprenti *m.*

apprise, *vb.* prévenir, informer.

approach, 1. *n.* approche *f.;* (make approaches to) faire des avances à. **2.** *vb.* s'approcher de.

approachable, *adj.* abordable, accessible.

approbation, *n.* approbation *f.*

appropriate, 1. *adj.* convenable. **2.** *vb.* s'approprier.

appropriation, *n.* appropriation *f.*

approval, *n.* approbation *f.*

approve, *vb.* approuver.

approximate, 1. *adj.* approximatif. **2.** *vb.* se rapprocher (de).

approximately, *adv.* approximativement, à peu près.

approximation, *n.* approximation *f.*

appurtenance, *n.* appartenance *f.,* dépendance *f.*

apricot, *n.* abricot *m.*

April, *n.* avril *m.*

apron, *n.* tablier *m.*

apropos, *adj.* à propos.

apse, *n.* abside *f.*

apt, *adj.* (likely to) sujet à; (suitable for) apte à; (appropriate) à propos; (clever) habile.

aptitude, *n.* aptitude *f.*

aquarium, *n.* aquarium *m.*

aquatic, *adj.* aquatique.

aqueduct, *n.* aqueduc *m.*

aqueous, *adj.* aqueux.

aquiline, *adj.* aquilin.

Arab, 1. *n.* Arabe *m.f.* **2.** *adj.* arabe.

Arabic, *adj. and n.* arabe *m.*

arable, *adj.* arable, labourable.

arbiter, *n.* arbitre *m.*

arbitrary, *adj.* arbitraire.

arbitrate, *vb.* arbitrer.

arbitration, *n.* arbitrage *m.*

arbitrator, *n.* arbitre *m.*

arbor, *n.* (bower) berceau *m.*

arboreal, *adj.* arboricole.

arc, *n.* arc *m.*

arcade, *n.* arcade *f.*

arch, 1. *n.* arc *m.;* (of bridge) arche *f.* **2.** *adj.* espiègle.

archaeology, *n.* archéologie *f.*

archaic, *adj.* archaïque.

archbishop, *n.* archevêque *m.*

archdiocese, *n.* archidiocèse *m.*

archduke, *n.* archiduc *m.*

archer, *n.* archer *m.*

archery, *n.* tir à l'arc *m.*

archipelago, *n.* archipel *m.*

architect, *n.* architecte *m.*

architectural, *adj.* architectural.

architecture, *n.* architecture *f.*

archives, *n.* archives *f.pl.*

archway, *n.* voûte *f.,* passage (sous une voûte) *m.*

arctic, *adj.* arctique.

ardent, *adj.* ardent.

ardor, *n.* ardeur *f.*

arduous, *adj.* difficile.

area, *n.* (geom.) aire *f.;* (locality) région *f.;* (surface) surface *f.*

area code, *n.* indicatif interurbain *m.*

arena, *n.* arène *f.*

argentine, *adj.* argentin.

argue, *vb.* (reason) argumenter; (indicate) prouver; (discuss) discuter.

argument, *n.* (reasoning) argument *m.;* (dispute) discussion *f.*

argumentative, *adj.* disposé à argumenter, raisonneur.

aria, *n.* air *m.,* chanson *f.*

arid, *adj.* aride.

arise, *vb.* (move upward) s'élever; (originate from) provenir de.

aristocracy, *n.* aristocratie *f.*

aristocrat, *n.* aristocrate *m.f.*

aristocratic, *adj.* aristocratique.

arithmetic, *n.* arithmétique *f.*

ark, *n.* arche *f.*

arm, *n.* 1. (limb) bras *m.;* (weapon) arme *f.* 2. *vb.* armer.

armament, *n.* armement *m.*

armchair, *n.* fauteuil *m.*

armed forces, *n.* forces armées *f.pl.*

armful, *n.* brassée *f.*

armhole, *n.* emmanchure *f.,* entournure *f.*

armistice, *n.* armistice *m.*

armor, *n.* armure *f.*

armory, *n.* (drill hall) salle *(f.)* d'exercice.

armpit, *n.* aisselle *f.*

arms, *n.* armes *f.pl.*

army, *n.* armée *f.*

arnica, *n.* arnica *f.*

aroma, *n.* arome *m.*

aromatic, *adj.* aromatique.

around, 1. *adv.* autour. 2. *prep.* autour de.

arouse, *vb.* (stir) soulever; (awake) réveiller.

arraign, *vb.* accuser, poursuivre en justice.

arrange, *vb.* arranger.

arrangement, *n.* arrangement *m.*

array, *n.* (military) rangs *m.pl.;* (display) étalage *m.*

array, *vb.* ranger.

arrear, *n.* arriéré *m.*

arrest, 1. *n.* (capture) arrestation *f.;* (military) arrêts *m.pl.;* (halt) arrêt *m.* 2. *vb.* arrêter.

arrival, *n.* arrivée *f.*

arrive, *vb.* arriver.

arrogance, *n.* arrogance *f.*

arrogant, *adj.* arrogant.

arrogate, *vb.* usurper, (to oneself) s'arroger.

arrow, *n.* flèche *f.*

arrowhead, *n.* pointe de flèche *f.;* (plant) sagittaire *m.*

arsenal, *n.* arsenal *m.*

arsenic, *n.* arsenic *m.*

arson, *n.* crime d'incendie *m.*

art, *n.* art *m.;* (fine arts) beaux-arts.

arterial, *adj.* artériel.

arteriosclerosis, *n.* artériosclérose *f.*

artery, *n.* artère *f.*

artesian well, *n.* puits artésien *m.*

artful, *adj.* (crafty) artificieux; (skillful) adroit.

arthritis, *n.* arthrite *f.*

artichoke, *n.* artichaut *m.*

article, *n.* article *m.*

articulate, *vb.* articuler.

articulation, *n.* articulation *f.*

artifice, *n.* artifice *m.*

artificial, *adj.* artificiel.

artificiality, *n.* nature artificielle *f.*

artillery, *n.* artillerie *f.*

artisan, *n.* artisan *m.*

artist, *n.* artiste *m.*

artistic, *adj.* artistique.

artistry, *n.* habileté *f.*

artless, *adj.* ingénu, naïf.

as, 1. *adv.* comme; (as . . . as) aussi . . . que; (as much as) autant que; (such as) tel que. 2. *conj.* (so . . . as) de façon à; (while) pendant que; (since) puisque; (progress) à mesure que. 3. *prep.* (as to) quant à.

asbestos, *n.* asbeste *m.*

ascend, *vb.* monter.

ascendancy, *n.* ascendant *m.*

ascendant, *adj.* ascendant, supérieur.

ascent, *n.* montée *f.;* (of a mountain) ascension *f.*

ascertain, *vb.* s'assurer (de).

ascetic, *n.* ascétique *m.*

ascribe, *vb.* attribuer.

ash, *n.* cendre *f.;* (tree) frêne *m.*

ashamed, *adj.* honteux; (be a. of) avoir honte de.

ashen, *adj.* cendré, gris pâle.

ashes, *n.* cendres *f.pl.*

ashore, *adv.* à terre; (go a.) débarquer.

ash-tray, *n.* cendrier *m.*

Asia, *n.* Asie *f.*

Asian, 1. *n.* Asiatique *m.f.* 2. *adj.* asiatique.

aside, *adv.* de côté.

ask, *vb.* demander à; (invite) inviter.

askance, *adv.* de travers, oblique-ment.

asleep, *adj.* endormi.

asparagus, *n.* asperges *f.pl.*

aspect, *n.* aspect *m.*

asperity, *n.* aspérité *f.*, rudesse *f.*

aspersion, *n.* aspersion *f.*

asphalt, *n.* asphalte *m.*

asphyxia, *n.* asphyxie *f.*

asphyxiate, *vb.* asphyxier.

aspirant, *n.* aspirant *m.*

aspirate, *vb.* aspirer.

aspiration, *n.* aspiration *f.*

aspirator, *n.* aspirateur *m.*

aspire, *vb.* aspirer.

aspirin, *n.* aspirine *f.*

ass, *n.* âne *m.*, ânesse *f.*

assail, *vb.* assaillir.

assailable, *adj.* attaquable.

assailant, *n.* assaillant *m.*

assassin, *n.* assassin *m.*

assassinate, *vb.* assassiner.

assassination, *n.* assassinat *m.*

assault, *n.* assaut *m.*

assay, **1.** *n.* essai *m.*, vérification *f.*, épreuve *f.* **2.** *vb.* essayer.

assemblage, *n.* assemblage *m.*

assemble, *vb.* assembler, *tr.*; s'assembler, *intr.*

assembly, *n.* assemblée *f.*

assent, **1.** *n.* assentiment *m.* **2.** *vb.* consentir.

assert, *vb.* affirmer.

assertion, *n.* assertion *f.*

assertive, *adj.* assertif.

assertiveness, *n.* qualité d'être assertif.

assess, *vb.* (tax) taxer; (evaluate) évaluer.

assessor, *n.* assesseur *m.*

assets, *n.pl.* (comm.) actif *m.*; (property) biens *m.pl.*

asseverate, *vb.* affirmer solennellement.

asseveration, *n.* affirmation *f.*

assiduous, *adj.* assidu.

assiduously, *adv.* assidûment.

assign, *vb.* assigner.

assignable, *adj.* assignable, transférable.

assignation, *n.* assignation *f.*, rendez-vous *m.*

assignment, *n.* (law) cession *f.*; (school) tâche *f.*

assimilate, *vb.* assimiler, *tr.*; s'assimiler, *intr.*

assimilation, *n.* assimilation *f.*

assimilative, *adj.* assimilatif, assimilateur.

assistance, *n.* aide *f.*

assistant, *n.* aide *m.f.*

assist in, *vb.* aider à.

associate, *vb.* associer, *tr.*; s'associer, *intr.*

association, *n.* association *f.*

assonance, *n.* assonance *f.*

assort, *vb.* assortir.

assorted, *adj.* assorti.

assortment, *n.* assortiment *m.*

assuage, *vb.* adoucir, apaiser.

assume, *vb.* (take) prendre; (appropriate) s'arroger; (feign) simuler; (suppose) supposer.

assuming, *adj.* prétentieux, arrogant.

assumption, *n.* supposition *f.*; (eccles.) Assomption *f.*

assurance, *n.* assurance *f.*

assure, *vb.* assurer.

assured, *adj.* assuré.

assuredly, *adv.* assurément.

aster, *n.* aster *m.*

asterisk, *n.* astérisque *m.*

astern, *adv.* à l'arrière, de l'arrière.

asteroid, *n.* astéroïde *m.*

asthma, *n.* asthme *m.*

astigmatism, *n.* astigmatisme *m.*

astir, *adj.* agité, debout.

astonish, *vb.* étonner.

astonishment, *n.* étonnement *m.*

astound, *vb.* stupéfier.

astral, *adj.* astral.

astray, *adj.* égaré; (go a.) s'égarer.

astride, *adv.* à califourchon.

astringent, *n. and adj.* astringent *m.*

astrology, *n.* astrologie *f.*

astronaut, *n.* astronaute *m.*

astronomy, *n.* astronomie *f.*

astute, *adj.* fin.

asunder, *adv.* (apart) écartés; (to pieces) en morceaux.

asylum, *n.* asile *m.*

asymmetry, *n.* asymétrie *f.*

at, *prep.* (time, place, price) à; (someone's house, shop, etc.) chez.

ataxia, *n.* ataxie *f.*

atheist, *n.* athée *m.f.*

athlete, *n.* athlète *m.f.*

athletic, *adj.* athlétique.

athletics, *n.* sports *m.pl.*

athwart, *adv.* de travers.
Atlantic, *adj.* atlantique.
Atlantic Ocean, *n.* océan Atlantique *m.*
atlas, *n.* atlas *m.*
atmosphere, *n.* atmosphère *f.*
atmospheric, *adj.* atmosphérique.
atoll, *n.* atoll *m.*
atom, *n.* atome *m.*
atomic, *adj.* atomique.
atomic bomb, *n.* bombe atomique *f.*
atomic energy, *n.* énergie atomique *f.*
atomic theory, *n.* théorie atomique *f.*
atomic warfare, *n.* guerre atomique *f.*
atomic weight, *n.* poids atomique *m.*
atonal, *adj.* atonal.
atone for, *vb.* expier.
atonement, *n.* expiation *f.*
atrocious, *adj.* atroce.
atrocity, *n.* atrocité *f.*
atrophy, *n.* atrophie *f.*
atropine, *n.* atropine *f.*
attach, *vb.* attcher.
attaché, *n.* attaché *m.*
attachment, *n.* attachement *m.;* (device) accessoire *m.*
attack, 1. *n.* attaque *f.* **2.** *vb.* attaquer.
attacker, *n.* agresseur *m.*
attain, *vb.* atteindre.
attainable, *adj.* qu'on peut atteindre.
attainment, *n.* (realization) réalisation *f.;* (knowledge) connaissance *f.*
attempt, *n.* tentative *f.*
attend, *vb.* (give heed to) faire attention à; (medical) soigner; (serve) servir; (meeting) assister à; (lectures) suivre; (see to) s'occuper de.
attendance, *n.* service *m.;* présence *f.*
attendant, *n.* serviteur *m.;* (retinue) suite *f.*
attention, *n.* attention *f.;* (pay attention to) faire attention à.
attentive, *adj.* attentif.
attentively, *adv.* attentivement.
attenuate, *vb.* atténuer.
attest, *vb.* attester.
attic, *n.* grenier *m.*

attire, 1. *n.* costume *m.* **2.** *vb.* parer, *tr.;* se parer, *intr.*
attitude, *n.* attitude *f.*
attorney, *n.* avoué *m.*
attract, *vb.* attirer.
attraction, *n.* attraction *f.*
attractive, *adj.* attrayant.
attributable, *adj.* attribuable, imputable.
attribute, *n.* attribut *m.*
attrition, *n.* attrition *f.*
attune, *vb.* accorder, mettre à l'unisson.
auction, *n.* vente (*f.*) aux enchères.
auctioneer, *n.* commissaire-priseur *m.*
audacious, *adj.* audacieux.
audacity, *n.* audace *f.*
audible, *adj.* intelligible.
audience, *n.* (listeners) auditoire *m.;* (interview) audience *f.*
audiovisual, *adj.* audiovisuel.
audit, 1. *vb.* vérifier (des comptes). **2.** *n.* vérification (des comptes) *f.*
audition, *n.* audition *f.*
auditor, *n.* vérificateur *m.,* censeur *m.*
auditorium, *n.* salle *f.*
auditory, *adj.* auditif.
auger, *n.* tarière *f.*
augment, *vb.* augmenter.
augur, *vb.* augurer.
August, *n.* août *m.*
aunt, *n.* tante *f.*
auspice, *n.* auspice *m.*
auspicious, *adj.* de bon augure.
austere, *adj.* austère.
austerity, *n.* austérité *f.*
Australia, *n.* Australie *f.*
Australian, 1. *n.* Australien *m.* **2.** *adj.* australien.
Austria, *n.* Autriche *f.*
Austrian, 1. *n.* Autrichien *m.* **2.** *adj.* autrichien.
authentic, *adj.* authentique.
authenticate, *vb.* authentiquer, valider.
authenticity, *n.* authenticité *f.*
author, *n.* auteur *m.*
authoritarian, *adj.* autoritaire.
authoritative, *adj.* autoritaire.
authoritatively, *adv.* avec autorité, en maître.
authority, *n.* autorité *f.*
authorization, *n.* autorisation *f.*

authorize, *vb.* autoriser.
auto, *n.* auto *f.*
autobiography, *n.* autobiographie *f.*
autocracy, *n.* autocratie *f.*
autocrat, *n.* autocrate *m.*
autograph, 1. *n.* autographe *m.* **2.** *vb.* autographier.
automatic, *adj.* automatique.
automatically, *adv.* automatiquement.
automobile, *n.* automobile *f.*
automotive, *adj.* automoteur.
autonomously, *adv.* d'une manière autonome.
autonomy, *n.* autonomie *f.*
autopsy, *n.* autopsie *f.*
autumn, *n.* automne *m.*
auxiliary, *adj.* auxiliaire.
avail, *vb.* servir; (be of no a.) ne servir à rien.
available, *adj.* disponible.
avalanche, *n.* avalanche *f.*
avarice, *n.* avarice *f.*
avariciously, *adv.* avec avarice.
avenge, *vb.* venger.
avenger, *n.* vengeur *m.*, vengeresse *f.*
avenue, *n.* avenue *f.*
average, 1. *n.* moyenne *f.* **2.** *adj.* moyen.
averse, *adj.* opposé.
aversion, *n.* aversion *f.*
avert, *vb.* détourner.
aviary, *n.* volière *f.*
aviation, *n.* aviation *f.*
aviator, *n.* aviateur *m.*
aviatrix, *n.* aviatrice *f.*
avid, *adj.* avide.
avocation, *n.* distraction *f.*, profession *f.*, métier *m.*
avoid, *vb.* éviter.
avoidable, *adj.* évitable.
avoidance, *n.* action d'éviter *f.*
avow, *vb.* avouer.
avowal, *n.* aveu *m.*
avowed, *adj.* avoué, confessé.
avowedly, *adj.* de son propre aveu, ouvertement.
await, *vb.* attendre.
awake, *vb.* éveiller, *tr.*; s'éveiller, *intr.*
awaken, *vb. see* awake.
award, 1. *n.* (prize) prix *m.*; (law) sentence *f.* **2.** *vb.* décerner.
aware, *adj.* (be a.) savoir; (not to be a.) ignorer.

awash, *adv.* dans l'eau.
away, *adv.* loin; (go a.) s'en aller; (a. from) absent de.
awe, *n.* crainte *f.*
awesome, *adj.* inspirant du respect.
awful, *adj.* terrible.
awhile, *adv.* pendant quelque temps.
awkward, *adj.* (clumsy) gauche; (embarrassing) embarrassant.
awning, *n.* tente *f.*
awry, *adv.* de travers.
ax, *n.* hache *f.*
axiom, *n.* axiome *m.*
axis, *n.* axe *m.*
axle, *n.* essieu *m.*
ayatollah, *n.* ayatollah *m.*
azure, *n.* azur *m.*
azure, *adj.* azuré.

B

babble, *vb.* babiller.
babbler, *n.* babillard *m.*
babe, *n.* enfant *m. or f.*
baboon, *n.* babouin *m.*
baby, *n.* bébé *m.*
babyish, *adj.* enfantin.
bachelor, *n.* célibataire *m.*
bacillus, *n.* bacille *m.*
back, 1. *n.* dos *m.* **2.** *vb.* (b. up, go b.) reculer; (uphold) soutenir. **3.** *adv.* en arrière.
backbone, *n.* épine dorsale *f.*
backer, *n.* partisan *m.*
backfire, *vb.* donner des retours de flamme, retomber (sur).
background, *n.* fond *m.*
backhand, *adj.* donné avec le revers de la main.
backing, *n.* soutien *m.*
backlash, *n.* réaction conservatrice *f.*
backlog, *n.* réserve *f.*
back out, *vb.* se retirer.
backpack, *n.* sac tyrolien *m.*
backstage, *adv.* dans les coulisses.
backward, *adv.* en arrière.
backwardness, *n.* retard *m.*
backwards, *adv.* en arrière.
backwater, 1. *n.* eau stagnante *f.* **2.** *vb.* aller en arrière (dans l'eau).
backwoods, *n.* forêts vierges *f.pl.*

bacon, n. porc (m.) salé et fumé.
bacteriologist, n. bactériologue m.
bacteriology, n. bactériologie f.
bacterium, n. bactérie f.
bad, adj. mauvais; (wicked) méchant.
badge, n. insigne m.
badger, vb. ennuyer.
badness, n. mauvaise qualité f.; (wickedness) méchanceté f.
baffle, vb. déconcerter.
bafflement, n. confusion f.
bag, n. sac m.; (suitcase) valise f.
baggage, n. bagage m.
baggage cart, n. (airport) chariot m.
baggage claim, n. bulletin de bagage m.
baggy, adj. bouffant.
bagpipe, n. cornemuse f.
bail, 1. n. (law) caution f. **2.** vb. (b. out water) vider (l'eau).
bailiff, n. huissier m.
bait, n. appât m.
bake, vb. faire cuire au four, tr.
baker, n. boulanger m.
bakery, n. boulangerie f.
baking, n. boulangerie f.
balance, 1. n. (equilibrium) équilibre m.; (bank) solde m.; (account, scales) balance f. **2.** vb. balancer, tr.
balcony, n. balcon m.; (theater) galerie f.
bald, adj. chauve.
baldness, n. calvitie f.; (fig.) sécheresse f.
bale, n. balle f.
balk, vb. frustrer.
balky, adj. regimbé.
ball, n. (games, bullet) balle f.; (round object) boule f.; (dance) bal m.
ballad, n. (song) romance f.; (poem) ballade f.
ballast, n. lest m.
ball bearing, n. roulement à billes m.
ballerina, n. ballérina f.
ballet, n. ballet m.
balloon, n. ballon m.
ballot, n. scrutin m.
ballroom, n. salon de bal m.
balm, n. baume m.
balmy, adj. embaumé; doux.
balsa, n. balsa f.

balsam, n. baume m.
balustrade, n. balustrade f.
bamboo, n. bambou m.
ban, 1. n. ban m. **2.** vb. mettre au ban, tr.
banal, adj. banal.
banana, n. banane f.
band, n. bande f.; (music) orchestre m.
bandage, n. bandage m.
band-aid, n. pansement adhésif m.
bandanna, n. foulard m.
bandbox, n. carton (de modiste) m.
bandit, n. bandit m.
bandmaster, n. chef de musique m.
bandsman, n. musicien m.
bandstand, n. kiosque m.
baneful, adj. pernicieux.
bang, vb. frapper.
bang, n. coup m.
banish, vb. bannir.
banishment, n. bannissement m.
banister, n. rampe f.
bank, n. banque f.; (river) rive f.
bankbook, n. livret de banque m.
banker, n. banquier m.
banking, n. banque f., affaires de banque f.pl.
bank note, n. billet de banque m.
bankrupt, adj. and n. failli m.
bankruptcy, n. faillite f.
banner, n. bannière f.
banquet, n. banquet m.
banter, 1. n. badinage m. **2.** vb. badiner, railler.
baptism, n. baptême m.
baptismal, adj. baptismal.
Baptist, n. Baptiste m.
baptistery, n. baptistère m.
baptize, vb. baptiser.
bar, n. (drinks) bar m.; (metal) barre f.; (law) barreau m.
barb, n. barbillon m.
barbarian, barbarous, adj. and n. barbare m.f.
barbarism, n. barbarie f.; (gramm.) barbarisme m.
barber, n. coiffeur m.
barbiturate, n. barbiturat m.
bare, 1. adj. nu. **2.** vb. découvrir.
bareback, adv. à dos nu.
barefoot, adv. nu-pieds.
barely, adv. à peine.
bareness, n. nudité f.
bargain, n. marché m.

bargain, vb. marchander.

barge, n. chaland m.

barium, n. barium m.

bark, 1. n. (tree) écorce f.; (dog) aboiement m. **2.** vb. (dog) aboyer.

barley, n. orge f.

barn, n. (grain) grange f.; (livestock) étable f.

barnacle, n. anatife (shellfish) m.; barnache (goose) f.

barnyard, n. basse-cour f.

barometer, n. baromètre m.

barometric, adj. barométrique.

baron, n. baron m.

baroness, n. baronne f.

baronial, adj. baronnial, seigneurial.

baroque, adj. baroque.

barracks, n. caserne f.

barrage, n. barrage m.

barred, adj. barré, empêché, exclus, défendu.

barrel, n. tonneau m.

barren, adj. stérile.

barrenness, n. stérilité f.

barricade, n. barricade f.

barrier, n. barrière f.

barroom, n. buvette f., comptoir m., bar m.

bartender, n. barman m.

barter, n. troc m.

base, 1. n. base f. **2.** adj. bas m., basse f.

baseball, n. baseball m.

baseboard, n. moulure de base f.

basement, n. sous-sol m.

baseness, n. bassesse f.

bashful, adj. timide.

bashfully, adv. timidement, modestement.

bashfulness, n. timidité f., modestie f.

basic, adj. fondamental.

basin, n. (wash) cuvette f.; (river) bassin m.

basis, n. base f.

bask, se chauffer intr.

basket, n. (with handle) panier m.; (without handle) corbeille f.

bass, n. (music) basse f.; (fish) bar m.

bassinet, n. bercelonnette f.

bassoon, n. basson m.

bastard, n. bâtard m., (law) enfant naturel m.

baste, vb. (cooking) arroser; (sewing) faufiler.

bat, n. (animal) chauve-souris f.; (baseball) batte f.

batch, n. fournée f.

bate, vb. rabattre, diminuer.

bath, n. bain m.

bathe, vb. se baigner.

bather, n. baigneur m.

bathrobe, n. peignoir (m.) de bain.

bathroom, n. salle (f.) de bain.

bathtub, n. baignoire f.

baton, n. bâton m.

battalion, n. bataillon m.

batter, n. (cooking) pâte f.

battery, n. (military) batterie f.; (electric) pile f.

battle, n. bataille f.

battle, vb. lutter.

battlefield, n. champ (m.) de bataille.

battleship, n. cuirassé m.

bauxite, n. bauxite f.

bawl, vb. brailler.

bay, n. (geography) baie f.; (plant) laurier m.

bayonet, n. baïonnette f.

bazaar, n. bazar m.

be, vb. être.

beach, n. plage f.

beachhead, n. (haut de) plage f.

beacon, n. phare m.

bead, n. perle f.

beading, n. ornement de grains m.

beady, adj. comme un grain, couvert de grains.

beak, n. bec m.

beaker, n. gobelet m., coupe f.

beam, 1. n. (construction) poutre f.; (light) rayon m. **2.** vb. rayonner.

beaming, adj. rayonnant.

bean, n. haricot m.

bear, 1. n. ours m. **2.** vb. (carry) porter; (endure) supporter; (birth) enfanter.

bearable, adj. supportable.

beard, n. barbe f.

bearded, adj. barbu.

beardless, adj. imberbe.

bearer, n. porteur m.

bearing, n. (person) maintien m.; (machinery) coussinet m.; (naut.) relèvement m.

bearskin, n. peau d'ours f.

beast, n. bête f.

beat, 1. vb. battre. 2. n. battement m.

beaten, adj. battu.

beatify, vb. béatifier.

beating, n. battement m., rossée f.

beau, n. galant m.

beautiful, adj. beau (bel) m., belle f.

beautifully, adv. admirablement.

beautify, vb. embellir.

beauty, n. beauté f.

beauty parlor, n. salon (m.) de beauté.

beaver, n. castor m.

becalm, vb. calmer, apaiser; (naut.) abriter.

because, conj. parce que.

beckon, vb. faire signe (à).

become, vb. devenir.

becoming, adj. convenable; (dress) seyant.

bed, n. lit m.

bedbug, n. punaise f.

bedclothes, n. couvertures f.pl.

bedding, n. literie f.

bedfellow, n. camarade de lit m.

bedizen, vb. parer, attifer.

bedridden, adj. alité.

bedrock, n. roche solide f.

bedroom, n. chambre (f.) à coucher.

bedside, n. bord du lit m.

bedspread, n. dessus (m.) de lit.

bedstead, n. bois de lit m.

bedtime, n. heure (f.) de se coucher.

bee, n. abeille f.

beef, n. bœuf m.

beefsteak, n. bifteck m.

beehive, n. ruche f.

beer, n. bière f.

beeswax, n. cire jaune f.

beet, n. betterave f.

beetle, n. scarabée m.

befall, vb. arriver (à).

befit, vb. convenir (à).

befitting, adj. convenable.

before, 1. adv. (place) en avant; (time) avant. 2. prep. (place) devant; (time) avant. 3. conj. avant que.

beforehand, adv. d'avance.

befriend, vb. aider; traiter en ami.

befuddle, vb. embrouiller, déconcerter.

beg, vb. (of beggar) mendier; (ask) prier.

beget, vb. engendrer, produire.

beggar, n. mendiant m.

beggarly, adj. chétif, misérable.

begin, vb. commencer.

beginner, n. commençant m.

beginning, n. commencement m.

beguile, vb. tromper, séduire.

behalf, n. (on b. of) de la part de; (in b. of) en faveur de.

behave, vb. se conduire.

behavior, n. conduite f.

behead, vb. décapiter.

behind, adv. and prep. derrière.

behind, n. derrière m.

behold, 1. vb. voir. 2. interj. voici.

beige, adj. beige.

being, n. être m.

bejewel, vb. orner de bijoux.

belated, adj. attardé.

belch, vb. éructer.

belfry, n. clocher m., beffroi m.

Belgian, 1. n. Belge m.f. 2. adj. belge.

Belgium, n. Belgique f.

belie, vb. démentir.

belief, n. croyance f.; (confidence) confiance f.

believable, adj. croyable.

believe, vb. croire.

believer, n. croyant m.

belittle, vb. rabaisser.

bell, n. (house) sonnette f.; (church) cloche f.

bellboy, n. chasseur m.

bell buoy, n. bouée sonore f.

belligerence, n. belligérance f.

belligerent, adj. and n. belligérant m.

belligerently, adv. d'une manière belligérante.

bellow, vb. mugir.

bellows, n. soufflet m.

bell-tower, n. clocher m.

belly, n. ventre m.

belongings, n. effets, m.pl.

belong to, vb. appartenir (à).

beloved, adj. and n. chéri m.

below, 1. adv. en bas. 2. prep. au-dessous de.

belt, n. ceinture f.

bench, n. banc m.

bend, vb. plier; (curve) courber tr.

beneath, see below.

benediction, n. bénédiction f.

benefactor, n. bienfaiteur m.

benefactress, n. bienfaitrice f.

beneficent, adj. bienfaisant.

beneficial, adj. salutaire.

beneficiary, n. bénéficiaire f.

benefit, 1. (favor) bienfait m.; (advantage) bénéfice m.

benevolence, n. bienveillance f.

benevolent, adj. bienveillant.

benevolently, adv. bénévolement.

benign, adj. bénin m. bénigne f.

benignity, n. bénignité f.

bent, n. penchant m.

benzene, n. benzène m.

benzine, n. benzine f.

bequeath, vb. léguer.

bequest, n. legs m.

berate, vb. gronder.

bereave, vb. priver (de).

bereavement, n. privation f., perte f., deuil m.

beriberi, n. béribéri m.

berry, n. baie f.

berth, n. couchette f.

beseech, vb. supplier.

beseechingly, adv. en suppliant.

beset, vb. attaquer, presser, assiéger.

beside, prep. à côté de.

besides, adv. en outre.

besiege, vb. assiéger.

besieged, adj. assiégé.

besieger, n. assiégeant m.

besmirch, vb. tacher, salir.

best, 1. adj. (le) meilleur. **2.** adv. (le) mieux.

bestial, adj. bestial.

bestir, vb. remuer.

best man, n. garçon d'honneur (at weddings) m.

bestow, vb. accorder.

bestowal, n. dispensation f.

bet, 1. n. pari m. **2.** vb. parier.

betake (oneself), vb. se rendre.

betray, vb. trahir.

betroth, vb. fiancer.

betrothal, n. fiançailles f.pl.

better, 1. adj. meilleur. **2.** adv. mieux.

between, prep. entre.

bevel, 1. adj. en biseau. **2.** vb. biaiser.

beverage, n. boisson f.

bewail, vb. lamenter, pleurer.

beware of, vb. prendre garde à.

bewilder, vb. égarer.

bewildered, adj. égaré.

bewildering, adj. déconcertant.

bewilderment, n. égarement m.

bewitch, vb. ensorceler.

beyond, 1. adv. au delà. **2.** prep. au delà de.

biannual, adj. semestriel.

bias, n. (slant) biais m.; (prejudice) prévention f.

bib, n. bavette f.

Bible, n. Bible f.

biblical, adj. biblique.

bibliography, n. bibliographie f.

bicarbonate, n. bicarbonat m.

bicentennial, adj. and adj. bicentenaire m.

biceps, n. biceps m.

bicker, vb. se quereller, se chamailler.

bicycle, n. bicyclette f.

bicyclist, n. cycliste m.

bid, 1. n. (auction) enchère f.; (bridge) appel m. **2.** vb. (order) ordonner; (invite) inviter.

bidder, n. enchérisseur m.

bide, vb. (live) demeurer; (wait) attendre.

bier, n. corbillard m., civière f.

bifocal, adj. bifocal.

big, adj. grand.

bigamy, n. bigamie f.

bigot, n. bigot m.

bigotry, n. bigoterie f.

bilateral, adj. bilatéral.

bile, n. bile f.

bilingual, adj. bilingue.

bilious, adj. bilieux.

bill, n. (restaurant) addition f.; (hotel, profession) note f.; (money) billet (m.) de banque; (poster) affiche f.; (politics) projet (m.) de loi; (b. of fare) carte (f.) du jour; (bird) bec m.

billet, n. (mil.) billet de logement m.

billfold, n. portefeuille m.

billiard balls, n.pl. billes n.pl.

billiards, n. billard m.

billion, n. billion m.

bill of health, n. patente de santé f.

bill of lading, n. connaissement m.

bill of sale, n. lettre de vente f., acte de propriété m.

billow, *n.* grande vague *f.*, lame *f.*

bimetallic, *adj.* bimétallique.

bimonthly, *adj. and adv.* bimensuel.

bin, *n.* coffre *m.*

bind, *vb.* lier; (books) relier.

bindery, *n.* atelier de reliure *f.*

binding, **1.** *n.* (book) reliure *f.* **2.** *adj.* obligatoire.

binocular, *adj.* binoculaire.

biochemistry, *n.* biochimie *f.*

biodegradable, *adj.* sujet à la putréfaction.

biofeedback, *n.* biofeedback *m.*, information reçue par un organisme pendant un processus biologique *f.*

biographer, *n.* biographe *m.*

biographical, *adj.* biographique.

biography, *n.* biographie *f.*

biological, *adj.* biologique.

biologically, *adv.* biologiquement.

biology, *n.* biologie *f.*

bipartisan, *adj.* représentant les deux partis.

biped, *n.* bipède *m.*

bird, *n.* oiseau *m.*

birdlike, *adj.* comme un oiseau.

bird of prey, *n.* oiseau de proie *m.*

birth, *n.* naissance *f.*

birth control, *n.* contrôle des naissances *m.*

birthday, *n.* anniversaire *(m.)* de naissance.

birthmark, *n.* tache de naissance *f.*

birthplace, *n.* lieu *(m.)* de naissance.

birth rate, *n.* natalité *f.*

birthright, *n.* droit d'aînesse *m.*

biscuit, *n.* (hard) biscuit *m.*; (soft) petit pain *(m.)* au lait.

bisect, *vb.* couper en deux.

bishop, *n.* évêque *m.*

bishopric, *n.* évêché *m.*

bismuth, *n.* bismuth *m.*

bison, *n.* bison *m.*

bit, *n.* (piece) morceau *m.*; (a b. of)) un peu (de); (harness) mors *m.*; unité unique d'information *f.*

bitch, *n.* chienne *f.*

bite, **1.** *n.* morsure *f.* **2.** *vb.* mordre.

biting, *adj.* mordant.

bitter, *adj.* amer.

bitterly, *adv.* amèrement, avec amertume.

bitterness, *n.* amertume *f.*

bivouac, *n.* bivouac *m.*

biweekly, *adj. and adv.* tous les quinze jours.

black, *adj.* noir.

Black, *n. and adj.* (for person) noir *m.*; noire *f.*

blackberry, *n.* mûre *(f.)* de ronce.

blackbird, *n.* merle *m.*

blackboard, *n.* tableau *(m.)* noir.

blacken, *vb.* noircir.

black eye, *n.* œil poché *m.*

blackguard, *n.* gredin *m.*, polisson *m.*, salaud *m.*

blackmail, *n.* chantage *m.*

black market, *n.* marché noir *m.*

blackout, *n.* blackout *m.*

blacksmith, *n.* forgeron *m.*

bladder, *n.* vessie *f.*

blade, *n.* (sword, knife) lame *f.*; (grass) brin *m.*

blame, **1.** *n.* blâme *m.* **2.** *vb.* blâmer.

blameless, *adj.* innocent, sans tache.

blanch, *vb.* blanchir, pâlir.

bland, *adj.* doux *m.*, douce *f.*

blank, **1.** *n.* (space) blanc *m.*; (void) vide *m.*; (printing) tiret *m.* **2.** *adj.* (page) blanc *m.*, blanche *f.*; (empty) vide.

blanket, *n.* couverture *f.*

blare, *n.* son (de la trompette) *m.*, rugissement *m.*

blare, *vb.* retentir, *intr.*

blaspheme, *vb.* blasphémer.

blasphemer, *n.* blasphémateur *m.*

blasphemous, *adj.* blasphématoire.

blasphemy, *n.* blasphème *m.*

blast, *n.* (wind) rafale *f.*; (mine) explosion *f.*

blatant, *adj.* criard, bruyant.

blaze, **1.** *n.* flambée *f.* **2.** *vb.* flamber.

blazing, *adj.* enflammé, flamboyant.

bleach, *vb.* décolorer, *tr.*

bleak, *adj.* morne.

bleakness, *n.* froidure *f.*

bleed, *vb.* saigner.

blemish, *n.* défaut *m.*

blend, **1.** *n.* mélange *m.* **2.** *vb.* mêler *tr.*

blended, *adj.* mélangé.

bless, *vb.* bénir.

blessed, *adj.* béni.

blessing, *n.* bénédiction *f.*

blight, 1. *vb.* flétrir, détruire, nieller, brouir. **2.** *n.* brouissure *f.*, flétrissure *f.*

blind, 1. *n.* store *m.* **2.** *adj.* aveugle; **(b. alley)** cul-de-sac *m.*

blindfold, *adj. and adv.* les yeux bandés.

blinding, *adj.* aveuglant.

blindly, *adv.* aveuglément.

blindness, *n.* cécité *f.*

blink, *vb.* clignoter.

bliss, *n.* béatitude *f.*

blissful, *adj.* bienheureux.

blissfully, *adv.* heureusement.

blister, *n.* ampoule *f.*

blithe, *adj.* gai, joyeux.

blizzard, *n.* tempête *(f.)* de neige.

bloat, *vb.* boursoufler.

bloc, *n.* bloc *m.*

block, 1. *n.* bloc *m.;* **(houses)** pâté *m.* **2.** *vb.* bloquer.

blockade, *n.* blocus *m.*

blond, *adj. and n.* blond *m.*

blood, *n.* sang *m.*

bloodhound, *n.* limier *m.*

bloodless, *adj.* exsangue, sans effusion de sang.

blood plasma, *n.* plasma du sang *m.*

blood poisoning, *n.* empoisonnement du sang *m.*

blood pressure, *n.* tension artérielle *f.*

bloodshed, *n.* effusion *(f.)* de sang.

bloodshot, *adj.* injecté de sang.

bloodthirsty, *adj.* sanguinaire.

bloody, *adj.* sanglant.

bloom, 1. *n.* fleur *f.* **2.** *vb.* fleurir.

blooming, 1. *n.* floraison *f.* **2.** *adj.* fleurissant.

blossom, *see* bloom.

blot, 1. *n.* tache *f.* **2.** *vb.* **(spot)** tacher; **(dry ink)** sécher l'encre.

blotch, *n.* tache *f.*

blotchy, *adj.* couvert de taches.

blotter, *n.* buvard *m.*

blouse, *n.* blouse *f.*

blow, 1. *n.* coup *m.* **2.** *vb.* souffler; **(b. out)** éteindre; **(b. over)** passer; **(b. up)** faire sauter, *tr.*

blowout, *n.* éclatement *(m.)* de pneu.

blubber, 1. *vb.* pleurer comme un veau. **2.** *n.* graisse de baleine *f.*

bludgeon, 1. *n.* matraque *f.* **2.** *vb.* donner des coups de matraque.

blue, *adj.* bleu.

blue jeans, *n.* blue jeans *m.pl.*

blueprint, *n.* dessin négatif *m.*

bluff, *n.* bluff *m.*

bluffer, *n.* bluffeur *m.*

blunder, *n.* bévue *f.*

blunderer, *n.* maladroit *m.*

blunt, *adj.* **(blade)** émoussé; **(person)** brusque.

bluntly, *adv.* brusquement.

bluntness, *n.* brusquerie *f.*

blur, *vb.* **(smear)** barbouiller.

blush, 1. *n.* rougeur *f.* **2.** *vb.* rougir.

bluster, *n.* fanfaronnade *f.*

boar, *n.* **(wild)** sanglier *m.*

board, *n.* **(plank)** planche *f.;* **(daily meals)** pension *f.;* **(boat)** bord *m.;* **(politics)** ministère *m.;* **(administration)** conseil *m.*

boarder, *n.* pensionnaire *m.*

boarding pass, *n.* carte *(f.)* d'embarquement.

boast (of), *vb.* se vanter (de).

boaster, *n.* vantard *m.*

boastful, *adj.* vantard.

boastfulness, *n.* vantardise *f.*

boat, *n.* bateau *m.*

boathouse, *n.* abri *(m.)* à bateaux.

boatswain, *n.* maître d'équipage *m.*

bob, *vb.* **(hair)** couper court.

bobbin, *n.* bobine *f.*

bode, *vb.* présager.

bodice, *n.* corsage *m.*

bodily, *adj.* corporel.

body, *n.* corps *m.*

bodyguard, *n.* garde *(f.)* du corps.

bog, 1. *n.* marécage *m.* **2.** *vb.* embourber.

Bohemia, *n.* (geographical) Bohême *f.;* *(fig.)* bohème *f.*

Bohemian, 1. *n.* (geographical) Bohémien *m.;* *(fig.)* bohème *m.f.* **2.** *adj.* (geographical) bohémien; *(fig.)* bohème.

boil, 1. *vb.* bouillir, *intr.;* faire bouillir, *tr.* **2.** *n.* *(med.)* furoncle *m.,* (popular) clou *m.*

boiler, *n.* chaudière *f.*

boisterous, *adj.* **(person)** bruyant.

boisterously, *adv.* bruyamment.

bold, *adj.* hardi.

boldface, adj. (type) caractères gras m.pl.

boldly, adv. hardiment, avec audace.

boldness, n. hardiesse f.

bologna, n. saucisson (m.) de Bologne.

bolster, n. traversin m.

bolster up, vb. soutenir.

bolt, 1. n. verrou m. **2.** vb. verrouiller.

bomb, n. bombe f.

bombard, vb. bombarder.

bombardier, n. bombardier m.

bombardment, n. bombardement m.

bomber, n. avion (m.) de bombardement.

bombproof, adj. à l'épreuve des bombes.

bombshell, n. bombe f.

bombsight, n. viseur de lancement m.

bonbon, n. bonbon m.

bond, n. lien m.; (law, finance) obligation f.

bondage, n. servitude f.

bonded, adj. entreposé.

bone, n. os m.

boneless, adj. sans os.

bonfire, n. feu (m.) de joie.

bonnet, n. chapeau m.

bonus, n. gratification f.

bony, adj. osseux.

book, n. livre m.

bookbindery, n. atelier de reliure m.

bookcase, n. bibliothèque f.

bookkeeper, n. teneur (m.) de livres.

bookkeeping, n. comptabilité f.

booklet, n. opuscule m.

bookseller, n. libraire m.; (second-hand) bouquiniste m.

bookstore, bookshop, n. librairie f.

boon, n. bienfait m., don m.

boor, n. rustre m.

boorish, adj. rustre.

boost, vb. (push) pousser; (praise) louer.

boot, n. bottine f.

bootblack, n. cireur m.

booth, n. (fair) baraque f.; (telephone) cabine f.

booty, n. butin m.

border, n. bord m.; (of country) frontière f.

borderline, adj. touchant (à), avoisinant.

bore, vb. (make a hole) forer; (annoy) ennuyer.

boredom, n. ennui m.

boric acid, n. acide borique m.

born, 1. adj. né. **2.** vb. (be b.) naître.

born-again, adj. rené.

borough, n. (administration) circonscription électorale f.; (large village) bourg m.

borrower, n. emprunteur m.

borrow from, vb. emprunter à.

bosom, n. sein m.

boss, 1. n. patron m. **2.** vb. diriger.

bossy, adj. comme un patron, impérieux.

botanical, adj. botanique.

botany, n. botanique f.

botch, 1. n. ravaudage m. **2.** vb. ravauder, faire une mauvaise besogne.

both, adj. and pron. tous (les) deux m., toutes (les) deux f.

bother, 1. n. ennui m. **2.** vb. gêner.

bothersome, adj. gênant.

bottle, n. bouteille f.

bottom, n. fond m.

bottomless, adj. sans fond.

bough, n. branche f.

bouillon, n. bouillon m.

boulder, n. galet m.

boulevard, n. boulevard m.

bounce, vb. (ball) rebondir.

bound, 1. n. (limit) borne f.; (jump) bond m. **2.** vb. (limit) borner; (jump) bondir.

boundary, n. frontière f.

bound for, adj. en route pour.

boundless, adj. sans bornes, illimité.

boundlessly, adv. sans bornes.

bounteous, adj. généreux, bienfaisant.

bounty, n. largesse f.; (premium) prime f.

bouquet, n. bouquet m.

bourgeois, adj. bourgeois.

bout, n. (fever) accès m.

bovine, n. bovine f.; adj. bovin.

bow, n. (weapon) arc m.; (violin)

archet *m.*; (curtsy) révérence *f.*; (ship) avant *m.*

bow, *vb.* incliner, *tr.*

bowels, *n.* entrailles *f.pl.*

bowl, 1. *n.* bol *m.* **2.** *vb.* jouer aux boules.

bowlegged, *adj.* à jambes arquées.

bowler, *n.* joueur de boule *m.*

box, *n.* boîte *f.*; (theater) loge *f.*

boxcar, *n.* wagon de marchandises *m.*

boxer, *n.* boxeur *m.*

boxing, *n.* boxe *f.*

box office, *n.* bureau *(m.)* de location.

boy, *n.* garçon *m.*

boycott, *vb.* boycotter.

boyhood, *n.* première jeunesse *f.*

boyish, *adj.* enfantin, puéril.

boyishly, *adv.* comme un gamin.

brace, 1. *n.* fortifier. **2.** *n.* vilebrequin (tool) *m.*, paire *f.*, couple *m.*

bracelet, *n.* bracelet *m.*

bracket, *n.* (wall) console *f.*; (printing) crochet *m.*

brag, *vb.* se vanter.

braggart, *n.* fanfaron *m.*

braid, *n.* (hair) tresse *f.*; (sewing) galon *m.*

brain, *n.* cerveau *m.*; (brains) cervelle *f.*

brainy, *adj.* intelligent.

brake, *n.* frein *m.*

bran, *n.* son *m.*

branch, *n.* branche *f.*

brand, *n.* marque *f.*

brandish, *vb.* brandir.

brand-new, *adj.* tout neuf.

brandy, *n.* eau-de-vie *f.*

brash, *adj.* impertinent.

brass, *n.* cuivre (*m.*) jaune.

brassiere, *n.* soutien-gorge *m.*

brat, *n.* gosse *m.f.*

bravado, *n.* bravade *f.*

brave, *adj.* courageux.

bravery, *n.* courage *m.*

brawl, *n.* rixe *f.*

brawn, *n.* partie charnue *f.*, muscles *m.pl.*

bray, *vb.* braire.

brazen, *adj.* (person) effronté.

Brazil, *n.* Brésil *m.*

breach, *n.* infraction *f.*; *(mil.)* brèche *f.*

bread, *n.* pain *m.*

breadth, *n.* largeur *f.*

break, 1. *n.* rupture *f.*; (pause) interruption *f.* **2.** *vb.* rompre, briser, casser.

breakable, *adj.* cassable.

breakage, *n.* cassure *f.*, rupture *f.*

breakfast, *n.* (petit) déjeuner *m.*

breakwater, *n.* brise-lames *m.*, jetée *f.*

breast, *n.* poitrine *f.*, sein *m.*

breath, *n.* haleine *f.*; *(fig.,* wind) souffle *m.*

breathe, *vb.* respirer.

breathless, *adj.* (out of breath) essoufflé.

breathlessly, *adv.* hors d'haleine.

bred, *adj.* élevé.

breeches, *n.* pantalon *m.sg.*

breed, *vb.* produire; (livestock) élever.

breeder, *n.* (raiser) éleveur *m.*

breeding, *n.* (manners) éducation *f.*; (animals) élevage *m.*

breeze, *n.* brise *f.*

breezy, *adj.* (windy) venteux; (manner) dégagé.

brevity, *n.* brièveté *f.*

brew, *vb.* (beer) brasser; (tea) faire infuser *tr.*

brewery, *n.* brasserie *f.*

briar, *n.* ronce *f.*

bribe, *vb.* corrompre.

briber, *n.* corrupteur *m.*

bribery, *n.* corruption *f.*

brick, *n.* brique *f.*

bricklaying, *n.* maçonnerie *f.*

bricklike, *adj.* comme une brique.

bridal, *adj.* nuptial.

bride, *n.* mariée *f.*

bridegroom, *n.* marié *m.*

bridesmaid, *n.* demoiselle (*f.*) d'honneur.

bridge, *n.* pont *m.*; (boat) passerelle *f.*; (cards) bridge *m.*

bridged, *adj.* lié.

bridgehead, *n.* tête de pont *f.*

bridle, *n.* bride *f.*

brief, *adj.* bref *m.*, brève *f.*

brief case, *n.* serviette *f.*

briefly, *adv.* brièvement.

briefness, *n.* brièveté *f.*

brier, *n.* bruyère *f.*, ronces *f.pl.*

brig, *n.* brick *m.*

brigade, *n.* brigade *f.*

bright, *adj.* vif *m.*, vive *f.*; intelligent.

brighten, vb. faire briller, tr.

brightness, n. éclat m.

brilliance, n. éclat m.

brilliant, adj. brillant.

brim, n. bord m.

brine, n. saumure f.

bring, vb. (thing) apporter; (person) amener; **(b. about)** amener, causer.

brink, n. bord m.

briny, adj. salé.

brisk, adj. vif m., vive f.

brisket, n. poitrine (meat) f.

briskly, adv. vivement.

briskness, n. vivacité f.

bristle, n. soie f.

bristly, adj. hérissé (de), poilu.

British, adj. britannique.

British Empire, n. Empire Britannique m.

British Isles, n. Îles Britanniques f.pl.

brittle, adj. fragile.

broad, adj. large.

broadcast, vb. radiodiffuser.

broadcast, n. radio-émission f.

broadcaster, n. speaker m.

broadcloth, n. drap (m.) fin.

broaden, vb. élargir.

broadly, adv. largement.

broadminded, adj. large d'esprit.

broadside, n. côte f., bordée f.

brocade, n. brocart m.

brocaded, adj. de brocart.

broil, vb. griller.

broiler, n. gril m.

broken-hearted, adj. qui a le coeur brisé.

broker, n. courtier m.; **(stock-b.)** agent (m.) de change.

brokerage, n. courtage f.

bronchial, adj. bronchique.

bronchitis, n. bronchite f.

bronze, n. bronze m.

brooch, n. broche f.

brood, 1. n. couvée f. 2. vb. couver.

brook, n. ruisseau m.

broom, n. balai m.

broomstick, n. manche à balai m.

broth, n. bouillon m.

brothel, n. bordel m., maison mal famée f.

brother, n. frère m.

brotherhood, n. fraternité f.

brother-in-law, n. beau-frère m.

brotherly, adj. fraternel.

brow, n. front m.

brown, adj. brun.

browse, vb. (animals) brouter; (books) feuilleter (des livres).

bruise, 1. n. meurtrissure f. 2. vb. meurtrir.

brunette, adj. and n. brune f.

brunt, n. choc m.

brush, n. brosse f.; **(paint-b.)** pinceau m.

brushwood, n. broussailles f.pl.

brusque, adj. brusque.

brusquely, adv. brusquement.

brutal, adj. brutal.

brutality, n. brutalité f.

brutalize, vb. abrutir.

brute, n. brute f.

bubble, 1. n. bulle f. 2. vb. bouillonner.

buck, n. daim m.; (male) mâle m.

bucket, n. seau m.

buckle, n. boucle f.

buckram, n. bougran m.

buckshot, n. chevrotine f.

buckwheat, n. sarrasin m., blé noir m.

bud, 1. n. bourgeon m. 2. vb. bourgeonner.

budding, adj. en herbe.

budge, vb. bouger.

budget, n. budget m.

buffalo, n. buffle m.

buffer, n. tampon m.

buffet, n. (sideboard) buffet m.

buffoon, n. bouffon m.

bug, n. insecte m.

bugle, n. clairon m.

build, vb. bâtir.

builder, n. (buildings) entrepreneur m.; (ships) constructeur m.

building, n. bâtiment m.

bulb, n. (electricity) ampoule f.; (botany) bulbe m.

bulge, n. bosse f.

bulk, n. masse f.

bulkhead, n. cloison étanche f.

bulky, adj. volumineux.

bull, n. taureau m.

bulldog, n. bouledogue m.

bulldozer, n. machine à refouler f.

bullet, n. balle f.

bulletin, n. bulletin m.

bulletproof, adj. à l'épreuve des balles.

bullfinch, n. bouvreuil m.

bullion, n. lingot m.

bully, vb. rudoyer.

bulwark, n. rempart m.

bum, n. fainéant m.

bumblebee, n. bourdon m.

bump, **1.** n. (blow) coup m.; (protuberance) bosse f. **2.** vb. cogner.

bumper, n. (auto) pare-chocs m.

bun, n. brioche f.

bunch, n. (flowers) bouquet m.; (grapes) grappe f.; (keys) trousseau m.

bundle, n. paquet m.

bungle, vb. bousiller.

bunion, n. cor m.

bunk, n. couchette f.

bunny, n. lapin m.

bunting, n. drapeaux m.pl.

buoy, n. bouée f.

buoyant, adj. qui a du ressort.

burden, n. fardeau m.

burdensome, adj. onéreux.

bureau, n. (office) bureau m.; (chest of drawers) commode f.

burglar, n. cambrioleur m.

burglarize, vb. cambrioler.

burglary, n. vol (m.) avec effraction.

burial, n. enterrement m.

burlap, n. gros canevas m.

burly, adj. corpulent.

burn, vb. brûler.

burner, n. bec m.

burning, adj. brûlant.

burnish, vb. brunir, polir.

burrow, n. terrier m.

burst, vb. éclater.

bury, vb. enterrer.

bus, n. autobus m.

bush, n. buisson m.

bushel, n. boisseau m.

bushy, adj. buissonneux; (hair) touffu.

busily, adv. activement.

business, n. affaire f.; (comm.) affaires f.pl.

businesslike, adj. pratique.

businessman, n. homme (m.) d'affaires.

business-woman, n. femme (f.) d'affaires.

bust, n. buste m.

bustle, vb. se remuer.

busy, adj. occupé.

busybody, n. officieux m.

but, conj. mais; (only) ne . . . que; (except) sauf.

butcher, n. boucher m.

butchery, n. tuerie f., massacre m.

butler, n. maître (m.) d'hôtel.

butt, n. bout m., (of jokes) plastron m.

butter, n. beurre m.

buttercup, n. bouton d'or m.

butterfly, n. papillon m.

buttermilk, n. babeurre m.

butterscotch, n. caramel au beurre m.

buttock, n. fesse f.

button, n. bouton m.

buttonhole, n. boutonnière f.

buttress, n. contrefort m.; (flying b.) arc-boutant m.

buxom, adj. (of women) aux formes rebondies.

buy, vb. acheter.

buyer, n. acheteur m.

buzz, **1.** n. bourdonnement m. **2.** vb. bourdonner.

buzzard, n. buse f.

buzzer, n. trompe f., sirène f.

by, prep. (through) par; (near) près de.

by-and-by, adv. bientôt.

bygone, adj. passé, d'autrefois.

bylaw, n. règlement local m.

by-pass, **1.** n. route d'évitement f. **2.** vb. faire un détour.

by-product, n. sous-produit m.

bystander, n. spectateur m.

byte, n. unité fondamentale de données f.

byway, n. sentier détourné m.

C

cab, n. (taxi) taxi m.; (horse) fiacre m.

cabaret, n. cabaret m.

cabbage, n. chou m.

cabin, n. (hut) cabane f.; (boat) cabine f.

cabinet, n. cabinet m.

cabinetmaker, n. ébéniste m.

cable, **1.** n. câble m. **2.** vb. câbler.

cablegram, n. câblogramme m.

cachet, n. cachet m.

cackle, **1.** n. caquet m. **2.** vb. caqueter.

cacophony, n. cacophonie f.

cactus, n. cactus m.

cad, n. mufle m.

cadaver, n. cadavre m.

cadaverous, adj. cadavérique.

cadence, *n.* cadence *f.*
cadet, *n.* cadet *m.*
cadmium, *n.* cadmium *m.*
cadre, *n.* cadre *m.*
café, *n.* café, (-restaurant) *m.*
cafeteria, *n.* restaurant *m.*
caffeine, *n.* caféine *f.*
cage, *n.* cage *f.*
caged, *adj.* mis en cage.
caisson, *n.* caisson *m.*
cajole, *vb.* cajoler.
cake, *n.* gâteau *m.*
calamitous, *adj.* calamiteux, désastreux.
calamity, *n.* calamité *f.*
calcify, *vb.* calcifier.
calcium, *n.* calcium *m.*
calculable, *adj.* calculable.
calculate, *vb.* calculer.
calculating, *adj.* qui fait des calculs.
calculation, *n.* calcul *m.*
calculus, *n.* calcul *m.*
caldron, *n.* chaudron *m.*
calendar, *n.* calendrier *m.*
calender, *n.* calandre *f.*
calf, *n.* veau *m.*
calfskin, *adj.* en peau de veau.
caliber, *n.* calibre *m.*
calico, *n.* calicot *m.*
calisthenic, *adj.* callisthénique.
calisthenics, *n.* callisthénie *f.*
calk, *vb.* ferrer à glace.
call, 1. *n.* appel *m.;* (visit) visite *f.* **2.** *vb.* appeler; (call on) faire visite à.
calligraphy, *n.* calligraphie *f.*
calling, *n.* vocation *f.,* profession *f.*
calling card, *n.* carte de visite *f.*
callously, *adv.* d'une manière insensible.
callousness, *n.* insensibilité *f.*
callow, *adj.* blanc-bec.
callus, *n.* callosité *f.*
calm, 1. *adj.* calme. **2.** *vb.* calmer.
calmly, *adv.* calmement.
calmness, *n.* calme *m.,* tranquillité *f.*
caloric, *adj.* calorique.
calorie, *n.* calorie *f.*
calorimeter, *n.* calorimètre *m.*
calumniate, *vb.* calomnier.
calumny, *n.* calomnie *f.*
Calvary, *n.* Calvaire *m.*
calve, *vb.* vêler.
calyx, *n.* calice *m.*

camaraderie, *n.* camaraderie *f.*
cambric, *n.* batiste *f.*
camel, *n.* chameau *m.*
camellia, *n.* camélia *m.*
camel's hair, *n.* poil de chameau *m.*
cameo, *n.* camée *m.*
camera, *n.* appareil photographique *m.*
camouflage, *vb.* camoufler.
camouflaged, *adj.* camouflé.
camouflaging, *adj.* camouflant.
camp, 1. *n.* camp *m.;* (holiday camp) camping **m. 2.** *vb.* camper.
campaign, *n.* campagne *f.*
camper, *n.* qui fait du camping.
camphor, *n.* camphre *m.*
camphor ball, *n.* balle de camphre *f.*
campus, *n.* terrains *(m.pl.)* de l'université.
can, 1. *n.* (food) boîte *f.;* (general) bidon *m.* **2.** *vb.* (be able) pouvoir; (put in a can) conserver.
Canada, *n.* Canada *m.*
Canadian, 1. *n.* Canadien *m.* **2.** *adj.* canadien.
canal, *n.* canal *m.*
canalize, *vb.* canaliser.
canapé, *n.* canapé *m.*
canard, *n.* canard *m.*
canary, *n.* serin *m.*
Canary Islands, *n.* Îles Canaries *f.pl.*
cancel, *vb.* annuler; (erase) biffer.
cancellation, *n.* annulation *f.*
cancer, *n.* cancer *m.*
candelabrum, *n.* candélabre *m.*
candid, *adj.* sincère.
candidacy, *n.* candidature *f.*
candidate, *n.* candidat *m.*
candidly, *adv.* franchement.
candidness, *n.* candeur *f.*
candied, *adj.* candi.
candle, *n.* bougie *f.;* (church) cierge *m.*
candler, *n.* fabricant de chandelles *m.*
candlestick, *n.* chandelier *m.*
candor, *n.* sincérité *f.*
candy, *n.* bonbon *m.*
cane, *n.* canne *f.*
canine, *adj.* canin.
canister, *n.* boîte à thé *f.*
canker, *n.* chancre *m.*

cankerworm, *n.* ver rongeur *m.*

canned, *adj.* conservé en boîtes (de fer blanc).

canner, *n.* travailleur dans une conserverie *m.*

cannery, *n.* conserverie *f.*

cannibal, *adj. and n.* cannibale *m.f.*

canning, *n.* mise en conserve, en boîtes (de fer blanc) *f.*

cannon, *n.* canon *m.*

cannonade, *n.* canonnade *f.*

cannoneer, *n.* canonier *m.*

cannot, *vb.* ne peut pas.

canny, *adj.* avisé, rusé.

canoe, *n.* canot *m.*

canon, *n.* chanoine *m.*; canon (rule) *m.*

canonical, *adj.* canonique.

canonize, *vb.* canoniser.

canopy, *n.* dais *m.*

cant, *n.* hypocrisie *f.*

can't, *vb.* ne peut pas.

cantaloupe, *n.* melon *m.*, cantaloup *m.*

canteen, *n.* cantine *f.*; bidon *m.*

canter, 1. *n.* petit galop *f.* 2. *vb.* aller au petit galop.

cantonment, *n.* cantonnement *m.*

canvas, *n.* toile *f.*

canvass, 1. *n.* sollicitation *f.* 2. *vb.* solliciter; (discuss) débattre.

canyon, *n.* gorge *f.*, défilé *m.*

cap, *n.* bonnet *m.*; (peaked) casquette *f.*

capability, *n.* capacité *f.*

capable, *adj.* capable.

capably, *adv.* capablement.

capacious, *adj.* ample, spacieux.

capacity, *n.* capacité *f.*

caparison, 1. *n.* caparaçon *m.* 2. *vb.* caparaçonner.

cape, *n.* (geography) cap *m.*; (cloak) cape *f.*

caper, 1. *n.* bond *m.*; (plant) câpre *f.* 2. *vb.* bondir.

capillary, *adj.* capillaire.

capital, *adj.* capital.

capital, *n.* (finance) capital *m.*; (city) capitale *f.*; (letter) majuscule *f.*; (architecture) chapiteau *m.*

capitalism, *n.* capitalisme *m.*

capitalist, *n.* capitaliste *m.f.*

capitalistic, *adj.* capitaliste.

capitalization, *n.* capitalisation *f.*

capitalize, *vb.* capitaliser.

capitulate, *vb.* capituler.

capon, *n.* chapon *m.*

caprice, *n.* caprice *m.*

capricious, *adj.* capricieux.

capriciously, *adv.* capricieusement.

capriciousness, *n.* caractère capricieux *m.*, humeur fantasque *f.*

capsize, *vb.* chavirer, *intr.*; faire chavirer, *tr.*

capsule, *n.* capsule *f.*

captain, *n.* capitaine *m.*

caption, *n.* en-tête *m.*

captious, *adj.* chicaneur.

captivate, *vb.* captiver.

captivating, *adj.* séduisant.

captive, *adj. and n.* captif *m.*

captivity, *n.* captivité *f.*

captor, *n.* capteur *m.*

capture, 1. *n.* capture *f.* 2. *vb.* capturer.

car, *n.* (auto) voiture *f.*; (train) wagon *m.*

caracul, *n.* caracul *m.*

carafe, *n.* carafe *f.*

caramel, *n.* caramel *m.*

carat, *n.* carat *m.*

caravan, *n.* caravane *f.*

caraway, *n.* carvi *m.*, cumin (des prés) *m.*

carbide, *n.* carbure *m.*

carbine, *n.* carabine *f.*

carbohydrate, *n.* carbohydrate *m.*

carbon, *n.* carbone *m.*

carbon dioxide, *n.* acide carbonique *m.*

carbon monoxide, *n.* oxyde de carbone *m.*

carbon paper, *n.* papier carbone *m.*

carbuncle, *n.* escarboucle *f.*, charbon (med.) *m.*

carburetor, *n.* carburateur *m.*

carcass, *n.* carcasse *f.*

carcinogenic, *adj.* cancérogène.

card, *n.* carte *f.*

cardboard, *n.* carton *m.*

cardiac, *adj.* cardiaque.

cardigan, *n.* gilet de tricot *m.*

cardinal, *n.* cardinal *m.*

care, *n.* (worry) souci *m.*; (attention) attention *f.*; (take c.!) faites attention!; (charge) soin *m.*; (take c. of) prendre soin de. 2. *vb.* (c. about) se soucier de; (c. for) aimer; (look after) soigner.

careen, *vb.* caréner.

career, *n.* carrière *f.*

carefree, *adj.* insouciant.

careful, *adj.* soigneux.

carefully, *adv.* soigneusement, attentivement.

carefulness, *n.* soin *m.,* attention *f.*

careless, *adj.* insouciant.

carelessly, *adv.* nonchalamment, négligemment.

carelessness, *n.* insouciance *f.,* négligence *f.*

caress, 1. *n.* caresse *f.* **2.** *vb.* caresser.

caretaker, *n.* concierge *m.f.*

cargo, *n.* cargaison *f.*

caricature, *n.* caricature *f.*

caries, *n.* carie *f.*

carillon, *n.* carillon *m.*

carload, *n.* voiturée *f.*

carnal, *adj.* charnel.

carnation, *n.* œillet *m.*

carnival, *n.* carnaval *m.*

carnivorous, *adj.* carnivore.

carol, *n.* **(Xmas c.)** noël *m.*

carouse, *vb.* faire la fête.

carpenter, *n.* charpentier *m.*

carpet, *n.* tapis *m.*

carpeting, *n.* pose de tapis *f.*

car pool, *n.* groupe de personnes qui voyagent régulièrement ensemble en auto *m.*

carriage, *n.* (vehicle) voiture *f.;* (bearing) maintien *m.;* (transport) transport *m.*

carrier, *n.* porteur *m.,* messager *m.*

carrier pigeon, *n.* pigeon voyageur *m.*

carrot, *n.* carotte *m.*

carrousel, *n.* carrousel *m.*

carry, *vb.* porter; **(c. on)** continuer; **(c. out)** exécuter; **(c. through)** mener à bonne fin.

cart, *n.* charrette *f.*

cartage, *n.* charriage *m.,* transport *m.*

cartel, *n.* cartel *m.*

carter, *n.* charretier *m.*

cartilage, *n.* cartilage *m.*

carton, *n.* carton *m.*

cartoon, *n.* dessin satirique *m.*

cartoonist, *n.* caricaturiste *m.*

cartridge, *n.* cartouche *f.*

carve, *vb.* (art) sculpter; (meat) découper.

carver, *n.* découpeur *m.,* sculpteur *m.*

carving, *n.* découpage *m.,* sculpture *f.*

cascade, *n.* cascade *f.*

case, *n.* (instance, state of things) cas *m.;* (law) cause *f.;* (packing) caisse *f.;* (holder) étui *m.;* **(in any c.)** en tout cas.

cash, 1. *n.* espèces *f.pl.;* (C.O.D.) livraison contre remboursement *f.* **2.** *vb.* **(c. a check)** toucher.

cashier, *n.* caissier *m.*

cashmere, *n.* cachemire *m.*

casing, *n.* revêtement *m.,* enveloppe *f.*

casino, *n.* casino *m.*

cask, *n.* tonneau *m.*

casket, *n.* cassette *f.*

casserole, *n.* casserole *f.*

cassette, *n.* cassette *f.*

cast, 1. *n.* (throw) coup *m.;* (characteristic) trempe *f.;* (theater) distribution *f.;* (c. from mold) moulage *m.;* (hue) nuance *f.* **2.** *vb.* (throw) jeter; (metal) couler.

castaway, *n.* naufragé *m.,* rejeté *m.*

caste, *n.* caste *f.*

caster, *n.* fondeur *m.*

castigate, *vb.* châtier, punir.

cast iron, *n.* fonte *f.*

castle, *n.* château *m.*

castoff, *adj.* abandonné.

casual, *adj.* (accidental) casuel; (person) insouciant.

casually, *adv.* fortuitement, en passant.

casualness, *n.* nonchalance *f.*

casualties, *n.* (mil.) pertes *f.pl.*

cat, *n.* chat *m.,* chatte *f.*

cataclysm, *n.* cataclysme *m.*

catacomb, *n.* catacombe *f.*

catalogue, *n.* catalogue *m.*

catapult, *n.* catapulte *f.*

cataract, *n.* cataracte *f.*

catarrh, *n.* catarrhe *m.*

catastrophe, *n.* catastrophe *f.*

catch, *vb.* attraper; (seize, understand) saisir.

catcher, *n.* qui attrape.

catchword, *n.* mot d'ordre *m.*

catchy, *adj.* (musical air) facile à retenir; (question) insidieuse.

catechism, *n.* catéchisme *m.*

catechize, *vb.* catéchiser.

categorical, *adj.* catégorique.

category, *n.* catégorie *f.*

cater, *vb.* pourvoir à.

caterpillar, *n.* chenille *f.*

catgut, *n.* corde à boyau *f.*

catharsis, *n.* catharsis *f.,* (med.) purgation *f.*

cathartic, *adj.* cathartique, purgatif.

cathedral, *n.* cathédrale *f.*

cathode, *n.* cathode *f.*

Catholic, *adj.* catholique.

Catholic Church, *n.* Église catholique *f.*

Catholicism, *n.* catholicisme *m.*

cat nap, *n.* somme *m.*

catsup, *n.* sauce piquante *f.*

cattle, *n.* bétail *m.,* bestiaux *m.pl.*

cattleman, *n.* éleveur de bétail *m.*

catwalk, *n.* coursive *f.*

cauliflower, *n.* chou-fleur *m.*

causation, *n.* causation *f.*

cause, *n.* cause *f.*

causeway, *n.* chaussée *f.*

caustic, *adj.* caustique.

cauterize, *vb.* cautériser.

cautery, *n.* cautère *m.*

caution, 1. *n.* prudence *f.*

caution, *vb.* avertir.

cautious, *adj.* prudent.

cavalcade, *n.* cavalcade *f.*

cavalier, *adj. and n.* cavalier *m.*

cavalry, *n.* cavalerie *f.*

cave, *n.* caverne *f.*

cave-in, *n.* effondrement *m.*

cavern, *n.* caverne *f.*

caviar, *n.* caviar *m.*

cavity, *n.* cavité *f.*

cease, *vb.* cesser (de).

ceaseless, *adj.* incessant, continuel.

cedar, *n.* cèdre *m.*

cede, *vb.* céder.

ceiling, *n.* plafond *m.*

celebrant, *n.* célébrant *m.*

celebrate, *vb.* célébrer.

celebration, *n.* célébration *f.*

celebrity, *n.* célébrité *f.*

celerity, *n.* célérité *f.,* vitesse *f.*

celery, *n.* céleri *m.*

celestial, *adj.* céleste.

celibacy, *n.* célibat *m.*

celibate, *adj.* célibataire.

cell, *n.* cellule *f.*

cellar, *n.* cave *f.*

cellist, *n.* violoncelliste *m.*

cello, *n.* violoncelle *m.*

cellophane, *n.* cellophane *f.*

cellular, *adj.* cellulaire.

celluloid, *n.* celluloïd *m.*

cellulose, *n.* cellulose *f.*

Celtic, *adj.* celtique.

cement, 1. *n.* ciment *m.* **2.** *vb.* cimenter.

cemetery, *n.* cimetière *m.*

censor, 1. *n.* censeur *m.* **2.** *vb.* censurer.

censorious, *adj.* critique, hargneux.

censorship, *n.* censure *f.*

censure, *n.* censure *f.*

census, *n.* recensement *m.*

cent, *n.* cent *m.; (per c.)* pour cent.

centenary, centennial, *adj. and n.* centenaire *m.*

center, *n.* centre *m.*

centerfold, *n.* pages centrales *f.pl.*

centerpiece, *n.* pièce de milieu *f.*

centigrade, *adj.* centigrade.

centigrade thermometer, *n.* thermomètre centigrade *m.*

central, *adj.* central.

centralize, *vb.* centraliser.

century, *n.* siècle *m.*

century plant, *n.* agave d'Amérique *m.*

ceramic, *adj.* céramique.

ceramics, *n.* céramique *f.*

cereal, *adj. and n.* céréale *f.*

cerebral, *adj.* cérébral.

ceremonial, *adj. and n.* cérémonial *m.*

ceremonious, *adj.* cérémonieux.

ceremony, *n.* cérémonie *f.*

certain, *adj.* certain.

certainly, *adv.* certainement.

certainty, *n.* certitude *f.*

certificate, *n.* certificat *m.; (birth c.)* acte de naissance.

certification, *n.* certification *f.*

certified, *adj.* certifié, diplômé, breveté.

certifier, *n.* (personne) qui certifie.

certify, *vb.* certifier.

certitude, *n.* certitude *f.*

cervical, *adj.* cervical.

cervix, *n.* cervix *m.*

cessation, *n.* cessation *f.,* suspension *f.*

cession, *n.* cession *f.*

cesspool, *n.* fosse d'aisances *f.*

chafe, *vb.* frictionner.

chaff, 1. *n.* menue paille *f.*; (*colloq.*) blague *f.* **2.** *vb.* blaguer.

chafing dish, *n.* réchaud *m.*

chagrin, *n.* chagrin *m.*

chain, *n.* chaîne *f.*

chain reaction, *n.* réaction caténaire *f.*

chain store, *n.* succursale de grand magasin *f.*

chair, *n.* chaise *f.*; (**arm-c.**) fauteuil *m.*

chairman, *n.* président *m.*

chairmanship, *n.* présidence *f.*

chairperson, *n.* président *m.*; présidente *f.*

chairwoman, *n.* présidente *f.*

chalice, *n.* calice *m.*

chalk, *n.* craie *f.*

chalky, *adj.* de craie, calcaire.

challenge, *n.* défi *m.*

challenge, *vb.* défier; (dispute) contester.

challenger, *n.* qui fait un défi, prétendant *m.*

chamber, *n.* chambre *f.*

chamberlain, *n.* chambellan *m.*

chambermaid, *n.* femme de chambre *f.*

chamber music, *n.* musique de chambre *f.*

chameleon, *n.* caméléon *m.*

chamois, *n.* chamois *m.*

champ, *vb.* ronger, mâcher.

champion, *n.* champion *m.*

championship, *n.* championnat *m.*

chance, *n.* chance *f.*; (**by c.**) par hasard.

chancel, *n.* sanctuaire *m.*, choeur *m.*

chancellery, *n.* chancellerie *f.*

chancellor, *n.* chancelier *m.*

chandelier, *n.* lustre *m.*

change, 1. *n.* changement *m.*; (money) monnaie *f.*; (exchange) change *m.* **2.** *vb.* changer.

changeable, *adj.* changeant.

changeability, *n.* variabilité *f.*

changer, *n.* changeur *m.*

channel, *n.* canal *m.*; (**the English C.**) la Manche *f.*

chant, 1. *n.* chant *m.* **2.** *vb.* chanter.

chaos, *n.* chaos *m.*

chaotic, *adj.* chaotique.

chap, *n.* (on skin) gerçure *f.*; (young man) gars *m.*

chapel, *n.* chapelle *f.*

chaperon, *n.* (person) duègne *f.*; chaperon *m.*

chaplain, *n.* aumônier *m.*

chapman, *n.* colporteur *m.*

chapped, *adj.* gercé.

chapter, *n.* chapitre *m.*

char, *vb.* carboniser.

character, *n.* caractère *m.*; (in fiction) personnage *m.*; (role) rôle *m.*

characteristic, 1. *n.* trait caractéristique *m.* **2.** *adj.* caractéristique.

characteristically, *adv.* d'une manière caractéristique.

characterization, *n.* action de caractériser *f.*

characterize, *vb.* caractériser.

charcoal, *n.* charbon *(m.)* de bois.

charge, 1. *n.* (guns, legal, office) charge *f.*; (price) prix *m.*; (care) soin *m.* **2.** *vb.* charger; (**c. with**) charger de; (price) demander.

charger, *n.* grand plat *m.*; cheval de bataille *m.*

chariot, *n.* char *m.*, chariot *m.*

charioteer, *n.* conducteur de chariot *m.*

charisma, *n.* charisme *m.*

charitable, *adj.* charitable.

charitableness, *n.* bienveillance *f.*

charitably, *adv.* charitablement.

charity, *n.* charité *f.*

charlatan, *n.* charlatan *m.*

charlatanism, *n.* charlatanisme *m.*

charm, 1. *n.* charme *m.* **2.** *vb.* charmer.

charmer, *n.* charmeur *m.*, enchanteur *m.*

charming, *adj.* charmant.

charred, *adj.* carbonisé.

chart, *n.* (map) carte *f.*; (graph) graphique *m.*

charter, 1. *n.* charte *f.* **2.** *vb.* (boat) affréter.

charter flight, *n.* vol frété *m.*; charter *m.*

charwoman, *n.* femme de journée *f.*, femme de ménage *f.*

chase, 1. *n.* chasse *f.* **2.** *vb.* chasser.

chaser, *n.* chasseur *m.*; ciseleur *m.*

chasm, *n.* abîme *m.*

chassis, *n.* chassis *m.*

chaste, *adj.* chaste.

chasten, *vb.* châtier, corriger.

chasteness, *n.* pureté *f.*

chastise, *vb.* châtier.

chastisement, *n.* châtiment *m.*

chastity, *n.* chasteté *f.*

chat, 1. *n.* causette *f.* **2.** *vb.* causer.

chateau, *n.* château *m.*

chattel, *n.* bien *m.*, meuble *m.*

chatter, 1. *n.* bavardage *m.* **2.** *vb.* bavarder.

chatterbox, *n.* bavard *m.*

chauffeur, *n.* chauffeur *m.*

cheap, *adj.* (inexpensive) bon marché, (mean) de peu de valeur.

cheapen, *vb.* déprécier.

cheaply, *adv.* à bon marché.

cheapness, *n.* bon marché *m.*, bas prix *m.*; basse qualité *f.*

cheat, *vb.* tromper; (at games) tricher.

cheater, *n.* tricheur *m.*, trompeur *m.*

check, 1. *n.* (restraint) frein *m.*; (verification) vérification *f.*; (stub) ticket *m.*; (bill) addition *f.*; (bank draft) chèque *m.* **2.** *vb.* (stop) arrêter; (restrain) modérer; (verify) vérifier; (luggage) enregistrer.

checker, *n.* enregistreur *m.*, contrôleur *m.*

checkers, *n.* jeu de dames *m.*

checkmate, 1. *n.* échec et mat *m.* **2.** *vb.* mater.

cheek, *n.* joue *f.*

cheer, 1. *n.* (applause) hourra *m.* **2.** *vb.* (acclaim) acclamer; **(c. up,** *tr.)* réjouir.

cheerful, cheery, *adj.* gai.

cheerfully, *adv.* gaiement, de bon cœur.

cheerfulness, *n.* gaieté *f.*, bonne humeur *f.*

cheerless, *adj.* triste, morne, sombre.

cheery, *adj.* gai, joyeux.

cheese, *n.* fromage *m.*

cheesecloth, *n.* gaze *f.*

cheesy, *adj.* fromageux.

chemical, *adj.* chimique.

chemically, *adv.* chimiquement.

chemist, *n.* chimiste *m.f.*

chemistry, *n.* chimie *f.*

chemotherapy, *n.* chimiothérapie *f.*

chenille, *n.* chenille *f.*

cherish, *vb.* chérir.

cherry, *n.* cerise *f.*

cherub, *n.* chérubin *m.*

chess, *n.* échecs *m.pl.*

chessman, *n.* pièce *f.*

chest, *n.* (box) coffre *m.*; (body) poitrine *f.*; **(c. of drawers)** commode *f.*

chestnut, *n.* châtaigne *f.*

chevron, *n.* chevron *m.*

chew, *vb.* mâcher.

chewer, *n.* mâcheur *m.*

chic, *adj.* chic.

chicanery, *n.* chicane *f.*, chicanerie *f.*

chick, *n.* poussin *m.*

chicken, *n.* poulet *m.*

chicken-hearted, *adj.* peureux.

chicken-pox, *n.* varicelle *f.*

chicle, *n.* chiclé *m.*

chicory, *n.* chicorée *f.*

chide, *vb.* gronder, réprimander.

chief, 1. *n.* chef *m.* **2.** *adj.* principal.

chiefly, *adv.* surtout, principalement.

chieftain, *n.* chef de clan *m.*

chiffon, *n.* chiffon *m.*

chilblain, *n.* engelure *f.*

child, *n.* enfant *m.f.*

childbirth, *n.* enfantement *m.*

childhood, *n.* enfance *f.*

childish, *adj.* enfantin.

childishness, *n.* puérilité *f.*, enfantillage *m.*

childless, *adj.* sans enfant.

childlessness, *n.* l'état d'être sans enfants.

childlike, *adj.* comme un enfant, en enfant.

Chile, *n.* Chili *m.*

Chilean, 1. *n.* Chilien *m.* **2.** *adj.* chilien.

chili, *n.* piment *m.*

chill, 1. *n.* froid *m.*; (shiver) frisson *m.* **2.** *vb.* refroidir.

chilliness, *n.* froid *m.*, frisson *m.*

chilly, *adj.* un peu froid.

chime, 1. *n.* carillon *m.* **2.** *vb.* carillonner.

chimney, *n.* cheminée *f.*

chimney sweep, *n.* ramoneur *m.*

chimpanzee, *n.* chimpanzé *m.*

chin, *n.* menton *m.*

China, n. Chine f.

china, n. (ware) porcelaine f.

chinchilla, n. chinchilla m.

Chinese, 1. n. (person) Chinois m.; (language) chinois m. **2.** adj. chinois.

chink, n. fente f., crevasse f.

chintz, n. perse f.

chip, n. éclat m.; **(potato c.s)** frites m.pl.

chipmunk, n. tamias m.

chiropodist, n. pédicure m.

chiropractor, n. chiropracteur m.

chirp, vb. pépier, gazouiller.

chisel, 1. vb. ciseler. **2.** n. ciseau m.

chivalrous, adj. chevaleresque.

chivalry, n. chevalerie f.

chive, n. ciboulette f.

chloride, n. chlorure m.

chlorine, n. chlore m.

chloroform, n. chloroforme m.

chlorophyll, n. chlorophylle m.

chockfull, adj. plein comme un œuf.

chocolate, n. chocolat m.

choice, n. choix m.

choir, n. chœur m.

choke, vb. étouffer.

choker, n. foulard m.

cholera, n. choléra m.

choleric, adj. cholérique.

choose, vb. choisir.

chop, 1. n. (meat) côtelette f. **2.** vb. couper.

chopper, n. couperet m.

choppy, adj. (sea) clapoteux.

chopstick, n. baguette f., bâtonnet m.

choral, adj. choral.

chord, n. (music) accord m.

chore, n. travail (m.) de ménage.

choreography, n. chorégraphie f.

chorister, n. choriste m. enfant de chœur m.

chortle, vb. glousser de joie.

chorus, n. chœur m.

chowder, n. (sorte de) bouillabaisse f.

christen, vb. baptiser.

Christendom, n. chrétienté f.

christening, n. baptême m.

Christian, adj. and n. chrétien m.

Christianity, n. christianisme m.

Christmas, n. Noël m.

chromatic, adj. chromatique.

chromium, n. chrome m.

chromosome, n. chromosome m.

chronic, adj. chronique.

chronically, adv. chronologiquement.

chronicle, n. chronique f.

chronological, adj. chronologique.

chronology, n. chronologie f.

chrysalis, n. chrysalide f.

chrysanthemum, n. chrysanthème m.

chubby, adj. joufflu.

chuck, n. petite tape f., glousse-ment (de volaille) m.

chuckle, vb. rire tout bas.

chug, 1. n. souffle m. (d'une machine à vapeur). **2.** vb. souffler.

chum, n. camarade m., copain m.

chummy, adj. familier, intime.

chunk, n. gros morceau m.

chunky, adj. en gros morceaux.

church, n. église f.

churchman, n. homme d'église m., ecclésiastique m.

churchyard, n. cimetière m.

churn, vb. baratter.

chute, n. glissière f.

chutney, n. chutney m.

cicada, n. cigale f.

cider, n. cidre m.

cigar, n. cigare m.

cigarette, n. cigarette f.

cilia, n. cils m.pl.

ciliary, adj. ciliaire.

cinch, n. (it's a c.) c'est facile.

cinchona, n. quinquina m.

cinder, n. cendre f.

cinema, n. cinéma m.

cinematic, adj. cinématographique.

cinnamon, n. cannelle f.

cipher, n. chiffre m.; (nought) zéro m.

circle, 1. n. cercle m. **2.** vb. entourer (de).

circuit, n. circuit m.

circuitous, adj. détourné, sinueux.

circuitously, adv. d'une manière détournée, par des détours.

circular, adj. circulaire.

circularize, vb. envoyer des circulaires.

circulate, vb. circuler, tr.; faire circuler, intr.

circulation, n. circulation f.

circulator, n. circulateur m.

circulatory, adj. circulaire, circulatoire.

circumcise, vb. circoncire.

circumcision, n. circoncision f.

circumference, n. circonférence f.

circumlocution, n. circonlocution f.

circumscribe, vb. circonscrire.

circumspect, adj. conspect.

circumstance, n. (condition) circonstance f.; (financial) moyens m.pl.

circumstantial, adj. circonstanciel.

circumstantially, adv. en détail.

circumvent, vb. circonvenir.

circumvention, n. circonvention f.

circus, n. cirque m.

cirrhosis, n. cirrhose f.

cistern, n. citerne f.

citadel, n. citadelle f.

citation, n. citation f.

cite, vb. citer.

citizen, n. citoyen m.

citizenry, n. tous les citoyens m.pl.

citizenship, n. droit (m.) de cité.

citric acid, n. acide citrique m.

city, n. ville f.; cité f.

civic, adj. civique.

civics, n. instruction (f.) civique.

civil, adj. civil; (polite) poli; (c. servant) fonctionnaire m.

civilian, n. civil m.

civility, n. civilité f., politesse f.

civilization, n. civilisation f.

civilize, vb. civiliser.

civilized, adj. civilisé.

civil service, n. administration (civile) f.

civil war, n. guerre civile f.

clad, adj. habillé, vêtu.

claim, 1. n. (demand) demande f.; (right) droit m. **2.** vb. (demand) réclamer, prétendre; (insist) soutenir.

claimant, n. réclamateur m., prétendant m.

clairvoyance, n. clairvoyance f.

clairvoyant, n. voyant m.

clam, n. palourde f., mollusque m.

clamber, vb. grimper.

clammy, adj. visqueux, moite.

clamor, n. clameur f.

clamorous, adj. bruyant.

clamp, 1. n. (metal) crampon m.; (carpentry) serre-joint m. **2.** vb. cramponner, serrer.

clan, n. clan m., clique f., coterie f.

clandestine, adj. clandestin.

clandestinely, adv. clandestinement.

clang, 1. n. cliquetis m., son métallique m. **2.** vb. résonner.

clangor, n. cliquetis m.

clannish, adj. de clan.

clap, vb. (applaud) applaudir.

clapboard, n. bardeau m.

clapper, n. claqueur m., battant (of a bell) m.

claque, n. claque f.

claret, n. vin rouge de Bordeaux m.

clarification, n. clarification f.

clarify, vb. (lit.) clarifier; (fig.) éclaircir.

clarinet, n. clarinette f.

clarinetist, n. clarinettiste m.

clarion, n. clairon m.

clarity, n. clarté f.

clash, 1. vb. choquer, tr.; s'entrechoquer, intr. **2.** n. choc m.

clasp, 1. n. agrafe f.; (embrace) étreinte f. **2.** vb. agrafer, étreindre.

class, n. classe f.

classic, classical, adj. classique.

classicism, n. classicisme m.

classifiable, adj. classifiable.

classification, n. classification f.

classify, vb. classifier, classer.

classmate, n. camarade (m.) de classe.

classroom, n. salle (f.) de classe.

clatter, n. bruit m.

clause, n. clause f.

claustrophobia, n. claustrophobie f.

claw, n. griffe f.

claw-hammer, n. marteau à dent m.

clay, n. argile f., glaise f.

clean, 1. adj. propre. **2.** vb. nettoyer.

clean-cut, adj. net, fin.

cleaner, n. (dry-c.) teinturier m.

cleanliness, cleanness, n. propreté f.

cleanse, vb. nettoyer, curer.

cleanser, n. chose qui nettoie f., détersif m., cureur m.

clear, 1. *adj.* clair. 2. *vb.* (c. up) déblayer; (profit) gagner; (get over) franchir; (weather, *intr.*) s'éclaircir.

clear-cut, *adj.* nettement dessiné.

clearing, *n.* (open place) clairière *f.*, éclaircissement *m.*, (comm.) acquittement *m.*, (woods) éclaircie *f.*

clearing house, *n.* banque de virement *f.*, chambre de compensation *f.*

clearly, *adv.* clairement, nettement, évidemment.

clearness, *n.* clarté *f.*, netteté *f.*

cleat, *n.* fer *m.*, (naut.) taquet *m.*

cleavage, *n.* fendage *m.*, scission *f.*

cleave, *vb.* (split) fendre; (adhere) adhérer.

cleaver, *n.* fendeur (person) *m.*, fendoir *m.*, couperet (instrument) *m.*

cleft, *n.* fente *f.*

clemency, *n.* clémence *f.*

clench, *vb.* serrer.

clergy, *n.* clergé *m.*

clergyman, *n.* ecclésiastique *m.*

clerical, *adj.* (clergy) clérical; (business) de bureau.

clericalism, *n.* cléricalisme *m.*

clerk, *n.* (business) employé *m.*; (store) commis *m.*; (law, eccles.) clerc *m.*

clerkship, *n.* place de clerc *f.*, place de commis *f.*

clever, *adj.* habile.

cleverly, *adv.* habilement.

cleverness, *n.* adresse *f.*

clew, *n.* fil *m.*

cliché, *n.* cliché *m.*

click, 1. *n.* cliquetis *m.*, déclic *m.* 2. *vb.* cliqueter.

client, *n.* client *m.*

clientele, *n.* clientèle *f.*

cliff, *n.* falaise *f.*

climactic, *adj.* arrivé à son apogée.

climate, *n.* climat *m.*

climatic, *adj.* climatique.

climax, *n.* comble *m.*

climb, 1. *n.* montée *f.* 2. *vb.* monter, grimper.

climber, *n.* grimpeur *m.*, ascensioniste *m.*

clinch, *vb.* river; (settle) conclure.

cling, *vb.* s'accrocher.

clinging, *adj.* qui se cramponne, qui s'accroche (à).

clinic, *n.* clinique *f.*

clinical, *adj.* clinique.

clinically, *adv.* d'une manière clinique.

clip, 1. *vb.* couper. 2. *n.* pince *f.*

clipper, *n.* rogneur *m.*, tondeuse (instrument) *f.*, (naut.) fin voilier *m.*

clipping, *n.* coupure *f.*

clique, *n.* clique *f.*

cloak, *n.* manteau *m.*; (cloakroom) vestiaire *m.*

clock, *n.* horloge *f.*; (two o'clock) deux heures.

clockwise, *adv.* dans le sens des aiguilles d'une montre.

clockwork, *n.* mouvement (*m.*) d'horlogerie.

clod, *n.* motte (*f.*) de terre; (person) lourdaud *m.*

clog, *vb.* entraver.

cloister, *n.* cloître *m.*

clone, *n.* reproduction exacte *f.*

close, 1. *adj.* (closed) fermé; (narrow) étroit; (near) proche; (secret) réservé. 2. *vb.* fermer. 3. *adv.* tout près. 4. *prep.* (c. to) près de.

closely, *adv.* de près, étroitement.

closeness, *n.* proximité *f.*, lourdeur (of weather) *f.*, réserve *f.*

closet, *n.* (room) cabinet *m.*; (clothes) placard *m.*

clot, *n.* (blood) caillot *m.*

cloth, *n.* étoffe *f.*

clothe, *vb.* vêtir (de); habiller.

clothes, *n.* habits *m.pl.*

clothes hanger, *n.* cintre *m.*

clothespin, *n.* pince *f.*

clothier, *n.* drapier *m.*, tailleur *m.*

clothing, *n.* vêtements *m.pl.*

cloud, *n.* nuage *m.*

cloudburst, *n.* trombe *f.*, rafale de pluie *f.*

cloudiness, *n.* état nuageux *m.*, obscurité *f.*

cloudless, *adj.* sans nuage.

cloudy, *adj.* nuageux, couvert.

clout, 1. *n.* gifle *f.*, tape *f.* 2. *vb.* gifler, taper.

clove, *n.* clou (*m.*) de girofle.

clover, *n.* trèfle *m.*

clown, *n.* bouffon *m.*

clownish, *adj.* rustre, grossier, de payan.

cloy, *vb.* rassasier.

club, *n.* (society) club *m.,* société *f.;* cercle *m.;* (stick) massue *f.;* (golf) crosse *f.;* (cards) trèfle *m.*

clubfoot, *n.* pied bot *m.*

clue, *n.* fil *m.*

clump, *n.* (trees) bosquet *m.;* massif *m.*

clumsiness, *n.* gaucherie *f.,* maladresse *f.*

clumsy, *adj.* gauche.

cluster, 1. *n.* (people) groupe *m.;* (fruit) grappe *f.;* (flowers, trees) bouquet *m.* **2.** *vb.* se grouper.

clutch, 1. *n.* (claw) griffe *f.;* (auto) embrayage *m.* **2.** *vb.* saisir.

clutter, *vb.* encombrer.

coach, 1. *n.* (carriage) carrosse *m.;* (train) wagon *m.;* (sports) entraîneur *m.* **2.** *vb.* (sports) entraîner; (school) donner des leçons particulières à.

coachman, *n.* cocher *m.*

coagulate, *vb.* se coaguler.

coagulation, *n.* coagulation *f.*

coal, *n.* charbon *(m.)* de terre, houille *f.*

coalesce, *vb.* se fondre, se fusionner, s'unir.

coalition, *n.* coalition *f.*

coal tar, *n.* goudron de houille *m.*

coarse, *adj.* grossier.

coarsen, *vb.* rendre plus grossier.

coarseness, *n.* grossièreté *f.*

coast, *n.* côte *f.*

coastal, *adj.* de la côte, littoral.

coaster, *n.* caboteur *m.;* dessous de carafe *m.*

coast guard, *n.* garde-côtes *m.*

coat, 1. *n.* (man) pardessus *m.;* (woman) manteau *m.;* (paint) couche *f.* **2.** *vb.* **(c. with)** revêtir de.

coating, *n.* couche *f.,* enduit *m.,* étoffe pour habits *f.*

coat of arms, *n.* écusson *m.,* cotte d'armes *f.*

coax, *vb.* cajoler.

cobalt, *n.* cobalt *m.*

cobbler, *n.* savetier *m.,* cordonnier *m.*

cobblestone, *n.* pierre du pavé *f.*

cobra, *n.* cobra *m.*

cobweb, *n.* toile *(f.)* d'araignée.

cocaine, *n.* cocaïne *f.*

cock, 1. *n.* (fowl) coq *m.;* (male) mâle *m.* **2.** *vb.* faire de l'œil.

cocker spaniel, *n.* épagneul cocker *m.*

cockeyed, *adj.* louche.

cockhorse, *n.* dada *m.*

cockroach, *n.* blatte *f.*

cocksure, *adj.* sûr et certain.

cocktail, *n.* cocktail *m.*

cocky, *adj.* suffisant.

cocoa, *n.* cacao *m.*

coconut, *n.* noix *(f.)* de coco.

cocoon, *n.* cocon *m.*

cod, *n.* morue *f.*

coddle, *vb.* dorloter.

code, *n.* code *m.*

codeine, *n.* codéine *f.*

codfish, *n.* morue *f.*

codify, *vb.* codifier.

cod-liver oil, *n.* huile de foie de morue *f.*

coeducation, *n.* enseignement mixte *m.*

coequal, *adj.* égal.

coerce, *vb.* contraindre.

coercion, *n.* coercition *f.,* contrainte *f.*

coercive, *adj.* coercitif.

coexist, *vb.* coexister.

coffee, *n.* café *m.*

coffee shop, *n.* cafétéria *f.*

coffer, *n.* coffre *m.*

coffin, *n.* cercueil *m.*

cog, *n.* dent *f.*

cogent, *adj.* puissant, fort.

cogitate, *vb.* méditer, penser.

cognizance, *n.* connaissance *f.*

cognizant, *adj.* instruit, *(law)* compétent.

cogwheel, *n.* roue d'engrenage *f.*

coherent, *adj.* cohérent.

cohesion, *n.* cohésion *f.*

cohesive, *adj.* cohésif.

cohort, *n.* cohorte *f.*

coiffure, *n.* coiffure *f.*

coil, *n.* rouleau *m.*

coin, *n.* pièce *(f.)* de monnaie.

coinage, *n.* monnayage *m.,* monnaie *f.*

coincide, *vb.* coïncider.

coincidence, *n.* coïncidence *f.*

coincident, *adj.* coïncident.

coincidental, *adj.* coïncident, d'accord (avec).

coincidentally, *adv.* par coïncidence.

colander, *n.* passoire *f.*

cold, 1. n. (temperature) froid m.; (medical) rhume m. 2. adj. froid; (it is cold) il fait froid; (feel cold) avoir froid.

cold-blooded, adj. de sang froid.

coldly, adv. froidement.

coldness, n. froideur f.

collaborate, vb. collaborer.

collaboration, n. collaboration f.

collaborator, n. collaborateur m.

collapse, 1. n. effondrement m.; (med.) affaissement m. 2. vb. s'effondrer; (med.) s'affaisser.

collar, n. col m.; (dog) collier m.

collarbone, n. clavicule f.

collate, vb. collationner, comparer.

collateral, adj. and n. collatéral m.

collation, n. collation f., comparaison f., repas froid m.

colleague, n. collègue m.f.

collect, vb. rassembler.

collection, n. collection f.; (money) collecte f.

collective, adj. collectif.

collectively, adv. collectivement.

collector, n. (art) collectionneur m.; (tickets) contrôleur m.

college, n. collège m.; (higher education) université f.

collegiate, adj. de collège, collégial.

collide, vb. se heurter (contre).

colliery, n. houillère f., mine de charbon f.

collision, n. collision f.

colloquial, adj. familier.

colloquialism, n. expression de style familier f.

colloquially, adv. en style familier.

colloquy, n. colloque m., entretien m.

collusion, n. collusion f., connivence f.

colon, n. (gramm.) deux points m.pl.

colonel, n. colonel m.

colonial, adj. colonial.

colonist, n. colon m.

colonization, n. colonisation f.

colonize, vb. coloniser.

colony, n. colonie f.

color, 1. n. couleur f. 2. vb. colorer, tr.

coloration, n. coloris m.

colored, adj. coloré, de couleur; colorié.

colorful, adj. coloré, pittoresque.

coloring, n. coloris m., couleur f.

colorless, adj. sans couleur, incolore, terne.

colossal, adj. colossal.

colt, n. poulain m.

colter, n. coutre m.

column, n. colonne f.

columnist, n. journaliste (qui a sa rubrique à lui) m.

coma, n. coma m.

comb, 1. n. peigne m. 2. vb. peigner.

combat, n. combat m.

combatant, adj. and n. combattant m.

combative, adj. combatif.

combination, n. combinaison f.

combination lock, n. serrure à combinaisons f.

combine, vb. combiner, tr.

combustible, adj. and n. combustible m.

combustion, n. combustion f.

come, vb. venir; (c. about) arriver; (c. across) rencontrer; (c. away) partir; (c. back) revenir; (c. down) descendre; (c. in) entrer; (c. out) sortir; (c. up) monter.

comedian, n. comédien m.

comedienne, n. comédienne f.

comedy, n. comédie f.

comely, adj. avenant.

comet, n. comète f.

comfort, 1. n. (mental) consolation f.; (material) confort m. 2. vb. consoler.

comfortable, adj. commode.

comfortably, adv. confortablement, commodément.

comforter, n. consolateur m.

comfortingly, adv. d'une manière réconfortante.

comfortless, adj. sans consolation, inconsolable, désolé.

comic, comical, adj. comique.

comic strip, n. dessin comique m.

coming, n. venue f., arrivée f., approche f.

comma, n. virgule f.

command, 1. n. commandement m. 2. vb. commander (à).

commandeer, vb. réquisitionner.

commander, n. commandant m.

commander in chief, n. généralissime m.

commandment, n. commandement m.

commemorate, vb. commémorer.

commemoration, n. célébration f., commémoration f.

commemorative, adj. commémoratif.

commence, vb. commencer.

commencement, n. (school) distribution (f.) des diplômes.

commend, vb. (entrust) recommander; (praise) louer.

commendable, adj. louable, recommandable.

commendably, adv. d'une manière louable.

commendation, n. louange f.

commensurate, adj. proportionné.

comment, 1. n. commentaire m. **2.** vb. commenter.

commentator, n. commentateur m.

commerce, n. commerce m.

commercial, adj. commercial.

commercialism, n. commercialisme m.

commercialize, vb. commercialiser.

commercially, adv. commercialement.

commiserate, vb. plaindre, avoir pitié de.

commissary, n. (person) commissaire m.; (supply store) dépôt (m.) de vivres.

commission, n. (assignment) commande f.; (officer) brevet m.; (committee, percentage) commission f.

commissioner, n. commissaire m.

commit, vb. commettre.

commitment, n. engagement m.

committee, n. comité m.

commodious, adj. spacieux.

commodity, n. produit m., commodité f., denrée f.

common, adj. commun; (vulgar) vulgaire.

common law, n. droit coutumier m.

commonly, adv. communément, ordinairement.

commonness, n. vulgarité f.

commonplace, n. lieu-commun m.

commonwealth, n. état m.

commotion, n. agitation f.

communal, adj. communal.

commune, n. commune f.

communicable, adj. communicable.

communicant, n. communiant m.

communicate, vb. communiquer.

communication, n. communication f.

communicative, adj. communicatif.

communion, n. communion f.

communiqué, n. communiqué m.

communism, n. communisme m.

communist, adj. and n. communiste m.f.

communistic, adj. communiste.

community, n. communauté f.

commutation, n. commutation f.

commute, vb. changer, (law) commuer.

commuter, n. voyageur de banlieue m.

compact, 1. n. (agreement) accord m.; (cosmetic) poudrier m. **2.** adj. compact.

compactness, n. compacité f.

companion, n. compagnon m., compagne f.

companionable, adj. sociable.

companionship, n. camaraderie f.

company, n. compagnie f.

comparable with, adj. comparable à.

comparative, adj. and n. comparatif m.

comparatively, adv. comparativement, relativement.

compare, vb. comparer.

comparison, n. comparaison f.

compartment, n. compartiment m.

compass, n. (naut.) boussole f.; (geom.) compas m.

compassion, n. compassion f.

compassionate, adj. compatissant.

compassionately, adv. avec compassion.

compatible, adj. compatible.

compatriot, n. compatriote m.f.

compel, vb. forcer.

compensate, vb. compenser.

compensation, n. compensation f.

compensatory, *adj.* compensateur.

compete, *vb.* rivaliser.

competence, *n.* compétence *f.*

competent, *adj.* capable.

competently, *adv.* convenablement, avec compétence.

competition, *n.* concurrence *f.*

competitor, *n.* concurrent *m.*

compile, *vb.* compiler.

complacency, *n.* contentement (*m.*) de soi-même.

complacent, *adj.* content de soi-même.

complacently, *adv.* avec un air (un ton) suffisant.

complain, *vb.* se plaindre.

complainer, *n.* plaignant *m.,* réclameur *m.*

complainingly, *adv.* d'une manière plaignante.

complaint, *n.* plainte *f.*

complement, *n.* complément *m.*

complete, *adj.* complet.

completely, *adv.* complètement, tout à fait.

completeness, *n.* état complet *m.,* perfection *f.*

completion, *n.* achèvement *m.*

complex, *adj. and n.* complexe *m.*

complexion, *n.* teint *m.*

complexity, *n.* complexité *f.*

compliance, *n.* acquiescement *m.*

compliant, *adj.* complaisant, accommodant.

complicate, *vb.* compliquer.

complicated, *adj.* compliqué.

complication, *n.* complication *f.*

complicity, *n.* complicité *f.*

compliment, *n.* compliment *m.*

complimentary, *adj.* flatteur, de félicitations.

comply with, *vb.* se conformer à.

component, *adj. and n.* composant *m.*

comport, *vb.* s'accorder (avec), convenir (à).

compose, *vb.* composer.

composed, *adj.* composé, calme, tranquille.

composer, *n.* compositeur *m.*

composite, *adj.* composé.

composition, *n.* composition *f.*

compost, *n.* compost *m.,* terreau *m.*

composure, *n.* calme *m.,* tranquillité *f.,* sang-froid *m.*

compote, *n.* compote *f.*

compound, 1. *adj. and n.* composé *m.* **2.** *vb.* composer.

comprehend, *vb.* comprendre.

comprehensible, *adj.* compréhensible, intelligible.

comprehension, *n.* compréhension *f.*

comprehensive, *adj.* compréhensif.

compress, 1. *n.* compresse *f.* **2.** *vb.* comprimer, *tr.*

compressed, *adj.* comprimé.

compression, *n.* compression *f.*

compressor, *n.* compresseur *m.*

comprise, *vb.* comprendre.

compromise, 1. *n.* compromis *m.* **2.** *vb.* compromettre.

compromiser, *n.* comprometteur *m.*

compulsion, *n.* contrainte *f.*

compulsive, *adj.* coercitif, obligatoire.

compulsory, *adj.* obligatoire.

compunction, *n.* componction *f.*

computation, *n.* supputation *f.*

compute, *vb.* supputer.

computer, *n.* ordinateur *m.*

computerize, *vb.* informatiser.

computer science, *n.* informatique *f.*

comrade, *n.* camarade *m.f.*

comradeship, *n.* camaraderie *f.*

concave, *adj.* concave.

conceal, *vb.* cacher.

concealment, *n.* action (*f.*) de cacher.

concede, *vb.* concéder.

conceit, *n.* vanité *f.*

conceited, *adj.* vaniteux, suffisant.

conceivable, *adj.* concevable.

conceivably, *adv.* d'une manière concevable.

conceive, *vb.* concevoir.

concentrate, *vb.* concentrer *tr.*

concentration camp, *n.* camp de concentration *m.*

concept, *n.* concept *m.*

conception, *n.* conception *f.*

concern, 1. *n.* (what pertains to one) affaire *f.;* (*comm.*) entreprise *f.;* (solicitude) souci *m.* **2.** *vb.* concerner; (**c. oneself with**) s'intéresser à; (**be c.ed about**) s'inquiéter de.

concerning, *prep.* concernant.

concert, n. concert m.

concerted, adj. concerté.

concession, n. concession f.

conciliate, vb. concilier.

conciliation, n. conciliation f.

conciliator, n. conciliateur m.

conciliatory, adj. conciliant, conciliatoire.

concise, adj. concis.

concisely, adv. avec concision, succinctement.

conciseness, n. concision f.

conclave, n. conclave m.

conclude, vb. conclure.

conclusion, n. conclusion f.

conclusive, adj. concluant.

conclusively, adv. d'une manière concluante.

concoct, vb. préparer.

concomitant, 1. adj. concomitant. **2.** n. accessoire m.

concord, n. concorde f.

concordat, n. concordat m.

concourse, n. concours m., affluence f.

concrete, 1. n. béton m. **2.** adj. concret.

concretely, adv. d'une manière concrète.

concreteness, n. état concret m.

concubine, n. concubine f.

concur, vb. (events) concourir; (persons) être d'accord.

concurrence, n. assentiment m., concours m.

concurrent, adj. concourant.

concussion, n. secousse f., ébranlement m.

condemn, vb. condamner.

condemnable, adj. condamnable.

condemnation, n. condamnation f.

condensation, n. condensation f.

condense, vb. condenser, tr.

condenser, n. condenseur m.

condescend, vb. condescendre.

condescendingly, adv. avec condescendance.

condescension, n. condescendance f.

condiment, n. condiment m., assaisonnement m.

condition, 1. n. condition f. **2.** vb. conditionner.

conditional, adj. and n. conditionnel m.

conditionally, adv. conditionnellement.

condolence, n. condoléance f.

condole with, vb. faire ses condoléances à.

condominium, n. condominium m.

conducive, adj. favorable.

conduct, 1. n. conduite f. **2.** vb. conduire.

conductivity, n. conductivité f.

conductor, n. conducteur m.; (bus) receveur m.; (rail) chef (m.) de train; (music) chef (m.) d'orchestre.

conduit, n. conduit m., tuyau m.

cone, n. cône m.

confection, n. confection f.; (sweet) bonbon m.

confectioner, n. confiseur m.

confectionery, n. confiserie f.

confederacy, confederation, n. confédération f.

confederate, adj. and n. confédéré m.

confer, vb. conférer.

conference, n. (meeting) entretien m.; (congress) congrès m.

confess, vb. avouer; (eccles.) confesser, tr.

confession, n. confession f.

confessional, n. confessional m.

confessor, n. confesseur m.

confetti, n. confetti m.

confidant, n. confident m.

confidante, n. confidente f.

confide, vb. confier (à), tr.

confidence, n. (trust) confiance f.; (secret) confidence f.

confident, adj. confiant.

confidential, adj. confidentiel.

confidentially, adv. confidentiellement.

confidently, adv. avec confiance.

confine, vb. (banish) confiner; (limit) limiter.

confirm, vb. confirmer.

confirmation, n. confirmation f.

confirmed, adj. invétéré, incorrigible.

confiscate, vb. confisquer.

confiscation, n. confiscation f.

conflagration, n. conflagration f., incendie m.

conflict, n. conflit m.

conform, vb. conformer, tr.

conformation, *n.* conformation *f.,* conformité *f.*

conformer, *vb.* conformiste *m.*

conformist, *n.* conformiste *m.*

conformity, *n.* conformité *f.*

confound, *vb.* confondre; **(c. him!)** que le diable l'emporte!

confront, *vb.* confronter.

confuse, *vb.* confondre.

confusion, *n.* confusion *f.*

congeal, *vb.* congeler, *tr.*

congealment, *n.* congélation *f.*

congenial, *adj.* (person) sympathique; (thing) convenable.

congenital, *adj.* congénital.

congenitally, *adv.* d'une manière congénitale.

congestion, *n.* (med.) congestion *f.;* (traffic) encombrement *m.*

conglomerate, *adj.* congloméré.

conglomeration, *n.* conglomération *f.*

congratulate, *vb.* féliciter (de).

congratulation, *n.* félicitation *f.*

congratulatory, *adj.* de félicitation.

congregate, *vb.* rassembler, *r.*

congregation, *n.* assemblée *f.*

congress, *n.* congrès *m.*

congressional, *adj.* congressionnel.

conic, *adj.* conique.

conjecture, *n.* conjecture *f.*

conjugal, *adj.* conjugal.

conjugate, *vb.* conjuguer.

conjugation, *n.* conjugaison *f.*

conjunction, *n.* conjonction *f.*

conjunctive, *adj.* conjonctif.

conjunctivitis, *n.* conjonctivite *f.*

conjure, *vb.* conjurer.

connect, *vb.* joindre.

connection, *n.* connexion *f.;* (social) relations *f.pl.;* (train) correspondance *f.*

connivance, *n.* connivence *f.*

connive, *vb.* conniver (à).

connoisseur, *n.* connaisseur *m.*

connotation, *n.* connotation *f.*

connote, *vb.* signifier, vouloir dire.

connubial, *adj.* conjugal, du mariage.

conquer, *vb.* conquérir.

conquerable, *adj.* qui peut être vaincu, domptable.

conqueror, *n.* conquérant *m.*

conquest, *n.* conquête *f.*

conscience, *n.* conscience *f.*

conscientious, *adj.* consciencieux.

conscientiously, *adv.* consciencieusement.

conscious, *adj.* conscient.

consciously, *adv.* sciemment, en parfaite connaissance.

consciousness, *n.* conscience *f.*

conscript, *adj. and n.* conscrit *m.*

conscription, *n.* conscription *f.*

consecrate, *vb.* consacrer.

consecration, *n.* consécration *f.*

consecutive, *adj.* consécutif.

consecutively, *adv.* consécutivement, de suite.

consensus, *n.* consensus *m.,* assentiment général *m.*

consent, 1. *n.* consentement *m.* **2.** *vb.* consentir.

consequence, *n.* conséquence *f.*

consequent, *adj.* conséquent.

consequential, *adj.* conséquent, logique.

consequently, *adv.* par conséquent.

conservation, *n.* conservation *f.*

conservatism, *n.* conservatisme *m.*

conservative, *adj.* (politics) conservateur; (comm.) prudent.

conservatively, *adv.* d'une manière conservatrice.

conservatory, *n.* conservatoire *m.*

conserve, *vb.* conserver.

consider, *vb.* considérer.

considerable, *adj.* considérable.

considerably, *adv.* considérablement.

considerate, *adj.* plein d'égards.

considerately, *adv.* avec égards, avec indulgence.

consideration, *n.* considération *f.*

considering, *prep.* vu que, attendu que.

consign, *vb.* consigner.

consignment, *n.* expédition *f.,* consignation *f.*

consistency, *n.* consistance *f.*

consistent, *adj.* consistant.

consist of, *vb.* consister en.

consolation, *n.* consolation *f.*

console, *vb.* consoler.

consolidate, *vb.* consolider.

consommé, *n.* consommé *m.*

consonant, *n.* consonne *f.*

consort, 1. n. compagnon m., épous m. 2. vb. s'associer (à).
conspicuous, adj. en évidence.
conspicuously, adv. visiblement, éminemment.
conspicuousness, n. éclat m., position éminente f.
conspiracy, n. conspiration f.
conspirator, n. conspirateur m.
conspire, vb. conspirer.
conspirer, n. conspirateur m.
constancy, n. constance f., fermeté f.
constant, adj. constant.
constantly, adv. constamment.
constellation, n. constellation f.
consternation, n. consternation f.
constipation, n. constipation f.
constituency, n. circonscription électorale f.
constituent, adj. constituant.
constitute, vb. constituer.
constitution, n. constitution f.
constitutional, adj. constitutionnel.
constrain, vb. contraindre.
constrained, adj. contraint.
constraint, n. contrainte f., gêne f.
constrict, vb. resserrer.
construct, vb. construire.
construction, n. construction f.
constructive, adj. constructif.
constructively, adv. constructivement, par induction.
constructor, n. constructeur m.
construe, vb. interpréter.
consul, n. consul m.
consular, adj. consulaire.
consulate, n. consulat m.
consult, vb. consulter.
consultant, n. conseiller m.
consultation, n. consultation f.
consume, vb. consumer.
consumer, n. consommateur m.
consummate, 1. adj. consommé. 2. vb. consommer.
consummation, n. consommation f.
consumption, n. consommation f.; (med.) phtisie f.
consumptive, adj. poitrinaire, tuberculeux.
contact, n. contact m.
contagion, n. contagion f.
contagious, adj. contagieux.
contain, vb. contenir.

container, n. récipient m.
contaminate, vb. contaminer.
contaminated, adj. contaminé.
contemplate, vb. contempler.
contemplation, n. contemplation f.
contemplative, adj. contemplatif.
contemporary, adj. contemporain.
contempt, n. mépris m.
contemptible, adj. méprisable.
contemptuous, adj. méprisant.
contemptuously, adv. avec mépris, dédaigneusement.
contend, vb. (struggle) lutter; (maintain) soutenir.
contender, n. compétiteur m.
content, n. (satisfaction) contentement m.; (c.s) contenu m.
contented with, adj. content de.
contention, n. contention f., lutte f.
contentment, n. contentement m.
contest, 1. n. (struggle) lutte f.; (competition) concours m. 2. vb. contester.
contestable, adj. contestable.
contestant, n. concurrent m., disputant m.
context, n. contexte m.
contiguous, adj. contigu.
continence, n. continence f., retenue f.
continent, adj. and n. continent m.
continental, adj. continental.
contingency, n. contingence f.
contingent, adj. contingent.
continual, adj. continuel.
continuation, n. continuation f.
continue, vb. continuer.
continuity, n. continuité f.
continuous, adj. continu.
continuously, adv. continûment, sans interruption.
contort, vb. tordre, défigurer.
contortionist, n. contortionniste m.
contour, n. contour m.
contraband, n. contrebande f.
contraception, n. limitation des naissances f., contraception f.
contraceptive, n. contraceptif f.
contract, 1. n. contrat m. 2. vb. contracter, tr.
contracted, adj. contracté, resserré.

contraction, n. contraction f.

contractor, n. entrepreneur m.

contradict, vb. contredire.

contradictable, adj. qui peut être contredit.

contradiction, n. contradiction f., démenti m.

contradictory, adj. contradictoire.

contraption, n. machin m.

contrary, adj. and n. contraire m.; **(on the c.)** au contraire.

contrast, 1. n. contraste m. **2.** vb. mettre en contraste, tr.; contraster, intr.

contribute, vb. contribuer.

contribution, n. contribution f.

contributive, adj. contributif.

contributor, n. contribuant m.

contributory, adj. contributaire.

contrite, adj. contrit, pénitent.

contrition, n. contrition f.

contrivance, n. combinaison f., invention f., artifice m.

contrive, vb. inventer, imaginer, arranger.

control, 1. n. autorité f.; (machinery) commande f. **2.** vb. gouverner; (check) contrôler.

controllable, adj. vérifiable, gouvernable.

controller, n. contrôleur m.

controversial, adj. de controverse, polémique.

controversy, n. controverse f.

contusion, n. contusion f.

conundrum, n. devinette f., énigme f.

convalescence, n. convalescence f.

convalescent, adj. convalescent.

convene, vb. assembler, tr.

convenience, n. convenance f.; (comfort) commodité f.

convenient, adj. commode.

conveniently, adv. commodément.

convent, n. couvent m.

convention, n. convention f.

conventional, adj. conventionnel.

conventionally, adv. par convention.

converge, vb. converger.

convergence, n. convergence f.

convergent, adj. convergent.

conversant, adj. versé (dans), familier (avec).

conversation, n. conversation f.

conversational, adj. de conversation.

conversationalist, n. causeur m.

converse, vb. converser.

conversely, adv. réciproquement.

convert, vb. convertir, tr.

converter, n. convertisseur m.

convertible, adj. convertible (of things), convertissable (of persons).

convex, adj. convexe.

convey, vb. (transport) transporter; (transmit) transmettre.

conveyance, n. transport m.

conveyor, n. transporteur m., conducteur (électrique) m.

convict, 1. n. forçat m. **2.** vb. condamner.

conviction, n. (condemnation) condamnation f.; (persuasion) conviction f.

convince, vb. convaincre.

convincing, adj. convaincant.

convincingly, adv. d'une manière convaincante.

convivial, adj. jovial, joyeux.

convocation, n. convocation f.

convoke, vb. convoquer.

convoy, n. convoi m.

convulse, vb. convulser, bouleverser.

convulsion, n. convulsion f.

convulsive, adj. convulsif.

cook, 1. n. cuisinier m. **2.** vb. cuire, intr.; faire cuire, tr.

cookbook, n. livre de cuisine m.

cookie, n. gâteau sec m.

cool, adj. frais m., fraîche f.

cooler, n. rafraîchissoir m., réfrigérant m., (motor) radiateur m.

coolness, n. fraîcheur f.

coop, n. cage (f.) à poules.

coöperate, vb. coopérer.

coöperation, n. coopération f.

coöperative, 1. n. coopérative f. **2.** adj. coopératif.

coöperatively, adj. d'une manière coopérative.

coördinate, vb. coordonner.

coördination, n. coordination f.

coördinator, n. coordinateur m.

cop, 1. n. (slang) flic m. **2.** vb. (colloquial) attraper, pincer.

cope with, vb. tenir tête à.

copier, n. machine à copier f.

copious, adj. copieux.
copiously, adv. copieusement.
copiousness, n. abondance f.
copper, n. cuivre m.
copperplate, n. cuivre plané m.; taille-douce f.
copy, 1. n. copie f. **2.** vb. copier.
copyist, n. copiste m., imitateur m.
copyright, n. droit (m.) d'auteur.
coquetry, n. coquetterie f.
coquette, n. coquette f.
coral, n. corail m.; pl. coraux.
cord, n. corde f.
cordial, adj. and n. cordial m.
cordiality, n. cordialité f.
cordially, adv. cordialement.
cordon, n. cordon m.
cordovan, adj. cordovan.
corduroy, m. velours côtelé m.
core, n. cœur m.
cork, n. (botany) liège m.; (stopper) bouchon m.
corkscrew, n. tire-bouchon m.
corn, n. maïs m.
cornea, n. cornée f.
corner, n. coin m.
cornerstone, n. pierre angulaire f.
cornet, n. cornet m.
cornetist, n. cornettiste m.
cornice, n. corniche f.
cornucopia, n. corne d'abondance f.
corollary, n. corollaire m.
coronary, adj. coronaire.
coronation, n. couronnement m.
coroner, n. coroner m.
coronet, n. (petite) couronne f.
corporal, n. (mil.) caporal m.
corporate, adj. de corporation.
corporation, n. corporation f.
corps, n. corps m.
corpse, n. cadavre m.
corpulent, adj. corpulent, gros.
corpuscle, n. corpuscule m.
corral, n. corral m.
correct, 1. adj. correct. **2.** vb. corriger.
correction, n. correction f.
corrective, 1. adj. correctif. **2.** n. correctif m.
correctly, adv. correctement, justement.
correctness, n. correction f.
correlate, vb. être en corrélation, intr.; mettre en corrélation, tr.
correlation, n. corrélation f.

correspond, vb. correspondre.
correspondence, n. correspondance f.
correspondent, n. correspondant m.
corridor, n. couloir m.
corroborate, vb. corroborer.
corroboration, n. corroboration f., confirmation f.
corroborative, adj. coroboratif.
corrode, vb. corroder.
corrosion, n. corrosion f.
corrugate, vb. rider, plisser.
corrupt, 1. adj. corrompu. **2.** vb. corrompre.
corruptible, adj. corruptible.
corruption, n. corruption f.
corruptive, adj. corruptif.
corsage, n. corsage m.
corset, n. corset m.
cortege, n. cortège m.
corvette, n. corvette f.
cosmetic, adj. and n. cosmétique m.
cosmic, adj. cosmique.
cosmic rays, n. rayons cosmiques m.pl.
cosmopolitan, adj. and n. cosmopolite m.f.
cosmos, n. cosmos m.
cost, 1. n. coût m. **2.** vb. coûter.
costliness, n. haut prix m., somptuosité f.
costly, adj. coûteux.
costume, n. costume m.
costumer, n. costumier m.
cot, n. (berth) couchette f.; (folding) lit-cage m.
coterie, n. coterie f., clique f.
cotillion, n. cotillon m.
cottage, n. chaumière f.
cotton, n. coton m.
cottonseed, n. graine de coton f.
couch, n. divan m.
cougar, n. couguar m.
cough, 1. n. toux f. **2.** vb. tousser.
could, vb. pouvait, pourrait.
council, n. conseil m.
councilman, n. conseiller m.
counsel, 1. n. conseil m. **2.** vb. conseiller.
counselor, n. conseiller m.
count, 1. n. (calculation) compte m.; (title) comte m. **2.** vb. compter.
countenance, n. expression f.

counter, 1. n. (shop) comptoir m. **2.** adv. **(c. to)** à l'encontre de.

counteract, vb. neutraliser.

counteraction, n. action contraire f.

counterattack, n. contre-attaque f.

counterbalance, 1. n. contrepoids m. **2.** vb. contre-balancer.

counterfeit, 1. adj. (money) faux m., fausse f. **2.** vb. contrefaire.

countermand, vb. contremander.

counteroffensive, n. contre-offensive f.

counterpart, n. contre-partie f.

countess, n. comtesse f.

countless, adj. innombrable.

country, n. (nation) pays m.; (opposed to town) campagne f.; (native c.) patrie f.

countryman, n. (of same c.) compatriote m.f.; (rustic) campagnard m.

county, n. comté m.

coupé, n. coupé m.

couple, 1. n. couple f. **2.** vb. coupler.

coupon, n. coupon m.

courage, n. courage m.

courageous, adj. courageux.

courier, n. courrier m.

course, n. cours m.; (of c.) bien entendu; (route) route f.; (meal) service m.

court, 1. n. cour f. **2.** vb. faire la cour à.

courteous, adj. courtois.

courtesy, n. courtoisie f.

courthouse, n. palais de justice m.

courtier, n. courtisan m.

courtly, adj. de cour, élégant, courtois.

courtmartial, n. conseil de guerre m.

courtroom, n. salle d'audience f.

courtship, n. cour f.

courtyard, n. cour f.

cousin, n. cousin m., cousine f.

covenant, n. pacte m.

cover, 1. n. (book, comm., blanket) couverture f.; (pot) couvercle m.; (shelter) abri m.; (envelope) pli m.; (mil.) couvert m. **2.** vb. couvrir.

coverage, n. couverture f.

covering, n. couverture f., enveloppe f.

covet, vb. convoiter.

covetous, adj. avide, avaricieux.

cow, n. vache f.

coward, adj. lâche.

cowardice, n. lâcheté f.

cowboy, n. (U.S.A.) cowboy m.

cower, vb. se blottir.

cow hand, n. vacher m.

cowhide, n. peau (f.) de vache.

coxswain, n. patron de chaloupe m., barreur m.

coy, adj. timide.

cozy, adj. confortable.

crab, n. crabe m.

crab apple, n. pomme sauvage f.

crack, 1. n. (fissure) fente f.; (noise) craquement m. **2.** vb. tr. (glass, china) fêler; (nuts) casser; (noise) faire craquer. **3.** vb. intr. (split) se fendiller; (noise) craquer.

cracked, adj. fendu, fêlé.

cracker, n. biscuit m.

cracking, n. craquement m., claquement m.

crackup, n. crach m.

cradle, n. berceau f.

craft, n. (skill) habileté f.; (trade) métier m.; (boat) embarcation f.

craftsman, n. artisan m.

craftsmanship, n. habileté, technique f.

crafty, adj. rusé, astucieux.

crag, n. rocher à pic m., rocher escarpé m.

cram, vb. remplir, farcir.

cramp, n. (med.) crampe f.; (mechanical) crampon m.

cranberry, n. canneberge f., airelle f.

crane, n. grue f.

cranium, n. crâne m.

crank, n. manivelle f.

cranky, adj. d'humeur difficile.

cranny, n. crevasse f., fente f.

craps, n. (slang) jeu de dés m.

crapshooter, n. (slang) joueur aux dés m.

crash, 1. n. (noise) fracas m.; (accident) accident m. **2.** vb. tomber avec fracas, intr.

crate, n. caisse f.

crater, n. cratère m.

crave for, vb. désirer ardemment.

craven, adj. lâche, poltron.

craving, *n.* désir ardent *m.*, besoin impérieux *m.*

crawl, *vb.* (reptiles) ramper; (persons) se traîner.

crayon, *n.* pastel *m.*

crazed, *adj.* fou, dément.

crazy, *adj.* fou *m.*, folle *f.*

creak, *vb.* grincer.

creaky, *adj.* qui crie, qui grince.

cream, *n.* crème *f.*

creamery, *n.* crêmerie *f.*

creamy, *adj.* crémeux, de crème.

crease, 1. *n.* pli *m.* **2.** *vb.* froisser, *tr.*

create, *vb.* créer.

creation, *n.* création *f.*

creative, *adj.* créateur *m.*, créatrice *f.*

creator, *n.* créateur *m.*, créatrice *f.*

creature, *n.* créature *f.*

credence, *n.* créance *f.*, croyance *f.*

credentials, *n.* lettres (*f.pl.*) de créance; (student, servant) certificat *m.*

credibility, *n.* crédibilité *f.*

credible, *adj.* croyable.

credit, *n.* crédit *m.*; (merit) honneur *m.*

creditable, *adj.* estimable.

creditably, *adv.* honorablement.

credit card, *n.* carte de crédit *f.*

creditor, *n.* créancier *m.*

credo, *n.* credo *m.*

credulity, *n.* crédulité *f.*

credulous, *adj.* crédule.

creed, *n.* (belief) croyance *f.*, (theology) credo *m.*

creek, *n.* ruisseau *m.*

creep, *vb.* (reptiles, insects, plants) ramper; (persons) se glisser.

cremate, *vb.* incinérer.

crematory, *n.* crématorium *m.*

creosote, *n.* créosote *f.*

crepe, *n.* crêpe *m.*

crescent, *n.* croissant *m.*

crest, *n.* crête *f.*

crestfallen, *adj.* abattu, découragé.

cretonne, *n.* cretonne *f.*

crevice, *n.* crevasse *f.*

crew, *n.* (boat) équipage *m.*; (gang) équipe *f.*

crib, *n.* (child's bed) lit (*m.*) d'enfant; (manger) mangeoire *f.*

cricket, *n.* (insect) grillon *m.*; (game) cricket *m.*

crier, *n.* crieur *m.*, huissier *m.*

crime, *n.* crime *m.*

criminal, *adj.* criminel.

criminologist, *n.* criminologue *m.*

criminology, *n.* criminologie *f.*

crimson, *adj. and n.* cramoisi *m.*

cringe, *vb.* faire des courbettes, se tapir, s'humilier.

crinkle, 1. *n.* pli *m.*, sinuosité *f.* **2.** *vb.* serpenter, former en zigzag.

cripple, 1. *n.* estropié *m.* **2.** *vb.* estropier.

crisis, *n.* crise *f.*

crisp, *adj.* (food) croquant; (manner) tranchant.

crispness, *n.* frisure *f.*

crisscross, *adj. and adv.* entrecroisé.

criterion, *n.* critérium *m.*

critic, *n.* critique *m.*

critical, *adj.* critique.

criticism, *n.* critique *f.*

criticize, *vb.* critiquer.

critique, *n.* critique *f.*

croak, *vb.* (frogs) coasser; (crows, persons) croasser.

crochet, 1. *vb.* broder au crochet. **2.** *m.* crochet *m.*

crock, *n.* pot (*m.*) de terre.

crockery, *n.* faïence *f.*

crocodile, *n.* crocodile *m.*

crocodile tears, *n.* larmes de crocodiles *f.pl.*

crone, *n.* vieille femme *f.*

crony, *n.* vieux camarade *m.*, compère *m.*

crook, *n.* (thief) escroc *m.*, voleur *m.*

crooked, *adj.* tortu.

croon, *vb.* chantonner, fredonner.

crop, *n.* récolte *f.*

croquet, *n.* (jeu de) croquet *m.*

croquette, *n.* croquette *f.*

cross, 1. *n.* croix *f.* **2.** *adj.* maussade. **3.** *vb.* croiser, *tr.*; (**c. oneself**) se signer; (**c. out**) rayer; (**go across**) traverser.

crossbreed, *n.* race croisée *f.*

cross-examine, *vb.* contre-examiner.

cross-eye, *adj.* louche.

cross-fertilization, *n.* croisement *m.*

cross-purpose, *n.* opposition *f.*,

contradiction *f.*, malentendu *m.*

cross section, *n.* coupe en travers *f.*

crossword puzzle, *n.* mots croisés *m.pl.*

crotch, *n.* fourche *f.*, fourchet *m.*

crouch, *vb.* s'accroupir.

croup, *n.* croupe *f.*; *(med.)* croup *m.*

croupier, *n.* croupier *m.*

crouton, *n.* crouton *m.*

crow, 1. *n.* (bird) corneille *f.*; **(cock-c.)** chant *(m.)* du coq. **2.** *vb.* chanter.

crowd, *n.* foule *f.*

crowd, *vb.* serrer, *tr.*; **(c. with)** remplir de.

crowded, *adj.* (streets, etc.) encombré.

crown, 1. *n.* couronne *f.*; (of head) sommet *m.*; (of hat) calotte *f.* **2.** *vb.* couronner.

crown prince, *n.* prince héritier *m.*

crow's-foot, *n.* patte d'oie (near the eye) *f.*; *(naut.)* araignée *f.*

crucial, *adj.* crucial.

crucible, *n.* creuset *m.*

crucifix, *n.* crucifix *m.*

crucifixion, *n.* crucifixion *f.*, crucifiement *m.*

crucify, *vb.* crucifier.

crude, *adj.* (unpolished) grossier; (metals, etc.) brut.

crudeness, *n.* crudité *f.*

cruel, *adj.* cruel.

cruelty, *n.* cruauté *f.*

cruet, *n.* burette *f.*

cruise, *n.* croisière *f.*

cruiser, *n.* croiseur *m.*

crumb, *n.* (small piece) miette *f.*; (not crust) mie *f.*

crumble, *vb.* émietter, *tr.*

crumple, *vb.* chiffonner, *tr.*

crunch, 1. *vb.* croquer, broyer, **2.** *n.* grincement *m.*

crusade, *n.* croisade *f.*

crusader, *n.* croisé *m.*

crush, *vb.* écraser.

crust, *n.* croûte *f.*

crustacean, *adj.* crustacé.

crusty, *adj.* couvert d'une croûte; *(fig.)* bourru, maussade.

crutch, *n.* béquille *f.*

cry, 1. *n.* cri *m.* **2.** *vb.* (shout) crier; (weep) pleurer.

crying, *adj.* criant.

cryosurgery, *n.* cryochirurgie *f.*

crypt, *n.* crypte *f.*

cryptic, *adj.* occulte, secret.

cryptography, *n.* cryptographie *f.*

crystal, *n.* cristal *m.*

crystalline, *adj.* cristallin.

crystallize, *vb.* cristalliser, *tr.*

cub, *n.* petit de *m.* (d'un animal).

Cuba, *n.* Cuba *m.*

Cuban, 1. *n.* Cubain *m.* **2.** *adj.* cubain.

cube, *n.* cube *m.*

cubic, *adj.* cubique.

cubicle, *n.* compartiment *m.*, cabine *f.*

cubic measure, *n.* mesures de volume *f.pl.*

cubism, *n.* cubisme *m.*

cuckoo, *n.* coucou *m.*; *(fig.)* niais *m.*

cucumber, *n.* concombre *m.*

cud, *n.* bol alimentaire *m.*, panse *f.*, chique (of tobacco) *f.*

cuddle, *vb.* serrer (dans ses bras), *tr.*

cudgel, 1. *n.* bâton *m.*, gourdin *m.*, trique *f.* **2.** *vb.* bâtonner.

cue, *n.* (theater) réplique *f.*; (hint) mot *m.*

cuff, *n.* poignet *m.*

cuisine, *n.* cuisine *f.*

culinary, *adj.* culinaire, de cuisine.

cull, *vb.* cueillir, recueillir.

culminate, *vb.* culminer.

culmination, *n.* point culminant *m.*

culpable, *adj.* coupable.

culprit, *n.* coupable *m.f.*

cult, *n.* culte *m.*

cultivate, *vb.* cultiver.

cultivated, *adj.* cultivé.

cultivation, *n.* culture *f.*

cultivator, *n.* cultivateur *m.*

cultural, *adj.* cultural.

culture, *n.* culture *f.*

cumbersome, *adj.* encombrant.

cumulative, *adj.* cumulatif.

cunning, 1. *n.* (guile) ruse *f.*; (skill) adresse *f.* **2.** *adj.* rusé; (attractive) charmant.

cup, *n.* tasse *f.*

cupboard, *n.* armoire *f.*

cupidity, *n.* cupidité *f.*

curable, *adj.* guérissable.

curator, *n.* conservateur *m.*
curb, 1. *n.* (horse) gourmette *f.;* (pavement) bord *m.* **2.** *vb.* (horse) gourmer; *(fig.)* brider.
curbstone, *n.* garde-pavé *m.*
curd, *n.* lait caillé *m.*
curdle, *vb.* cailler.
cure, 1. *n.* (healing) guérison *f.;* (remedy) remède *m.* **2.** *vb.* guérir.
curfew, *n.* couvre-feu *m.*
curio, *n.* curiosité *f.*
curiosity, *n.* curiosité *f.*
curious, *adj.* curieux.
curl, 1. *n.* boucle *f.* **2.** *vb.* friser.
curly, *adj.* frisé.
currant, *n.* groseille *f.*
currency, *n.* monnaie *f.*
current, *adj.* and *n.* courant *m.*
currently, *adv.* couramment.
curriculum, *n.* programme d'études *m.,* plan d'études *m.*
curry, *n.* cari *m.*
curse, 1. *n.* (malediction) malédiction *f.;* (oath) juron *m.;* (scourge) fléau *m.* **2.** *vb.* maudire; (swear) jurer.
cursed, *adj.* maudit.
cursory, *adj.* rapide, superficiel.
curt, *adj.* brusque.
curtail, *vb.* raccourcir.
curtain, *n.* rideau *m.*
curtsy, *n.* révérence *f.*
curvature, *n.* courbure *f.*
curve, 1. *n.* courbe *f.* **2.** *vb.* courber, *tr.*
cushion, *n.* coussin *m.*
cuspidor, *n.* crachoir *m.*
custard, *n.* crème *f.*
custodian, *n.* gardien *m.*
custody, *n.* (care) garde *f.;* (arrest) détention *f.*
custom, *n.* coutume *f.*
customary, *adj.* habituel.
customer, *n.* client *m.*
custom-house, customs, *n.* douane *f.*
customs-officer, *n.* douanier *m.*
cut, 1. *n.* (wound) coupure *f.;* (clothes, hair) coupe *f.;* (reduction) réduction *f.* **2.** *vb.* couper.
cutaneous, *adj.* cutané.
cute, *adj.* gentil *m.,* gentille *f.*
cut glass, *n.* cristal *m.*
cuticle, *n.* cuticule *f.*
cutlery, *n.* coutellerie *f.*
cutlet, *n.* côtelette *f.*

cutout, *n.* découpage *m.,* coupe *f.*
cutter, *n.* coupeur *m.,* coupeuse *f.*
cutthroat, *n.* coupe-jarret *m.*
cutting, 1. *n.* incision *f.* **2.** *adj.* incisif, tranchant.
cyclamate, *n.* cyclamate *m.*
cycle, 1. *n.* cycle *m.* **2.** *vb.* faire de la bicyclette.
cyclist, *n.* cycliste *m.*
cyclone, *n.* cyclone *m.*
cyclotron, *n.* cyclotron *m.*
cylinder, *n.* cylindre *m.*
cylindrical, *adj.* cylindrique.
cymbal, *n.* cymbale *f.*
cynic, *n.* cynique *m.*
cynical, *adj.* cynique.
cynicism, *n.* cynisme *m.*
cypress, *n.* cyprès *m.*
cyst, *n.* kyste *m.*

D

dab, 1. *n.* coup léger *m.,* tape *f.* **2.** *vb.* toucher légèrement.
dabble, *vb.* humecter, faire l'amateur.
dad, *n.* papa *m.*
daffodil, *n.* narcisse *m.*
daffy, *adj.* niais, sot.
dagger, *n.* poignard *m.*
dahlia, *n.* dahlia *m.*
daily, *adj.* quotidien.
daintiness, *n.* délicatesse *f.*
dainty, *adj.* délicat.
dairy, *n.* laiterie *f.*
dairyman, *n.* crémier *m.*
dais, *n.* estrade *f.*
daisy, *n.* marguerite *f.*
dale, *n.* vallon *m.,* vallée *f.*
dam, *n.* digue *f.*
damage, 1. *n.* dommage *m.* **2.** *vb.* endommager.
damask, *n.* damas *m.*
damnation, *n.* damnation *f.*
damp, *adj.* humide.
dampen, *vb.* humecter.
dampness, *n.* humidité *f.,* moiteur *f.*
damsel, *n.* demoiselle *f.,* jeune fille *f.*
dance, 1. *n.* danse *f.* **2.** *vb.* danser.
dancer, *n.* danseur *m.*
dandelion, *n.* pissenlit *m.*
dandruff, *n.* pellicules *f.pl.*
dandy, 1. *n.* dandy *m.* **2.** *adj.* élégant.

danger, *n.* danger *m.*

dangerous, *adj.* dangereux.

dangle, *vb.* pendiller, *intr.*

Dane, *n.* Danois *m.*

Danish, *adj. and n.* danois *m.*

dapper, *adj.* pimpant, petit et vif.

dappled, *adj.* pommelé.

dare, *vb.* oser.

daredevil, *n.* casse-cou *m.*

daring, *adj.* audacieux.

dark, *adj.* sombre.

darken, *vb.* obscurcir, *tr.*

dark horse, *n.* tocard *m.*

darkness, *n.* obscurité *f.*

darkroom, *n.* chambre noire *f.*

darling, *adj. and n.* chéri *m.*

darn, 1. *n.* reprise *f.* 2. *vb.* repriser.

darning needle, *n.* aiguille à repriser *f.*

dart, 1. *n.* dard *m.;* (sewing) pince *f.* 2. *vb.* se précipiter.

dash, 1. *n.* (energy) fougue *f.;* (pen) trait *m.* 2. *vb.* (throw) lancer; (destroy) détruire; (rush) se précipiter.

dashboard, *n.* tablier *m.*

dashing, *adj.* fougueux, brillant, superbe.

data, *n.* données *f.pl.*

data processing, *n.* élaboration *f.*

date, 1. *n.* date *f.;* (appointment) rendez-vous *m.;* (fruit) datte *f.* 2. *vb.* dater.

date line, *n.* ligne de changement de date *f.*

daub, 1. *n.* barbouillage *m.* 2. *vb.* barbouiller.

daughter, *n.* fille *f.*

daughter-in-law, *n.* belle-fille *f.*

daunt, *vb* intimider.

dauntless, *adj.* intrépide, indomptable.

dauntlessly, *adv.* d'une manière intrépide.

davenport, *n.* divan *m.*

dawdle, *vb.* flâner, muser.

dawn, *n.* aube *f.*

day, *n.* jour *m.;* (span of day) journée *f.*

daydream, *n.* rêverie *f.*

daylight, *n.* lumière (*f.*) du jour.

daylight-saving time, *n.* l'heure d'été *f.*

daze, *vb.* étourdir.

dazzle, *vb.* éblouir.

deacon, *n.* diacre *m.*

dead, *adj.* mort.

deaden, *vb.* amortir.

dead end, *n.* cul de sac *m.,* impasse *f.*

dead letter, *n.* lettre morte *f.*

deadline, *n.* ligne de délimitation *f.*

deadlock, *n.* impasse *f.*

deadly, *adj.* mortel.

deadwood, *n.* bois mort *m.*

deaf, *adj.* sourd.

deafen, *vb.* assourdir.

deaf-mute, *adj.* sourd-muet.

deafness, *n.* surdité *f.*

deal, 1. *n.* (great d.) beaucoup; (business) affair *f.;* (cards) donne *f.* 2. *vb.* (d. with) traiter; (d. out) distribuer.

dealer, *n.* marchand *m.*

dean, *n.* doyen *m.*

dear, *adj. and n.* cher *m.*

dearly, *adv.* chèrement.

dearth, *n.* disette *f.*

death, *n.* mort *f.*

deathless, *adj.* impérissable.

deathly, *adj.* mortel.

debacle, *n.* débâcle *f.*

debase, *vb.* avilir.

debatable, *adj.* discutable.

debate, 1. *n.* débat *m.* 2. *vb.* discuter.

debater, *n.* orateur parlementaire *m.,* argumentateur *m.*

debauch, 1. *n.* débauche *f.* 2. *vb.* débaucher, corrompre.

debenture, *n.* obligation *f.*

debilitate, *vb.* débiliter, affaiblir.

debit, *n.* débit *m.*

debonair, *adj.* courtois et jovial.

debris, *n.* débris *m.pl.*

debt, *n.* dette *f.*

debtor, *n.* débiteur *m.*

debunk, *vb.* dégonfler.

debut, *n.* début *m.*

debutante, *n.* débutante *f.*

decade, *n.* période (*f.*) de dix ans.

decadence, *n.* décadence *f.*

decadent, *adj.* décadent.

decaffeinated, *adj.* décaféiné.

decalcomania, *n.* décalcomanie *f.*

decanter, *n.* carafe *f.*

decapitate, *vb.* décapiter.

decay, 1. *n.* décadence *f.;* (state of ruin) délabrement *m.;* (teeth) carie *f.* 2. *vb.* tomber en décadence.

deceased, *adj.* défunt.

deceit, *n.* tromperie *f.*
deceitful, *adj.* trompeur.
deceive, *vb.* tromper.
deceiver, *n.* imposteur.
December, *n.* décembre *m.*
decency, *n.* décence *f.*
decent, *adj.* décent.
decentralization, *n.* décentralisation *f.*
decentralize, *vb.* décentraliser.
deception, *n.* tromperie *f.,* duperie *f.*
deceptive, *adj.* décevant, trompeur.
decibel, *n.* décibel *m.*
decide, *vb.* décider.
decided, *adj.* décidé, prononcé.
deciduous, *adj.* à feuillage caduc.
decimal, *adj.* décimal.
decimate, *vb.* décimer.
decipher, *vb.* déchiffrer.
decision, *n.* décision *f.*
decisive, *adj.* décisif.
deck, *n.* (boat) pont *m.;* (cards) paquet *m.*
deck hand, *n.* matelot de pont *m.*
declaim, *vb.* déclamer.
declamation, *n.* déclamation *f.*
declaration, *n.* déclaration *f.*
declarative, *adj.* explicatif, (law) déclaratif.
declare, *vb.* déclarer.
declension, *n.* déclinaison *f.*
decline, *vb.* décliner.
decode, *vb.* déchiffrer.
décolleté, *adj.* décolleté.
decompose, *vb.* décomposer, *tr.*
decongestant, *adj.* décongestionnant.
decor, *n.* décor *m.*
decorate, *vb.* décorer.
decoration, *n.* décoration *f.*
decorative, *adj.* décoratif.
decorator, *n.* décorateur *m.*
decorous, *adj.* bienséant, convenable.
decorum, *n.* décorum *m.*
decoy, 1. *n.* leurre *m.* **2.** *vb.* leurrer.
decrease, 1. *n.* diminution *f.* **2.** *vb.* diminuer.
decree, *n.* décret *m.*
decrepit, *adj.* décrépit.
decry, *vb.* décrier, dénigrer.
dedicate, *vb.* dédier.
dedication, *n.* dédicace *f.*
deduce, *vb.* déduire.

deduct, *vb.* déduire.
deduction, *n.* déduction *f.*
deductive, *adj.* déductif.
deed, *n.* action *f.;* (law) acte *(m.)* notarié.
deem, *vb.* juger.
deep, *adj.* profond.
deepen, *vb.* approfondir, *tr.*
deep freeze, *n.* surgélateur *m.*
deeply, *adv.* profondément.
deep-rooted, *adj.* enraciné.
deer, *n.* cerf *m.*
deerskin, *n.* peau de daim *f.*
deface, *vb.* défigurer.
defamation, *n.* diffamation *f.*
defame, *vb.* diffamer.
default, *n.* défaut *m.*
defeat, 1. *n.* défaite *f.* **2.** *vb.* vaincre.
defeatism, *n.* défaitisme *m.*
defect, *n.* défaut *m.*
defection, *n.* défection *f.*
defective, *adj.* défectueux.
defend, *vb.* défendre.
defendant, *n.* défendeur *m.*
defender, *n.* défenseur *m.*
defense, *n.* défense *f.*
defenseless, *adj.* sans défense.
defensible, *adj.* défendable, soutenable.
defensive, *adj.* défensif.
defer, *vb.* (put off) différer; (show deference) déférer.
deference, *n.* déférence *f.*
deferential, *adj.* plein de déférence, respectueux.
defiance, *n.* défi *m.*
defiant, *adj.* de défi.
deficiency, *n.* insuffisance *f.*
deficient, *adj.* insuffisant.
deficit, *n.* déficit *m.*
defile, *vb.* souiller.
define, *vb.* définir.
definite, *adj.* défini.
definitely, *adv.* d'une manière déterminée.
definition, *n.* définition *f.*
definitive, *adj.* définitif.
deflate, *vb.* dégonfler.
deflation, *n.* dégonflement *m.*
deflect, *vb.* faire dévier, détourner.
deform, *vb.* déformer.
deformity, *n.* difformité *f.*
defraud, *vb.* frauder.
defray, *vb.* payer.
defrost, *vb.* déglacer.

defroster, n. déglaceur m.
deft, adj. adroit.
defy, vb. défier.
degenerate, vb. dégénérer.
degeneration, n. dégénérescence f.
degradation, n. dégradation f.
degrade, vb. dégrader.
degree, n. degré m.
dehydrate, vb. déshydrater.
deify, vb. déifier.
deign, vb. daigner.
deity, n. divinité f.
dejected, adj. abattu.
dejection, n. abattement m.
delay, 1. n. retard m. **2.** vb. retarder, tr.; tarder, intr.
delectable, adj. délectable.
delegate, 1. n. délégué m. **2.** vb. déléguer.
delegation, n. délégation f.
delete, vb. rayer, biffer.
deliberate, 1. adj. délibéré. **2.** vb. délibérer.
deliberately, adv. de propos délibéré.
deliberation, n. délibération f.
deliberative, adj. délibératif.
delicacy, n. délicatesse f.
delicate, adj. délicat.
delicatessen, n. charcuterie f.
delicious, adj. délicieux.
delight, 1. n. délices f.pl. **2.** vb. enchanter.
delightful, adj. charmant.
delineate, vb. esquisser, dessiner.
delinquency, n. délit m.
delinquent, adj. and n. délinquant m.
delirious, adj. délirant.
deliver, vb. délivrer; (speech) prononcer.
deliverance, n. délivrance f.
delivery, n. (child) accouchement m.; (speech) débit m.; (goods) livraison f.; (letters) distribution f.; (general d.) poste restante f.
delouse, vb. épouiller.
delude, vb. tromper.
deluge, n. déluge m.
delusion, n. illusion f.
de luxe, adv. de luxe.
delve, vb. creuser, pénétrer.
demagogue, n. démagogue m.
demand, 1. n. demande f. **2.** vb. demander; (as right) exiger.
demarcation, n. démarcation f.

demean, vb. comporter.
demeanor, n. maintien m.
demented, adj. fou m., folle f.
demerit, n. démérite m.
demigod, n. demi-dieu n.
demilitarize, vb. démilitariser.
demise, n. décès m., mort f.
demobilization, n. démobilisation f.
demobilize, vb. démobiliser.
democracy, n. démocratie f.
democrat, n. démocrate m.f.
democratic, adj. démocratique.
demolish, vb. démolir.
demolition, n. démolition f.
demon, n. démon m.
demonstrable, adj. démonstrable.
demonstrate, vb. démontrer.
demonstration, n. démonstration f.
demonstrative, adj. démonstratif.
demonstrator, n. démonstrateur m.
demoralize, vb. démoraliser.
demote, vb. réduire à un grade inférieur.
demur, vb. hésiter, s'opposer à.
demure, adj. posé, d'une modestie affectée.
den, n. antre m., repaire m.
denature, vb. dénaturer.
denaturalize, vb. dénaturaliser.
denial, n. dénégation f.; (refusal) refus m.
denim, n. treillis m.
Denmark, n. Danemark m.
denomination, n. dénomination f.; (religion) confession f.
denominator, n. dénominateur m.
denote, vb. dénoter.
denouement, n. dénouement m.
denounce, vb. dénoncer.
dense, adj. dense; (stupid) bête.
density, n. densité f.
dent, n. bosselure f.
dental, adj. dentaire; (gramm.) dental.
dentifrice, n. dentifrice f.
dentist, n. dentiste m.
dentistry, n. art du dentiste m., dentisterie f.
denture, n. dentier m., râtelier m.
denude, vb. dénuder.
denunciation, n. dénonciation f.
deny, vb. nier.
deodorant, n. désodorisant m.

deodorize, *vb.* désodoriser, désinfecter.

depart, *vb.* partir, s'en aller, quitter.

department, *n.* département *m.;* (government) ministère *m.;* (**d. store**) grand magasin *m.*

departmental, *adj.* départemental.

departure, *n.* départ *m.*

depend on, *vb.* dépendre de; (rely) compter sur.

dependability, *n.* confiance que l'on inspire *f.*

dependable, *adj.* digne de confiance.

dependence, *n.* dépendance *f.,* confiance *f.*

dependent, *adj.* dépendant.

depict, *vb.* peindre.

depiction, *n.* description *f.*

deplete, *vb.* épuiser.

deplorable, *adj.* déplorable.

deplore, *vb.* déplorer.

depopulate, *vb.* dépeupler.

deport, *vb.* déporter.

deportation, *n.* déportation *f.*

deportment, *n.* maintien *m.*

depose, *vb.* déposer.

deposit, 1. *n.* dépôt *m.* **2.** *vb.* déposer.

depositor, *n.* déposant *m.*

depository, *n.* dépôt *m.,* dépositaire *m.*

depot, *n.* dépôt *m.,* gare *f.*

deprave, *vb.* dépraver, corrompre.

depravity, *n.* dépravation *f.,* corruption *f.*

deprecate, *vb.* désapprouver, s'opposer à.

depreciate, *vb.* déprécier.

depreciation, *n.* dépréciation *f.*

depredation, *n.* déprédation *f.,* pillage *m.*

depress, *vb.* (lower) abaisser; *(fig.)* abattre.

depressed, *adj.* abattu, bas.

depression, *n.* dépression *f.;* (personal) abattement *m.;* (comm.) crise *f.*

deprive, *vb.* priver.

depth, *n.* profondeur *f.*

depth charge, *n.* grenade sous-marine *f.*

deputy, *n.* délégué *m.;* (politics) député *m.*

derail, *vb.* dérailler.

derange, *vb.* déranger.

deranged, *adj.* dérangé, troublé.

derelict, 1. *n.* vaisseau abandonné *m.,* épave *f.* **2.** *adj.* abandonné, délaissé.

dereliction, *n.* abandon *m.*

deride, *vb.* tourner en dérision.

derision, *n.* dérision *f.*

derisive, *adj.* dérisoire.

derivation, *n.* dérivation *f.,* origine *f.*

derivative, *n.* dérivatif.

derive, *vb.* dériver.

dermatology, *n.* dermatologie *f.*

derogatory, *adj.* dérogatoire.

derrick, *n.* grue *f.*

descend, *vb.* descendre.

descendant, *n.* descendant *m.*

descent, *n.* descente *f.*

describe, *vb.* décrire.

description, *n.* description *f.*

descriptive, *adj.* descriptif.

desecrate, *vb.* profaner.

desensitize, *vb.* désensibiliser.

desert, 1. *n.* (place) désert *m.;* (merit) mérite *m.* **2.** *vb.* déserter.

deserter, *n.* déserteur *m.*

desertion, *n.* abandon *m.;* (military) désertion *f.*

deserve, *vb.* mériter.

deserving, *adj.* méritoire, de mérite.

design, 1. *n.* (project) dessein *m.;* (architecture) projet *m.* **2.** *vb.* dessiner; (**d. for**) destiner à.

designate, *vb.* désigner.

designation, *n.* désignation *f.*

designedly, *adv.* à dessein.

designer, *n.* dessinateur *m.*

designing, *adj.* intrigant, artificieux.

desirable, *adj.* désirable.

desire, 1. *n.* désir *m.* **2.** *vb.* désirer.

desirous, *adj.* désireux.

desist, *vb.* cesser.

desk, *n.* (office) bureau *m.;* (school) pupitre *m.*

desolate, *adj.* désolé.

desolation, *n.* désolation *f.*

despair, 1. *n.* désespoir *m.* **2.** *vb.* désespérer.

desperado, *n.* désespéré *m.,* cerveau brûlé *m.*

desperate, *adj.* désespéré.

desperation, *n.* désespoir *m.*

despicable, *adj.* méprisable.
despise, *vb.* mépriser.
despite, *prep.* en dépit de.
despondent, *adj.* découragé.
despot, *n.* despote *m.*
despotic, *adj.* despotique.
despotism, *n.* despotisme *m.*
dessert, *n.* dessert *m.*
destination, *n.* destination *f.*
destine, *vb.* destiner.
destiny, *n.* destin *m.*
destitute, *adj.* (deprived) dénué; (poor) indigent.
destitution, *n.* destitution *f.*
destroy, *vb.* détruire.
destroyer, *n.* destructeur *m.*; (naval) contre-torpilleur *m.*
destructible, *adj.* destructible.
destruction, *n.* destruction *f.*
destructive, *adj.* destructif.
desultory, *adj.* à bâtons rompus, décousu.
detach, *vb.* détacher.
detachment, *n.* détachement *m.*
detail, *n.* détail *m.*
detain, *vb.* retenir; (in prison) détenir.
detect, *vb.* découvrir.
detection, *n.* découverte *f.*
detective, *n.* agent (*m.*) de la police secrète; **(d. novel)** roman policier.
detente, *n.* détente *f.*
detention, *n.* détention *f.*
deter, *vb.* détourner, empêcher (de), dissuader (de).
detergent, *n.* détersif *m.*
deteriorate, *vb.* détériorer, *tr.*
deterioration, *n.* détérioration *f.*
determination, *n.* détermination *f.*
determine, *vb.* déterminer.
determined, *adj.* déterminé.
determinism, *n.* déterminisme *m.*
deterrence, *n.* préventif *m.*
deterrent, *n. and adj.* préventif *m.*
detest, *vb.* détester.
dethrone, *vb.* détrôner.
detonate, *vb.* détoner.
detour, *n.* détour *m.*
detract, *vb.* enlever, ôter (à), dénigrer, déroger (à).
detriment, *n.* détriment *m.*, préjudice *m.*
detrimental, *adj.* préjudiciable, nuisible (à).

devaluate, *vb.* dévaluer, déprécier.
devastate, *vb.* dévaster.
develop, *vb.* développer, *tr.*
developer, *n.* (photography) révélateur *m.*
developing nation, *n.* nation en cours de développement *f.*
development, *n.* développement *m.*
deviate, *vb.* dévier, s'écarter (de).
deviation, *n.* déviation *f.*, écart *m.*
device, *n.* expédient *m.*
devil, *n.* diable *m.*
devilish, *adj.* diabolique.
devious, *adj.* détourné.
devise, *vb.* (plan) combiner; (plot) tramer.
devitalize, *vb.* dévitaliser.
devoid, *adj.* dépourvu.
devote, *vb.* consacrer.
devoted, *adj.* dévoué.
devotee, *n.* dévot *m.*, dévote *f.*
devotion, *n.* (religious) dévotion *f.*; (to person or thing) dévouement *m.*
devour, *vb.* dévorer.
devout, *adj.* dévot.
dew, *n.* rosée *f.*
dewy, *adj.* de rosée.
dexterity, *n.* dextérité *f.*
dexterous, *adj.* adroit.
diabetes, *n.* diabète *m.*
diabolic, *adj.* diabolique.
diadem, *n.* diadème *m.*
diagnose, *vb.* diagnostiquer.
diagnosis, *n.* diagnose *f.*
diagnostic, *adj.* diagnostique.
diagonal, *adj.* diagonal.
diagonally, *adv.* diagonalement.
diagram, *n.* diagramme *m.*
dial, 1. *n.* cadran *m.* 2. *vb.* **(d. a number)** composer.
dialect, *n.* dialecte *m.*
dialogue, *n.* dialogue *m.*
diameter, *n.* diamètre *m.*
diametrical, *adj.* diamétral.
diamond, *n.* diamant *m.*; (shape) losange *m.*; (cards) carreau *m.*
diaper, *n.* (babies) couche *f.*
diaphragm, *n.* diaphragme *m.*
diarrhea, *n.* diarrhée *f.*
diary, *n.* journal *m.*
diathermy, *n.* diathermie *f.*
diatribe, *n.* diatribe *f.*
dice, *n.* dés *m.pl.*
dicker, *vb.* marchander.

dictaphone, n. machine à dicter f.

dictate, vb. dicter.

dictation, n. dictée f.

dictator, n. dictateur m.

dictatorial, adj. dictatorial.

dictatorship, n. dictature f.

diction, n. diction f.

dictionary, n. dictionnaire m.

didactic, adj. didactique.

die, 1. n. dé m. **2.** vb. mourir.

die-hard, n. intransigeant m., ultra m.

diet, n. régime m.

dietary, adj. diététique.

dietetics, n. diététique f.

dietitian, n. diététicien m.

differ, vb. différer.

difference, n. différence f.

different, adj. différent.

differential, adj. différentiel.

difficult, adj. difficile.

difficulty, n. difficulté f.

diffident, adj. hésitant, timide.

diffuse, adj. diffus.

diffusion, n. diffusion f.

dig, vb. bêcher; (hole) creuser.

digest, vb. digérer.

digestible, adj. digestible.

digestion, n. digestion f.

digestive, adj. and n. digestif m.

digital, adj. (in watches, etc.) digital.

digitalis, n. digitaline f.

dignified, adj. plein de dignité.

dignify, vb. honorer, élever.

dignitary, n. dignitaire m.

dignity, n. dignité f.

digress, vb. faire une digression.

digression, n. digression f.

dike, n. (ditch) fossé m.; (dam) digue f.

dilapidated, adj. délabré.

dilapidation, n. délabrement m.

dilate, vb. dilater, tr.

dilatory, adj. dilatoire, lent, négligent.

dilemma, n. dilemme m.

dilettante, n. dilettante m., amateur m.

diligence, n. diligence f.

diligent, adj. diligent.

dill, n. aneth m.

dilute, vb. diluer.

dim, adj. (light, sight) faible; (color) terne.

dime, n. un dixième de dollar m.

dimension, n. dimension f.

diminish, vb. diminuer.

diminution, n. diminution f.

diminutive, 1. adj. tout petit. **2.** n. (gramm.) diminutif m.

dimness, n. (weakness) faiblesse f.; (darkness) obscurité f.

dimple, n. (face) fossette f.

din, n. tapage m.

dine, vb. dîner.

diner, dining-car, n. wagon-restaurant m.

dingy, adj. défraîchi.

dining room, n. salle (f.) à manger.

dinner, n. dîner m.; (d. jacket) smoking m.

dinosaur, n. dinosaurien m.

diocese, n. diocèse m.

dip, vb. plonger.

diphtheria, n. diphtérie f.

diploma, n. diplôme m.

diplomacy, n. diplomatie f.

diplomat, n. diplomate m.

diplomatic, adj. diplomatique.

dipper, n. cuiller (f.) à pot.

dire, adj. affreux.

direct, vb. (guide) diriger; (address) adresser.

direct, adj. direct.

direct current, n. courant continu m.

direction, n. direction f.; (orders) instructions f.pl.

directional, adj. de direction.

directive, 1. n. directif m. **2.** adj. dirigeant.

directly, adv. directement.

directness, n. rectitude f.; (frankness) franchise f.

director, n. directeur m.

directorate, n. conseil d'administration m.

directory, n. annuaire m.

dirge, n. chant funèbre m.

dirigible, adj. and n. dirigeable m.

dirt, n. saleté f.

dirty, adj. sale.

disability, n. incapacité f.

disable, vb. mettre hors de combat, tr.

disabled, adj. invalide.

disabuse, vb. désabuser.

disadvantage, n. désavantage m.

disagree, vb. être en désaccord.

disagreeable, adj. désagréable.

disagreement, n. désaccord m.

disappear, vb. disparaître.

disappearance, *n.* disparition *f.*

disappoint, *vb.* désappointer.

disappointment, *n.* désappointement *m.*

disapproval, *n.* désapprobation *f.*

disapprove, *vb.* désapprouver.

disarm, *vb.* désarmer.

disarmament, *n.* désarmement *m.*

disarray, *n.* désarroi *m.*, désordre *m.*

disassemble, *vb.* démonter, désassembler.

disaster, *n.* désastre *m.*

disastrous, *adj.* désastreux.

disavow, *vb.* désavouer.

disavowal, *n.* désaveu *m.*

disband, *vb.* congédier, *tr.;* se débander, *intr.*

disbar, *vb.* rayer du tableau des avocats.

disbelieve, *vb.* ne pas croire, refuser de croire.

disburse, *vb.* débourser.

discard, *vb.* mettre de côté.

discern, *vb.* discerner.

discerning, *adj.* judicieux, éclairé.

discernment, *n.* discernement *m.*

discharge, 1. *n.* décharge *f.; (mil.)* congé *m.* 2. *vb.* décharger; *(mil.)* congédier.

disciple, *n.* disciple *m.*

disciplinarian, *n.* disciplinaire *m.*

disciplinary, *adj.* disciplinaire.

discipline, *n.* discipline *f.*

disclaim, *vb.* désavouer, nier.

disclaimer, *n.* désaveu *m.*

disclose, *vb.* révéler.

disclosure, *n.* révélation *f.*

disco, *adj.* disco.

discolor, *vb.* décolorer.

discomfiture, *n.* défaite *f.*, déroute *f.*

discomfort, *n.* malaise *m.*

disconcert, *vb.* déconcerter.

disconnect, *vb.* désunir.

disconnected, *adj.* (electricity) hors circuit.

disconsolate, *adj.* désolé.

discontent, *n.* mécontentement *m.*

discontented, *adj.* mécontent.

discontinue, *vb.* discontinuer.

discord, *n.* discorde *f.*

discordant, *adj.* discordant, en désaccord.

discotheque, *n.* discothèque *f.*

discount, *n.* escompte *m.; (reduction)* remise *f.*

discourage, *vb.* décourager.

discouragement, *n.* découragement *m.*

discourse, *n.* discours *m.*

discourteous, *adj.* impoli.

discourtesy, *n.* impolitesse *f.*

discover, *vb.* découvrir.

discoverer, *n.* découvreur *m.*

discovery, *n.* découverte *f.*

discredit, 1. *n.* discrédit *m.* 2. *vb.* discréditer.

discreditable, *adj.* déshonorant, peu honorable.

discreet, *adj.* discret.

discrepancy, *n.* contradiction *f.*

discretion, *n.* discrétion *f.*

discriminate, *vb.* distinguer.

discrimination, *n.* discernement *m.*, jugement *m.*

discursive, *adj.* discursif, sans suite.

discuss, *vb.* discuter.

discussion, *n.* discussion *f.*

disdain, *n.* dédain *m.*

disdainful, *adj.* dédaigneux.

disease, *n.* maladie *f.*

disembark, *vb.* débarquer.

disembody, *vb.* dépouiller du corps.

disenchantment, *n.* désenchantement *m.*

disengage, *vb.* dégager.

disentangle, *vb.* démêler.

disfavor, *n.* défaveur *f.*

disfigure, *vb.* défigurer, enlaidir.

disfranchise, *vb.* priver du droit de vote.

disgorge, *vb.* dégorger.

disgrace, *n.* disgrâce *f.*

disgraceful, *adj.* honteux.

disgruntled, *adj.* mécontent, de mauvaise humeur.

disguise, 1. *n.* déguisement *m.* 2. *vb.* dégoûter.

dish, *n.* plat *m.; (wash the dishes)* laver la vaisselle.

dishcloth, *n.* torchon *m.*

dishearten, *vb.* décourager.

dishonest, *adj.* malhonnête.

dishonesty, *n.* malhonnêteté *f.*

dishonor, *n.* déshonneur *m.*

dishonorable, *adj.* (action) déshonorant.

disillusion, *n.* désillusion *f.*

disinfect, *vb.* désinfecter.

disinfectant, *n.* désinfectant *m.*

disinherit, *vb.* déshériter.

disintegrate, *vb.* désagréger.

disinterested, *adj.* désintéressé.

disjointed, *adj.* désarticulé, disloqué.

disk, *n.* disque *m.*

dislike, **1,** *n.* aversion *f.* **2.** *vb.* ne pas aimer.

dislocate, *vb.* disloquer.

dislodge, *vb.* déloger.

disloyal, *adj.* infidèle.

disloyalty, *n.* infidélité *f.*, perfidie *f.*

dismal, *adj.* sombre.

dismantle, *vb.* dépouiller (de).

dismay, *n.* consternation *f.*

dismember, *vb.* démembrer.

dismiss, *vb.* congédier.

dismissal, *n.* renvoi *m.*

dismount, *vb.* descendre.

disobedience, *n.* désobéissance *f.*

disobedient, *adj.* désobéissant.

disobey, *vb.* désobéir à.

disorder, *n.* désordre *m.*

disorderly, *adj.* désordonné.

disorganize, *vb.* désorganiser.

disown, *vb.* désavouer.

disparage, *vb.* déprécier, dénigrer.

disparate, *adj.* disparate.

disparity, *n.* inégalité *f.*

dispassionate, *adj.* calme.

dispatch, **1.** *n.* (business) expédition *f.*; (speed) promptitude *f.*; (message) dépêche *f.* **2.** *vb.* expédier.

dispatcher, *n.* expéditeur *m.*

dispel, *vb.* dissiper.

dispensable, *adj.* dont on peut se passer.

dispensary, *n.* dispensaire *m.*

dispensation, *n.* dispensation *f.*

dispense, *vb.* distribuer, dispenser.

dispersal, *n.* dispersion *f.*

disperse, *vb.* disperser.

displace, *vb.* déplacer.

displaced person, *n.* réfugié *m.*

displacement, *n.* déplacement *m.*

display, **1.** *n.* (show) exposition *f.*; (shop, ostentation) étalage *m.* **2.** *vb.* étaler.

displease, *vb.* déplaire à.

disposable, *adj.* disponible.

disposal, *n.* disposition *f.*

dispose, *vb.* disposer.

disposition, *n.* disposition *f.*; (character) caractère *m.*

dispossess, *vb.* déposséder, exproprier.

disproportion, *n.* disproportion *f.*

disproportionate, *adj.* disproportionné.

disprove, *vb.* réfuter.

disputable, *adj.* contestable, disputable.

dispute, **1.** *n.* (discussion) discussion *f.*; (quarrel) dispute *f.* **2.** *vb.* (se) disputer.

disqualify, *vb.* (sports) disqualifier.

disregard, *vb.* ne tenir aucun compte de.

disrepair, *n.* délabrement *m.*

disreputable, *adj.* déshonorant, honteux.

disrespect, *n.* irrévérence *f.*

disrespectful, *adj.* irrespectueux.

disrobe, *vb.* déshabiller, dévêtir.

disrupt, *vb.* faire éclater, rompre.

dissatisfaction, *n.* mécontentement *m.*

dissatisfy, *vb.* mécontenter.

dissect, *vb.* disséquer.

dissemble, *vb.* dissimuler.

disseminate, *vb.* disséminer.

dissension, *n.* dissension *f.*

dissent, *vb.* différer.

dissertation, *n.* dissertation *f.*, discours *m.*

disservice, *n.* mauvais service rendu *m.*

dissimilar, *adj.* dissemblable.

dissipate, *vb.* dissiper.

dissipated, *adj.* dissipé.

dissipation, *n.* dissipation *f.*

dissociate, *vb.* désassocier, dissocier.

dissolute, *adj.* dissolu.

dissolution, *n.* dissolution *f.*

dissolve, *vb.* dissoudre, *tr.*

dissonance, *n.* dissonance *f.*, désaccord *m.*

dissonant, *adj.* dissonant.

dissuade, *vb.* dissuader.

distance, *n.* distance *f.*

distant, *adj.* distant.

distaste, *n.* dégoût *m.*

distasteful, *adj.* désagréable.

distemper, **1.** *n.* maladie des chiens *f.* **2.** peindre en détrempe.

distend, *vb.* dilater, gonfler.

distill, vb. distiller.

distillation, n. distillation f.

distiller, n. distillateur m.

distillery, n. distillerie f.

distinct, adj. distinct.

distinction, n. distinction f.

distinctive, adj. distinctif.

distinctly, adv. distinctement, clairement.

distinguish, vb. distinguer.

distinguished, adj. distingué.

distort, vb. déformer.

distract, vb. (divert) distraire; (upset) affoler.

distracted, adj. affolé, bouleversé.

distraction, n. (diversion) distraction f.; (madness) folie f.

distraught, adj. affolé, éperdu, hors de soi.

distress, 1. n. détresse f. **2.** vb. affliger.

distressing, adj. affligeant, pénible, désolant.

distribute, vb. distribuer.

distribution, n. distribution f.

distributor, n. distributeur m.

district, n. (region) contrée f.; (administration) district m.; (town) quartier m.

distrust, 1. n. méfiance f. **2.** vb. se méfier de.

distrustful, adj. méfiant.

disturb, vb. déranger.

disturbance, n. dérangement m.

disunite, vb. désunir.

disuse, n. désuétude f.

ditch, n. fossé m.

ditto, adv. idem, de même.

diva, n. diva f.

divan, n. divan m.

dive, vb. plonger.

dive bomber, n. avion de bombardement qui fait des vols piqués m.

diver, n. plongeur m.

diverge, vb. diverger.

divergence, n. divergence f.

divergent, adj. divergent.

diverse, adj. divers.

diversion, n. (amusement) divertissement m.

diversity, n. diversité f.

divert, vb. (turn aside) détourner; (amuse) divertir.

divest, vb. ôter, dépouiller, priver.

divide, vb. diviser.

divided, adj. divisé, séparé.

dividend, n. dividende m.

divine, adj. divin.

divinity, n. divinité f.

divisible, adj. divisible.

division, n. division f.

divisive, adj. qui divise, qui sépare.

divorce, 1. n. divorce m. **2.** vb. divorcer.

divorcee, n. divorcé m., divorcée f.

divulge, vb. divulguer.

dizziness, n. vertige m.

dizzy, adj. pris de vertige.

do, vb. faire; **(how d. you d.?)** comment allez-vous?

docile, adj. docile.

dock, n. bassin m.

docket, n. registre m., bordereau m.

dockyard, n. chantier de construction de navires m.

doctor, n. docteur m.

doctorate, n. doctorat m.

doctrinaire, adj. doctrinaire.

doctrine, n. doctrine f.

document, n. document m.

documentary, adj. documentaire.

documentation, n. documentation f.

dodge, vb. esquiver, éluder.

doe, n. daine f.

doeskin, n. peau de daim f.

dog, n. chien m.

dogfight, n. combat de chiens m., mêlée générale f.

dogged, adj. obstiné, tenace.

doggerel, n. poésie burlesque f.

doghouse, n. chenil m.

dogma, n. dogme m.

dogmatic, adj. dogmatique.

dogmatism, n. dogmatisme m.

doily, n. petit napperon m.

doldrum, n. (naut.) zone des calmes f., cafard m.

dole, 1. n. pitance f.; aumone f. **2.** vb. distribuer parcimonieusement.

doleful, adj. lugubre.

doll, n. poupée f.

dollar, n. dollar m.

dolorous, adj. douloureux.

dolphin, n. dauphin m.

domain, n. domaine m.

dome, n. dôme m.

domestic, *adj.* domestique.
domesticate, *vb.* domestiquer, apprivoiser.
domicile, *n.* domicile *m.*
dominance, *n.* dominance *f.*, prédominance *f.*
dominant, *adj.* dominant.
dominate, *vb.* dominer.
domination, *n.* domination *f.*
domineer, *vb.* se montrer tyrannique.
domineering, *adj.* impérieux.
dominion, *n.* domination *f.*; (territory) possessions *f.pl.*
domino, *n.* domino *m.*
don, *vb.* endosser, revêtir.
donate, *vb.* donner.
donation, *n.* donation *f.*
done, *vb.* fait.
donkey, *n.* âne *m.*
don't, *vb.* ne faites pas!, ne fais pas!
doom, *vb.* condamner.
doomsday, *n.* (jour du) jugement dernier *m.*
door, *f.* porte *f.*; (d.-keeper) concierge *m.f.*
doorman, *n.* portier *m.*
doorstep, *n.* seuil *m.*, pas de la porte *m.*
doorway, *n.* (baie de) porte *f.*, encadrement de la porte *m.*
dope, *n.* stupéfiant *m.*
dormant, *adj.* endormi, assoupi.
dormer, *n.* lucarne *f.*
dormitory, *n.* maison (*f.*) d'étudiants.
dosage, *n.* dosage *m.*
dose, *n.* dose *f.*
dossier, *n.* dossier *m.*
dot, *n.* point *m.*
dotage, *n.* radotage *m.*
dote, *vb.* radoter; (d. on) aimer excessivement.
double, 1. *adj. and n.* double *m.* **2.** *vb.* doubler.
double-breasted, *adj.* croisé.
double-cross, *vb.* duper, tromper.
double-dealing, *n.* duplicité *f.*
double time, *n.* pas gymnastique *m.*
doubly, *adv.* doublement.
doubt, 1. *n.* doute *m.* **2.** *vb.* douter (de).
doubtful, *adj.* douteux.
doubtless, *adv.* sans doute.
dough, *n.* pâte *f.*

doughnut, *n.* pet (*m.*) de nonne.
dour, *adj.* austère.
douse, *vb.* plonger, tremper.
dove, *n.* colombe *f.*
dowager, *n.* douairière *f.*
dowdy, *adj.* dans élégance, qui manque de chic.
dowel, 1. *n.* goujon *m.* **2.** *vb.* goujonner.
down, 1. *n.* duvet *m.* **2.** *adv.* en bas. **3.** *prep.* (along) le long de.
downcast, *adj.* (look) baissé.
downfall, *n.* chute *f.*
downhearted, *adj.* découragé, déprimé.
downhill, 1. *n.* descente *f.* **2.** *adj.* en pente, incliné.
downpour, *n.* averse *f.*
downright, *adv.* tout à fait.
downstairs, *adv.* en bas.
downtown, *adv.* en ville.
downtrodden, *adj.* opprimé, piétiné.
downward, *adj.* descendant.
downy, *adj.* duveteux.
dowry, *n.* dot *f.*
doze, *vb.* sommeiller.
dozen, *n.* douzaine *f.*
drab, *adj.* (color) gris; (dull) terne.
draft, 1. *n.* (drawing) dessin *m.*; (mil.) conscription *f.*; (air) courant (*m.*) d'air. **2.** *vb.* (mil.) appeler sous le drapeau.
draftee, *n.* conscrit *m.*
draftsman, *n.* dessinateur *m.*
drafty, *adj.* plein de courante d'air.
drag, *vb.* traîner.
dragnet, *n.* drague *f.*, seine *f.*, chalut *m.*
dragon, *n.* dragon *m.*
drain, *vb.* drainer, *tr.*; s'écouler, *intr.*
drainage, *n.* drainage *m.*
dram, *n.* drachme *f.*, goutte *f.*
drama, *n.* drame *m.*
dramatic, *adj.* dramatique.
dramatics, *n.* théâtre *m.*
dramatist, *n.* dramaturge *m.*
dramatize, *vb.* dramatiser.
dramaturgy, *n.* dramaturgie *f.*
drape, *vb.* draper.
drapery, *n.* draperie *f.*
drastic, *adj.* drastique.
draught, *n.* traction *f.*; trait *m.*

draw, *vb.* (pull) tirer; (sketch) dessiner.

drawback, *n.* inconvénient *m.*

drawbridge, *n.* pont-levis *m.*

drawer, *n.* tiroir *m.*

drawing, *n.* dessin *m.*

drawl, 1. *n.* voix (*f.*) traînante. **2.** *vb.* traîner la voix.

dray, *n.* camion *m.*

drayman, *n.* camionneur *m.*

dread, 1. *n.* crainte *f.* **2.** *vb.* redouter.

dreadful, *adj.* affreux.

dreadfully, *adv.* terriblement, affreusement.

dream, *n.* rêve *m.*

dreamer, *n.* rêveur *m.*

dreamy, *adj.* rêveur *m.*, rêveuse *f.*

dreary, *adj.* morne.

dredge, *vb.* draguer.

dreg, *n.* lie *f.*

drench, *vb.* tremper.

dress, 1. *n.* robe *f.* **2.** *vb.* habiller, *tr.;* s'habiller, *intr.*

dresser, *n.* commode *f.*

dressing, *n.* toilette *f.;* (surgical) pansement *m.*

dressing gown, *n.* robe de chambre *f.*, peignoir *m.*

dressmaker, *n.* couturière *f.*

dress rehearsal, *n.* répétition générale *f.*

drier, *n.* sécheur *m.*, dessécheur *m.*

drift, *vb.* (boat) dériver; (person) se laisser aller.

driftwood, *n.* bois flottant *m.*

drill, 1. *n.* (tool) foret *m.;* (exercise) exercice *m.* **2.** *vb.* (hole) forer; (exercise) exercer, *tr.;* faire l'exercice, *intr.*

drink, 1. *n.* boisson *f.* **2.** *vb.* boire.

drinkable, *adj.* potable.

drip, *vb.* dégoutter.

dripping, 1. *n.* dégouttement *m.* **2.** *adj.* ruisselant.

drive, 1. *n.* promenade (*f.*) en voiture; (energy) énergie *f.* **2.** *vb.* (auto, animals) conduire; (force) pousser.

drivel, *n.* bave *f.*

driver, *n.* (auto) chauffeur *m.*

drizzle, 1. *n.* bruine *f.* **2.** *vb.* bruiner.

dromedary, *n.* dromadaire *m.*

drone, 1. *n.* abeille mâle *f.;* bour-

donnement *m.* **2.** *vb.* bourdonner.

droop, *vb.* pencher.

drop, 1. *n.* goutte *f.;* (fall) chute *f.* **2.** *vb.* tomber, *intr.;* laisser tomber, *tr.*

dropout, *n.* étudiant qui quitte l'école avant de recevoir son diplôme *m.*

dropper, *n.* compte-gouttes *m.*

dropsy, *n.* hydropisie *f.*

drought, *n.* sécheresse *f.*

drove, *n.* troupeau *m.*

drown, *vb.* noyer, *tr.*

drowse, *vb.* s'assoupir.

drowsiness, *n.* somnolence *f.*

drowsy, *adj.* somnolent.

drudge, *vb.* s'éreinter.

drug, *n.* drogue *f.*

druggist, *n.* pharmacien *m.*

drug store, *n.* pharmacie *f.*

drum, *n.* tambour *m.;* (ear) tympan *m.*

drum major, *n.* tambour-major *m.*

drummer, *n.* tambour *m.*

drumstick, *n.* baguette de tambour *f.*

drunk, *adj.* ivre.

drunkard, *n.* ivrogne *m.*

drunkenness, *n.* ivresse *f.;* (habitual) ivrognerie *f.*

dry, 1. *adj.* sec *m.*, sèche *f.* **2.** *vb.* sécher.

dry-clean, *vb.* nettoyer à sec.

dry cleaner, *n.* teinturier *m.*

dry dock, 1. *n.* cale sèche *f.* **2.** *vb.* mettre en cale sèche.

dry goods, *n.* articles de nouveautés *m.pl.*

dryness, *n.* sécheresse *f.*

dual, *adj.* double.

dualism, *n.* dualisme *m.*

dubious, *adj.* douteux.

duchess, *n.* duchesse *f.*

duchy, *n.* duché *m.*

duck, *n.* canard *m.*

duct, *n.* conduit *m.*

ductile, *adj.* ductile.

dud, 1. *adj.* incapable. **2.** *n.* obus qui a raté *m.*

due, *adj.* dû *m.*, due *f.*

duel, *n.* duel *m.*

duelist, *n.* duelliste *m.*

duet, *n.* duo *m.*

duffel bag, *n.* sac pour les vêtements de rechange *m.*

dugout, n. abri-caverne m.

duke, n. duc m.

dukedom, n. duché m.

dulcet, adj. doux, suave.

dull, adj. (boring) ennuyeux.

dullard, n. lourdaud m.

dullness, n. (monotony) monotonie f.

duly, adv. dûment.

dumb, adj. muet m., muette f.; (stupid) sot m., sotte f.

dumbwaiter, n. monte-plats m.

dumfound, vb. abasourdir, interdire.

dummy, n. (dressmaking) mannequin m.; (cards) mort m.

dump, n. voirie f.

dumpling, n. boulette (de pâte) f.

dun, vb. importuner, talonner.

dunce, n. crétin m.

dunce cap, n. bonnet d'âne m.

dune, n. dune f.

dung, n. fiente f.; (agriculture) fumier m.

dungaree, n. salopette f., bleus m.pl.

dungeon, n. cachot m.

dupe, 1. n. dupe f. **2.** vb. duper.

duplex, adj. double.

duplicate, 1. n. double m. **2.** vb. faire le double de.

duplication, n. duplication f.

duplicity, n. duplicité f.

durable, adj. durable.

durability, n. durabilité f.

duration, n. durée f.

duress, n. contrainte f., coercition f.

during, prep. pendant.

dusk, n. crépuscule m.

dusky, adj. sombre.

dust, 1. n. poussière f. **2.** vb. épousseter.

dustpan, n. ramasse-poussière m.

dust storm, n. tourbillon de poussière m.

dusty, adj. poussièreux.

Dutch, adj. and n. hollandais m.

Dutchman, n. Hollandais m.

dutiful, adj. respectueux, fidèle.

dutifully, adv. avec soumission.

duty, n. (moral, legal) devoir m.; (tax) droit m.; **(be on d.)** être de service.

duty-free, adj. exempt de droits.

dwarf, adj. and n. nain m.

dwell, vb. demeurer.

dwindle, vb. diminuer.

dye, 1. n. teinture f. **2.** vb. teindre.

dyer, n. teinturier m.

dyestuff, n. matière colorante f.

dynamic, adj. dynamique.

dynamics, n. dynamique f.

dynamite, n. dynamite f.

dynamo, n. dynamo f.

dynasty, n. dynastie f.

dysentery, n. dysenterie f.

dyslexia, n. dyslexie f.

dyspepsia, n. dyspepsie f.

dyspeptic, adj. dyspeptique.

E

each, 1. adj. chaque. **2.** pron. chacun m., chacune f.; **(e. other)** l'un l'autre.

eager, adj. ardent.

eagerly, adv. ardemment, avidement.

eagerness, n. empressement m.

eagle, n. (bird) aigle m.; (mil.) aigle f.

eaglet, n. aiglon m.

ear, n. oreille f.

earache, n. mal d'oreille m.

eardrum, n. tympan m.

earl, n. comte m.

early, 1. adj. (of morning) matinal; (first) premier. **2.** adv. de bonne heure; tôt.

earmark, 1. n. marque distinctive f. **2.** vb. marquer, assigner.

earn, vb. gagner.

earnest, adj. sérieux.

earnestly, adv. sérieusement, sincèrement.

earnestness, n. gravité f., sérieux m.

earnings, n. salaire m.

earphone, n. casque (téléphonique) m.

earring, n. boucle (f.) d'oreille.

earshot, n. portée de voix f.

earth, n. terre f.

earthenware, n. poterie f., argile cuite f.

earthly, adj. terrestre.

earthquake, n. tremblement (m.) de terre.

earthworm, n. ver de terre m.

earthy, adj. terreux.

ease, n. aise f.; **(with e.)** avec facilité.

easel, n. chevalet m.

easily, adv. facilement.

easiness, n. facilité f.

east, n. est m.

Easter, n. Pâques m.

easterly, adj. d'est, vers l'est.

eastern, adj. de l'est, oriental.

eastward, adv. vers l'est.

easy, adj. facile; (of manners) aisé.

easygoing, adj. insouciant, peu exigeant, accommodant.

eat, vb. manger.

eaves, n. avant-toit m.

eavesdrop, vb. écouter aux portes.

ebb, n. (water) reflux m.; (decline) déclin m.

ebony, n. ébène m.

ebullient, adj. bouillonnant.

eccentric, adj. excentrique.

eccentricity, n. excentricité f.

ecclesiastic, adj. and n. ecclésiastique m.

ecclesiastical, adj. ecclésiastique.

echelon, n. échelon m.

echo, n. écho m.

eclipse, n. éclipse f.

ecological, adj. écologique.

ecology, n. écologie f.

economic, adj. économique.

economical, adj. (person) économe.

economics, n. économie (f.) politique.

economist, n. économiste m.

economize, vb. économiser.

economy, n. économie f.

ecru, n. écru m.

ecstasy, n. (religious) extase f.; (fig.) transport m.

ecumenical, adj. œcuménique.

eczema, n. eczéma m.

eddy, n. remous m.

edge, n. bord m.; (blade) fil m.

edging, n. pose f., bordure f.

edgy, adj. d'un air agacé.

edible, adj. comestible.

edict, n. édit m.

edifice, n. édifice m.

edify, vb. édifier.

edition, n. édition f.

editor, n. (text) éditeur m.; (paper) rédacteur m.

editorial, n. article (m.) de fond.

educate, vb. (upbringing) élever; (knowledge) instruire.

education, n. éducation f.; (schooling) instruction f.

educator, n. éducateur m.

eel, n. anguille f.

efface, vb. effacer.

effect, 1. n. effet m. **2.** vb. effectuer.

effective, adj. (having effect) efficace; (in effect) effectif f.

effectively, adv. efficacement, effectivement.

effectiveness, n. efficacité f.

effectual, adj. efficace.

effeminate, adj. efféminé.

effervesce, vb. être en effervescence, pétiller d'animation.

effete, adj. épuisé, caduc.

efficacious, adj. efficace.

efficacy, n. efficacité f.

efficiency, n. (person) compétence f.; (machine) rendement m.

efficient, adj. (person) capable.

efficiently, adv. efficacement, avec compétence.

effigy, n. effigie f.

effort, n. effort m.

effortless, adj. sans effort.

effrontery, n. effronterie f.

effulgent, adj. resplendissant.

effusive, adj. démonstratif.

egg, n. œuf m.; (boiled e.) œuf à la coque; (fried e.) œuf sur le plat; (poached e.) œuf poché; (scrambled e.) œuf brouillé.

eggplant, n. aubergine f.

egoism, n. égoïsme m.

egotism, n. égotisme m.

egotist, n. égotiste m.

Egypt, n. Égypte m.

Egyptian, 1. n. Égyptien m. **2.** adj. égyptien.

eight, adj. and n. huit m.

eighteen, adj. and n. dix-huit m.

eighteenth, adj. and n. dix-huitième m.f.

eighth, adj. and n. huitième m.f.

eightieth, adj. quatre-vingtième.

eighty, adj. and n. quatre-vingts m.

either, 1. adj. (each of two) chaque; (one or other) l'un ou l'autre. **2.** pron. chacun; l'un ou l'autre. **3.** conj. (e. . . . or) ou . . . ou . . .

ejaculate, vb. éjaculer, prononcer.

eject, vb. (throw) jeter.

ejection, n. jet m., éjection f., expulsion f.

eke, vb. suppléer à, subsister pauvrement.

elaborate, 1. adj. minutieux. **2.** vb. élaborer.

elapse, vb. (time) s'écouler.

elastic, adj. and n. élastique m.

elasticity, n. élasticité f.

elate, vb. exalter, transporter.

elated, adj. exalté.

elation, n. exaltation f.

elbow, n. coude m.

elbowroom, n. aisance des coudes f.

elder, adj. and n. aîné m.

elderberry, n. baie de sureau f.

elderly, adj. d'un certain âge.

eldest, adj. aîné.

elect, vb. élire.

election, n. élection f.

electioneer, vb. faire une campagne électorale.

elective, adj. électif.

electorate, n. électorat m., les votants m.pl.

electric, electrical, adj. électrique.

electric chair, n. fauteuil électrique m.

electric eel, n. anguille électrique f.

electrician, n. électricien m.

electricity, n. électricité f.

electrocardiogram, n. électrocardiogramme m.

electrocute, vb. électrocuter.

electrode, n. électrode f.

electrolysis, n. électrolyse f.

electron, n. électron m.

electronics, n. électronique f.

electroplate, 1. vb. plaquer. **2.** adj. plaqué.

elegance, n. élégance f.

elegant, adj. élégant.

elegiac, adj. élégiaque.

elegy, n. élégie f.

element, n. élément m.

elemental, elementary, adj. élémentaire.

elephant, n. éléphant m.

elephantine, adj. éléphantin.

elevate, vb. élever.

elevation, n. élévation f.

elevator, n. ascenseur m.

eleven, adj. and n. onze m.

eleventh, adj. and n. onzième m.f.

elf, n. elfe m.

elfin, adj. d'elfe.

elicit, vb. tirer, faire jaillir.

eligibility, n. éligibilité f.

eligible, adj. éligible.

eliminate, vb. éliminer.

elimination, n. élimination f.

elixir, n. élixir m.

elk, n. élan m.

elm, n. orme m.

elocution, n. élocution f.

elongate, vb. allonger, étendre.

elope, vb. s'enfuir.

eloquence, n. éloquence f.

eloquent, adj. éloquent.

eloquently, adv. d'une manière éloquente.

else, 1. adj. autre; (someone e.) quelqu'un d'autre. **2.** adv. autrement.

elsewhere, adv. ailleurs.

elucidate, vb. élucider, éclaircir.

elude, vb. éluder.

elusive, adj. évasif, insaisissable.

emaciated, adj. émacié.

emanate, vb. émaner.

emancipate, vb. émanciper.

emancipation, n. émancipation f.

emancipator, n. émancipateur m.

emasculate, vb. émasculer.

embalm, vb. embaumer.

embankment, n. levée f.

embargo, n. embargo m.

embark, vb. embarquer, tr.

embarrass, vb. embarrasser.

embarrassing, adj. embarrassant.

embarrassment, n. embarras m.

embassy, n. ambassade f.

embellish, vb. embellir.

embellishment, n. embellissement m.

ember, n. braise f., charbon ardent m.

embezzle, vb. détourner.

embitter, vb. aigrir, envenimer.

emblazon, vb. blasonner.

emblem, n. emblème m.

emblematic, adj. emblématique.

embody, vb. incarner, incorporer.

emboss, vb. graver en relief, travailler en bosse.

embrace, 1. n. étreinte f. **2.** vb. embrasser.

embroider, vb. broder.

embroidery, n. broderie f.

embroil, vb. embrouiller.

embryo, *n.* embryon *m.*

embryology, *n.* embryologie *f.*

embryonic, *adj.* embryonnaire.

emerald, *n.* émeraude *f.*

emerge, *vb.* émerger.

emergency, *n.* circonstance *(f.)* critique; **(e. exit)** sortie *(f.)* de secours.

emergent, *adj.* émergent.

emery, *n.* émeri *m.*

emetic, *n.* émétique *m.*

emigrant, *n.* émigrant *m.*

emigrate, *vb.* émigrer.

emigration, *n.* émigration *f.*

eminence, *n.* éminence *f.*

eminent, *adj.* éminent.

emissary, *n.* émissaire *m.*

emission control, *n.* appareil pour limiter l'émission de vapeurs nuisibles *m.*

emit, *vb.* émettre.

emollient, *adj.* émollient.

emolument, *n.* traitement *m.*

emotion, *n.* émotion *f.*

emotional, *adj.* émotif; (excitable) émotionnable.

emperor, *n.* empereur *m.*

emphasis, *n.* (impressiveness) force *f.*; (stress) accent *m.*

emphasize, *vb.* mettre en relief.

emphatic, *adj.* (manner) énergique.

empire, *n.* empire *m.*

empirical, *adj.* empirique.

employ, *vb.* employer.

employee, *n.* employé *m.*

employer, *n.* patron *m.*

employment, *n.* emploi *m.*

empower, *vb.* autoriser.

empress, *n.* impératrice *f.*

emptiness, *n.* vide *m.*

empty, 1. *adj.* vide. **2.** *vb.* vider.

emulate, *vb.* émuler.

emulsion, *n.* émulsion *f.*

enable, *vb.* mettre à même (de).

enact, *vb.* (law) décréter; (play) jouer.

enactment, *n.* promulgation *f.*, acte législatif *m.*

enamel, *n.* émail *m.*, *pl.* émaux.

enamor, *vb.* amouracher.

encamp, *vb.* camper, faire camper.

encampment, *n.* campement *m.*

encephalitis, *n.* encéphalite *f.*

encephalon, *n.* encéphale *m.*

enchant, *vb.* enchanter.

enchanting, *adj.* ravissant.

enchantment, *n.* enchantement *m.*

encircle, *vb.* entourer.

enclose, *vb.* enclore; (in letter) joindre.

enclosure, *n.* enclos *m.*; (in letter) pièce *(f.)* jointe.

encompass, *vb.* entourer.

encounter, *vb.* rencontrer.

encourage, *vb.* encourager.

encouragement, *n.* encouragement *m.*

encroach, *vb.* empiéter.

encumber, *vb.* encombrer.

encyclical, *n.* encyclique *f.*

encyclopedia, *n.* encyclopédie *f.*

end, 1. *n.* fin *f.*; (extremity) bout *m.*; (aim) but *m.* **2.** *vb.* finir.

endanger, *vb.* mettre en danger.

endear, *vb.* rendre cher.

endearment, *n.* charme *m.*, attrait *m.*

endeavor, 1. *n.* effort *m.* **2.** *vb.* s'efforcer.

endemic, *adj.* endémique.

ending, *n.* terminaison *f.*

endless, *adj.* sans fin.

endocrine gland, *n.* glande endocrine *f.*

endorse, *vb.* (sign) endosser; (support) appuyer.

endorsement, *n.* (signing) endossement *m.*; (approval) approbation *f.*

endow, *vb.* doter.

endowment, *n.* dotation *f.*, fondation *f.*

endurance, *n.* résistance *f.*

endure, *vb.* supporter.

enduring, *adj.* durable.

enema, *n.* lavement *m.*

enemy, *adj. and n.* ennemi *m.*

energetic, *adj.* énergique.

energy, *n.* énergie *f.*

enervate, *vb.* énerver, affaiblir.

enervation, *n.* affaiblissement *m.*

enfold, *vb.* envelopper.

enforce, *vb.* imposer; (law) exécuter.

enfranchise, *vb.* affranchir, accorder le droit de vote.

engage, *vb.* engager, *tr.*; **(become e.d,** to be married) se fiancer.

engaged, *adj.* occupé, pris; fiancé.

engagement, *n.* engagement *m.;* (marriage) fiançailles *f.pl.*

engaging, *adj.* attrayant, séduisant.

engender, *vb.* engendrer.

engine, *n.* machine *f.;* (train) locomotive *f.;* (motor) moteur *m.*

engineer, *n.* (profession) ingénieur *m.;* (engine operator) mécanicien *m.;* (mil.) soldat (*m.*) du génie.

engineering, *n.* génie *m.*

England, *n.* Angleterre *f.*

English, *adj. and n.* anglais *m.*

Englishman, *n.* Anglais *m.*

Englishwoman, *n.* Anglaise *f.*

engrave, *vb.* graver.

engraver, *n.* graveur *m.*

engraving, *n.* gravure *f.*

engross, *vb.* (absorb) absorber.

engrossing, *adj.* absorbant.

enhance, *vb.* rehausser.

enigma, *n.* énigme *f.*

enigmatic, *adj.* énigmatique.

enjoin, *vb.* enjoindre.

enjoy, *vb.* jouir de; (e. oneself) s'amuser.

enjoyable, *adj.* agréable.

enjoyment, *n.* jouissance *f.*

enlace, *vb.* enlacer.

enlarge, *vb.* agrandir, *tr.*

enlargement, *n.* agrandissement *m.*

enlarger, *n.* agrandisseur *m.,* amplificateur *m.*

enlighten, *vb.* éclairer.

enlightenment, *n.* éclaircissement *m.*

enlist, *vb.* enrôler, *tr.*

enlisted man, *n.* gradé *m.*

enlistment, *n.* enrôlement *m.*

enliven, *vb.* animer.

enmesh, *vb.* engrener, embarrasser.

enmity, *n.* inimitié *f.*

ennoble, *vb.* anoblir.

ennui, *n.* ennui *m.*

enormity, *n.* énormité *f.*

enormous, *adj.* énorme.

enough, *adj. and adv.* assez (de).

enrage, *vb.* faire enrager.

enrapture, *vb.* ravir, enchanter.

enrich, *vb.* enrichir.

enroll, *vb.* enrôler.

enrollment, *n.* enrôlement *m.*

ensemble, *n.* ensemble *m.*

enshrine, *vb.* enchâsser.

ensign, *n.* (navy) enseigne *m.*

enslave, *vb.* asservir.

ensnare, *vb.* prendre au piège.

ensue, *vb.* s'ensuivre.

entail, *vb.* (involve) entraîner; (law) substituer.

entangle, *vb.* empêtrer.

enter, *vb.* entrer (dans).

enterprise, *n.* entreprise *f.*

enterprising, *adj.* entreprenant.

entertain, *vb.* (amuse) amuser; (receive) recevoir.

entertainment, *n.* amusement *m.*

enthrall, *vb.* captiver, ensorceler.

enthusiasm, *n.* enthousiasme *m.*

enthusiast, *n.* enthousiaste *m.f.*

enthusiastic, *adj.* enthousiaste.

entice, *vb.* attirer.

entire, *adj.* entier.

entirely, *adv.* entièrement.

entirety, *n.* totalité *f.*

entitle, *vb.* donner droit à; (book) intituler.

entomb, *vb.* enterrer, ensevelir.

entrails, *n.* entrailles *f.pl.*

entrain, *vb.* embarquer en chemin de fer.

entrance, *n.* entrée *f.*

entrant, *n.* débutant *m.,* inscrit *m.*

entrap, *vb.* attraper, prendre au piège.

entreat, *vb.* supplier.

entreaty, *n.* instance *f.*

entrench, *vb.* retrancher.

entrust to, *vb.* confier à.

entry, *n.* (entrance) entrée *f.;* (recording) inscription *f.*

enumerate, *vb.* énumérer.

enumeration, *n.* énumération *f.*

enunciate, *vb.* énoncer.

enunciation, *n.* énonciation *f.*

envelop, *vb.* envelopper.

envelope, *n.* enveloppe *f.*

enviable, *adj.* enviable.

envious, *adj.* envieux.

environment, *n.* milieu *m.*

environmentalist, *n.* écologiste *m.;* environmentaliste *m.*

environmental protection, *n.* protection de l'environment *f.*

environs, *n.* environs *m.pl.,* alentours *m.pl.*

envisage, *vb.* envisager.

envoy, *n.* envoyé *m.*

envy, 1. n. envie f. 2. vb. envier.

eon, n. éon m.

ephemeral, adj. éphémère.

epic, 1. n. épopée f. 2. adj. épique.

epicure, n. gourmet m.

epidemic, n. épidémie f.

epidermis, n. épiderme m.

epigram, n. épigramme f.

epilepsy, n. épilepsie f.

epilogue, n. épilogue m.

episode, n. épisode m.

epistle, n. épître f.

epitaph, n. épitaphe f.

epithet, n. épithète f.

epitome, n. épitomé m., résumé m.

epitomize, vb. résumer, abréger.

epoch, n. époque f.

equable, adj. uniforme, régulier.

equal, adj. égal; (be. e. to) être à la hauteur de.

equality, n. égalité f.

equalize, vb. égaliser, tr.

equanimity, n. tranquillité d'esprit f., équanimité f., sérénité f.

equate, vb. égaler, mettre en équation.

equation, n. équation f.

equator, n. équateur m.

equatorial, adj. équatorial.

equestrian, adj. équestre.

equidistant, adj. équidistant.

equilateral, adj. équilatéral.

equilibrium, n. équilibre m.

equinox, n. équinoxe f.

equip, vb. équiper.

equipment, n. équipement m.

equitable, adj. équitable, juste.

equity, n. équité f.

equivalent, adj. and n. équivalent m.

equivocal, adj. équivoque.

equivocate, vb. équivoquer.

era, n. ère f.

eradicate, vb. déraciner.

eradicator, n. effaceur m., grattoir m.

erase, vb. effacer.

eraser, n. gomme f.

erasure, n. rature f.

erect, adj. droit.

erection, n. érection f., construction f.

erectness, n. attitude droite f.

ermine, n. hermine f.

erode, vb. éroder, ronger.

erosion, n. érosion f.

erosive, adj. érosif.

erotic, adj. érotique.

err, vb. errer.

errand, n. course f.

errant, adj. errant.

erratic, adj. irrégulier, excentrique.

erring, adj. égaré, dévoyé.

erroneous, adj. erroné.

error, n. erreur f.

erudite, adj. érudit.

erudition, n. érudition f.

erupt, vb. entrer en éruption.

eruption, n. éruption f.

escalate, vb. escalader.

escalator, n. escalier roulant m.

escapade, n. escapade f.

escape, 1. n. fuite f. 2. vb. échapper.

escapism, n. évasion f., échappement m.

eschew, vb. éviter, s'abstenir.

escort, n. (mil.) escorte f.; (to a lady) cavalier m.

esculent, adj. comestible.

escutcheon, n. écusson m.

esoteric, adj. ésotérique.

especial, adj. spécial.

espionage, n. espionnage m.

espousal, n. adoption f., adhésion (à) f.

espouse, vb. épouser, embrasser (une cause).

Eskimo, 1. n. Esquimau m., Esquimaude f. 2. adj. esquimau m., esquimaude f.

esquire, n. écuyer m.; titre honorifique d'un "gentleman" m.

essay, 1. n. essai m.; (school) composition f. 2. vb. essayer.

essayist, n. essayiste m.

essence, n. essence f.

essential, adj. essentiel.

essentially, adv. essentiellement.

establish, vb. établir.

establishment, n. établissement m.

estate, n. (condition, class) état m.; (wealth) biens m.pl.; (land) propriété f.

esteem, 1. n. estime f. 2. vb. estimer.

estimable, adj. estimable.

estimate, 1. n. estimation f.; (comm.) devis m. 2. vb. estimer.

estimation, n. (opinion) jugement m.

estrange, vb. aliéner.

estuary, n. estuaire m.

etching, n. gravure (f.) à l'eau-forte.

eternal, adj. éternel.

eternity, n. éternité f.

ether, n. éther m.

ethereal, adj. éthéré.

ethical, adj. moral.

ethics, n. éthique f.

Ethiopia, n. Éthiopie f.

ethnic, adj. ethnique.

etiquette, n. étiquette f.

Etruscan, 1. n. Étrusque m.f. 2. adj. étrusque.

etymology, n. étymologie f.

eucalyptus, n. eucalyptus m.

eugenic, adj. eugénésique.

eugenics, n. eugénisme m., eugénique f.

eulogize, vb. faire l'éloge de.

eulogy, n. panégyrique m.

eunuch, n. eunuque m.

euphonious, adj. mélodieux, euphonique.

Europe, n. Europe f.

European, 1. n. Européen m. 2. adj. européen.

euthanasia, n. euthanasie f.

evacuate, vb. évacuer.

evacuee, n. évacué m.

evade, vb. éluder.

evaluate, vb. évaluer.

evaluation, n. évaluation f.

evanescent, adj. évanescent, éphémère.

evangelist, n. évangéliste m.

evaporate, vb. évaporer, tr.

evaporation, n. évaporation f.

evasion, n. subterfuge f.

evasive, adj. évasif.

eve, n. veille f.

even, 1. adj. égal; (number) pair. 2. adv. même.

evening, n. soir m.; (span of e.) soirée f.

evenness, n. égalité f.

event, n. événement m.; (eventuality) cas m.

eventful, adj. plein d'événements.

eventual, adj. (ultimate) définitif; (contingent) éventuel.

ever, adv. (at all times) toujours; (at any time) jamais.

everglade, n. région marécageuse (de la Floride) f.

evergreen, adj. à feuilles persistantes, toujours vert.

everlasting, adj. éternel.

every, adj. (each) chaque; (all) tous les m.; toutes les f.

everybody, everyone, pron. tout le monde; chacun.

everyday, adj. de tous les jours.

everything, pron. tout.

everywhere, adv. partout.

evict, vb. évincer.

eviction, n. éviction f.; expulsion f.

evidence, n. évidence f.; (proof) preuve f.

evident, adj. évident.

evidently, adv. évidemment.

evil, n. mal m.

evil, adj. mauvais.

evince, vb. démontrer.

eviscerate, vb. éviscérer.

evoke, vb. évoquer.

evolution, n. évolution f.

evolutionist, n. évolutionniste m.

evolve, vb. évoluer, développer.

ewe, n. agnelle f.

exact, adj. exact.

exacting, adj. (person) exigeant.

exactly, adv. exactement.

exaggerate, vb. exagérer.

exaggerated, adj. exagéré.

exaggeration, n. exagération f.

exalt, vb. exalter; (raise) élever.

exaltation, n. exaltation f.

examination, n. examen m.

examine, vb. examiner.

example, n. exemple m.

exasperate, vb. exaspérer.

exasperation, n. exaspération f.

excavate, vb. creuser.

exceed, vb. excéder.

exceedingly, adv. extrêmement.

excel, vb. exceller, intr.

excellence, excellency, n. excellence f.

excellent, adj. excellent.

excelsior, n. copeaux d'emballage m.pl.

except, 1. vb. excepter. 2. prep. excepté, sauf.

exception, n. exception f.

exceptional, adj. exceptionnel.

excerpt, n. extrait m.

excess, n. excès m.; (surplus) excédent m.

excessive, *adj.* excessif.
exchange, 1. *n.* échange *m.;* (money) change *m.* **2.** *vb.* échanger.
exchangeable, *adj.* échangeable.
excise, *n.* contribution indirecte *f.,* régie *f.*
excitable, *adj.* émotionnable, excitable.
excite, *vb.* exciter.
excitement, *n.* agitation *f.*
exclaim, *vb.* s'écrier.
exclamation, *n.* exclamation *f.*
exclamation point or **mark,** *n.* point d'exclamation *m.*
exclude, *vb.* exclure.
exclusion, *n.* exclusion *f.*
exclusive, *adj.* exclusif; (stylish) sélect.
excommunicate, *vb.* excommunier.
excommunication, *n.* excommunication *f.*
excoriate, *vb.* excorier, écorcher.
excrement, *n.* excrément *m.*
excruciating, *adj.* atroce, affreux.
exculpate, *vb.* disculper, exonérer.
excursion, *n.* excursion *f.*
excusable, *adj.* excusable.
excuse, 1. *n.* excuse *f.* **2.** *vb.* excuser.
execrable, *adj.* exécrable, abominable.
execute, *vb.* exécuter.
execution, *n.* exécution *f.*
executioner, *n.* bourreau *m.*
executive, *adj. and n.* exécutif *m.*
executive mansion, *n.* maison présidentielle *f.*
executor, *n.* exécuteur *m.*
exemplary, *adj.* exemplaire.
exemplify, *vb.* expliquer par des exemples.
exempt, 1. *adj.* exempt. **2.** *vb.* exempter.
exercise, 1. *n.* exercice *m.* **2.** *vb.* exercer.
exert, *vb.* employer; (e. oneself) s'efforcer de.
exertion, *n.* effort *m.*
exhale, *vb.* exhaler.
exhaust, 1. *n.* (machines) échappement *m.* **2.** *vb.* épuiser.
exhaustion, *n.* épuisement *m.*
exhaustive, *adj.* complet, approfondi.

exhibit, *vb.* (pictures, etc.) exposer; (show) montrer.
exhibition, *n.* exposition *f.*
exhibitionism, *n.* exhibitionnisme *m.*
exhilarate, *vb.* égayer.
exhort, *vb.* exhorter.
exhortation, *n.* exhortation *f.*
exhume, *vb.* exhumer.
exigency, *n.* exigence *f.*
exile, 1. *n.* exil *m.;* (person) exilé *m.* **2.** *vb.* exiler.
exist, *vb.* exister.
existence, *n.* existence *f.*
existent, *adj.* existant.
exit, *n.* sortie *f.*
exodus, *n.* exode *m.*
exonerate, *vb.* exonérer.
exorbitant, *adj.* exorbitant.
exorcise, *vb.* exorciser.
exotic, *adj.* exotique.
expand, *vb.* étendre, *tr.;* (dilate) dilater, *tr.*
expanse, *n.* étendue *f.*
expansion, *n.* expansion *f.*
expansive, *adj.* expansif.
expatiate, *vb.* discourir.
expatriate, *vb.* expatrier.
expect, *vb.* s'attendre à; (await) attendre.
expectancy, *n.* attente *f.*
expectation, *n.* attente *f.;* (hope) espérance *f.*
expectorate, *vb.* expectorer.
expediency, *n.* convenance *f.*
expedient, *n.* expédient *m.*
expedite, *vb.* activer, accélérer.
expedition, *n.* expédition *f.*
expel, *vb.* expulser.
expend, *vb.* (money) dépenser; (use up) épuiser.
expenditure, *n.* dépense *f.*
expense, *n.* dépense *f.;* (expenses) frais *m.pl.*
expensive, *adj.* coûteux, cher.
expensively, *adv.* coûteusement.
experience, 1. *n.* expérience *f.* **2.** *vb.* éprouver.
experienced, *adj.* expérimenté.
experiment, *n.* expérience *f.*
experimental, *adj.* expérimental.
expert, *adj. and n.* expert *m.*
expiate, *vb.* expier.
expiration, *n.* expiration *f.*
expire, *vb.* expirer.
explain, *vb.* expliquer.
explanation, *n.* explication *f.*

explanatory, adj. explicatif.
expletive, n. explétif m.
explicit, adj. explicite.
explode, vb. (burst) éclater, intr.
exploit, 1. n. exploit m. **2.** vb. exploiter.
exploitation, n. exploitation f.
exploration, n. exploration f.
exploratory, adj. exploratif.
explore, vb. explorer.
explorer, n. explorateur m.
explosion, n. explosion f.
explosive, adj. and n. explosif m.
exponent, n. interprète m.
export, 1. n. (exportation) exportation f.; (exported object) article (m.) d'exportation. **2.** vb. exporter.
exportation, n. exportation f.
expose, vb. exposer.
exposé, n. exposé m.
exposition, n. exposition f.
expository, adj. explicatif.
expostulate, vb. faire des remontrances à.
exposure, n. exposition f.
expound, vb. exposer.
express, 1. adj. exprès. **2.** vb. exprimer.
expressage, n. frais d'expédition m.pl.
expression, n. expression f.
expressive, adj. expressif.
expressly, adv. expressément.
expressman, n. agent de messageries m.
expropriate, vb. exproprier.
expulsion, n. expulsion f.
expunge, vb. effacer, rayer.
expurgate, vb. expurger, épurer.
exquisite, adj. exquis.
extant, adj. existant.
extemporaneous, adj. improvisé, impromptu.
extend, vb. étendre; (prolong) prolonger.
extension, n. extension f.
extensive, adj. étendu.
extensively, adv. largement, considérablement.
extent, n. étendue f.; (to some e.) jusqu'à un certain point.
extenuate, vb. (tire out) exténuer; (diminish) atténuer.
exterior, adj. and n. extérieur m.
exterminate, vb. exterminer.

extermination, n. extermination f.
external, adj. externe.
extinct, adj. éteint.
extinction, n. extinction f.
extinguish, vb. éteindre.
extol, vb. vanter.
extort, vb. extorquer.
extortion, n. extorsion f.
extortioner, n. extorqueur m.
extra, adj. (additional) supplémentaire; (spare) de réserve.
extra-, prefix. (outside of) en dehors de; (intensive) extra-.
extract, 1. n. extrait m. **2.** vb. extraire.
extraction, n. extraction f.
extradite, vb. extrader.
extraneous, adj. étranger à.
extraordinary, adj. extraordinaire.
extravagance, n. extravagance f.; (money) prodigalité f.
extravagant, adj. extravagant; (money) prodigue.
extravaganza, m. œuvre fantaisiste f.
extreme, adj. and n. extrême m.
extremity, n. extrémité f.
extricate, vb. dégager, tirer.
extrovert, n. extroverti m.
exuberant, adj. exubérant.
exude, vb. exsuder.
exult, vb. exulter.
exultant, adj. exultant, joyeux.
eye, n. œil m., pl. yeux.
eyeball, n. globe (m.) de l'œil.
eyebrow, n. sourcil m.
eyeglass, n. lorgnon m.
eyeglasses, n. lunettes f.pl.
eyelash, n. cil m.
eyelet, n. œillet m.
eyelid, n. paupière f.
eye shadow, n. fard (m.) à paupières.
eyesight, n. vue f.
eyewitness, n. témoin oculaire m.

F

fable, n. fable f.
fabric, n. (structure) édifice m.; (cloth) tissu m.
fabricate, vb. fabriquer.
fabrication, n. fabrication f.
fabulous, adj. fabuleux.

façade, *n.* façade *f.*

face, 1. *n.* figure *f.* **2.** *vb.* faire face à.

facet, *n.* facette *f.*

facetious, *adj.* facétieux.

face value, *n.* valeur nominale *f.*

facial, *adj.* facial.

facile, *adj.* facile.

facilitate, *vb.* faciliter.

facility, *n.* facilité *f.*

facing, *n.* revêtement *m.,* revers *m.*

facsimile, *n.* fac-similé *m.*

fact, *n.* fait *m.;* **(as a matter of f.)** en effet.

faction, *n.* faction *f.*

factor, *n.* facteur *m.*

factory, *n.* fabrique *f.*

factual, *adj.* effectif, positif.

faculty, *n.* faculté *f.*

fad, *n.* marotte *f.*

fade, *vb. intr.* se faner; (color) se décolorer; **(f. away)** s'évanouir.

fagged, *adj.* épuisé, fatigué.

fail, *vb.* manquer; (not succeed) échouer.

failing, 1. *n.* manquement *m.* **2.** *adj.* faiblissant. **3.** *prep.* au défaut de.

faille, *n.* faille *f.*

failure, *n.* (lack) défaut *m.;* (want of success) insuccès *m.*

faint, 1. *adj.* faible. **2.** *vb.* s'évanouir.

faintly, *adv.* faiblement, timidement, légèrement.

fair, 1. *n.* foire *f.* **2.** *adj.* (beautiful) beau *m.,* belle *f.;* (blond) blond; (honest) juste; (pretty good) passable.

fairly, *adv.* honnêtement, impartialement.

fairness, *n.* (honesty) honnêteté *f.*

fairy, *n.* fée *f.*

fairyland, *n.* pays des fées *m.*

faith, *n.* foi *f.*

faithful, *adj.* fidèle.

faithless, *adj.* infidèle.

fake, *vb.* truquer.

faker, *n.* truqueur *m.*

falcon, *n.* faucon *m.*

falconry, *n.* fauconnerie *f.*

fall, 1. *n.* chute *f.;* (autumn) automne *m.* **2.** *vb.* tomber.

fallacious, *adj.* fallacieux.

fallacy, *n.* fausseté *f.*

fallen, *adj.* tombé, déchu.

fallible, *adj.* faillible.

fallout, *n.* pluie radioactive *f.*

fallow, *adj.* en jachère.

false, *adj.* faux *m.,* fausse *f.*

falsehood, *n.* mensonge *m.*

falseness, *n.* fausseté *f.*

falsetto, *n.* and *adj.* fausset *m.*

falsification, *n.* falsification *f.*

falsify, *vb.* falsifier.

falter, *vb.* hésiter.

fame, *n.* renommée *f.*

famed, *adj.* célèbre, renommé, fameux.

familiar, *adj.* familier.

familiarity, *n.* familiarité *f.*

familiarize, *vb.* familiariser.

family, *n.* famille *f.*

famine, *n.* (food) disette *f.;* (general) famine *f.*

famished, *adj.* affamé.

famous, *adj.* célèbre.

fan, *n.* éventail *m.;* (mechanical) ventilateur *m.*

fanatic, *adj.* and *n.* fanatique *m.*

fanatical, *adj.* fanatique.

fanaticism, *n.* fanatisme *m.*

fanciful, *adj.* fantastique, fantaisiste.

fancy, 1. *n.* fantaisie *f.* **2.** *vb.* se figurer.

fanfare, *n.* fanfare *f.*

fang, *n.* croc (of a dog) *m.,* crochet (of a snake) *m.*

fantastic, *adj.* fantastique.

fantasy, *n.* fantaisie *f.*

far, *adv.* loin; **(so f.)** jusqu'ici; **(as f. as)** autant que; (much) beaucoup; **(by f.)** de beaucoup.

faraway, *adj.* lointain.

farce, *n.* farce *f.*

farcical, *adj.* bouffon.

fare, 1. *n.* (price) prix *m.;* (food) chère *f.* **2.** *vb.* aller.

farewell, *interj.* and *n.* adieu *m.*

far-fetched, *adj.* forcé.

far-flung, *adj.* très étendu, vaste.

farina, *n.* farine *f.*

farm, *n.* ferme *f.*

farmer, *n.* fermier *m.*

farmhouse, *n.* maison (*f.*) de ferme.

farming, *n.* culture *f.*

farmyard, *n.* cour de ferme *f.*

far-reaching, *adj.* de grande envergure.

far-sighted, *adj.* clairvoyant.

farther, 1. adj. plus éloigné. **2.** adv. plus loin.

farthest, adj. and adv. le plus lointain.

fascinate, vb. fasciner.

fascination, n. fascination f.

fascism, n. fascisme m.

fashion, n. mode f.; (manner) manière f.

fashionable, adj. à la mode.

fast, 1. n. jeûne m. **2.** adj. (speedy) rapide; (firm) en avance; (of clock) en avance. **3.** vb. jeûner. **4.** adv. (quickly) vite; (firmly) ferme.

fasten, vb. attacher, tr.

fastener, n. fermeture f.

fastening, n. attache f.

fastidious, adj. difficile.

fat, adj. gras m., grasse f.

fatal, adj. fatal; (deadly) mortel.

fatality, n. fatalité f.

fatally, adv. fatalement, mortellement.

fate, n. destin m.

fateful, adj. fatal.

father, n. père m.

fatherhood, n. paternité f.

father-in-law, n. beau-père m.

fatherland, n. patrie f.

fatherless, adj. sans père.

fatherly, adj. paternel.

fathom, 1. n. (naut.) brasse f. **2.** vb. sonder.

fatigue, n. fatigue f.

fatten, vb. engraisser.

fatty, adj. graisseux.

fatuous, adj. sot.

faucet, n. robinet m.

fault, n. (mistake) faute f.; (defect) défaut m.

faultfinding, n. disposition à critiquer f.

faultless, adj. sans défaut.

faultlessly, adv. d'une manière impeccable.

faulty, adj. défectueux.

favor, 1. n. faveur f. **2.** vb. favoriser.

favorable, adj. favorable.

favored, adj. favorisé.

favorite, adj. and n. favori m., favorite f.

favoritism, n. favoritisme m.

fawn, n. faon m.

faze, vb. bouleverser.

fear, 1. n. crainte f. **2.** vb. craindre.

fearful, adj. (person) craintif; (thing) effrayant.

fearless, adj. intrépide.

fearlessness, n. intrépidité f.

feasible, adj. faisable.

feast, n. fête f.; (banquet) festin m.

feat, n. exploit m.

feather, n. plume f.

feathered, adj. emplumé.

feathery, adj. plumeux.

feature, n. trait m.

February, n. février m.

fecund, adj. fécond.

federal, adj. fédéral.

federation, n. fédération f.

fedora, n. chapeau mou m.

fee, n. (for professional services) honoraires m.pl.; (school) frais m.pl.

feeble, adj. faible.

feeble-minded, adj. d'esprit faible.

feebleness, n. faiblesse f.

feed, 1. n. nourriture f. **2.** vb. nourrir, tr.

feedback, n. action de contrôle en retour f.

feel, vb. sentir, tr.; (touch) tâter.

feeling, n. sentiment m.

feign, vb. feindre.

felicitate, vb. féliciter.

felicitous, adj. heureux.

felicity, n. félicité f.

feline, adj. félin.

fell, adj. funeste.

fellow, n. (general) homme m., garçon m.; (companion) compagnon m.

fellowship, n. camaraderie f.; (university) bourse (f.) universitaire.

felon, n. criminel m.

felony, n. crime m.

felt, n. feutre m.

female, 1. n. (person) femme f.; (animals, plants) femelle f. **2.** adj. féminin, femelle.

feminine, adj. féminin.

femininity, n. féminéité f.

fence, 1. n. clôture f. **2.** vb. (enclose) enclore; (sword, foil) faire de l'escrime.

fencer, n. escrimeur m.

fencing, n. escrime f.

fender, *n.* garde-boue *m.;* (fireplace) garde-feu *m.*

ferment, *vb.* fermenter.

fermentation, *n.* fermentation *f.*

fern, *n.* fougère *f.*

ferocious, *adj.* féroce.

ferociously, *adv.* d'une manière féroce.

ferocity, *n.* férocité *f.*

ferry, *n.* passage *(m.)* en bac; (f. boat) bac *m.*

fertile, *adj.* fertile.

fertility, *n.* fertilité *f.*

fertilization, *n.* fertilisation *f.*

fertilize, *vb.* fertiliser.

fervency, *n.* ardeur *f.*

fervent, *adj.* fervent.

fervently, *adv.* ardemment.

fervid, *adj.* fervent.

fervor, *n.* ferveur *f.*

fester, *vb.* suppurer.

festival, *n.* fête *f.*

festive, *adj.* de fête.

festivity, *n.* réjouissance *f.*

festoon, 1. *n.* feston *m.* **2.** *vb.* festonner.

fetal, *adj.* foetal.

fetch, *vb.* (go and get) aller chercher; (bring) apporter.

fetching, *adj.* attrayant.

fete, *vb.* fêter.

fetid, *adj.* fétide.

fetish, *n.* fétiche *m.*

fetlock, *n.* fanon *m.*

fetter, 1. *n.* lien *m.,* chaîne *f.* **2.** *vb.* enchaîner.

fetus, *n.* fœtus *m.*

feud, *n.* inimitié *f.;* (historical) fief *m.*

feudal, *adj.* féodal.

feudalism, *n.* régime féodal *m.*

fever, *n.* fièvre *f.*

feverish, *adj.* fiévreux.

feverishly, *adv.* fébrilement, fiévreusement.

few, 1. *adj.* peu de; (a f.) quelques. **2.** *pron.* peu; (a f.) quelques-uns.

fiancé, *n.* fiancé *m.*

fiasco, *n.* fiasco *m.*

fiat, *n.* décret *m.*

fib, *n.* petit mensonge *m.*

fiber, *n.* fibre *f.*

fiberboard, *n.* fibre de bois *m.*

fibrous, *adj.* fibreux.

fickle, *adj.* volage.

fickleness, *n.* inconstance *f.*

fiction, *n.* fiction *f.;* (literature) romans *m.pl.*

fictional, *adj.* de romans.

fictitious, *adj.* fictif, imaginaire.

fictitiously, *adv.* d'une manière factice.

fiddle, 1. *n.* violon *m.* **2.** *vb.* jouer du violon.

fiddlesticks, *interj.* quelle blague!

fidelity, *n.* fidélité *f.*

fidget, *vb.* se remuer.

field, *n.* champ *m.*

fiend, *n.* démon *m.*

fiendish, *adj.* diabolique, infernal.

fierce, *adj.* féroce.

fiery, *adj.* ardent.

fiesta, *n.* fête *f.*

fife, *n.* fifre *m.*

fifteen, *adj. and n.* quinze *m.*

fifteenth, *adj. and n.* quinzième *m.*

fifth, *adj. and n.* cinquième *m.*

fifty, *adj. and n.* cinquante *m.*

fight, 1. *n.* combat *m.;* (struggle) lutte *f.;* (quarrel) dispute *f.* **2.** *vb.* combattre; se disputer.

fighter, *n.* combattant *m.*

figment, *n.* invention *f.*

figurative, *adj.* figuré.

figuratively, *adv.* au figuré.

figure, 1. *n.* figure *f.;* (of body) tournure *f.;* (math.) chiffre *m.* **2.** *vb.* figurer; calculer.

figured, *adj.* à dessin.

figurehead, *n.* homme de paille *m.*

figure of speech, *n.* façon de parler *f.*

figurine, *n.* figurine *f.*

filigree, *n.* filigrane *f.*

filings, *n.* limaille *f.*

fill, *vb.* remplir, *tr.*

fillet, 1. *n.* (band) bandeau *m.;* (meat, fish) filet *m.*

filling, *n.* remplissage *m.*

filling station, *n.* poste d'essence *m.*

filament, *n.* filament *m.*

filch, *vb.* escamoter.

file, 1. *n.* (tool) lime *f.;* (row) file *f.;* (papers) liasse *f.;* (for papers, etc.) classeur *m.;* (f.s) archives *f.pl.* **2.** *vb.* (tool) limer; (papers) classer; (f. off) défiler.

filial, *adj.* filial.

film, n. (cinema) film m.; (photo) pellicule f.

filmy, adj. couvert d'une pellicule.

filter, 1. n. filtre m. **2.** vb. filtrer.

filth, n. ordure f.

filthy, adj. immonde; obscène.

fin, n. nageoire f.

final, adj. final.

finale, n. finale m.

finalist, n. finaliste m.

finality, n. finalité f.

finally, adv. finalement, enfin.

finance, 1. n. finance f. **2.** vb. financer.

financial, adj. financier.

financier, n. financier m.

find, vb. trouver.

fine, 1. n. amende f. **2.** adj. (beautiful) beau m., belle f.; (pure, thin) fin. **3.** vb. mettre à l'amende.

fine arts, n. beaux arts m.pl.

finery, n. parure f.

finesse, 1. n. finesse f. **2.** vb. finasser.

finger, n. doigt m.

finger bowl, n. rince-bouche m.

fingernail, n. ongle m.

fingerprint, n. empreinte digitale f.

finicky, adj. affété.

finish, vb. finir.

finished, adj. fini, achevé.

finite, adj. fini.

Finland, n. Finlande f.

Finn, n. Finlandais, Finnois m.

Finnish, 1. n. finnois m. **2.** adj. finlandais, finnois.

fir, n. sapin m.

fire, 1. n. feu m.; (burning of house, wood) incendie m. **2.** vb. (weapon) tirer.

fire alarm, n. avertisseur d'incendie m.

firearm, n. arme (f.) à feu.

firedamp, n. grisou m.

fire engine, n. pompe à incendie f.

fire escape, n. échelle de sauvetage f.

fire extinguisher, n. extincteur m.

firefly, n. luciole f.

fireman, n. pompier m.

fireplace, n. cheminée f.

fireproof, adj. à l'épreuve du feu.

fireside, n. coin du feu m.

firewood, n. bois de chauffage m.

fireworks, n. feu (m.) d'artifice.

firm, 1. n. maison (f.) de commerce. **2.** adj. ferme.

firmness, n. fermeté f.

first, 1. adj. premier. **2.** adv. d'abord.

first-aid, n. premiers secours m.pl.

first-class, adj. de premier ordre.

first-hand, adj. de première main.

first-rate, adj. de premier ordre.

fiscal, adj. fiscal.

fish, 1. n. poisson m. **2.** vb. pêcher.

fisherman, n. pêcheur m.

fishery, n. pêcherie f.

fishhook, n. hameçon m.

fishing, n. pêche f.

fishmonger, n. marchand de poisson m.

fishwife, n. marchande de poisson f.

fishy, adj. de poisson; (slang) louche.

fission, n. fission f.

fissure, n. fente f.

fist, n. poing m.

fistic, adj. au poing.

fit, 1. n. accès m. **2.** adj. (suitable) convenable; (capable) capable; (**f. for**) propre à. **3.** vb. (befit) convenir à; (clothes) aller à; (adjust) ajuster, tr.

fitful, adj. agité, irrégulier.

fitness, n. à-propos m.; (person) aptitude f.

fitting, 1. n. ajustage m. **2.** adj. convenable.

five, adj. and n. cinq m.

fix, 1. n. embarras m. **2.** vb. fixer; (repair) réparer.

fixation, n. fixation f.

fixed, adj. fixe.

fixture, n. object (m.) d'attache.

flabby, adj. flasque.

flaccid, adj. flasque.

flag, n. drapeau m.; (stone) dalle f.

flagellate, vb. flageller.

flagging, 1. n. relâchement m. **2.** adj. qui s'affaiblit.

flagon, n. flacon m.

flagpole, n. mât de drapeau m.

flagrant, adj. flagrant.

flagrantly, adv. d'une manière flagrante.

flagship, *n.* vaisseau amiral *m.*

flagstone, *n.* dalle *f.*

flail, 1. *n.* fléau *f.* **2.** *vb.* battre au fléau.

flair, *n.* flair *m.*

flake, *n.* (snow) flocon *m.*

flamboyant, *adj.* flamboyant.

flame, 1. *n.* flamme *f.* **2.** *vb.* flamboyer.

flame thrower, *n.* lanceur de flammes *m.*

flaming, *adj.* flamboyant.

flamingo, *n.* flamant *m.*

flank, *n.* flanc *m.*

flannel, *n.* flanelle *f.*

flap, 1. *n.* (wing) coup *m.;* (pocket) patte *f.;* (table) battant *m.* **2.** *vb.* battre.

flare, *vb.* flamboyer.

flare-up, 1. *n.* emportement *m.* **2.** *vb.* s'emporter.

flash, *n.* éclair *m.*

flashcube, *n.* flash-cube *m.*

flashiness, *n.* faux brillant *m.,* éclat superficiel *m.*

flashlight, *n.* (lighthouse) feu *(m.)* à éclats; (pocket) lampe *(f.)* de poche.

flashy, *adj.* voyant.

flask, *n.* gourde *f.*

flat, 1. *n.* appartement *m.;* (tire) pneu *(m.)* crevé. **2.** *adj.* plat *m.,* platte *f.*

flatcar, *n.* wagon en plateforme *m.*

flatness, *n.* (evenness) égalité *f.;* (dullness) platitude *f.*

flatten, *vb.* aplatir.

flatter, *vb.* flatter.

flatterer, *n.* flatteur *m.*

flattery, *n.* flatterie *f.*

flattop, *n.* porte-avion *m.*

flaunt, *vb.* parader, étaler.

flavor, *n.* (taste) saveur *f.;* (fragrance) arome *m.*

flavoring, *n.* assaisonnement *m.*

flavorless, *adj.* fade.

flaw, *n.* défaut *m.*

flawless, *adj.* sans défaut, parfait.

flawlessly, *adv.* d'une manière impeccable.

flax, *n.* lin *m.*

flay, *vb.* écorcher.

flea, *n.* puce *f.*

fleck, 1. *n.* tache *f.* **2.** *vb.* tacheter.

fledgling, *n.* oisillon *m.*

flee, *vb.* s'enfuir.

fleece, *n.* toison *f.*

fleecy, *adj.* laineux, moutonneux.

fleet, *n.* flotte *f.*

fleeting, *adj.* fugitif.

flesh, *n.* chair *f.*

fleshy, *adj.* charnu.

flex, *vb.* fléchir.

flexibility, *n.* flexibilité *f.*

flexible, *adj.* flexible.

flicker, 1. *n.* lueur *(f.)* vacillante. **2.** *vb.* trembloter.

flier, *n.* aviateur *m.*

flight, *n.* (flying) vol *m.;* (fleeing) fuite *f.*

flight attendant, *n.* hôtesse de l'air *f.*

flighty, *adj.* étourdi.

flimsy, *adj.* sans solidité.

flinch, *vb.* reculer, broncher.

fling, *vb.* jeter.

flint, *n.* (lighter) pierre *(f.)* à briquet; (mineral) silex *m.*

flippant, *adj.* léger.

flippantly, *adv.* légèrement.

flirt, *vb.* flirter.

flirtation, *n.* flirt *m.*

float, *vb.* flotter.

flock, 1. *n.* troupeau *m.* **2.** *vb.* accourir.

flog, *vb.* fouetter.

flood, *n.* inondation *f.*

floodgate, *n.* écluse *f.*

floodlight, *n.* lumière à grand flots *f.*

floor, *n.* plancher *m.;* **(take the f.)** prendre la parole; (story) étage *m.*

flooring, *n.* plancher *m.,* parquet *m.*

floorwalker, *n.* inspecteur du magasin *m.*

flop, 1. *vb.* faire plouf, s'effondrer. **2.** *n.* fiasco *m.*

floral, *adj.* floral.

florid, *adj.* fleuri, vermeil.

florist, *n.* fleuriste *m.f.*

flounce, 1. *n.* volant *m.* **2.** *vb.* se démener.

flounder, *n.* flet *m.*

flour, *n.* farine *f.*

flourish, *vb.* prospérer.

flow, *vb.* couler.

flower, 1. *n.* fleur *f.* **2.** *vb.* fleurir.

flowerpot, *n.* pot à fleurs *m.*

flowery, *adj.* fleuri.

fluctuate, *vb.* osciller.

fluctuation, *n.* fluctuation *f.*

flue, *n.* tuyau de cheminée *m.*
fluency, *n.* facilité *f.*
fluent, *adj.* (be a f. speaker of . . .) parler . . . couramment.
fluid, *adj and n.* fluide *m.*
fluidity, *n.* fluidité *f.*
flunk, *vb.* coller, recaler.
flunkey, *n.* laquais *m.*
fluorescent lamp, *n.* lampe fluorescente *f.*
fluoroscope, *n.* fluoroscope *m.*
flurry, **1.** *n.* agitation *f.* **2.** *vb.* agiter.
flush, *n.* (redness) rougeur *f.;* (plumbing) chasse *f.*
flute, *n.* flûte *f.*
flutter, **1.** *n.* (bird) voltigement *m.;* (agitation) agitation *f.* **2.** *vb.* s'agiter; (heart) palpiter.
flux, *n.* flux *m.*
fly, **1.** *n.* mouche *f.* **2.** *vb.* voler.
foam, *n.* écume *f.*
focal, *adj.* focal.
focus, **1.** *n.* foyer *m.;* (in f.) au point. **2.** *vb.* (photo) mettre au point.
fodder, *n.* fourrage *m.*
foe, *n.* ennemi *m.*
fog, *n.* brouillard *m.*
foggy, *adj.* brumeux.
foil, *n.* (sheet) feuille *f.;* (set-off) repoussoir *m.;* (fencing) fleuret *m.*
foist, *vb.* fourrer.
fold, **1.** *n.* pli *m.* **2.** *vb.* plier.
folder, *n.* (booklet) prospectus *m.*
foliage, *n.* feuillage *m.*
folio, *n.* in-folio *m.*
folk, *n.* gens *m.f.pl.*
folklore, *n.* folk-lore *m.*
follicle, *n.* follicule *m.*
follow, *vb.* suivre.
follower, *n.* disciple *m.*
folly, *n.* folie *f.*
foment, *vb.* fomenter.
fond, *adj.* tendre; (be f. of) aimer.
fondant, *n.* fondant *m.*
fondle, *vb.* caresser.
fondly, *adv.* tendrement.
fondness, *n.* tendresse *f.*
food, *n.* nourriture *f.*
foodstuff, *n.* comestible *m.*
fool, *n.* sot *m.,* sotte *f.;* (jester) bouffon *m.*
foolhardiness, *n.* témérité *f.*
foolhardy, *adj.* téméraire.
foolish, *adj.* sot *m.,* sotte *f.*

foolproof, *adj.* à toute épreuve.
foolscap, *n.* papier écolier *m.*
foot, *n.* pied *m.*
footage, *n.* métrage *m.*
football, *n.* football *m.,* ballon *m.*
foothill, *n.* colline basse *f.*
foothold, *n.* point d'appui *m.*
footing, *n.* pied *m.,* point d'appui *m.*
footlights, *n.* rampe *f.*
footnote, *n.* note *f.*
footprint, *n.* empreinte de pas *f.*
footsore, *adj.* aux pieds endoloris.
footstep, *n.* pas *m.*
footstool, *n.* tabouret *m.*
footwork, *n.* jeu de pieds *m.*
fop, *n.* fat *m.*
for, **1.** *prep.* pour. **2.** *conj.* car.
forage, **1.** *n.* fourrage *m.* **2.** *vb.* fourrager.
foray, *n.* razzia *f.*
forbear, *vb.* (avoid) s'abstenir de; (be patient) montrer de la patience.
forbearance, *n.* patience *f.*
forbid, *vb.* défendre (à).
forbidding, *adj.* rébarbatif.
force, **1.** *n.* force *f.* **2.** *vb.* forcer.
forced, *adj.* forcé.
forceful, *adj.* énergique.
forcefulness, *n.* énergie *f.,* vigueur *f.*
forceps, *n.* forceps *m.*
forcible, *adj.* forcé.
ford, **1.** *n.* gué *m.* **2.** *vb.* traverser à gué.
fore, *adj.* antérieur, de devant.
fore, *n.* avant *m.*
fore and aft, *adv.* de l'avant à l'arrière.
forearm, *n.* avant-bras *m.*
forebears, *n.* ancêtres *m.pl.*
forebode, *vb.* présager.
foreboding, **1.** *n.* mauvais augure *m.,* pressentiment *m.* **2.** *adj.* qui présage le mal.
forecast, **1.** *n.* prévision *f.* **2.** *vb.* prévoir.
forecaster, *n.* pronostiqueur *m.*
forecastle, *n.* gaillard *m.*
foreclose, *vb.* exclure, forclore.
forefather, *n.* ancêtre *m.*
forefinger, *n.* index *m.*
forefront, *n.* premier rang *m.*
foregone, *adj.* décidé d'avance.
foreground, *n.* premier plan *m.*

forehead, *n.* front *m.*

foreign, *adj.* étranger.

foreign aid, *n.* aide aux pays étrangers *f.*

foreigner, *n.* étranger *m.*

foreleg, *n.* jambe antérieure *f.*

foreman, *n.* contremaître *m.*

foremost, *adj.* premier.

forenoon, *n.* matinée *f.*

forensic, *adj.* judiciaire.

forerunner, *n.* avant-coureur *m.*

foresee, *vb.* prévoir.

foreseeable, *adj.* que l'on peut prévoir.

foreshadow, *vb.* présager.

foresight, *n.* prévoyance *f.*

forest, *n.* forêt *f.*

forestall, *vb.* anticiper, devancer.

forester, *n.* forestier *m.*

forestry, *n.* sylviculture *f.*

foretaste, *n.* avant-goût *m.*

foretell, *vb.* prédire.

forever, *adv.* pour toujours.

forevermore, *adv.* à jamais.

forewarn, *vb.* prévenir.

foreword, *n.* avant-propos *m.*

forfeit, *vb.* forfaire.

forfeiture, *n.* perte par confiscation *f.*, forfaiture *f.*

forgather, *vb.* se réunir.

forge, **1.** *n.* forge *f.* **2.** *vb.* forger; (signature, money) contrefaire.

forger, *n.* faussaire *m.*, falsificateur *m.*

forgery, *n.* faux *m.*

forget, *vb.* oublier.

forgetful, *adj.* oublieux.

forget-me-not, *n.* myosotis *m.*

forgive, *vb.* pardonner (à).

forgiveness, *n.* pardon *m.*

forgo, *vb.* renoncer à.

fork, *n.* fourchette *f.*; (tool, road) fourche *f.*

forlorn, *adj.* (hopeless) désespéré; (forsaken) abandonné.

form, **1.** *n.* forme *f.*; (blank) formule *f.* **2.** *vb.* former.

formal, *adj.* formel.

formaldehyde, *n.* formaldéhyde *f.*

formality, *n.* formalité *f.*

formally, *adv.* formellement.

format, *n.* format *m.*

formation, *n.* formation *f.*

formative, *adj.* formatif.

former, **1.** *adj.* précédent; (with latter) premier. **2.** *pron.* le premier.

formerly, *adv.* autrefois, jadis, auparavant.

formidable, *adj.* formidable.

formless, *adj.* informe.

formula, *n.* formule *f.*

formulate, *vb.* formuler.

formulation, *n.* formulation *f.*

forsake, *vb.* abandonner.

forsythia, *n.* forsythie *f.*

fort, *n.* fort *m.*

forte, *n.* fort *m.*

forth, *adv.* en avant; **(and so f.)** et ainsi de suite.

forthcoming, *adj.* à venir.

forthright, **1.** *adj.* tout droit. **2.** *adv.* carrément, nettement.

forthwith, *adv.* sur-le-champ, tout de suite.

fortieth, *adj. and n.* quarantième *m.*

fortification, *n.* fortification *f.*

fortify, *vb.* fortifier, renforcer.

fortissimo, *adv.* fortissimo.

fortitude, *n.* courage *m.*

fortnight, *n.* quinzaine *f.*

fortress, *n.* forteresse *f.*

fortuitous, *adj.* fortuit.

fortunate, *adj.* heureux.

fortune, *n.* fortune *f.*

fortuneteller, *n.* diseur de bonne aventure *m.*

forty, *adj. and n.* quarante *m.*

forum, *n.* (Roman) forum *m.*

forward, **1.** *adj.* en avant; (advanced) avancé; (bold) hardi. **2.** *adv.* en avant. **3.** *vb.* (letter) faire suivre.

forwardness, *n.* empressement *m.*, effronterie *f.*

fossil, *n.* fossile *m.*

fossilize, *vb.* fossiliser.

foul, *adj.* (dirty) sale; (disgusting) dégoûtant; (obscene) ordurier; (abominable) infâme.

found, *vb.* fonder.

foundation, *n.* fondation *f.*; (theory) fondement *m.*

founder, *n.* fondateur *m.*

foundling, *n.* enfant trouvé.

foundry, *n.* fonderie *f.*

fountain, *n.* fontaine *f.*

fountainhead, *n.* source *f.*

fountain pen, *n.* stylo-(graphe) *m.*

four, *adj. and n.* quatre *m.*

four-in-hand, *n.* attelage à quatre *m.*

fourscore, *adj.* quatre-vingts.
foursome, *n.* à quatre.
fourteen, *adj. and n.* quatorze *m.*
fourth, *adj. and n.* quatrième *m.*; (fraction) quart *m.*
fourth estate, *n.* quatrième état *m.*
fowl, *n.* volaille *f.*
fox, *n.* renard *m.*
foxglove, *n.* digitale *f.*
foxhole, *n.* renardière *f.*
fox terrier, *n.* fox-terrier *m.*
fox trot, *n.* fox-trot *m.*
foxy, *adj.* rusé.
foyer, *n.* foyer *m.*
fracas, *n.* fracas *m.*
fraction, *n.* fraction *f.*
fracture, *n.* fracture *f.*
fragile, *adj.* fragile.
fragment, *n.* fragment *m.*
fragmentary, *adj.* fragmentaire.
fragrance, *n.* parfum *m.*
fragrant, *adj.* parfumé.
frail, *adj.* frêle.
frailty, *n.* faiblesse *f.*
frame, *n.* (picture) cadre *m.*; (structure) structure *f.*
frame-up, **1.** *n.* coup monté *m.* **2.** *vb.* monter un coup.
framework, *n.* charpente *f.*
France, *n.* France *f.*
franchise, *n.* droit (*m.*) électoral.
frank, *adj.* franc *m.*, franche *f.*
frankfurter, *n.* saucisse (*f.*) de Francfort.
frankincense, *n.* encens *m.*
frankly, *adv.* franchement.
frankness, *n.* franchise *f.*
frantic, *adj.* frénétique.
fraternal, *adj.* fraternel.
fraternally, *adv.* fraternellement.
fraternity, *n.* fraternité *f.*
fraternization, *n.* fraternisation *f.*
fraternize, *vb.* fraterniser.
fratricide, *n.* fratricide *m.*
fraud, *n.* fraude *f.*; (person) imposteur *m.*
fraudulent, *adj.* frauduleux.
fraudulently, *adv.* frauduleusement.
fraught, *adj.* chargé (de), plein, gros.
fray, **1.** *n.* bagarre *f.* **2.** *vb.* érailler.
freak, *n.* (whim) caprice *m.*; (abnormality) phénomène *m.*
freckle, *n.* tache de rousseur *f.*

freckled, *adj.* taché de rousseur.
free, **1.** *adj.* libre; (without cost) gratuit. **2.** *vb.* libérer, affranchir.
freedom, *n.* liberté *f.*
free lance, *n.* journaliste ou politicien indépendant *m.* **2.** *vb.* faire du journalisme indépendant.
freestone, *n.* pêche dont la chair n'adhère pas au noyau *f.*
free verse, *n.* vers libre *m.*
free will, *n.* libre arbitre *m.*
freeze, *vb.* geler.
freezer, *n.* glacière *f.*; congélateur *m.*
freezing point, *n.* point de congélation *m.*
freight, *n.* fret *m.*
freightage, *n.* frètement *m.*
freighter, *n.* affréteur *m.*
French, *adj. and n.* français *m.*
French leave, *n.* filer à l'anglaise.
Frenchman, *n.* Français *m.*
French toast, *n.* tranche de pain frite *f.*
Frenchwoman, *n.* Française *f.*
frenzied, *adj.* affolé, frénétique.
frenzy, *n.* frénésie *f.*
frequency, *n.* fréquence *f.*
frequent, **1.** *adj.* fréquent. **2.** *vb.* fréquenter.
frequently, *adv.* fréquemment.
fresco, *n.* fresque *f.*
fresh, *adj.* frais *m.*, fraîche *f.*; (new, recent) nouveau; nouvel *m.*, nouvelle *f.*
freshen, *vb.* refraîchir.
freshman, *n.* étudiant de première année *m.*
freshness, *n.* fraîcheur *f.*
fresh-water, *adj.* d'eau douce.
fret, *vb.* ronger, *tr.*
fretful, *adj.* chagrin.
fretfully, *adv.* avec irritation.
fretfulness, *n.* irritabilité *f.*
friar, *n.* moine *m.*, frère religieux *m.*
fricassee, *n.* fricassée *f.*
friction, *n.* friction *f.*
Friday, *n.* vendredi *m.*
friend, *n.* ami *m.*, amie *f.*
friendless, *adj.* sans amis.
friendliness, *n.* disposition (*f.*) amicale.
friendly, *adj.* amical.
friendship, *n.* amitié *f.*
fright, *n.* effroi *m.*
frighten, *vb.* effrayer.

frightful, *adj.* affreux.

frigid, *adj.* glacial.

Frigid Zone, *n.* zone glaciale *f.*

frill, 1. *n.* volant *m.*; affectation *f.* **2.** *vb.* plisser.

frilly, *adj.* froncé, ruché.

fringe, *n.* frange *f.*

frisky, *adj.* folâtre.

frivolity, *n.* frivolité *f.*

frivolous, *adj.* frivole.

frivolousness, *n.* frivolité *f.*

frock, *n.* robe *f.*; (monk's) froc *m.*

frog, *n.* grenouille *f.*

frolic, *vb.* folâtrer.

from, *prep.* de; (time) depuis.

front, *n.* front *m.*; (front part) devant *m.*; (in f. of) devant.

frontage, *n.* étendue de devant *f.*

frontal, *adj.* frontal, de face.

frontier, *n.* frontière *f.*

frost, *n.* gelée *f.*

frostbite, *n.* gelure *f.*

frosting, *n.* glaçage *m.*

frosty, *adj.* gelé, glacé.

froth, 1. *n.* écume *f.* **2.** *vb.* écumer.

frown, *vb.* froncer les sourcils.

frowzy, *adj.* mal tenu, peu soigné.

frozen, *adj.* gelé.

fructify, *vb.* fructifier.

frugal, *adj.* frugal.

frugality, *n.* frugalité *f.*

fruit, *n.* fruit *m.*

fruitful, *adj.* fructueux.

fruition, *n.* réalisation *f.*, jouissance *f.*, fructification *f.*

fruitless, *adj.* infructueux.

frustrate, *vb.* faire échouer.

frustration, *n.* frustration *f.*

fry, *vb.* frire, *intr.;* faire frire, *tr.*

fryer, *n.* casserole *f.*

fuchsia, *n.* fuchsia *m.*

fudge, 1. *n.* espèce de fondant américain. **2.** *interj.* bah!

fuel, *n.* combustible *m.*

fugitive, *adj.* fugitif.

fugue, *n.* fugue *f.*

fulcrum, *n.* pivot *m.*, point d'appui *m.*

fulfill, *vb.* accomplir.

fulfillment, *n.* accomplissement *m.*

full, *adj.* plein.

fullback, *n.* arrière *m.*

full dress, *adj.* en tenue de cérémonie.

fullness, *n.* plénitude *f.*

fully, *adv.* pleinement.

fulminate, *vb.* fulminer.

fulmination, *n.* fulmination *f.*

fumble, *vb.* tâtonner.

fume, *n.* fumée *f.*

fumigate, *vb.* désinfecter.

fumigator, *n.* fumigateur *m.*

fun, *n.* (amusement) amusement *m.*; (have f.) s'amuser; (joke) plaisanterie *f.*; (make f. of) se moquer de.

function, *n.* fonction *f.*

functional, *adj.* fonctionnel.

functionary, *n.* fonctionnaire *m.*

fund, *n.* fonds *m.*

fundamental, *adj.* fondamental.

funeral, *n.* funérailles *f.pl.*

funereal, *adj.* funèbre, funéraire.

fungicide, *n.* fongicide *m.*

fungus, *n.* fongus *m.*

funnel, *n.* entonnoir *m.*; (smoke-stack) cheminée *f.*

funny, *adj.* drôle.

fur, *n.* fourrure *f.*

furious, *adj.* furieux.

furlong, *n.* furlong *m.*

furlough, *n.* permission *f.*

furnace, *n.* fourneau *m.*

furnish, *vb.* fournir; (house) meubler.

furnishings, *n.* ameublement *m.*

furniture, *n.* meubles *m.pl.*

furor, *n.* fureur *f.*

furred, *adj.* fourré.

furrier, *n.* fourreur *m.*

furrow, *n.* sillon *m.*

furry, *adj.* qui ressemble à la fourrure.

further, 1. *adj.* ultérieur. **2.** *adv.* (distance) plus loin; (extent) davantage.

furtherance, *n.* avancement *m.*

furthermore, *adv.* en outre.

fury, *n.* furie *f.*

fuse, *vb.* fondre.

fuselage, *n.* fuselage *m.*

fusillade, *n.* fusillade *f.*

fusion, *n.* fusion *f.*, fusionnement *m.*

fuss, *n.* (make a f.) faire des histoires.

fussy, *adj.* difficile.

futile, *adj.* futile.

futility, *n.* futilité *f.*

future, 1. *n.* avenir *m.*; (gramm.) futur *m.* **2.** *adj.* futur.

futurity, *n.* avenir *m.*

futurology, *n.* futurologie *f.*

fuzz, *n.* duvet *m.,* flou *m.*

fuzzy, *adj.* flou, frisotté.

G

gab, *vb.* jaser.

gabardine, *n.* gabardine *f.*

gable, *n.* pignon *m.*

gadabout, *n.* coureur *m.*

gadfly, *n.* taon *m.*

gadget, *n.* truc *m.*

gag, 1. *vb.* bâillonner. **2.** *n.* blague *f.,* bobard *m.;* bâillon *m.*

gaiety, *n.* gaieté *f.*

gaily, *adv.* gaiement.

gain, 1. *n.* gain *m.* **2.** *vb.* gagner.

gainful, *adj.* profitable, rémunérateur.

gainfully, *adv.* profitablement.

gainsay, *vb.* contredire.

gait, *n.* allure *f.*

gala, *n.* fête de gala *f.*

galaxy, *n.* galaxie *f.,* assemblée brillante *f.*

gale, *n.* grand vent *m.*

gall, *n.* (bile) fiel *m.;* (sore) écorchure *f.*

gallant, *adj.* (brave) vaillant; (with ladies) galant.

gallantly, *adv.* galamment.

gallantry, *n.* vaillance *f.,* galanterie *f.*

gall bladder, *n.* vésicule biliaire *f.*

galleon, *n.* galion *m.*

gallery, *n.* galerie *f.*

galley, *n.* galère *f., (naut.)* cuisine *f.,* (typographic) galée *f.*

galley proof, *n.* épreuve en première *f.*

Gallic, *adj.* gaulois.

gallivant, *vb.* courailler.

gallon, *n.* gallon *m.*

gallop, 1. *n.* galop *m.* **2.** *vb.* galoper.

gallows, *n.* potence *f.*

gallstone, *n.* calcul biliaire *m.*

galore, *adv.* à foison, à profusion.

galosh, *n.* galoche *f.*

galvanize, *vb.* galvaniser.

gamble, 1. *n.* jeu *(m.)* de hasard. **2.** *vb.* jouer.

gambler, *n.* joueur *m.*

gambling, *n.* jeu *m.*

gambol, 1. *n.* gambade *f.* **2.** *vb.* gamboler.

game, *n.* jeu *m.;* (hunting) gibier *m.*

gamely, *adv.* courageusement, crânement.

gameness, *n.* courage *m.,* crânerie *f.*

gamin, *n.* gamin *m.*

gamut, *n.* gamme *f.*

gamy, *adj.* giboyeux.

gander, *n.* jars *m.*

gang, *n.* bande *f.;* (workers) équipe *f.*

gangling, *adj.* dégingandé.

gangplank, *n.* passerelle *f.*

gangrene, *n.* gangrène *f.*

gangrenous, *adj.* gangreneux.

gangster, *n.* gangster *m.*

gangway, *n.* passage *m.*

gap, *n.* (opening) ouverture *f.;* (empty space) vide *m.*

gape, *vb.* rester bouche bée.

garage, *n.* garage *m.*

garb, 1. *n.* vêtement *m.,* costume *m.* **2.** *vb.* vêtir, habiller.

garbage, *n.* ordures *f.pl.*

garble, *vb.* tronquer, altérer.

garden, *n.* jardin *m.*

gardener, *n.* jardinier *m.*

gardenia, *n.* gardénia *m.*

gargle, 1. *n.* gargarisme *m.* **2.** *vb.* se gargariser.

gargoyle, *n.* gargouille *f.*

garish, *adj.* voyant.

garland, *n.* guirlande *f.*

garlic, *n.* ail *m.*

garment, *n.* vêtement *m.*

garner, *vb.* mettre en grenier.

garnet, *n.* grenat *m.*

garnish, *vb.* garnir.

garnishee, *n.* tiers-saisi *m.*

garnishment, *n.* saisie-arrêt *f.*

garret, *n.* mansarde *f.*

garrison, *n.* garnison *f.*

garrote, 1. *n.* garrotte *f.* **2.** *vb.* garrotter.

garrulous, *adj.* bavard, loquace.

garter, *n.* jarretière *f.*

gas, *n.* gaz *m.;* (g. station) poste *(m.)* d'essence.

gaseous, *adj.* gazeux.

gash, 1. *n.* coupure *f.,* entaille *f.* **2.** *vb.* couper, entailler.

gasket, *n.* garcette *f.*

gasless, *adj.* sans gaz.

gas mask, *n.* masque à gaz *m.*

gasohol, *n.* essence *(f.)* fabriquée avec de l'alcool.

gasoline, n. essence f.

gasp, vb. (astonishment) sursauter; (lack of breath) haleter.

gassy, adj. gazeux, bavard.

gastric, adj. gastrique.

gastric juice, n. suc gastrique m.

gastritis, n. gastrite f.

gastronomically, adv. d'une manière gastronomique.

gastronomy, n. gastronomie f.

gate, n. (city) porte f.; (with bars) barrière f.; (wrought-iron) grille f.

gateway, n. porte f., entrée f.

gather, vb. rassembler, tr.; recueillir, tr.

gathering, n. rassemblement m.

gaudily, adv. de manière voyante.

gaudiness, n. éclat criard m., ostentation f.

gaudy, adj. voyant.

gaunt, adj. décharné.

gauntlet, n. gantelet m.

gauze, n. gaze f.

gavel, n. marteau m.

gavotte, n. gavotte f.

gawky, adj. dégingandé.

gay, 1. adj. gai; (homosexual) homosexuel. **2.** n. homosexuel m.

gaze, vb. regarder fixement.

gazelle, n. gazelle f.

gazette, n. gazette f.

gazetteer, n. gazetier m., répertoire géographique m.

gear, n. (implements, device) appareil m.; (machines) engrenage m.; (in g.) engrené; (g. change) changement (m.) de vitesse.

gearing, n. engrenage m.

gearshift, n. changement de vitesse m.

gelatin, n. gélatine f.

gelatinous, adj. gélatineux.

geld, vb. châtrer.

gelding, n. animal châtré m.

gem, n. pierre (f.) précieuse.

gender, n. genre m.

gene, n. déterminant d'hérédité m.

genealogical, adj. généalogique.

genealogy, n. généalogie f.

general, adj. and n. général m.

generality, n. généralité f.

generalization, n. généralisation f.

generalize, vb. généraliser.

generally, adv. généralement.

generalship, n. stratégie f.

generate, vb. engendrer, générer.

generation, n. génération f.

generic, adj. générique.

generosity, n. générosité f.

generous, adj. généreux.

generously, adv. généreusement.

genetic, adj. génétique.

genetics, n. génétique f.

genial, adj. sympathique.

geniality, n. jovialité f., bienveillance f.

genially, adv. affablement.

genital, adj. génital.

genitals, n. organes génitaux m.pl.

genitive, n. and adj. génitif m.

genius, n. génie m.

genocide, n. génocide m.

genre, n. genre m.

genteel, adj. de bon ton.

gentian, n. gentiane f.

gentile, n. gentil m.

gentility, n. prétention à la distinction f.

gentle, adj. doux m., douce f.

gentleman, n. monsieur m., pl. messieurs; (character) galant homme m.

gentlemanly, adj. comme il faut, bien élevé.

gentlemen's agreement, n. convention verbale f.

gentleness, n. douceur f.

gently, adv. doucement.

gentry, n. petite noblesse f.

genuflect, vb. faire des génuflexions.

genuine, adj. véritable.

genuinely, adv. véritablement.

genuineness, n. authenticité f.

genus, n. genre m.

geographer, n. géographe m.

geographical, adj. géographique.

geography, n. géographie f.

geometric, adj. géométrique.

geometry, n. géométrie f.

geopolitics, n. géopolitique f.

geranium, n. géranium m.

germ, n. germe m.

German, 1. n. (person) Allemand m.; (language) allemand m. **2.** adj. allemand.

germane, adj. approprié.

Germanic, adj. allemand, germanique.

German measles, *n.* rougeole bénigne *f.*

Germany, *n.* Allemagne *f.*

germicide, *n.* microbicide *m.*

germinal, *adj.* germinal.

germinate, *vb.* germer.

gestate, *vb.* enfanter.

gestation, *n.* gestation *f.*

gesticulate, *vb.* gesticuler.

gesticulation, *n.* gesticulation *f.*

gesture, *n.* geste *m.*

get, *vb.* (obtain) obtenir; (receive) recevoir; (take) prendre; (become) devenir; (arrive) arriver; **(g. in)** entrer; **(g. off)** descendre; **(g. on, agree)** s'entendre; **(g. on,** go up) monter; **(g. out)** sortir; **(g. up)** se lever.

getaway, *n.* fuite *f.*

geyser, *n.* geyser *m.*

ghastly, *adj.* horrible.

ghost, *n.* (specter) revenant *m.;* **(Holy G.)** Saint-Esprit *m.*

ghost writer, *n.* collaborateur anonyme *m.,* nègre *m.*

ghoul, *n.* goule *f.,* vampire *m.*

giant, *n.* géant *m.*

gibberish, *n.* baragouin *m.*

gibbon, *n.* gibbon *m.*

gibe, 1. *n.* raillerie *f.* **2.** *vb.* railler.

giblet, *n.* abatis (de volaille) *m.*

giddy, *adj.* étourdi.

gift, *n.* don *m.;* (present) cadeau *m.*

gifted, *adj.* doué.

gigantic, *adj.* géant, gigantesque.

giggle, *vb.* rire nerveusement, glousser.

gigolo, *n.* gigolo *m.*

gild, *vb.* dorer.

gill, *n.* ouïes (of fish) *f.pl.*

gilt, 1. *n.* dorure *f.* **2.** *adj.* doré.

gilt-edged, *adj.* doré sur tranche.

gimcrack, *1. n.* camelote *f.* **2.** *adj.* de camelote.

gimlet, *n.* vrille *f.*

gin, *n.* genièvre *m.*

ginger, *n.* gingembre *m.*

ginger ale, *n.* boisson gazeuse au gingembre *f.*

gingerly, *adv.* avec précaution.

gingersnap, *n.* biscuit au gingembre *m.*

gingham, *n.* guingan *m.*

giraffe, *n.* girafe *f.*

gird, *vb.* ceindre.

girder, *n.* support *m.*

girdle, *n.* gaine *f.*

girl, *n.* jeune fille *f.*

girlish, *adj.* de jeune fille.

girth, *n.* sangle *f.,* circonférence *f.,* corpulence *f.*

gist, *n.* fond *m.,* essence *f.*

give, *vb.* donner; **(g. back)** rendre; **(g. in)** céder; **(g. out)** distribuer; **(g. up)** renoncer à.

give-and-take, *adv.* donnant donnant.

given, *adj.* donné.

given name, *n.* nom de baptême *m.*

giver, *n.* donneur *m.*

gizzard, *n.* gésier *m.*

glacé, *adj.* glacé.

glacial, *adj.* glaciaire.

glacier, *n.* glacier *m.*

glad, *adj.* heureux.

gladden, *vb.* réjouir.

glade, *n.* clairère *f.,* éclaircie *f.*

gladiolus, *n.* glaïeul *m.*

gladly, *adv.* volontiers.

gladness, *n.* joie *f.*

Gladstone bag, *n.* sac américain *m.*

glamour, *n.* éclat *m.*

glance, *n.* coup (*m.*) d'œil.

gland, *n.* glande *f.*

glandular, *adj.* glandulaire.

glare, 1. *n.* (light) clarté *f.;* (stare) regard *m.*) enflammé. **2.** *vb.* (shine) briller; (look) jeter des regards enflammés.

glaring, *adj.* éclatant, flagrant, voyant, manifeste.

glass, *n.* verre *m.*

glass-blowing, *n.* soufflage *m.*

glasses, *n.* lunettes *f.pl.*

glassful, *n.* verre *m.,* verrée *f.*

glassware, *n.* verrerie *f.*

glassy, *adj.* vitreux.

glaucoma, *n.* glaucome *m.*

glaze, 1. *n.* lustre *m.* **2.** *vb.* vitrer.

glazier, *n.* vitrier *m.*

gleam, 1. *n.* lueur *f.* **2.** *vb.* luire.

glee, *n.* allégresse *f.*

glee club, *n.* chœur d'hommes *m.*

gleeful, *adj.* joyeux, allègre.

glen, *n.* vallon *m.,* ravin *m.*

glib, *adj.* spécieux.

glide, *vb.* glisser; (plane) planer.

glider, *n.* planeur *m.*

glimmer, 1. *n.* faible lueur *f.* **2.** *vb.* jeter une faible lueur.

glimmering, adj. faible, vacillant.

glimpse, vb. entrevoir.

glint, 1. n. éclair m., reflet m. **2.** vb. entreluire, étinceler.

glitter, vb. étinceler.

gloat, vb. se régaler de.

global, adj. global.

globe, n. globe m.

globetrotter, n. globe trotter m.

globular, adj. globulaire, globuleux.

globule, n. globule m.

glockenspiel, n. glockenspiel m.

gloom, n. (darkness) ténèbres f.pl.; (sadness) tristesse f.

gloomy, adj. sombre.

glorification, n. glorification f.

glorify, vb. glorifier.

glorious, adj. glorieux; (weather) radieux.

glory, n. gloire f.

gloss, 1. n. lustre m., vernis m., glose f. **2.** vb. lustrer, glacer.

glossary, n. glossaire m.

glossy, adj. lustré, glacé.

glove, n. gant m.

glow, n. (light) lumière f.; (heat) chaleur f.

glowing, adj. embrasé, rayonnant.

glowingly, adv. en termes chaleureux.

glowworm, n. ver luisant m.

glucose, n. glucose f.

glue, 1. n. colle (f.) forte. **2.** vb. coller.

glum, adj. maussade.

glumness, n. air maussade m., tristesse f.

glut, 1. n. assouvissement m., excès m., pléthore f. **2.** vb. assouvir, rassasier, gorger.

glutinous, adj. glutineux.

glutton, n. gourmand m.

gluttonous, adj. gourmand, goulu.

glycerin, n. glycérine f.

gnarl, n. loupe f., nœud m.

gnash, vb. grincer.

gnat, n. moucheron m.

gnaw, vb. ronger.

gnu, n. gnou m.

go, vb. aller; (g. away) s'en aller; (g. back) retourner; (g. by) passer; (g. down) descendre; (g. in) entrer; (g. on) continuer; (g. out) sortir; (g. up) monter; (g. without) se passer de.

goad, 1. n. aiguillon m. **2.** vb. aiguillonner, piquer.

goal, n. but m.

goat, n. chèvre f.

goatee, n. barbiche f.

goatherd, n. chevrier m.

goatskin, n. peau de chèvre f.

gobble, vb. avaler goulûment, dévorer.

gobbler, n. avaleur m.; dindon m.

go-between, n. intermédiaire m.

goblet, n. gobelet m.

goblin, n. gobelin m., lutin m.

God, n. Dieu m.

godchild, n. filleul m.

goddess, n. déesse f.

godfather, n. parrain m.

godless, adj. athée, impie, sans Dieu.

godlike, adj. comme un dieu, divin.

godly, adj. dévot, pieux, saint.

godmother, n. marraine f.

godsend, n. aubaine f., bienfait du ciel m.

Godspeed, interj. bon voyage!

go-getter, n. homme d'affaires énergique m., arriviste m.

goiter, n. goitre m.

gold, n. or m.

gold brick, n. attrape-niais m.

golden, adj. d'or.

goldenrod, n. solidage m.

golden rule, n. règle par excellence f.

gold-filled, adj. aurifié, en (or) doublé.

goldfinch, n. chardonneret m.

goldfish, n. poisson rouge m.

gold leaf, n. feuille d'or f., or battu m.

goldsmith, n. orfèvre m.

gold standard, n. étalon or m.

golf, n. golf m.

gondola, n. gondole f.

gondolier, n. gondolier m.

gone, adj. disparu, parti.

gong, n. gong m.

gonorrhea, n. gonorrhée f., blennorrhagie f.

good, adj. bon m., bonne f.

good, n. bien m.; (goods) marchandises f.pl.

good-bye, n. and interj. adieu m.

Good Friday, *n.* Vendredi Saint *m.*

good-hearted, *adj.* qui a un bon cœur, compatissant.

good-humored, *adj.* de bonne humeur, plein de bonhomie.

good-looking, *adj.* beau, joli.

good-natured, *adj.* au bon naturel, accommodant.

goodness, *n.* bonté *f.*

good will, *n.* bonne volonté *f.*

goose, *n.* oie *f.*

gooseberry, *n.* groseille verte *f.*

gooseneck, *n.* col de cygne *m.*

goose step, *n.* pas d'oie *m.*

gore, 1. *n.* (dress) chanteau *m.;* soufflet *m.;* (blood) sang coagulé *m.* **2.** *vb.* corner.

gorge, *n.* gorge *f.*

gorgeous, *adj.* splendide.

gorilla, *n.* gorille *m.*

gory, *adj.* sanglant, ensanglanté.

gosling, *n.* oison *m.*

gospel, *n.* évangile *m.*

gossamer, *n.* filandre *f.*, gaze légère *f.*

gossip, 1. *n.* bavardage *m.* **2.** *vb.* bavarder.

Gothic, *adj.* gothique.

gouge, 1. *n.* gouge *f.* **2.** *vb.* gouger.

gourd, *n.* gourde *f.*, courge *f.*

gourmand, *n.* gourmand *m.*

gourmet, *n.* gourmet *m.*

govern, *vb.* gouverner.

governess, *n.* gouvernante *f.*

government, *n.* gouvernement *m.*

governmental, *adj.* gouvernemental.

governor, *n.* gouvernant *m.*

governorship, *n.* fonctions de gouverneur *f.pl.*, temps de gouvernement *m.*

gown, *n.* robe *f.*

grab, *vb.* saisir.

grace, *n.* grâce *f.*

graceful, *adj.* gracieux.

gracefully, *adv.* avec grâce.

graceless, *adj.* sans grâce, gauche.

gracious, *adj.* gracieux; (merciful) miséricordieux.

grackle, *n.* mainate *m.*

grade, 1. *n.* grade *m.;* (quality) qualité *f.* **2.** *vb.* classer.

grade crossing, *n.* passage à niveau *m.*

gradual, *adj.* graduel.

gradually, *adv.* graduellement.

graduate, *vb.* graduer; (school) prendre ses grades.

graft, *n.* corruption *f.*

grail, *n.* graal *m.*

grain, *n.* grain *m.*

gram, *n.* gramme *f.*

grammar, *n.* grammaire *f.*

grammarian, *n.* grammairien *m.*

grammar school, *n.* école primaire *f.*

grammatical, *adj.* grammatical.

gramophone, *n.* phonographe.

granary, *n.* grenier *m.*

grand, *adj.* grandiose; (in titles) grand; (fine, *colloq.*) épatant.

grandchild, *n.* petit-fils *m.;* petite-fille *f.;* petits-enfants *m.pl.*

granddaughter, *n.* petite-fille *f.*

grandee, *n.* grand *m.*

grandeur, *n.* grandeur *f.*

grandfather, *n.* grand-père *m.*

grandiloquent, *adj.* grandiloquent.

grandiose, *adj.* grandiose.

grand jury, *n.* jury d'accusation *m.*

grandly, *adv.* grandement, magnifiquement.

grandmother, *n.* grand-mère *f.*

grand opera, *n.* grand opéra *m.*

grandson, *n.* petit-fils *m.*

grandstand, *n.* grande tribune *f.*

granger, *n.* régisseur *m.*

granite, *n.* granit *m.*

granny, *n.* bonne-maman *f.*

grant, 1. *n.* concession *f.;* (money) subvention *f.* **2.** *vb.* accorder; (admit) admettre.

granular, *adj.* en grains, granulé.

granulate, *vb.* granuler, grener.

granulation, *n.* granulation *f.*

granule, *n.* granule *m.*

grape, *n.* raisin *m.*

grapefruit, *n.* pamplemousse *f.*

grapeshot, *n.* mitraille *f.*

grapevine, *n.* treille *f.*

graph, *n.* courbe *f.*

graphic, *adj.* graphique, pittoresque.

graphite, *n.* graphite *m.*

graphology, *n.* graphologie *f.*

grapple, 1. *n.* grappin *m.;* lutte *f.* **2.** *vb.* accrocher; en venir aux prises.

grasp, 1. n. (hold) prise f. **2.** vb. saisir.

grasping, adj. avide, cupide.

grass, n. herbe f.

grasshopper, n. sauterelle f.

grassy, adj. herbeux, verdoyant.

grate, 1. n. grille f. **2.** vb. (cheese, etc.) râper; (make noise) grincer.

grateful, adj. reconnaissant.

gratify, vb. contenter, satisfaire.

grating, 1. n. grille f. **2.** vb. grinçant, discordant.

gratis, adv. gratis, gratuitement.

gratitude, n. gratitude f.

gratuitous, adj. gratuit.

gratuity, n. (tip) pourboire m.

grave, 1. n. tombe f. **2.** adj. grave.

gravel, n. gravier m.

gravely, adv. gravement, sérieusement.

gravestone, n. pierre sépulcrale f., tombe f.

graveyard, n. cimetière m.

gravitate, vb. graviter.

gravitation, n. gravitation f.

gravity, n. gravité f.

gravure, n. gravure f.

gravy, n. jus m.

gray, adj. gris.

grayish, adj. grisâtre.

gray matter, n. substance grise f., cendrée f.

graze, vb. paître.

grazing, n. pâturage m.

grease, 1. n. graisse f. **2.** vb. graisser.

great, adj. grand.

Great Dane, n. grand Danois m.

greatness, n. grandeur f.

Greece, n. Grèce f.

greediness, n. gourmandise f.

greedy, adj. gourmand.

Greek, 1. n. (person) Grec m., Grecque f.; (language) grec m. **2.** adj. grec m., grecque f.

green, adj. vert.

greenery, n. verdure f.

greenhouse, n. serre f.

greet, vb. saluer.

greeting, n. salutation f.; (reception) accueil m.

gregarious, adj. grégaire.

grenade, n. grenade f.

grenadine, n. grenadine f.

greyhound, n. lévrier m.

grid, n. grill m.

griddle, n. gril m.

gridiron, n. gril m.

grief, n. chagrin m.

grievance, n. grief m.

grieve, vb. affliger, tr.; chagriner, tr.

grievous, adj. douloureux.

grill, 1. n. gril m. **2.** vb. griller.

grillroom, n. grill-room m.

grim, adj. sinistre.

grimace, n. grimace f.

grime, n. saleté f., noirceur f.

grimy, adj. sale, noirci, encrassé.

grin, n. large sourire m.

grind, vb. (crush) moudre; (sharpen) aiguiser.

grindstone, n. meule f.

gringo, n. Anglo-américain m.

grip, n. prise f.

gripe, vb. saisir, empoigner; grogner.

grisly, adj. hideux, horrible.

grist, n. blé à moudre m., mouture f.

gristle, n. cartilage m.

grit, n. grès m., sable m.; (fig.) cran m., courage m.

grizzled, adj. grison, grisonnant.

groan, 1. n. gémissement m. **2.** vb. gémir.

grocer, n. épicier m.

grocery, n. épicerie f.

grog, n. grog m.

groggy, adj. gris, titubant.

groin, n. aine f.

groom, 1. n. (horses) palefrenier m.; (bridegroom) nouveau marié m. **2.** vb. (horses) panser.

groove, n. rainure f.

grope, vb. tâtonner.

grosgrain, adj. de grosgrain.

gross, adj. (bulky) gros m., grosse f.; (coarse) grossier; (comm.) brut.

grossly, adv. grossièrement.

grossness, n. grossièreté f., énormité f.

grotesque, adj. and n. grotesque m.

grotto, n. grotte f.

grouch, 1. n. maussaderie f.; grogneur m. **2.** vb. grogner.

ground, n. (earth) terre f.; (territory) terrain m.; (reason) raison f.; (background) fond m.

ground hog, n. marmotte d'Amérique f.

groundless, adj. sans fondement.

ground swell, n. houle f., lame de fond f.

groundwork, n. fondement m., fond m., base f.

group, 1. n. groupe m. **2.** vb. grouper, tr.

groupie, n. groupie f.; membre d'un groupe de jeunes filles m.

grouse, 1. n. tétras m. **2.** vb. grogner.

grove, n. bocage m., bosquet m.

grovel, vb. ramper, se vautrer.

grow, vb. croître; (persons) grandir; (become) devenir; (cultivate) cultiver.

growl, vb. grogner.

grown, adj. fait, grand.

grownup, adj. and n. grand m., adulte m.f.

growth, n. croissance f.; (increase) accroissement m.

grub, 1. n. larve f., ver blanc m.; (slang) nourriture f. **2.** vb. défricher, fouiller.

grubby, adj. véreux, (fig.) sale.

grudge, n. rancune f.

gruel, n. gruau m.

gruesome, adj. lugubre, terrifiant.

gruff, adj. bourru.

grumble, vb. grommeler.

grumpy, adj. bourru, morose.

grunt, 1. n. grognement m. **2.** vb. grogner.

guarantee, 1. n. garantie f. **2.** vb. garantir.

guarantor, n. garant m.

guaranty, n. garantie f.

guard, 1. n. garde f. **2.** vb. garder.

guarded, adj. prudent, circonspect, réservé.

guardhouse, n. corps de garde m., poste m.

guardian, n. gardien m.; (law) tuteur m.

guardianship, n. tutelle f.

guardsman, n. garde m.

guava, n. goyave f.

gubernatorial, adj. du gouverneur, du gouvernement.

guerrilla, n. guérilla f.

guess, 1. n. conjecture f. **2.** vb. deviner.

guesswork, n. conjecture f.

guest, n. invité m.

guffaw, 1. n. gros rire m. **2.** vb. s'esclaffer.

guidance, n. direction f.

guide, 1. n. guide m. **2.** vb. guider.

guidebook, n. guide m.

guidepost, n. poteau indicateur m.

guild, n. corporation f., corps de métier m.

guile, n. astuce f., artifice m.

guillotine, n. guillotine f.

guilt, n. culpabilité f.

guiltily, adv. criminellement.

guiltless, adj. innocent.

guilty, adj. coupable.

guimpe, n. guimpe f.

guinea fowl, n. pintade f.

guinea pig, n. cobaye m.

guise, n. guise f., façon f.

guitar, n. guitare f.

gulch, n. ravin m.

gulf, n. (geog.) golfe m.; (fig.) gouffre m.

gull, n. mouette f.

gullet, n. gosier m.

gullible, adj. crédule, facile à duper.

gully, n. ravin m.

gulp, 1. n. goulée f., gorgée f., trait m. **2.** vb. avaler, gober.

gum, n. gomme f.; (teeth) gencive f.

gumbo, n. gombo m.

gummy, adj. gommeux.

gun, n. (cannon) canon m.; (rifle) fusil m.

gunboat, n. canonnière f.

gunman, n. partisan armé m., voleur armé m., bandit m.

gunner, n. artilleur m.

gunpowder, n. poudre (f.) à canon.

gunshot, n. portée de fusil f.

gunwale, n. plat-bord m.

gurgle, vb. faire glouglou, gargouiller.

guru, n. gourou m.

gush, 1. n. jaillissement m. **2.** vb. jaillir.

gusher, n. source jaillissante f., personne exubérante f.

gusset, n. gousset m., soufflet m.

gust, n. (wind) rafale f.

gustatory, adj. gustatif.

gusto, n. goût m., délectation f., verve f.

gusty, adv. venteux, orageux.

gut, 1. n. boyau m., intestin m. **2.** vb. éventrer, vider.

gutter, *n.* (roof) gouttière *f.;* (street) ruisseau *m.*

guttural, *adj.* guttural.

guy, **1.** *n.* type *m.,* individu *m.* **2.** *vb.* se moquer de.

guzzle, *vb.* ingurgiter, boire avidement.

gym, *n.* gymnase *m.*

gymnasium, *n.* gymnase *m.*

gymnast, *n.* gymnaste *m.*

gymnastic, *adj.* gymnastique.

gymnastics, *n.* gymnastique *f.*

gynecology, *n.* gynécologie *f.*

gypsum, *n.* gypse *m.*

gypsy, *n.* gitane *m.f.*

gyrate, *vb.* tournoyer.

gyroscope, *n.* gyroscope *m.*

H

habeas corpus, *n.* habeas corpus *m.*

haberdasher, *n.* chemisier *m.,* mercier *m.*

haberdashery, *n.* chemiserie *f.,* mercerie *f.*

habiliment, *n.* habillement *m.,* apprêt *m.*

habit, *n.* habitude *f.*

habitable, *adj.* habitable.

habitat, *n.* habitat *m.*

habitation, *n.* habitation *f.*

habitual, *adj.* habituel.

habituate, *vb.* habituer, accoutumer.

habitué, *n.* habitué *m.*

hack, **1.** *n.* (tool) pioche *f.;* (horse) cheval (*m.*) de louage; (vehicle) voiture (*f.*) de louage. **2.** *vb.* (**h. up**) hacher; (notch) entailler.

hackneyed, *adj.* banal, rebattu.

hacksaw, *n.* scie à métaux *f.*

haddock, *n.* aigle fin *m.*

haft, *n.* manche *m.,* poignée *f.*

hag, *n.* vielle sorcière *f.*

haggard, *adj.* hagard.

haggle, *vb.* marchander.

hagridden, *adj.* tourmenté par le cauchemar.

hail, **1.** *n.* grêle *f.* **2.** *vb.* (weather) grêler; (salute) saluer; (come from) venir de. **3.** *interj.* salut.

Hail Mary, *n.* Ave Maria *m.*

hailstone, *n.* grêlon *m.*

hailstorm, *n.* tempête de grêle *f.*

hair, *n.* cheveux *m.pl.;* (single, on head) cheveu *m.;* (on body, animals) poil *m.*

haircut, *n.* coupe (*f.*) de cheveux.

hairdo, *n.* coiffure *f.*

hairdresser, *n.* coiffeur *m.*

hairline, *n.* délié *m.*

hairpin, *n.* épingle (*f.*) à cheveux.

hair-raising, *adj.* horripilant, horrifique.

hair's-breadth, *n.* l'épaisseur d'un cheveu *f.*

hairspray, *n.* laque *f.*

hairy, *adj.* velu, poilu.

halcyon, **1.** *n.* alcyon *m.* **2.** *adj.* calme.

hale, *adj.* sain.

half, **1.** *n.* moitié *f.* **2.** *adj.* demi. **3.** *adv.* à moitié.

half-and-half, *n.* moitié de l'un, moitié de l'autre *f.*

halfback, *n.* demi-arrière *m.*

half-baked, *adj.* à moitié cuit, inexpérimenté, incomplet.

half-breed, *n.* métis *m.*

half brother, *n.* frère de père *m.,* frère de mère *m.*

half dollar, *n.* demi-dollar *m.*

half-hearted, *adj.* sans enthousiasme.

half-mast, *adv.* à mi-mât.

halfpenny, *n.* petit sou *m.*

halfway, *adv.* à mi-chemin.

half-wit, *n.* niais *m.,* sot *m.*

halibut, *n.* flétan *m.*

hall, *n.* (large room) salle *f.;* (entrance) vestibule *m.*

hallmark, *n.* contrôle *m.*

hallow, *vb.* sanctifier.

Halloween, *n.* la veille de la Toussaint *f.*

hallucination, *n.* hallucination *f.*

hallway, *n.* corridor *m.,* vestibule *m.*

halo, *n.* auréole *f.*

halt, **1.** *n.* halte *f.* **2.** *vb.* arrêter, *tr.*

halter, *n.* licou *m.,* longe *f.,* corde *f.*

halve, *vb.* diviser en deux, partager en deux.

halyard, *n.* drisse *f.*

ham, *n.* jambon *m.*

hamlet, *n.* hameau *m.*

hammer, **1.** *n.* marteau *m.* **2.** *vb.* marteler.

hammock, *n.* hamac *m.*

hamper, 1. *n.* panier *m.* **2.** *vb.* embarrasser, gêner.
hamstring, *vb.* couper le jarret à, couper les moyens à.
hand, *n.* main *f.*
handball, *n.* balle *f.*
handbook, *n.* manuel *m.*
handcuff, 1. *n.* menotte *f.* **2.** *vb.* mettre les menottes à.
handful, *n.* poignée *f.*
handicap, *n.* handicap *m.*, désavantage *m.*
handicraft, *n.* métier *m.*
handiwork, *n.* main-d'œuvre *f.*
handkerchief, *n.* mouchoir *m.*
handle, 1. *n.* manche *m.* **2.** *vb.* manier.
handle bar, *n.* guidon *m.*
handmade, *adj.* fait à la main, fabriqué à la main.
handmaid, *n.* servante *f.*
hand organ, *n.* orgue portatif *m.*, orgue de Barbarie *f.*
handout, *n.* aumône *f.*; compte rendu communiqué à la presse *m.*
hand-pick, *vb.* trier à la main, éplucher à la main.
handsome, *adj.* beau *m.*, belle *f.*
hand-to-hand, *adj.* corps à corps.
handwriting, *n.* écriture *f.*
handy, *adj.* (person) adroit; (thing) commode; (at hand) sous la main.
handy man, *n.* homme à tout faire *m.*, bricoleur *m.*, factotum *m.*
hang, *vb.* pendre.
hangar, *n.* hangar *m.*
hangdog, *adj.* avec une mine patibulaire, avec un air en dessous.
hanger-on, *n.* dépendant *m.*, parasite *m.*
hang glider, *n.* glisseur duquel l'usager pend *m.*
hanging, 1. *n.* suspension *f.*, pendaison *f.* **2.** *adj.* suspendu, pendant.
hangman, *n.* bourreau *m.*
hangnail, *n.* envie *f.*
hangout, *n.* repaire *m.*, nid *m.*
hang-over, *n.* reste *m.*, reliquat *m.*
hangup, *n.* difficulté psychologique *f.*
hank, *n.* écheveau *m.*, torchette *f.*
hanker, *vb.* désirer vivement, convoiter.

haphazard, *adv.* au hasard.
happen, *vb.* (take place) arriver; (chance to be) se trouver.
happening, *n.* événement *m.*
happily, *adv.* heureusement.
happiness, *n.* bonheur *m.*
happy, *adj.* heureux.
happy-go-lucky, *adj.* sans souci, insouciant.
harakiri, *n.* hara-kiri *m.*
harangue, 1. *n.* harangue *f.* **2.** *vb.* haranguer.
harass, *vb.* harceler, tracasser.
harbinger, *n.* avant-coureur *m.*, précurseur *m.*
harbor, *n.* (refuge) asile *m.*; (port) port *m.*
hard, 1. *adj.* dur; (difficult) difficile. **2.** *adv.* fort.
hard-bitten, *adj.* tenace dur à cuire.
hard-boiled, *adj.* dur, tenace, boucané.
hard coal, *n.* anthracite *m.*
harden, *vb.* durcir.
hard-headed, *adj.* pratique, positif.
hard-hearted, *adj.* insensible, impitoyable, au cœur dur.
hardiness, *n.* robustesse *f.*, vigueur *f.*
hardly, *adv.* (in a hard manner) durement; (scarcely) à peine; (h. ever) presque jamais.
hardness, *n.* dureté *f.*; (difficulty) difficulté *f.*
hardship, *n.* privation *f.*
hardtack, *n.* galette *f.*, biscuit de mer *m.*
hardware, *n.* quincaillerie *f.*
hardwood, *n.* bois dur *m.*
hardy, *adj.* robuste.
hare, *n.* lièvre *m.*
harebrained, *adj.* écervelé, étourdi.
harelip, *n.* bec-de-lièvre *m.*
harem, *n.* harem *m.*
hark, 1. *vb.* prêter l'oreille à. **2.** *interj.* écoutez!
Harlequin, *n.* Arlequin *m.*
harlot, *n.* prostituée *f.*, fille de joie *f.*
harm, 1. *n.* mal *m.* **2.** *vb.* nuire à.
harmful, *adj.* nuisible.
harmless, *adj.* inoffensif.
harmonic, *adj.* harmonique.
harmonica, *n.* harmonica *m.*

harmonious, adj. harmonieux.

harmonize, vb. harmoniser.

harmony, n. harmonie f.

harness, 1. n. harnais m. **2.** vb. harnacher.

harp, n. harpe f.

harpoon, 1. n. harpon m. **2.** vb. harponner.

harridan, n. vieille sorcière f., vieille mégère f.

harrow, vb. herser; (fig.) tourmenter.

harry, vb. harceler.

harsh, adj. rude.

harshness, n. rudesse f.

harvest, 1. n. moisson f. **2.** vb. moissoner.

hash, 1. n. hachis m., émincé m. **2.** vb. hacher (de la viande).

hashish, n. hachisch m.

hasn't, vb. n'a pas.

hassle, 1. vb. harceler. **2.** n. harcèlement m.

hassock, n. agenouilloir m.

haste, n. hâte f.

hasten, vb. hâter, tr.

hastily, adv. à la hâte.

hasty, adj. précipité.

hat, n. chapeau m.

hatch, vb. (hen) couver; (egg) éclore.

hatchery, n. établissement de pisiculture m.

hatchet, n. hachette f.

hate, vb. haïr.

hateful, adj. odieux.

hatred, n. haine f.

haughtiness, n. arrogance f., hauteur f.

haughty, adj. hautain.

haul, vb. traîner.

haunch, n. hanche f., cuissot m.

haunt, vb. hanter.

have, vb. avoir; (h. to, necessity) devoir.

haven, n. havre m.; (refuge) asile m.

haven't, vb. n'ont pas.

havoc, n. ravage m.

hawk, n. faucon m.

hawker, n. colporteur m., marchand ambulant m.

hawser, n. haussière f., amarre f.

hawthorn, n. aubépine f.

hay, n. foin m.

hay fever, n. fièvre des foins f.

hayfield, n. champs de foin m.

hayloft, n. fenil m., grenier m.

haystack, n. meule de foin f.

hazard, 1. n. hasard m. **2.** vb. hasarder, risquer.

hazardous, adj. hasardeux.

haze, n. brume (f.) légère.

hazel, n. noisetier m.; couleur de noisette f.

hazy, adj. brumeux, nébuleux.

he, pron. il; (alone, stressed, with another subject) lui.

head, n. tête f.

headache, n. mal (m.) de tête.

headband, n. bandeau m.

headfirst, adv. la tête la première.

headgear, n. garniture de tête f., coiffure f.

head-hunting, n. chasse aux têtes f.

heading, n. rubrique f.

headlight, n. phare m., projecteur m.

headlong, adv. la tête la première.

headman, n. chef m.

headmaster, n. directeur m., principal m.

head-on, adj. and adv. de front.

headquarters, n. (mil.) quartier (m.) général; (comm.) bureau (m.) principal.

headstone, n. pierre angulaire f.

headstrong, adj. volontiare, têtu, entêté.

headwaters, n. cours supérieur (d'une rivière) m., eau d'amont f.

headway, n. progrès m.

headwork, n. travail de tête m., travail intellectuel m.

heady, adj. impétueux, capiteux.

heal, vb. guérir.

health, n. santé f.

healthful, adj. salubre.

healthy, adj. sain.

heap, 1. n. tas m. **2.** vb. entasser.

hear, vb. entendre.

hearing, n. audition f.; ouïe f.

hearsay, n. ouï-dire m.

hearse, n. catafalque m., corbillard m.

heart, n. cœur m.

heartache, n. chagrin m., peine de cœur f.

heartbreak, n. déchirement de cœur m.

heartbroken, adj. avec le cœur brisé, navré.

heartburn, *n.* brûlures d'estomac *f.pl.,* aigreur *f.*

heartfelt, *adj.* sincère, qui va au cœur.

hearth, *n.* foyer *m.,* âtre *m.*

heartless, *adj.* sans cœur, insensible, sans pitié.

heart-rending, *adj.* à fendre le cœur, navrant, déchirant.

heartsick, *adj.* écœuré.

heart-stricken, *adj.* frappé au cœur, navré.

heart-to-heart, *adj.* à cœur ouvert, intime.

hearty, *adj.* cordial.

heat, 1. *n.* chaleur *f.* **2.** *vb.* chauffer.

heated, *adj.* chaud, chauffé, animé.

heath, *n.* bruyère *f.,* lande *f.*

heathen, *adj. and n.* païen *m.,* païenne *f.*

heather, *n.* bruyère *f.,* brande *f.*

heatstroke, *n.* coup de chaleur *m.*

heat wave, *n.* vague de chaleur *f.,* onde calorifique *f.*

heave, *vb.* (lift) lever; (utter) pousser; (rise) se soulever, *intr.*

heaven, *n.* ciel *m.,* *pl.* cieux.

heavenly, *adj.* céleste.

heavy, *adj.* lourd.

heavyweight, *n.* poids lourd *m.*

Hebrew, 1. *n.* (language) hébreu *m.* **2.** *adj.* hébreu.

heckle, *vb.* poser des questions embarrassantes.

hectare, *n.* hectare *m.*

hectic, *adj.* (restless) agité.

hectograph, 1. *n.* hectographe *m.,* autocopiste *m.* **2.** *vb.* hectographier, autocopier.

hedge, *n.* haie *f.*

hedgehog, *n.* hérisson *m.*

hedgehop, *vb.* voler à ras de terre.

hedgerow, *n.* bordure de haies *f.*

hedonism, *n.* hédonisme *m.*

heed, 1. *n.* attention *f.* **2.** *vb.* faire attention à.

heedless, *adj.* étourdi, imprudent, insouciant.

heel, *n.* talon *m.*

hefty, *adj.* fort, solide, costaud.

hegemony, *n.* hégémonie *f.*

heifer, *n.* génisse *f.*

height, *n.* hauteur *f.*

heighten, *vb.* rehausser, augmenter.

heinous, *adj.* odieux, atroce, abominable.

heir, *n.* héritier *m.*

heir apparent, *n.* héritier présomptif *m.*

heirloom, *n.* meuble *m.* (or bijou *m.*) de famille.

heir presumptive, *n.* héritier présomptif *m.*

helicopter, *n.* hélicoptère *m.*

heliocentric, *adj.* héliocentrique.

heliograph, *n.* héliographe *m.*

heliotrope, *n.* héliotrope *m.*

helium, *n.* hélium *m.*

hell, *n.* enfer *m.*

Hellenism, *n.* hellénisme *m.*

hellish, *adj.* infernal, diabolique.

hello, *interj.* (telephone) allô.

helm, *n.* barre (*f.*) du gouvernail.

helmet, *n.* casque *m.*

helmsman, *n.* homme de barre *m.,* timonier *m.*

help, 1. *n.* aide *f.* **2.** *vb.* aider; (at table) servir. **3.** *interj.* au secours!

helper, *n.* aide *m.f.*

helpful, *adj.* (person) serviable; (thing) utile.

helpfulness, *n.* serviabilité *f.,* utilité *f.*

helping, 1. *n.* portion *f.* **2.** *adj.* secourable.

helpless, *adj.* (forlorn) délaissé; (powerless) impuissant.

helter-skelter, *adv.* pêle-mêle, en désordre.

hem, 1. *n.* ourlet *m.* **2.** *vb.* ourler.

hematite, *n.* hématite *f.*

hemisphere, *n.* hémisphère *m.*

hemlock, *n.* ciguë *f.*

hemoglobin, *n.* hémoglobine *f.*

hemophilia, *n.* hémophilie *f.*

hemorrhage, *n.* hémorragie *f.*

hemorrhoid, *n.* hémorroïde *f.*

hemp, *n.* chanvre *m.*

hemstitch, 1. *n.* ourlet *m.* **2.** *vb.* ourler.

hen, *n.* poule *f.*

hence, *adv.* (time, place) d'ici; (therefore) de là.

henceforth, *adv.* désormais.

henchman, *n.* homme de confiance *m.,* acolyte *m.,* satellite *m.*

henequen, *n.* henequen *m.*

henna, 1. *n.* henné *m.* **2.** *vb.* teindre au henné.

henpeck, vb. mener par le bout du nez.

hepatic, adj. hépatique.

hepatica, n. hépatique f.

her, 1. adj. son m., sa f., ses pl. **2.** pron. (direct) la; (indirect) lui; (alone, stressed, with prep.) elle.

herald, n. héraut m.

heraldic, adj. héraldique.

heraldry, n. l'héraldique f.

herb, n. herbe f.

herbaceous, adj. herbacé.

herbarium, n. herbier m.

herculean, adj. herculéen.

herd, n. troupeau m.

here, adv. ici; **(h. is)** voici.

hereabout, adv. par ici, près d'ici.

hereafter, adv. dorénavant.

hereby, adv. par ceci, par ce moyen, par là.

hereditary, adj. héréditaire.

heredity, n. hérédité f.

herein, adv. ici; **(h. enclosed)** ci-enclus.

heresy, n. hérésie f.

heretic, n. hérétique m.f.

heretical, adj. hérétique.

hereto, adv. ci-joint.

heretofore, adv. jusqu'ici.

herewith, adv. avec ceci, ci-joint.

heritage, n. héritage m., patrimoine m.

hermetic, adj. hermétique.

hermit, n. ermite m.

hermitage, n. ermitage m.

hernia, n. hernie f.

hero, n. héros m.

heroic, adj. héroïque.

heroically, adv. héroïquement.

heroin, n. héroïne f.

heroine, n. héroïne f.

heroism, n. héroïsme m.

heron, n. héron m.

herpes, n. herpès m.

herring, n. hareng m.

herringbone, n. arête de hareng f.

hers, pron. le sien m., la sienne f.

herself, pron. elle-même; (reflexive) se.

hertz, n. hertz m.

hesitancy, n. hésitation f., incertitude f.

hesitant, adj. hésitant, irrésolu.

hesitate, vb. hésiter.

hesitation, n. hésitation f.

heterodox, adj. hétérodoxe.

heterodoxy, n. hétérodoxie f.

heterogeneous, adj. hétérogène.

heterosexual, adj. hétérosexuel.

hew, vb. couper, tailler.

hexagon, n. hexagone m.

heyday, n. apogée m., beaux jours m.pl.

hiatus, n. lacune f.

hibernate, vb. hiberner, hiverner.

hibernation, n. hibernation f.

hibiscus, n. hibiscus m.

hiccup, 1. n. hoquet m. **2.** vb. hoqueter.

hickory, n. noyer (blanc) d'Amérique m.

hide, vb. cacher, tr.

hide, n. peau f.

hideous, adj. hideux.

hide-out, n. cachette f., lieu de retraite m.

hierarchical, adj. hiérarchique.

hierarchy, n. hiérarchie f.

hieroglyphic, adj. hiéroglyphique.

high, adj. haut.

highbrow, n. intellectuel m.

high fidelity, n. haute fidélité f.

high-handed, adj. arbitraire, tyrannique.

high-hat, vb. traiter de haut en bas.

highland, n. haute terre f.

highlight, 1. n. clou m. **2.** vb. mettre en relief.

highly, adv. extrêmement.

high-minded, adj. à l'esprit élevé, généreux.

Highness, n. (title) Altesse f.

high school, n. lycée m.

high seas, n. haute mer f.

high-strung, adj. nerveux, impressionable.

high tide, n. marée haute f.

highway, n. grande route f.

hijacker, n. pirate de l'air m.

hike, n. excursion (f.) à pied.

hilarious, adj. hilare.

hilariousness, n. hilarité f.

hilarity, n. hilarité f.

hill, n. colline f.

hilt, n. poignée f., garde f.

him, pron. (direct) le; (indirect) lui; (alone, stressed, with prep.) lui.

himself, pron. lui-même; (reflexive) se.

hinder, vb. (impede) gêner; (prevent) empêcher.

hindmost, adj. dernier.

hindquarter, *n.* arrière-main *m.*, arrière-train *m.*
hindrance, *n.* empêchement *m.*, obstacle *m.*, entrave *f.*
Hindu, 1. *n.* Hindou *m.* **2.** *adj.* hindou.
hinge, *n.* gond *m.*
hint, 1. *n.* allusion *f.* **2.** *vb.* insinuer.
hinterland, *n.* hinterland *m.*, arrière-pays *m.*
hip, *n.* hanche *f.*
hippodrome, *n.* hippodrome *m.*
hippopotamus, *n.* hippopotame *m.*
hire, *vb.* louer; (servant) engager.
hireling, *n.* mercenaire *m.*, stipendié *m.*
hirsute, *adj.* hirsute, velu.
his, 1. *adj.* son *m.*, sa *f.*, ses *pl.* **2.** *pron.* le sien *m.*, la sienne *f.*
Hispanic, *adj.* hispanique.
hiss, *vb.* siffler.
historian, *n.* historien *m.*
historic, *adj.* historique.
historical, *adj.* historique.
history, *n.* histoire *f.*
histrionic, *adj.* histrionique, théâtral.
histrionics, *n.* parade d'émotions *f.*, démonstration peu sincère *f.*
hit, 1. *n.* coup *m.*; (success) succès *m.* **2.** *vb.* frapper.
hitch, 1. *n.* (obstacle) anicroche *f.* **2.** *vb.* (fasten) accrocher, *tr.*
hither, 1. *adv.* ici. **2.** *adj.* le plus rapproché.
hitherto, *adj.* jusqu'ici.
hive, *n.* ruche *f.*
hives, *n.* éruption *f.*, varicelle pustuleuse *f.*, urticaire *f.*
hoard, 1. *n.* amas *m.* **2.** *vb.* amasser; (money) thésauriser.
hoarse, *adj.* enroué.
hoax, *n.* mystification *f.*
hobble, *vb.* boitiller, clopiner, entraver.
hobbyhorse, *n.* dada *m.*, cheval de bois *m.*
hobgoblin, *n.* lutin *m.*, esprit follet *m.*
hobnail, 1. *n.* caboche *f.*, clou à ferrer *m.* **2.** *vb.* ferrer.
hobnob, *vb.* boire avec, fréquenter.
hobo, *n.* vagabond *m.*, clochard *m.*, ouvrier ambulant *m.*

hock, *n.* jarret *m.*
hockey, *n.* hockey *m.*
hocuspocus, *n.* passe-passe *m.*
hod, *n.* auge *f.*
hodgepodge, *n.* mélange confus *m.*
hoe, 1. *n.* houe *f.* **2.** *vb.* houer.
hog, *n.* porc *m.*
hogshead, *n.* tonneau *m.*, barrique *f.*
hog-tie, *vb.* lier les quatre pattes.
hoist, 1. *n.* treuil *m.*, grue *f.* **2.** *vb.* hisser.
hold, 1. *n.* prise *f.*; (ship) cale *f.* **2.** *vb.* tenir; (contain) contenir; (**h. back**) retenir; (**h. up**) arrêter, détenir, entraver.
holdup, *n.* arrêt *m.*, suspension *f.*; coup à main armée *m.*
hole, *n.* trou *m.*
holiday, *n.* jour (*m.*) de fête; fête *f.*; (**h.s**) vacances *f.pl.*
holiness, *n.* sainteté *f.*
Holland, *n.* les Pays-Bas *m.pl.*, Hollande *f.*
hollow, *adj.* and *n.* creux *m.*
holly, *n.* houx *m.*
hollyhock, *n.* passe-rose *f.*, rose-trémière *f.*
holocaust, *n.* holocauste *m.*
hologram, *n.* hologramme *m.*
holography, *n.* holographie *f.*
holster, *n.* étui *m.*
holy, *adj.* saint.
Holy See, *n.* Saint-Siège *m.*
Holy Spirit, *n.* Saint-Esprit *m.*
Holy Week, *n.* semaine sainte *f.*
homage, *n.* hommage *m.*
home, *n.* maison *f;* (hearth) foyer (*m.*) domestique; (**at h.**) à la maison, chez soi.
homeland, *n.* patrie *f.*
homeless, *adj.* sans foyer, sans asile, sans abri.
homelike, *adj.* qui ressemble au foyer domestique.
homely, *adj.* laid.
homemade, *adj.* fait à la maison.
home rule, *n.* autonomie *f.*
homesick, *adj.* nostalgique.
homespun, *adj.* (étoffe) de fabrication domestique, fait à la maison, simple.
homestead, *n.* ferme *f.*, bien de famille *m.*
homeward, *adj.* de retour.

homework, *n.* travail fait à la maison *m.*, devoirs *m.pl.*

homicide, *n.* homicide *m.*

homily, *n.* homélie *f.*

homing pigeon, *n.* pigeon messager *m.*

hominy, *n.* bouillie de farine de maïs *f.*, semoule de maïs *f.*

homogeneous, *adj.* homogène.

homonym, *n.* homonyme *m.*

homosexual, *n.* and *adj.* homosexuel *f.*, homosexuelle *f.*

Honduras, *n.* Honduras *m.*

hone, *vb.* aiguiser, affiler.

honest, *adj.* honnête.

honestly, *adv.* honnêtement, de bonne foi.

honesty, *n.* honnêteté *f.*

honey, *n.* miel *m.*

honeybee, *n.* abeille domestique *f.*

honeycomb, 1. *n.* rayon de miel *m.* **2.** *vb.* cribler, affouiller.

honeydew melon, *n.* melon *m.*

honeymoon, *n.* lune (*f.*) de miel.

honeysuckle, *n.* chèvre-feuille *m.*

honor, 1. *n.* honneur *m.* **2.** *vb.* honorer.

honorable, *adj.* honorable.

honorary, *adj.* honoraire.

hood, *n.* capuchon *m.*; (vehicle) capote *f.*

hoodlum, *n.* voyou *m.*

hoodwink, *vb.* tromper, bander les yeux à.

hoof, *n.* sabot *m.*

hook, 1. *n.* croc *m.*; (fishing) hameçon *m.* **2.** *vb.* accrocher.

hooked, *adj.* crochu, recourbé.

hooked rug, *n.* tapis à points noués simples *m.*

hookworm, *n.* ankylostome *m.*

hoop, *n.* cercle *m.*

hoop skirt, *n.* jupe à paniers *f.*, vertugadin *m.*

hoot, 1. *n.* ululation *f.*, hululement *m.*, huée *f.* **2.** *vb.* huluter, huer.

hop, 1. *n.* (plant) houblon *m.* **2.** *vb.* sautiller.

hope, 1. *n.* espérance *f.*, espoir *m.* **2.** *vb.* espérer.

hopeful, *adj.* plein d'espoir.

hopeless, *adj.* désespéré.

hopelessness, *n.* désespoir *m.*, état désespéré *m.*

hopscotch, *n.* marelle *f.*

horde, *n.* horde *f.*

horizon, *n.* horizon *m.*

horizontal, *adj.* horizontal.

hormone, *n.* hormone *f.*

horn, *n.* corne *f.*; (music) cor *m.*

hornet, *n.* frelon *m.*, guêpe-frelon *f.*

horny, *adj.* corné, calleux.

horoscope, *n.* horoscope *m.*

horrendous, *adj.* horrible, horripilant.

horrible, *adj.* horrible.

horrid, *adj.* affreux.

horrify, *vb.* horrifier.

horror, *n.* horreur *f.*

horse, *n.* cheval *m.*

horseback, *n.* **(on h.)** à cheval.

horsefly, *n.* taon *m.*

horsehair, *n.* crin *m.*

horseman, *n.* cavalier *m.*

horsemanship, *n.* équitation *f.*, manège *m.*

horseplay, *n.* jeu de mains *m.*, badinerie grossière *f.*

horsepower, *n.* puissance en chevaux *f.*

horseradish, *n.* raifort *m.*

horseshoe, *n.* fer à cheval *m.*

horsewhip, 1. *n.* cravache *f.* **2.** *vb.* cravacher, sangler.

hortatory, *adj.* exhortatif.

horticulture, *n.* horticulture *f.*

hose, *n.* (pipe) tuyau *m.*; (stockings) bas *m.pl.*

hosiery, *n.* bonneterie *f.*

hospitable, *adj.* hospitalier.

hospital, *n.* hôpital *m.*

hospitality, *n.* hospitalité *f.*

hospitalization, *n.* hospitalisation *f.*

hospitalize, *vb.* hospitaliser.

host, *n.* hôte *m.*

hostage, *n.* otage *m.*

hostel, *n.* hôtellerie *f.*, auberge *f.*

hostelry, *n.* hôtellerie *f.*, auberge *f.*

hostess, *n.* hôtesse *f.*

hostile, *adj.* hostile.

hostility, *n.* hostilité *f.*

hot, *adj.* chaud.

hotbed, *n.* couche *f.*, foyer ardent *m.*

hot dog, *n.* saucisse chaude.

hotel, *n.* hôtel *m.*

hot-headed, *adj.* impétueux, exalté, emporté.

hothouse, *n.* serre *f.*

hound, 1. *n.* chien (*m.*) de chasse. **2.** *vb.* poursuivre, pourchasser.

hour, *n.* heure *f.*

hourglass, *n.* sablier *m.*

hourly, *adv.* à chaque heure, à l'heure.

house, *n.* maison *f.*; (legislature) chambre *f.*

housefly, *n.* mouche domestique *f.*

household, *n.* (family) famille *f.*; (servants) domestiques *m.pl.*

housekeeper, *n.* gouvernante *f.*

housekeeping, *n.* ménage *m.*, économie domestique *f.*

housemaid, *n.* fille de service *f.*, bonne *f.*, femme de chambre *f.*

housewife, *n.* ménagère *f.*

housework, *n.* ménage *m.*

hovel, *n.* taudis *m.*, bicoque *f.*

hover, *vb.* planer.

hovercraft, *n.* aéroglisseur *m.*

how, *adv.* comment; (**h. much**) combien (de); (in exclamation) comme.

however, *adv.* (in whatever way) de quelque manière que; (with adj.) si . . . que; (nevertheless) cependant.

howitzer, *n.* obusier *m.*

howl, *vb.* hurler.

hub, *n.* moyeu *m.*, centre *m.*

hubbub, *n.* vacarme *m.*, tintamarre *m.*

huckleberry, *n.* airelle *f.*

huddle, 1. *n.* tas confus *m.*, fouillis *m.* **2.** *vb.* entasser.

hue, *n.* couleur *f.*

huff, 1. *n.* emportement *m.*, accès de colère *m.* **2.** *vb.* gonfler, enfler.

hug, 1. *n.* étreinte *f.* **2.** *vb.* serrer dans ses bras.

huge, *adj.* énorme.

hulk, *n.* carcasse *f.*, ponton *m.*

hull, *n.* coque *f.*, corps *m.*

hullabaloo, *n.* vacarme *m.*

hum, *vb.* (insect) bourdonner; (sing) fredonner.

human, humane, *adj.* humain.

humanism, *n.* humanisme *m.*

humanitarian, *adj.* humanitaire.

humanities, *n.* humanités *f.pl.*

humanity, *n.* humanité *f.*

humanly, *adv.* humainement.

humble, *adj.* humble.

humbug, *n.* blague *f.*, tromperie *f.*, fumisterie *f.*

humdrum, *adj.* monotone, assommant.

humid, *adj.* humide.

humidify, *vb.* humidifier.

humidor, *n.* boîte à cigares *f.*

humiliate, *adj.* humilier.

humiliation, *n.* humiliation *f.*

humility, *n.* humilité *f.*

humor, *n.* (wit) humour *m.*; (medical, mood) humeur *f.*

humorous, *adj.* (witty) humoristique; (funny) drôle.

hump, *n.* bosse *f.*

humpback, *n.* bossu *m.*

humus, *n.* humus *m.*, terreau *m.*

hunch, 1. *n.* bosse *f.*; pressentiment *m.* **2.** *vb.* arrondir, voûter.

hunchback, *n.* bossu *m.*

hundred, *adj. and n.* cent *m.*

hundredth, *n. and adj.* centième *m.*

Hungarian, 1. *n.* (person) Hongrois *m.*; (language) hongrois *m.* **2.** *adj.* hongrois.

Hungary, *n.* Hongrie *f.*

hunger, *n.* faim *f.*

hungry, *adj.* affamé; (**be h.**) avoir faim.

hunk, *n.* gros morceau *m.*

hunt, *vb.* chasser.

hunter, *n.* chasseur *m.*

hunting, *n.* chasse *f.*

huntress, *n.* chasseuse *f.*, chasseresse *f.*

hurdle, *n.* claie *f.*

hurl, *vb.* lancer.

hurricane, *n.* ouragan *m.*

hurry, 1. *n.* hâte *f.*; (**in a h.**) à la hâte. **2.** *vb.* presser, *tr.*; se presser, *intr.*

hurt, *vb.* faire mal (à).

hurtful, *adj.* nuisible, pernicieux, préjudiciable.

hurtle, *vb.* se choquer, se heurter.

husband, *n.* mari *m.*

husbandry, *n.* agriculture *f.*, économie *f.*

hush, 1. *interj.* chut! paix! **2.** *vb.* taire, imposer silence à.

husk, 1. *n.* cosse *f.*, gousse *f.* **2.** *vb.* écosser, éplucher.

husky, *adj.* cossu; rauque, enroué.

hustle, *vb.* bousculer, se presser.

hut, *n.* cabane *f.*

hutch, *n.* huche *f.*, clapier *m.*

hyacinth, *n.* jacinthe *f.*

hybrid, *n.* hybride *m.*

hydrangea, *n.* hortensia *f.*

hydrant, *n.* prise d'eau *f.*, bouche d'incendie *f.*

hydraulic, *adj.* hydraulique.

hydrochloric acid, *n.* acide chlorhydrique *m.*

hydroelectric, *adj.* hydroélectrique.

hydrogen, *n.* hydrogène *m.*

hydrophobia, *n.* hydrophobie *f.*

hydroplane, *n.* hydroplane *m.*

hydrotherapy, *n.* hydrothérapie *f.*

hyena, *n.* hyène *f.*

hygiene, *n.* hygiène *f.*

hygienic, *adj.* hygiénique.

hymn, *n.* (song, anthem) hymne *m.*; (church) hymne *f.*

hymnal, *n.* hymnaire *m.*, receuil d'hymnes *m.*

hyperacidity, *n.* hyperacidité *f.*

hyperbole, *n.* hyperbole *f.*

hypercritical, *adj.* hypercritique.

hypersensitive, *adj.* hypersensible.

hypertension, *n.* hypertension *f.*

hyphen, *n.* trait d'union *m.*

hyphenate, *vb.* mettre un trait d'union à.

hypnosis, *n.* hypnose *f.*

hypnotic, *adj.* hypnotique.

hypnotism, *n.* hypnotisme *m.*

hypnotize, *vb.* hypnotiser.

hypochondria, *n.* hypocondrie *f.*

hypochondriac, *n. and adj.* hypocondriaque *m.*

hypocrisy, *n.* hypocrisie *f.*

hypocrite, *n.* hypocrite *m.f.*

hypocritical, *adj.* hypocrite.

hypodermic, *adj.* hypodermique.

hypotenuse, *n.* hypoténuse *f.*

hypothesis, *n.* hypothèse *f.*

hypothetical, *adj.* hypothétique.

hysterectomy, *n.* hystérectomie *f.*

hysteria, *n.* hystérie *f.*

hysterical, *adj.* hystérique.

I

I, *pron.* je; (alone, stressed, with another subject) moi.

iambic, *adj.* iambique.

Iberia, *n.* Ibérie *f.*

ice, *n.* glace *f.*

iceberg, *n.* iceberg *m.*, gros bloc de glace *m.*

ice-box, *n.* glacière *f.*

ice cream, *n.* glace *f.*

ice skate, 1. *n.* patin à glace *m.* **2.** *vb.* patiner.

ichthyology, *n.* ichtyologie *f.*

icing, *n.* glacé *m.*

icon, *n.* icone *f.*

icy, *adj.* glacial.

idea, *n.* idée *f.*

ideal, *adj. and n.* idéal *m.*

idealism, *n.* idéalisme *m.*

idealist, *n.* idéaliste *m.f.*

idealistic, *adj.* idéaliste.

idealize, *vb.* idéaliser.

ideally, *adv.* idéalement, en idée.

identical (with), *adj.* identique (à).

identifiable, *adj.* identifiable.

identification, *n.* identification *f.*

identify, *vb.* identifier.

identity, *n.* identité *f.*

ideology, *n.* idéologie *f.*

idiocy, *n.* idiotie *f.*, idiotisme *m.*

idiom, *n.* (language) idiome *m.*; (peculiar expression) idiotisme *m.*

idiot, *adj. and n.* idiot *m.*

idiotic, *adj.* idiot.

idle, *adj.* (unoccupied) désœuvré; (lazy) paresseux; (futile) vain.

idleness, *n.* oisiveté *f.*

idol, *n.* idole *f.*

idolatry, *n.* idolâtrie *f.*

idolize, *vb.* idolâtrer.

idyl, *n.* idylle *f.*

idyllic, *adj.* idyllique.

if, *conj.* si.

ignite, *vb.* feindre d'ignorer.

ignition, *n.* ignition *f.*, allumage *m.*

ignoble, *adj.* ignoble; (low birth) plébéien.

ignominious, *adj.* ignominieux.

ignoramus, *n.* ignorant *m.*, ignare *m.*

ignorance, *n.* ignorance *f.*

ignorant, *adj.* ignorant; **(be i. of)** ignorer.

ignore, *vb.* feindre d'ignorer.

ill, 1. *n.* mal *m.* **2.** *adj.* (sick) malade; (bad) mauvais. **3.** *adv.* mal.

illegal, *adj.* illégal.

illegible, *adj.* illisible.

illegibly, *adv.* illisiblement.

illegitimacy, *n.* illégitimité *f.*

illegitimate, *adj.* illégitime.

illicit, *adj.* illicite.

illiteracy, *n.* analphabétisme *m.*

illiterate, *adj.* illettré.

illness, *n.* maladie *f.*

illogical, *adj.* illogique.

illuminate, *vb.* illuminer.

illumination, *n.* illumination *f.,* enluminure *f.*

illusion, *n.* illusion *f.*

illusive, *adj.* illusoire.

illustrate, *vb.* illustrer.

illustration, *n.* illustration *f.;* (example) exemple *m.*

illustrative, *adj.* explicatif, qui éclaircit.

illustrious, *adj.* illustre.

ill will, *adj.* mauvais vouloir *m.,* malveillance *f.*

image, *n.* image *f.*

imagery, *n.* images *f.pl,* langage figuré *m.*

imaginable, *adj.* imaginable.

imaginary, *adj.* imaginaire.

imagination, *n.* imagination *f.*

imaginative, *adj.* imaginatif.

imagine, *vb.* imaginer, *tr.*

imam, *n.* imam *m.*

imbecile, *n.* imbécile *m.*

imitate, *vb.* imiter.

imitation, *n.* imitation *f.*

imitative, *adj.* imitatif.

immaculate, *adj.* immaculé, sans tache.

immanent, *adj.* immanent.

immaterial, *adj.* immatériel, incorporel, sans conséquence.

immature, *adj.* pas mûr, prématuré.

immediate, *adj.* immédiat.

immediately, *adv.* immédiatement, tout de suite.

immense, *adj.* immense.

immerse, *vb.* immerger, plonger.

immigrant, *n.* immigrant *m.,* immigré *m.*

immigrate, *vb.* immigrer.

imminent, *adj.* imminent.

immobile, *adj.* fixe, immobile.

immobilize, *vb.* immobiliser.

immoderate, *adj.* immodéré, intempéré, outré.

immodest, *adj.* immodeste, impudique, présomptueux.

immoral, *adj.* immoral.

immorality, *n.* immoralité *f.*

immorally, *adv.* immoralement.

immortal, *adj. and n.* immortel *m.*

immortality, *n.* immortalité *f.*

immortalize, *vb.* immortaliser.

immovable, *adj.* fixe, immuable, inébranlable.

immunity, *n.* exemption *f.,* immunité *f.*

immunize, *vb.* immuniser.

immutable, *adj.* immuable, inaltérable.

impact, *n.* choc *m.,* impact *m.*

impair, *vb.* affaiblir, altérer, compromettre.

impale, *vb.* empaler.

impart, *vb.* donner, communiquer, transmettre.

impartial, *adj.* impartial.

impatience, *n.* impatience *f.*

impatient, *adj.* impatient.

impeach, *vb.* attaquer, accuser, récuser.

impede, *vb.* entraver, empêcher.

impediment, *n.* entrave *f.,* obstacle *m.,* empêchement *f.*

impel, *vb.* pousser, forcer.

impenetrable, *adj.* impénétrable.

impenitent, *adj.* impénitent.

imperative, 1. *n. (gramm.)* impératif *m.* **2.** *adj.* impératif *(gramm.);* urgent, impérieux.

imperceptible, *adj.* imperceptible.

imperfect, *adj. and n.* imparfait *m.*

imperfection, *n.* imperfection *f.*

imperial, *adj.* impérial.

imperialism, *n.* impérialisme *m.*

imperil, *vb.* mettre en péril, exposer au danger.

imperious, *adj.* impérieux, arrogant.

impersonate, *vb.* personnifier, représenter.

impersonation, *n.* personnification *f.,* incarnation *f.*

impersonator, *n.* personnificateur *m.*

impertinence, *n.* impertinence *f.*

impervious, *adj.* impénétrable, imperméable.

impetuous, *adj.* impétueux.

impetus, *n.* élan *m.,* vitesse acquise *f.*

impinge, *vb.* se heurter à, empiéter sur.

implacable, *adj.* implacable.

implant, *vb.* inculquer, implanter.

implement, *n.* outil *m.*

implicate, vb. impliquer, entre-mêler.

implication, n. implication f.

implicit, adj. implicite.

implied, adj. implicite, tacite.

implore, vb. implorer.

imply, vb. impliquer.

impolite, adj. impoli.

imponderable, adj. impondérable.

import, 1. n. article (m.) d'importation; importation f. 2. vb. importer.

importance, n. importance f.

important, adj. important.

importation, n. importation f.

importune, vb. importuner.

impose (on), vb. imposer (à).

imposition, n. imposition f.

impossibility, n. impossibilité f.

impossible, adj. impossible.

impotence, n. impuissance f.

impotent, adj. impuissant.

impoverish, vb. appauvrir.

impregnable, adj. imprenable, inexpugnable.

impregnate, vb. imprégner, féconder.

impresario, n. imprésario m.

impress, vb. (imprint) imprimer; (affect) faire une impression à.

impression, n. impression f.

impressive, adj. impressionnant.

imprison, vb. emprisonner.

imprisonment, n. emprisonnement m.

improbable, adj. improbable.

impromptu, adv., adj. and n. impromptu m.

improper, adj. (inaccurate) impropre; (unbecoming) malséant.

improve, vb. améliorer, tr.

improvement, n. amélioration f.

improvise, vb. improviser.

impudent, adj. insolent, effronté, impertinent.

impugn, vb. attaquer, contester, impugner.

impulse, n. impulsion f.

impulsion, n. impulsion f.

impulsive, adj. impulsif.

impunity, n. impunité f.

impure, adj. impur.

impurity, n. impureté f.

impute, vb. imputer.

in, prep. en; (with art. or adj.) dans; (town) à.

inadvertent, adj. inattentif, négligent, involontaire.

inalienable, adj. inaliénable.

inane, adj. inepte, niais, bête.

inaugural, adj. inaugural.

inaugurate, vb. inaugurer.

inauguration, n. inauguration f.

Inca, n. Inca m.

incandescence, n. incandescence f.

incandescent, adj. incandescent.

incantation, n. incantation f., conjuration f.

incapacitate, vb. rendre incapable, priver de capacité légale.

incarcerate, vb. incarcérer, emprisonner.

incarnate, 1. vb. incarner. 2. adj. incarné, fait chair.

incarnation, n. incarnation f.

incendiary, 1. n. incendiaire m. 2. adj. incendiaire, séditieux.

incense, n. encens m.

incentive, n. stimulant m., aiguillon m.

inception, n. commencement m., début m.

incessant, adj. incessant, continuel.

incest, n. inceste m.

inch, n. pouce m.

incidence, n. incidence f.

incident, n. incident m.

incidental, adj. fortuit.

incidentally, adv. incidemment, en passant.

incinerator, n. incinérateur m.

incipient, adj. naissant, qui commence.

incision, n. incision f., entaille f.

incisive, adj. incisif, tranchant.

incisor, n. incisive f.

incite, vb. inciter, instiguer.

inclination, n. inclinaison f., penchant m.

incline, vb. incliner.

inclose, see enclose.

include, vb. comprendre.

inclusive, adj. inclusif.

incognito, adj. and adv. incognito.

income, n. revenu m.

incomparable, adj. incomparable.

inconvenience, 1. n. inconvénient m. 2. vb. incommoder.

inconvenient, adj. incommode.

incorporate, vb. incorporer.

incorrigible, adj. incorrigible.
increase, 1. n. augmentation f. **2.** vb. augmenter.
incredible, adj. incroyable.
incredulity, n. incrédulité f.
incredulous, adj. incrédule.
increment, n. augmentation f., accroissement m.
incriminate, vb. incriminer.
incrimination, n. incrimination f.
incrust, vb. incruster.
incubator, n. incubateur m.
inculcate, vb. inculquer.
incumbency, n. période d'exercice f., charge f.
incumbent, 1. n. titulaire m., bénéficiare m. **2.** adj. couché, posé, appuyé.
incur, vb. encourir.
incurable, adj. incurable.
indebted, adj. endetté.
indeed, adv. en effet.
indefatigable, adj. infatigable, lassable.
indefinite, adj. indéfini.
indefinitely, adv. indéfiniment.
indelible, adj. indélébile, ineffaçable.
indemnify, vb. garantir, indemniser, dédommager.
indemnity, n. garantie f., indemnité f., dédommagement m.
indent, vb. denteler, découper, entailler.
indentation, n. découpage m., renfoncement m., entendement m.
independence, n. indépendance f.
independent, adj. indépendant.
in-depth, adj. profond.
index, n. index m.
India, n. Inde f.
Indian, 1. n. Indien m. **2.** adj. indien.
indicate, vb. indiquer.
indication, n. indication f.
indicative, adj. and n. indicatif m.
indicator, n. indicateur m.
indict, vb. accuser, inculper.
indictment, n. accusation f., inculpation f., réquisitoire m.
indifference, n. indifférence f.
indifferent, adj. indifférent.
indigenous, adj. indigène.
indigent, adj. indigent, pauvre.
indigestion, n. dyspepsie f., indigestion f.

indignant, adj. indigné.
indignation, n. indignation f.
indignity, n. indignité f., affront m.
indirect, adj. indirect.
indiscreet, adj. indiscret.
indiscretion, n. imprudence f.
indiscriminate, adj. aveugle, qui ne fait pas de distinction.
indispensable, adj. indispensable.
indisposed, adj. peu enclin, peu disposé, indisposé, souffrant.
individual, 1. n. individu m. **2.** adj. individuel.
individuality, n. individualité f.
individually, adv. individuellement.
indivisible, adj. indivisible.
indoctrinate, vb. endoctriner, instruire.
indolent, adj. indolent, paresseux.
Indonesia, n. Indonésie f.
indoor, adj. d'intérieur.
indoors, adv. à la maison.
indorse, vb. endosser, appuyer, sanctionner.
induce, vb. (persuade) persuader; (produce) produire.
induct, vb. installer, conduire.
induction, n. induction f.; installation f.
inductive, adj. inductif.
indulge, vb. contenter, favoriser.
indulgence, n. indulgence f.
indulgent, adj. indulgent.
industrial, adj. industriel.
industrialist, n. industriel m.
industrious, adj. travailleur.
industry, n. industrie f.; (diligence) assiduité f.
ineligible, adj. inéligible.
inept, adj. inepte, mal à propos.
inert, adj. inerte, apathique.
inertia, n. inertie f.
inevitable, adj. inévitable.
inexplicable, adj. inexplicable.
infallible, adj. infaillible.
infamous, adj. infâme.
infamy, n. infamie f.
infancy, n. (première) enfance f.
infant, n. enfant m.f.
infantile, adj. enfantin, infantile.
infantryman, n. soldat d'infanterie m., fantassin m.
infatuated, adj. infauté, entiché.
infect, vb. infecter.

infection, n. infection f.

infectious, adj. infectieux, infect, contagieux.

infer, vb. déduire.

inference, n. inférence f.

inferior, adj. and n. inférieur m.

inferiority complex, n. complexe d'infériorité f.

infernal, adj. infernal.

inferno, n. enfer m.

infest, vb. infester.

infidel, n. infidèle m., incroyant m.

infidelity, n. infidélité f.

infiltrate, vb. infiltrer.

infinite, adj. and n. infini m.

infinitesimal, adj. infinitésimal.

infinitive, n. infinitif m.

infinity, n. infinité f.

infirm, adj. infirme, faible, maladif.

infirmary, n. infirmerie f.

infirmity, n. infirmité f.

inflame, vb. enflammer, tr.

inflammable, adj. inflammable.

inflammation, n. inflammation f.

inflammatory, adj. incendiaire, inflammatoire.

inflate, vb. gonfler.

inflation, n. (currency) inflation f.

inflection, n. inflection f.

inflict, vb. (penalty) infliger.

infliction, n. infliction f., châtiment m.

influence, n. influence f.

influential, adj. influent.

influenza, n. grippe f., influenza f.

inform, vb. (tell) informer.

informal, adj. (without formality) sans cérémonie.

information, n. renseignements m.pl.

infringe, vb. enfreindre, violer.

infuriate, vb. rendre furieux.

ingenious, adj. ingénieux.

ingenuity, n. ingéniosité f.

ingredient, n. ingrédient m.

inhabit, vb. habiter.

inhabitant, n. habitant m.

inhale, vb. inhaler, aspirer, humer.

inherent, adj. inhérent.

inherit, vb. hériter.

inheritance, n. héritage m.

inhibit, vb. empêcher; (psychology) inhiber.

inhibition, n. inhibition f., défense expresse f., prohibition f.

inhuman, adj. inhumain.

inimical, adj. ennemi, hostile, défavorable.

inimitable, adj. inimitable.

iniquity, n. iniquité f.

initial, 1. n. initiale f. **2.** adj. initial.

initiate, vb. (begin) commencer; (admit) initier.

initiation, n. commencement m., début m., initiation f.

initiative, n. initiative f.

inject, vb. injecter.

injection, n. injection f.

injunction, n. injonction f., ordre m.

injure, vb. (harm) nuire à; (wound) blesser; (damage) abîmer.

injurious, adj. (harmful) nuisible; (offensive) injurieux.

injury, n. (person) préjudice m.; (body) blessure f.; (thing) dommage m.

injustice, n. injustice f.

ink, n. encre f.

inland, adj. and n. intérieur m.

inlet, n. entrée f., admission f., débouché m.

inmate, n. habitant m., hôte m., pensionnaire m.

inn, n. auberge f.

inner, adj. intérieur.

innocence, n. innocence f.

innocent, adj. innocent.

innocuous, adj. inoffensif.

innovation, n. innovation f.

innuendo, n. (person) insinuation f., allusion malveillante f.

innumerable, adj. innombrable.

inoculate, vb. inoculer.

inoculation, n. inoculation f., vaccination préventive f.

input, n. informations fournies à un informateur f.pl.

inquest, n. enquête f.

inquire (about), vb. se renseigner (sur).

inquiry, n. (investigation) recherche f.; (question) demande f.; (official) enquête f.

inquisition, n. Inquisition f.; enquête f., recherche f.

inquisitive, *adj.* curieux, questionneur, indiscret.

inroad, *n.* incursion *f.,* invasion *f.* empiètement *m.*

insane, *adj.* fou *m.,* folle *f.*

insanity, *n.* folie *f.,* insanité *f.,* démence *f.*

inscribe, *vb.* inscrire, graver.

inscription, *n.* inscription *f.*

insect, *n.* insecte *m.*

insecticide, *n.* insecticide *m.*

inseparable, *adj.* inséparable.

insert, *vb.* insérer.

insertion, *n.* insertion *f.*

inside, 1. *n.* dedans *m.* **2.** *adj.* intérieur. **3.** *prep.* à l'intérieur de. **4.** *adv.* (en) dedans.

insidious, *adj.* insidieux.

insight, *n.* perspicacité *f.,* pénétration *f.*

insignia, *n.* insignes *m.pl.*

insignificance, *n.* insignifiance *f.*

insignificant, *adj.* insignifiant.

insinuate, *vb.* insinuer.

insinuation, *n.* insinuation *f.*

insipid, *adj.* insipide, fade.

insist, *vb.* insister.

insistence, *n.* insistance *f.*

insistent, *adj.* qui insiste, importun.

insolence, *n.* insolence *f.*

insolent, *adj.* insolent.

insomnia, *n.* insomnie *f.*

inspect, *vb.* examiner, inspecter.

inspection, *n.* inspection *f.*

inspector, *n.* inspecteur *m.*

inspiration, *n.* inspiration *f.*

inspire, *vb.* inspirer.

install, *vb.* installer.

installation, *n.* installation *f.,* montage *m.*

installment, *n.* acompte *m.,* versement partiel *m.,* payement à compte *m.*

instance, *n.* exemple *m.*

instant, *n.* instant *m.*

instantaneous, *adj.* instantané.

instantly, *adv.* à l'instant.

instead, *adv.* au lieu de cela.

instead of, *prep.* au lieu de.

instigate, *vb.* instiguer.

instill, *vb.* instiller, faire pénétrer, inculquer.

instinct, *n.* instinct *m.*

instinctive, *adj.* instinctif.

institute, *vb.* instituer.

institution, *n.* institution *f.*

instruct, *vb.* instruire.

instruction, *n.* instruction *f.*

instructive, *adj.* instructif.

instructor, *n.* *(mil.)* instructeur *m.;* (university) chargé *(m.)* de cours.

instrument, *n.* instrument *m.*

instrumental, *adj.* instrumental, contributif (à).

insufferable, *adj.* insupportable, intolérable.

insufficient, *adj.* insuffisant.

insular, *adj.* insulaire.

insulate, *vb.* isoler.

insulation, *n.* isolement *m.*

insulator, *n.* isolant *m.,* isolateur *m.*

insulin, *n.* insuline *f.*

insult, 1. *vb.* insulter. **2.** *n.* insulte *f.*

insuperable, *adj.* insurmontable.

insurance, *n.* assurance *f.*

insure, *vb.* assurer.

insurgent, *adj. and n.* insurgé *m.*

insurrection, *n.* insurrection *f.,* soulèvement *m.*

intact, *adj.* intact.

intangible, *adj.* intangible, impalpable.

integral, *adj.* intégrant.

integrate, *vb.* intégrer, compléter, rendre entier.

integrity, *n.* intégrité *f.*

intellect, *n.* (mind) esprit *m.;* (faculty) intellect *m.*

intellectual, *adj. and n.* intellectuel *m.*

intelligence, *n.* intelligence *f.;* (information) renseignements *m.pl.*

intelligent, *adj.* intelligent.

intelligentsia, *n.* l'intelligence *f.*

intelligible, *adj.* intelligible.

intend, *vb.* avoir l'intention de; (destine for) destiner à.

intense, *adj.* intense.

intensity, *n.* intensité *f.*

intensive, *adj.* intensif.

intent, *adj.* (i. on) (absorbed in) absorbé dans; (determined to) déterminé à.

intention, *n.* intention *f.*

intentional, *adj.* intentionnel, voulu, fait exprès.

intercede, *vb.* intervenir, intercéder.

intercept, *vb.* intercepter, capter.

intercourse, n. commerce m., relations f.pl., rapports m.pl.
interdict, vb. interdire, prohiber.
interest, 1. n. intérêt m. 2. vb. intéresser.
interesting, adj. intéressant.
interface, n. entreface f.
interfere, vb. (person) intervenir (dans); (i. with, hinder) gêner.
interference, n. (person) intervention f.
interim, adv. entre temps, en attendant.
interior, adj. and n. intérieur m.
interject, vb. lancer, émettre.
interjection, n. interjection f.
interlude, n. intermède m., interlude m.
intermarry, vb. se marier.
intermediary, n. intermédiaire m.f.
intermediate, adj. and n. intermédiaire m.f.
interment, n. enterrement m.
intermission, n. interruption f., relâche f.; (theater) entr'acte m.
intermittent, adj. intermittent.
intern, 1. n. interne m. 2. vb. interner.
internal, adj. interne.
international, adj. international.
internationalism, n. internationalisme m.
interne, n. interne m.
interpose, vb. interposer, tr.
interpret, vb. interpréter.
interpretation, n. interprétation f.
interpreter, n. interprète m.f.
interrogate, vb. interroger, questionner.
interrogation, n. interrogation f.
interrogative, 1. adj. interrogateur. 2. n. interrogatif m.
interrupt, vb. interrompre.
interruption, n. interruption f.
intersect, vb. entrecouper, intersecter, entrecroiser.
intersection, n. intersection f.
intersperse, vb. entremêler, parsemer, intercaler.
interval, n. intervalle m.
intervene, vb. intervenir.
intervention, n. intervention f.
interview, n. entrevue f.; (press) interview m. or f.
intestine, n. intestin m.
intimacy, n. intimité f.

intimate, adj. intime.
intimidate, vb. intimider.
intimidation, n. intimidation f.
into, prep. en; (with art. or adj.) dans.
intonation, n. intonation f.
intone, vb. entonner, psalmodier.
intoxicate, vb. enivrer.
intoxication, n. intoxication f., ivresse f.
intravenous, adj. intraveineux.
intrepid, adj. intrépide, brave, courageux.
intricacy, n. complexité f., nature compliquée f.
intricate, adj. compliqué.
intrigue, n. intrigue f.
intrinsic, adj. intrinsèque.
introduce, vb. (bring in) introduire; (present) présenter.
introduction, n. introduction f.; (presenting) présentation f.
introductory, adj. introductoire, d'introduction.
introspection, n. introspection f., recueillement m.
introvert, n. introverti m.
intrude on, vb. importuner.
intruder, n. intrus m.
intuition, n. intuition f.
intuitive, adj. intuitif.
inundate, vb. inonder.
invade, vb. envahir.
invader, n. envahisseur m., transgresseur m.
invalid, adj. and n. infirme m.f.
invariable, adj. invariable.
invasion, n. invasion f.
invective, n. invective f.
inveigle, vb. attirer, séduire, leurrer.
invent, vb. inventer.
invention, n. invention f.
inventive, adj. inventif, trouveur.
inventor, n. inventeur m.
inventory, n. inventaire m.
invertebrate, 1. n. invertébré m. 2. adj. invertébré.
invest, vb. investir; (money) placer.
investigate, vb. faire des recherches (sur).
investigation, n. investigation f.
investment, n. placement m.
inveterate, adj. invétéré, enraciné.

invidious, *adj.* odieux, haïssable, ingrat.
invigorate, *vb.* fortifier, vivifier.
invincible, *adj.* invincible.
invisible, *adj.* invisible.
invitation, *n.* invitation *f.*
invite, *vb.* inviter.
invocation, *n.* invocation *f.*
invoice, *n.* facture *f.*
invoke, *vb.* invoquer.
involuntary, *adj.* involontaire.
involve, *vb.* (implicate) impliquer; (entail) entraîner.
invulnerable, *adj.* invulnérable.
inward, *adj.* intérieur.
iodine, *n.* iode *f.*
Iran, *n.* Iran *m.*
Iraq, *n.* Irak *m.*
irate, *adj.* en colère, courroucé, furieux.
Ireland, *n.* Irlande *f.*
iridium, *n.* iridium *m.*
iris, *n.* iris *m.*
Irish, *adj.* irlandais.
Irishman, *n.* Irlandais *m.*
irk, *vb.* ennuyer.
iron, *n.* fer *m.*
ironworks, *n.* fonderie de fonte *f.*, usine métallurgique *f.*
irony, *n.* ironie *f.*
irrational, *adj.* irrationnel, déraisonnable, absurde.
irrefutable, *adj.* irréfutable, irrécusable.
irregular, *adj.* irrégulier.
irregularity, *n.* irrégularité *f.*
irrelevant, *adj.* non pertinent, hors de propos.
irresistible, *adj.* irrésistible.
irresponsible, *adj.* irresponsable.
irreverent, *adj.* irrévérent, irrévérencieux.
irrevocable, *adj.* irrévocable.
irrigate, *vb.* irriguer, arroser.
irrigation, *n.* irrigation *f.*
irritability, *n.* irritabilité *f.*
irritable, *adj.* irritable, irascible.
irritant, *n.* irritant *m.*
irritate, *vb.* irriter.
irritation, *n.* irritation *f.*
Islam, *n.* Islam *m.*
Islamic, *adj.* islamique.
island, *n.* île *f.*
isolate, *vb.* isoler.
isolation, *n.* isolement *m.*
isolationist, *n.* isolationniste *m.*
isosceles, *adj.* isoscèle.

Israel, *n.* Israël *m.*
Israeli, *n.* Israëli *m.*
issuance, *n.* délivrance *f.*
issue, 1. *n.* (way out, end) issue *f.*; (result) résultat *m.*; (question) question *f.*; (money, bonds) émission *f.* **2.** *vb.* (come out) sortir; (publish) publier; (money) émettre.
isthmus, *n.* isthme *m.*
it, *pron.* (subject) il *m.*; elle *f.*; (object) le *m.*, la *f.*; (of it) en; (in it, to it) y.
Italian, 1. *n.* (person) Italien *m.*; (language) italien *m.* **2.** *adj.* italien.
Italy, *n.* Italie *f.*
itch, 1. *n.* démangeaison *f.* **2.** *vb.* démanger.
item, *n.* (article) article *m.*; (detail) détail *m.*
itemize, *vb.* détailler.
itinerant, *adj.* ambulant.
itinerary, *n.* itinéraire *m.*
its, 1. *adj.* son *m.*, sa *f.*, ses *pl.* **2.** *pron.* le sien *m.*, la sienne *f.*
itself, *pron.* lui-même *m.*, elle-même *f.*; (reflexive) se.
ivory, *n.* ivoire *f.*
ivy, *n.* lierre *m.*

J

jab, *n.* coup *m.*, coup sec *m.* **2.** *vb.* piquer, donner un coup sec.
jackal, *n.* chacal *m.*
jackass, *n.* âne *m.*; idiot *m.*
jacket, *n.* (man) veston *m.*; (woman) jaquette *f.*
jackknife, *n.* couteau de poche *m.*
jack-of-all-trades, *n.* maître Jacques *m.*, factotum *m.*, homme à tous les métiers *m.*
jade, *n.* rosse *f.*, haridelle *f.*; drôlesse *f.*, coureuse *f.*; jade *m.*
jaded, *adj.* surmené, éreinté, blasé, fatigué.
jagged, *adj.* déchiqueté, entaillé, dentelé.
jaguar, *n.* jaguar *m.*
jail, *n.* prison *f.*
jailer, *n.* gardien *m.*, geôlier *m.*
jam, 1. *n.* foule *f.*, presse *f.*, embouteillage *m.*; confiture *f.* **2.** *vb.* serrer, presser.

jamb, *n.* jambage *m.,* montant *m.,* chambranle *m.*

jangle, 1. *n.* querelle *f.,* chamaille *f.;* cliquetis *m.* **2.** *vb.* se quereller, se chamailler; cliqueter.

janitor, *n.* concierge *m.*

January, *n.* janvier *m.*

Japan, *n.* Japon *m.*

Japanese, 1. *n.* (person) Japonais *m.;* (language) japonais *m.* **2.** *adj.* japonais.

jar, 1. *n.* (container) pot *m.;* (sound) son *(m.)* discordant; (shock) secousse *f.* **2.** *vb.* secouer, heurter.

jargon, *n.* jargon *m.*

jasmine, *n.* jasmin *m.*

jaundice, *n.* jaunisse *f.*

jaunt, *n.* petite excursion *f.,* balade *f.*

javelin, *n.* javelot *m.,* javeline *f.*

jaw, *n.* mâchoire *f.*

jay, *n.* geai *m.*

jaywalk, *vb.* se promener d'une façon distraite ou imprudente.

jazz, *n.* jazz *m.*

jealous, *adj.* jaloux.

jealousy, *n.* jalousie *f.*

jeans, *n.* jeans *m.pl.*

jeer, 1. *n.* raillerie *f.;* moquerie *f.,* huée *f.* **2.** *vb.* se moquer de, huer.

jelly, *n.* gelée *f.*

jellyfish, *n.* méduse *f.*

jeopardize, *vb.* exposer au danger, mettre en danger, hasarder.

jeopardy, *n.* danger *m.,* péril *m.*

jerk, *n.* saccade *f.*

jerkin, *n.* justaucorps *m.,* pourpoint *m.*

jerky, *adj.* saccadé, coupé.

jersey, *n.* jersey *m.,* tricot de laine *m.*

Jerusalem, *n.* Jérusalem *m.*

jest, 1. plaisanterie *f.,* raillerie *f.,* badinage *m.* **2.** *vb.* plaisanter, railler, badiner.

jester, *n.* railleur *m.,* farceur *m.,* bouffon *m.*

Jesuit, *n.* jésuite *m.*

Jesus, *n.* Jésus *m.*

jet, *n.* (mineral) jais *m.;* (water, gas) jet *m.;* (j. plane) avion *(m.)* à réaction.

jet lag, *n.* désorientation physiologique produite par le décalage d'heures.

jetsam, *n.* épaves *f.pl.*

jettison, *vb.* se délester.

jetty, *n.* jetée *f.,* môle *m.*

Jew, *n.* Juif *m.,* Juive *f.*

jewel, *n.* bijou *m.*

jeweler, *n.* bijoutier *m.,* jouaillier *m.*

jewelry, *n.* bijouterie *f.*

Jewish, *adj.* juif *m.,* juive *f.*

jib, *n.* foc *m.*

jibe, *vb.* être en accord, s'accorder.

jiffy, *n.* instant *m.,* clin d'œil *m.*

jig, 1. *n.* gigue *f.;* calibre *m.,* gabarit *m.* **2.** danser la gigue, sautiller.

jilt, *vb.* délaisser, plaquer, planter.

jingle, 1. *n.* tintement *m.,* cliquetis *m.* **2.** *vb.* tinter, cliqueter.

jinx, *n.* porte-malheur *m.*

jittery, *adj.* très nerveux.

job, *n.* (work) travail *m.;* (employment) emploi *m.*

jobber, *n.* intermédiaire *m.,* marchandeur *m.,* sous-traitant *m.*

jockey, *n.* jockey *m.*

jocular, *adj.* facétieux, jovial, rieur.

jocund, *adj.* enjoué.

jodhpurs, *n.* pantalon d'équitation *m.*

jog, 1. *n.* coup *m.,* secousse *f.,* cahot *m.* **2.** *vb.* pousser, secouer, cahoter.

joggle, 1. *n.* petite secousse *f.* **2.** *vb.* secouer légèrement.

join, *vb.* (things) joindre; (group, etc.) se joindre à.

joiner, *n.* menuisier *m.*

joint, 1. *n.* joint *m.* **2.** *adj.* (in common) commun; (in partnership) co-.

jointly, *adv.* ensemble, conjointement.

joist, *n.* solive *f.,* poutre *f.*

joke, 1. *n.* plaisanterie *f.* **2.** *vb.* plaisanter.

joker, *n.* farceur *m.,* blagueur *m.;* joker *m.*

jolly, *adj.* joyeux.

jolt, 1. *n.* cahot *m.,* choc *m.,* secousse *f.* **2.** *vb.* cahoter, secouer, ballotter.

jonquil, *n.* jonquille *f.*

jostle, *vb.* coudoyer *tr.*

jounce, 1. *n.* cahot *m.,* secousse *f.* **2.** *vb.* cahoter.

journal, n. journal m.
journalism, n. journalisme m.
journalist, n. journaliste m.
journey, 1. n. voyage m. **2.** vb. voyager.
journeyman, n. compagnon m.
jovial, adj. jovial, gai.
jowl, n. mâchoire f.
joy, n. joie f.
joyful, adj. joyeux.
joyous, adj. joyeux.
jubilant, adj. réjoui, jubilant, exultant.
jubilee, n. jubilé m.
Judaism, n. judaïsme m.
judge, 1. n. juge m. **2.** vb. juger.
judgment, n. jugement m.
judicial, adj. judiciaire.
judiciary, adj. judiciaire.
judicious, adj. judicieux, sensé.
jug, n. cruche f.
juggle, vb. jongler.
jugular, adj. jugulaire.
juice, n. jus m.
juicy, adj. juteux.
July, n. juillet m.
jumble, 1. n. brouillamini m., fouillis m., fatras m. **2.** vb. brouiller, mêler confusément.
jump, 1. n. saut m. **2.** vb. sauter.
junction, n. jonction f.; (rail) embranchement m.
juncture, n. jointure f., jonction f., conjoncture f.
June, n. juin m.
jungle, n. jungle f., brousse f.
junior, adj. and n. (age) cadet m.; (rank) subalterne m.
juniper, n. genévrier m., genièvre m.
junk, n. (waste) rebut m.
junket, n. jonchée f.; festin m., partie de plaisir f.
jurisdiction, n. juridiction f.
jurisprudence, n. jurisprudence f.
jurist, n. juriste m., légiste m.
juror, m. juré m., membre du jury m.
jury, n. jury m.
just, 1. adj. juste. **2.** adv. (exactly) juste; (barely) à peine; (have j.) venir de.
justice, n. justice f.
justifiable, adj. justifiable, justifié.
justification, n. justification f.
justify, vb. justifier.

jut, vb. être en saillie.
jute, n. jute m.
juvenile, adj. juvénile.

K

kale, n. chou m.
kaleidoscope, n. kaléidoscope m.
kangaroo, n. kangourou m.
karakul, n. karakul m., caracul m.
karat, n. carat m.
karate, n. karaté m.
keel, n. quille f.
keen, adj. (edge) aiguisé; (pain, point) aigu; (look, mind) pénétrant; **(k. on)** enthousiaste de.
keep, vb. tenir; (reserve, protect, retain) garder; (remain) rester; (continue) continuer à.
keeper, n. gardien m.
keepsake, n. souvenir m.
keg, n. caque f., barillet m., tonnelet m.
kennel, n. chenil m.
kerchief, n. fichu m., mouchoir m.
kernel, n. (grain) grain m.; (nut) amande f.; (fig.) noyau m.
kerosene, n. pétrole m.
ketchup, n. sauce piquante à base de tomates f.
kettle, n. bouilloire f.
kettledrum, n. timbale f.
key, n. clef, clé f.; (piano, typewriter) touche f.
keyhole, n. entrée de clef f.
khaki, n. kaki m.
kick, 1. n. coup (m.) de pied; (gun) recul m. **2.** vb. donner un coup de pied à.
kid, n. (animal, skin) chevreau m.; (child) gosse m.f.
kidnap, vb. enlever de vive force.
kidnaper, n. auteur de l'enlèvement m., ravisseur m.
kidney, n. rein m.; (food) rognon m.
kidney bean, n. haricot nain m.
kill, vb. tuer.
killer, n. tueur m., meurtrier m.
kiln, n. four (céramique) m., séchoir m.
kilocycle, n. kilocycle m.
kilohertz, n. kilohertz m.
kilowatt, n. kilowatt m.
kilt, n. kilt m.

kimono, *n.* kimono *m.*

kin, *n.* (relation) parent *m.*

kind, 1. *n.* genre *m.* **2.** *adj.* aimable.

kindergarten, *n.* jardin d'enfants *m.,* école maternelle *f.*

kindle, *vb.* allumer, *tr.*

kindling, *n.* allumage *m.,* bois d'allumage *m.*

kindly, *adv.* avec bonté.

kindness, *n.* bonté *f.*

kindred, 1. *n.* parenté *f.,* affinité *f.* **2.** *adj.* analogue.

kinetic, *adj.* cinétique *f.*

king, *n.* roi *m.*

kingdom, *n.* royaume *m.*

kink, 1. *n.* nœud *m.,* tortillement *m.* **2.** *vb.* se nouer.

kiosk, *n.* kiosque *m.*

kipper, *n.* kipper *m.,* hareng légèrement salé et fumé *m.*

kiss, 1. *n.* baiser *m.* **2.** *vb.* baiser.

kitchen, *n.* cuisine *f.*

kite, *n.* cerf-volant *m.*

kitten, *n.* petit chat *m.*

kleptomania, *n.* kleptomanie *f.*

kleptomaniac, *n.* kleptomane *m.*

knack, *n.* tour de main *m.,* talent *m.,* truc *m.*

knapsack, *n.* havresac *m.*

knead, *vb.* pétrir, malaxer.

knee, *n.* genou *m.*

kneecap, *n.* genouillère *f.*

kneel, *vb.* s'agenouiller.

knell, *n.* glas *m.*

knickers, *n.* pantalon *m.,* culotte *f.*

knife, *n.* couteau *m.*

knight, *n.* chevalier *m.*

knit, *vb.* (with needles) tricoter.

knock, 1. *n.* coup *m.* **2.** *vb.* frapper.

knot, *n.* nœud *m.*

knotty, *adj.* plein de nœuds.

know, *vb.* savoir; (be acquainted with) connaître.

knowledge, *n.* connaissance *f.;* (learning) savoir *m.*

knuckle, *n.* articulation du doigt *f.,* jointure du doigt *f.*

kodak, *n.* kodak *m.*

Korea, *n.* Corée *f.*

L

label, *n.* étiquette *m.*

labor, 1. *n.* travail *m.;* (workers) ouvriers *m.pl.* **2.** *vb.* peiner.

laboratory, *n.* laboratoire *m.*

laborer, *n.* travailleur *m.*

laborious, *adj.* laborieux.

labor union, *n.* syndicat *m.*

laburnum, *n.* cytise *m.*

labyrinth, *n.* labyrinthe *m.*

lace, *n.* dentelle *f.;* (string) lacet *m.*

lacerate, *vb.* lacérer, déchirer.

laceration, *n.* lacération *f.*

lack, 1. *n.* manque *m.* **2.** *vb.* manquer de.

lackadaisical, *adj.* affecté.

laconic, *adj.* laconique.

lacquer, *n.* vernis-laque *m.*

lactic, *adj.* lactique.

lactose, *n.* lactose *f.*

lacy, *adj.* de dentelle.

ladder, *n.* échelle *f.*

ladle, *n.* cuiller à pot *f.*

lady, *n.* dame *f.*

ladybug, *n.* coccinelle *f.*

lag behind, *vb.* rester en arrière.

lagoon, *n.* lagune *f.*

laid-back, *adj.* décontracté.

lair, *n.* tanière *f.,* repaire *m.*

laissez faire, *n.* laissez faire *m.*

laity, *n.* les laïques *m.pl.*

lake, *n.* lac *m.*

lamb, *n.* agneau *m.*

lame, *adj.* boiteux.

lament, *vb.* se lamenter (sur); (mourn) pleurer.

lamentable, *adj.* lamentable, déplorable.

lamentation, *n.* lamentation *f.*

laminate, *vb.* laminer, écacher.

lamp, *n.* lampe *f.*

lampoon, 1. *n.* pasquinade *f.,* satire *f.* **2.** *vb.* lancer des satires.

lance, *n.* lance *f.*

land, 1. *n.* terre *f.* **2.** *vb.* (boat) débarquer; (plane) atterrir.

landholder, *n.* propriétaire foncier *m.*

landing, *n.* débarquement *m.,* mise à terre *m.*

landlord, *n.* propriétaire *m.f.*

landmark, *n.* borne *f.*

landscape, *n.* paysage *m.*

landslide, *n.* éboulement *m.*

landward, *adv.* vers la terre.

lane, *n.* (country) sentier *m.;* (town) ruelle *f.*

language, *n.* langue *f.;* (form of expression) langage *m.*

languid, *adj.* languissant.

languish, *vb.* languir.

languor, *n.* langueur *f.*

lanky, *adj.* grand et maigre.

lanolin, *n.* lanoline *f.*

lantern, *n.* lanterne *f.*

lap, *n.* genoux *m.pl.*

lapel, *n.* revers *m.*

lapin, *n.* lapin *m.*

lapse, 1. *n.* (of time) laps *m.;* (error) faute *f.* **2.** *vb.* passer.

larceny, *n.* larcin *m.,* vol *m.*

lard, *n.* saindoux *m.*

large, *adj.* grand.

largely, *adv.* en grande partie.

largo, *n.* largo *m.*

lariat, *n.* lasso *m.*

lark, *n.* alouette *f.*

larkspur, *n.* pied d'alouette *m.,* delphinium *m.*

larva, *n.* larve *f.*

laryngitis, *n.* laryngite *f.*

larynx, *n.* larynx *m.*

lascivious, *adj.* lascif.

laser, *n.* laser *m.*

lash, 1. *n.* (whip) lanière *f.;* (blow) coup *(m.)* de fouet. **2.** *vb.* fouetter.

lass, *n.* jeune fille *f.*

lassitude, *n.* lassitude *f.*

lasso, *n.* lasso *m.*

last, 1. *adj.* dernier; (at l.) enfin. **2.** *vb.* durer.

lasting, *adj.* durable.

latch, *n.* loquet *m.*

late, *adj. and adv.* (on in day, etc.) tard; (after due time) en retard; (dead) feu; (recent) dernier.

lately, *adv.* dernièrement.

latent, *adj.* latent, caché.

lateral, *adj.* latéral.

lath, *n.* latte *f.*

lathe, *n.* tour *m.*

lather, *n.* (soap) mousse *f.;* (horse) écume *f.*

Latin, 1. *n.* (person) Latin *m.;* (language) latin *m.* **2.** *adj.* latin.

latitude, *n.* latitude *f.*

latrine, *n.* latrine *f.*

latter, *adj. and pron.* dernier.

lattice, *n.* treillis *m.*

laud, *vb.* louer.

laudable, *adj.* louable.

laudanum, *n.* laudanum *m.*

laudatory, *adj.* élogieux.

laugh, laughter, *n.* rire *m.*

laugh (at), *vb.* rire (de).

laughable, *adj.* risible.

launch, 1. *n.* (boat) chaloupe *f.* **2.** *vb.* lancer, *tr.*

launder, *vb.* blanchir.

laundry, *n.* (works) blanchisserie *f.;* (washing) lessive *f.*

laundryman, *n.* blanchisseur *m.*

laureate, *adj. and n.* lauréat *m.f.*

laurel, *n.* laurier *m.*

lava, *n.* lave *f.*

lavaliere, *n.* lavallière *f.*

lavatory, *n.* lavabo *m.;* cabinet *(m.)* de toilette.

lavender, *n.* lavande *f.*

lavish, 1. *adj.* (person) prodigue; (thing) somptueux. **2.** *vb.* prodiguer.

law, *n.* loi *f.;* (jurisprudence) droit *m.*

lawful, *adj.* légal.

lawless, *adj.* sans loi.

lawn, *n.* pelouse *f.*

lawsuit, *n.* procès *m.*

lawyer, *n.* (counselor) avocat *m.;* (attorney) avoué *m.;* (jurist) jurisconsulte *m.*

lax, *adj.* lâche, mou, relâché.

laxative, *n.* laxatif *m.*

laxity, *n.* relâchement *m.*

lay, *vb.* poser.

layer, *n.* couche *f.*

layman, *n.* laïque *m.*

lazy, *adj.* paresseux.

lead, 1. *n.* (metal) plomb *m.;* (pencil) mine *f.* **2.** *vb.* mener, conduire.

leaden, *adj.* de plomb.

leader, *n.* chef *m.*

lead pencil, *n.* crayon à la mine de plomb *m.*

leaf, *n.* feuille *f.*

leaflet, *n.* feuillet *m.*

leafy, *adj.* feuillu.

league, *n.* (compact) ligue *f.;* (measure) lieue *f.*

League of Nations, *n.* La Société des Nations *f.*

leak, 1. *n.* (liquid) fuite *f.;* (boat) voie *(f.)* d'eau. **2.** *vb.* fuir; faire eau.

leakage, *n.* fuite d'eau *f.*

leaky, *adj.* qui coule, qui fait eau.

lean, 1. *adj.* maigre. **2.** *vb. intr.* (**l. against**) s'appuyer sur; (stoop) se pencher. **3.** *vb.tr.* appuyer.

leap, *vb.* sauter.

leap year, *n.* année bissextile f.

learn, *vb.* apprendre.

learned, *adj.* savant, docte.

learning, *n.* science f., instruction f., érudition f.

lease, *n.* bail m.

leash, *n.* laisse f., attache f.

least, 1. *n.* moins m. **2.** *adj.* (le) moindre. **3.** *adv.* (le) moins.

leather, *n.* cuir m.

leathery, *adj.* coriace.

leave, 1. *n.* permission f. **2.** *vb.* laisser; (go away from) quitter.

leaven, 1. *n.* levain m. **2.** *vb.* faire lever, modifier.

lecherous, *adj.* lascif, libertin.

lecture, *n.* conférence f.

lecturer, *n.* conférencier m.

ledge, *n.* bord m.; (of rocks) chaîne f.

ledger, *n.* grand livre m.

lee, *n.* côté m.; (l.) sous le vent.

leech, *n.* sangsue f.

leek, *n.* poireau m.

leer, 1. *n.* œillade f., regard de côté m. **2.** *vb.* lorgner.

leeward, *adj. and adv.* sous le vent.

left, *adj. and n.* gauche f.; (**on, to the l.**) à gauche.

leftist, *n.* gaucher m.

left wing, *n.* l'aile gauche f.

leg, *n.* (man, horse) jambe f.; (most animals) patte f.

legacy, *n.* legs m.

legal, *adj.* légal.

legalize, *vb.* rendre légal.

legation, *n.* légation f.

legend, *n.* légende f.

legendary, *adj.* légendaire.

legible, *adj.* lisible.

legion, *n.* légion f.

legislate, *vb.* faire les lois.

legislation, *n.* législation f.

legislator, *n.* législateur m.

legislature, *n.* législature f.

legitimate, *adj.* légitime.

legume, *n.* légume m.

leisure, *n.* loisir m.

leisurely, *adv.* à loisir.

lemon, *n.* citron m.

lemonade, *n.* citron (m.) pressé.

lend, *vb.* prêter.

length, *n.* (dimension) longueur f.; (time) durée f.

lengthen, *vb.* allonger, tr.

lengthwise, *adv.* en long.

lengthy, *adj.* assez long.

lenient, *adj.* indulgent.

lens, *n.* lentille f.; (camera) objectif m.

Lent, *n.* carême m.

Lenten, *adj.* de carême.

lentil, *n.* lentille f.

leopard, *n.* léopard m.

leper, *n.* lépreux m.

leprosy, *n.* lèpre f.

lesbian, 1. *adj.* lesbien. **2.** *n.* lesbienne f.; tribade f.

lesion, *n.* lésion f.

less, 1. *adj.* (smaller) moindre; (not so much) moins de. **2.** *adv.* (l. than) moins (de).

lessen, *vb.* diminuer.

lesser, *adj.* moindre.

lesson, *n.* leçon f.

lest, *conj.* de peur que . . . (ne).

let, *vb.* laisser; (lease) louer.

letdown, *n.* déception f.

lethal, *adj.* mortel.

lethargic, *adj.* léthargique.

lethargy, *n.* léthargie f.

letter, *n.* lettre f.

letterhead, *n.* en-tête de lettre m.

lettuce, *n.* laitue f.

levee, *n.* lever m.

level, 1. *adj.* (flat) égal; (l. with) au niveau de. **2.** *n.* niveau m.

lever, *n.* levier m.

levity, *n.* légèreté f.

levy, 1. *n.* levée f. **2.** *vb.* lever.

lewd, *adj.* impudique.

lexicon, *n.* lexique m.

liability, *n.* responsabilité f.

liable, *adj.* (responsible for) responsable de; (subject to) sujet à.

liar, *n.* menteur m.

libation, *n.* libation f.

libel, *n.* diffamation f.

libelous, *adj.* diffamatoire.

liberal, *adj.* libéral; (generous) généreux.

liberalism, *n.* libéralisme m.

liberality, *n.* libéralité f.

liberate, *vb.* libérer.

libertine, 1. *n.* libre-penseur m. **2.** *adj.* libertin.

liberty, *n.* liberté f.

libidinous, *adj.* libidineux.

libido, n. libido m.
librarian, n. bibliothécaire m.
library, n. bibliothèque f.
libretto, n. livret m.
license, n. permis m.; (tradesmen) patente f.; (abuse of freedom) licence f.
licentious, adj. licencieux.
lick, vb. lécher.
licorice, n. réglisse f.
lid, n. couvercle m.
lie, 1. n. mensonge f. **2.** vb. (lib) mentir; (recline) être couché; (l. down) se coucher; (be situated) se trouver.
lien, n. privilège m.
lieutenant, n. lieutenant m.
life, n. vie f.
lifeboat, n. bateau de sauvetage m.
life buoy, n. bouée de sauvetage m.
lifeguard, n. garde du corps m.
life insurance, n. assurance sur la vie f.
lifeless, adj. sans vie.
life preserver, n. appareil de sauvetage m.
life style, n. manière de vivre f.
lifetime, n. vie f., vivant m.
lift, vb. lever.
ligament, n. ligament m.
ligature, n. ligature f.
light, 1. n. lumière f. **2.** adj. (not heavy) léger; (not dark) clair. **3.** vb. allumer, tr.
lighten, vb. (relieve) alléger, tr.; (brighten) éclairer, tr.
lighter, n. (cigaret) briquet m.
lighthouse, n. phare m.
lightly, adv. légèrement.
lightness, n. légèreté f.
lightning, n. (flash of) éclair m.
lignite, n. lignite m.
likable, adj. agréable.
like, 1. adj. pareil. **2.** vb. aimer; plaire à. **3.** prep. comme.
likelihood, n. probabilité f.
likely, adj. probable.
liken, vb. comparer.
likeness, n. ressemblance f.
likewise, adv. de même.
lilac, n. lilas m.
lilt, 1. n. forte cadence f. **2.** vb. chanter gaiement.
lily, n. lis m.; (l. of the valley) muguet m.

limb, n. membre m.; (tree) grosse branche f.
limber, 1. adj. souple, flexible. **2.** vb. assouplir.
limbo, n. limbes m.pl.
lime, n. (mineral) chaux f.; (tree) tilleul m.; (fruit) lime f.
limelight, n. lumière oxhydrique f.
limestone, n. pierre à chaux f., calcaire m.
limewater, n. eau de chaux f.
limit, 1. n. limite f. **2.** vb. limiter.
limitation, n. limitation f.
limitless, adj. sans limite, sans bornes.
limousine, n. limousine f.
limp, 1. adj. flasque. **2.** vb. boiter.
limpid, adj. limpide.
linden, n. tilleul m.
line, n. ligne f.
lineage, n. lignée f., race f.
lineal, adj. linéaire.
linen, n. (cloth) toile f.; (sheets, etc.) linge m.
linger, vb. s'attarder.
lingerie, n. lingerie f.
linguist, n. linguiste m.
linguistic, adj. linguistique.
linguistics, n. linguistique f.
liniment, n. liniment m.
lining, n. (clothes) doublure f.
link, 1. n. (chain) chaînon m.; (fig.) lien m. **2.** vb. (re)lier.
linoleum, n. linoléum m.
linseed, n. graine de lin f.
lint, n. charpie f.
lion, n. lion m.
lip, n. lèvre f.
lipstick, n. rouge (m.) à lèvres.
liquefy, vb. liquéfier.
liqueur, n. liqueur f.
liquid, adj. and n. liquide m.
liquidate, vb. liquider.
liquidation, n. liquidation f., acquittement m.
liquor, n. boisson (f.) alcoolique.
lisp, vb. zézayer.
list, 1. n. liste f. **2.** vb. enregistrer.
listen (to), vb. écouter.
listless, adj. inattentif.
litany, n. litanie f.
literacy, n. degré d'aptitude à lire et à écrire m.
literal, adj. littéral.
literary, adj. littéraire.
literate, adj. lettré.

literature, n. littérature f.

lithe, adj. flexible, pliant.

lithograph, vb. lithographier.

lithography, n. lithographie f.

litigant, n. plaideur m.

litigation, n. litige m.

litmus, n. tournesol m.

litter, n. (vehicle, animals' bedding) litière f.; (disorder) fouillis m.; (animals' young) portée f.

little, 1. n. and adv. peu m. **2.** adj. (small) petit; (not much) peu (de).

liturgical, adj. liturgique.

liturgy, n. liturgie f.

live, vb. vivre.

livelihood, n. vie f., subsistance f., gagne-pain m.

lively, adj. vif m., vive f.

liven, vb. animer, activer.

liver, n. foie m.

livery, n. livrée f.

livestock, n. bétail m.

livid, adj. livide, blême.

lizard, n. lézard m.

llama, n. lama m.

lo, interj. voilà.

load, 1. n. (cargo) charge f.; (burden) fardeau m. **2.** vb. charger.

loaf, 1. n. pain m. **2.** vb. flâner.

loafer, n. fainéant m.

loam, n. terre grasse f.

loan, 1. n. (thing) prêt m.; (borrowing) emprunt m. **2.** vb. prêter.

loath, adj. fâché, peiné.

loathe, vb. détester.

loathing, n. dégoût m.

loathsome, adj. dégoûtant.

lobby, n. (hall) vestibule m.

lobe, n. lobe m.

lobster, n. homard m.

local, adj. local.

locale, n. localité f., scène f.

locality, n. localité f.

localize, vb. localiser.

locate, vb. localiser.

location, n. placement m.

lock, 1. n. (door) serrure f.; (hair) mèche f. **2.** vb. fermer à clef.

locker, n. armoire f.; (baggage) consigne automatique f.

locket, n. médaillon m.

lockjaw, n. tétanos m.

locksmith, n. serrurier m.

locomotion, n. locomotion f.

locomotive, n. locomotive f.

locust, n. sauterelle f.

locution, n. locution f.

lode, n. filon m.

lodge, vb. loger.

lodger, n. locataire m.

lodging, n. logement m.

loft, n. grenier m.

lofty, adj. élevé; (proud) hautain.

log, n. (wood) bûche f.; (boat) loch m.

loge, n. loge f.

logic, n. logique f.

logical, adj. logique.

loins, n. reins m.pl.

loiter, vb. flâner.

lollipop, n. sucre d'orge m.

London, n. Londres m.

lone, lonely, lonesome, adj. solitaire.

loneliness, n. solitude f.

long, 1. adj. long m., longue f. **2.** adv. longtemps.

longevity, n. longévité f.

long for, vb. désirer ardemment.

longing, n. désir ardent m.

longitude, n. longitude f.

longitudinal, adj. longitudinal.

look, 1. n. regard m.; aspect m. **2.** vb. (l. at) regarder; (l. for) chercher; (l. after) soigner; (seem) paraître.

looking glass, n. miroir m.

loom, 1. n. métier m. **2.** vb. se dessiner.

loop, n. boucle f.

loophole, n. meurtrière f., échappatoire f.

loose, adj. (not tight) lâche; (detached) détaché; (morals) relâché.

loosen, vb. desserrer.

loot, 1. n. butin m. **2.** vb. piller.

lop, vb. élaguer, ébrancher.

loquacious, adj. loquace.

lord, n. seigneur m.; (title) lord m.

lordship, n. seigneurie f.

lorgnette, n. lorgnette f.

lose, vb. perdre.

loss, n. perte f.

lot, n. (fortune) sort m.; (land) terrain m.; (much) beaucoup.

lotion, n. lotion f.

lottery, n. loterie f.

lotus, n. lotus m., lotos m.

loud, 1. adj. fort; (noisy) bruyant. **2.** adv. haut.

lounge, 1. n. sofa m.; hall m. **2.** vb. flâner.
louse, n. pou m.
lout, n. rustre m.
louver, n. auvent m.
lovable, adj. aimable.
love, 1. n. amour m. **2.** vb. aimer.
lovely, adj. beau m., belle f.
lover, n. amoureux m.
low, adj. bas m., basse f.
lowboy, n. commode basse f.
lowbrow, adj. terre à terre.
lower, vb. baisser.
lowly, adj. humble.
loyal, adj. loyal.
loyalist, n. loyaliste m.
loyalty, n. loyauté f.
lozenge, n. pastille f.
lubricant, n. lubrifiant m.
lubricate, vb. lubrifier.
lucid, adj. lucide.
luck, n. chance f.
lucky, adj. (person) heureux.
lucrative, adj. lucratif.
ludicrous, adj. risible.
lug, vb. traîner, tirer.
luggage, n. bagages m.pl.
lukewarm, adj. tiède.
lull, n. moment (m.) de calme.
lullaby, n. berceuse f.
lumbago, n. lumbago m.
lumber, n. bois (m.) de charpente.
luminous, adj. lumineux.
lump, n. (gros) morceau m.
lumpy, adj. grumeleux.
lunacy, n. folie f.
lunar, adj. lunaire.
lunatic, n. aliéné m.
lunch, 1. n. déjeuner m. **2.** vb. déjeuner.
luncheon, n. déjeuner m.
lung, n. poumon m.
lunge, 1. n. botte f. **2.** vb. se fendre.
lurch, 1. n. embardée f. **2.** vb. faire une embardée.
lure, vb. (animal) leurrer; (attract) attirer.
lurid, adj. blafard, sombre.
lurk, vb. se cacher.
luscious, adj. délicieux.
lush, adj. luxuriant.
lust, n. luxure f.
luster, n. lustre m.
lustful, adj. lascif, sensuel.
lustrous, adj. brillant, lustré.

lusty, adj. vigoreux.
lute, n. luth m.
Lutheran, n. Luthérien m.
luxuriant, adj. exubérant.
luxurious, adj. (thing) luxueux.
luxury, n. luxe m.
lying, n. mensonge m.
lymph, n. lymphe f.
lynch, vb. lyncher.
lyre, n. lyre f.
lyric, adj. lyrique.
lyricism, n. lyrisme m.

M

macaroni, n. macaroni m.
machine, n. machine f.
machine gun, n. mitrailleuse f.
machinery, n. machines f.pl; (fig.) mécanisme m.
machinist, n. machiniste m.
machismo, n. phallocratie f.
macho, 1. adj. phallocrate. **2.** n. homme phallocrate m.
mackerel, n. maquereau m.
mackinaw, n. mackinaw m.
mad, adj. fou m., folle f.
madam, n. madame f.
madcap, n. and adj. écervelé.
madden, vb. exaspérer.
made, adj. fait, fabriqué.
mafia, n. mafia f.
magazine, n. revue f.
magic, 1. n. magie f. **2.** adj. magique.
magician, n. magicien m.
magistrate, n. magistrat m.
magnanimous, adj. magnanime.
magnate, n. magnat m.
magnesium, n. magnésium m.
magnet, n. aimant m.
magnetic, adj. magnétique.
magnificence, n. magnificence f.
magnificent, adj. magnifique.
magnify, vb. grossir.
magnitude, n. grandeur f.
mahogany, n. acajou m.
maid, n. (servant) bonne f.; (old m.) vieille fille f.
maiden, adj. de jeune fille.
mail, 1. n. courrier m. **2.** vb. envoyer par la poste.
mailbox, n. boîte (f.) aux lettres.
mailman, n. facteur m.
maim, vb. estropier, mutiler.
main, adj. principal.

mainframe, *n.* partie centrale d'un informateur *f.*

mainland, *n.* terre (*f.*) ferme.

mainspring, *n.* grand ressort *m.;* mobile essentiel *m.*

maintain, *vb.* maintenir; (support) soutenir.

maintenance, *n.* entretien *m.*

maize, *n.* maïs *m.*

majestic, *adj.* majestueux.

majesty, *n.* majesté *f.*

major, 1. *n. (mil.)* commandant *m.;* (school) sujet (*m.*) principal. **2.** *adj.* majeur.

majority, *n.* majorité *f.*

major scale, mode, or key, *n.* ton majeur *m.,* mode majeur *m.*

make, 1. *n.* fabrication *f.* **2.** *vb.* faire.

make-believe, 1. *n.* trompe l'œil *m.* **2.** *vb.* feindre.

maker, *n.* fabricant *m.*

makeshift, *n.* expédient *m.*

make-up, *n.* (face) maquillage *m.*

maladjusted, *adj.* mal adapté, mal ajusté.

maladjustment, *n.* mauvaise adaptation *f.*

malady, *n.* maladie *f.*

malaria, *n.* malaria *f.*

male, *adj. and n.* mâle *m.*

malevolent, *adj.* malveillant.

malice, *n.* méchanceté *f.*

malicious, *adj.* méchant.

malign, *vb.* calomnier.

malignant, *adj.* malin *m.,* maligne *f.*

malleable, *adj.* malléable.

malnutrition, *n.* mauvaise hygiène (*f.*) alimentaire.

malpractice, *n.* méfait *m.*

malt, *n.* malt *m.*

mammal, *n.* mammifère *m.*

man, *n.* homme *m.*

manage, 1. *vb. tr.* (administer) gérer; (conduct) diriger; (person, animal) dompter. **2.** *vb. intr.* se tirer d'affaire; **(m. to)** réussir à.

management, *n.* direction *f.*

manager, *n.* directeur *m.;* (household) ménager *m.*

mandate, *n.* (politics) mandat *m.*

mandatory, *adj.* obligatoire.

mandolin, *n.* mandoline *f.*

mane, *n.* crinière *f.*

maneuver, *n.* manœuvre *f.*

manganese, *n.* manganèse *m.*

manger, *n.* mangeoire *f.*

mangle, *vb.* mutiler.

manhood, *n.* virilité *f.*

mania, *n.* (craze) manie *f.;* (madness) folie *f.*

maniac, *adj. and n.* fou *m.,* folle *f.*

manicure, *n.* (person) manucure *m.f.;* (care of hands) soin (*m.*) des mains.

manifest, 1. *adj.* manifeste. **2.** *vb.* manifester.

manifesto, *n.* manifeste *m.*

manifold, *adj.* (varied) divers; (numerous) nombreux.

manipulate, *vb.* manipuler.

mankind, *n.* genre (*m.*) humain.

manly, *adj.* viril.

manner, *n.* manière *f.;* (customs) mœurs *f.pl.*

mannerism, *n.* maniérisme *m.,* affectation *f.*

mansion, *n.* (country) château *m.;* (town) hôtel *m.*

manslaughter, *n.* homicide involontaire *m.*

mantel, *n.* (framework) manteau *m.;* (shelf) tablette *f.*

mantle, *n.* manteau *f.*

manual, *adj. and n.* manuel *m.*

manufacture, 1. *n.* manufacture *f.;* (product) produit (*m.*) manufacturé. **2.** *vb.* fabriquer.

manufacturer, *n.* fabricant *m.*

manure, *n.* fumier *m.*

manuscript, *adj. and n.* manuscrit *m.*

many, 1. *adj.* beaucoup de, un grand nombre de; **(too m.)** trop de; **(so m.)** tant de; **(how m.)** combien de. **2.** *pron.* beaucoup.

map, *n.* carte (*f.*) géographique.

maple, *n.* érable *m.*

mar, *vb.* gâter.

marble, *n.* marbre *m.*

march, 1. *n.* marche *f.* **2.** *vb.* marcher.

March, *n.* mars *m.*

mare, *n.* jument *f.*

margarine, *n.* margarine *f.*

margin, *n.* marge *f.*

marijuana, *n.* marijuana *f.;* marie-jeanne *f.*

marinate, *vb.* faire mariner.

marine, 1. *n.* (ships) marine *f.;* (soldier) fusilier (*m.*) marin. **2.** *adj.* marin; (insurance) maritime.

mariner, *n.* marin *m.*

marionette, *n.* marionnette *f.*

marital, *adj.* matrimonial.

maritime, *adj.* maritime.

mark, 1. *n.* marque *f.*; (target) but *m.*; (school) point *m.* **2.** *vb.* marquer.

market, *n.* marché *m.*

market place, *n.* place (*f.*) du marché.

marmalade, *n.* confiture *f.*

maroon, 1. *adj. and n.* rouge (*m.*) foncé. **2.** *vb.* abandonner (dans une île déserte).

marquee, *n.* (tente) marquise *f.*

marquis, *n.* marquis *m.*

marriage, *n.* mariage *m.*

married, *adj.* marié.

marrow, *n.* moelle *f.*

marry, *vb.* épouser; se marier (avec).

marsh, *n.* marais *m.*

marshal, *n.* maréchal *m.*

marshmallow, *n.* guimauve (plant) *f.*

martial, *adj.* martial.

martinet, *n.* officier strict sur la discipline *m.*

martyr, *n.* martyr *m.*

martyrdom, *n.* martyre *m.*

marvel, 1. *n.* merveille *f.* **2.** *vb.* (**m. at**) s'étonner de.

marvelous, *adj.* merveilleux.

mascara, *n.* mascara *m.*

mascot, *n.* mascotte *f.*

masculine, *adj.* masculin.

mash, *n.* (food) purée *f.*

mask, 1. *n.* masque *m.* **2.** *vb.* masquer.

mason, *n.* maçon *m.*

masquerade, *n.* mascarade *f.*, bal masqué *m.*

mass, *n.* masse *f.*

Mass, *n.* messe *f.*

massacre, 1. *n.* massacre *m.* **2.** *vb.* massacrer.

massage, *n.* massage *m.*

masseur, *n.* masseur *m.*

massive, *adj.* massif.

mass meeting, *n.* réunion *f.*

mast, *n.* mât *m.*

master, 1. *n.* maître *m.* **2.** *vb.* maîtriser.

masterpiece, *n.* chef-d'œuvre *m.*

mastery, *n.* maîtrise *f.*

masticate, *vb.* mâcher.

mat, *n.* (door) paillasson *m.*

match, 1. *n.* (for fire) allumette *f.*; (equal) égal *m.*; (marriage) mariage *m.*; (person to marry) parti *m.*; (sport) partie *f.* **2.** *vb.* assortir, *tr.*

mate, *n.* (fellow-worker) camarade *m.f.*; (of pair) compagnon *m.*; compagne *f.*; (boat) officier *m.*

material, 1. *n.* matière *f.*; (cloth) étoffe *f.* **2.** *adj.* matériel.

materialism, *n.* matérialisme *m.*

materialize, *vb.* matérialiser, *tr.*; se réaliser, *intr.*

maternal, *adj.* maternel.

maternity, *n.* maternité *f.*

mathematical, *adj.* mathématique.

mathematics, *n.* mathématiques *f.pl.*

matinee, *n.* matinée *f.*

matriarch, *n.* femme qui porte les chausses *f.*

matrimony, *n.* mariage *m.*

matron, *n.* (institution) intendante *f.*

matter, 1. *n.* (substance) matière *f.*; (subject) sujet *m.*; (question, business) affaire *f.*; (**what is the m.?**) qu'est-ce qu'il y a? **2.** *vb.* importer.

mattress, *n.* matelas *m.*

mature, 1. *adj.* mûr. **2.** *vb.* mûrir.

maturity, *n.* maturité *f.*; (comm.) échéance *f.*

maudlin, *adj.* larmoyant.

mausoleum, *n.* mausolée *m.*

maxim, *n.* maxime *f.*

maximum, *n.* maximum *m.*

may, *vb.* pouvoir.

May, *n.* mai *m.*

maybe, *adv.* peut-être.

mayhem, *n.* mutilation *f.*

mayonnaise, *n.* mayonnaise *f.*

mayor, *n.* maire *m.*

maze, *n.* labyrinthe *m.*

me, *pron.* (unstressed direct and indirect) me; (alone, stressed, with *prep.*) moi.

meadow, *n.* (small) pré *m.*; (large) prairie *f.*

meager, *adj.* maigre.

meal, *n.* (repast) repas *m.*; (grain) farine *f.*

mean, 1. *n.* (math.) moyenne *f.*; (m.s, financial) moyens *m.pl.*; (m.s, way to do) moyen *m.* **2.**

adj. humble; (stingy) avare; (contemptible) méprisable. 3. *vb.* (signify) vouloir dire; (purpose) se proposer (de); (destine) destiner (à).

meaning, *n.* sens *m.*
meantime, meanwhile, *adv.* sur ces entrefaites.
measles, *n.* rougeole *f.*
measure, 1. *n.* mesure *f.* 2. *vb.* mesurer.
measurement, *n.* mesurage *m.*
meat, *n.* viande *f.*
mechanic, *n.* mécanicien *m.*
mechanical, 1. *adj.* mécanique. 2. *(fig.)* machinal.
mechanism, *n.* mécanisme *m.*
mechanize, *vb.* mécaniser.
medal, *n.* médaille *f.*
meddle, *vb.* se mêler (de).
media, *n.* organes de communication *m.pl.*
median, *adj.* médian.
mediate, *vb.* agir en médiateur.
medical, *adj.* médical.
medicate, *vb.* médicamenter.
medicine, *n.* médecine *f.*
medieval, *adj.* médiéval.
mediocre, *adj.* médiocre.
mediocrity, *n.* médiocrité *f.*
meditate, *vb.* méditer.
meditation, *n.* méditation *f.*
Mediterranean, 1. *adj.* méditerrané. 2. *n.* **(M. Sea)** Méditerranée *f.*
medium, 1. *n.* milieu *m.;* (agent) intermédiaire *m.;* (psychic person) médium *m.* 2. *adj.* moyen.
medley, *n.* mélange *m.*
meek, *adj.* doux *m.,* douce *f.*
meekness, *n.* douceur *f.*
meet, *vb.* rencontrer, *tr.;* (become acquainted with) faire la connaissance de; (expenses) faire face à.
meeting, *n.* réunion *f.*
megahertz, *n.* mégahertz *m.*
megaphone, *n.* mégaphone *m.*
melancholy, *n.* mélancolie *f.*
mellow, *adj.* moelleux.
melodious, *adj.* mélodieux.
melodrama, *n.* mélodrame *m.*
melody, *n.* mélodie *f.*
melon, *n.* melon *m.*
melt, *vb.* fondre.
meltdown, *n.* fusion *f.*
member, *n.* membre *m.*

membrane, *n.* membrane *f.*
memento, *n.* mémento *m.*
memoir, *n.* mémoire *m.*
memorable, *adj.* mémorable.
memorandum, *n.* mémorandum *m.*
memorial, 1. *n.* souvenir *m.,* monument *m.* 2. *adj.* commémoratif.
memorize, *vb.* apprendre par cœur.
memory, *n.* mémoire *f.*
menace, 1. *n.* menace *f.* 2. *vb.* menacer.
menagerie, *n.* ménagerie *f.*
mend, *vb.* (clothes) raccommoder; (correct) corriger.
mendacious, *adj.* menteur.
mendicant, *n. and adj.* mendiant *m.*
menial, *adj.* servile.
menstruation, *n.* menstruation *f.*
menswear, *n.* habillements masculins *m.pl.*
mental, *adj.* mental.
mentality, *n.* mentalité *f.*
menthol, *n.* menthol *m.*
mention, 1. *n.* mention *f.* 2. *vb.* mentionner; (don't m. it) il n'y a pas de quoi.
menu, *n.* menu *m.*
mercantile, *adj.* mercantile.
mercenary, *adj. and n.* mercenaire *m.*
merchandise, *n.* marchandise(s) *f.(pl.)*
merchant, 1. *n.* négociant *m.* 2. *adj.* marchand.
merchant marine, *n.* marine marchande *f.*
merciful, *adj.* miséricordieux.
merciless, *adj.* impitoyable.
mercury, *n.* mercure *m.*
mercy, *n.* miséricorde *f.;* (at the m. of) à la merci de.
mere, *adj.* simple.
merely, *adv.* simplement.
merge, *vb.* fusionner.
merger, *n.* fusion *f.*
merit, 1. *n.* mérite *m.* 2. *vb.* mériter.
meritorious, *adj.* (person) méritant; (deed) méritoire.
mermaid, *n.* sirène *f.*
merriment, *n.* gaieté *f.*
merry, *adj.* gai.
merry-go-round, *n.* carrousel *m.*

mesh, *n.* maille *f.*

mesmerize, *vb.* magnétiser.

mess, 1. *n.* (muddle) fouillis *m.;* gâchis *m.;* (mil.) popote *f.* **2.** *vb.* gâcher.

message, *n.* message *m.*

messenger, *n.* messager *m.*

messy, *adj.* (dirty) malpropre.

metabolism, *n.* métabolisme *m.*

metal, *n.* métal *m.*

metallic, *adj.* métallique.

metamorphosis, *n.* métamorphose *f.*

metaphysics, *n.* métaphysique *f.*

meteor, *n.* météore *m.*

meter, 1. *n.* (measure) mètre *m.;* (device) compteur *m.*

method, *n.* méthode *f.*

meticulous, *adj.* méticuleux.

metric, *adj.* métrique.

metropolis, *n.* métropole *f.*

metropolitan, *adj.* métropolitain.

mettle, *n.* ardeur *f.*

Mexican, 1. *n.* Mexicain *f.* **2.** *adj.* mexicain.

Mexico, *n.* Mexique *m.*

mezzanine, *n.* mezzanine *f.*

microbe, *n.* microbe *m.*

microfiche, *n.* microfiche *f.*

microfilm, *n.* microfilm *m.*

microform, *n.* microforme *f.*

microphone, *n.* microphone *m.*

microscope, *n.* microscope *m.*

microscopic, *adj.* microscopique.

mid, *adj.* mi-.

middle, 1. *n.* milieu *m.* **2.** *adj.* du milieu.

middle-aged, *adj.* d'un certain âge.

Middle Ages, *n.* moyen âge *m.*

middle class, *n.* classe moyenne *f.*, bourgeoisie *f.*

Middle East, *n.* Moyen Orient *m.*

midget, *n.* nain *m.*

midnight, *n.* minuit *m.*

midriff, *n.* diaphragme *m.*

midwife, *n.* sage-femme *f.*

mien, *n.* mine *f.*, air *m.*

might, *n.* puissance *f.*

mighty, *adj.* puissant.

migrate, *vb.* émigrer.

migration, *n.* migration *f.*

mild, *adj.* doux *m.*, douce *f.*

mildew, *n.* rouille *f.*

mile, *n.* mille *m.*

mileage, *n.* kilométrage *m.*

milestone, *n.* borne routière *f.*

militarism, *n.* militarisme *m.*

military, *adj.* militaire.

militia, *n.* milice *f.*

milk, *n.* lait *m.*

milkman, *n.* laitier *m.*

milky, *adj.* laiteux.

mill, 1. *n.* (grinding) moulin *m.;* (spinning) filature *f.;* (factory) usine *f.* **2.** *vb.* (grind) moudre; (crowd) fourmiller.

miller, *n.* meunier *m.*

millimeter, *n.* millimètre *m.*

milliner, *n.* modiste *f.*

millinery, *n.* modes *f.pl.*

million, *n.* million *m.*

millionaire, *adj. and n.* millionnaire *m.f.*

mimic, 1. *n.* mime *m.* **2.** *adj.* mimique. **3.** *vb.* imiter.

mince, *vb.* (chop) hacher.

mind, 1. *n.* esprit *m.;* (opinion) avis *m.;* (desire) envie *f.* **2.** *vb.* (heed) faire attention à; (listen to) écouter; (apply oneself to) s'occuper de; (take care) prendre garde; (look after) garder; (never m.) n'importe.

mindful, *adj.* attentif.

mine, 1. *n.* mine *f.* **2.** *pron.* le mien *m.*, la mienne *f.*

mine field, *n.* champ de mines *m.*

miner, *n.* mineur *m.*

mineral, *adj. and n.* minéral *m.*

mine sweeper, *n.* dragueur de mines *m.*

mingle, *vb.* mêler, *tr.*

miniature, *n.* miniature *f.*

miniaturize, *vb.* miniaturiser.

minimize, *vb.* réduire au minimum.

minimum, *n.* minimum *m.*

minimum wage, *n.* salaire minimum *m.*

mining, *n.* exploitation minière *f.*, pose de mines *f.*

minister, *n.* ministre *m.*

ministry, *n.* ministère *m.*

mink, *n.* vison *m.*

minnow, *n.* vairon *m.*

minor, *adj. and n.* mineur *m.*

minority, *n.* minorité *f.*

minstrel, *n.* ménestrel *m.*

mint, *n.* (plant) menthe *f.;* (place) Hôtel (*m.*) de la Monnaie.

minute, 1. *n.* minute *f.;* (of meeting) procès-verbal *m.* **2.** *adj.*

(very small) minuscule; (detailed) minutieux.

miracle, n. miracle m.

miraculous, adj. miraculeux.

mirage, n. mirage m.

mire, n. boue f., bourbier m.

mirror, n. miroir m.

mirth, n. gaieté f.

misadventure, n. mésaventure f., contretemps m.

misappropriate, vb. détourner, dépréder.

misbehave, vb. se mal conduire.

miscellaneous, adj. divers.

mischief, n. (harm) mal m.; (mischievousness) malice f.

mischievous, adj. espiègle; (wicked) méchant.

misconstrue, vb. mal interpréter, tourner en mal.

misdemeanor, n. délit m.

miser, n. avare m.f.

miserable, adj. (unhappy) malheureux; (wretched) misérable.

miserly, adj. avare.

misery, n. (affliction) souffrance(s) f.(pl.); (poverty) misère f.

misfit, n. vêtement manqué m.; inadapté, inapte m.

misfortune, n. malheur m.

misgiving, n. doute m.

mishap, n. mésaventure f.

mislead, vb. tromper, égarer.

misplace, vb. mal placer.

mispronounce, vb. mal prononcer, estropier.

miss, vb. manquer; **(I m. you)** vous me manquez.

Miss, n. mademoiselle f.

missile, n. projectile m.

mission, n. mission f.

missionary, adj. and n. missionnaire m.f.

misspell, vb. mal orthographier.

mist, n. brume f.

mistake, 1. n. erreur f. **2.** vb. (misunderstand) comprendre mal; (make a mistake) se tromper (de).

mister, n. monsieur m.

mistletoe, n. gui m.

mistreat, vb. maltraiter.

mistress, n. maîtresse f.

mistrust, 1. n. méfiance f. **2.** vb. se méfier de.

misty, adj. brumeux.

misunderstand, vb. mal comprendre.

misuse, vb. (misapply) faire mauvais usage (de); (maltreat) maltraiter.

mite, n. denier m., obole f.

mitigate, vb. adoucir.

mitten, n. moufle f.

mix, vb. mêler, tr.

mixture, n. mélange m.

mix-up, n. embrouillement m.

moan, 1. n. gémissement m. **2.** vb. gémir.

moat, n. fossé m.

mob, n. foule f.; (pejorative) populace f.

mobile, adj. mobile.

mobilization, n. mobilisation f.

mobilize, vb. mobiliser.

mock, vb. (m. at) se moquer de; (imitate) singer.

mockery, n. moquerie f.

mod, adj. à la mode.

mode, n. mode m.

model, n. modèle m.

moderate, 1. adj. modéré. **2.** vb. modérer.

moderation, n. modération f.

modern, adj. moderne.

modernize, vb. moderniser.

modest, adj. modeste.

modesty, n. modestie f.

modify, vb. modifier.

modish, adj. à la mode.

modulate, vb. moduler.

moist, adj. moite.

moisten, vb. humecter.

moisture, n. humidité f.

molar, n. and adj. molaire f.

molasses, n. mélasse f.

mold, 1. n. (casting) moule m.; (mildew) moisissure f. **2.** vb. (shape) mouler; (get moldy) moisir.

moldy, adj. moisi.

mole, n. (animal) taupe f.; (spot grain (m.) de beauté.

molecule, n. molécule f.

molest, vb. molester.

mollify, vb. adoucir, apaiser.

molten, adj. fondu, coulé.

moment, n. moment m.

momentary, adj. momentané.

momentous, adj. important.

monarch, n. monarque m.

monarchy, n. monarchie f.

monastery, n. monastère m.

Monday, n. lundi m.
monetary, adj. monétaire.
money, n. argent m.; (comm.) monnaie f.
mongrel, n. métis m.
monitor, n. moniteur m.
monk, n. moine m.
monkey, n. singe m.
monologue, n. monologue m.
monoplane, n. monoplan m.
monopolize, vb. monopoliser.
monopoly, n. monopole m.
monosyllable, n. monosyllabe f.
monotone, n. monotone m.
monotonous, adj. monotone.
monotony, n. monotonie f.
monsoon, n. mousson f.
monster, n. monstre m.
monstrosity, n. monstruosité f.
monstrous, adj. monstrueux.
month, n. mois m.
monthly, adj. mensuel.
monument, n. monument m.
monumental, adj. monumental.
mood, n. humeur f.; (gramm.) mode m.
moody, adj. de mauvaise humeur.
moon, n. lune f.
moonlight, n. clair (m.) de lune.
moor, n. lande f.
mooring, n. amarrage m.
moot, adj. discutable.
mop, n. balai (m.) à laver.
moped, n. cyclomoteur m.
moral, 1. n. morale f.; (morals) moralité f. **2.** adj. moral.
morale, n. moral m.
moralist, n. moraliste m.f.
morality, n. moralité f.; (ethics) morale f.
morally, adv. moralement.
morbid, adj. morbide.
more, 1. pron. en . . . davantage. **2.** adj.; adv. plus; (**m. than**) plus de; (**no m.**) ne . . . plus.
moreover, adv. de plus.
mores, n. mœurs f.pl.
morgue, n. morgue f.
morning, n. matin m.; (length of m.) matinée f.; (**good m.**) bonjour.
moron, n. idiot m.
morose, adj. morose.
Morse code, n. l'alphabet Morse m.
morsel, n. morceau m.

mortal, adj. and n. mortel m.
mortality, n. mortalité f.
mortar, n. mortier m.
mortgage, 1. n. hypothèque f. **2.** vb. hypothéquer.
mortician, n. entrepreneur de pompes funèbres m.
mortify, vb. mortifier.
mortuary, adj. mortuaire.
mosaic, 1. n. mosaïque f. **2.** adj. en mosaïque.
Moscow, n. Moscou m.
Moslem, adj. and n. musulman m.
mosquito, n. moustique m.
moss, n. mousse f.
most, 1. n. le plus. **2.** adj. le plus (de); la plupart (de). **3.** adv. (with adj. and vb.) le plus; (intensive) très.
mostly, adv. pour la plupart; (time) la plupart du temps.
moth, n. (clothes) mite f.
mother, n. mère f.
mother-in-law, n. belle-mère f.
motif, n. motif m.
motion, n. mouvement m.; (gesture) signe m.; (proposal) motion f.
motionless, adj. immobile.
motion-picture, n. film m.
motivate, vb. motiver.
motive, n. motif m.
motley, 1. adj. bigarré. **2.** n. livrée de bouffon m.
motor, n. moteur m.
motorboat, n. canot (m.) automobile.
motorist, n. automobiliste m.
motto, n. devise f.
mound, n. tertre m.
mount, 1. n. (hill) mont m.; (horse, structure) monture f. **2.** vb. monter.
mountain, n. montagne f.
mountaineer, n. montagnard m., Alpiniste m.
mountainous, adj. montagneux.
mountebank, n. saltimbanque m., charlatan m.
mourn, vb. pleurer.
mournful, adj. triste.
mourning, n. deuil m.
mouse, n. souris f.
mouth, n. bouche f.
mouthpiece, n. embouchure f., embout m.

movable, adj. mobile.

move, vb. mouvoir, tr.; remuer; (stir) bouger; (affect with emotion) émouvoir; (change residence) déménager; (propose) proposer.

movement, n. mouvement m.

moving, 1. n. déménagement m. **2.** adj. touchant.

mow, vb. faucher; (lawn) tondre.

Mr., n. M. m. (abbr. for Monsieur).

Mrs., n. Mme. f. (abbr. for Madame).

much, adj., pron. and adv. beaucoup (de); **(too m.)** trop (de); **(so m.)** tant (de); **(how m.)** combien (de).

mucilage, n. mucilage m.

muck, n. fumier m.

mucous, adj. muqueux.

mud, n. boue f.

muddy, adj. boueux.

muff, n. manchon m.

muffin, n. petit pain m.

muffle, vb. emmitoufler.

mug, n. gobelet m., pot m.

mulatto, n. mulâtre m.

mule, n. mulet m.

mullah, n. mollah m.

multicolored, adj. multicolore.

multinational, adj. multinational.

multiple, adj. multiple.

multiplication, n. multiplication f.

multiplicity, n. multiplicité f.

multiply, vb. multiplier, tr.

multitude, n. multitude f.

mummy, n. momie f.; maman f.

mumps, n. oreillons m.pl.

munch, vb. mâcher.

municipal, adj. municipal.

munificent, adj. munificent.

munition, n. munition(s) f.

mural, n. (painting) peinture (f.) murale.

murder, n. meurtre m.

murderer, n. meurtrier m.

murmur, 1. n. murmure m. **2.** vb. murmurer.

muscle, n. muscle m.

muscular, adj. musculaire; (strong) musculeux.

muse, 1. n. muse f. **2.** vb. méditer.

museum, n. musée m.

mushroom, n. champignon m.

music, n. musique f.

musical, adj. musical; (person) musicien.

musical comedy, n. comédie musicale f.

musician, n. musicien m.

Muslim, adj. and n. musulman m.

muslin, n. mousseline f.

must, vb. devoir; falloir (used impersonally, il faut que).

mustache, n. moustache f.

mustard, n. moutarde f.

muster, vb. rassembler, tr.

musty, adj. moisi, suranné.

mutation, n. mutation f.

mute, adj. muet.

mutilate, vb. mutiler.

mutiny, n. mutinerie f.

mutter, vb. grommeler.

mutton, n. mouton m.

mutual, adj. mutuel.

muzzle, n. muselière f.

my, adj. mon m., ma f., mes pl.

myopia, n. myopie f.

myriad, n. myriade f.

myself, pron. moi-même; (reflexive) me.

mysterious, adj. mystérieux.

mystery, n. mystère m.

mystic, adj. mystique.

mystify, vb. mystifier.

myth, n. mythe m.

mythical, adj. mythique.

mythology, n. mythologie f.

N

nag, vb. gronder.

nail, 1. n. (person, animal) ongle m.; (metal) clou m.; **(n. polish)** vernis m. à ongles. **2.** vb. clouer.

naïve, adj. naïf m., naïve f.

naked, adj. nu.

name, 1. n. nom m. **2.** vb. nommer.

namesake, n. homonyme m.

nap, n. petit somme m.

napkin, n. serviette f.

narcissus, n. narcisse m.

narcotic, adj. and n. narcotique m.

narrate, vb. raconter.

narrative, n. récit m.

narrow, adj. étroit.

nasal, adj. nasal.

nasty, adj. désagréable.

natal, adj. natal.

nation, n. nation f.
national, adj. national.
nationalism, n. nationalisme m.
nationality, n. nationalité f.
nationalization, n. nationalisation f.
nationalize, vb. nationaliser.
native, 1. n. natif m.; (primitive inhabitant, etc.) indigène m.f. **2.** adj. natif; (place) natal; (language) maternel.
nativity, n. naissance f.
natural, adj. naturel.
naturalist, n. naturaliste m.
naturalize, vb. naturaliser.
naturalness, n. naturel m.
nature, n. nature f.
naughty, adj. méchant.
nausea, n. nausée f.
nauseous, adj. nauséeux.
nautical, adj. marin.
naval, adj. naval.
nave, n. nef f.
navigable, adj. navigable.
navigate, vb. naviguer.
navigation, n. navigation f.
navigator, n. navigateur m.
navy, n. marine f.
navy yard, n. arsenal maritime m.
near, 1. adj. proche. **2.** adv. près. **3.** prep. près de.
nearly, adv. de près; (almost) presque.
near-sighted, adj. myope.
neat, adj. propre.
neatness, n. propreté f.
nebula, n. nébuleuse f.
nebulous, adj. nébuleux.
necessary, adj. nécessaire.
necessity, n. nécessité f.
neck, n. cou m.
necklace, n. collier m.
necktie, n. cravate f.
nectar, n. nectar m.
need, 1. n. besoin m. **2.** vb. avoir besoin de.
needful, adj. nécessaire.
needle, n. aiguille f.
needle point, n. pointe d'aiguille f.
needless, adj. inutile.
needy, adj. nécessiteux.
nefarious, adj. infâme.
negative, adj. négatif.
neglect, 1. n. négligence f. **2.** vb. négliger (de).
negligee, n. négligée f.

negligent, adj. négligent.
negligible, adj. négligeable.
negotiate, vb. négocier.
negotiation, n. négociation f.
Negro, adj. and n. nègre m.
neighbor, n. voisin m.; (fellow man) prochain m.
neighborhood, n. voisinage m.
neither, 1. adj. and pron. ni l'un ni l'autre. **2.** adv. non plus. **3.** conj. **(n. . . . nor)** ni . . . ni.
neon, n. néon m.
neophyte, n. néophyte m.
nephew, n. neveu m.
nepotism, n. népotisme m.
nerve, n. nerf m.
nervous, adj. nerveux.
nervous system, n. système nerveux m.
nest, n. nid m.
nestle, vb. se nicher.
net, 1. n. filet m. **2.** adj. net m., nette f.
Netherlands, the, n. les Pays-Bas m.pl., Hollande f.
network, n. réseau m.
neuralgia, n. névralgie f.
neurology, n. neurologie f.
neurotic, adj. and n. névrosé m.
neutral, adj. and n. neutre m.
neutron, n. neutron m.
neutron bomb, n. bombe à neutrons f.
never, adv. jamais.
nevertheless, adv. néanmoins.
new, adj. nouveau m., nouvelle f.; (not used) neuf m., neuve f.
news, n. (piece of news) nouvelle f.
newsboy, n. vendeur (m.) de journaux.
newscast, n. journal parlé m., informations f.pl.
newspaper, n. journal m.
newsreel, n. film d'actualité m.
New Testament, n. le Nouveau Testament m.
new year, n. nouvel an m.
next, 1. adj. prochain. **2.** adv. ensuite. **3.** prep. auprès de.
nibble, vb. grignoter.
nice, adj. (person) gentil; (thing) joli.
nick, n. entaille f.
nickel, n. nickel m.
nickname, n. surnom m.
nicotine, n. nicotine f.

niece, *n.* nièce *f.*

niggardly, *adj.* chiche.

night, *n.* nuit *f.;* (evening) soir *m.*

night club, *n.* boîte de nuit *f.,* établissement de nuit *m.*

nightgown, *n.* chemise (*f.*) de nuit.

nightingale, *n.* rossignol *m.*

nightly, *adv.* tous les soirs; toutes les nuits.

nightmare, *n.* cauchemar *m.*

nimble, *adj.* agile.

nine, *adj.* and *n.* neuf *m.*

nineteen, *adj.* and *n.* dix-neuf *m.*

ninety, *adj.* and *n.* quatre-vingt-dix *m.*

ninth, *adj.* and *n.* neuvième *m.*

nip, 1. *n.* pincement *m.,* pinçade *f.* **2.** *vb.* pincer.

nipple, *n.* mamelon *m.*

nitrogen, *n.* nitrogène *m.*

no, 1. *adj.* pas de. **2.** *interj.; adv.* non.

nobility, *n.* noblesse *f.*

noble, *adj.* noble.

nobleman, *n.* gentilhomme *m.*

nobly, *adv.* noblement.

nobody, *pron.* personne.

nocturnal, *adj.* nocturne.

nod, 1. *n.* signe (*m.*) de la tête. **2.** *vb.* incliner la tête.

node, *n.* nœud *m.*

no-frills, *adj.* simple.

noise, *n.* bruit *m.*

noiseless, *adj.* silencieux.

noisome, *n.* puant, fétide.

noisy, *adj.* bruyant.

nomad, *n.* nomade *m.* and *f.*

nominal, *adj.* nominal.

nominate, *vb.* (appoint) nommer; (propose) désigner.

nomination, *n.* (appointment) nomination *f.;* (proposal) désignation *f.*

nominee, *n.* personne nommée *f.,* candidat choisi *m.*

nonaligned, *adj.* (in politics) non-aligné.

nonchalant, *adj.* nonchalant.

noncombatant, *adj.* and *n.* non-combatant *m.*

noncommissioned, *adj.* sans brevet.

noncommittal, *adj.* qui n'engage à rien.

nondescript, *adj.* indéfinissable.

none, *pron.* aucun.

nonentity, *n.* nullité *f.*

non-proliferation, *n.* non-proliferation *m.*

nonresident, *n.* and *adj.* non-résident *m.*

nonsense, *n.* absurdité *f.*

nonstop, *adj.* sans arrêt.

noodles, *n.* nouilles *f.pl.*

nook, *n.* coin *m.,* recoin *m.*

noon, *n.* midi *m.*

noose, *n.* nœud coulant *m.*

nor, *conj.* ni; (and not) et ne . . . pas.

normal, *adj.* normal.

normally, *adv.* normalement.

north, *n.* nord *m.*

North America, *n.* Amérique (*f.*) du Nord.

northeast, *n.* nord-est *m.*

northern, *adj.* du nord.

North Pole, *n.* pôle nord *m.*

northwest, *n.* nord-ouest *m.*

Norway, *n.* Norvège *f.*

Norwegian, 1. *n.* (person) Norvégien *m.;* (language) norvégien *m.* **2.** *adj.* norvégien.

nose, *n.* nez *m.*

nosebleed, *n.* saignement du nez *m.*

nose dive, *n.* vol piqué *m.*

nostalgia, *n.* nostalgie *f.*

nostril, *n.* narine *f.;* (animals) naseau *m.*

nostrum, *n.* panacée *f.,* remède de charlatan *m.*

not, *adv.* (ne) pas.

notable, *adj.* and *n.* notable *m.*

notation, *n.* notation *f.*

note, 1. *n.* note *f.;* (letter, finance) billet *m.;* (distinction) marque *f.* **2.** *vb.* noter.

notebook, *n.* (small) carnet *m.;* (large) cahier *m.*

noted, *adj.* célèbre.

notepaper, *n.* papier à notes *m.*

noteworthy, *adj.* remarquable, mémorable.

nothing, *pron.* rien.

notice, 1. *n.* (announcement) avis *m.;* (attention) attention *f.;* (forewarning) préavis *m.* **2.** *vb.* remarquer.

noticeable, *adj.* remarquable; apparent.

notification, *n.* notification *f.*

notify, *vb.* avertir.

notion, *n.* idée *f.*

notoriety, *n.* notoriété *f.*
notorious, *adj.* notoire.
notwithstanding, 1. *adv.* tout de même. **2.** *prep.* malgré.
noun, *n.* substantif *m.*
nourish, *vb.* nourrir.
nourishment, *n.* nourriture *f.*
novel, *n.* roman *m.*
novelist, *n.* romancier *m.*
novelty, *n.* nouveauté *f.*
November, *n.* novembre *m.*
novice, *n.* novice *m.f.*
now, *adv.* maintenant; **(n. and then)** de temps en temps.
nowhere, *adv.* nulle part.
nozzle, *n.* ajutage *m.,* jet *m.*
nuance, *n.* nuance *f.*
nuclear, *adj.* nucléaire.
nuclear physics, *n.* physique nucléaire *f.*
nuclear warhead, *n.* cône de charge nucléaire *m.*
nuclear waste, *n.* déchets nucléaires *m.pl.*
nucleus, *n.* noyau *m.*
nude, *adj. and n.* nu *m.*
nugget, *n.* pépite *f.*
nuisance, *n.* (thing) ennui *m.;* (person) peste *f.*
nuke, 1. *n.* arme nucléaire *f.* **2.** *vb.* détruire avec des armes nucléaires.
nullify, *vb.* annuler, nullifier.
number, 1. *n.* nombre *m.;* (in a series, street, etc.) numéro *m.* **2.** *vb.* compter, numéroter.
numerical, *adj.* numérique.
numerous, *adj.* nombreux.
nun, *n.* religieuse *f.*
nuncio, *n.* nonce *m.*
nuptial, *adj.* nuptial.
nurse, 1. *n.* (hospital) infirmière *f.;* (wet-n.) nourrice *f.* **2.** *vb.* soigner; (suckle) allaiter.
nursery, *n.* (children) chambre (*f.*) des enfants; (plants) pépinière *f.*
nurture, 1. *n.* nourriture *f.* **2.** *vb.* nourrir, entretenir.
nut, *n.* noix *f.;* (metal) écrou *m.*
nutcracker, *n.* casse-noix *m.*
nutrition, *n.* nutrition *f.*
nutritious, *adj.* nutritif.
nutshell, *n.* coquille de noix *f.;* (in a n.) en deux mots.
nylon, *n.* nylon *m.*
nymph, *n.* nymphe *f.*

O

oak, *n.* chêne *m.*
oar, *n.* rame *f.*
oasis, *n.* oasis *f.*
oath, *n.* serment *m.;* (curse) juron *m.*
oatmeal, *n.* farine d'avoine *f.*
oats, *n.* avoine *f.*
obdurate, *adj.* obstiné, têtu.
obedience, *n.* obéissance *f.*
obedient, *adj.* obéissant.
obeisance, *n.* salut *m.*
obelisk, *n.* obélisque *m.*
obey, *vb.* obéir à.
obituary, *n.* nécrologe *m.*
object, 1. *n.* objet *m.* **2.** *vb.* objecter.
objection, *n.* objection *f.*
objectionable, *adj.* répréhensible.
objective, *adj. and n.* objectif *m.*
obligation, *n.* obligation *f.*
obligatory, *adj.* obligatoire.
oblige, *vb.* obliger.
oblivion, *n.* oubli *m.*
obnoxious, *adj.* odieux.
obscene, *adj.* obscène.
obscure, *adj.* obscur.
obsequious, *adj.* obséquieux.
observance, *n.* observance *f.*
observation, *n.* observation *f.*
observe, *vb.* observer.
observer, *n.* observateur *m.*
obsession, *n.* obsession *f.*
obsolete, *adj.* désuet.
obstacle, *n.* obstacle *m.*
obstetrician, *n.* médecin-accoucheur *m.*
obstinate, *adj.* obstiné.
obstreperous, *adj.* tapageur.
obstruct, *vb.* obstruer.
obstruction, *n.* obstruction *f.*
obtain, *vb.* obtenir.
obtrude, *vb.* mettre en avant.
obviate, *vb.* prévenir, éviter.
obvious, *adj.* évident.
occasion, *n.* occasion *f.*
occasional, *adj.* (not regular) de temps en temps.
occult, *adj.* occulte.
occupant, *n.* occupant *m.*
occupation, *n.* occupation *f.;* (vocation) métier *m.*
occupy, *vb.* occuper.
occur, *vb.* (happen) avoir lieu; (come to the mind) se présenter à l'esprit.

occurrence, *n.* occurrence *f.*

ocean, *n.* océan *m.*

o'clock, *see* clock.

octagon, *n.* octogone *m.*

octave, *n.* octave *f.*

October, *n.* octobre *m.*

octopus, *n.* poulpe *m.*

ocular, *adj.* oculaire.

oculist, *n.* oculiste *f.*

odd, *adj.* (not even) impair; (unmatched) dépareillé; (strange) bizarre.

oddity, *n.* singularité *f.*

odds, *n.* inégalité *f.,* (betting) cote *f.*

odious, *adj.* odieux.

odor, *n.* odeur *f.*

of, *prep.* de.

off, 1. *adv.* (away) à . . . de distance; (cancelled) rompu. **2.** *prep.* de.

offend, *vb.* offenser; **(o. against the law)** enfreindre la loi.

offender, *n.* offenseur *m.;* (law) délinquant *m.*

offense, *n.* offense *f.;* (transgression) délit *m.*

offensive, 1. *n.* offensive *f.* 2. *adj. (mil.,* etc.) offensif; (word, etc.) offensant.

offer, 1. *n.* offre *f.* 2. *vb.* offrir.

offering, *n.* offre *f.,* offrande *f.*

offhand, 1. *adj.* spontané. **2.** *adv.* sans préparation.

office, *n.* (service) office *m.;* (function) fonctions *f.pl.;* (room) bureau *m.*

officer, *n.* (mil.) officier *m.;* (public) fonctionnaire *m.*

official, *adj.* officiel.

officiate, *vb.* officier.

officious, *adj.* officieux.

offshore, 1. *adv.* vers le large. **2.** *adj.* du côté de la terre.

offspring, *n.* descendant *m.*

often, *adv.* souvent.

oil, *n.* huile *f.*

oilcloth, *n.* toile cirée *f.*

oily, *adj.* huileux.

ointment, *n.* onguent *m.*

okay, *interj.* très bien.

old, *adj.* vieux (vieil) *m.,* vieille *f.;* **(how o. are you?)** quel âge avez-vous?

old-fashioned, *adj.* démodé.

Old Testament, *n.* l'Ancien Testament *m.*

olfactory, *adj.* olfactif.

oligarchy, *n.* oligarchie *f.*

olive, *n.* (tree) olivier *m.;* (fruit) olive *f.*

ombudsman, *n.* (in France) médiateur *m.;* (in Quebec) protecteur du citoyen *m.*

omelet, *n.* omelette *f.*

omen, *n.* présage *m.*

ominous, *adj.* de mauvais augure.

omission, *n.* omission *f.*

omit, *vb.* omettre.

omnibus, *n.* omnibus *m.*

omnipotent, *adj.* omnipotent, tout-puissant.

on, *prep.* sur.

once, *adv.* une fois; (formerly) autrefois; **(at o., without delay)** tout de suite; **(at o., at the same time)** à la fois.

one, 1. *adj.* un; (only) seul. **2.** *n.* un *m.* **3.** *pron.* un; (indefinite subject) on, (indefinite object) vous; **(the o.)** celui; **(this o.)** celui-ci; **(that o.)** celui-là; **(which o.)** lequel.

oneself, *pron.* soi-même; (reflexive) se.

one-sided, *adj.* unilatéral.

onion, *n.* oignon *m.*

onionskin, *n.* pelure d'oignon *f.,* (paper) papier pelure *m.*

only, 1. *adj.* seul. **2.** *adv.* seulement.

onslaught, *n.* assaut *m.*

onward, *adj. and adv.* en avant.

opal, *n.* opale *f.*

opaque, *adj.* opaque.

open, 1. *adj.* ouvert. **2.** *vb.* ouvrir.

opening, *n.* ouverture *f.*

opera, *n.* opéra *m.*

opera glasses, *n.* jumelles *f.pl.*

operate, *vb.* opérer; (put into operation) actionner.

operatic, *adj.* d'opéra.

operation, *n.* opération *f.;* (functioning) fonctionnement *m.*

operator, *n.* opérateur *m.;* (telephone) standardiste *f.*

operetta, *n.* opérette *f.*

opinion, *n.* opinion *f.*

opponent, *n.* adversaire *m.f.*

opportunism, *n.* opportunisme *m.*

opportunity, *n.* occasion *f.*

oppose, *vb.* (put in opposition) opposer; (resist) s'opposer à.

opposite, 1. *adj.* opposé. **2.** *adv.* vis-à-vis. **3.** *prep.* en face de.
opposition, *n.* opposition *f.*
oppress, *vb.* opprimer.
oppression, *n.* oppression *f.*
oppressive, *adj.* oppressif; (heat, etc.) accablant.
optic, *adj.* optique.
optician, *n.* opticien *m.*
optimism, *n.* optimisme *m.*
optimistic, *adj.* optimiste.
option, *n.* option *f.*
optional, *adj.* facultatif.
optometry, *n.* optométrie *f.*
opulent, *adj.* opulent, riche.
or, *conj.* ou; (with negative) ni.
oracle, *n.* oracle *m.*
oral, *adj.* oral.
orange, *n.* orange *f.*
orangeade, *n.* orangeade *f.*
oration, *n.* discours *m.*
orator, *n.* orateur *m.*
oratory, *n.* art (*m.*) oratoire.
orbit, *n.* orbite *f.*
orchard, *n.* verger *m.*
orchestra, *n.* orchestre *m.*
orchid, *n.* orchidée *f.*
ordain, *vb.* ordonner.
ordeal, *n.* épreuve *f.*
order, 1. *n.* ordre *m.;* (comm.) commande *f.* **2.** *vb.* ordonner; (comm.) commander.
orderly, *adj.* ordonné.
ordinance, *n.* ordonnance *f.*
ordinary, *adj. and n.* ordinaire *m.*
ordination, *n.* ordination *f.*
ore, *n.* minerai *m.*
organ, *n.* (music) orgue *m.;* (body) organe *m.*
organdy, *n.* organdi *m.*
organic, *adj.* organique.
organism, *n.* organisme *m.*
organist, *n.* organiste *m.f.*
organization, *n.* organisation *f.*
organize, *vb.* organiser.
orgy, *n.* orgie *f.*
orient, *vb.* orienter.
Orient, *n.* Orient *m.*
Oriental, 1. *n.* Oriental *m.* **2.** *adj.* oriental.
orientation, *n.* orientation *f.*
origin, *n.* origine *f.*
original, *adj.* (new, unique) original; (from the origin) originel.
originality, *n.* originalité *f.*
ornament, *n.* ornement *m.*
ornamental, *adj.* ornemental.

ornate, *adj.* orné.
ornithology, *n.* ornithologie *f.*
orphan, *n.* orphelin *m.*
orphanage, *n.* orphelinat *m.*
orthodox, *adj.* orthodoxe.
orthopedics, *n.* orthopédie *f.*
osmosis, *n.* osmose *f.*
ostensible, *adj.* prétendu.
ostentation, *n.* ostentation *f.*
ostentatious, *adj.* plein d'ostentation.
ostracize, *vb.* ostraciser.
ostrich, *n.* autruche *f.*
other, *adj. and pron.* autre.
otherwise, *adv.* autrement.
ought, *vb.* devoir.
ounce, *n.* once *f.*
our, *adj.* notre *sg.,* nos *pl.*
ours, *pron.* le nôtre.
ourself, *pron.* nous-même; (reflexive) nous.
oust, *vb.* évincer.
ouster, *n.* éviction *f.*
out, *adv.* dehors.
outbreak, *n.* (beginning) commencement *m.;* (insurrection) révolte *f.*
outburst, *n.* éruption *f.*
outcast, *n.* paria *m.*
outcome, *n.* résultat *m.*
outdoors, *adv.* dehors.
outer, *adj.* extérieur.
outfit, *n.* équipement *m.*
outgrowth, *n.* conséquence *f.*
outing, *n.* promenade *f.*
outlandish, *adj.* bizarre.
outlaw, *vb.* proscrire.
outlet, *n.* issue *f.*
outline, 1. *n.* contour *m.;* (general idea) aperçu *m.* **2.** *vb.* (drawing) tracer; (plan) exposer à grands traits.
out of, *prep.* hors de; (because of) par; (without) sans.
out-of-date, *adj.* suranné.
output, *n.* rendement *m.*
outrage, *n.* outrage *m.*
outrageous, *adj.* outrageant.
outrank, *vb.* occuper un rang supérieur.
outright, *adv.* complètement.
outrun, *vb.* dépasser.
outside, 1. *adv.* dehors. **2.** *prep.* en dehors de.
outskirts, *n.* limites *f.pl.*
outward, *adj.* extérieur.

oval, *adj. and n.* ovale *m.*

ovation, *n.* ovation *f.*

oven, *n.* four *m.*

over, 1. *prep.* (on) sur; (above) au-dessus de; (beyond) au delà de; (more than) plus de. **2.** *adv.* (all over) partout; (more) davantage; (finished) fini; (with *adj.*) trop.

overbearing, *adj.* arrogant.

overcoat, *n.* pardessus *m.*

overcome, *vb.* vaincre; (**be o. by**) succomber à.

overdue, *adj.* arriéré, échu.

overflow, *vb.* déborder.

overhaul, *vb.* examiner en détail, remettre au point.

overhead, 1. *adj.* (comm.) général. **2.** *adv.* en haut.

overkill, *n.* exagération rhétorique *f.*

overlook, *vb.* (look on to) avoir vue sur; (neglect) négliger.

overnight, *adv.* pendant la nuit.

overpower, *vb.* (subdue) subjuguer; (crush) accabler.

overrule, *vb.* décider contre.

overrun, *vb.* envahir.

oversee, *vb.* surveiller.

oversight, *n.* inadvertance *f.*

overstuffed, *adj.* rembourré.

overt, *adj.* manifeste.

overtake, *vb.* rattraper; (accident, etc.) arriver à.

overthrow, *vb.* renverser.

overtime, *n.* heures (*f.pl.*) supplémentaires.

overture, *n.* ouverture *f.*

overturn, *vb.* renverser, tr.

overview, *n.* vue d'ensemble *f.*

overweight, *n.* excédent *m.*

overwhelm, *vb.* accabler (de).

overwork, *vb.* surmener, tr.

owe, *vb.* devoir.

owing, 1. *prep.* à cause de, en raison de. **2.** *adj.* dû.

owl, *n.* hibou *m.*

own, 1. *adj.* propre. **2.** *vb.* posséder; (admit) avouer; (acknowledge) reconnaître.

owner, *n.* propriétaire *m.f.*

ox, *n.* bœuf *m.*

oxygen, *n.* oxygène *m.*

oxygen mask, *n.* masque d'oxygène *m.*

oyster, *n.* huître *f.*

P

pace, 1. *n.* (step) pas *m.;* (gait) allure *f.* **2.** *vb.* arpenter.

Pacific Ocean, *n.* océan Pacifique *m.*

pacific, *adj.* pacifique.

pacifism, *n.* pacifisme *m.*

pacify, *vb.* pacifier.

pack, 1. *n.* paquet *m.;* (animals, persons) bande *f.* **2.** *vb.* emballer; (crowd) entasser.

package, *n.* paquet *m.*

pact, *n.* pacte *m.,* contrat *m.*

pad, 1. *n.* (stuffing) bourrelet *m.;* (cotton, ink) tampon *m.;* (paper) bloc *m.* **2.** *vb.* (clothes) ouater; (stuff) bourrer.

padding, *n.* remplissage *m.,* rembourrage *m.*

paddle, *n.* pagaie *f.*

paddock, *n.* enclos *m.*

pagan, *adj. and n.* païen *m.*

page, 1. *n.* (book) page *f.;* (attendant) page *m.*

pageant, *n.* spectacle *m.*

pagoda, *n.* pagode *f.*

pail, *n.* seau *m.*

pain, 1. *n.* douleur *f.;* (trouble) peine *f.* **2.** *vb.* (hurt) faire mal (à); (distress) faire de la peine (à).

painful, *adj.* douloureux.

painstaking, *adj.* soigneux.

paint, 1. *n.* peinture *f.* **2.** *vb.* peindre.

painter, *n.* peintre *m.*

painting, *n.* peinture *f.*

pair, *n.* paire *f.*

pajamas, *n.* pyjama *m.*

palace, *n.* palais *m.*

palatable, *adj.* d'un goût agréable, agréable au palais.

palate, *n.* palais *m.*

palatial, *adj.* qui ressemble à un palais, magnifique.

pale, *adj.* pâle.

paleness, *n.* pâleur *f.*

palette, *n.* palette *f.*

pall, 1. *n.* drap funéraire *m.* **2.** *vb.* s'affadir.

pallbearer, *n.* porteur (d'un cordon du poêle) *m.*

pallid, *adj.* pâle, blême.

palm, *n.* (tree) palmier *m.;* (branch) palme *f.;* (hand) paume *f.*

palpitate, *vb.* palpiter.
paltry, *adj.* mesquin.
pamper, *vb.* choyer.
pamphlet, *n.* brochure *f.*
pan, *n.* (cooking) casserole *f.*
panacea, *n.* panacée *f.*
Pan-American, *adj.* panaméricain.
pancake, *n.* crêpe *f.*
pane, *n.* (window) vitre *f.*
panel, *n.* panneau *m.*
pang, *n.* angoisse *f.*
panic, *n.* panique *f.*
panorama, *n.* panorama *m.*
pant, *vb.* haleter.
pantomime, *n.* pantomime *m.*
pantry, *n.* office *f.*
pants, *n.* pantalon *m.*
panty hose, *n.* collant *m.*
papal, *adj.* papal.
paper, *n.* papier *m.*
paperback, *n.* livre broché *m.*
par, *n.* pair *m.,* égalité *f.*
parable, *n.* parabole *f.*
parachute, *n.* parachute *m.*
parade, *n.* parade *f.*
paradise, *n.* paradis *m.*
paradox, *n.* paradoxe *m.*
paraffin, *n.* paraffine *f.*
paragraph, *n.* alinéa *m.*
parakeet, *n.* perruche *f.*
parallel, 1. *n.* (line) parallèle *f.;* (geography, comparison) parallèle *m.* **2.** *adj.* parallèle.
paralyze, *vb.* paralyser.
paramedic, *n.* assistant médical *m.*
parameter, *n.* paramètre *m.*
paramount, *adj.* souverain.
paraphrase, *vb.* paraphraser.
parasite, *n.* parasite *m.*
parcel, *n.* paquet *m.;* **(p. post)** colis postal *m.*
parch, *vb.* dessécher, *tr.*
parchment, *n.* parchemin *m.*
pardon, 1. *n.* pardon *m.* **2.** *vb.* pardonner.
pare, *vb.* (fruit) peler.
parent, *n.* père *m.;* mère *f.;* **(parents)** parents *m.pl.*
parentage, *n.* naissance *f.*
parenthesis, *n.* parenthèse *f.*
parish, *n.* paroisse *f.*
Parisian, 1. *n.* Parisien *m.* **2.** *adj.* parisien.
parity, *n.* parité *f.,* égalité *f.*

park, 1. *n.* parc *m.* **2.** *vb.* stationner.
parley, *n.* conférence *f.,* pourparler *m.*
parliament, *n.* parlement *m.*
parliamentary, *adj.* parlementaire.
parlor, *n.* petit salon *m.*
parochial, *adj.* paroissial; (limited in outlook) de clocher.
parody, *n.* parodie *f.*
parole, 1. *n.* parole *f.* **2.** *vb.* libérer conditionnellement.
paroxysm, *n.* paroxysme *m.*
parrot, *n.* perroquet *m.*
parsley, *n.* persil *m.*
parson, *n.* pasteur *m.*
part, 1. *n.* (of a whole) partie *f.;* (share) part *f.* **2.** *vb.* (divide) diviser; (share) partager; (of people) se séparer.
partake of, *vb.* participer à.
partial, *adj.* partiel; (favoring) partial.
participant, *adj.* and *n.* participant *m.*
participate, *vb.* participer.
participation, *n.* participation *f.*
participle, *n.* participe *m.*
particle, *n.* particule *f.*
particular, 1. *n.* détail *m.* **2.** *adj.* particulier; (person) exigeant.
parting, *n.* séparation *f.;* (hair) raie *f.*
partisan, *n.* partisan *m.*
partition, *n.* partage *m.;* (wall) cloison *f.*
partly, *adv.* en partie.
partner, *n.* associé *m.*
part of speech, *n.* partie *(f.)* du discours.
partridge, *n.* perdrix *f.*
party, *n.* (faction) parti *m.;* (social) réception *f.;* (group of people) groupe *m.;* (law) partie *f.*
pass, 1. *n.* (mountain) col *m.;* (permission) laissez-passer *m.* **2.** *vb.* passer.
passable, *adj.* traversable, passable, assez bon.
passage, *n.* passage *m.*
passenger, *n.* (land) voyageur *m.;* (sea, air) passager *m.*
passer-by, *n.* passant *m.*
passion, *n.* passion *f.*
passionate, *adj.* passionné. .
passive, *adj.* and *n.* passif *m.*

passport, n. passeport m.
past, 1. adj. and n. passé m. **2.** prep. (beyond) au delà de; (more than) plus de; **(half p. four)** quatre heures et demie.
paste, 1. n. pâte f.; (glue) colle f. **2.** vb. coller.
pasteurize, vb. pasteuriser.
pastime, n. passe-temps m.
pastor, n. pasteur m.
pastry, n. pâtisserie f.
pasture, n. pâturage m.
pasty, adj. empâté, pâteux.
pat, vb. taper.
patch, 1. n. pièce f. **2.** vb. rapiécer.
patchwork, n. ouvrage fait de pièces disparates m.
patent, n. brevet (m.) d'invention.
patent leather, n. cuir (m.) verni.
paternal, adj. paternel.
paternity, n. paternité f.
path, n. sentier m.
pathetic, adj. pathétique.
pathology, n. pathologie f.
pathos, n. pathétique m.
patience, n. patience f.
patient, 1. n. malade m.f. **2.** adj. patient.
patio, n. patio m.
patriarch, n. patriarche m.
patriot, n. patriote m.f.
patriotic, adj. patriotique.
patriotism, n. patriotisme m.
patrol, n. patrouille f.
patrolman, n. agent (de police) m., patrouilleur m.
patron, n. protecteur m.; (comm.) client m.
patronize, vb. protéger.
pattern, n. modèle m.; (design) dessin m.
pauper, n. indigent m., pauvre m., mendiant m.
pause, n. pause f.
pave, vb. paver.
pavement, n. pavé m.; (sidewalk) trottoir m.
pavilion, n. pavillon m.
paw, n. patte f.
pawn, 1. n. pion m. **2.** vb. mettre en gage, engager.
pay, 1. n. salaire m. **2.** vb. payer.
payment, n. payement m.
pea, n. pois m.
peace, n. paix f.
peaceable, peaceful, adj. paisible.
peach, n. pêche f.

peacock, n. paon m.
peak, n. sommet m.
peal, 1. n. retentissement m. **2.** vb. sonner, retentir.
peanut, n. arachide f.
pear, n. poire f.
pearl, n. perle f.
peasant, n. paysan m.
pebble, n. caillou m.
peck, vb. becqueter.
peculiar, adj. particulier; (unusual) singulier.
pecuniary, adj. pécuniaire.
pedagogue, n. pédagogue m.
pedagogy, n. pédagogie f.
pedal, n. pédale f.
pedant, n. pédant m.
peddle, vb. colporter.
peddler, n. colporteur m.
pedestal, n. piédestal m.
pedestrian, n. piéton m.
pediatrician, n. pédiatre m.
pedigree, n. généalogie f.
peek, 1. n. coup d'œil furtif m. **2.** vb. regarder à la dérobée.
peel, 1. n. pelure f. **2.** vb. peler.
peep, vb. regarder furtivement.
peer, 1. n. pair m. **2.** vb. regarder.
peevish, adj. irritable.
peg, n. cheville f.
pelt, 1. n. peau f., fourrure f. **2.** vb. lancer, jeter.
pelvis, n. bassin m.
pen, n. plume f.; (ballpoint) stylo (m.) à bille.
penalty, n. peine f.
penance, n. pénitence f.
penchant, n. penchant m.
pencil, n. crayon m.
pending, prep. pendant.
penetrate, vb. pénétrer.
penetration, n. pénétration f.
peninsula, n. péninsule f.
penitent, 1. adj. pénitent, contrit. **2.** n. pénitent m.
penknife, n. canif m.
penniless, adj. sans le sou.
penny, n. sou m.
pension, n. pension f.
pensive, adj. pensif.
pent-up, adj. refoulé.
penury, n. pénurie f.
people, 1. n. gens m.f.pl.; (of a country) peuple m. **2.** vb. peupler.
pepper, n. poivre m.

perambulator, n. voiture d'enfant f.

perceive, vb. apercevoir, tr.

percent, pour cent.

percentage, n. pourcentage m.

perceptible, adj. perceptible.

perception, n. perception f.

perch, 1. n. (for birds) perchoir m.; (fish) perche f. **2.** vb. se percher.

perdition, n. perte f.

peremptory, adj. péremptoire.

perennial, adj. perpétuel; (plant) vivace.

perfect, adj. parfait.

perfection, n. perfection f.

perforation, n. perforation f.

perform, vb. accomplir; (theater) jouer.

performance, n. (task) accomplissement m.; (theater) représentation f.

perfume, n. parfum m.

perfunctory, adj. fait pour la forme, superficiel.

perhaps, adv. peut-être.

peril, n. péril m.

perilous, adj. périlleux.

perimeter, n. périmètre m.

period, n. période f.; (full stop) point m.

periodic, adj. périodique.

periodical, n. périodique m.

periphery, n. périphérie f.

perish, vb. périr.

perishable, adj. périssable.

perjury, n. parjure m.

permanent, adj. permanent.

permeate, vb. filtrer.

permissible, adj. admissible.

permission, n. permission f.

permit, 1. n. permis m. **2.** vb. permettre.

pernicious, adj. pernicieux.

perpendicular, adj. perpendiculaire, vertical.

perpetrate, vb. perpétrer.

perpetual, adj. perpétuel.

perplex, vb. mettre dans la perplexité.

perplexity, n. perplexité f., embarras m.

persecute, vb. persécuter.

persecution, n. persécution f.

perseverance, n. persévérance f.

persevere, vb. persévérer.

persist, vb. persister.

persistent, adj. persistant.

person, n. personne f.

personage, n. personnage m.

personal, adj. personnel.

personality, n. personnalité f.

personally, adv. personnellement.

personnel, n. personnel m.

perspective, n. perspective f.

perspiration, n. transpiration f.

perspire, vb. transpirer.

persuade, vb. persuader.

persuasive, adj. persuasif.

pertain, vb. appartenir.

pertinent, adj. pertinent.

perturb, vb. troubler.

peruse, vb. lire attentivement.

pervade, vb. pénétrer.

perverse, adj. entêté (dans l'erreur).

perversion, n. perversion f.

pessimism, n. pessimisme m.

pestilence, n. pestilence f.

pet, n. (animal) animal (m.) familier.

petal, n. pétale m.

petition, n. pétition f.

petroleum, n. pétrole m.

petticoat, n. jupon m.

petty, adj. insignifiant.

phantom, n. fantôme m.

pharmacist, n. pharmacien m.

pharmacy, n. pharmacie f.

phase, n. phase f.

phenomenal, adj. phénoménal.

phenomenon, n. phénomène m.

philanthropy, n. philanthropie f.

philosopher, n. philosophe m.

philosophical, adj. philosophique.

philosophy, n. philosophie f.

phobia, n. phobie f.

phonograph, n. phonographe m.

photocopier, n. photocopieur m.

photocopy, n. photocopie f.

photograph, photography, n. photographie f.

phrase, n. phrase f.

physical, adj. physique.

physician, n. médecin m.

physics, n. physique f.

pianist, n. pianiste m.f.

piano, n. piano m.

pick, vb. (choose) choisir; (gather) cueillir.

pickles, n. conserves (f.pl.) au vinaigre.

picnic, n. pique-nique m.

picture, *n.* tableau *m.; (motion picture)* film *m.*

picturesque, *adj.* pittoresque.

pie, *n.* tarte *f.*

piece, *n.* morceau *m.*

pier, *n.* jetée *f.;* quai *m.*

pierce, *vb.* percer.

piety, *n.* piété *f.*

pig, *n.* cochon *m.*

pigeon, *n.* pigeon *m.*

pigeonhole, *n. (for papers, etc.)* case *f.*

pile, 1. *n. (construction)* pieu *m.; (heap)* tas *m.* **2.** *vb.* entasser.

pilgrim, *n.* pèlerin *m.*

pilgrimage, *n.* pèlerinage *m.*

pill, *n.* pilule *f.*

pillar, *n.* pilier *m.*

pillow, *n.* oreiller *m.*

pilot, *n.* pilote *m.*

pimple, *n.* bouton *m.*

pin, 1. *n.* épingle *f.* **2.** *vb.* épingler.

pinch, *vb.* pincer.

pine, 1. *n.* pin *m.* **2.** *vb.* languir.

pineapple, *n.* ananas *m.*

pink, *adj. and n.* rose *m.*

pinnacle, *n.* pinacle *m.*

pint, *n.* pinte *f.*

pioneer, *n.* pionnier *m.*

pious, *adj.* pieux.

pipe, *n.* tuyau *m.; (smoking)* pipe *f.*

piper, *n. (bagpipe)* joueur *(m.)* de cornemuse.

piquant, *adj.* piquant.

pirate, *n.* pirate *m.*

pistol, *n.* pistolet *m.*

piston, *n.* piston *m.*

pit, *n.* fosse *f.*

pitch, 1. *n. (substance)* poix *f.; (throw)* jet *m.; (height)* hauteur *f.; (music)* ton *m.* **2.** *vb. (throw)* lancer.

pitcher, *n. (vessel)* cruche *f.; (baseball)* lanceur *m.*

pitfall, *n.* trappe *f.*

pitiful, *adj.* pitoyable.

pitiless, *adj.* impitoyable.

pity, 1. *n.* pitié *f.; (what a p.!)* quel dommage! **2.** *vb.* plaindre.

pivot, *n.* pivot *m.,* axe *m.*

pizza, *n.* pizza *f.*

place, 1. *n.* endroit *m.; (locality)* lieu *m.; (position occupied)* place *f.* **2.** *vb.* mettre.

placid, *adj.* placide.

plague, *n. (disease)* peste *f.; (fig.)* fléau *m.*

plaid, *n. (blanket)* plaid *m.; (textile)* tartan *m.*

plain, 1. *n.* plaine *f.* *adj. (clear)* clair; *(simple)* simple; *(of person)* quelconque.

plaintiff, *n.* demandeur *m.*

plan, 1. *n.* plan *m.* **2.** *vb.* faire le plan de.

plane, *n. (surface)* plan *m.; (tool)* rabot *m.; (tree)* platane *m.; (airplane)* avion *m.*

planet, *n.* planète *f.*

plank, *n.* planche *f.*

plant, 1. *n.* plante *f.* **2.** *vb.* planter.

plantation, *n.* plantation *f.*

planter, *n.* planteur *m.*

plasma, *n.* plasma *m.*

plaster, *n.* plâtre *m.*

plastic, *adj.* plastique.

plate, *n.* plaque *f.; (for eating)* assiette *f.*

plateau, *n.* plateau *m.*

platform, *n.* plate-forme *f.; (railroad)* quai *m.*

platter, *n.* plat *m.*

plausible, *adj.* plausible.

play, 1. *n.* jeu *m.; (drama)* pièce *(f.)* de théâtre. **2.** *vb.* jouer; *(game)* jouer à; *(instrument)* jouer de.

player, *n.* jouer *m.; (theater)* acteur *m.*

playful, *adj.* enjoué.

playground, *n. (children)* terrain *(m.)* de jeu.

playmate, *n.* camarade *(m.f.)* de jeu.

playwright, *n.* dramaturge *m.*

plea, *n.* défense *f.; (excuse)* excuse *f.*

plead, *vb.* plaider; *(allege)* alléguer.

pleasant, *adj.* agréable.

please, *vb.* plaire à; *(satisfy)* contenter; **(if you p.)** s'il vous plaît.

pleasure, *n.* plaisir *m.*

pleat, *n.* pli *m.*

pledge, *n.* gage *m.; (promise)* engagement *m.*

plentiful, *adj.* abondant.

plenty, *n.* abondance *f.*

pliable, *adj.* pliable.

pliers, *n.* pinces *f.pl.*

plight, *n.* état *m.*

plot, *n.* (literature) intrigue *f.;* (conspiracy) complot *m.*

plow, 1. *n.* charrue *f.* **2.** *vb.* labourer.

pluck, *n.* courage *m.*

plug, *n.* tampon *m.;* (electric) prise (*f.*) de courant.

plum, *n.* prune *f.*

plumber, *n.* plombier *m.*

plume, *n.* panache *m.*

plump, *adj.* grassouillet *m.*

plunder, *vb.* piller.

plunge, 1. *n.* plongeon *m.* **2.** *vb.* plonger.

plural, *adj. and n.* pluriel *m.*

plus, *n.* plus *m.*

pneumonia, *n.* pneumonie *f.*

poach, *vb.* (of eggs) pocher.

poacher, *n.* braconnier *m.*

pocket, *n.* poche *f.*

pocketbook, *n.* sac (*m.*) à main.

poem, *n.* poésie *f.;* (long) poème *f.*

poet, *n.* poète *m.*

poetic, *adj.* poétique.

poetry, *n.* poésie *f.*

poignant, *adj.* poignant.

point, 1. *n.* point *m.;* (sharp end) pointe *f.* **2.** *vb.* (gun, etc.) pointer; (indicate) désigner.

pointed, *adj.* pointu; (ironical) mordant.

poise, *n.* équilibre *m.*

poison, 1. *n.* poison *m.* **2.** *vb.* empoisonner.

poisonous, *adj.* empoisonné; (plant) vénéneux; (animal) venimeux.

Poland, *n.* Pologne *f.*

polar, *adj.* polaire.

polar bear, *n.* ours (*m.*) blanc.

Pole, *n.* Polonais *m.*

pole, *n.* (geography) pôle *m.;* (wood) perche *f.*

police, *n.* police *f.*

policeman, *n.* agent (*m.*) de police.

policy, *n.* politique *f.;* (insurance) police *f.*

Polish, *adj. and n.* polonais *m.*

polish, *vb.* polir; (shoes) cirer.

polite, *adj.* poli.

politic, political, *adj.* politique.

politician, *n.* politicien *m.*

politics, *n.* politique *f.*

poll, *n.* (voting) scrutin *m.*

pollen, *n.* pollen *m.*

pollute, *vb.* polluer.

polygamy, *n.* polygamie *f.*

pomp, *n.* pompe *f.*

pompous, *adj.* pompeux.

pond, *n.* étang *m.*

ponder, *vb.* réfléchir.

ponderous, *adj.* pesant.

pony, *n.* poney *m.*

pool, *n.* mare *f.;* (swimming) piscine *f.*

poor, *adj.* pauvre.

pop, *n.* petit bruit (*m.*) sec.

pope, *n.* pape *m.*

popular, *adj.* populaire.

popularity, *n.* popularité *f.*

population, *n.* population *f.*

porch, *n.* véranda *f.*

pore, 1. *n.* pore *m.* **2.** *vb.* **(p. over)** s'absorber dans.

pork, *n.* porc *m.*

pornography, *n.* pornographie *f.*

porous, *adj.* poreux.

port, *n.* (harbor) port *m.;* (naut.) bâbord *m.;* (wine) porto *m.*

portable, *adj.* portatif.

portal, *n.* portail *m.*

portfolio, *n.* portefeuille *m.*

portion, *n.* portion *f.*

portrait, *n.* portrait *m.*

portray, *vb.* (paint) peindre; (describe) dépeindre.

Portugal, *n.* Portugal *m.*

Portuguese, 1. *n.* (person) Portugais *m.;* (language) portugais *m.* **2.** *adj.* portugais.

pose, 1. *n.* pose *f.* **2.** *vb.* poser.

position, *n.* position *f.*

positive, 1. *n.* positif *m.* **2.** *adj.* positif.

possess, *vb.* posséder.

possession, *n.* possession *f.*

possibility, *n.* possibilité *f.*

possible, *adj.* possible.

possibly, *adv.* il est possible que . . .; (perhaps) peut-être.

post, 1. *n.* (mail) poste *f.;* (wood) poteau *m.;* (place) poste *m.* **2.** *vb.* (mail) mettre à la poste; (placard) afficher.

postage, *n.* affranchissement *m.*

postal, *adj.* postal.

post card, *n.* carte (*f.*) postale.

poster, *n.* affiche *f.*

posterior, *adj.* postérieur.

posterity, *n.* postérité *f.*

post office, *n.* bureau (*m.*) de poste.

postpone, vb. remettre.

postscript, n. post-scriptum m.

posture, n. posture f.

pot, n. pot m.; (saucepan) marmite f.; (marijuana) herbe f., kif m.

potato, n. pomme (f.) de terre.

potent, adj. puissant.

potential, adj. and n. potentiel m.

pottery, n. poterie f.

pouch, n. sac m.

poultry, n. volaille f.

pound, n. livre f.

pour, vb. verser; (rain) tomber à verse.

poverty, n. pauvreté f.

powder, n. poudre f.

power, n. pouvoir m.; (nation, mathematics) puissance f.

powerful, adj. puissant.

powerless, adj. impuissant.

practical, adj. pratique.

practically, adv. pratiquement.

practice, 1. n. (exercise) exercice m.; (habit) habitude f.; (not theory) pratique f. **2.** vb. pratiquer; (piano, etc.) s'exercer (à).

practiced, adj. expérimenté.

prairie, n. savane f.

praise, 1. n. éloge m. **2.** vb. louer.

prank, n. fredaine f.

pray, vb. prier.

prayer, n. prière f.

preach, vb. prêcher.

preacher, n. prédicateur m.

precarious, adj. précaire.

precaution, n. précaution f.

precede, vb. précéder.

precedent, n. précédent m.

precept, n. précepte m.

precious, adj. précieux.

precipice, n. précipice m.

precipitate, vb. précipiter.

precise, adj. précis.

precision, n. précision f.

preclude, vb. empêcher.

precocious, adj. précoce.

predecessor, n. prédécesseur m.

predestination, n. prédestination f.

predicament, n. situation (f.) difficile.

predict, vb. prédire.

predispose, vb. prédisposer.

predominant, adj. prédominant.

prefabricate, vb. préfabriquer.

preface, n. préface f.

prefer, vb. préférer.

preferable, adj. préférable.

preference, n. préférence f.

prefix, n. préfixe m.

pregnant, adj. enceinte.

prejudice, n. préjugé m.

preliminary, adj. préliminaire.

prelude, n. prélude m.

premature, adj. prématuré.

premeditate, vb. préméditer.

premier, n. premier ministre m.

première, n. première f.

premise, n. (place) lieux m.pl.; (logic) prémisse f.

premium, n. prix m.

preparation, n. préparation f.; préparatifs m.pl.

preparatory, adj. préparatoire.

prepare, vb. préparer, tr.

preponderant, adj. prépondérant.

preposition, n. préposition f.

preposterous, adj. absurde.

prerequisite, n. nécessité (f.) préalable.

prescribe, vb. prescrire.

prescription, n. prescription f.; (medical) ordonnance f.

presence, n. présence f.

present, 1. adj. and n. présent m. **2.** vb. présenter.

presentable, adj. présentable.

presentation, n. présentation f.

presently, adv. tout à l'heure.

preservative, adj. and n. préservatif m.

preserve, 1. n. (jam) confiture f. **2.** vb. (protect) préserver; (keep) conserver.

preside, vb. présider.

president, n. président m.

press, 1. n. presse f. **2.** vb. presser; (iron) repasser.

pressure, n. pression f.

prestige, n. prestige m.

presume, vb. présumer.

presumptuous, adj. présomptueux.

pretend, vb. (claim, aspire) prétendre; (feign) simuler.

pretense, n. faux semblant m.

pretentious, adj. prétentieux.

pretext, n. prétexte m.

pretty, adj. joli.

prevail, vb. prévaloir; **(p. upon)** décider.

prevalent, adj. répandu.

prevent, vb. (impede) empêcher; (forestall) prévenir.

prevention, n. empêchement m.

preventive, adj. préventif.

previous, adj. antérieur.

prey, n. proie f.

price, n. prix m.

priceless, adj. inestimable.

prick, 1. n. piqûre f. **2.** vb. piquer.

pride, n. orgueil m.

priest, n. prêtre m.

prim, adj. affecté.

primary, adj. premier; (school, geology) primaire.

prime, 1. n. comble m. **2.** adj. premier, de première qualité. **3.** vb. amorcer.

primitive, adj. primitif.

prince, n. prince m.

princess, n. princesse f.

principal, adj. principal.

principle, n. principe m.

print, 1. n. (mark) empreinte f.; (book) impression f.; (photo) épreuve f. **2.** vb. imprimer.

printout, n. feuille imprimée produite par un ordinateur f.

priority, n. priorité f.

prism, n. prisme m.

prison, n. prison f.

prisoner, n. prisonnier m.

privacy, n. retraite f.

private, adj. particulier; (not public) privé.

privation, n. privation f.

privilege, n. privilège m.

prize, n. prix m.

probability, n. probabilité f.

probable, adj. probable.

probe, vb. sonder.

problem, n. problème m.

procedure, n. procédé m.

proceed, vb. procéder; (advance) avancer.

process, n. (method) procédé m.; (progress) développement m.

procession, n. cortège m.; (religious) procession f.

proclaim, vb. proclamer.

proclamation, n. proclamation f.

procure, vb. procurer.

prodigal, adj. and n. prodigue m.

prodigy, n. prodige m.

produce, vb. produire.

product, n. produit m.

production, n. production f.

productive, adj. productif.

profane, adj. profane.

profess, vb. professer.

profession, n. profession f.

professional, adj. professionnel.

professor, n. professeur m.

proficient, adj. capable.

profile, n. profil m.

profit, 1. n. profit m. **2.** vb. profiter.

profitable, adj. profitable.

profound, adj. profond.

profuse, adj. (of thing) profus; (of person) prodigue.

program, n. programme m.

progress, n. progrès m.; (motion forward) marche f.

progressive, adj. progressif.

prohibit, vb. défendre.

prohibition, n. défense f.

prohibitive, adj. prohibitif.

project, 1. n. projet m. **2.** vb. projeter; (jut out) faire saillie.

projection, n. projection f.; (jutting out) saillie f.

projector, n. projecteur m.

proliferation, n. prolifération f.

prolong, vb. prolonger.

prominent, adj. saillant.

promiscuous, adj. (indiscriminate) sans distinction.

promise, 1. n. promesse f. **2.** vb. promettre.

promote, vb. (raise) promouvoir; (encourage) encourager.

promotion, n. promotion f.

prompt, adj. prompt.

pronoun, n. pronom m.

pronounce, vb. prononcer.

pronunciation, n. prononciation f.

proof, n. (evidence) preuve f.; (test) épreuve f.

prop, n. appui m.

propaganda, n. progagande f.

propagate, vb. propager, tr.

propeller, n. hélice f.

proper, adj. propre; (respectable, fitting) convenable.

property, n. propriété f.

prophecy, n. prophétie f.

prophesy, vb. prophétiser.

prophet, n. prophète m.

prophetic, adj. prophétique.

proportion, n. proportion f.

proportionate, adj. proportionné.

proposal, n. proposition f.; demande (f.) en mariage.

propose, *vb.* proposer, *tr.*

proposition, *n.* (proposal, grammar) proposition *f.*; (undertaking) affaire *f.*

proprietor, *n.* propriétaire *m.f.*

prosaic, *adj.* prosaïque.

proscribe, *vb.* proscrire.

prose, *n.* prose *f.*

prosecute, *vb.* poursuivre.

prospect, *n.* perspective *f.*

prospective, *adj.* en perspective.

prosper, *vb.* prospérer.

prosperity, *n.* prospérité *f.*

prosperous, *adj.* prospère.

prostitute, 1. *n.* prostituée *f.* 2. *vb.* prostituer.

prostrate, *adj.* prosterné.

protect, *vb.* protéger.

protection, *n.* protection *f.*

protective, *adj.* protecteur.

protector, *n.* protecteur *m.*

protégé, *n.* protégé *m.*

protein, *n.* protéine *f.*

protest, 1. *n.* protestation *f.*; (comm.) protêt *m.* 2. *vb.* protester.

Protestant, *adj. and n.* protestant *m.*

protocol, *n.* protocole *m.*

protrude, *vb.* saillir.

prove, *vb.* prouver; (test) éprouver.

proverb, *n.* proverbe *m.*

provide (with) *vb.* pourvoir (de), *tr.*

providence, *n.* (foresight) prévoyance *f.*; (divine) providence *f.*

province, *n.* province *f.*

provincial, *adj. and n.* provincial *m.*

provision, *n.* (stock) provision *f.*

provocation, *n.* provocation *f.*

provoke, *vb.* provoquer; (irritate) irriter.

prowess, *n.* prouesse *f.*

prowl, *vb.* rôder.

proximity, *n.* proximité *f.*

prudence, *n.* prudence *f.*

prudent, *adj.* prudent.

prune, *n.* pruneau *m.*

Prussia, *n.* Prusse *f.*

Prussian, 1. *n.* Prussien *m.* 2. *adj.* prussien.

pry, *vb.* fureter.

psalm, *n.* psaume *m.*

psychedelic, *adj.* psychédélique.

psychiatry, *n.* psychiatrie *f.*

psychoanalysis, *n.* psychanalyse *f.*

psychology, *n.* psychologie *f.*

psychological, *adj.* psychologique.

ptomaine, *n.* ptomaïne *f.*

public, 1. *n.* public *m.* 2. *adj.* public *m.*, publique *f.*

publication, *n.* publication *f.*

publicity, *n.* publicité *f.*

publish, *vb.* publier.

publisher, *n.* éditeur *m.*

pudding, *n.* pouding *m.*

puddle, *n.* flaque *f.*

puff, *n.* (smoke etc.) bouffée *f.*

pull, *vb.* tirer.

pulley, *n.* poulie *f.*

pulp, *n.* pulpe *f.*

pulpit, *n.* chaire *f.*

pulsar, *n.* pulsar *m.*

pulsate, *vb.* battre.

pulse, *n.* pouls *m.*

pump, 1. *n.* pompe *f.* 2. *vb.* pomper.

pumpkin, *n.* potiron *m.*

pun, *n.* calembour *m.*

punch, *n.* (tool) poinçon *m.*; (blow) coup (*m.*) de poing; (beverage) punch *m.* 2. *vb.* (pierce) percer; (pummel) gourmer.

punctual, *adj.* ponctuel.

punctuate, *vb.* ponctuer.

puncture, *n.* piqûre *f.*

punish, *vb.* punir.

punishment, *n.* punition *f.*

pupil, *n.* (school) élève *m.f.*; (eye) pupille *f.*

puppet, *n.* marionnette *f.*

puppy, *n.* petit chien *m.*

purchase, 1. *n.* achat *m.* 2. *vb.* acheter.

pure, *adj.* pur.

puree, *n.* purée *f.*

purge, *vb.* purger.

purify, *vb.* purifier.

purity, *n.* pureté *f.*

purple, *adj.* violet.

purpose, *n.* but *m.*; (to the p.) à propos.

purposely, *adv.* exprès.

purse, *n.* bourse *f.*

pursue, *vb.* poursuivre.

pursuit, *n.* poursuite *f.*; (occupation) occupation *f.*; (p. plane) avion (*m.*) de chasse.

push, 1. *n.* poussée *f.* **2.** *vb.* pousser.

put, *vb.* mettre.

puzzle, 1. *n.* problème *m.* **2.** *vb.* embarrasser.

pyramid, *n.* pyramide *f.*

Q

quadraphonic, *adj.* quadriphonique.

quail, *n.* caille *f.*

quaint, *adj.* (strange) étrange.

quake, *vb.* trembler.

qualification, *n.* (reservation) réserve *f.;* (aptitude) compétence *f.;* (description) qualification *f.*

qualify, *vb.* qualifier; (modify) modifier.

quality, *n.* qualité *f.*

qualm, *n.* scrupule *m.*

quantity, *n.* quantité *f.*

quarantine, *n.* quarantaine *f.*

quarrel, 1. *n.* querelle *f.* **2.** *vb.* se quereller.

quarry, *n.* carrière *f.*

quarter, *n.* quart *m.;* (district, moon, beef) quartier *m.*

quarterly, *adj.* trimestriel.

quartet, *n.* quatuor *f.*

quartz, *n.* quartz *m.*

quasar, *n.* quasar *m.*

quaver, *vb.* chevroter.

queen, *n.* reine *f.*

queer, *adj.* bizarre.

quell, *vb.* réprimer.

quench, *vb.* éteindre.

query, *n.* question *f.*

quest, *n.* recherche *f.*

question, 1. *n.* question *f.* **2.** *vb.* interroger; (raise questions) mettre en doute.

questionable, *adj.* douteux.

question mark, *n.* point (*m.*) d'interrogation.

questionnaire, *n.* questionnaire *m.*

quick, 1. *adj.* rapide; (lively) vif. **2.** *adv.* vite.

quicken, *vb.* accélérer.

quiet, 1. *n.* tranquillité *f.* **2.** *adj.* tranquille.

quilt, *n.* courtepointe *f.*

quinine, *n.* quinine *f.*

quip, *n.* mot (*m.*) piquant.

quit, *vb.* quitter.

quite, *adv.* tout à fait.

quiver, *vb.* trembloter.

quiz, 1. *n.* petit examen *m.* **2.** *vb.* examiner.

quorum, *n.* quorum *m.*

quota, *n.* (share) quote-part *f.;* (immigration, etc.) contingent *m.*

quotation, *n.* citation *f.;* (comm.) cote *f.*

quote, *vb.* citer.

R

rabbi, *n.* rabbin *m.*

rabbit, *n.* lapin *m.*

rabble, *n.* tourbe *f.*

rabid, *adj.* enragé.

race, 1. *n.* (people) race *f.;* (contest) course *f.* **2.** *vb.* lutter à la course (avec).

race-track, *n.* piste *f.*

rack, *n.* râtelier *m.;* (torture) chevalet (*m.*) de torture.

racket, *n.* (tennis) raquette *f.;* (noise) tintamarre *m.*

radar, *n.* radar *m.*

radiance, *n.* éclat *m.*

radiant, *adj.* radieux.

radiate, *vb.* irradier.

radiation, *n.* rayonnement *m.*

radiator, *n.* radiateur *m.*

radical, *adj. and n.* radical *m.*

radio, *n.* télégraphie (*f.*) sans fil (*commonly* T.S.F.).

radioactive, *adj.* radio-actif.

radish, *n.* radis *m.*

radium, *n.* radium *m.*

radius, *n.* rayon *m.*

raft, *n.* radeau *m.*

rafter, *n.* chevron *m.*

rag, *n.* chiffon *m.*

rage, *n.* rage *f.*

ragged, *adj.* en haillons.

ragweed, *n.* ambroisie *f.*

raid, *n.* (police) descente *f.;* (mil.) raid *m.*

rail, *n.* (bar) barre *f.;* (railroad) rail *m.*

railroad, *n.* chemin (*m.*) de fer.

rain, 1. *n.* pluie *f.* **2.** *vb.* pleuvoir.

rainbow, *n.* arc-en-ciel *m.*

raincoat, *n.* imperméable *m.*

rainfall, *n.* chute (*f.*) de pluie.

rainy, *adj.* pluvieux.

raise, *vb.* (bring up, erect, promote) élever; (lift) lever; (plants) cultiver.

raisin, n. raisin (m.) sec.

rake, 1. n. râteau m. **2.** vb. râteler.

rally, n. (mil.) ralliement m.; (meeting) rassemblement m.

ram, n. bélier m.

ramble, vb. rôder; (speech) divaguer.

ramp, n. rampe f.

rampart, n. rempart m.

rancid, adj. rance.

random, n. hasard m.

range, n. (scope) étendue f.; (mountains) chaîne f.; (distance) portée f.; (stove) fourneau m.

rank, 1. n. rang m. **2.** vb. ranger, tr.

ransack, vb. (search) fouiller; (pillage) saccager.

ransom, n. rançon f.

rap, 1. n. coup m. **2.** vb. frapper.

rapid, adj. and n. rapide m.

rapture, n. ravissement m.

rare, adj. rare; (meat) saignant.

rascal, n. coquin m.

rash, 1. n. éruption f. **2.** adj. téméraire.

raspberry, n. framboise f.

rat, n. rat m.

rate, 1. n. taux m.; (speed) vitesse f.; (at any r.) en tous cas; (first-r.) de premier ordre. **2.** vb. estimer.

rather, adv. plutôt.

ratify, vb. ratifier.

ration, n. ration f.

rational, adj. raisonnable; (mathematics, philosophy) rationnel.

rattle, n. (toy) hochet m.; (noise) fracas m.

rave, vb. délirer; (r. about) s'extasier sur.

raven, n. corbeau m.

raw, adj. cru.

ray, n. rayon m.

rayon, n. rayonne f.

razor, n. rasoir m.

reach, 1. n. portée f. **2.** vb. atteindre; (extend) étendre, tr.; (arrive) arriver à.

react, vb. réagir.

reaction, n. réaction f.

reactionary, adj. réactionnaire.

read, vb. lire.

reader, n. (person) lecteur m.; (book) livre (m.) de lecture.

readily, adv. promptement.

ready, adj. prêt.

real, adj. réel.

realist, n. réaliste m.f.

reality, n. réalité f.

realization, n. réalisation f.

realize, vb. (notice) s'apercevoir de; (make real) réaliser, tr.

really, adv. vraiment.

realm, n. royaume m.

reap, vb. moissonner.

rear, 1. n. (hind part) queue f.; (mil.) arrière-garde f. **2.** adj. situé à l'arrière. **3.** vb. élever.

reason, 1. n. raison f. **2.** vb. raisonner.

reasonable, adj. raisonnable.

reassure, vb. rassurer.

rebate, n. rabais m.

rebel, 1. adj. and n. rebelle m.f. **2.** vb. se rebeller.

rebellion, n. rébellion f.

rebellious, adj. rebelle.

rebirth, n. renaissance f.

rebound, n. rebond m.

rebuke, 1. n. réprimande f. **2.** vb. réprimander.

rebuttal, n. réfutation f.

recall, vb. (call back) rappeler; (remember) se rappeler.

recede, vb. s'éloigner.

receipt, n. (for payment) quittance f.

receive, vb. recevoir.

receiver, n. (phone) récepteur m.

recent, adj. récent.

receptacle, n. réceptacle m.

reception, n. réception f.; (welcoming) accueil m.

receptive, adj. réceptif.

recess, n. recoin m.; (Parliament) vacances f.pl.; (school) récréation f.

recipe, n. recette f.

reciprocate, vb. payer de retour.

recite, vb. réciter.

reckless, adj. téméraire.

reckon, vb. compter.

reclaim, v. (person) corriger; (land) défricher.

recline, vb. reposer, tr.

recognition, n. reconnaissance f.

recognize, vb. reconnaître.

recoil, vb. reculer.

recollect, vb. se rappeler.

recommend, vb. recommander.

recommendation, n. recommandation f.

recompense, n. récompense f.

reconcile, vb. réconcilier.

record, 1. n. (register) registre m.; (mention) mention f.; (known facts of person) antécédents m.pl.; (sports) record m.; (phonograph) disque m. **2.** vb. enregistrer.

record player, n. tourne-disques m.

recount, vb. raconter.

recover, vb. recouvrer; (from illness) se rétablir.

recovery, n. recouvrement m.; (health) rétablissement m.

recruit, 1. n. recrue f. **2.** vb. recruter.

rectangle, n. rectangle m.

rectify, vb. rectifier.

recuperate, vb. se rétablir, intr.

recur, vb. revenir.

recycle, vb. recycler.

red, adj. and n. rouge m.

redeem, vb. racheter.

redemption, n. rachat m.; (theology) rédemption f.

redress, 1. n. justice f. **2.** vb. redresser, réparer; faire justice à.

reduce, vb. réduire.

reduction, n. réduction f.; (on price) remise f.

reed, n. roseau m.; (music) anche f.

reef, n. récif m.

reel, n. bobine f.

refer, vb. référer.

referee, n. arbitre m.

reference, n. référence f.

refill, vb. remplir (à nouveau).

refine, vb. raffiner.

refinement, n. raffinement m.

reflect, vb. réfléchir.

reflection, n. réflexion f.

reform, 1. n. réforme f. **2.** vb. réformer, tr.

reformation, n. réforme f.

refractory, adj. réfractaire.

refrain from, vb. se retenir de.

refresh, vb. rafraîchir.

refreshment, n. rafraîchissement m.

refrigerator, n. frigidaire m.

refuge, n. refuge m.

refugee, n. réfugié m.

refund, 1. n. remboursement m. **2.** vb. rembourser.

refusal, n. refus m.

refuse, 1. n. rebut m. **2.** vb. refuser.

refute, vb. réfuter.

regain, vb. regagner.

regal, adj. royal.

regard, 1. n. égard m.; (regards, compliments) amitiés f.pl. **2.** vb. regarder.

regardless, adj. sans se soucier de.

regent, adj. and n. régent m.

regime, n. régime m.

regiment, n. régiment m.

region, n. région f.

register, 1. n. registre m. **2.** vb. enregistrer; (letter) recommander.

registration, n. enregistrement m.

regret, 1. n. regret m. **2.** vb. regretter.

regular, adj. régulier.

regularity, n. regularité f.

regulate, vb. régler.

regulation, n. règlement m.

regulator, n. régulateur m.

rehabilitate, vb. réhabiliter.

rehearse, vb. répéter.

reign, 1. n. règne m. **2.** vb. régner.

rein, n. rêne f.

reindeer, n. renne m.

reinforce, vb. renforcer.

reinforcement, n. renfort m.

reject, vb. rejeter.

rejoice, vb. réjouir, tr.

rejoin, vb. (join again) rejoindre; (reply) répliquer.

relapse, n. rechute f.

relate, vb. raconter; (have reference to) se rapporter (à), **(relate to)** entrer en rapport avec.

relation, n. relation f.; (relative) parent m.

relative, 1. n. parent m. **2.** adj. relatif.

relax, vb. relâcher.

relay, 1. n. relais m. **2.** vb. relayer.

release, 1. n. délivrance f. **2.** vb. libérer.

relent, vb. se laisser attendrir.

relevant, adj. pertinent.

reliability, n. sûreté f.

reliable, adj. digne de confiance.

reliant, adj. confiant.

relic, n. relique f.

relief, *n.* (ease) soulagement *m.;* (help) secours *m.;* (projection) relief *m.*

relieve, *vb.* (ease) soulager; (help) secourir.

religion, *n.* religion *f.*

religious, *adj.* religieux.

relinquish, *vb.* abandonner.

relish, 1. *n.* goût *m.* **2.** *vb.* goûter.

reluctant, *adj.* peu disposé (à).

rely upon, *vb.* compter sur.

remain, *vb.* rester.

remainder, *n.* reste *m.*

remark, 1. *n.* remarque *f.* **2.** *vb.* remarquer.

remarkable, *adj.* remarquable.

remedy, 1. *n.* remède *m.* **2.** *vb.* rémédier à.

remember, *vb.* se souvenir de.

remembrance, *n.* souvenir *m.*

remind of, *vb.* rappeler à (person recalling).

reminisce, *vb.* raconter ses souvenirs.

remit, *vb.* remettre.

remnant, *n.* reste *m.,* vestige *m.,* (of cloth) coupon *m.*

remorse, *n.* remords *m.*

remote, *adj.* éloigné; (vague) vague.

removable, *adj.* transportable.

removal, *n.* enlèvement *m.*

remove, *vb.* enlever.

rend, *vb.* déchirer.

render, *vb.* rendre.

rendezvous, *n.* rendez-vous *m.*

renew, *vb.* renouveler.

renewal, *n.* renouvellement *m.*

renounce, *vb.* (give up) renoncer à; (repudiate) répudier.

renovate, *vb.* renouveler.

renown, *n.* renommée *f.*

rent, 1. *n.* loyer *m.* **2.** *vb.* louer.

repair, 1. *n.* réparation *f.* **2.** *vb.* réparer.

repay, *vb.* (give back) rendre; (refund) rembourser.

repeat, *vb.* répéter.

repel, *vb.* repousser.

repent, *vb.* se repentir (de).

repentance, *n.* repentir *m.*

repertoire, *n.* répertoire *m.*

repetition, *n.* répétition *f.*

replace, *vb.* (place again) replacer; (take place of) remplacer.

reply, 1. *n.* réponse *f.* **2.** *vb.* répondre.

report, 1. *n.* rapport *m.;* (rumor) bruit *m.* **2.** *vb.* rapporter; (inform against) dénoncer.

repose, *n.* repos *m.*

represent, *vb.* représenter.

representation, *n.* représentation *f.*

representative, 1. *n.* représentant *m.;* (politics) député *m.* **2.** *adj.* représentatif.

repress, *vb.* réprimer.

reprimand, *n.* réprimande *f.*

reproach, 1. *n.* reproche *m.* **2.** *vb.* faire des reproches à.

reproduce, *vb.* reproduire, *tr.*

reproduction, *n.* reproduction *f.*

reproof, *n.* réprimande *f.*

reprove, *vb.* réprimander.

reptile, *n.* reptile *m.*

republic, *n.* république *f.*

republican, *adj. and n.* républicain *m.*

repulsive, *adj.* répulsif.

reputation, *n.* réputation *f.*

repute, 1. *n.* renom *m.* **2.** *vb.* réputer.

request, 1. *n.* requête *f.* **2.** *vb.* demander.

require, *vb.* exiger.

requirement, *n.* exigence *f.*

requisite, *adj.* nécessaire.

requisition, *n.* réquisition *f.*

rescue, 1. *n.* délivrance *f.* **2.** *vb.* délivrer.

research, *n.* recherche *f.*

resemble, *vb.* ressembler à.

resent, *vb.* être froissé de.

reservation, *n.* réserve *f.*

reserve, 1. *n.* réserve *f.* **2.** *vb.* réserver.

reservoir, *n.* réservoir *m.*

reside, *vb.* résider.

residence, *n.* résidence *f.*

resident, 1. *n.* habitant *m.* **2.** *adj.* résidant.

resign, *vb.* résigner; (from post) se démettre (de).

resignation, *n.* résignation *f.;* (from post) démission *f.*

resist, *vb.* résister (à).

resistance, *n.* résistance *f.*

resolute, *adj.* résolu.

resolution, *n.* résolution *f.*

resolve, *vb.* résoudre.

resonant, *adj.* résonnant.

resort, 1. *n.* (resource) ressource *f.*; (recourse) recours *m.*; (place) lieu *(m.)* de séjour. **2.** *vb.* avoir recours.

resound, *vb.* résonner.

resource, *n.* ressource *f.*

respect, 1. *n.* respect *m.*; (reference) rapport *m.* **2.** *vb.* respecter.

respectable, *adj.* respectable.

respectful, *adj.* respectueux.

respective, *adj.* respectif.

respiration, *n.* respiration *f.*

respite, *n.* répit *m.*

respond, *vb.* répondre.

response, *n.* réponse *f.*

responsibility, *n.* responsabilité *f.*

responsible, *adj.* responsable.

rest, 1. *n.* (repose) repos *m.*; (remainder) reste *m.*; **(the r.,** the others) les autres *m.f.pl.* **2.** *vb.* se reposer.

restaurant, *n.* restaurant *m.*

restful, *adj.* qui repose.

restless, *adj.* (anxious) inquiet.

restoration, *n.* restauration *f.*

restore, *vb.* remettre; (repair) restaurer.

restrain, *vb.* contenir.

restraint, *n.* contrainte *f.*

restrict, *vb.* restreindre.

result, 1. *n.* résultat *m.* **2.** *vb.* résulter.

resume, *vb.* reprendre.

résumé, *n.* résumé *m.*

resurrect, *vb.* ressusciter.

retail, *n.* détail *m.*

retain, *vb.* retenir.

retaliate, *vb.* user de représailles.

retard, *vb.* retarder.

reticent, *adj.* réservé.

retina, *n.* rétine *f.*

retire, *vb.* se retirer.

retort, *n.* riposte *f.*

retreat, 1. *n.* retraite *f.* **2.** *vb.* se retirer.

retrieve, *vb.* recouvrer.

retrospect, *n.* renvoi *m.*, (in retrospect) coup d'œil rétrospectif *m.*

return, 1. *n.* retour *m.*; (returns, comm.) recettes *f.pl.* **2.** *vb.* (give back) rendre: (go back) retourner; (come back) revenir.

reunion, *n.* réunion *f.*

reveal, *vb.* révéler.

revel, *vb.* s'ébattre.

revelation, *n.* révélation *f.*

revelry, *n.* bacchanale *f.*

revenge, 1. *n.* vengeance *f.* **2.** *vb.* **(r. oneself)** se venger.

revenue, *n.* revenu *m.*

reverberate, *vb.* réverbérer, réfléchir; répercuter.

revere, *vb.* révérer.

reverence, *n.* révérence *f.*

reverend, *adj.* révérend.

reverent, *adj.* respectueux.

reverie, *n.* rêverie *f.*

reverse, 1. *n.* (opposite) contraire *m.*; (defeat, medal) revers *m.*; (gear) marche *(f.)* arrière. **2.** *vb.* renverser.

revert, *vb.* revenir.

review, *n.* revue *f.*

revise, *vb.* réviser.

revision, *n.* révision *f.*

revival, *n.* renaissance *f.*; (religious) réveil *m.*

revive, *vb.* revivre, *intr.*; faire revivre, *tr.*

revoke, *vb.* révoquer.

revolt, 1. *n.* révolte *f.* **2.** *vb.* se révolter.

revolution, *n.* révolution *f.*

revolutionary, *adj.* révolutionnaire.

revolve, *vb.* tourner, *intr.*

revolver, *n.* revolver *m.*

reward, 1. *n.* récompense *f.* **2.** *vb.* récompenser.

rheumatism, *n.* rhumatisme *m.*

rhinoceros, *n.* rhinocéros *m.*

rhubarb, *n.* rhubarbe *f.*

rhyme, 1. *n.* rime *f.* **2.** *vb.* rimer.

rhythm, *n.* rythme *m.*

rhythmical, *adj.* rythmique.

rib, *n.* côte *f.*

ribbon, *n.* ruban *m.*

rice, *n.* riz *m.*

rich, *adj.* riche.

rid, *vb.* débarrasser.

riddle, *n.* énigme *f.*

ride, 1. *n.* promenade *f.* **2.** *vb.* (horse) aller à cheval; (vehicle) aller en voiture.

rider, *n.* (on horse) cavalier *m.*

ridge, *n.* crête *f.*

ridicule, 1. *n.* ridicule *m.* **2.** *vb.* se moquer de.

ridiculous, *adj.* ridicule.

rifle, *n.* fusil *m.*

rig, 1. *n.* (vessel) gréement *m.*; (outfit) tenue *f.* **2.** *vb.* gréer.

right, 1. *n.* droit *m.*; (not left) droite *f.* **2.** *adj.* (straight, not left) droit; (correct, proper) juste; **(be r.,** of person) avoir raison; **(all r.)** c'est bien. **3.** *adv.* (straight) droit; (not left) à droite; (justly) bien.

righteous, *adj.* juste.

righteousness, *n.* justice *f.*

right of way, *n.* droit de passage *m.,* (automobiles) priorité de passage *f.*

rigid, *adj.* rigide.

rigor, *n.* rigueur *f.*

rigorous, *adj.* rigoureux.

rim, *n.* bord *m.;* (wheel) jante *f.*

ring, 1. *n.* anneau *m.;* (ornament) bague *f.;* (circle) cercle *m.;* (arena) arène *f.;* (sound) son *m.;* (phone) coup *(m.)* de téléphone. **2.** *vb.* sonner.

rinse, *vb.* rincer.

riot, *n.* émeute *f.*

rip, 1. *n.* fente *f.* **2.** *vb.* fendre, tr.

ripe, *adj.* mûr.

ripen, *vb.* mûrir.

ripoff, 1. *n.* vol *m.* **2.** *vb.* voler.

ripple, 1. *n.* (on water) ride *f.* **2.** *vb.* rider, tr.

rise, 1. *n.* (ground) montée *f.;* (increase) augmentation *f.;* (rank) avancement *m.* **2.** *vb.* se lever.

risk, 1. *n.* risque *m.* **2.** *vb.* risquer.

rite, *n.* rite *m.*

ritual, *adj.* rituel.

rival, 1. *adj. and n.* rival *m.* **2.** *vb.* rivaliser avec.

rivalry, *n.* rivalité *f.*

river, *n.* fleuve *m.*

rivet, *n.* rivet *m.*

road, *n.* route *f.*

roam, *vb.* errer (par).

roar, *vb.* (person) hurler; (lion) rugir; (bull, sea) mugir; (thunder, cannon) gronder; (laughter) éclater de.

roast, 1. *n.* rôti *m.* **2.** *vb.* rôtir.

rob, *vb.* voler.

robber, *n.* voleur *m.*

robbery, *n.* vol *m.*

robe, *n.* robe *f.*

robin, *n.* rouge-gorge *m.*

robot, *n.* automate *m.*

robust, *adj.* robuste.

rock, 1. *n.* rocher *m.* **2.** *vb.* balancer; (child) bercer. **3.** *adj.* (musique) rock.

rocker, *n.* (chair) chaise *(f.)* à bascule.

rocket, *n.* fusée *f.*

rocky, *adj.* rocheux.

rod, *n.* verge *f.*

rodent, *adj. and n.* rongeur *m.*

roe, *n.* (animal) chevreuil *m.;* (of fish) œufs *(m.pl.)* de poisson.

rogue, *n.* coquin *m.*

roguish, *adj.* coquin.

role, *n.* rôle *m.*

roll, **1.** *n.* rouleau *m.;* (bread) petit pain *m.;* (list) liste *f.;* **(r.-call)** appel *m.;* (boat) roulis *m.* **2.** *vb.* rouler.

roller, *n.* rouleau *m.*

Roman, 1. *n.* Romain *m.* **2.** *adj.* romain.

romance, *n.* roman *(m.)* de chevalerie.

romantic, *adj.* romanesque; (poetry, music) romantique.

romp, 1. *n.* tapage *m.* **2.** *vb.* batifoler.

roof, *n.* toit *m.*

room, *n.* (space) place *f.;* (private use) chambre *f.;* (public use) salle *f.*

roommate, *n.* camarade *(m.f.)* de chambre.

rooster, *n.* coq *m.*

root, **1.** *n.* racine *f.;* (source) source *f.* **2.** *vb.* enraciner, tr.

rope, *n.* corde *f.*

rosary, *n.* rosaire *m.*

rose, *n.* rose *f.*

rosin, *n.* colophane *f.*

rosy, *adj.* de rose.

rot, 1. *n.* pourriture *f.* **2.** *vb.* pourrir.

rotary, *adj.* rotatoire.

rotate, *vb.* tourner.

rotation, *n.* rotation *f.*

rotten, *adj.* pourri.

rouge, *n.* rouge *m.*

rough, *adj.* rude; (sea weather) gros *m.,* grosse *f.*

round, 1. *adj.* rond; **(r. trip)** l'aller *(m.)* et le retour. **2.** *n.* rond *m.;* (circuit) tournée *f.*

rouse, *vb.* (wake) réveiller; (stir up) secouer.

rout, *n.* (mil.) déroute *f.*

route, *n.* route *f.*

routine, *n.* routine *f.*

rove, *vb.* errer (par).

rover, *n.* rôdeur *m.*

row, 1. *n.* rang *m.;* dispute *f.* **2.** *vb.* ramer.

rowboat, *n.* barque *f.*

rowdy, *adj.* tapageur.

royal, *adj.* royal.

royalty, *n.* royauté *f.;* (of author) droits *(m.pl.)* d'auteur.

rub, *vb.* frotter.

rubber, *n.* caoutchouc *m.*

rubbish, *n.* rebuts *m.pl.;* (nonsense) bêtises *f.pl.*

ruby, *n.* rubis *m.*

rudder, *n.* gouvernail *m.*

ruddy, *adj.* rouge.

rude, *adj.* (rough) rude; (impolite) impoli.

rudiment, *n.* rudiment *m.*

rue, *vb.* regretter.

ruffian, *n.* bandit *m.*

ruffle, *n.* (frill) fraise *f.*

rug, *n.* tapis *m.*

rugged, *adj.* (rough) rude; (uneven) raboteux.

ruin, 1. *n.* ruine *f.* **2.** *vb.* ruiner.

ruinous, *adj.* ruineux.

rule, 1. *n.* règle *f.;* (authority) autorité *f.* **2.** *vb.* gouverner; (decide) décider.

ruler, *n.* souverain *m.;* (for lines) règle *f.*

rum, *n.* rhum *m.*

Rumania, *n.* Roumanie *f.*

Rumanian, 1. *n.* (person) Roumain *m.;* (language) roumain *m.* **2.** *adj.* roumain.

rumba, *n.* rumba *f.*

rumble, *vb.* gronder.

rumor, *n.* rumeur *f.*

run, *vb. intr.* courir; (of engine) marcher; (of colors) déteindre; (of liquids) couler; **(r. away)** s'enfuir.

run-down, *adj.* épuisé.

rung, *n.* échelon *m.*

runner, *n.* (person) coureur *m.;* (table) chemin *(m.)* de table.

rupture, *n.* rupture *f.*

rural, *adj.* rural.

rush, 1. *n.* (haste) hâte *f.;* (onrush) ruée *f.;* (air, water) coup *m.;* (plant) jonc *m.* **2.** *vb.* se précipiter, *intr.*

Russia, *n.* Russie *f.*

Russian, 1. *n.* (person) Russe *m.f.;* (language) russe *m.* **2.** *adj.* russe.

rust, 1. *n.* rouille *f.* **2.** *vb.* rouiller, *tr.*

rustic, *adj.* rustique.

rustle, *n.* (leaves) bruissement *m.;* (skirt) frou-frou *m.*

rusty, *adj.* rouillé.

rut, *n.* ornière *f.*

ruthless, *adj.* impitoyable.

rye, *n.* seigle *m.*

S

Sabbath, *n.* sabbat *m.*

saber, *n.* sabre *m.*

sable, *n.* zibeline *f.*

sabotage, 1. *n.* sabotage *m.* **2.** *vb.* saboter.

saboteur, *n.* saboteur *m.*

saccharin, *n.* saccharine *f.*

sachet, *n.* sachet *m.*

sack, 1. *n.* sac *m.* **2.** *vb.* saccager.

sacrament, *n.* sacrement *m.*

sacred, *adj.* sacré.

sacrifice, 1. *n.* sacrifice *m.* **2.** *vb.* sacrifier.

sacrilege, *n.* sacrilège *m.*

sad, *adj.* triste.

sadden, *vb.* attrister, *tr.*

saddle, *n.* selle *f.*

sadism, *n.* sadisme *m.*

safe, 1. *n.* coffre-fort *n.* **2.** *adj.* sûr; **(s. and sound)** sain et sauf; **(s. from)** à l'abri de.

safeguard, *vb.* sauvegarder.

safety, *n.* sûreté *f.,* sécurité *f.*

safety pin, *n.* épingle *(f.)* anglaise.

sage, *n.* (person) sage *m.;* (plant) sauge *f.*

sail, 1. *n.* voile *f.* **2.** *vb.* naviguer; (depart) partir.

sailboat, *n.* canot *(m.)* à voiles.

sailor, *n.* marin *m.*

saint, *adj. and n.* saint *m.*

sake, *n.* **(for the s. of)** pour l'amour de.

salad, *n.* salade *f.*

salary, *n.* appointements *m.pl.*

sale, *n.* vente *f.*

salesman, *n.* vendeur *m.*

sales tax, *n.* impôt sur les ventes *m.*

saliva, *n.* salive *f.*

salmon, *n.* saumon *m.*

salt, 1. *n.* sel *m.* **2.** *vb.* saler.

salute, 1. *n.* salut *m.* **2.** *vb.* saluer.

salvage, *n.* sauvetage *m.*

salvation, n. salut m.

salve, vb. sanctifier.

same, 1. adj. and pron. même. **2.** adv. de même.

sample, n. échantillon m.

sanatorium, n. sanatorium m.

sanctify, vb. sanctifier.

sanction, n. sanction f.

sanctity, n. sainteté f.

sanctuary, n. sanctuaire m.

sand, n. sable m.

sandal, n. sandale f.

sandwich, n. sandwich m.

sandy, adj. sablonneux.

sane, adj. sain d'esprit.

sanitary, adj. sanitaire.

sanitary napkin, n. serviette (f.) hygiènique.

sanitation, n. hygiène f.

sanity, n. santé (f.) d'esprit.

Santa Claus, n. Père Noël m.

sap, n. sève f.

sapphire, n. saphir m.

sarcasm, n. sarcasme m.

sardine, n. sardine f.

sash, n. ceinture f.

satellite, n. satellite m.

satin, n. satin m.

satire, n. satire f.

satisfaction, n. satisfaction f.

satisfactory, adj. satisfaisant.

satisfy, vb. satisfaire.

saturate, vb. saturer.

Saturday, n. samedi m.

sauce, n. sauce f.

saucer, n. soucoupe f.

saucy, adj. impertinent.

sausage, n. saucisse f.

savage, adj. and n. sauvage m.f.

save, vb. sauver; (put aside) mettre de côté; (economize) épargner.

savior, n. sauveur m.

savor, n. saveur f.

savory, adj. savoureux.

saw, 1. n. scie f. **2.** vb. scier.

say, vb. dire.

scab, n. croûte f., gale f.

scaffold, n. échafaud m.

scald, vb. échauder.

scale, 1. n. (fish) écaille f.; (balance) balance f.; (series, graded system, map) échelle f.; (music) gamme f. **2.** vb. escalader.

scalp, 1. n. cuir (m.) chevelu. **2.** vb. scalper.

scan, vb. (examine) scruter; (verse) scander.

scandal, n. scandale m.

scandalous, adj. scandaleux.

Scandinavia, n. Scandinavie f.

Scandinavian, 1. n. Scandinave m.f. **2.** adj. scandinave.

scant(y), adj. limité, faible.

scar, n. cicatrice f.

scarce, adj. rare.

scare, vb. effrayer.

scarf, n. écharpe f.

scarlet, adj. and n. écarlate f.; (s. fever) scarlatine f.

scathing, adj. cinglant.

scatter, vb. éparpiller.

scavenger, n. boueur m.

scenario, n. scénario m.

scene, n. scène f.

scenery, n. (theater) décors m.pl.; (landscape) paysage m.

scent, 1. n. parfum m., odeur f. **2.** vb. flairer, sentir.

schedule, n. plan m.

scheme, n. plan m.

scholar, n. savant m.

scholarship, n. (school) bourse f.

school, n. école f.

sciatica, n. sciatique f.

science, n. science f.

science fiction, n. science-fiction f.

scientist, n. scientifique m.f.

scissors, n. ciseaux m.pl.

scoff at, vb. se moquer de.

scold, vb. gronder.

scoop out, vb. évider.

scope, n. (extent) portée f.; (outlet) carrière f.

scorch, vb. roussir.

score, n. (games) points m.pl.; (twenty) vingtaine f.; (music) partition f.

scorn, 1. n. mépris m. **2.** vb. mépriser.

scornful, adj. dédaigneux.

Scotch, Scottish, adj. écossais.

Scotchman, Scotsman, n. Écossais m.

Scotch tape, n. ruban adhésif m.

Scotland, n. Écosse f.

scour, vb. nettoyer.

scourge, n. fléau m.

scout, n. éclaireur m.; (boy s.) boy-scout m.

scowl, vb. se renfrogner.

scramble, vb. avancer péniblement.

scrap, 1. n. petit morceau m. **2.** vb. mettre au rebut.

scrape, scratch, 1. n. égratignure f. **2.** vb. gratter.

scream, 1. n. cri m. **2.** vb. crier.

screen, n. écran m.; (folding s.) paravent m.

screw, 1. n. vis f. **2.** vb. visser, tr.

screwdriver, n. tournevis m.

scribble, vb. griffonner.

scroll, n. rouleau m.

scrub, vb. frotter.

scruple, n. scrupule m.

scrupulous, adj. scrupuleux.

scrutinize, vb. scruter.

sculptor, n. sculpteur m.

sculpture, n. sculpture f.

scythe, n. faux f.

sea, n. mer f.

seabed, n. lit de la mer f.

seacoast, n. littoral m.

seal, 1. n. (animal) phoque m.; (stamp) sceau m. **2.** vb. sceller.

seam, n. couture f.

seaport, n. port (m.) de mer.

search, 1. n. recherche f. **2.** vb. chercher.

seasickness, n. mal (m.) de mer.

season, 1. n. saison f. **2.** vb. assaisonner.

seat, 1. n. siège m. **2.** vb. asseoir.

second, 1. n. seconde f. **2.** adj. second, deuxième.

secondary, adj. secondaire.

secret, adj. and n. secret m.

secretary, n. secrétaire m.f.

sect, n. secte f.

section, n. section f.

sectional, adj. régional.

secular, adj. (church) séculier; (time) séculaire.

secure, 1. adj. sûr. **2.** vb. (make s.) mettre en sûreté; (make fast) fixer; (obtain) obtenir.

security, n. sûreté f.; (comm., law) caution f.; (finance, pl.) valeurs f.pl.

sedative, adj. and n. sédatif m.

seduce, vb. séduire.

see, vb. voir.

seed, n. semence f.; (vegetables, etc.) graine f.

seek, vb. chercher.

seem, vb. sembler.

seep, vb. suinter.

segment, n. segment m.

segregate, vb. séparer.

seize, vb. saisir.

seldom, adv. rarement.

select, vb. choisir.

selection, n. sélection f.

self, n. moi m., personne f.

selfish, adj. égoïste.

selfishness, n. égoïsme m.

sell, vb. vendre, tr.

semantics, n. sémantique f.

semester, n. semestre m.

semicircle, n. demi-cercle m.

semicolon, n. point (m.) et virgule (f.).

seminary, n. séminaire m.

senate, n. sénat m.

senator, n. sénateur m.

send, vb. envoyer; **(s. back)** renvoyer.

senile, adj. sénile.

senior, adj. and n. (age) aîné m.; (rank) supérieur m.

senior citizen, n. personne du troisième âge f.

sensation, n. sensation f.

sensational, adj. sensationnel.

sense, n. sens m.

sensible, adj. (wise) sensé; (appreciable) sensible.

sensitive, adj. sensible.

sensual, adj. sensuel.

sentence, 1. n. (gramm.) phrase f.; (law) sentence f.

sentiment, n. sentiment m.

sentimental, adj. sentimental.

separate, 1. adj. séparé. **2.** vb. séparer, tr.

separation, n. séparation f.

September, n. septembre m.

sequence, n. suite f.

serenade, n. sérénade f.

serene, adj. serein.

sergeant, n. sergent m.

serial, n. roman-feuilleton m.

series, n. série f.

serious, adj. sérieux.

sermon, n. sermon m.

serpent, n. serpent m.

serum, n. sérum m.

servant, n. (domestic) domestique m.f.; (public) employé m.

serve, vb. servir.

service, n. service m.; (church) office m.

servitude, n. servitude f.

session, n. session f.

set, 1. n. ensemble m. **2.** adj. fixe; (decided) résolu. **3.** vb. tr. (put) mettre; (regulate) régler; (jewels) monter; (fix) fixer. **4.** vb. intr. (sun, etc.) se coucher; **(s. about)** se mettre à.

settle, vb. (establish) établir, tr.; (fix) fixer; (decide) décider; (arrange) arranger; (pay) payer; **(s. down to,** intr.) se mettre à.

settlement, n. (colony) colonie f.; (accounts) règlement m.

settler, n. colon m.

seven, adj. and n. sept m.

seventeen, adj. and n. dix-sept m.

seventh, adj. and n. septième f.

seventy, adj. and n. soixante-dix m.

sever, vb. séparer, couper.

several, adj. and pron. plusieurs.

severe, adj. sévère.

severity, n. sévérité f.

sew, vb. coudre.

sewer, n. égout m.

sex, n. sexe m.

sexism, n. sexisme m.

sexist, adj. sexiste.

sexual, adj. sexuel.

shabby, adj. (clothes) usé; (person) mesquin.

shade, 1. n. ombre f.; (colors) nuance f.; (window) store m. **2.** vb. ombrager.

shadow, n. ombre f.

shady, adj. ombragé; (not honest) louche.

shaft, n. (mine) puits m.

shaggy, adj. poilu, hirsute.

shake, vb. tr. secouer; trembler; **(s. hands)** serrer la main à.

shallow, adj. peu profond.

shame, n. honte f.

shameful, adj. honteux.

shampoo, n. schampooing m.

shape, 1. n. forme f. **2.** vb. former.

share, 1. n. part f.; (finance) action f. **2.** vb. partager.

shark, n. requin m.

sharp, adj. (cutting) tranchant; (clever) fin; (piercing) perçant; (music) dièse.

sharpen, vb. aiguiser.

shatter, vb. briser.

shave, vb. raser, tr.

shaving brush, n. blaireau m.

shaving cream, n. crème à raser f.

shawl, n. châle m.

she, pron. elle.

sheaf, n. (grain) gerbe f.

shear, vb. tondre.

shears, n. cisailles f.pl.

sheath, n. étui m.

shed, 1. n. hangar m. **2.** vb. verser.

sheep, n. mouton m.

sheet, n. (bed) drap m.; (paper, metal) feuille f.

shelf, n. rayon m.

shell, n. (egg) coquille f.; (of building) carcasse f.; (explosive) obus m.

shellac, n. laque f.

shellfish, n. coquillages m.pl.

shelter, 1. n. abri m. **2.** vb. abriter.

shepherd, n. berger m.

sherbet, n. sorbet m.

sherry, n. xérès m.

shield, n. bouclier m.

shift, 1. n. (change) changement m.; (workers) équipe f.; (expedient) expédient m.; (shirt) chemise f. **2.** vb. changer; **(s. gears)** changer de vitesse.

shine, vb. briller, intr.; (shoes) cirer.

shiny, adj. luisant.

ship, n. navire m.; vaisseau m.

shipment, n. envoi m.

shirk, vb. esquiver.

shirt, n. chemise f.

shiver, 1. n. frisson m. **2.** vb. frissonner.

shock, 1. n. choc m. **2.** vb. choquer.

shoe, n. soulier m.

shoelace, n. lacet m.

shoemaker, n. cordonnier m.

shoot, vb. tirer; (person) fusiller; (hit) atteindre; (rush) se précipiter.

shop, 1. n. boutique f.; (factory) atelier m. **2.** vb. faire des emplettes.

shore, n. rivage m.

short, adj. court.

shortage, n. manque m.

shorten, vb. raccourcir.

shorthand, n. sténographie f.

shot, n. coup m.

should, vb. devoir (in conditional).

shoulder, n. épaule f.

shout, 1. n. cri m. **2.** vb. crier.

shove, vb. pousser.

shovel, n. pelle f.

show, 1. n. (exhibition) exposition f.; (spectacle, performance) spectacle, performance) spectacle m.; (semblance) semblant m.; (display) parade f. **2.** vb. montrer, tr.

shower, n. averse f.

shrapnel, n. shrapnel m.

shrewd, adj. sagace.

shriek, n. cri (m.) perçant.

shrill, adj. aigu.

shrimp, n. crevette f.

shrine, n. châsse f.

shrink, vb. rétrécir, tr.

shroud, n. linceul m.

shrub, n. arbrisseau m.

shudder, 1. n. frisson m. **2.** vb. frissonner.

shun, vb. fuir.

shut, vb. fermer.

shutter, n. volet m.

shy, adj. timide.

sick, adj. malade.

sickness, n. maladie f.

side, n. côté f.

sidewalk, n. trottoir m.

siege, n. siège m.

sieve, n. tamis m.

sift, vb. cribler.

sigh, 1. n. soupir m. **2.** vb. soupirer.

sight, n. vue f.; (spectacle) spectacle m.

sightseeing, n. tourisme m.

sign, 1. n. signe m.; (placard) enseigne f. **2.** vb. signer.

signal, n. signal m.

signature, n. signature f.

significance, n. (meaning) signification f.; (importance) importance f.

significant, adj. significatif.

signify, vb. signifier.

silence, n. silence m.

silent, adj. silencieux.

silk, n. soie f.

silken, adj. de soie.

silly, adj. sot m., sotte f.

silver, 1. n. argent m. **2.** adj. d'argent.

silverware, n. argenterie f.

similar, adj. semblable.

simple, adj. simple.

simplicity, n. simplicité f.

simplify, vb. simplifier.

simply, adv. simplement.

simultaneous, adj. simultané.

sin, 1. n. péché m. **2.** vb. pécher.

since, 1. adv., prep. depuis. **2.** conj. (time) depuis que; (cause) puisque.

sincere, adj. sincère.

sincerity, n. sincérité f.

sinful, adj. (person) pécheur m., pécheresse f.; (act) coupable.

sing, vb. chanter.

singer, n. chanteur m.

single, adj. (only one) seul; (particular) particulier; (not married) célibataire.

singular, adj. and n. singulier m.

sinister, adj. sinistre.

sink, 1. n. évier m. **2.** vb. enfoncer, tr.; (vessel) couler au fond; (diminish, weaken) baisser.

sinner, n. pécheur m., pécheresse f.

sinus, n. sinus m.

sip, vb. siroter.

sir, n. monsieur m.; (title) Sir m.

sirloin, n. aloyau m.

sister, n. sœur f.

sister-in-law, n. belle-sœur f.

sit, vb. (**s. down**) s'asseoir; (be seated) être assis.

site, n. emplacement m.

situate, vb. situer.

situation, n. situation f.

six, adj. and n. six m.

sixteen, adj. and n. seize m.

sixteenth, adj. and n. seizième m.

sixth, adj. and n. sixième m.

sixty, adj. and n. soixante m.

size, n. grandeur f.; (person) taille f.; (shoes, gloves) pointure f.

skate, 1. n. patin m. **2.** vb. patiner.

skateboard, n. planche à roulettes f.

skeleton, n. squelette m.

skeptic, n. sceptique m.f.

skeptical, adj. sceptique.

sketch, 1. n. croquis m. **2.** vb. esquisser.

ski, 1. n. ski m. **2.** vb. faire du ski.

skill, n. adresse f.

skillful, adj. adroit.

skim, vb. (milk) écrémer; (book) feuilleter; (surface) effleurer.

skin, 1. n. peau f. **2.** vb. écorcher.

skip, vb. sauter.

skirt, n. jupe f.

skull, *n.* crâne *m.*

sky, *n.* ciel *m.*

skyscraper, *n.* gratte-ciel *m.*

slab, *n.* dalle *f.*

slack, *adj.* lâche.

slacken, *vb.* (slow up) ralentir; (loosen) relâcher.

slacks, *n.* pantalon *m.*

slander, 1. *n.* calomnie *f.* **2.** *vb.* calomnier.

slang, *n.* argot *m.*

slant, 1. *n.* (slope) pente *f.;* (bias) biais *m.* **2.** *vb.* incliner.

slap, *n.* claque *f.*

slash, *n.* taillade *f.*

slate, *n.* ardoise *f.*

slaughter, 1. *n.* (people) massacre *m.;* (animals) abattage *m.* **2.** *vb.* massacrer; abattre.

slave, *n.* esclave *m.f.*

slavery, *n.* esclavage *m.*

slay, *vb.* tuer.

sled, *n.* traîneau *m.*

sleep, 1. *n.* sommeil *m.;* (go to s.) s'endormir. **2.** *vb.* dormir.

sleeping bag, *n.* sac de couchage.

sleeping pill, *n.* somnifère *m.*

sleepy, *adj.* somnolent; (be s.) avoir sommeil.

sleet, 1. *n.* grésil *m.* **2.** *vb.* grésiller.

sleeve, *n.* manche *f.*

sleigh, *n.* traîneau *m.*

slender, *adj.* mince; svelte.

slice, *n.* tranche *f.*

slide, 1. *n.* (sliding) glissade *f.;* (microscope) lamelle *f.;* (lantern) plaque *(f.)* de projection. **2.** *vb.* glisser.

slight, *adj.* léger; mince.

sling, 1. *n.* fronde *f.;* (medical) écharpe *f.* **2.** *vb.* (throw) lancer; (hang) suspendre.

slip, 1. *n.* (sliding) glissade *f.;* (tongue, pen) lapsus *m.;* (mistake) faux pas *m.;* (paper) fiche *f.;* (garment) combinaison *f.* **2.** *vb.* glisser; (err) faire une faute.

slipper, *n.* pantoufle *f.*

slippery, *adj.* glissant.

slit, 1. *n.* fente *f.* **2.** *vb.* fendre.

slogan, *n.* mot *(m.)* d'ordre; (politics) cri *(m.)* de guerre.

slope, 1. *n.* pente *f.* **2.** *vb.* incliner.

sloppy, *adj.* mal soigné.

slot, *n.* fente *f.*

slow, *adj.* lent; (clock) en retard.

slowness, *n.* lenteur *f.*

sluggish, *adj.* paresseux.

slumber, *vb.* sommeiller.

sly, *adj.* (crafty) rusé; (secretive) sournois.

smack, *n.* (a bit) soupçon *m.;* (noise) claquement *m.*

small, *adj.* petit.

smallpox, *n.* petite vérole *f.*

smart, 1. *adj.* (clever) habile; (stylish) élégant. **2.** *vb.* cuire.

smash, *vb.* briser, *tr.*

smear, *vb.* tache *f.* salir.

smell, 1. *n.* odeur *f.* **2.** *vb.* sentir.

smelt, 1. *n.* éperlan *m.* **2.** *vb.* fondre.

smile, *n., vb.* sourire *m.*

smite, *vb.* frapper.

smoke, 1. *n.* fumée *f.* **2.** *vb.* fumer.

smolder, *vb.* couver.

smooth, 1. *adj.* lisse. **2.** *vb.* lisser.

smother, *vb.* étouffer.

smuggle, *vb.* faire passer en contrebande.

snack, *n.* casse-croute *m.*

snag, *n.* obstacle *(m.)* caché.

snail, *n.* escargot *m.*

snake, *n.* serpent *m.*

snap, 1. *n.* (bite) coup *(m.)* de dents; (sound) coup *(m.)* sec. **2.** *vb.tr.* (with teeth) happer; (sound) faire claquer.

snapshot, *n.* cliché *m.*

snare, *n.* piège *m.*

snarl, *vb.* grogner.

snatch, *vb.* saisir.

sneak, *vb.* se glisser furtivement.

sneakers, *n.* (shoes) tennis *m.*

sneer, *vb.* ricaner.

sneeze, 1. *n.* éternuement *m.* **2.** *vb.* éternuer.

snob, *n.* snob *m.*

snore, *vb.* ronfler.

snow, 1. *n.* neige *f.* **2.** *vb.* neiger.

snug, *adj.* confortable.

so, *adv.* si; tellement; (thus) ainsi; **(s. that)** de sorte que.

soak, *vb.* tremper.

soap, *n.* savon *m.*

soar, *vb.* prendre son essor.

sob, 1. *n.* sanglot *m.* **2.** *vb.* sangloter.

sober, *adj.* (sedate) sérieux; (not drunk) qui n'est pas ivre.

sociable, *adj.* sociable.

social, *adj.* social.

socialism, *n.* socialisme *m.*

socialist, *adj. and n.* socialiste *m.f.*

society, *n.* société *f.*

sociology, *n.* sociologie *f.*

sock, *n.* chaussette *f.*

socket, *n.* douille *f.*

sod, *n.* motte *f.*

soda, *n.* soude *f.; (s.-water)* eau (*f.*) de Seltz.

sofa, *n.* canapé *m.*

soft, *adj.* doux *m.,* douce *f.; (yielding)* mou *m.,* molle *f.*

soften, *vb.* amollir, *tr.*

soil, 1. *n.* terroir *m.* **2.** *vb.* souiller.

sojourn, 1. *n.* séjour *m.* **2.** *vb.* séjourner.

solace, *n.* consolation *f.*

solar, *adj.* solaire.

soldier, *n.* soldat *m.*

sole, *n.* (shoe) semelle *f.; (fish)* sole *f.*

solemn, *adj.* solennel.

solemnity, *n.* solennité *f.*

solicit, *vb.* solliciter.

solicitous, *adj.* empressé.

solid, *adj. and n.* solide *m.*

solidity, *n.* solidité *f.*

solitary, *adj.* solitaire.

solitude, *n.* solitude *f.*

solo, *n.* solo *m.*

solution, *n.* solution *f.*

solve, *vb.* résoudre.

solvent, *adj.* (comm.) solvable.

somber, *adj.* sombre.

some, 1. *adj.* quelque; (partitive) de. **2.** *pron.* certains; (with verb) en.

somebody, someone, *pron.* quelqu'un.

something, *pron.* quelque chose *m.*

some time, *adv.* (past) autrefois; (future) quelque jour.

sometimes, *adv.* quelquefois.

somewhat, *adv.* quelque peu.

somewhere, *adv.* quelque part.

son, *n.* fils *m.*

song, *n.* chant *m.; (light s.)* chanson *f.*

son-in-law, *n.* gendre *m.*

soon, *adv.* bientôt, tôt.

soot, *n.* suie *f.*

soothe, *vb.* calmer.

sophisticated, *adj.* blasé.

soprano, *n.* soprano *m.*

sordid, *adj.* sordide.

sore, *adj.* (aching) douloureux; **(have a s.** throat, etc.) avoir mal à. . . .

sorrow, *n.* douleur *f.*

sorrowful, *adj.* (person) affligé.

sorry, 1. *adj.* fâché; **(be s.)** regretter. **2.** *interj.* pardon!

sort, 1. *n.* sorte *f.* **2.** *vb.* trier.

soul, *n.* âme *f.*

sound, 1. *n.* son *m.* **2.** *adj.* (healthy) sain, solide. **3.** *vb.* sonner.

soup, *n.* potage *m.*

sour, *adj.* aigre.

source, *n.* source *f.*

south, *n.* sud *m.*

southeast, *n.* sud-est *m.*

southern, *adj.* du sud.

South Pole, *n.* pôle sud *m.*

southwest, *n.* sud-ouest *m.*

souvenir, *n.* souvenir *m.*

sow, *vb.* semer.

space, *n.* espace *m.*

space shuttle, *n.* navette spatiale *f.*

spacious, *adj.* spacieux.

spade, *n.* bêche *f.; (cards)* pique *m.*

Spain, *n.* Espagne *f.*

span, *n.* (hand) empan *m.; (bridge)* travée *f.*

Spaniard, *n.* Espagnol *m.*

Spanish, *adj. and n.* espagnol *m.*

spank, *vb.* fesser.

spanking, *n.* fessée *f.*

spare, 1. *adj.* (in reserve) de réserve. **2.** *vb.* épargner.

spark, *n.* étincelle *f.*

sparkle, *vb.* étinceler.

sparrow, *n.* moineau *m.*

spasm, *n.* spasme *m.*

speak, *vb.* parler.

speaker, *n.* (public) orateur *m.*

special, *adj.* spécial.

specialist, *n.* spécialiste *m.f.*

specially, *adv.* spécialement.

specialty, *n.* spécialité *f.*

species, *n.* espèce *f.*

specific, *adj.* spécifique.

specify, *vb.* spécifier.

specimen, *n.* spécimen *m.*

spectacle, *n.* spectacle *m.*

spectacular, *adj.* spectaculaire.

spectator, *n.* spectateur *m.*

speculate, *vb.* spéculer.

speculation, *n.* spéculation *f.*

speech, *n.* (address) discours *m.;* (utterance) parole *f.*

speed, *n.* vitesse *f.*

speedy, *adj.* rapide.

spell, 1. *n.* (incantation) charme *m.;* (period) période *f.* **2.** *vb.* épeler.

spend, *vb.* (money) dépenser; (time) passer.

sphere, *n.* sphère *f.*

spice, *n.* épice *f.*

spider, *n.* araignée *f.*

spike, *n.* pointe *f.*

spill, *vb.* répandre *tr.*

spin, *vb.* (thread) filer; (twirl) tourner.

spinach, *n.* épinards *m.pl.*

spine, *n.* épine *f.;* (backbone) épine (*f.*) dorsale.

spiral, *n.* spirale *f.* **2.** *adj.* spiral.

spirit, *n.* esprit *m.*

spiritual, *adj.* spirituel.

spiritualism, *n.* spiritisme *m.*

spit, 1. *n.* (saliva) crachat *m.;* (for roast) broche *f.* **2.** *vb.* cracher.

spite, *n.* dépit *m.;* (**in s. of**) malgré.

splash, *vb.* éclabousser.

splendid, *adj.* splendide.

splendor, *n.* splendeur *f.*

splinter, *n.* éclat *m.*

split, *vb.* fendre.

spoil, 1. *n.* butin *m.* **2.** *vb.* gâter.

sponge, *n.* éponge *f.*

sponsor, *n.* (law) garant *m.*

spontaneous, *adj.* spontané.

spontaneity, *n.* spontanéité *f.*

spool, *n.* bobine *f.*

spoon, *n.* cuiller *f.*

spoonful, *n.* cuillerée *f.*

sporadic, *adj.* sporadique.

sport, *n.* sport *m.;* (fun) jeu *m.*

spot, 1. *n.* (stain) tache *f.;* (place) endroit *m.* **2.** *vb.* tacher; (recognize) reconnaître.

spouse, *n.* époux *m.,* épouse *f.*

spout, 1. *n.* (teapot, etc.) bec *m.* **2.** *vb.* jaillir.

sprain, *n.* entorse *f.*

sprawl, *vb.* s'étaler.

spray, *n.* (sea) embrun *m.*

spread, 1. *n.* étendue *f.* **2.** *vb.* étendre, *tr.*

spree, *n.* (**be on a s.**) faire la noce.

sprightly, *adj.* éveillé.

spring, 1. *n.* (season) printemps

m.; (source) source *f.;* (leap) saut *m.;* (device) ressort *m.* **2.** *vb.* (leap) sauter; (water) jaillir.

sprinkle, *vb.* asperger.

spry, *adj.* alerte.

spur, 1. *n.* éperon *m.* **2.** *vb.* éperonner.

spurious, *adj.* faux *m.*

spurn, *vb.* repousser.

spurt, 1. *n.* jet *m.* **2.** *vb.* jaillir.

spy, *n.* espion *m.*

squad, *n.* escouade *f.*

squadron, *n.* escadron *m.*

squalid, *adj.* misérable.

squall, *n.* rafale *f.*

squander, *vb.* gaspiller.

square, 1. *n.* (geom.) carré *m.;* (in town) place *f.* **2.** *adj.* carré.

squat, *vb.* s'accroupir.

squeak, *vb.* crier.

squeeze, *vb.* serrer; (lemon) presser.

squirrel, *n.* écureuil *m.*

squirt, *vb.* seringuer.

stab, *vb.* poignarder.

stability, *n.* stabilité *f.*

stable, 1. *n.* écurie *f.* **2.** *adj.* stable.

stack, *n.* (hay) meule *f.;* (pile) pile *f.;* (chimney) souche *f.*

staff, *n.* (stick) bâton *m.;* (mil.) état-major *m.;* (personnel) personnel *m.*

stage, *n.* (theater) scène *f.;* (in development) période *f.;* (stopping-place) étape *f.*

stagflation, *n.* stagflation *f.*

stagger, *vb.* (totter) chanceler.

stagnant, *adj.* stagnant.

stain, 1. *n.* tache *f.* **2.** *vb.* (spot) tacher; (color) teinter.

stairs, *n.* escalier *m.*

stake, 1. *n.* (post) pieu *m.;* (at s.) en jeu. **2.** *vb.* (gaming) mettre au jeu.

stale, *adj.* (bread) rassis.

stalk, *n.* tige *f.*

stall, *n.* (stable, church) stalle *f.*

stamina, *n.* vigueur *f.*

stammer, *vb.* bégayer.

stamp, 1. *n.* timbre(-poste) *m.* **2.** *vb.* (letter) timbrer; (with foot) frapper du pied.

stampede, *n.* sauve-qui-peut *m.*

stand, 1. *n.* (position) position *f.;* (resistance) résistance *f.;* (stall) étalage *m.;* (vehicles) station *f.*

2. vb. tr. (put) poser; (endure) supporter. **3.** vb. intr. (upright) se tenir debout (be situated, be) se trouver; (stop) s'arrêter.

standard, n. (flag) étendard m.; (measure, etc.) étalon m.; (living, etc.) niveau m.

star, n. étoile f.; (movie) vedette f.

starch, n. amidon m.

stare, vb. regarder fixement.

stark, adj. pur.

start, 1. n. (beginning) commencement m.; (surprise, etc.) tressaillement m. **2.** vb. commencer, tressaillir.

startle, vb. effrayer.

starvation, n. faim f.

starve, vb. intr. mourir de faim.

state, 1. n. état m. **2.** vb. déclarer.

statement, n. déclaration f.

statesman, n. homme (m.) d'état.

static, adj. statique.

station, n. (railroad) gare f.; (bus, subway) station f.

stationary, adj. stationnaire.

stationery, n. papeterie f.

statistics, n. statistique f.

statue, n. statue f.

stature, n. stature f.

statute, n. statut m.

stay, vb. rester.

steady, adj. ferme; (constant) soutenu.

steak, n. bifteck m.

steal, vb. voler.

steam, n. vapeur f.

steamboat, n. bateau (m.) à vapeur.

steamship, n. vapeur m.

steel, n. acier m.

steep, adj. raide.

steeple, n. clocher m.

steer, 1. n. jeune bœuf m. **2.** vb. gouverner.

stem, n. (plant) tige f.

stenographer, n. sténographe m.f.

stenography, n. sténographie f.

step, n. pas m.; (of staircase) marche f.

stereophonic, adj. stéréophonique.

sterile, adj. stérile.

stern, adj. sévère.

stethoscope, n. stéthoscope m.

stew, n. ragoût m.

steward, n. (airline) garçon m.

stewardess, n. (airline) hôtesse de l'air f.

stick, 1. n. bâton m. **2.** vb. (paste) coller, tr.; (remain) rester.

sticky, adj. gluant.

stiff, adj. raide.

stiffness, n. raideur f.

stifle, vb. étouffer.

still, 1. adj. tranquille. **2.** adv. encore. **3.** conj. cependant.

stillness, n. tranquillité f.

stimulant, n. stimulant m.

stimulate, vb. stimuler.

stimulus, n. stimulant m.

sting, 1. n. piqûre f. **2.** vb. (prick) piquer; (smart) cuire.

stingy, adj. mesquin.

stir, 1. vb. remuer; (person, intr.) bouger. **2.** n. mouvement m.

stitch, 1. n. (sewing) point m.; (knitting) maille f. **2.** vb. coudre.

stock, n. (goods on hand) marchandises f.pl.; (finance) valeurs f.pl.

stockbroker, n. agent de change m.

stock exchange, n. Bourse f.

stocking, n. bas m.

stole, n. étole f.

stomach, n. estomac m.; **(s. ache)** mal (m.) à l'estomac.

stone, n. pierre f.

stool, n. escabeau m.

stoop, vb. se pencher.

stop, 1. n. arrêt m. **2.** vb. arrêter, tr.; (prevent) empêcher (de); (cease) cesser.

storage, n. emmagasinage m.

store, 1. n. (shop) magasin m.; (supply) provision f. **2.** vb. emmagasiner.

storm, n. orage m.

stormy, adj. orageux.

story, n. histoire f.; (floor) étage m.

stout, adj. gros m., grosse f.

stove, n. fourneau m.

straight, adj. and adv. droit.

straighten, vb. redresser.

strain, 1. n. effort m. **2.** vb. (stretch) tendre; (filter) passer.

strait, n. (geog.) détroit m.

strand, n. plage f.

strange, adj. étrange; (foreign) étranger.

stranger, n. étranger m.

strangle, vb. étrangler.

strap, n. courroie f.
strategic, adj. stratégique.
strategy, n. stratégie f.
straw, n. paille f.
strawberry, n. fraise f.
stray, adj. égaré.
streak, 1. n. raie f. 2. vb. rayer.
stream, n. courant m.; (small river) ruisseau m.
streamline, vb. caréner.
street, n. rue f.
strength, n. force f.
strengthen, vb. fortifier.
strenuous, adj. énergique.
streptococcus, n. streptocoque m.
stress, 1. n. force f.; tension f.; (gramm.) accent m. 2. vb. accentuer.
stretch, vb. étendre, tr.
stretcher, n. brancard m.
strict, adj. strict.
stride, n. enjambée f.
strife, n. lutte f.
strike, 1. n. grève f. 2. vb. frapper; (match, tr.) allumer; (clock) sonner; (workers) se mettre en grève.
string, n. ficelle f.; (music) corde f.
string bean, n. haricot vert m.
strip, 1. n. bande f. 2. vb. dépouiller.
stripe, n. bande f.; (mil.) galon m.
strive, vb. s'efforcer (de).
stroke, 1. n. coup m. 2. vb. caresser.
stroll, n. tour m.
strong, adj. fort.
structure, n. structure f.
struggle, 1. n. lutte f. 2. vb. lutter.
stub, n. souche f.
stubborn, adj. opiniâtre, obstiné, têtu.
student, n. étudiant m.
studio, n. atelier m.
studious, adj. studieux.
study, 1. n. étude f.; (room) cabinet (m.) de travail. 2. vb. étudier.
stuff, 1. n. (materials) matériaux m.pl.; (textile) étoffe f. 2. vb. bourrer; (cooking) farcir.
stuffing, n. bourre f.; (cooking) farce f.
stumble, vb. trébucher.
stump, n. (tree) souche f.
stun, vb. étourdir.
stunt, n. tour (m.) de force.

stupid, adj. stupide.
stupidity, n. stupidité f.
sturdy, adj. vigoureux.
stutter, vb. bégayer.
style, n. style m.
stylish, adj. élégant.
subconscious, adj. subconscient.
subdue, vb. subjuguer.
subject, 1. n. sujet m. 2. adj. (people, country) assujetti; (liable) sujet. 3. vb. assujettir.
sublimate, vb. sublimer.
sublime, adj. sublime.
submarine, adj. n. sous-marin m.
submerge, vb. submerger.
submission, n. soumission f.
submit, vb. soumettre.
subnormal, adj. sous-normal.
subordinate, adj. and n. subordonné m.
subscribe, vb. (consent, support) souscrire; (to paper, etc.) s'abonner.
subscription, n. souscription f.; (to paper, etc.) abonnement m.
subsequent, adj. subséquent.
subsidy, n. subvention f.
substance, n. substance f.
substantial, adj. substantiel; (well-to-do) aisé.
substitute, 1. n. remplaçant m. 2. vb. substituer.
substitution, n. substitution f.
subterfuge, n. subterfuge m., faux-fuyant m.
subtle, adj. subtil.
subtract, vb. soustraire.
suburb, n. faubourg m.
subversive, adj. subversif.
subway, n. métro(politain) m.
succeed, vb. (come after) succéder à; (be successful) réussir à.
success, n. succès m.
successful, adj. heureux.
succession, n. succession f.
successive, adj. successive.
successor, n. successeur m.
succumb, vb. succomber.
such, adj. tel; (intensive, **s. a** + adj.) un . . . aussi + adj.
suck, vb. sucer.
suction, n. succion f.
sudden, adj. soudain.
sue, vb. poursuivre.
suffer, vb. souffrir.
suffice, vb. suffire.
sufficient, adj. suffisant.

suffocate, vb. suffoquer.

sugar, n. sucre m.

suggest, vb. suggérer.

suggestion, n. suggestion f.

suicide, 1. n. suicide m. **2.** vb. **(commit s.)** se suicider, intr.

suit, 1. n. (law) procès m.; (clothes) (man's) complet m., (woman's) tailleur m.; (cards) couleur f. **2.** vb. convenir (à).

suitable, adj. convenable.

suitcase, n. valise f.

sum, n. somme f.

summary, 1. n. résumé m., abrégé m. **2.** adj. sommaire, immédiat.

summer, n. été m.

summon, vb. (convoke) convoquer; (bid to come) appeler.

sun, n. soleil m.

sunburn, n. hâle m.

Sunday, n. dimanche m.

sunny, adj. ensoleillé.

sunshine, n. soleil m.

superb, adj. superbe.

superficial, adj. superficiel.

superfluous, adj. superflu.

superintendent, n. surveillant m.

superior, adj. and n. supérieur m.

superiority, n. supériorité f.

supernatural, adj. and n. surnaturel m.

supersede, vb. remplacer.

superstar, n. superstar f.

superstition, n. superstition f.

superstitious, adj. superstitieux.

supervise, vb. surveiller.

supper, n. souper m.

supplement, n. supplément m.

supply, 1. n. approvisionnement m.; provision f. **2.** vb. fournir (de).

support, 1. n. appui m. **2.** vb. soutenir; (bear) supporter; (back up) appuyer.

suppose, vb. supposer.

suppress, vb. supprimer.

suppression, n. suppression f.

supreme, adj. suprême.

sure, adj. sûr.

surface, n. surface f.

surge, n. houle f.

surgeon, n. chirurgien m.

surgery, n. chirurgie f.

surpass, vb. surpasser.

surplus, n. surplus m.

surprise, 1. n. surprise f. **2.** vb. surprendre.

surrender, vb. rendre, tr.

surround, vb. entourer.

survey, vb. contempler; (investigate) examiner.

survival, n. survivance f.

survive, vb. survivre.

susceptible, adj. susceptible (de).

suspect, vb. soupçonner.

suspend, vb. suspendre.

suspense, n. incertitude f.; **(in s.)** en suspens.

suspension, n. suspension f.

suspicion, n. soupçon m.

suspicious, adj. soupçonneux; (questionable) suspect.

sustain, vb. soutenir.

swallow, 1. n. (bird) hirondelle f. **2.** vb. avaler.

swamp, n. marais m.

swan, n. cygne m.

swarm, n. essaim m.

sway, 1. n. (rule) domination f.; (motion) oscillation f. **2.** vb. gouverner.

swear, vb. jurer.

sweat, 1. n. sueur f. **2.** vb. suer.

Swede, n. Suédois m.

Sweden, n. Suède f.

Swedish, adj. and n. suédois m.

sweep, 1. n. (bend) courbe f.; (movement) mouvement (m.) circulaire. **2.** vb. balayer.

sweepstakes, n. poule f.

sweet, adj. doux m., douce f.; sucré.

sweetheart, n. amant m., amante f.

sweetness, n. douceur f.

swell, vb. gonfler, tr.; enfler, intr.

swift, adj. rapide.

swim, vb. nager.

swimsuit, n. maillot de bain m.

swindle, vb. escroquer.

swine, n. cochon m.

swing, vb. balancer, tr.

Swiss, 1. n. Suisse m. **2.** adj. suisse, helvétique.

switch, n. (elect.) interrupteur m.

Switzerland, n. Suisse f.

sword, n. épée f.

syllable, n. syllabe f.

symbol, n. symbole m.

symbolic, adj. symbolique.

sympathetic, adj. compatissant.

sympathy, n. compassion f.

symphony, n. symphonie f.

symptom, n. symptôme m.

synchronize, vb. synchroniser, tr.

syndicate, n. syndicat m.

syndrome, n. syndrome m.

synonym, n. synonyme m.

synthetic, adj. synthétique.

syringe, n. seringue f.

syrup, n. sirop m.

system, n. système m.

systematic, adj. systématique.

T

tabernacle, n. tabernacle m.

table, n. table f.

tablecloth, n. nappe f.

tablespoon, n. cuiller à soupe.

tablet, n. tablette f.

tack, 1. n. (nail) broquette f. **2.** vb. clouer.

tact, n. tact m.

tag, n. étiquette f.

tail, n. queue f.

tailor, n. tailleur m.

take, vb. prendre; (lead) conduire; (carry) porter.

tale, n. conte m.

talent, n. talent m.

talk, 1. n. conversation f. **2.** vb. parler.

talkative, adj. bavard.

tall, adj. grand.

tame, adj. (animal) apprivoisé.

tamper, vb. toucher à.

tampon, n. tampon m.

tan, n. (leather) tan m.; (skin) hâle m.

tangible, adj. tangible.

tangle, n. embrouillement m.

tank, n. réservoir m.; (mil.) char (m.) d'assaut.

tap, 1. n. (water) robinet m.; (knock) petit coup m. **2.** vb. frapper légèrement.

tape, n. ruban m.

tape recorder, n. magnétophone m.

tapestry, n. tapisserie f.

tar, n. goudron m.

target, n. cible f.

tariff, n. tarif m.

tarnish, vb. ternir, tr.

task, n. tâche f.

taste, 1. n. goût m. **2.** vb. goûter.

tasty, adj. savoureux.

taut, adj. raide.

tavern, n. taverne f.

tax, 1. n. impôt m. **2.** vb. imposer.

taxi, n. taxi m.

taxpayer, n. contribuable m.

tea, n. thé m.

teach, vb. enseigner; (to do) apprendre à.

teacher, n. instituteur m.; (school) professeur m.

team, n. (animals) attelage m.; (people) équipe f.

teapot, n. théière f.

tear, 1. n. larme f.; (rip) déchirure f. **2.** vb. déchirer.

tease, vb. taquiner.

teaspoon, n. cuiller (f.) à thé.

technical, adj. technique.

technique, n. technique f.

tedious, adj. ennuyeux.

telegram, n. télégramme m.

telegraph, n. télégraphe m.

telephone, 1. n. téléphone m. **2.** vb. téléphoner.

telescope, n. télescope m.

televise, vb. téléviser.

television, n. télévision f.

tell, vb. dire; (story, etc.) raconter.

teller, n. (bank) caissier m.

temper, n. (humor) humeur f.; (lose one's t.) s'emporter; (anger) colère f.; (metals) trempe f.

temperament, n. tempérament m.

temperamental, adj. instable.

temperance, n. tempérance f.

temperate, adj. (habit) sobre; (climate) tempéré.

temperature, n. température f.

tempest, n. tempête f.

temple, n. temple m.; (forehead) tempe f.

temporary, adj. temporaire.

tempt, vb. tenter.

temptation, n. tentation f.

ten, adj. dix m.

tenant

tend,

tentative, *adj.* tentatif, expérimental.

tenth, *adj.* and *n.* dixième *m.*

term, *n.* terme *m.;* (school) trimestre *m.;* (conditions) conditions *f.pl.*

terrace, *n.* terrasse *f.*

terrible, *adj.* terrible.

terrify, *vb.* terrifier.

territory, *n.* territoire *m.*

terror, *n.* terreur *f.*

test, 1. *n.* épreuve *f.* **2.** *vb.* mettre à l'épreuve.

testament, *n.* testament *m.*

testify, *vb.* témoigner (de); (declare) affirmer.

testimony, *n.* témoignage *m.*

text, *n.* texte *m.*

textile, *adj.* textile.

texture, *n.* texture *f.*

than, *conj.* que; (with numerals) de.

thank, *vb.* remercier; **(t. you)** merci.

thankful, *adj.* reconnaissant.

that *sg.,* **those** *pl.* **1.** *adj.* ce, cet *m.,* cette *f.,* ces *pl.;* (opposed to *this*) ce . . . -là, *etc.* **2.** *demonstrative pron.* celui-là *m.,* celle-là *f.,* ceux-là *m.pl.,* celles-là *f.pl.;* (object not named) cela, *abbr.* ça; **(what is t.?)** qu'est-ce que c'est que ça? **3.** *relative pron.* qui (subject); que (object). **4.** *conj.* que; (purpose) pour que.

the, *art.* le *m.,* la *f.,* les *pl.*

theater, *n.* théâtre *m.*

theft, *n.* vol *m.*

their, *adj.* leur *sg.,* leurs *pl.*

theirs, *pron.* le leur *m.,* la leur *f.,* les leurs *pl.*

them, *pron.* eux *m.,* elles *f.;* (unstressed, with verb) les (direct), leur (indirect).

theme, *n.* thème *m.*

themselves, *pron.* eux-mêmes *m.,* elles-mêmes *f.;* (reflexive) se.

then, *adv.* alors; (after that) ensuite.

**   ce,** *adv.* (place) de là; (reason) pour cette raison.

**   ** théologie *f.*

**   ** théorique.

**   **) y.

thermometer, *n.* thermomètre *m.*

these, *see* **this.**

they, *pron.* ils *m.,* elles *f.*

thick, *adj.* épais.

thicken, *vb.* épaissir, *tr.*

thickness, *n.* épaisseur *f.*

thief, *n.* voleur *m.*

thigh, *n.* cuisse *f.*

thimble, *n.* dé *m.*

thin, *adj.* mince.

thing, *n.* chose *f.*

think (of), *vb.* penser (à).

thinker, *n.* penseur *m.*

third, 1. *n.* tiers *m.* **2.** *adj.* troisième.

Third World, *n.* Tiers Monde *m.*

thirst, *n.* soif *f.*

thirsty, *adj.* **(be t.)** avoir soif.

thirteen, *adj.* and *n.* treize *m.*

thirty, *adj.* and *n.* trente *m.*

this, *sg.* **these** *pl.* **1.** *adj.* ce, cet *m.,* cette *f.,* ces *pl.;* (opposed to *that*) ce . . . -ci, *etc.* **2.** *demonstrative pron.* celui-ci *m.,* celle-ci *f.,* ceux-ci *m.pl.,* celles-ci *f.pl.;* (object not named) ceci.

thorough, *adj.* complet.

those, *see* **that.**

though, *conj.* quoique.

thought, *n.* pensée *f.*

thoughtful, *adj.* pensif.

thousand, *adj.* and *n.* mille *m.*

thread, *n.* fil *m.*

threat, *n.* menace *f.*

threaten, *vb.* menacer.

three, *adj.* and *n.* trois *m.*

thrift, *n.* économie *f.*

thrill, 1. *n.* tressaillement *m.* **2.** *vb.* tressaillir, *intr.;* faire frémir, *tr.*

thrive, *vb.* prospérer.

throat, *n.* gorge *f.*

throne, *n.* trône *m.*

through, *prep.* and *adv.* à travers; **(be t.)** avoir fini.

throughout, *adv.* partout.

throw, *vb.* jeter.

thrust, *vb.* pousser.

thumb, *n.* pouce *m.*

thunder, 1. *n.* tonnerre *m.* **2.** *vb.* tonner.

Thursday, *n.* jeudi *m.*

thus, *adv.* ainsi.

thwart, *vb.* contrarier.

ticket, *n.* billet *m.*

tickle, *vb.* chatouiller.

ticklish, *adj.* chatouilleux.

tide, *n.* marée *f.*

tidy, *adj.* ordonné, en ordre.

tie, 1. *n.* lien *m.;* (neck-t.) cravate *f.* **2.** *vb.* attacher; (bind) lier; (knot) nouer.

tier, *n.* gradin *m.*

tiger, *n.* tigre *m.*

tight, *adj.* serré; (drunk) gris.

tighten, *vb.* serrer.

tile, *n.* (roof) tuile *f.*

till, 1. *prep.* jusqu'à. **2.** *conj.* jusqu'à ce que.

tilt, *vb.* pencher.

timber, *n.* (building) bois *(m.)* de construction.

time, *n.* temps *m.;* (occasion) fois *f.;* (clock) heure *f.;* (what t. is it?) quelle heure est-il?; (have a good t.) s'amuser bien.

timetable, *n.* horaire *m.*

timid, *adj.* timide.

timidity, *n.* timidité *f.*

tin, *n.* étain *m.*

tint, *n.* teinte *f.*

tiny, *adj.* tout petit.

tip, 1. *n.* (money) pourboire *m.;* (end) bout *m.* **2.** *vb.* (money) donner un pourboire à; (t. over) renverser.

tire, 1. *n.* (car, etc.) pneumatique *(abbr.* pneu) *m.* **2.** *vb.* fatiguer.

tired, *adj.* fatigué.

tissue, *n.* tissu *m.*

title, *n.* titre *m.*

to, *prep.* à; (in order t.) pour.

tobacco, *n.* tabac *m.*

today, *adv.* aujourd'hui.

toe, *n.* orteil *m.*

together, *adv.* ensemble.

toil, *vb.* travailler dur.

toilet, *n.* toilette *f.;* (t. paper) papier *(m.)* hygiénique.

token, *n.* témoignage *m.;* (coin) jeton *m.*

tolerance, *n.* tolérance *f.*

tolerant, *adj.* tolérant.

tolerate, *vb.* tolérer.

tomato, *n.* tomate *f.*

tomb, *n.* tombeau *m.*

tomorrow, *adv.* demain.

ton, *n.* tonne *f.*

tone, *n.* ton *m.*

tongue, *n.* langue *f.*

tonic, *adj. and n.* tonique *m.*

tonight, *adv.* cette nuit; (evening) ce soir.

tonsil, *n.* amygdale *f.*

too, *adv.* trop; (also) aussi.

tool, *n.* outil *m.*

tooth, *n.* dent *m.*

toothache, *n.* mal *(m.)* de dents.

toothbrush, *n.* brosse *(f.)* à dents.

toothpaste, *n.* dentifrice *m.*

top, *n.* (mountain, etc.) sommet *m.;* (table) dessus *m.*

topcoat, *n.* pardessus *m.*

topic, *n.* sujet *m.*

torch, *n.* torche *f.*

torment, 1. *n.* tourment *m.* **2.** *vb.* tourmenter.

torrent, *n.* torrent *m.*

torture, 1. *n.* torture *f.* **2.** *vb.* torturer.

toss, *vb.* (throw) jeter; s'agiter.

total, *adj. and n.* total *m.*

totalitarian, *adj.* totalitaire.

touch, 1. *n.* (touching) attouchement *m.;* (sense) toucher *m.;* (small amount) pointe *f.;* (contact) contact *m.* **2.** *vb.* toucher.

tough, *adj.* dur.

tour, *n.* tour *m.*

tourist, *n.* touriste *m.f.*

tournament, *n.* tournoi *m.*

tow, *vb.* remorquer.

toward, *prep.* (place, time) vers; (feelings, etc.) envers.

towel, *n.* serviette *f.*

tower, *n.* tour *f.*

town, *n.* ville *f.*

toy, *n.* jouet *m.*

trace, *n.* trace *f.*

track, *n.* piste *f.;* (railroad) voie *f.*

tract, *n.* (space) étendue *f.*

tractor, *n.* tracteur *m.*

trade, 1. *n.* commerce *m.;* (job) métier *m.* **2.** *vb.* commercer.

trader, *n.* commerçant *m.*

tradition, *n.* tradition *f.*

traditional, *adj.* traditionnel.

traffic, *n.* circulation *f.*

tragedy, *n.* tragédie *f.*

tragic, *adj.* tragique.

trail, *n.* trace *f.*

train, 1. *n.* train *m.;* (dress) traîne *f.;* (retinue) suite *f.* **2.** *vb.* (sports) entraîner, *tr.;* (mil.) exercer, *tr.*

traitor, *n.* traître *m.*

tramp, *n.* (steps) bruit *(m.)* de pas; (person) chemineau *m.*

tranquil, *adj.* tranquille.

tranquillity, *n.* tranquillité *f.*

transaction, *n.* opération *f.*

transfer, 1. n. transport m.; (ticket) billet (m.) de correspondance. **2.** vb. transférer, tr.

transform, vb. transformer.

transfusion, n. transfusion f.

transition, n. transition f.

translate, vb. traduire.

translation, n. traduction f.

transmit, vb. transmettre.

transparent, adj. transparent.

transport, transportation, 1. n. transport m. **2.** vb. transporter.

transsexual, adj. transsexuel.

transvestite, adj. travesti.

trap, 1. n. piège m. **2.** vb. prendre au piège.

trash, n. (rubbish) rebut m.

travel, 1. n. voyage m. **2.** vb. voyager.

traveler, n. voyageur m.

traveler's check, n. chèque de voyage n.

tray, n. plateau m.

treacherous, adj. traître.

tread, vb. marcher.

treason, n. trahison f.

treasure, n. trésor m.

treasurer, n. trésorier m.

treasury, n. trésor m.

treat, vb. traiter.

treatment, n. traitement m.

treaty, n. traité m.

tree, n. arbre m.

tremble, vb. trembler.

tremendous, adj. terrible.

trench, n. tranchée f.

trend, n. tendance f.

trespass, vb. empiéter.

triage, n. présélection f.

trial, 1. n. (law) procès m.; (test) épreuve f.

triangle, n. triangle m.

tribulation, n. tribulation f.

tributary, 1. n. (river) affluent m. **2.** adj. tributaire.

tribute, n. tribut m.

trick, 1. n. ruse f. **2.** vb. duper.

tricky, adj. astucieux.

trifle, n. bagatelle f.

trigger, n. détente f.

trim, 1. adj. soigné. **2.** vb. (put in order) arranger; (adorn) garnir; (cut) tailler.

trinket, n. breloque f.

trip, 1. n. voyage m. **2.** vb. trébucher.

triple, adj. and n. triple m.

trite, adj. rebattu.

triumph, n. triomphe m.

triumphant, adj. triomphant.

trivial, adj. trivial.

trolley-car, n. tramway m.

troop, n. troupe f.

trophy, n. trophée m.

tropic, n. tropique m.

trot, 1. n. trot m. **2.** vb. intr. trotter.

trouble, 1. n. (misfortune) malheur m.; (difficulty) difficulté f.; (inconvenience, medical) dérangement m. **2.** vb. (worry) inquiéter, tr.; (inconvenience) déranger; (afflict) affliger.

troublesome, adj. gênant.

trough, n. auge f.

trousers, n. pantalon m.

trousseau, n. trousseau f.

trout, n. truite f.

truce, n. trêve f.

truck, n. camion m.

true, adj. vrai.

truly, adv. vraiment.

trumpet, n. trompette f.

trunk, n. (clothes) malle f.; (body, tree) tronc m.

trust, 1. n. confiance f.; (business) trust m. **2.** vb. se confier à; (entrust) confier.

trustworthy, adj. digne de confiance.

truth, n. vérité f.

truthful, adj. sincère.

try, vb. essayer; (law) mettre en jugement.

tryst, n. rendez-vous m.

T-shirt, n. maillot m.

tub, n. baignoire f.

tube, n. tube m.

tuberculosis, n. tuberculose f.

tuck, n. (fold) pli m.

Tuesday, n. mardi m.

tug, 1. n. (boat) remorqueur m. **2.** vb. (pull) tirer; (boat) remorquer.

tuition, n. (prix de l')enseignement m.

tulip, n. tulipe f.

tumble, vb. (fall) tomber.

tumor, n. tumeur f.

tumult, n. tumulte m.

tuna, n. thon m.

tune, 1. n. air m.; (concord, harmony) accord m. **2.** vb. accorder.

tunnel, n. tunnel m.

turban, n. turban m.

turf, n. gazon m.

Turk, n. Turc m., Turque f.

turkey, n. dindon m.

Turkey, n. Turquie f.

Turkish, 1. n. turc m. 2. adj. turc m., turque f.

turmoil, n. tumulte m.

turn, 1. n. tour m.; (road) détour m. 2. vb. tourner.

turnip, n. navet m.

turret, n. tourelle f.

turtle, n. tortue f.

tutor, n. précepteur m.

twelfth, adj. and n. douzième m.

twelve, adj. and n. douze m.

twentieth, adj. and n. vingtième m.

twenty, adj. and n. vingt m.

twice, adv. deux fois.

twig, n. brindille f.

twilight, n. crépuscule m.

twin, adj. and n. jumeau m., jumelle f.

twine, n. ficelle f.

twinkle, vb. scintiller.

twist, vb. tordre.

two, adj. and n. deux m.

type, 1. n. type m.; (printing) caractère m. 2. vb. taper à la machine.

typewriter, n. machine (f.) à écrire.

typhoid fever, n. fièvre (f.) typhoïde.

typical, adj. typique.

typist, n. dactylo(graphe) m.f.

tyranny, n. tyrannie f.

tyrant, n. tyran m.

U

udder, n. mamelle f.

ugliness, n. laideur f.

ugly, adj. laid.

ulcer, n. ulcère m.

ulterior, adj. ultérieur.

ultimate, adj. dernier.

umbrella, n. parapluie m.

umpire, n. arbitre m.f.

unable, adj. incapable; (u. to) dans l'impossibilité de.

unanimous, adj. unanime.

uncertain, adj. incertain.

uncle, n. oncle m.

unconscious, 1. n. inconscient m.

2. adj. (aware) inconscient; (faint) sans connaissance; (u. of) sans conscience de.

uncover, vb. découvrir.

under, 1. prep. sous. 2. adv. au-dessous.

underestimate, vb. sous-estimer.

undergo, vb. subir.

underground, adj. souterrain.

underline, vb. souligner.

underneath, adv. en dessous.

undershirt, n. gilet (m.) de dessous.

understand, vb. comprendre.

undertake, vb. entreprendre.

undertaker, n. entrepreneur (m.) de pompes funèbres.

underwear, n. vêtements (m.pl.) de dessous.

undo, vb. défaire.

undress, vb. déshabiller, tr.

uneasy, adj. gêné.

uneven, adj. inégal.

unexpected, adj. inattendu.

unfair, adj. injuste.

unfit, adj. peu propre (à).

unfold, vb. déplier.

unforgettable, adj. inoubliable.

unfortunate, adj. malheureux.

unhappy, adj. malheureux.

uniform, adj. and n. uniforme m.

unify, vb. unifier.

union, n. union f.

unique, adj. unique.

unisex, adj. unisexuel.

unit, n. unité f.

unite, vb. unir, tr.

United Nations, n. Nations Unies f.pl.

United States, n. États-Unis m.pl.

unity, n. unité f.

universal, adj. universel.

universe, n. univers m.

university, n. université f.

unleaded, adj. sans plomb.

unless, conj. à moins que . . . ne.

unlike, adj. dissemblable.

unload, vb. décharger.

unlock, vb. ouvrir.

untie, vb. dénouer.

until, conj. jusqu'à ce que.

unusual, adj. insolite.

up, prep. vers le haut de.

uphold, vb. soutenir.

upholster, vb. tapisser.

upon, prep. sur.

upper, adj. supérieur.

upright, adj. droit.

uproar, n. vacarme m.

upset, vb. renverser.

upstairs, adv. en haut.

uptight, adj. tendu.

upward, 1. adj. dirigé en haut. **2.** adv. en montant.

urge, vb. (beg) prier.

urgency, n. urgence f.

urgent, adj. urgent.

us, pron. nous.

use, 1. n. usage m. **2.** vb. employer; se servir de.

useful, adj. utile.

useless, adj. inutile.

usher, n. huissier m.

usual, adj. usuel.

utensil, n. ustensile m.

utilize, vb. utiliser, se servir de.

utmost, 1. n. le plus; (all one can) tout son possible. **2.** adj. (greatest) le plus grand.

utter, 1. adj. absolu. **2.** vb. prononcer; (cry) pousser.

utterance, n. émission f.

V

vacancy, n. vide m., vacance f.

vacant, adj. vide.

vacate, vb. quitter, évacuer.

vacation, n. vacances f.pl.

vaccinate, vb. vacciner.

vaccine, n. vaccin m.

vacuum, n. vide m.; (v. cleaner) aspirateur m.

vagrant, adj. vagabond.

vague, adj. vague.

vain, adj. vain.

valiant, adj. vaillant.

valid, adj. valide.

valise, n. valise f.

valley, n. vallée f.

valor, n. valeur f.

valuable, adj. de valeur.

value, 1. n. valeur f. **2.** vb. évaluer.

value-added tax, n. taxe à la valeur ajoutée f.

valve, n. soupape f.

vandal, n. vandale m.f.

vanguard, n. avant-garde f.

vanilla, n. vanille f.

vanish, vb. s'évanouir.

vanity, n. vanité f.

vanquish, vb. vaincre.

vapor, n. vapeur, f.

variation, n. variation f.

varied, adj. varié.

variety, n. variété f.

various, adj. divers.

varnish, n. vernis m.

vary, vb. varier.

vase, n. vase m.

vasectomy, n. vasectomie f.

vassal, n. vassal m.

vast, adj. vaste.

vat, n. cuve f.

vault, n. voûte f.

vegetable, n. légume m.

vehement, adj. véhément.

vehicle, n. véhicule m.

veil, n. voile m.

vein, n. veine f.

velocity, n. vitesse f.

velvet, n. velours m.

vengeance, n. vengeance f.

vent, n. ouverture f.

ventilate, vb. ventiler.

venture, 1. n. aventure f. **2.** vb. hasarder, tr.

verb, n. verbe m.

verbose, adj. verbeux.

verdict, n. verdict m.

verge, n. bord m.

verify, vb. vérifier.

versatile, adj. versatile.

verse, n. vers m.pl.; (line of poetry) vers m.

version, n. version f.

vertical, adj. vertical.

very, adv. très.

vessel, n. vaisseau m.

vest, n. gilet m.

veteran, n. vétéran m.

veto, n. véto m.

vex, vb. vexer.

viaduct, n. viaduc m.

vibrate, vb. vibrer.

vibration, n. vibration f.

vice, n. vice m.

vicinity, n. voisinage m.

vicious, adj. méchant.

victim, n. victime f.

victor, n. vainqueur m.

victorious, adj. victorieux.

victory, n. victoire f.

videodisc, n. vidéodisque m.

videotape, n. bande vidéo f.

view, n. vue f.

vigil, n. veille f.

vigilant, adj. vigilant.

vigor, *n.* vigueur *f.*
vile, *adj.* vil, abominable.
village, *n.* village *m.*
villain, *n.* scélérat *m.*
vindicate, *vb.* défendre.
vine, *n.* vigne *f.*
vinegar, *n.* vinaigre *m.*
vineyard, *n.* vigne *f.*
vintage, *n.* (grapes gathered) vendange *f.*; (year of wine) année *f.*
violate, *vb.* violer.
violation, *n.* violation *f.*
violence, *n.* violence *f.*
violent, *adj.* violent.
violet, 1. *n.* violette *f.* **2.** *adj.* violet.
violin, *n.* violon *m.*
virgin, *n.* vierge *f.*
virile, *adj.* viril.
virtual, *adj.* vrai.
virtue, *n.* vertu *f.*
virtuous, *adj.* vertueux.
virus, *n.* virus *m.*
visa, *n.* visa *m.*
visible, *adj.* visible.
vision, *n.* vision *f.*
visit, 1. *n.* visite *f.* **2.** *vb.* visiter.
visitor, *n.* visiteur *m.*
visual, *adj.* visuel.
vital, *adj.* vital.
vitality, *n.* vitalité *f.*
vitamin, *n.* vitamine *f.*
vivacious, *adj.* vif *m.*, vive *f.*
vivid, *adj.* vif *m.*, vive *f.*
vocabulary, *n.* vocabulaire *m.*
vocal, *adj.* vocal.
vogue, *n.* vogue *f.*
voice, *n.* voix *f.*
void, *adj.* (law) nul.
volcano, *n.* volcan *m.*
volume, *n.* volume *m.*
voluntary, *adj.* volontaire.
volunteer, 1. *n.* volontaire *m.* **2.** *vb.* s'engager.
vomit, *vb.* vomir.
vote, 1. *n.* vote *m.* **2.** *vb.* voter.
voter, *n.* votant *m.*
vouch for, *vb.* répondre de.
vow, *n.* vœu *m.*
vowel, *n.* voyelle *f.*
voyage, *n.* voyage *m.*
vulgar, *adj.* vulgaire.
vulnerable, *adj.* vulnérable.

W

wade, *vb.* traverser à gué.
waffle, *n.* gaufre (américaine) *f.*
wag, *vb.* agiter.
wage, *vb.* (war) faire la guerre.
wages, *n.* salaire *m.*
wagon, *n.* chariot *m.*
wail, *vb.* gémir.
waist, *n.* taille *f.*
wait (for), *vb.* attendre.
waiter, *n.* garçon *m.*
waitress, *n.* serveuse *f.*
wake (up), *vb.* réveiller, *tr.*; s'éveiller, *intr.*
walk, 1. *n.* promenade *f.* **2.** *vb.* marcher; **(take a w.)** se promener.
wall, *n.* mur *m.*
wallcovering, *n.* tenture *f.*
wallet, *n.* portefeuille *m.*
wallpaper, *n.* papier peint *m.*; papier à tapisser *m.*
walnut, *n.* noix *f.*
walrus, *n.* morse *m.*
waltz, *n.* valse *f.*
wander, *vb.* errer.
want, 1. *n.* besoin *m.* **2.** *vb.* vouloir.
war, *n.* guerre *f.*
ward, *n.* (hospital) salle *f.*; (charge) pupille *m.f.*
ware, *n.* marchandises *f.pl.*
warlike, *adj.* guerrier.
warm, 1. *adj.* chaud; **(be w.)** avoir chaud. **2.** *vb.* chauffer.
warmth, *n.* chaleur *f.*
warn, *vb.* avertir.
warning, *n.* avertissement *m.*
warp, *vb.* détourner.
warrant, 1. *n.* mandat *m.* **2.** *vb.* garantir.
warrior, *n.* guerrier *m.*
warship, *n.* navire (*m.*) de guerre.
wash, *vb.* laver, *tr.*
washing machine, *n.* laveuse mécanique *f.*
washroom, *n.* salle de bain *f.*
wasp, *n.* guêpe *f.*
waste, 1. *n.* (money) gaspillage *m.*; (time) perte *f.*; (rubbish) déchets *m.pl.* **2.** *vb.* gaspiller, perdre.
watch, 1. *n.* (timepiece) montre *f.*; (guard) garde *f.* **2.** *vb.* veiller.
watchful, *adj.* vigilant.

watchmaker, *n.* horloger *m.*
watchman, *n.* gardien *m.*
water, *n.* eau *f.*
waterbed, *n.* aqualit *m.*
water color, *n.* aquarelle *f.*
waterfall, *n.* chute (*f.*) d'eau.
waterproof, *adj.* imperméable.
wave, 1. *n.* (sea) vague *f.;* (sound) onde *f.;* **(permanent w.)** ondulation (*f.*) permanente. **2.** *vb.* agiter; (hair) onduler.
waver, *vb.* vaciller.
wax, *n.* cire *f.*
way, *n.* (road) chemin *m.;* (distance) distance *f.;* (direction) côté *m.;* (manner) manière *f.*
we, *pron.* nous.
weak, *adj.* faible.
weaken, *vb.* affaiblir.
weakness, *n.* faiblesse *f.*
wealth, *n.* richesse, *f.*
wealthy, *adj.* riche.
weapon, *n.* arme *f.*
wear, *vb.* porter.
weary, *adj.* las.
weasel, *n.* belette *f.*
weather, *n.* temps *m.*
weave, *vb.* tisser.
weaver, *n.* tisserand *m.*
web, *n.* (fabric) tissu *m.;* (spider) toile *f.*
wedding, *n.* noces *f.pl.*
wedge, *n.* coin *m.*
Wednesday, *n.* mercredi *m.*
weed, *n.* mauvaise herbe *f.*
week, *n.* semaine *f.*
weekday, *n.* jour (*m.*) de semaine.
week end, *n.* week-end *m.,* fin de semaine *f.*
weekly, *adj.* hebdomadaire.
weep, *vb.* pleurer.
weigh, *vb.* peser.
weight, *n.* poids *m.*
weird, *adj.* mystérieux.
welcome, *adj.* bienvenu.
welfare, *n.* bien-être *m.*
well, 1. *n.* (water) puits *m.* **2.** *adv.* bien.
well-known, *adj.* bien connu.
west, *n.* ouest *m.*
western, *adj.* de l'ouest.
westward, *adv.* vers l'ouest.
wet, 1. *adj.* mouillé; (weather) pluvieux. **2.** *vb.* mouiller.
whale, *n.* baleine *f.*
what, 1. *adj.* quel. **2.** *pron.* (relative, that which) ce qui (subject),

ce que (object); (interrogative) qu'est-ce qui; quoi. **3.** *interj.* quoi!
whatever, 1. *adj.* quelque . . . qui (subject), . . . que (object). **2.** *pron.* quoi qui (subject), . . . que (object).
wheat, *n.* blé *m.*
wheel, *n.* roue *f.*
wheel chair, *n.* fauteuil (*m.*) roulant.
when, *conj.* quand.
whenever, *conj.* toutes les fois que.
where, *conj.* où.
wherever, *conj.* partout où.
whether, *conj.* soit que; (if) si.
which, 1. *adj.* quel. **2.** *pron.* (relative) qui; lequel; (interrogative) lequel.
whichever, *pron.* n'importe lequel.
while, *conj.* pendant que; (whereas) tandis que.
whim, *n.* caprice *m.,* lubie *f.*
whip, *n.* fouet *m.*
whirl, *vb.* faire tourner, *tr.;* tourner sur soi, *intr.*
whirlpool, *n.* tourbillon *m.*
whirlwind, *n.* tornade *f.*
whisker, *n.* (man) favori *m.;* (animals) moustache *f.*
whiskey, *n.* whiskey *m.*
whisper, *vb.* chuchoter.
whistle, 1. *n.* sifflet *m.* **2.** *vb.* siffler.
white, *adj.* blanc *m.,* blanche *f.*
who, *pron.* qui.
whoever, *pron.* qui que.
whole, *adj.* entier.
wholesale, *adj. and adv.* en gros.
wholesome, *adj.* sain.
wholly, *adv.* entièrement.
whom, *pron.* (relative) que; lequel; (interrogative) qui.
whose, *pron.* (relative) dont; (interrogative) de qui.
why, *adv.* pourquoi.
wicked, *adj.* méchant.
wickedness, *n.* méchanceté *f.*
wide, *adj.* large.
widen, *vb.* élargir, *tr.*
widespread, *adj.* répandu.
widow, *n.* veuve *f.*
widower, *n.* veuf *m.*
width, *n.* largeur *f.*
wield, *vb.* manier.

wife, *n.* femme *f.*

wig, *n.* perruque *f.*

wild, *adj.* sauvage.

wilderness, *n.* désert *m.*

wildlife, *n.* faune *f.*

will, 1. *n.* volonté *f.;* **(last w.)** testament *m.* **2.** *vb.* vouloir; (bequeath) léguer.

willful, *adj.* obstiné.

willing, *adj.* bien disposé.

wilt, *vb.* flétrir.

win, *vb.* gagner.

wind, *n.* vent *m.*

windshield, *n.* pare-brise *m.*

window, *n.* fenêtre *f.*

windy, *adj.* venteux.

wine, *n.* vin *m.*

wing, *n.* aile *f.*

wink, 1. *n.* clin *(m.)* d'œil. **2.** *vb.* clignoter.

winner, *n.* gagnant *m.*

winter, *n.* hiver *m.*

wipe, *vb.* essuyer.

wire, *n.* fil *(m.)* de fer.

wireless, *n.* télégraphie *(f.)* sans fil *(abbr.* T.S.F.*)*.

wisdom, *n.* sagesse *f.*

wise, *adj.* sage.

wish, 1. *n.* désir *m.* **2.** *vb.* désirer.

wit, *n.* esprit *m.*

witch, *n.* sorcière *f.*

with, *prep.* avec.

withdraw, *vb.* retirer, *tr.*

wither, *vb.* flétrir.

withhold, *vb.* refuser.

within, *adv.* dedans.

without, *prep.* sans.

witness, *n.* témoin *m.*

witty, *adj.* spirituel.

wizard, *n.* sorcier *m.*

woe, *n.* malheur *m.*

wolf, *n.* loup *m.*

woman, *n.* femme *f.*

womb, *n.* matrice *f.*

wonder, *vb.* (ask oneself) se demander; (be surprised) être étonné.

wonderful, *adj.* merveilleux.

woo, *vb.* faire la cour à.

wood, *n.* bois *m.*

wooden, *adj.* de bois.

wool, *n.* laine *f.*

woolen, *adj.* de laine.

word, *n.* mot *m.*

work, 1. *n.* travail *m.* **2.** *vb.* travailler.

worker, *n.* travailleur *m.*

workman, *n.* ouvrier *m.*

world, *n.* monde *m.*

worldly, *adj.* mondain.

world-wide, *adj.* mondial.

worm, *n.* ver *m.*

worn, *adj.* usé.

worry, 1. *n.* souci *m.* **2.** *vb.* tracasser, préoccuper, *tr.*

worse, *adj.* pire. **2.** *adv.* pis.

worship, 1. *n.* culte *m.* **2.** *vb.* adorer.

worst, 1. *adj.* (le) pire. **2.** *adv.* (le) pis.

worth, *n.* valeur *f.;* (be w. while to) valoir la peine de.

worthless, *adj.* indigne; (without value) sans valeur.

worthy, *adj.* digne.

would, *vb.* vouloir.

wound, 1. *n.* blessure *f.* **2.** *vb.* blesser.

wrap, *vb.* envelopper.

wrapping, *n.* couverture *f.*

wrath, *n.* courroux *m.*

wreath, *n.* couronne *f.*

wreck, *n.* (ship) naufrage *m.;* (remains) débris *m.pl.*

wrench, *vb.* tordre.

wrestle, *vb.* lutter.

wretched, *adj.* misérable.

wring, *vb.* tordre.

wrinkle, *n.* ride *f.*

wrist, *n.* poignet *m.*

wrist watch, *n.* montre-bracelet *f.*

write, *vb.* écrire.

writer, *n.* écrivain *m.*

writhe, *vb.* se tordre.

wrong, 1. *n.* tort *m.* **2.** *adj.* faux *m.,* fausse *f.;* **(be w.)** avoir tort.

X, Y, Z

x-rays, *n.* rayons X *m.pl.*

xylophone, *n.* xylophone *m.*

yacht, *n.* yacht *m.*

yam, *n.* igname *f.*

yard, *n.* (house, etc.) cour *f.;* (lumber, etc.) chantier *m.;* (measure) yard *m.*

yarn, *n.* fil *m.*

yawn, 1. *n.* bâillement *m.* **2.** *vb.* bâiller.

year, *n.* an *m.;* (duration) année *f.*

yearly, *adj.* annuel.

yearn for, *vb.* soupirer après.

yell, *vb.* hurler.

yellow, *adj. and n.* jaune *m.*

yes, *adv.* oui; (after negative question) si.

yesterday, *adv.* hier.

yet, 1. *adv.* encore. **2.** *conj.* néanmoins.

yield, *vb.* (resign, submit) céder; (produce) produire.

yogurt, *n.* yaourt *m.*

yoke, *n.* joug *m.*

yolk, *n.* jaune *m.*

you, *pron.* vous; (familiar, *sg.*) tu.

young, *adj.* jeune.

your, *adj.* votre *sg.,* vos *pl.;* (familiar form) ton *m.sg.,* ta *f.sg.,* tes *pl.*

yours, *pron.* le vôtre; (familiar form) le tien *m.,* la tienne *f.*

yourself, *pron.* vous-même; (familiar form) toi-même; (reflexive) vous, te.

youth, *n.* jeunesse *f.*

youthful, *adj.* (young) jeune; (of youth) de jeunesse.

zap, *vb.* frapper d'une façon soudaine et inattendue.

zeal, *n.* zèle *m.*

zealous, *adj.* zélé.

zebra, *n.* zèbre *m.*

zero, *n.* zéro *m.*

zest, *n.* entrain *m.;* (taste) saveur *f.*

zip code, *n.* code postal *m.*

zipper, *n.* fermeture *f.* éclair.

zone, *n.* zone *f.*

zoo, *n.* jardin *(m.)* zoologique.

zucchini, *n.* courgette *f.*

Food Terms

lemonade	citron pressé
lettuce	laitue
liver	foie
lobster	homard
meat	viande
melon	melon
milk	lait
mushroom	champignon
noodles	nouilles
nut	noix
omelet	omelette
onion	oignon
orange	orange
peach	pêche
pear	poire
pepper	poivre
pie	tarte
pork	porc
potato	pomme de terre
rice	riz
roast beef	rosbif
roasted	rôti
salad	salade
salmon	saumon
salt	sel
sandwich	sandwich
scrambled eggs	oeufs brouillés
shrimp	crevette
soda	soude
sole	sole
soup	potage
spinach	épinard
steak	bifteck
strawberry	fraise
stuffed	farci
sugar	sucre
tea	thé
tomato	tomate
trout	truite
turkey	dindon
veal	veau
vegetable	légume
water	eau
wine	vin

Useful Words and Phrases

Good day. Bonjour.
Good afternoon. Bonjour.
Good evening. Bonsoir.
Good night. Bonne nuit.
Good bye. Au revoir.
How are you? Comment allez-vous?
Fine, thank you. Très bien, merci.
Glad to meet you. Enchanté de faire votre connaissance.
Thank you very much. Merci beaucoup.
You're welcome. Pas de quoi.
Please. S'il vous plaît.
Good luck. Bonne chance.
To your health. A votre santé.
I am lost. Je me suis égaré(e).

Please help me. Aidez-moi, s'il vous plaît.
Do you understand? Comprenez-vous?
I don't understand. Je ne comprends pas.
Speak slowly, please. Parlez lentement, s'il vous plaît.
Please repeat. Répétez, s'il vous plaît.
I don't speak French. Je ne parle pas français.
Do you speak English? Parlez-vous anglais?
Does anyone here speak English? Y a-t-il quelqu'un qui parle anglais?
How do you say...in French? Comment dit-on...en français?
What do you call this? Comment appelle-t-on ceci?

What is your name? Comment vous appelez-vous?
My name is... Je m'appelle...
I am an American. Je suis américain.
May I introduce... Permettez-moi de vous présenter...

How is the weather? Quel temps fait-il?
What time is it? Quelle heure est-il?
What is it? Qu'est-ce que c'est?

I would like... Je voudrais...
Please give me... S'il vous plaît, donnez-moi...
Please bring me... S'il vous plaît, apportez-moi...
How much does this cost? Combien est ceci?
It is too expensive. C'est trop cher.
May I see something cheaper? Pourrais-je voir quelque chose à meilleur marché?
May I see something better? Pourrais-je voir quelque chose de meilleur?
It is not exactly what I want. Ce n'est pas exactement ce que je cherche.
I want to buy... Je voudrais acheter...
Do you accept traveler's checks? Acceptez-vous les chèques de voyage?

I want to eat. Je voudrais manger.
Can you recommend a restaurant? Pouvez-vous recommander un restaurant?
I am hungry. J'ai faim.
I am thirsty. J'ai soif.
May I see the menu? Pourrais-je voir le menu?
Check, please. L'addition, s'il vous plaît.
Is service included in the bill? Le service est-il compris?
Where can I get a taxi? Où pourrais-je trouver un taxi?
What is the fare to... Quel est le tarif jusqu'à...?
Please take me to this address. Veuillez me conduire à cette adresse.
I have a reservation. J'ai une réservation.
Where is the nearest drugstore? Où est la pharmacie la plus proche?
Is there a hotel here? Y a-t-il un hôtel ici?

Where is...? Où est...?
Where is the men's (women's) room? Où est la toilette pour messieurs (dames)?
What is the way to...? Quelle est la route de...?
Take me to... Conduisez-moi à...
I need... J'ai besoin de...
I am ill. Je suis malade.
Please call a doctor. Appelez un docteur, s'il vous plaît.
Is there any mail for me? Y a-t-il du courrier pour moi?
Please call the police. Appelez la police, s'il vous plaît.
I want to send a telegram. Je voudrais envoyer un télégramme.
Where can I change money? Où puis-je changer de l'argent?
Where is the nearest bank? Où est la banque la plus proche?
Will you accept checks? Acceptez-vous des chèques?
What is the postage? Quel est l'affranchissement?
Where can I mail this letter? Où est-ce que je peux mettre cette lettre à la poste?
Please help me with my luggage. S'il vous plaît, aidez-moi avec mes bagages.

Right away. Tout de suite.
Help! Au secours!
Who is it? Qui est-ce que c'est?
Come in. Entrez.
Stop. Arrêtez.
Hurry. Dépêchez-vous.
Go on. Continuez.
Right. A droite.
Left. A gauche.
Straight ahead. Tout droit.
Hello! (*on telephone*) Allô!
As soon as possible. Aussitôt que possible.
Pardon me. Pardon *or* Pardonnez-moi *or* Je m'excuse.
Look out! Attention! *or* Faites attention!
Just a minute! Un instant!

Signs

Attention	Caution	**Ralentir**	Go Slow
Danger	Danger	**Défense de fumer**	No smoking
Sortie	Exit	**Défense d'entrer**	No admittance
Entrée	Entrance	**Dames**	Women
Halte, Arrêtez	Stop	**Hommes**	Men
Fermé	Closed	**Lavabos, toilettes**	Lavatory
Ouvert	Open		

Food Terms

apple	pomme
artichoke	artichaut
asparagus	asperges
bacon	porc salé et fumé
baked	au four
banana	banane
bean	haricot
beer	bière
beet	betterave
biscuit	petit pain
boiled	bouilli
bread	pain
broiled	grillé
butter	beurre
cake	gâteau
carrot	carotte
cauliflower	chou-fleur
celery	céleri
cheese	fromage
chicken	poulet
chocolate	chocolat
coffee	café
cognac	cognac
cookie	gâteau sec
crab	crabe
cream	crème
cucumber	concombre
dessert	dessert
duck	canard
egg	oeuf
fillet	filet
fish	poisson
fowl	volaille
fried	frit
fruit	fruit
goose	oie
grape	raisin
grapefruit	pamplemousse
ham	jambon
hamburger	hamburger
ice cream	glace
jelly	gelée
juice	jus
lamb	agneau